HIPAA Compliance Handbook

2016 Edition

by Patricia I. Carter

HIPAA Compliance Handbook is intended for HIPAA coordinators, project managers, privacy officers, compliance professionals, health care record managers, and others who have the responsibility for implementing the HIPAA Privacy and Security Regulations. It contains easy-to-understand explanations of the legal and regulatory provisions.

Highlights of the 2016 Edition

The 2016 edition provides the following benefits:

- New separate chapter on Breach Notification, with expanded content (see Chapter 5)

- Updates on HIPAA enforcement by State Attorneys General (see § 6.01[C])

- Analysis of new resolution agreements between HHS and covered entities and lessons learned (see § 6.05)

- Incorporates new guidance from OCR, including guidance on the status of workplace wellness programs (see § 7.02)

- Updated State-by-State Guide to Medical Privacy Statutes (see Appendix I)

12/15

For questions concerning this shipment, billing, or other customer service matters, call our Customer Service Department at 1-800-234-1660.

For toll-free ordering, please call 1-800-638-8437.

HIPAA COMPLIANCE HANDBOOK

2016 Edition

Patricia I. Carter, J.D.

 Wolters Kluwer

Copyright © 2016 CCH Incorporated. All Rights Reserved.

No part of this publication may be reproduced or transmitted in any form or by any means, including electronic, mechanical, photocopying, recording, or utilized by any information storage or retrieval system, without written permission from the publisher. For information about permissions or to request permissions online, visit us at *http://www.wklawbusiness.com/footer-pages/permissions*, or a written request may be faxed to our permissions department at 212-771-0803.

Published by Wolters Kluwer in New York.

Wolters Kluwer Legal & Regulatory Solutions U.S. serves customers worldwide with CCH, Aspen Publishers and Kluwer Law International products.

Printed in the United States of America

1 2 3 4 5 6 7 8 9 0

ISBN 978-1-4548-5632-0

About Wolters Kluwer Legal & Regulatory Solutions U.S.

Wolters Kluwer Legal & Regulatory Solutions U.S. delivers expert content and solutions in the areas of law, corporate compliance, health compliance, reimbursement, and legal education. Its practical solutions help customers successfully navigate the demands of a changing environment to drive their daily activities, enhance decision quality and inspire confident outcomes.

Serving customers worldwide, its legal and regulatory solutions portfolio includes products under the Aspen Publishers, CCH Incorporated, Kluwer Law International, ftwilliam.com and MediRegs names. They are regarded as exceptional and trusted resources for general legal and practice-specific knowledge, compliance and risk management, dynamic workflow solutions, and expert commentary.

WOLTERS KLUWER SUPPLEMENT NOTICE

This product is updated on a periodic basis with supplements and/or new editions to reflect important changes in the subject matter.

If you would like information about enrolling this product in the update service, or wish to receive updates billed separately with a 30-day examination review, please contact our Customer Service Department at 1-800-234-1660 or email us at: *customer.service@wolterskluwer.com*. You can also contact us at:

Wolters Kluwer
Distribution Center
7201 McKinney Circle
Frederick, MD 21704

Important Contact Information

- To order any title, go to *www.wklawbusiness.com* or call 1-800-638-8437.

- To reinstate your manual update service, call 1-800-638-8437.

- To contact Customer Service, e-mail *customer.service@wolterskluwer.com*, call 1-800-234-1660, fax 1-800-901-9075, or mail correspondence to: Order Department—Wolters Kluwer, PO Box 990, Frederick, MD 21705.

- To review your account history or pay an invoice online, visit *www.WKLawBusiness.com/payinvoices*.

ABOUT THE AUTHOR

PATRICIA I. CARTER, J.D., is Senior Counsel for an integrated not-for-profit health system, which includes hospitals, medical and dental clinics, online health services, wellness programs, health insurance plans, and a third-party administrator of self-funded health plans. Ms. Carter advises the health system on HIPAA and other privacy- and security-related issues, as well as providing general health law services. Ms. Carter has been a frequent lecturer and writer on HIPAA privacy and security since 1998.

Ms. Carter was previously a partner with a large law firm in Minneapolis, Minnesota. She earned her J.D., *magna cum laude*, from Hamline University School of Law and her B.A., *magna cum laude*, from the University of Minnesota. Prior to becoming an attorney, Ms. Carter had a successful 14-year career in health plan administration, including 10 years as an information systems manager, trainer, and consultant for health plan administrators.

CONTENTS

A complete table of contents for each chapter is included at the beginning of the chapter.

Chapter 1

BASIC PRINCIPLES OF HEALTH INFORMATION AND ADMINISTRATIVE SIMPLIFICATION

Hellm
Plen Corpols
Clephone

§ 1.01 ADMINISTRATIVE SIMPLIFICATION—BACKGROUND

When the Health Insurance Portability and Accountability Act (HIPAA)[1] was originally passed in 1996, it was aimed at improving the efficiency and effectiveness of the health care system in the United States. The section of HIPAA called "Administrative Simplification,"[2] which is the focus of this book, was originally added to HIPAA to implement national standards for electronic health care transactions, such as claims and eligibility verification, and otherwise facilitate electronic data interchange. This standardization was intended to improve the Medicare and Medicaid programs and the efficiency and effectiveness of the health care system generally.[3] Because of concerns that, with increased electronic exchange of health information, breaches of confidentiality could happen on a previously inconceivable scale, privacy and security measures were added to the Administrative Simplification provisions.[4]

In February 2009, Congress passed the American Recovery and Reinvestment Act of 2009 (ARRA),[5] commonly referred to as the Stimulus Bill. The Stimulus Bill contains a section called the Health Information Technology for Economic and Clinical Health Act (HITECH Act). As with the original HIPAA legislation, the HITECH Act once again links the expansion of nationwide electronic exchange of health information with enhanced privacy and security requirements. The HITECH Act calls for an investment of $20 billion in health information technology infrastructure and Medicare and Medicaid incentives to encourage health care providers to use health information technology to electronically exchange patient health information. In addition, the HITECH Act requires the government to lead an effort to develop standards that allow for the nationwide electronic exchange and use of health information to improve quality and coordination of care. Combined with these incentives, the HITECH Act includes provisions strengthening federal privacy and security laws to protect individually identifiable health information from misuse as the health care sector increases its use of health information technology.[6] The privacy and security changes arising from the HITECH Act and its implementing regulations ("HITECH Regulations") are summarized in **Appendix A** and are addressed at appropriate points throughout this book. In 2010, the Patient Protection and Affordable Care Act (also known as the ACA or Health Care Reform Bill) made some additional changes related to electronic health information transactions.[7] These are addressed in **Chapter 2.**

The HIPAA Administrative Simplification provisions require the Department of Health and Human Services (HHS) to develop and implement standards for the electronic transmission of certain health information and to protect the privacy and security of individually identifiable health information.[8] To this end, HHS has issued the following sets of federal regulations (the *Administrative Simplification Regulations*):

- *Transactions*: Standards for the content and format of certain electronic transactions, including standard code sets and identifiers (the *Transaction Standards*).[9]

---

[1] Pub. L. No. 104-191, 110 Stat. 1936 (codified in scattered sections of 18, 26, 29, and 42 U.S.C.).

[2] Pub. L. No. 104-191, Title II, Subpt. F.

[3] Pub. L. No. 104-191, § 261.

[4] 65 Fed. Reg. 82,474 (Dec. 28, 2000).

[5] Pub. L. No. 111-005.

[6] House Ways and Means Committee HITECH Fact Sheet, formerly available at http://waysandmeans.house.gov/media/pdf/110/hit2.pdf.

[7] Patient Protection and Affordable Care Act (ACA), Pub. L. No. 111-148, Title I, Sec. 1104 (2010).

[8] Pub. L. No. 104-191, §§ 263, 264 (codified at 42 U.S.C. §§ 1320d-2–1320d-8).

[9] 45 C.F.R. Pts. 160 and 162; 65 Fed. Reg. 50,311 (Aug. 17, 2000); 65 Fed. Reg. 70,507 (Nov. 24, 2000) (correcting certain minor errors); 68 Fed. Reg. 8381 (Feb. 20, 2003) (modifications); 74 Fed. Reg. 3296 (Jan. 16, 2009) (Version 5010 standards); 74 Fed. Reg. 3328 (Jan. 16, 2009) (ICD-10 codes); 76 Fed. Reg. 40,458 (July 8, 2011) (operating rules, eligibility/claim status); 77 Fed. Reg. 1556 (Jan. 10, 2012) (standards for electronic funds transfers and remittance advice); 77 Fed. Reg. 48,008 (Aug. 10, 2012) (operating rules, EFT/remittance advice); 77 Fed. Reg. 54,664 (Sept. 5, 2012) (health plan ID, code sets; ICD-10 compliance date); 79 Fed. Reg. 45128 (Aug. 4, 2014) (ICD-10 compliance date).

- *Privacy*: Regulations safeguarding the privacy of an individual's health care information and establishing certain individual rights with respect to that information (the *Privacy Regulations*).[10]

- *Security*: Standards for assuring the confidentially, integrity, and accessibility of electronic health information (the *Security Regulations*).[11]

- *Breach*: Regulations issued under HITECH, establishing notification requirements in the event of certain privacy breaches (the *Breach Regulations*).[12]

- *Enforcement*: Regulations regarding enforcement of the Administrative Simplification Regulations, including civil and criminal penalties (the *Enforcement Regulations*).[13]

Chapter 1 of this book addresses some issues common to all of the Administrative Simplification Regulations. **Chapters 2 through 6** discuss each set of regulations in more detail. **Chapter 7** addresses the special issues applicable to group health plans.

§ 1.02   TO WHOM DO THE ADMINISTRATIVE SIMPLIFICATION REGULATIONS APPLY?

The Administrative Simplification Regulations originally applied only to "covered entities"—health plans, health care providers, and clearinghouses, as defined below. Business associates of the covered entities had certain contractual obligations to covered entities arising from "business associate agreements" required by the Privacy and Security Regulations. A significant change under the HITECH Act was to make these business associates directly liable for violation of certain provisions of the Privacy and Security Regulations. The following sections define covered entities and business associates in greater detail.

[A]   Covered Entities

All of the Administrative Simplification Regulations apply directly to the following three types of health care entities (the *covered entities*):[14]

[1]   Health Plan

A health plan is an individual or group plan that provides, or pays the cost of, medical care. Health plans include public and private plans offered, for example, through health insurers, health maintenance organizations (HMOs), Medicare, Medicaid, Medicare Prescription Drug Plans (PDPs), and most group health plans, whether insured or self-insured.[15]

There is an exception for a group health plan that has fewer than 50 participants and is administered by the employer that sponsors the plan. (See **Chapter 7** for special information about group health plans.)

---

[10] 45 C.F.R. Pts. 160 and 164; 65 Fed. Reg. 82,462 (Dec. 28, 2000); 66 Fed. Reg. 12,434 (Feb. 26, 2001) (changing compliance date); 67 Fed. Reg. 53,182 (Aug. 14, 2002) (elimination of consent requirement and other changes); 78 Fed. Reg. 5566 (Jan. 25, 2013) (HITECH Regulations, including revisions to the *Privacy Regulations*).

[11] 45 C.F.R. Pts. 160 and 164; 68 Fed. Reg. 8334 (Feb. 20, 2003); 78 Fed. Reg. 5566 (Jan. 25, 2013) (HITECH Regulations, including revisions to the *Security Regulations*).

[12] 74 Fed. Reg. 42,740 (Aug. 24, 2009) (interim final breach notification rule); 78 Fed. Reg. 5566 (Jan. 25, 2013) (HITECH Regulations, including revisions to *Breach Regulations*).

[13] 74 Fed. Reg. 56,123 (Oct. 30, 2009) (interim final enforcement rule); 78 Fed. Reg. 5566 (Jan. 25, 2013) (HITECH Regulations, including revisions to *Enforcement Regulations*).

[14] 42 U.S.C. § 1320d-1(a); 45 C.F.R. §§ 160.102–160.103; 45 C.F.R. § 164.104. See also "Are You a Covered Entity?" available at http://www.cms.gov/Regulations-and-Guidance/HIPAA-Administrative-Simplification/HIPAAGenInfo/AreYouaCoveredEntity.html.

[15] 45 C.F.R. § 160.103.

[2] Health Care Provider

A health care provider is a covered entity if two tests are satisfied. The provider must (1) meet the HIPAA definition of health care provider and (2) conduct certain electronic transactions.

Health care provider is broadly defined as a provider of medical or health services described under Medicare Part A or Part B (which together encompass most typical health care services), or any other person or organization that furnishes, bills, or is paid for health care in the normal course of business.[16]

Whether a provider is a covered entity also depends on its conduct of certain transactions. A provider that *electronically* transmits or receives any of the enumerated standard transactions (e.g., transmitting or receiving billing/encounter information) is a covered entity. See **§ 2.01** for a list of these transactions.

[3] Health Care Clearinghouse

A health care clearinghouse is a public or private entity, such as a billing service, repricing company, or value-added network, that either (1) processes or facilitates the processing of health information received from another entity in a nonstandard format or containing nonstandard data content into a standard transaction or (2) receives a standard transaction from another entity and processes or facilitates the processing of health information into a nonstandard format or nonstandard data content for the receiving entity.[17]

Although a clearinghouse is a covered entity, it is generally also a business associate of a provider or health plan (or both). The discussion of clearinghouses in this book is generally limited to their business associate role. (See **§ 1.02[B]**.)

[B] Business Associates

The 1996 HIPAA statute applied only to covered entities, but HHS knew that covered entities use a variety of contractors, professional service providers, and other businesses in carrying out their health care activities. HHS had concerns that covered entities could circumvent the Privacy Regulations by contracting out for these health care functions, and the protected health information or "PHI" (as defined in **§ 1.03[A]**) that was shared with these "business associates" would not be protected.[18] To address this issue, the Privacy Regulations permit covered entities to disclose PHI to business associates or allow business associates to create, receive, maintain, or transmit PHI on behalf of the covered entity when necessary to help the covered entities carry out their health care functions, but not for the independent purposes of these business associates.[19] The covered entity is required to obtain satisfactory written assurances (a "business associate agreement") that the business associates will use the PHI only for the purposes for which they are engaged by the covered entity, will safeguard the PHI from misuse, and will cooperate with and help the covered entity comply with the covered entity's responsibilities under the Privacy Regulations.[20]

The HITECH Act fundamentally changed this approach and for the first time imposes direct statutory obligations on business associates.[21] The 2013 HITECH Regulations further clarify the direct liability of business associates under the Privacy, Security, and Breach Regulations.[22] A business associate was always required to adhere to the terms of the business associate agreement as a contractual obligation; under HITECH, this

---

[16] 45 C.F.R. § 160.103.

[17] 45 C.F.R. § 160.103.

[18] 65 Fed. Reg. 82,640–82,641 (Dec. 28, 2000).

[19] 45 C.F.R. §§ 164.103, 165.502(e), and 164.504(e).

[20] 45 C.F.R. §§ 164.103, 165.502(e), and 164.504(e); see also HHS OCR Guidance on the Privacy Regulations, available at http://www.hhs.gov/ocr/privacy/hipaa/understanding/coveredentities/privacyguidance.html (hereinafter OCR Guidance). For more information on business associate agreements, see **§ 3.06**.

[21] HITECH Act §§ 13401, 13404.

[22] 78 Fed. Reg. 5598 (Jan. 25, 2013).

becomes a statutory and regulatory obligation as well.[23] See **Chapter 6** for information about HIPAA's criminal and civil penalties, now applicable to business associates, as well as covered entities.

Liability attaches when the arrangement meets the definition of a business associate relationship, whether or not a business associate agreement has been signed.[24] Business associates now have direct liability for:

- Uses and disclosures of PHI, except those permitted or required by the business associate agreement or as required by law;[25]

- Uses and disclosures of PHI that would violate the Privacy Regulations if done by the covered entity (with the exception of certain permitted uses and disclosures of PHI for the proper management and administration of the business associate, or to provide certain data aggregation services for the covered entity);[26]

- Failure to provide a required breach notification to the covered entity;[27]

- Failure to provide access to a copy of electronically maintained PHI requested by an individual (to be provided to the covered entity, or directly to the individual or a designated third party, as specified in the business associate agreement);[28]

- Failure to disclose PHI when required by HHS to investigate or determine business associate's compliance with the Privacy and Security Regulations;[29]

- If the business associate knows of a pattern or practice of a subcontractor business associate that is a material breach or violation of the subcontractor's obligations under its business associate agreement, failure to take reasonable steps to cure the breach or end the violation (or, if such steps are unsuccessful, terminate the agreement);[30]

- Failure to provide an accounting of disclosures;[31] and

- Failure to comply with the Security Regulations.[32]

Although business associates are required to comply with essentially all of the Security Regulations, they are not, however, required to comply with all requirements of the Privacy Regulations. For example, a business associate is not required to have a notice of privacy practices or a privacy officer. A covered entity may delegate functions, such as distribution of its notice of privacy practices, to a business associate under the terms of their business associate agreement. That would, however, be a contractual obligation for the business associate and not create direct liability for that function under the Privacy Regulations.[33]

The Privacy Regulations, as updated by the HITECH Regulations, do not always state throughout that particular limitations on uses and disclosures of PHI apply to business associates. HHS determined this to be unnecessary, because of the basic principle that the business associate may not use or disclose PHI in any way that would not be permitted if done by the covered entity, so any such limitations automatically apply to the business associate.[34]

---

[23] HITECH Act § 13404(a); 78 Fed. Reg. 5599 (Jan. 25, 2013).

[24] 78 Fed. Reg. 5598 (Jan. 25, 2013).

[25] 45 C.F.R. § 164.502(a)(3); 78 Fed. Reg. 5598 (Jan. 25, 2013). A business associate's use or disclosure is considered impermissible if the business associate does not apply the minimum necessary standard, as described in **§ 3.01[A]**. 78 Fed. Reg. 5599 (Jan. 25, 2013).

[26] 45 C.F.R. § 164.502(a)(3); 78 Fed. Reg. 5597, 5598 (Jan. 25, 2013). See **§ 3.06[A]** for additional explanation of these exceptions.

[27] 45 C.F.R. § 164.410(a); 78 Fed. Reg. 5598 (Jan. 25, 2013). See **§ 3.06** regarding breach notification.

[28] 45 C.F.R. § 164.502(a)(4)(ii); 78 Fed. Reg. 5598-5599, 5632 (Jan. 25, 2013). See **§ 3.02[B][3]** regarding electronic copies of PHI.

[29] 45 C.F.R. § 164.502(a)(4)(i); 78 Fed. Reg. 5599 (Jan. 25, 2013).

[30] 45 C.F.R. § 164.504(e)(1)(iii).

[31] HITECH Act § 13405; see also proposed rule at 76 Fed. Reg. 31426 (May 31, 2011). See **§ 3.02[D]** regarding accounting for disclosures.

[32] HITECH Act § 13401(a); 45 C.F.R. Subpart C; 78 Fed. Reg. 5599 (Jan. 25, 2013). See **Chapter 4**.

[33] 78 Fed. Reg. 5601 (Jan. 25, 2013).

[34] 78 Fed. Reg. 5597 (Jan. 25, 2013).

[1] Who Is a Business Associate?

Not all outside vendors or service providers that have relationships with a covered entity are *business associates* for purposes of the Privacy and Security Regulations. A business associate is a person or an entity that creates, receives, maintains, or transmits PHI for payment or health care operations activities of the covered entity (or other functions or activities governed by the Privacy Regulations).[35] Examples of such services that give rise to a business associate relationship if they are performed on behalf of a covered entity and involve PHI include:

- Claims processing or administration;
- Data analysis, processing, or administration;
- Utilization review, quality assurance;
- Patient safety activities;
- Billing;
- Benefit management;
- Practice management; and
- Repricing.[36]

In addition, if the following types of services involve the disclosure of PHI from the covered entity, they would give rise to a business associate relationship:

- Legal;
- Actuarial;
- Accounting;
- Consulting; and
- Data aggregation.[37]

The HITECH Act clarifies how the business associate definition applies in certain specific situations. For example, anyone who provides data transmission services (involving PHI) for a covered entity and who requires access to PHI on a routine basis is a business associate of the covered entity. Such organizations include health information organizations and e-prescribing gateways.[38] Entities that manage the exchange of PHI through a network, including providing record locator services and performing oversight and governance functions for electronic health information exchanges, have more than random or infrequent access to PHI and are therefore business associates.[39] Data transmission organizations that do not require access to PHI on a routine basis, however, would not be considered business associates.[40]

HHS has long said that a person or an organization that acts merely as a "conduit" for PHI (e.g., the U.S. Postal Service, private couriers, and electronic equivalents such as Internet service providers) is not a business associate. These "conduits" simply transport information without accessing it other than on a random or

---

[35] 45 C.F.R. § 160.103; 78 Fed. Reg. 5570 (Jan. 25, 2013); 78 Fed. Reg. 5575 (Jan. 25, 2013). A covered entity may be the business associate of another covered entity. 45 C.F.R. § 160.103.

[36] 45 C.F.R. § 160.103 (see 42 C.F.R. § 3.20 for definition of patient safety activities).

[37] 45 C.F.R. § 160.103 (see 45 C.F.R. § 164.501 for definition of data aggregation).

[38] HITECH § 30408; 45 C.F.R. § 164.501. A health information organization (referred to as a health information exchange under the HITECH Act) is not formally defined but is described as "an organization that oversees and governs the exchange of health-related information among organizations." 78 Fed. Reg. 5571 (Jan. 25, 2013).

[39] 78 Fed. Reg. 5571 (Jan. 25, 2013).

[40] 78 Fed. Reg. 5570 (Jan. 25, 2013).

infrequent basis as may be necessary for the performance of the transportation service or as required by law. Because no disclosure is intended by the covered entity and the probability of exposure to any PHI is small, no business associate relationship exists for HIPAA purposes.[41] HHS clarifies in the HITECH Regulations that this "conduit exception" is meant to be construed narrowly and provides additional examples for guidance.[42] A telecommunications company that transmits PHI, and has only occasional random access for reviewing whether the data is transmitting properly, would not be a business associate. However, a health information organization that uses a record locator service to manage the exchange of PHI among covered entities would be a business associate because it requires access to PHI to perform the service.[43]

A significant clarification under the HITECH Regulations is that HHS considers the conduit exception to apply to transmission services but not to storage services. If an entity maintains (stores) PHI on behalf of a covered entity, that entity is a business associate, even if it never actually views the PHI. For example, a data storage company that has access to PHI (whether paper or electronic) is a business associate, even if it does not view the PHI or does so only on a random or infrequent basis. If the entity is storing the PHI, it does not matter whether it actually views the PHI it holds.[44] HHS recognizes that both the transmission service and the storage service create the opportunity to access the PHI. It makes a distinction, however, in what it calls the "transient versus persistent nature of the opportunity."[45] Storage companies have greater opportunities than transmission services to access the PHI, so the greater protections of a business associate agreement are required.

Also specifically included in the definition of business associate are vendors of personal health records (PHR) who offer the PHR to individuals on behalf of a covered entity.[46] If a covered entity hires a vendor to provide and manage a PHR service for the benefit of the covered entities' patients or members, and supplies the vendor with PHI for this purpose, the PHR vendor would be providing the service "on behalf of" the covered entity and would be a business associate. However, a PHR vendor offering the service directly to individuals may not be a business associate, even if the PHR vendor enters into a relationship with the covered entity for the electronic exchange of PHI.[47]

[2] Who Is Not a Business Associate?

An equally important question is "Who is *not* a business associate?" Persons or organizations with functions, activities, or services that do not involve the use or disclosure of PHI, and where any access to PHI by such persons would be incidental, are not business associates. For example, a health care provider is not required to enter into a business associate agreement with its janitorial service, because the performance of such service does not involve the use or disclosure of PHI, even though some minimal access to PHI may occur. In this case, where a janitor has contact with PHI incidentally, such disclosure is permissible as an incidental disclosure (see § 3.03[E]), provided reasonable safeguards are in place.[48]

Any member of the covered entity's workforce, which includes employees, volunteers, trainees, and other persons under the direct control of a covered entity, whether paid or unpaid, is not a business associate. In a situation where the assigned workstation of an independent contractor is on the covered entity's premises and such person performs a substantial proportion of his or her activities at that location, the covered entity may choose to treat this person either as a business associate or as part of its workforce. If there is no business associate agreement, it will be assumed that this person is a member of the covered entity's workforce.[49]

---

[41] 65 Fed. Reg. 82,573 (Dec. 28, 2000); see also 75 Fed. Reg. 40,868, 40,873 (July 14, 2010) and 78 Fed. Reg. 5571–5572 (Jan. 25, 2013).

[42] 78 Fed. Reg. 5571–5572 (Jan. 25, 2013).

[43] 78 Fed. Reg. 5572 (Jan. 25, 2013).

[44] 78 Fed. Reg. 5572 (Jan. 25, 2013).

[45] 78 Fed. Reg. 5572 (Jan. 25, 2013).

[46] 45 C.F.R. § 160.103.

[47] 45 C.F.R. § 160.103. 78 Fed. Reg. 5572 (Jan. 25, 2013).

[48] 67 Fed. Reg. 53,252–53,253 (Aug. 14, 2002); OCR Guidance (Business Associates).

[49] 45 C.F.R. § 160.103; 65 Fed. Reg. 82,480 (Dec. 28, 2000).

Originally, HIPAA included some specific exceptions to the business associate requirements, which were characterized as exceptions to the requirement to have a business associate agreement, leaving open the question as to whether these persons or entities were still business associates (even though an agreement was not required). When the HITECH Act extended liability to business associates, this question had to be answered. The HITECH Regulations answer this question by moving the following three exceptions into the definition of business associate, which means they are *not* business associates and not subject to the direct liability as business associates.[50] The term "business associate" does *not* include:

1. A health care provider, where the disclosures of PHI to the health care provider by the covered entity are for the treatment of an individual[51] (e.g., a primary care clinic disclosing PHI to a radiologist who is under contract to provide services on behalf of the clinic).

2. A plan sponsor, with respect to disclosures to the plan sponsor from a group health plan (or from a health insurer or HMO with respect to a group health plan), provided the plan document is amended and certain other requirements are met.[52]

3. A government agency, with respect to determining eligibility for, or enrollment in, a government health plan that provides public benefits and is administered by another government agency, or collecting PHI for such purposes, to the extent such activities are authorized by law.[53]

If a covered entity participating in an organized health care arrangement (OHCA) (discussed in § 1.02[C][3]) provides services with respect to the OHCA that would otherwise create a business associate relationship, it does not become a business associate to the OHCA by merely providing those services.[54] The fact that covered entities participate in an OHCA does not make the participants each other's business associates. Covered entities in an OHCA participate in joint activities or pursue common goals through joint activities, but this does not mean that one participant is providing services to, or on behalf of, the other participants.[55] An OHCA may, however, establish business associate relationships with nonparticipants, subject to the same requirements that apply to a covered entity entering into an arrangement with a business associate.

A bank or other financial institution that does no more than process consumer-conducted financial transactions by debit, credit, or other payment card; clear checks; initiate or process electronic funds transfers; or conduct any other activity that directly facilitates or effects the transfer of funds is not a business associate.[56]

A researcher who receives disclosures for research purposes permitted by the Privacy Regulations is not a business associate. Even if a covered entity hires an external researcher to perform research, the researcher is not a business associate, because it is not performing a function or activity covered by the Privacy Regulations, such as payment or health care operations, or providing one of the enumerated functions under the definition of business associate.[57] For the same reason, an Institutional Review Board (IRB) is not a business associate when it performs research review, approval, and oversight functions.[58] In some cases, however, a researcher may be a business associate. The researcher will be a business associate if it is performing health care operations functions, such as quality assessment and improvement activities, or using PHI to create de-identified data or limited data sets for the covered entity (see **§ 1.03[B]** and **[C]** for a discussion of de-identification and limited data sets).[59]

---

[50] 45 C.F.R. § 160.103; 78 Fed. Reg. 5574 (Jan. 25, 2013).
[51] 45 C.F.R. § 160.103.
[52] 45 C.F.R. § 164.103. See 45 C.F.R. § 164.504(f) and **Chapter 7** regarding the group health plan requirements.
[53] 45 C.F.R. § 164.103.
[54] 45 C.F.R. § 164.103.
[55] 65 Fed. Reg. 82,476 (Dec. 28, 2000).
[56] 65 Fed. Reg. 82,504–82,505 (Dec. 28, 2000); 78 Fed. Reg. 5575 (Jan. 25, 2013).
[57] 67 Fed. Reg. 53,252 (Aug. 14, 2002); 78 Fed. Reg. 5574–5575 (Jan. 25, 2013).
[58] 78 Fed. Reg. 5575 (Jan. 25, 2013).
[59] 78 Fed. Reg. 5575 (Jan. 25, 2013).

An insurer does not become a business associate when a covered entity purchases an insurance product, such as medical liability insurance, from the insurer. However, the insurer could become a business associate, if it provides additional services not directly related to the provision of the insurance benefits, such as risk management, risk assessment, or legal services, for the covered entity that involve access to PHI.[60]

Finally, as discussed in **§ 1.02[B][1]**, certain services fall under the "conduit exception" and do not create business associate relationships.

[3] Business Associate Subcontractors

One of the most significant changes in the HITECH Regulations is the inclusion of subcontractors in the definition of "business associate." In the original Privacy Regulations, HHS created the business associate concept so that PHI would continue to be protected even if the covered entity contracted out for certain health care-related services. The HITECH Regulations extend these protections "downstream" if a business associate subcontracts all or part of those services.[61]

A subcontractor is defined as a person to whom a business associate delegates a function, activity, or service other than in the capacity of a member of the workforce of such business associate.[62] Now, under the HITECH Regulations, a subcontractor that creates, receives, maintains, or transmits PHI on behalf of a business associate is itself a business associate (a "subcontractor business associate").[63] Although the term "subcontractor" implies the existence of a written contract, as with other business associate relationships, the defined relationship can exist even in the absence of a written contract.[64]

The HITECH Act extended direct liability for civil and criminal penalties under the Privacy and Security Regulations to business associates. The inclusion of subcontractors in the definition of business associate means that a subcontractor is subject to these civil and criminal penalties in the same manner as other business associates. In addition, subcontractors can have subcontractors who are also, by definition, business associates if the subcontracted service involves PHI.[65] This approach extends the obligations all the way downstream, as illustrated in Figure 1 below.

Covered entities are required to have business associate agreements with their "primary business associates" but not with subcontractors. This is handled downstream between each business associate and its subcontractors.[66] Previously, subcontractor agreements were required to contain certain written assurances, but under the HITECH Regulations, these agreements must meet all the specific requirements of a business associate agreement.[67]

[4] Business Associate Agreements

A person or entity that meets the definition of business associate has all the obligations and liabilities of a business associate. This is true even if the business associate does not enter into a business associate agreement with the covered entity (or, in the case of a subcontractor, with its upstream business associate).[68] Nevertheless, business associate agreements are required by the Regulations. **Section 3.07[A]** describes the content requirements for business associate agreements.

---

[60] 78 Fed. Reg. 5575 (Jan. 25, 2013). Similarly, a reinsurer does not become a business associate *solely* by selling a reinsurance policy to a group health plan and paying claims under the policy. Each entity is acting on its own behalf. OCR HIPAA FAQ, available at http://www.hhs.gov/ocr/privacy/hipaa/faq/business_associates/255.html.

[61] 78 Fed. Reg. 5572–5573 (Jan. 25, 2013).

[62] 45 C.F.R. § 164.103; 78 Fed. Reg. 5572–5573 (Jan. 25, 2013).

[63] 45 C.F.R. § 164.103; 78 Fed. Reg. 5572–74 (Jan. 25, 2013).

[64] 78 Fed. Reg. 5572 (Jan. 25, 2013).

[65] 78 Fed. Reg. 5574 (Jan. 25, 2013).

[66] 78 Fed. Reg. 5573 (Jan. 25, 2013).

[67] 78 Fed. Reg. 5602 (Jan. 25, 2013).

[68] 78 Fed. Reg. 5574 (Jan. 25, 2013).

FIGURE 1

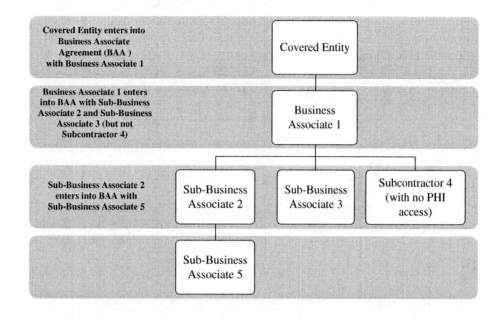

[C] Organizational Structures for Covered Entities

A covered entity has some options under the Privacy Regulations in terms of how it establishes its organizational structure for compliance purposes.

[1] Hybrid Entity

A hybrid entity is a single legal entity whose business activities include both "covered functions" and "noncovered functions" and that chooses to elect hybrid status by designating and documenting its health care component.[69] *Covered functions* are defined as those functions of a covered entity the performance of which makes the entity a health plan, health care provider, or health care clearinghouse.[70] A hybrid entity might include, for example, a residential services organization (generally performing noncovered functions) that incidentally provides certain health care services (covered functions) to its residents; a drugstore that includes both a pharmacy (covered function) and a store that sells general merchandise (noncovered function); or a college (generally noncovered functions) that operates a student health clinic (covered function).

For purposes of establishing a hybrid covered entity, the designated health care component must include any component that would meet the definition of a covered entity if it were a separate legal entity. Originally, the Privacy Regulations gave hybrid covered entities the choice of whether or not to include divisions or components with business associate functions in the health care component. Under the HITECH Regulations, the health care component must include any division or component that performs activities that would make it a business associate if it were a separate legal entity.[71] Otherwise, the business associate functions could avoid direct liability under the Privacy and Security Regulations.[72] Nevertheless, such a business associate division or component is only subject to the Privacy and Security Regulations with respect to the PHI it maintains, uses, or

---

[69] 45 C.F.R. §§ 164.103, 164.105(a).
[70] 45 C.F.R. § 164.103.
[71] 45 C.F.R. § 164.105(a)(iii); 78 Fed. Reg. 5588 (Jan. 25, 2013).
[72] 78 Fed. Reg. 5588 (Jan. 25, 2013).

discloses on behalf of the covered entity's health care component, and not to other information.[73] To comply with the HITECH Regulations, hybrid entities that previously had excluded business associate components from the health care component need to integrate those business-associate functions into their compliance programs and update their documentation of what is included in the "health care component."

Figure 2 illustrates the component parts of a hybrid entity.

FIGURE 2

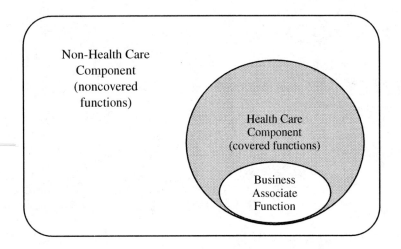

If the covered entity designates itself as a hybrid entity, the Privacy, Security and Breach Regulations apply to only the health care component. The covered entity must ensure that the health care component complies with the applicable requirements of the regulations.[74] A hybrid entity is required to create adequate separation in the form of "firewalls" between the health care component and other components of the entity. Transfer of protected health information (PHI) from the health care component to other components of the hybrid entity is a disclosure under the Privacy Regulations and therefore allowed only to the same extent such a disclosure is permitted to a separate entity.[75]

If the covered entity does not not choose to elect hybrid status by designating health care component(s), the entire entity is subject to the Privacy, Security, and Breach Regulations. If a covered entity does not choose to be a hybrid entity, it is not required to erect firewalls around its health care functions; however, the entity is still only allowed to use PHI as permitted by the Privacy Regulations. For example, workforce members may be permitted access to PHI only as necessary to carry out their duties with respect to the entity's covered functions.[76]

[2] Affiliated Covered Entities

Legally separate covered entities that are affiliated (i.e., under common ownership or control) may designate themselves as a single covered entity for purposes of compliance with the Privacy and Security Regulations.[77] Common ownership exists if an entity or entities possess an ownership or equity interest of 5 percent or more in another entity. Common control exists if an entity has the power, whether directly or indirectly, to significantly influence or direct the actions or policies of another entity.[78]

---

[73] 78 Fed. Reg. 5588 (Jan. 25, 2013).

[74] 45 C.F.R. § 164.105(a).

[75] 45 C.F.R. § 164.105(a)(ii); 67 Fed. Reg. 53,205 (Aug. 14, 2002).

[76] 67 Fed. Reg. 53,205 (Aug. 14, 2002).

[77] 45 C.F.R. §§ 164.105(b) and 164.103.

[78] 45 C.F.R. § 164.103 (definitions).

This designation as an Affiliated Covered Entity, or ACE, must be in writing, and this documentation must be kept on file. This written designation could, for example, be in the form of written resolutions of the Boards of Directors of the affected entities. The list of entities included in the ACE may change over time; these changes must also be documented.

If an ACE combines the covered functions of a health plan and the covered functions of a provider (and/or clearinghouse), the "multiple covered functions rule" applies just as it does to a single covered entity.[79] That is, each covered function must comply with the requirements applicable to its type of covered entity.[80] For example, the provider function within the ACE must obtain an acknowledgement of the notice of privacy practices from the individual, but the health plan function need not do so. Furthermore, the health plan function within the ACE must provide individuals with reminders about the notice every three years, but the provider function does not need to do this.[81]

In addition, the "multiple covered function rule" imposes some limits on the internal use of PHI within the ACE. A covered entity (or ACE, which acts as a single covered entity) that performs "multiple covered functions" must limit the disclosures from one "function" to the other. A covered entity or ACE may not share the PHI of individuals who receive services from one covered function (e.g., health care provider) with another covered function (e.g., health plan) if the individual is not involved with the other function.[82] This means, for example, that an ACE that has both a health plan function and provider function can share PHI of individuals within the ACE, even for treatment, payment, and health care operations, *only if* the individual is both a health plan member and a patient. Furthermore, if the ACE includes a component that is a health care clearinghouse, the clearinghouse must implement policies and procedures that protect the clearinghouse PHI from unauthorized access by the rest of the ACE.[83]

[3] Organized Health Care Arrangement

"Organized health care arrangement" (OHCA) describes certain permitted arrangements that involve clinical or operational integration among legally separate covered entities in which it is often necessary to share PHI for the joint management and operations of the arrangement and to benefit the common enterprise. A key component of these arrangements is that individuals who obtain services from them have an expectation that these arrangements are integrated and that the participants jointly manage the OHCA operations.[84]

The definition of an OHCA includes only the following five types of arrangements:

1. A clinically integrated care setting in which individuals typically receive health care from more than one health care provider (e.g., a hospital and its medical staff);

2. An organized system of health care in which more than one covered entity participates, and in which the participating covered entities hold themselves out to the public as participating in a joint arrangement, and they participate in joint activities that include at least one of the following:

    (a) utilization review, performed by other participating entities or a third party on behalf of the participating entities,

    (b) quality assessment and improvement activities, assessed by other participating entities or a third party on behalf of the participating entities,

---

[79] See § **3.01[D]** for more information about the multiple covered functions rule.

[80] 45 C.F.R. §§ 164.103 (definitions), 164.105(b), and 164.504(g).

[81] See § **3.02** for more information about the notice of privacy practices.

[82] 45 C.F.R. §§ 164.504(g); Office for Civil Rights (OCR) Summary of the Privacy Rule (Organizational Options), available at http://www.hhs.gov/ocr/privacy/hipaa/understanding/summary/index.html.

[83] 45 C.F.R. § 164.308(a)(4)(ii)(A).

[84] 45 C.F.R. § 160.103; 65 Fed. Reg. 82,494 (Dec. 28, 2000).

(c) payment activities, if the financial risk for delivering care is shared by the participating covered entities through the joint arrangement and if protected health information created or received by a covered entity is reviewed by other participating covered entities or by a third party on behalf of the joint arrangement for the purpose of administering the sharing of financial risk.

3. A group health plan and a health insurance issuer or HMO with respect to such group health plan, but only with respect to the group health plan members' PHI;

4. Multiple group health plans maintained by the same plan sponsor; or

5. Group health plans and the health insurance issuers or HMOs through which such plans are funded and administered.[85]

An OHCA is a limited purpose arrangement. It does not mean that the covered entities are combined for all purposes. The main benefit of an OHCA is that it permits use of a joint notice of privacy practices (and acknowledgments).[86] See **§ 3.02[A]** for further information about notices of privacy practices. The other benefit of the OHCA is that a covered entity that participates in an OHCA may disclose PHI about an individual to the other participants in the OHCA for joint health care operations activities of the OHCA.[87]

§ 1.03 PROTECTED HEALTH INFORMATION; DE-IDENTIFIED INFORMATION; LIMITED DATA SETS

[A] Protected Health Information

The type of information protected under the Privacy and Security Regulations is called *protected health information* (PHI). It is broadly defined as individually identifiable information, including demographic information, related to the past, present, or future physical or mental health or condition, the provision of health care to an individual,[88] or the past, present, or future payment for such health care, which is created or received by a covered entity. The form of the PHI is irrelevant. It may be oral or recorded in any medium, including electronic data, paper records, or any other form.[89]

PHI specifically excludes educational and other records that are covered (or are excluded) under the Family Education Rights and Privacy Act of 1974 (FERPA)[90] and any employment records maintained by a covered entity in its capacity as an employer.[91]

The HITECH Regulations clarify that PHI includes genetic information.[92] Although this may have been generally understood, it was included as a clarification, because the HITECH Regulations also implement certain limitations on the use of genetic information for underwriting purposes, as required by the Genetic Information Nondiscrimination Act of 2008 (GINA) (discussed in **§ 3.04[D]**).[93] A definition of "genetic information"

---

[85] 45 C.F.R. § 160.103.

[86] 45 C.F.R. § 164.520(d). The HITECH Regulations modified this provision to clarify that the participants in the OHCA need not all be covered entities, because health care providers who are not covered entities could be included in a clinically integrated care setting. 78 Fed. Reg. 5638 (Jan. 25, 2013).

[87] 45 C.F.R. § 164.506(c)(5).

[88] The term *individual* is used in the Privacy and Security Regulations and this book to refer to the person who is the subject of this PHI. 45 C.F.R. § 164.103.

[89] 45 C.F.R. § 160.103.

[90] 20 U.S.C. § 1232g, as amended. HHS and the Department of Education have jointly released guidance to explain the relationship between HIPAA and FERPA and to "address apparent confusion on the part of school administrators, health care professionals, and others as to how these two laws apply to records maintained on students." "Joint Guidance on the Application of the Family Educational Rights and Privacy Act (FERPA) and the Health Insurance Portability and Accountability Act of 1996 (HIPAA) to Student Health Records" (Nov. 2008), available at http://www.hhs.gov/ocr/privacy/hipaa/understanding/coveredentities/hipaaferpajointguide.pdf.

[91] 45 C.F.R. § 160.103.

[92] 45 C.F.R. § 160.103.

[93] 78 Fed. Reg. 5661 (Jan. 25, 2013).

(and definitions of certain terms used in that definition) has also been added, consistent with the GINA definitions.[94]

The HITECH Regulations made one further change affecting the definition of PHI. PHI no longer includes information relating to individuals who have been deceased for more than 50 years.[95] The purposes of the change were to (1) reduce the burdens on covered entities and on those seeking such information by eliminating the need to locate a personal representative who could authorize the disclosure, and (2) benefit family members, researchers, and historians seeking medical information for personal and public interest reasons.[96] This change does not require covered entities to keep PHI on decedents for 50 years after the individual's death.[97] Nor does it mandate disclosures of this information, once it ceases to be PHI. Finally, although the Privacy and Security Regulations will not apply, covered entities will remain subject to any other applicable legal or ethical requirements with regard to the information of these deceased individuals.

The Privacy Regulations have been in effect for more than a decade, but confusion still arises about how much information it takes to make information into "PHI." HHS provided some helpful guidance on this point in the HITECH Regulations. First, in the context of explaining when liability attaches to a business associate, HHS discussed the scope of "PHI." HHS states that PHI need not necessarily include diagnosis-specific information, such as information about the individual's treatment. It may be demographic or other information that contains no indication of the type of health care services provided to the individual. Nevertheless, if the information is tied to a covered entity, then it is PHI, because it indicates the individual received health care services or benefits from the covered entity.[98] Similarly, the 2012 guidance issued by OCR regarding methods of de-identifying information stated that while identifiers such as names and addresses are not PHI if listed in a publically available source, such as a phone book, if they are combined with "an indication that the individual was treated at a certain clinic, then this information would be PHI."[99]

Furthermore, the HITECH Regulations provided some additional guidance on the meaning of "demographic information," a term not formally defined in the Regulations but used, for example, in the context of describing the types of PHI that are permitted to be used for fundraising (see § 3.04[A]). Demographic information includes (but is not necessarily limited to) names, addresses, other contact information, age, gender, and dates of birth.[100] HHS had previously identified "insurance status" as demographic information but now states that insurance status does not fit in the category of demographic information.[101]

[B]   De-Identified Information

To be *individually identifiable*, PHI must either identify the individual or there must be a *reasonable basis* to believe that the information can be used to identify the individual.[102] *De-identified information* is not PHI and not protected by the Privacy and Security Regulations. This concept of de-identification is of great practical significance, because to the extent de-identified information can be used or disclosed in lieu of PHI, the Privacy and Security Regulations do not apply. As described in more detail below, PHI can be de-identified by either of two methods: by expert determination using the expert/statistical method or by the safe harbor method.[103] With

---

[94] 45 C.F.R. § 160.103.

[95] 45 C.F.R. § 160.103.

[96] 78 Fed. Reg. 5683 (Jan. 25, 2013).

[97] 78 Fed. Reg. 5614 (Jan. 25, 2013).

[98] 78 Fed. Reg. 5598 (Jan. 25, 2013).

[99] OCR, "Guidance Regarding Methods for De-Identification of Protected Information in Accordance with the Health Insurance Portability and Accountability Act (HIPAA) Privacy Rule" (Nov. 12, 2012), Section 1.1, available at http://www.hhs.gov/ocr/privacy/hipaa/understanding/coveredentities/De-identification/guidance.html (hereinafter "De-Identification Guidance").

[100] 78 Fed. Reg. 5621–5622 (Jan. 25, 2013).

[101] 78 Fed. Reg. 5622 (Jan. 25, 2013).

[102] 45 C.F.R. § 160.103.

[103] 45 C.F.R. §§ 164.502(d) and 164.514(a)–(b).

either of these methods a small risk of identification remains, but this information is considered de-identified for purposes of the Privacy and Security Regulations.[104]

Re-identification is a process involving the assignment of a unique code to the de-identified data set to permit later re-identification by the covered entity. This requires that (1) the re-identification code (or other means of re-identification) is not derived from or related to information about the individual and is not otherwise capable of being translated so as to identify the individual, and (2) the covered entity does not use or disclose the code for any other purpose and does not disclose the mechanism for re-identification.[105] Disclosure of a re-identification code is considered a disclosure of PHI.[106] Once information is re-identified, it is once again PHI and protected by the Privacy and Security Regulations.

[1] Expert Determination/Statistical Method

The statistical or expert determination method requires a formal determination by a qualified expert. This requires that a person with appropriate knowledge and experience of generally accepted statistical methods for rendering information into a form that is not individually identifiable applies those methods and principles and determines that the risk is very small that the information could be used alone, or in combination with other reasonably available information, by an anticipated recipient to identify an individual who is a subject of the information. The expert must document the methods used and the results of this analysis that justify a determination that the information is de-identifed.[107]

As required by the HITECH Act, HHS issued guidance on the de-identification of PHI.[108] This guidance is intended to further explain de-identification methods and clarify guidelines on the expert/statistical method so as to reduce covered entities' reliance on the safe harbor method.[109] The guidance covers questions such as:

- What qualifications are required for a person to be an "expert"?

- What is the standard for a "very small" risk of identification?

- How long are expert determinations good for?

The guidance also provides an overview of the workflow for an expert determination.[110]

[2] Safe Harbor Method

The safe harbor method requires that the following data elements identifying the individual (or relatives, employers, or household members of the individual) be removed, and that the covered entity does not have *actual knowledge* that the remaining information could be used alone or in combination with other information to identify the individual:

- Names;

- All geographic subdivisions smaller than a state, including street address, city, county, precinct, zip code, and equivalent codes. The first three digits of the zip code may be retained if certain conditions are met (i.e., the zip code area is not too sparsely populated);

---

[104] De-Identification Guidance, Section 1.3.

[105] 45 C.F.R. § 164.514(c).

[106] De-Identification Guidance, Section 1.4.

[107] 45 C.F.R. § 164.514(b)(1).

[108] HITECH Act § 13424(c). OCR, "Guidance Regarding Methods for De-Identification of Protected Information in Accordance with the Health Insurance Portability and Accountability Act (HIPAA) Privacy Rule" (Nov. 12, 2012), available at http://www.hhs.gov/ocr/privacy/hipaa/understanding/coveredentities/De-identification/guidance.html.

[109] U.S. Government Accountability Office, Report to Congressional Committees, "Prescription Drug Data: HHS Has Issued Health Privacy and Security Regulations but Needs to Improve Guidance and Oversight," GAO-12-605, at 18 (June 2012) (hereinafter June 2012 GAO Report).

[110] De-Identification Guidance, Section 2.

- All elements of dates (except year) if the date is directly related to an individual, including birth date, admission date, discharge date, service date, and date of death, as well as all ages over 89 and all elements of dates (including year) indicative of such age, except that such ages and elements may be aggregated into a single category of age 90 or older;

- Telephone numbers;

- Fax numbers;

- E-mail addresses;

- Social Security numbers;

- Medical record numbers;

- Health plan beneficiary numbers;

- Account numbers;

- Certificate/license numbers;

- Vehicle identifiers and serial numbers, including license plate numbers;

- Device identifiers and serial numbers;

- Web addresses—Universal Resource Locators (URLs);

- Internet Protocol (IP) address numbers;

- Biometric identifiers, including fingerprints and voice prints;

- Full-face photographic images and any comparable images; and

- Any other unique identifying number, characteristic, or code (except a re-identification code).

The de-identification guidance issued by HHS provides some additional information as to what might be included in the last item: "any other unique identifying number, characteristic or code." Identifying numbers could include, for example, a clinical trial record number. An identifying code could include a barcode embedded into an electronic health record or an electronic prescribing system, if that barcode is unique to a patient or service event. An identifying characteristic could be anything that distinguishes an individual (e.g., occupation, if rare or unique, such as "President of the United States").[111]

Information derived from any of the listed identifiers, or parts of the listed identifiers, are not permitted. For example, the individuals' initials or the last four digits of their Social Security Numbers may not be used under the Safe Harbor Method.[112]

The Safe Harbor Method requires that the covered entity not have "actual knowledge" that, after removing the listed identifiers, the remaining information could be used alone or in combination with other information to identify the individual. Actual knowledge means "clear and direct knowledge" that the remaining information could be used to identify the individual. That is, the covered entity is aware that the information is not actually de-identified.[113] Refer to the guidance for additional examples, such as situations involving unique data that would identify an individual, or a particular recipient that would have special knowledge or re-identification tools that would permit identification.

---

[111] De-Identification Guidance, Section 3.5.
[112] De-Identification Guidance, Section 3.2.
[113] De-Identification Guidance, Section 3.5.

[C]   Limited Data Sets

Due to concerns that the de-identification standard was so stringent that it might curtail important research, public health, and health care operations activities, HHS developed the "limited data set" approach for these purposes.

As with the de-identification safe harbor provisions, the Privacy Regulations specify the direct identifiers that must be removed for a data set to qualify as a limited data set. As with de-identified information, the direct identifiers listed apply to PHI about the individual or about relatives, employers, or household members of the individual. The direct identifiers that must be excluded for a limited data set are:

- Name;

- Street address—postal address information, other than town/city, state, and zip code;

- Telephone numbers;

- Fax numbers;

- E-mail addresses;

- Social Security numbers;

- Medical record numbers;

- Health plan beneficiary numbers;

- Account numbers;

- Certificate/license numbers;

- Vehicle identifiers and serial numbers, including license plate numbers;

- Device identifiers and serial numbers;

- Web addresses—Universal Resource Locators (URLs);

- Internet Protocol (IP) address numbers;

- Biometric identifiers, including fingerprints and voiceprints; and

- Full-face photographic images and any other comparable images.[114]

Unlike the list for de-identified information, the list of data elements to be excluded from the limited data set is an exhaustive list. Moreover, in contrast to de-identified data, the limited data set may retain more detailed geographic information (down to the county, city/town, or precinct level and five-digit zip codes) and dates (such as dates of admission and discharge, and dates of birth and death for the individual).[115] Because of this additional information, a limited data set is still PHI.

A covered entity may use or disclose a limited data set only for the purposes of research, public health, and health care operations, and only if the covered entity obtains satisfactory assurances in the form of a data use agreement that the recipient will only use or disclose the limited data set for these limited purposes.[116] See § 3.06[B] for more information about the requirements for data use agreements.

---

[114] 45 C.F.R. § 164.514(e)(2).

[115] 67 Fed. Reg. 53,235 (Aug. 14, 2002).

[116] 45 C.F.R. § 164.514(e)(3)–(e)(4).

§ 1.04 PREEMPTION

In general, the Privacy Regulations will not preempt or be preempted by most other federal or state laws regarding privacy, but a preemption analysis is required to make this determination. Covered entities and business associates will need to comply with a combination of the Privacy Regulations and other relevant state and federal law, including statutes, regulations, and case law. The required preemption analysis is complex, and legal counsel should be consulted; only a summary of the process is included here.

In most cases, state law will be preempted by the Privacy Regulations only if (1) the state law is "contrary to" HIPAA (i.e., it is impossible to comply with both or the state law creates an obstacle to the accomplishment of the full purposes of the Privacy Regulations); and (2) the state law relates to individually identifiable health information and is less stringent than the Privacy Regulations.[117] In comparing state law to the Privacy Regulations, the state law will normally be considered more stringent if it prohibits or restricts a use or disclosure that would be permitted under the Privacy Regulations, permits greater rights of access or amendment to the individual, provides more information to the individual (as in a notice of privacy practices), narrows the scope or duration or otherwise increases the privacy protections of an authorization, requires record keeping in more detail or for longer duration, or, in general, provides more privacy protections for the individual.[118]

For example, some states have laws providing special protections for mental health records. If these are more stringent than the Privacy Regulations, then the state law is not preempted and covered entities must comply with both. A careful analysis of state laws regarding privacy will be required to determine the applicable combination of HIPAA and state requirements.

The Security Regulations generally supersede contrary provisions of state law, including state laws that require medical or health plan records to be maintained or transmitted in written rather than electronic formats.[119]

Other federal laws regarding privacy of health information will generally still apply. Conflicting statutes will be interpreted, where possible, to give effect to both. There should be few instances where there is such a conflict under federal law. However, a covered entity will need to review other applicable federal laws to determine what impact HIPAA will have on compliance. Some of these federal laws include the following:

- Medicare conditions of participation applicable to certain health care providers;[120]

- Federal law regarding confidentiality of substance abuse treatment;[121]

---

[117] 45 C.F.R. §§ 160.202–160.203. State law may also be saved from preemption if the Secretary of HHS determines the state law provision is necessary to prevent fraud and abuse related to the provision of or payment for health care; to ensure appropriate regulation of insurance and health plans; for state reporting on health care delivery costs; for purposes related to a compelling public health and welfare need; or its principal purpose is the regulation of a controlled substance. State laws providing for the reporting of disease, or injury, child abuse, birth, death, or for public health surveillance, investigation, or intervention are also not preempted. Finally, state laws requiring health plans to provide information for management or financial audits, program monitoring and evaluation, or license or certification of facilities or individuals are not preempted. 45 C.F.R. § 160.203. The process of requesting an exception from preemption from the Secretary of HHS is outlined in an HHS OCR Notice. 68 Fed. Reg. 11,554 (Mar. 11, 2003).

[118] 45 C.F.R. § 160.202. HHS has stated that the Administrative Simplification Regulations do not create a federal evidentiary privilege nor give effect to State physician-patient privilege laws or provisions of State law relating to the privacy of individually identifiable health information for use in Federal court proceedings. Therefore, consistent with the Supremacy Clause, any State law that was preempted prior to HIPAA because of conflicts with a Federal law would continue to be preempted. Nothing in HIPAA or its implementing regulations is intended to expand the scope of State laws, regardless of whether they are more or less stringent than Federal law. 75 Fed. Reg. 40,874–75.

[119] 68 Fed. Reg. 8362 (Feb. 20, 2003).

[120] See http://www.cms.hhs.gov/CFCsAndCoPs/ for a list of links according to the type of health care organization.

[121] 42 U.S.C. § 290dd-2; 42 C.F.R. Pt. 2. The HHS Substance Abuse and Mental Health Services Administration (SAMHSA) Center for Substance Abuse Treatment has issued guidance regarding the Privacy Regulations and alcohol and substance abuse programs, The Confidentiality of Alcohol and Drug Abuse Patient Records Regulation and the HIPAA Privacy Rule: Implications for Alcohol and Substance Abuse Programs, available at http://store.samhsa.gov/product/The-Confidentiality-of-Alcohol-and-Drug-Abuse-Patient-Records-Regulation-and-the-HIPAA-Privacy-Rule/PHD1083. Further guidance has been issued by the SAMHSA Legal Action Center and HHS,

- Employee Retirement Security Act of 1974 (ERISA), relating to group health plans;[122]

- Family Educational Rights and Privacy Act (FERPA), relating to school health records;[123]

- Gramm-Leach-Bliley Act (GLBA),[124] imposing privacy requirements on financial institutions, including health insurance companies;

- The Privacy Act of 1974[125] and the Freedom of Information Act,[126] regarding records maintained by federal agencies;

- The Food, Drug, and Cosmetic Act;[127]

- Federal Information Security Management Act of 2002 (FISMA);[128] and

- Genetic Information Nondiscrimination Act of 2008 (GINA).[129]

§ 1.05 COMPLIANCE DATES

This section details the compliance dates for the Privacy Regulations, Security Regulations, and Transaction Standards.

[A] Original Privacy and Security Regulations

The Privacy Regulations were first published December 28, 2000, with revisions published August 14, 2002, and a compliance date of April 14, 2003.[130] The Security Regulations were issued on February 20, 2003, with a compliance date of April 20, 2005.[131]

[B] HITECH Compliance Dates

The HITECH Act was enacted February 17, 2009. Under the terms of the statute, the HITECH Act's privacy and security provisions took effect February 18, 2010, unless otherwise specified. Some of the exceptions include changes to the enforcement regulations, which were effective for violations occurring immediately after

---

titled "Applying Substance Abuse Confidentiality Regulations to Health Information Exchange (HIE)," available at http://www.samhsa.gov/HealthPrivacy/docs/EHR-FAQs.pdf. These regulations were last updated in 1987. In May 2014, SAMHSA announced a public hearing to consider possible changes to these regulations, regarding their applicability, consent requirements, managing redisclosures, medical emergency situations, qualified service organizations, research, and potential issues with electronic prescribing. 79 Fed. Reg. 26929 (May 12, 2014).

[122] Pub. L. No. 93-406. ERISA preemption analysis is not expected to be affected by the Privacy Regulations preemption analysis. 65 Fed. Reg. 82,582 (Dec. 28, 2000).

[123] 20 U.S.C. § 1232g. HHS and the Department of Education have jointly released guidance to explain the relationship between HIPAA and FERPA and to "address apparent confusion on the part of school administrators, health care professionals, and others as to how these two laws apply to records maintained on students." "Joint Guidance on the Application of the Family Educational Rights and Privacy Act (FERPA) and the Health Insurance Portability and Accountability Act of 1996 (HIPAA) to Student Health Records" (Nov. 2008), available at http://www.hhs.gov/ocr/privacy/hipaa/understanding/coveredentities/hipaaferpajointguide.pdf.

[124] Pub. L. No. 106-102.

[125] 5 U.S.C. § 552a.

[126] 5 U.S.C. § 552.

[127] 21 U.S.C. § 301 *et seq.*

[128] 44 U.S.C. § 3541 *et seq.*

[129] H.R. 493, 110th Cong. (2008); Pub. L. No. 110-233; 75 Fed. Reg. 68,912 (Nov. 9, 2010) (final regulations).

[130] 65 Fed. Reg. 82462 (Dec. 28, 2000); 67 Fed. Reg. 53181 (Aug. 4, 2002); 45 C.F.R. § 164.534 (original compliance dates). The Privacy Regulations contained "transition provisions," which grandfathered in certain prior business associate agreements and authorizations or consents already in effect. 45 C.F.R. § 164.532.

[131] 68 Fed. Reg. 8334 (Feb. 20, 2003). 45 C.F.R. § 164.318 (original compliance dates).

enactment of the HITECH statute. Also, interim final rules regarding breach notification were issued in 2009, with compliance required September 23, 2009.[132] For most of the HITECH Act requirements, final regulations were not published until after the statutory compliance date.

In its 2010 proposed HITECH Regulations, HHS acknowledged that compliance with the HITECH Act requirements would be difficult without final implementing regulations from HHS.[133] Therefore, HHS provides covered entities and business associates with 180 days beyond the effective date of the final regulations to come into compliance with most of the regulatory provisions.[134] Although this is a clear signal from HHS regarding its own enforcement intentions, it remains unclear what weight other enforcement actions, such as through the State Attorneys General, will give to the statutory (versus regulatory) compliance dates.

The HITECH Regulations were effective March 26, 2013.[135] Covered entities and business associates may choose to rely on the regulations as of that date. For example, if a covered entity wishes to expand the information it uses in targeted fundraising (see § 3.04[A][2]) or modify its consent practices with regard to student immunization records (see § 3.03[D][2]), it may do so as of March 26, 2013. In addition, the HITECH Regulations that modify the enforcement provisions are effective March 26, 2013.[136]

Compliance with all of the HITECH privacy and security standards is required by September 23, 2013, except that an extension of up to one year applies to certain business associate agreements and data use agreements. The regulatory obligations of business associates (and subcontractor business associates) took effect March 26, 2013; the additional time only applied to the documentation requirements of the business associate agreements. In some cases, covered entities and business associates may prefer to prepare amendments to existing business associate agreements rather than replace them entirely.

Business associate agreements (BAA) entered into before January 25, 2013:

An extension of the compliance date applies if a covered entity, or a business associate with respect to a subcontractor, prior to January 25, 2013, entered into and was operating under a BAA that complied with the BAA standards at the time, and does not renew or modify the BAA between March 26, 2013, and September 23, 2013. These BAAs will be deemed compliant until the earlier of September 22, 2014, or the date on or after September 23, 2013 that the BAA is renewed or modified.[137]

Data use agreements (DUA) involving remuneration, entered into before January 25, 2013:

An extension of the compliance date applies if a covered entity entered into and was operating under a DUA before January 25, 2013. Even if that DUA involves remuneration that would not be permitted under the new HITECH prohibitions on the sale of PHI, the covered entity may nevertheless continue to disclose limited data set information under that DUA, but only until the earlier of September 22, 2014, or the date on or after September 23, 2013 that the DUA is renewed or modified.[138]

The revised Breach Regulations under the HITECH Regulations took effect September 23, 2013. From September 23, 2009, through September 22, 2013, the requirements of the 2009 Breach Regulations apply.[139]

---

[132] 78 Fed. Reg. 5569 (Jan. 25, 2013); see also 74 Fed. Reg. 42740 (Aug. 24, 2009)(IFR breach notification).

[133] 75 Fed. Reg. 40,871 (July 14, 2010).

[134] 78 Fed. Reg. 5569 (Jan. 25, 2013). This 180-day period will be the compliance period for future amendments to privacy and security standards as well, unless a longer compliance period is deemed necessary and expressly stated in the regulation. 78 Fed. Reg. 5569 (Jan. 25, 2013). See § 3.06 for information about business associate agreements.

[135] 78 Fed. Reg. 5569 (Jan. 25, 2013). This effective date applies to all covered entities and business associates; there is no additional compliance period under the HITECH Regulations for small health plans (see § 1.05[D]).

[136] 78 Fed. Reg. 5569 (Jan. 25, 2013).

[137] 45 C.F.R. § 164.532(d)–(e).

[138] 45 C.F.R. § 164.532(f). See § 3.06[B] regarding data use agreements.

[139] 78 Fed. Reg. 5570 (Jan. 25, 2013). See **Chapter 5** regarding breach notification requirements.

[C]   Transaction Standards and Code Sets

The Transaction Standards were published August 17, 2000, and compliance was required by October 16, 2002 (or October 16, 2003, if an extension was requested under the Administrative Simplification Compliance Act).[140] Compliance with the Version 5010 standards was required January 1, 2012, but enforcement was delayed until after June 30, 2012.[141] The ICD-10 code implementation was required October 1, 2013, but a one-year extension was adopted, making the compliance date October 1, 2014.[142] The ICD-10 compliance date was further extended by the Protecting Access to Medicare Act of 2014, with compliance required by October 1, 2015.[143] Many other standards and regulations have been issued with regard to transactions, operating rules, identifiers, and code sets. More information on these standards and regulations, and their compliance dates, can be found in **Chapter 2**.

[D]   Special Rule for Small Health Plans

For small health plans (i.e., health plans with $5 million or less in annual receipts), an additional 12 months was added to each original compliance date for the Privacy, Security, and Standard Transaction Regulations.[144] Compliance dates for subsequent Administrative Simplification Regulations sometimes still provide extra time for small health plans, so this definition of them remains relevant.

HHS issued the following guidance in interpreting what receipts to use to determine whether a health plan qualifies as a small health plan.

Health plans that file certain federal tax returns and report receipts on those returns should use the following guidance provided by the Small Business Administration at 13 C.F.R. § 121.104 to calculate annual receipts. Receipts means "total income" (or in the case of a sole proprietorship, "gross income") plus "cost of goods sold" as these terms are defined or reported on Internal Revenue Service (IRS) federal tax return forms; Form 1120 for corporations; Form 1120S for Subchapter S corporations; Form 1065 for partnerships; and Form 1040, Schedule F for farm or Schedule C for sole proprietorships. However, the term "receipts" excludes net capital gains or losses, taxes collected for and remitted to a taxing authority if included in gross or total income, proceeds from the transactions between a concern and its domestic or foreign affiliates (if also excluded from gross or total income on a consolidated return filed with the IRS), and amounts collected for another by a travel agent, real estate agent, advertising agent, conference management service provider, freight forwarder or customs broker. In calculating receipts under this guidance, health plans should use the definitions and process described at 13 C.F.R. § 121.104(a)(2)-(3) and § 121.104(b).[145]

---

[140] 45 C.F.R. § 162.900 (setting the original Oct. 16, 2002, compliance date). The 2001 Administrative Simplification Compliance Act (ASCA), Pub. L. No. 107-105, extended the compliance date to October 16, 2003, for covered entities that applied for an extension.

[141] CMS Statement (Mar. 15, 2012), formerly available at https://www.cms.gov/Medicare/Coding/ICD10/downloads//Enforcement DiscretionAnnouncement.pdf.

[142] 45 C.F.R. § 162.1002; 77 Fed. Reg. 54,665 (Sep. 5, 2012).

[143] Protecting Access to Medicare Act of 2014 ("PAMA") (Pub. L. No. 113-93) stated that HHS may not adopt the ICD-10 standard prior to October 1, 2015. HHS subsequently issued a final rule, setting October 1, 2015, as the new compliance date and requiring covered entities to continue use of the ICD-9 codes until then. 79 Fed. Reg. 45,128 (Aug. 4, 2014).

[144] 45 C.F.R. § 160.103 (definition of Small Health Plan); 45 C.F.R. § 164.318 (Security Regulations); 45 C.F.R. § 164.534 (Privacy Regulations); 45 C.F.R. § 162.900 (Transaction Standards). The $5 million figure originally came from the Small Business Administration's (SBA's) definition of a "small business concern." The SBA has since modified this definition to include entities with $6 million or less in annual receipts. This change does not affect the HIPAA definition, because the SBA definition was not specifically adopted by HIPAA but only used as guidance. CMS HIPAA FAQ #1212, formerly available at http://questions.cms.hhs.gov.

[145] CMS HIPAA FAQ #1183, formerly available at http://questions.cms.hhs.gov; OCR HIPAA FAQ, available at http://www.hhs.gov/ocr/privacy/hipaa/faq/covered_entities/368.html.

Generally, *group health plans* will not fall within the above rule. Group health plans, which include ERISA group health plans sponsored by an employer, should instead use "proxy" measures to determine their annual receipts, as follows:

Fully insured health plans should use the amount of total premiums which they paid for health insurance benefits during the plan's last full fiscal year.

Self-insured health plans, both funded and unfunded, should use the total amount paid for health care claims by the employer, plan sponsor or benefit fund, as applicable to their circumstances, on behalf of the plan during the plan's last full fiscal year.

Those plans that provide health benefits through a mix of purchased insurance and self-insurance should combine the proxy measures to determine their total annual receipts.[146]

That is, a "mixed" health plan should add the insurance premiums for the insured portion and the claims paid for the self-insured portion to determine the total annual receipts. Premiums for stop-loss insurance purchased for self-insured plans are not included in calculating receipts.

For an employer who is the sponsor of group health plans, a key aspect of the above calculation is determining how many separate health plans (i.e., how many covered entities) comprise the benefits offered to employees. Employers should review their plan documents and annual Form 5500 filings in making this determination.

---

[146] CMS HIPAA FAQ #1183, formerly available at http://questions.cms.hhs.gov; OCR HIPAA FAQ, available at http://www.hhs.gov/ocr/privacy/hipaa/faq/covered_entities/368.html.

CHAPTER 2

ELECTRONIC TRANSACTIONS AND HEALTH INFORMATION EXCHANGES

§ 2.01 THE TRANSACTIONS

The core of HIPAA Administrative Simplification is the standardization of common electronic transactions, identifiers, and code sets. When HIPAA was enacted in 1996, health plans and health care providers were struggling to move toward automating certain common transactions, because electronic data interchange (EDI) was believed to be faster and more cost-effective than paper-based transactions. One of the obstacles to EDI in health care was the fact that there were hundreds of custom formats for these transactions and little standardization. Congress enacted the Administrative Simplification provisions of HIPAA to address this problem. Under the HIPAA Transaction Standards, health plans must be prepared to accept the most common electronic transactions in standardized formats, using standardized identifiers and codes. Providers may continue to conduct such transactions on paper, but if the transactions are conducted electronically, the standards must be followed.[1] This need for standardization is well accepted today.

A complete and detailed description of the Transaction Standards is beyond the scope of this book, but a summary of the key provisions is provided below.

HIPAA defines a *transaction* as the "exchange of information between two parties to carry out financial or administrative activities related to health care."[2] In August 2000, final regulations for the content and format of the most common transactions (the first "standard transactions") were published.[3] Currently, standards have been established for the following health care–related standard transactions:[4]

Standard Transactions

ASC X12 837 D	Health care claims—Dental
ASC X12 837 P	Health care claims—Professional
ASC X12 837 I	Health care claims—Institutional
NCPDP D.0 and Version 1.2	Health care claims—Retail pharmacy drug
ASC X12 837 P and NCPDP D.0 and Version 1.2	Health care claims—Retail pharmacy supplies and professional services
NCPDP D.0 and Version 1.2	Coordination of Benefits—Retail pharmacy drug
ASC X12 837 D	Coordination of Benefits—Dental
ASC X12 837 P	Coordination of Benefits—Professional
ASC X12 837 I	Coordination of Benefits—Institutional
ASC X12 270/271	Eligibility for a health plan (request and response)—Dental, professional, and institutional
NCPDP D.0 and Version 1.2	Eligibility for a health plan (request and response)—Retail pharmacy drugs
ASC X12 276/277	Health care claim status (request and response)
ASC X12 834	Enrollment and disenrollment in a health plan
ASC X12 835	Health care payment and remittance advice (CCD+ Addenda)

---

[1] 45 C.F.R. §§ 160.923–160.930.
[2] 45 C.F.R. § 160.103.
[3] 65 Fed. Reg. 50,311 (Aug. 17, 2000) (codified, as amended, at 45 C.F.R. Pts. 160 and 162).
[4] 77 Fed. Reg. 48,010–48,011 (Aug. 10, 2012).

ASC X12 820	Health plan premium payment
ASC X12 278	Referral certification and authorization (request and response)—Dental, professional, and institutional
NCPDP D.0 and Version 1.2	Referral certification and authorization (request and response)—Retail pharmacy drugs
NCPDP 3.0	Medicaid pharmacy subrogation (batch standard).

By 2009, the original versions of the transaction standards were widely recognized by the health care industry as outdated and lacking needed functionality. In response to industry concerns and recommendations, the Department of Health and Human Services (HHS) issued revised standards for these transactions that address technical, business, and policy issues.[5] The updated standards are the ASCX12 Technical Reports Type 3 (TR), version 005010, and are simply referred to as "Version 5010." In addition, the last standard listed above is a new standard adopted for Medicaid pharmacy subrogation claims.

The compliance date for the Version 5010 standards was January 1, 2012. However, the Centers for Medicare & Medicaid Services (CMS) delayed enforcement until after June 30, 2012.[6] The compliance dates were intended to give the industry enough time for all necessary system updates, internal testing, and testing with trading partners. But CMS decided to delay enforcement because covered entities were having difficulty achieving full implementation.[7]

As of January 1, 2014, two new standards are effective with respect to electronic fund transfers (EFT) and remittance advice. One standard is for the format used when a health plan initiates an EFT with its financial institution, and the other specifies the data content.[8] In 2010, the Patient Protection and Affordable Care Act (ACA) required that HHS establish a standard for electronic fund transfers, to be effective no later than January 1, 2014.[9] A health plan's EFT to a provider may be sent separately from the remittance advice explaining the payment, making it difficult for the provider to match up the payment to the corresponding claim. HHS issued an interim final rule in January 2012, which is intended to solve this problem by requiring the use of a trace number that automatically matches the EFT and the remittance notice, and eliminating the current manual reconciliation process.[10] All health plans must comply with this new standard as of January 1, 2014.[11]

Standards for other transactions will be issued at a later date. These include a standard for claims attachments. A proposed rule setting standards for electronic health care claims attachments was published in September 2005 and was scheduled to be finalized in September 2008.[12] However, in response to industry comments that it would not be feasible to implement Version 5010 at the same time as a new claims attachment standard, HHS delayed publication of the claims attachment standard and stated that it would take these concerns into consideration when determining a new publication date for the claims attachment standards.[13] The

---

[5] 74 Fed. Reg. 3296 (Jan. 16, 2009).

[6] CMS Statement (Mar. 15, 2012), formerly available at http://www.cms.gov/Medicare/Coding/ICD10/downloads//Enforcement Discretion Announcement.pdf. The compliance date for the new Medicaid pharmacy subrogation standards was also January 1, 2012, with enforcement delayed to July 1, 2012 (for small health plans the compliance date is January 1, 2013).

[7] CMS Statement (Mar. 15, 2012), formerly available at http://www.cms.gov/Medicare/Coding/ICD10/downloads// EnforcementDiscretionAnnouncement.pdf.

[8] 77 Fed. Reg. 1556 (Jan. 10, 2012).

[9] Patient Protection and Affordable Care Act (ACA), Pub. L. No. 111-148, Title I, § 1104(c) (2010).

[10] HHS News Release, "Affordable Care Act Provision Cuts Red Tape, Saves Up to $4.5 Billion" (Jan. 5, 2012), available at https://wayback.archive-it.org/3926/20150121155608/http://www.hhs.gov/news/press/2012pres/01/20120105a.html.

[11] 77 Fed. Reg. 1556 (Jan. 10, 2012).

[12] 70 Fed. Reg. 55,990 (Sept. 23, 2005); HHS Regulatory Agenda, 72 Fed. Reg. 22,563 (Apr. 30, 2007).

[13] 74 Fed. Reg. 3306 (Jan. 16, 2009).

ACA, however, now requires HHS to issue regulations establishing the claims attachment standard, to be effective no later than January 1, 2016.[14]

Many of these transactions are defined, in part, by who the parties to the transaction are. For example, a health care payment is a transmission from a health plan to a health care provider. In 2009, HHS revised the descriptions of certain transactions (enrollment and disenrollment, referral certification and authorization, and claims status) to more clearly specify the senders and receivers.[15] This information can help in analyzing whether an entity is or is not conducting one of these transactions. For example, CMS has clarified that if an individual uses a debit card issued by a Health Flexible Spending Account plan to pay a co-pay or other out-of-pocket expense at a pharmacy or provider's office, this is not a standard transaction, because it is considered to be a transaction between the individual and the provider, not a payment from the health plan to the provider (even though the plan is reimbursing the expense through the use of the card). It is considered comparable to the individual using a conventional credit card.[16]

§ 2.02 IDENTIFIERS AND CODE SETS

Standard transactions require standardized identifiers and code sets.

[A] Identifiers

HIPAA requires the development of unique identifiers for health care providers, employers, health plans, and individuals for use in standard transactions.

[1] Providers

A standard unique national identifier for health care providers has been adopted—the National Provider Identifier (NPI).[17] The NPI is a 10-digit number with no embedded information regarding the provider.[18] The compliance date for covered entities to convert to the NPI was May 23, 2007 (May 23, 2008, for small health plans). The NPI is now the only provider identifier that may be used to identify the provider in a standard transaction.[19] *Legacy identifiers*, such as Unique Physician Identification Numbers (UPINs), Medicaid Provider Numbers, and Medicare Provider Numbers, may no longer be used as provider identifiers in standard transactions but may still be used for other purposes (e.g., internal records).[20] In addition to requiring use of the NPI on standard transactions, CMS has since 2006 required providers to report their NPIs on their Medicare enrollment applications. CMS has now extended this to Medicaid, requiring that providers who are eligible for an NPI include their NPIs on all Medicaid enrollment applications.[21]

Under the NPI regulations, only providers who are covered entities are required to obtain an NPI and disclose it for purposes of conducting standard transactions. This creates a problem for pharmacies when they need to include the NPI of the prescriber on a pharmacy claim and the pharmacy does not have the NPI because the provider is not a covered entity.[22] This situation most commonly arises with hospital-based providers who

---

[14] ACA, Pub. L. No. 111-148, Title I, § 1104(c) (2010).

[15] 74 Fed. Reg. 3301 (Jan. 16, 2009).

[16] CMS HIPAA FAQ #1821, formerly available at http://questions.cms.hhs.gov; CMS HIPAA FAQ # 2350, formerly available at http://questions.cms.hhs.gov.

[17] 69 Fed. Reg. 3434 (Jan. 23, 2004).

[18] 45 C.F.R. § 162.406. The NPI itself does not contain any information, such as provider specialty, state/location, etc.

[19] 45 C.F.R. §§ 162.404, 162.410, 162.412, and 162.414.

[20] CMS HIPAA FAQ #2632, formerly available at http://questions.cms.hhs.gov. Where a health care provider must be identified in a standard transaction for tax purposes, it would continue to use its Taxpayer Identification Number.

[21] 42 C.F.R. § 431.107; 75 Fed. Reg. 24,437 (May 5, 2010).

[22] 77 Fed. Reg. 54,665, 54,680 (Sept. 5, 2012).

staff emergency departments and clinics, medical residents and interns, and members of group practices whose services are billed under the group's NPI.[23] The NPI regulations were revised in 2012 to address this issue. Effective May 6, 2013, if an individual provider who *is not* a covered entity has a member, employee, or contractual relationship with an organizational provider that *is* a covered entity, and he or she writes prescriptions in the scope of that relationship, the organizational provider must require the individual provider to obtain an NPI and disclose it as needed to identify the prescriber in standard transactions.[24] It is left up to the organizational provider to determine how to accomplish this, but it could be addressed in the terms of employment or other contracts, or in the policies of the organizational provider, as appropriate.

Large and complex provider organizations may need to obtain separate NPIs for subparts of the organization. To assist providers with this process, CMS issued a white paper in January 2006, entitled "Medicare Expectations on Determinations of Subparts by Medicare Organization Health Care Providers Who Are Covered Entities Under HIPAA."[25] Although a health plan may require that its enrolled health care providers obtain and use NPIs, it may not require a health care provider with an NPI to obtain additional NPIs.[26] Once a health care provider receives its NPI, changes to the NPI application information, such as a change in location, must be reported within 30 days.[27]

CMS makes NPI records available through the new National Plan and Provider Enumeration System (NPPES).[28] Anyone may request data from NPPES. NPPES data are available on the Internet, both by an online searchable database and by downloadable files. All the data in NPPES about each enumerated provider are made public, with three exceptions: Social Security numbers, individual taxpayer identification numbers, and dates of birth. HHS believes that the remaining data elements are sufficient to match provider records.[29]

Because the NPI data are now publicly available through NPPES, health care entities, including health plans and large provider organizations that maintain NPIs for many providers, may freely disclose their NPI data to trading partners and others to conduct standard transactions. Furthermore, health plans and other health care entities may disclose NPIs in directories and listings for purposes of appropriately using the NPIs in standard transactions.[30]

[2] Employers

A final rule was published that adopts the Employer Identification Number (EIN) assigned by the Internal Revenue Service as the standard employer identifier for use in standard transactions, effective July 30, 2002.[31]

[3] Health Plans

The ACA set a new deadline for the long-delayed national identifier for health plans. Under the ACA, HHS was directed to issue a final regulation establishing a unique health plan identifier, to be effective no later

---

[23] 77 Fed. Reg. 54,681 (Sept. 5, 2012).

[24] 77 Fed. Reg. 54,665, 54,680 (Sept. 5, 2012); 45 C.F.R. § 162.410.

[25] Available at http://www.cms.gov/Regulations-and-Guidance/HIPAA-Administrative-Simplification/NationalProvIdentStand/downloads/Medsubparts01252006.pdf.

[26] 69 Fed. Reg. 3450 (Jan. 23, 2004); 45 C.F.R. § 162.4⌐⌐.

[27] 45 C.F.R. § 162.410(a)(4).

[28] 72 Fed. Reg. 22,546 (Apr. 30, 2007); 30,011 (May 30, 2007). Updates have since been made to the NPPES to create additional functionality.

[29] 72 Fed. Reg. 22,546 (Apr. 30, 2007); 30,012 (May 30, 2007). For the searchable files, see https://nppes.cms.hhs.gov. For the downloadable database, see http://nppes.viva-it.com/NPI_Files.html.

[30] Disclosure of National Provider Identifiers (NPIs) by Health Care Industry Entities to Other Health Care Industry Entities (hereinafter Disclosure Guidance), available at http://www.cms.gov/Regulations-and-Guidance/HIPAA-Administrative-Simplification/NationalProvIdentStand/downloads/NPIdisclosures.pdf.

[31] 45 C.F.R. §§ 162.600 *et seq.*; 67 Fed. Reg. 38,009 (May 31, 2002). Compliance date is 12 months later for small health plans.

than October 1, 2012.[32] On September 5, 2012, HHS issued a final regulation for standards for a national health plan identifier (HPID).[33] All covered entities are required to use an HPID when identifying a health plan in a standard transaction, effective November 7, 2016. Health plans are required to obtain an HPID by November 5, 2014.[34] An HPID can be obtained through the Health Plan and Other Entity Enumeration System (HPOES).[35]

HHS provides some flexibility as to how health plans are enumerated and establishes the concepts of "controlling health plans" (CHP) and "subhealth plans" (SHP) for certain related organizations. A CHP is a health plan that controls its own business activities or is controlled by an entity that is not a health plan. An SHP is a health plan with business activities that are controlled by a CHP.[36] A CHP is required to obtain an HPID. A SHP is eligible but not required to obtain an HPID.[37] HHS also establishes an optional "other entity identifier" (OEID) that can be used to identify third-party administrators, clearinghouses, and other non–health plan entities that may need to be identified in standard transactions.[38] To assist health plans, CMS published HPID FAQs that address questions that relate to what types of plans must obtain an HPID, the difference between a health plan and a payer, the use of the HPID in standard transactions, and more.[39]

Due to concerns about this HPID enumeration structure and the use of the HPID in transactions, the National Committee on Vital and Health Statistics (NCVHS), an advisory body to HHS, on September 23, 2014, recommended that HHS revise its rulemaking so that the HPID would not be used in standard transactions and clarify the use of the HPID. CMS announced an enforcement delay on October 31, 2014, for the HPID "until further notice," to consider this recommendation.[40] On May 29, 2015, CMS published a Request for Information requesting input from health plans to determine what changes would be advisable to existing requirements regarding HPID enumeration and the use of the HPID in standard transactions, before moving forward with implementation of the HPID.[41]

[4] Individuals

The development of the individual identifier has been indefinitely suspended due to privacy concerns. Congress has consistently passed appropriations bills that prohibit expenditures for the promulgation or adoption of a unique health care identifier for individuals, until Congress passes legislation specifically approving a particular standard.[42]

[B] Code Sets

The regulations also establish standard code sets, which are the codes to be used in the standard transactions to convey key information. Many of these code sets have already been adopted by the health care system. They include the following medical code sets:

- ICD-10-CM diagnosis codes;

---

[32] ACA, Pub. L. No. 111-148, Title I, § 1104(c) (2010).

[33] 77 Fed. Reg. 54,664 (Sept. 5, 2012).

[34] 45 C.F.R. §§ 162.103, 162.504, 162.510; 77 Fed. Reg. 54,664–54,665 (Sept. 5, 2012). "Small health plans" (see § 1.05[D]) have until November 5, 2015, to obtain an HPID.

[35] More information about this process is available from CMS at http://www.cms.gov/Regulations-and-Guidance/HIPAA-Administrative-Simplification/Affordable-Care-Act/Health-Plan-Identifier.html.

[36] 45 C.F.R. § 162.103.

[37] 45 C.F.R. § 162.512.

[38] 45 C.F.R. § 162.514.

[39] CMS, Frequently Asked Questions, available at https://questions.cms.gov/faq.php?id=5005&rtopic=1851&rsubtopic=8230.

[40] See the CMS "Statement of Enforcement Discretion" at http://www.cms.gov/regulations-and-guidance/HIPAA-Administrative-Simplification/affordable-care-act/Health-Plan-Identifier.html.

[41] 80 Fed. Reg. 30646 (May 29, 2015).

[42] See, e.g., 1999 Omnibus Appropriations Act, PL 105-277, Sec. 516; 2010 Consolidated Appropriations Act, PL 111-117, Sec. 511.

- ICD-10-PCS inpatient procedure codes;

- NDC national drug codes for drugs and biologics in retail pharmacy transactions;

- CDT dental procedure codes;

- HCPCS and CPT-4 service codes; and

- HCPCS supply/equipment codes.[43]

The original standard code sets for diagnoses and for inpatient hospital procedures will be changed to the ICD-10-CM and ICD-10-PCS coding systems, respectively. Originally, the ICD-10 compliance date was set at October 1, 2013, but it was delayed until October 1, 2014.[44] Congress delayed it further by a provision in the Protecting Access to Medicare Act of 2014 (PAMA), which states that HHS may not adopt the ICD-10 standard prior to October 1, 2015.[45] HHS confirmed this by issuing a final rule setting October 1, 2015, as the ICD-10 compliance date and requiring covered entities to continue using the ICD-9 codes until that date.[46]

There are also nonmedical code sets (e.g., provider taxonomy codes for identifying provider type and specialization, claims status codes, state abbreviation codes, and zip codes).[47]

§ 2.03 TRANSACTION REQUIREMENTS

The general rule is that if a covered entity conducts one of the transactions listed in § 2.01 with another covered entity (or within the same covered entity) using electronic media,[48] the covered entity must conduct the transaction as a standard transaction (i.e., according to the Transaction Standards).[49] The standards may not be modified by the covered entity engaged in the transaction. The following additional rules apply to health plans:

1. If an entity requests a health plan to conduct a transaction as a standard transaction, the health plan must do so.

2. A health plan may not delay or reject a transaction, or attempt to adversely affect the other entity or the transaction, because the transaction is a standard transaction.

3. A health plan may not reject a standard transaction on the basis that it contains data elements not needed or used by the health plan (e.g., coordination of benefits information).

4. A health plan may not offer an incentive for a health care provider to conduct a transaction as a direct data entry transaction.

5. A health plan that operates as a clearinghouse or requires an entity to use a clearinghouse to receive, process, or transmit a standard transaction may not charge fees or costs in excess of the fees or costs

---

[43] 45 C.F.R. Pt. 162, subpt. J.

[44] 74 Fed. Reg. 3328 (Jan. 16, 2009); 77 Fed. Reg. 54,664 (Sept. 5, 2012).

[45] Protecting Access to Medicare Act of 2014 (PAMA) (Pub. L. No. 113-93).

[46] 79 Fed. Reg. 45,128 (Aug. 4, 2014).

[47] CMS, HIPAA Information Series: 4. Overview of Electronic Transactions & Code Sets (May 2003), formerly available at http://www.cms.gov/Regulations-and-Guidance/HIPAA-Administrative-Simplification/EducationMaterials/downloads/Whateelectronictransactionsandcodesets-4.pdf.

[48] "Electronic media" means electronic storage material, such as computer hard drives and any removable or transportable digital memory medium, such as magnetic tape or disk, optical disk, or digital memory card; and transmission media used to exchange information already in electronic storage media, such as Internet, extranet, intranet, leased lines, dial-up lines, private networks, and physical movement of electronic storage media. 45 C.F.R. § 160.103; 78 Fed. Reg. 5575 (Jan. 25, 2013).

[49] 45 C.F.R. §§ 162.923–162.930.

for normal telecommunications that the entity incurs when it directly transmits or receives a standard transaction to or from a health plan.[50]

A health plan must also meet each of the following requirements regarding code sets: (1) accept and promptly process any standard transaction that contains codes that are valid (as defined by these regulations) and (2) keep code sets for the current billing period (and appeals periods still open to processing under the terms of the health plan's coverage).[51]

The HIPAA Implementation Guides contain detailed implementation specifications for each standard transaction and have been provided to assist covered entities with developing software to comply with the Transaction Standards.[52] There is a separate Implementation Guide for each of the standard transactions. These Implementation Guides are very detailed. They are essential to implementation of the Transaction Standards. The shortcomings of the original transaction standards caused industry-wide difficulties and led to the development of "companion guides" and proprietary workarounds in addition to the Implementation Guides. Version 5010, with its clearer situational rules, is intended to minimize the need for these companion guides. Under Version 5010, HHS does not prohibit, but strongly discourages, the use of companion guides.[53]

The transaction standards were designed to create uniformity but still be flexible; however, that flexibility led to inconsistencies in how the standard transactions were implemented. Health plans created their own unique "companion guides" to establish response times, system availability, communication protocols, security practices, hours of operation, and other business practices. Providers had to vary their practices accordingly, depending on the health plan with which the provider was conducting the standard transaction. Under the ACA, Congress requires HHS to adopt a single set of "operating rules" to accompany each transaction standard and create uniform business rules that make the companion guides unnecessary.[54] These operating rules address "the rights and responsibilities of all parties, security requirements, transmission formats, response times, liabilities, exception processing, error resolution, and more, in order to facilitate successful interoperability between data systems of different entities."[55]

The first operating rules were for health plan eligibility transactions and health care claims status transactions, with compliance required by January 1, 2013.[56] CMS published operating rules for the electronic fund transfer and remittance advice transactions in August 2012, with compliance required by January 1, 2014.[57] Additional operating rules will be issued for health care claims, health plan enrollments and disenrollment, health claims attachments, health plan premium payments, and referrals and authorizations.[58] Health plans will be required to certify compliance with the Transaction Standards and operating rules, or penalties may be assessed.[59]

---

[50] 45 C.F.R. § 162.925(a). In addition, if a health plan receives a standard transaction and coordinates benefits with another health plan (or another payer), it must store the coordination of benefits data it needs to forward the standard transaction to the other health plan (or other payer). 45 C.F.R. § 162.925(b).

[51] 45 C.F.R. § 162.925(c).

[52] See 45 C.F.R. § 162.920.

[53] 74 Fed. Reg. 3297–3298; 3307–3308 (Jan.16, 2009).

[54] 76 Fed. Reg. 40,460 (July 8, 2011).

[55] 76 Fed. Reg. 40,458 (July 8, 2011).

[56] 76 Fed. Reg. 40,458 (July 8, 2011). Because most providers were not ready on January 1, 2013, HHS delayed enforcement of these operating rules until March 31, 2013. "CMS Announces 90-Day Period of Enforcement Discretion for Compliance with Eligibility and Claims Status Operating Rules," available at http://www.cms.gov/Outreach-and-Education/Outreach/OpenDoorForums/Downloads/010213Sec1104ofACAAnnouncement.pdf.

[57] 77 Fed. Reg. 48,008 (Aug. 10, 2012).

[58] CMS, "Engagement with Standards and Operating Rules," available at http://www.cms.gov/Regulations-and-Guidance/HIPAA-Administrative-Simplification/Affordable-Care-Act/IndustryStakeholderEngagement.html.

[59] ACA, Pub. L. No. 111-148, Title I, § 1104(b) (2010). On January 2, 2014, HHS published a proposed rule relating to requirements for health plans to certify compliance. Initially, Controlling Health Plans would need to submit documentation demonstrating compliance with the adopted standards and operating rules for eligibility transactions, health care claims status, and EFT/remittance advice, on or before December 31, 2015. 79 Fed. Reg. 298 (Jan. 2, 2014). A final regulation may be issued in 2015 but will likely follow clarification of the health plan identifier requirements.

§ 2.04   TRADING PARTNERS

Those parties with whom a covered entity exchanges information in a HIPAA standard transaction are referred to as trading partners. Trading partners may enter into agreements regarding this exchange or transfer of information, but that agreement may not attempt to circumvent the Transaction Standards by establishing alternatives to the HIPAA-mandated format, content, identifiers, code sets, or operating rules.[60]

§ 2.05   ELECTRONIC MEDICARE CLAIMS

The Administrative Simplification Compliance Act (ASCA) requires that all Medicare claims be submitted to CMS electronically in a HIPAA-compliant manner as of October 16, 2003.[61] Certain exceptions apply, including an exception for small health care providers, defined as either (1) Medicare providers (e.g., hospitals or skilled nursing facilities) with fewer than 25 full-time equivalent employees or (2) Medicare suppliers (e.g., physician groups) with fewer than 10 full-time equivalent employees.[62]

ASCA's requirement of electronic submission of Medicare claims means that most providers cannot avoid covered entity status under HIPAA by submitting only paper claims. A health care provider is a covered entity under the Privacy Regulations and Security Regulations if it meets the regulations' definition of *health care provider* and also engages in at least one electronic transaction enumerated under the Transaction Standards. As a result, a health care provider who was not a covered entity, because it chose not to conduct any electronic transactions, is now required to bill Medicare electronically (unless it meets an exception). This electronic billing will bring the provider within the definition of *covered entity*, triggering the need to also comply with the Privacy Regulations and Security Regulations.[63]

---

[60] 45 C.F.R. § 162.915.

[61] Pub. L. No. 107-105; 42 C.F.R. § 424.32(d)(2).

[62] 42 C.F.R. §§ 424.32(d)(1)(viii), 424.32(d)(3)(ii), and 424.32(d)(4); see also Medicare Claims Processing Manual, Pub. L. No. 100-04, Ch. 24, §§ 90 and 90.5.1.

[63] CMS HIPAA FAQ #1572, formerly available at http://questions.cms.hhs.gov.

CHAPTER 3

PRIVACY REGULATIONS

§ 3.01 PURPOSE AND GENERAL PRINCIPLES

The Privacy Regulations provide the first comprehensive federal protection for the privacy of health care information and have had a profound effect on the operations of covered entities and business associates.[1] The Privacy Regulations control the internal uses and the external disclosures of protected health information (PHI).[2] Covered entities and business associates may not use or disclose an individual's PHI, except as permitted or required by the Privacy Regulations.[3] The Privacy Regulations also create certain individual rights, establish administrative requirements, and mandate that covered entities enter into contracts with their business associates to maintain protection of health information that is shared. The Department of Health and Human Services (HHS) explained the purpose of the Privacy Regulations this way:

> This regulation has three major purposes: (1) to protect and enhance the rights of consumers by providing them access to their health information and controlling the inappropriate use of that information; (2) to improve the quality of health care in the U.S. by restoring trust in the health care system among consumers, health care professionals, and the multitude of organizations and individuals committed to the delivery of care; and (3) to improve the efficiency and effectiveness of health care delivery by creating a national framework for health privacy protection that builds on efforts by states, health systems, and individual organizations and individuals.[4]

The 2013 HITECH Regulations made significant changes to the Privacy Regulations as part of the implementation of the HITECH Act and also under the general HIPAA rulemaking authority of HHS.[5] These changes are addressed, where applicable, throughout this chapter, and summarized in **Appendix A**.

Most of this chapter is dedicated to explaining the rights of individuals, and what uses and disclosures are permitted under the Privacy Regulations. But first, a discussion of some key principles that impact those uses and disclosures.

[A] Minimum Necessary

Reasonable steps must be taken by covered entities and business associates to limit uses and disclosures to the minimum amount of PHI required to accomplish the intended purpose.[6] The idea is to avoid using or disclosing more of the individual's health information than is truly necessary, and to make covered entities and business associates evaluate their practices and limit the amount of information used or disclosed as appropriate to the circumstances.

There are exceptions to the minimum necessary rule. The requirement does not apply to disclosures to a health care provider for treatment purposes, disclosures to individuals of their own PHI, uses or disclosures made in accordance with an individual's authorization, disclosures to HHS regarding compliance or enforcement, or uses and disclosures required by law.[7]

A covered entity or business associate must determine the persons or classes of persons within its workforce who need access to PHI to carry out their job duties, the categories or types of PHI needed, and conditions appropriate to such access. A covered entity must develop policies and procedures for uses and disclosures that identify the amount of information that is required. When access to the individual's entire medical record is necessary, the policy should state this explicitly and provide the justification. For routine and recurring disclosure situations, the policies and procedures may be standard protocols. For nonroutine uses and disclosures, the

---

[1] See **§ 1.02** for an explanation of who is a covered entity and who is, or is not, a business associate.

[2] See **§ 1.03[A]** for a definition of protected health information.

[3] 45 C.F.R. 164.502(a).

[4] 65 Fed. Reg. 82,463 (Dec. 28, 2000).

[5] 78 Fed. Reg. 5566 (Jan. 25, 2013).

[6] 45 C.F.R. § 164.502(b); HHS OCR Guidance on the Privacy Regulations, available at http://www.hhs.gov/ocr/privacy/hipaa/understanding/coveredentities/privacyguidance.html (hereinafter OCR Guidance).

[7] 45 C.F.R. § 164.502(b); OCR Guidance (Minimum Necessary).

covered entity must develop reasonable criteria for making the determination as to what will be considered the minimum necessary information for the specific purpose and review disclosures in accordance with these criteria.[8]

The HITECH Act provides that a covered entity is in compliance with the minimum necessary standard only if it makes reasonable efforts to limit uses, disclosures, and requests for PHI, to the extent practicable, to the limited data set (see § 1.03[C]) or, if needed by the covered entity, to the minimum necessary to accomplish the intended purpose of such use, disclosure, or request.[9] This "limited data set" standard is a new interim standard, and HHS will issue future guidance. In the meantime, this interim standard changes the process for determining what is the minimum necessary by requiring the use of the limited data set (which contains no direct identifiers) as the starting point, rather than taking a larger set of PHI as the starting point and paring it back to the minimum necessary.

The HITECH Regulations explicitly extend this requirement to business associates, stating that business associates are directly responsible for making reasonable efforts to limit PHI to the minimum necessary to accomplish the intended use, disclosure, or request.[10] HHS reasoned that, because a determination of the minimum necessary PHI is integral to the permissibility of a use or disclosure, the business associate would not be making a permitted use or disclosure if this standard were not applied, as appropriate.[11] The HITECH Act indicated that a business associate disclosing PHI was responsible for making the "minimum necessary" determination with respect to that disclosure.[12] Under the HITECH Regulations, HHS interpreted this to mean that the business associate's uses, disclosures, and requests must be consistent with the covered entity's minimum necessary policies and procedures.[13] HHS has promised to issue guidance with regard to a business associate's application of the minimum necessary standard.[14]

The Privacy Regulations provide that, in certain circumstances, a covered entity or business associate may rely on the judgment of the party requesting the disclosure as to the minimum amount of information needed. Such reliance must be reasonable under the particular circumstances of the request. This reliance is permitted when the request is made by:

- A public official, for a disclosure permitted under 45 C.F.R. § 164.512 (e.g., public health disclosures or disclosures for law enforcement) if the public official represents that the amount requested is the minimum required for the purpose;

- Another covered entity, because covered entities are required to limit their requests to what they determine to be the minimum necessary information for the purpose;

- A professional who is a workforce member or business associate of the covered entity, for the purpose of providing professional services to the covered entity, if the professional represents that the PHI requested is the minimum required for the stated purpose; or

- A researcher with appropriate documentation from an Institutional Review Board (IRB) or Privacy Board.[15]

---

[8] 45 C.F.R. § 164.514(d); OCR Guidance (Minimum Necessary).

[9] HITECH Act § 13405(b). The HITECH Act required HHS to issue guidance by August 17, 2010, on what constitutes "minimum necessary," which takes into consideration HHS guidance regarding de-identified information, and the information necessary to improve patient outcomes and to detect, prevent, and manage chronic disease. This "minimum necessary" guidance has been delayed, but once it is issued, the Act's use of the limited data set as the starting point of the minimum necessary analysis may no longer apply. HITECH Act § 13405(b).

[10] 45 C.F.R. 164.502(b); 78 Fed. Reg. 5591 (Jan. 25, 2013).

[11] 78 Fed. Reg. 5599 (Jan. 25, 2013).

[12] HITECH Act § 13405(b)(2).

[13] 78 Fed. Reg. 5599 (Jan. 25, 2013).

[14] 78 Fed. Reg. 5599 (Jan. 25, 2013).

[15] 45 C.F.R. § 164.514(d) 78 Fed. Reg. 5599 (Jan. 25, 2013).

The Privacy Regulations allow but do not require such reliance on another party's determination.[16]

[B] Verification of Identity

Prior to making a disclosure permitted under the Privacy Regulations, the covered entity must verify the identity and authority of the person requesting the PHI, whether it is an individual requesting access to his or her own records or another person asking for a disclosure of PHI.[17]

An exception is made for the disclosures to family and caregivers and facility directory disclosures described in **§ 3.03[C]**, if the covered entity relies on the exercise of professional judgment in making these disclosures.[18] In addition, the verification requirement is considered met in the case of a permitted disclosure made to avert a serious threat to health or safety (see **§ 3.03[D][10]**), if the covered entity acts on a good faith belief in making the disclosure.[19]

The covered entity should, based on the circumstances, obtain any necessary supporting representations, whether oral or written, associated with the request (e.g., proof of identity or proof of legal guardianship). If the disclosure requires particular representations or documentation, a covered entity may rely (if such reliance is reasonable) on statements or documentation that on its face meets the applicable requirements.[20] In particular, the documentation requirements for a law enforcement administrative request, such as a civil investigative demand (see **§ 3.03[D][6]**), may be satisfied by an administrative subpoena or similar process, or by a separate written statement that, on its face, demonstrates that the applicable requirements have been met.[21] For research purposes, the documentation required to demonstrate a waiver by an IRB or privacy board (see **§ 3.03[D][9]**) may be satisfied by one or more written statements that are appropriately dated and signed as required under the Privacy Regulations research provisions.[22]

With respect to verifying the identity of public officials, a covered entity may rely (if such reliance is reasonable under the circumstances) on any of the following to verify identity when the disclosure of PHI is to a public official or a person acting on behalf of the public official:

- If the request is made in person, presentation of an agency identification badge, other official credentials, or other proof of government status;

- If the request is in writing, the request is on appropriate government letterhead; or

- If the disclosure is to a person acting on behalf of a public official, a written statement on appropriate government letterhead that the person is acting under the government's authority or other evidence or documentation of agency, such as a contract for services, memorandum of understanding, or purchase order, that establishes that the person is acting on behalf of the public official.[23]

With respect to verifying the authority of public officials, a covered entity may rely (if such reliance is reasonable under the circumstances) on a written statement of the legal authority under which the information is

---

[16] 45 C.F.R. § 164.514(d); OCR Guidance (Minimum Necessary). The language of the HITECH Act appeared to limit the ability of a covered entity or business associate to rely on the minimum necessary determinations of others with regard to disclosures. HITECH Act § 13405(b). However, the HITECH Regulations preserved the former regulatory language, permitting reliance on minimum necessary determinations made by others, in certain circumstances, as described in this section. See 45 C.F.R. § 164.514(d). Future OCR guidance regarding "minimum necessary" issues may clarify this.

[17] 45 C.F.R. § 164.514(h).

[18] 45 C.F.R. § 164.514(h)(i) (stating verification not required for disclosures under 45 C.F.R. § 164.510); 45 C.F.R. § 164.514(h)(iv) (permitting reliance on professional judgment with regard to these disclosures).

[19] 45 C.F.R. § 164.514(h)(iv) (referring to 45 C.F.R. § 164.512(f)).

[20] 45 C.F.R. § 164.514(h).

[21] 45 C.F.R. § 164.514(h) (referring to the conditions in 45 C.F.R. § 164.512(f)(ii)(C)).

[22] 45 C.F.R. § 164.514(h) (referring to the IRB waiver provisions in 45 C.F.R. § 164.512(i)(2) and the signature requirements at 45 C.F.R. § 164.512(i)(2)(i) and (v)).

[23] 45 C.F.R. § 164.514(h)(2).

requested, or, if a written statement would be impracticable, an oral statement of such legal authority. If a request is made pursuant to legal process, warrant, subpoena, order, or other legal process issued by a grand jury or a judicial or administrative tribunal, it is presumed to constitute legal authority.[24]

The Privacy Regulations allow for verification in either oral or written form, unless written documentation is specifically required.[25] The covered entity or business associate disclosing PHI may, however, prefer written documentation for its records.

[C] Scalability and Flexibility

The Privacy Regulations are written as general standards, which are intended to be scalable and flexible. All covered entities must take appropriate steps to address the requirements of the Privacy Regulations, but in determining the scope and extent of their compliance activities, covered entities may weigh the costs and benefits of alternative approaches and scale their compliance activities to their structure, functions, and capabilities within the requirements of the regulations.[26] Covered entities will have different privacy needs, depending on their size and complexity. HHS recognizes that some organizations will need to implement more sophisticated policies and procedures than others.[27]

[D] Multiple Covered Functions

A covered entity may be a health care provider, or a health plan, or a clearinghouse; or it may be a combination of these. The activities or services that a covered entity performs that cause it to fit the HIPAA definition of a health care provider, a health plan, or a clearinghouse are called "covered functions." For example, the covered functions of a health plan involve paying for the cost of medical care. The covered functions of a health care provider involve the furnishing of health care services or supplies to individuals. If a covered entity performs the covered functions of more than one type of covered entity, the "multiple covered functions rule" applies to the covered entity's activities.

The "multiple covered functions rule" says that each covered function within the covered entity must comply with the requirements applicable to its type of covered entity.[28] For example, the provider function within the covered entity must follow the Regulations applicable to health care providers. This would include obtaining an acknowledgement of the notice of privacy practices from the individual. The health plan function within that covered entity must follow the Regulations as they apply to health plans. The health plan function does not need to obtain acknowledgement of the notice. Furthermore, the health plan function must provide individuals with reminders about the notice every three years (but the provider function does not need to do so).[29]

In addition, the "multiple covered functions rule" imposes some limits on the internal use of PHI within the covered entity. A covered entity that performs multiple covered functions must limit the exchanging of PHI from one "function" to the other and must segregate PHI accordingly. Specifically, a covered entity may not share the PHI of individuals who receive services from one covered function (e.g., health care provider) with another covered function (e.g., health plan) if the individual is not involved with the other function.[30] This means, for example, that a covered entity that has both a health plan function and provider function may share

---

[24] 45 C.F.R. § 164.514(h)(2).

[25] HHS, OCR, HIE Guidance, "Privacy and Security Framework: Safeguards," available at http://www.hhs.gov/ocr/privacy/hipaa/understanding/special/healthit.

[26] 65 Fed. Reg. 82,785 (Dec. 28, 2000).

[27] 65 Fed. Reg. 82,785 (Dec. 28, 2000).

[28] 45 C.F.R. §§ 164.103 (definitions), 164.105(b), and 164.504(g).

[29] See § 3.02 for more information about the notice of privacy practices.

[30] 45 C.F.R. §§ 164.504(g); 65 Fed. Reg. 82,509 (Dec. 28, 2000); Office for Civil Rights (OCR) Summary of the Privacy Rule (Organizational Options), available at http://www.hhs.gov/ocr/privacy/hipaa/understanding/summary/index.html.

PHI of individuals within the covered entity, even for treatment, payment, and health care operations, *only if* the individual is *both* a health plan member and a patient. HHS provides the following example: "an HMO may integrate data about health plan members and clinic services to members, but a health care system may not share information about a patient in its hospital with its health plan if the patient is not a member of the health plan."[31] This is summarized in the following chart.

Role of Individual in Relation to Covered Entity	Health Plan Member Only	Both a Health Plan Member and a Patient	Patient Only
Permitted Uses of PHI	For Health Plan function purposes only	Covered Entity may use, share, and integrate Individual's data between Health Plan functions and Provider functions	For Provider function purposes only

Another example, under the marketing rules (discussed in detail in **§ 3.04[C]**), is that a covered entity that has both health plan and provider functions, may not use its patient lists to market a new health plan product, to the extent the targeted patients are not also health plan members (i.e., have a relationship with the health plan function). The marketing by the health plan function must be limited to those patients who also have a relationship with the health plan function. Similarly, an integrated system that wishes to use combined patient data and member data for studies to improve the quality of care and reduce health care costs may be constrained by this multiple covered function rule. However, the impact of this rule may be minimal in a "closed model" integrated system, because there would be a 100% overlap (or nearly so) between the covered entity's health plan member population and its patient population.

Finally, if the covered entity includes a component that is a health care clearinghouse, the clearinghouse must implement policies and procedures that protect the clearinghouse PHI from unauthorized access by the rest of the covered entity.[32]

§ 3.02 INDIVIDUAL RIGHTS

Under the Privacy Regulations, individuals are given certain rights with respect to their health care information, as discussed below.

[A] Notice of Privacy Practices

A covered entity must prepare a notice of its privacy practices, which describes to the individual the uses and disclosures of PHI that may be made by the covered entity, the individual's rights, and the covered entity's legal duties with respect to PHI. There are requirements under the Privacy Regulations relating both to the content of the notice of privacy practices and the distribution of the notice. Moreover, direct treatment providers are required to make a good faith effort to obtain a written acknowledgment of the notice from the individual.[33]

---

[31] 65 Fed. Reg. 82,509 (Dec. 28, 2000).
[32] 45 C.F.R. § 164.308(a)(4)(ii)(A).
[33] 45 C.F.R. § 164.520.

[1] Content

The notice of privacy practices must be written in plain language and include all the required content elements listed below.[34] Changes arising from the HITECH Regulations are noted.

1. Header: The following statement as a header or otherwise prominently displayed: "THIS NOTICE DESCRIBES HOW MEDICAL INFORMATION ABOUT YOU MAY BE USED AND DISCLOSED AND HOW YOU CAN GET ACCESS TO THIS INFORMATION. PLEASE REVIEW IT CAREFULLY."

2. Uses and Disclosures: A description of the uses and disclosures the covered entity may make, including:

    • A description, including at least one example, of the types of uses and disclosures the covered entity is permitted by the Privacy Regulations to make for treatment, payment, and health care operations.[35] These descriptions must include sufficient detail to put the individual on notice of the permitted disclosures, and must reflect more stringent state law, if applicable. [Note: The examples selected should be illustrative and meaningful for the individual. Furthermore, the notice of privacy practices should make clear that these are examples only and not a complete list; therefore, using a small number of examples is generally advisable.]

    • A description of *each* of the other purposes for which the covered entity is permitted or required by these regulations to use or disclose PHI without the individual's written authorization. [Note: No examples are required here, but the descriptions must include sufficient detail to put the individual on notice of the required and permitted disclosures, and must reflect more stringent state law, if applicable.]

    • A description of certain types of uses and disclosures that do require an authorization, specifically, psychotherapy notes, marketing, and the sale of PHI. [This is a new requirement under the HITECH Regulations.[36]] This does not require a listing of all uses and disclosures requiring an authorization, but the notice must contain a statement that most uses and disclosures of psychotherapy notes, uses and disclosures of PHI for marketing purposes, and disclosures that constitute a sale of PHI will be made only with the individual's authorization.[37] If, however, a covered entity does not maintain psychotherapy notes, the statement about psychotherapy notes is not required.[38]

    • A statement that other uses and disclosures not described in the notice will be made only with the individual's written authorization and that the individual may revoke such authorization in writing at any time, except to the extent the covered entity has already relied on the authorization. [This is a clarification and restatement of a pre-HITECH requirement.]

    • If the covered entity intends to engage in any of the following activities, the description of uses and disclosures must include additional statements, as applicable:

       — *Fundraising*: Statement that the covered entity may contact the individual to raise funds for the covered entity, and that the individual has a right to opt out of receiving such communications [The affirmative statement of the opt-out is new with the HITECH Regulations.[39]];

---

[34] 45 C.F.R. § 164.520(b).

[35] See **§ 3.03[B]** for definitions of the key HIPAA terms *treatment, payment,* and *health care operations.*

[36] 45 C.F.R. § 164.520(b)(ii)(E).

[37] 78 Fed. Reg. 5624 (Jan. 25, 2013).

[38] 78 Fed. Reg. 5624 (Jan. 25, 2013).

[39] 45 C.F.R. § 164.520(b)(iii)(A). The mechanism for opting out need not be described in the notice, but the covered entity may choose to provide this additional detail. 78 Fed. Reg. 5624 (Jan. 25, 2013). See **§ 3.04[A]** for more information about uses and disclosures of PHI for fundraising.

— *Disclosures to Plan Sponsor*: Statement that a group health plan, or a health insurance issuer or HMO with respect to a group health plan, may disclose PHI to the sponsor of the plan;[40] and

— *Underwriting*: If the covered entity is a health plan that intends to use or disclose PHI for underwriting purposes, a statement that the health plan is prohibited from using or disclosing PHI that is genetic information for underwriting purposes. [This underwriting provision is new under the HITECH Regulations.[41]]

Prior to the HITECH Regulations, if the covered entity intended to provide appointment reminders or health-related information to individuals, the notice was required to include a statement that the covered entity might contact the individual to provide appointment reminders or information about treatment alternatives or other health-related benefits that might be of interest to the individual. Those statements are no longer required to be called out separately in the notice, but may be included if the covered entity chooses to do so.

3. Individual Rights: A statement of the individual's rights with respect to PHI and a brief description of how the individual may exercise these rights, as follows:

- The right to request restrictions on certain uses and disclosures of PHI. [Note: As a result of the HITECH Regulations, health plans and health care providers now have different obligations regarding drafting this part of the notice].[42]

    — For a health plan, the notice should continue to include a statement that the individual has the right to request restrictions on certain uses and disclosures of PHI, but the health plan is not required to agree to a requested restriction.

    — For health care providers, the notice must explain that the provider is required to agree to requested restrictions where the individual pays out-of-pocket for a health care service and requests that PHI related to the service not be disclosed to the individual's health plan.[43] The health care provider's notice should also state that it is not required to agree to *other* requested restrictions.

- The right to receive confidential communications of PHI;

- The right to inspect and copy PHI;

- The right to amend PHI;

- The right to receive an accounting of certain disclosures of PHI; and

- The right to obtain a paper copy of the notice of privacy practices from the covered entity upon request (even if the individual agreed to receive the notice electronically).

4. Covered Entity's Duties: A description of the covered entity's duties, including statements of the following:

- The covered entity is required by law to maintain the privacy of PHI and to provide individuals with notice of its legal duties and privacy practices with respect to PHI;

---

[40] The HITECH Regulations added a reference here to 45 C.F.R. § 164.504(f), which is the (unchanged) provision relating to disclosures to plan sponsors. For a health plan that will be disclosing PHI to a plan sponsor, the health plan will need to determine the extent of the PHI to be disclosed, whether plan documents need to be amended, and how much of this to explain in its notice of privacy practices. See **Chapter 7** for more information about disclosures to plan sponsors.

[41] 45 C.F.R. § 164.520(b)(iii)(C). This provision is not required for issuers of certain long-term care policies. See **§ 3.04[E]** for more information about uses and disclosures of PHI for underwriting.

[42] 78 Fed. Reg. 5624 (Jan. 25, 2013).

[43] 45 C.F.R. § 164.520(b)(iv)(A). See **§ 3.02[E][1]** for more information about these restriction requests in "self-pay" situations.

- The covered entity is required to abide by the terms of the notice of privacy practices currently in effect;

- The covered entity reserves the right to change the terms of its notice of privacy practices and to make the new notice provisions effective for all PHI that it maintains. The statement must also describe how it will provide individuals with a revised notice;

- The covered entity is required by law to notify affected individuals following a breach of unsecured PHI. [This provision is a new requirement under the Privacy Regulations.[44]]

5. Complaints: A statement that individuals may complain to the covered entity and to the Secretary of HHS if they believe their privacy rights have been violated, a brief description of how the individual may file a complaint with the covered entity, and a statement that the individual will not be retaliated against for filing a complaint.[45]

6. Contact: The name or title, and telephone number of a person or office to contact for further information.

7. Effective Date: The date on which the notice of privacy practices is first in effect, which may not be earlier than the date on which the notice is printed or otherwise published.

HHS has suggested using a *layered notice*—that is, a short statement summarizing the individual's rights and other information, with reference to an attached longer notice of privacy practices that contains all of the required elements.[46] This summary, however, is not a HIPAA notice and providing the summary by itself does not satisfy the notice requirement.

As noted above, if a State law imposes a more stringent standard on uses and disclosures, this must be reflected in the notice. Furthermore, State law may impose additional notice requirements. In some cases, these State requirements are satisfied by a separate notice, and in other cases, they require incorporation of State-specific language in the HIPAA notice.[47]

---

[44] 45 C.F.R. § 164.520(b)(v)(A). This provision is listed in the HITECH Regulations regarding notices of privacy practices under the "Covered Entity's Duties," but presumably, this could also be expressed as a right of the individual to receive breach notifications and placed in that section of the notice. A simple statement of this duty/right is all that is required. The covered entity may, but is not required to, define "breach" or "unsecured PHI," describe the risk assessment process, or go into detail about the notification process. 78 Fed. Reg. 5624–5625, 5644 (Jan. 25, 2013).

[45] The Privacy Regulations do not require that the covered entity provide HHS Office of Civil Rights (OCR) contact information in the Notice; however, if the covered entity chooses to do so, the appropriate OCR regional office should be identified. This information is available on the OCR website at http://www.hhs.gov/ocr/office/about/rgn-hqaddresses.html. The covered entity should have the OCR contact information available for individuals who request it. Many covered entities prefer to provide specific contact information in the notice only for internal reporting of complaints to give the covered entity an opportunity to resolve the complaint internally.

[46] 67 Fed. Reg. 53,243 (Aug. 14, 2002).

[47] For an example of a stand-alone State notice requirement (which preceded HIPAA), see the Minnesota statute at Minn. Stat. § 144.292, Subd.4. The Minnesota statute sets out requirements for content and distribution of the notice. For an example of a State law specifically requiring language to be included in the HIPAA notice, see Utah Code § 26-18-17. This is a new Utah statute requiring health care providers who participate in certain public health care programs (i.e., Medicaid and CHIP) to include in their HIPAA notices the information that the provider submits personally identifiable information about patients to the eligibility database for these programs. The Utah notice requirement was added in response to a massive data breach. In March 2012, hackers gained access to a Utah government server that stored Medicaid and CHIP program data, and compromised the data of nearly 800,000 individuals, including the Social Security numbers of up to 280,000 people. For information about the breach, see http://www.health.utah.gov/databreach/common-questions.html.

Health plans may also have notice obligations under the Gramm-Leach-Bliley regulations governing the privacy of consumer financial information. 16 C.F.R. 313.4–313.9. These requirements are beyond the scope of this book.

[2] Distribution

A covered entity must make the notice of privacy practices available to individuals in a variety of ways, as follows:[48]

- Special Rules for Health Plans

    Health plans must provide the notice of privacy practices to new enrollees at the time of enrollment. In addition, at least every three years, the health plan must notify enrollees that the notice is available and how to obtain a copy.

    A health plan may satisfy the distribution requirement by providing the notice to the named insured under the policy (and need not provide the notice to each covered dependent). If a health plan has more than one notice, it need only provide the notice that is relevant to the individual.[49] If the health plan maintains a website that provides information about the plan's benefits, the notice must be prominently posted on and available electronically through the website.[50]

    The notice-related obligations of a group health plan vary, depending on whether the plan is insured or self-insured and whether the plan creates or maintains PHI other than summary information and enrollment information. Refer to **Chapter 7** for additional information on group health plans.

- Special Rules for Direct Treatment Providers

    Definition: A direct treatment relationship means a treatment relationship between an individual and a health care provider that is not an indirect relationship, which in turn is defined as one where the provider delivers health care to the individual based on the orders of another health care provider, and typically provides services or products (or reports results) directly to another health care provider who is the one with direct contact with the individual.[51]

    Delivery of Notice: Providers in a direct treatment relationship with the individual must provide the notice of privacy practices no later than the date of the first service delivery. (In an emergency treatment situation, the notice must be provided as soon as reasonably practicable after the emergency.)[52]

    Written Acknowledgment: A direct treatment provider must make a good faith effort to obtain a written acknowledgment of receipt of the notice of privacy practices from the individual and, if not obtained, document the provider's good faith efforts to obtain such acknowledgment and the reason the acknowledgment was not obtained. In an emergency treatment situation, no acknowledgment is required.[53] The Privacy Regulations do not prescribe the form of the acknowledgment or the process for obtaining it. The individual's signature on the notice of privacy practices is not required; the provider could, instead, have the individual sign or initial a separate form or log sheet.[54] A provider that chooses to obtain consent from the individual could also design a form that combines the consent and the acknowledgment.[55]

    If the first service delivery is over the telephone, the provider may satisfy the notice and acknowledgment requirements by mailing the notice of privacy practices and acknowledgment form to the individual that same day and requesting that the individual sign the acknowledgment and mail it back to the provider. This would constitute the required good faith effort, even if the individual does not sign

---

[48] 45 C.F.R. § 164.520(c). The notice of privacy practices may be provided electronically under certain circumstances; see 45 C.F.R. § 164.520(c)(3). Also, inmates do not have a right to a notice of privacy practices. 45 C.F.R. § 164.520(a)(3).

[49] 45 C.F.R. § 164.520(c)(1).

[50] 45 C.F.R. § 164.520(c)(3).

[51] 45 C.F.R. § 164.501.

[52] 45 C.F.R. § 164.520(c)(2).

[53] 45 C.F.R. § 164.520(c)(2)(ii).

[54] 67 Fed. Reg. 53,240 (Aug. 14, 2002).

[55] 67 Fed. Reg. 53,240 (Aug. 14, 2002).

and return the acknowledgment form.[56] If the provider's first contact with the individual is just to schedule an appointment, the notice and acknowledgment can wait until the individual arrives for that appointment.[57]

Posting of Notice: If there is a physical service delivery site, the provider must post the notice of privacy practices at the site in a clear and prominent location where it is reasonable to expect individuals seeking services to be able to read it.[58] The provider must also have copies available for individuals to request and take with them. If the provider maintains a website that provides information about its services, the notice must be prominently posted on and available electronically through the website.[59]

- Notices Upon Request

    A covered entity's notice of privacy practices must also be available upon request (by anyone, not just the individual).[60]

Making the notice of privacy practices available on request, posting it at a facility or on a website, or placing copies on display does not substitute for physically providing the notice directly to the individual.[61]

[3] Revisions

The notice of privacy practices must be promptly revised and distributed whenever there is a material change to the covered entity's uses or disclosures, the individual's rights, the covered entity's legal duties, or other privacy practices stated in the notice. Also, changes in state law may require a revision of the notice.

Direct treatment providers must, as of the effective date of the revision, provide the revised notice to new patients (and obtain acknowledgment) according to the provider's usual process for distributing the notice to new patients. Also, if requested, the provider must give the revised notice to current patients (and anyone else). If there is a physical delivery site, the provider must post the revised notice in a clear and prominent location, on or before the effective date of the revision. Similarly, if the provider has a website, the revised notice must be posted there as well.[62]

For health plans, until September 23, 2013, the rule was that the new notice must be provided to enrollees within 60 days if there was a material change.[63] Under the HITECH Regulations, effective September 23, 2013, there are new rules for distribution of the notice if there is a material change, depending on whether the health plan posts its notice on its website:

- Health Plan That Posts Its Notice on Its Website: The health plan must prominently post a revised notice on its website by the effective date of the material change to the notice. In its next annual mailing to individuals covered by the plan, the health plan must provide the revised notice, or information about the material change and how to obtain a copy of the revised notice.[64]

---

[56] 67 Fed. Reg. 53,240 (Aug. 14, 2002).

[57] 67 Fed. Reg. 53,240–241 (Aug. 14, 2002).

[58] In the preamble to the HITECH Regulations, HHS states that providers may satisfy the requirement that they post the notice by posting a summary of the notice in a clear and prominent location and having the full notice immediately available for individuals to pick up "without any additional burden on their part" (e.g., without having to ask someone for a copy). 78 Fed. Reg. 5625 (Jan. 25, 2013). For example, HHS says, this would include posting the summary notice on the wall and having printed copies of the full notice on a table below the summary for individuals to pick up. Satisfying the requirement to post the notice by posting a summary of the notice is described by HHS as a clarification; yet the language of the Privacy Regulations does not include this method.

[59] 45 C.F.R. § 164.520(c)(iii).

[60] 45 C.F.R. § 164.520(c).

[61] 67 Fed. Reg. 53,243 (Aug. 14, 2002).

[62] 45 C.F.R. § 164.520(c)(2)(iv); 67 Fed. Reg. 53,241 (Aug. 14, 2002).

[63] 45 C.F.R. § 164.520(c)(1).

[64] 45 C.F.R. § 164.520(c)(2)(v)(A).

- Health Plan That Does Not Post Its Notice on a Website: The health plan must provide the revised notice, or information about the material change and how to obtain a copy of the revised notice, to individuals covered by the plan within 60 days of the material revision to the notice.[65]

Except when required by law, a material change to any term of the notice may not be implemented prior to the effective date of the notice in which such material change is reflected. The revision can only apply to PHI received or created by the covered entity after the revised notice is issued, unless the original notice includes the reservation of rights described in **§ 3.02[A][1]** above.[66] It is not necessary to obtain a new acknowledgment if the notice is revised.[67]

[4]   Revised Notices for HITECH Compliance

The HITECH Regulations clearly state that HHS considers changes to the content of notices required by the HITECH Regulations to be material changes.[68] Covered entities should carefully review their notices of privacy practices to make all necessary and appropriate changes. In summary, the key content changes under the HITECH Regulations are the inclusion of statements relating to:

- Most uses and disclosures for marketing purposes, for sale of PHI, and of psychotherapy notes require the individual's authorization.

- The individual may be contacted for fundraising purposes but has the right to opt out of such fundraising communications.

- The individual has the right to request restrictions on PHI disclosures to the individual's health plan for health services or items paid for out-of-pocket and in full, and the provider must comply with such request.

- The covered entity is required to notify the individual of any breach of the individual's unsecured PHI.

- A health plan may not use or disclose PHI that is genetic information for underwriting purposes.

Health plans and providers were required to have revised their notices of privacy practices by the compliance date of September 23, 2013.

Direct treatment providers, as of the effective date of the revisions (which must be September 23, 2013, or earlier), needed to provide the revised notice to new patients and make it available to others. The provider must also have posted the revised notice in a clear and prominent location at its physical delivery sites and on its website, if applicable.[69]

For a health plan that posts its notice on its website, the revised notice had to be posted there by the effective date of the revisions (which must be September 23, 2013 or earlier). In addition, the revised notice (or

---

[65] 45 C.F.R. § 164.520(c)(2)(v)(B).

[66] 45 C.F.R. § 164.520(b)(3).

[67] 67 Fed. Reg. 53,241 (Aug. 14, 2002).

[68] 78 Fed. Reg. 5625 (Jan. 25, 2013).

[69] For certain CLIA-certified and CLIA-exempt laboratories, with laboratory-specific notices of privacy practices, HHS delayed enforcement of the HITECH requirement that these labs provide the revised notice of privacy practices. Regulations were pending that would result in further material changes to the notices for these providers, with regard to individual access. HHS was allowing these providers to combine all the material changes in one revised notice. HHS, "Statement of Delay in Enforcement of HIPAA Requirement for Certain CLIA and CLIA-Exempt Laboratories to Revise their Notices of Privacy Practices" (Sept. 19, 2013), available at http://www.hhs.gov/ocr/privacy/hipaa/enforcement/clia-labs.html. These pending regulations were published in February 2014, and laboratories had until October 6, 2014, to make the necessary revisions to their notices of privacy practices. 79 Fed. Reg. 7289 (Feb. 6, 2014); HHS, "Reminder of End of NPP Enforcement Delay for CLIA Labs" (Oct. 3, 2014), available at http://www.hhs.gov/ocr/privacy/hipaa/enforcement/clia-labs.html.

information about the material changes and how to get a copy) had to be sent to the covered individuals in the health plan's next annual mailing after the effective date of the revisions.

For a health plan without a website, the health plan had to distribute the revised notice (or information about the material changes and how to get a copy) to covered individuals within 60 days of the effective date of the material change.

[5] Joint Notices

Participants in an organized health care arrangement (OHCA), as described in **§ 1.02[C][3]**, may use a single, joint notice of privacy practices, or each may have its own notice. If a joint notice is used, the covered entities participating in the OHCA must agree to abide by the terms of the notice with regard to PHI received or created in its role as a member of the OHCA.[70] Distribution of the notice must follow the applicable rules, but provision of the notice to the individual by any one participant in the OHCA will satisfy the notice-provision requirements for all participants in the OHCA.[71]

The joint notice should:

- Describe with reasonable specificity the covered entities, or classes of entities, to which the notice applies;

- Describe with reasonable specificity the service delivery sites, or classes of service delivery sites, to which the notice applies; and

- If applicable, state that the OHCA participants will share PHI with each other, as needed for treatment or payment purposes, or for health care operations relating to the OHCA.[72]

A covered entity that is a member of OHCA should verify that any joint notice includes all the elements applicable to its privacy practices. For example, a for-profit member of the OHCA might omit the fundraising provision from the notice, but that provision may be needed by a nonprofit member of the OHCA. If a covered entity is not satisfied with the joint notice and is unable to change it, it should provide its own separate notice.

[6] Other Notice Issues

All uses and disclosures of PHI by the covered entity, including those related to treatment, payment, and health care operations, must be consistent with the covered entity's notice of privacy practices.[73]

The notice of privacy practices may be used to inform individuals of certain requirements. For example, if the covered entity requires certain requests from individuals (e.g., requests for access or amendments) be in writing, this may be stated in the notice.

To provide additional assistance and guidance to covered entities, OCR and the Office of the National Coordinator for Health Information Technology (ONC) jointly developed model notices of privacy practices, which can be customized for covered entities to use. They were released on September 13, 2013, just before the HITECH deadline. There is a model for a health plan notice and a model for a provider notice. Each is available in multiple formats, and instructions are provided.[74] The models illustrate a level of plain language and lack of complexity and detail that OCR will still consider to be compliant with the Privacy Regulations. Absent

---

[70] 45 C.F.R. § 164.520(d)(1).

[71] 45 C.F.R. § 164.520(d)(3).

[72] 45 C.F.R. § 164.520(d)(2).

[73] See 67 Fed. Reg. 53,211 (Aug. 14, 2002).

[74] Available at http://www.hhs.gov/ocr/privacy/hipaa/modelnotices.html. ONC also sponsored a 2014 "digital privacy notice challenge" for the design of online notices of privacy practices. For more information, go to http://oncchallenges.ideascale.com/a/pages/digital-privacy-notice-challenge-winners.

guidance like this, covered entities have generally made their notices longer and more complex to ensure they were meeting all the requirements.

The Privacy Regulations contain no specific requirement to translate the notice of privacy practices into other languages. However, Title VI of the Civil Rights Act of 1964 may require the covered entity to provide materials in the primary language of persons with limited English proficiency within the service area.[75] OCR has made available model notices of privacy practices in Spanish for providers and health plans.[76] In addition, if the covered entity is required to comply with the Americans with Disabilities Act or Section 504 of the Rehabilitation Act of 1973, the covered entity has an obligation to take steps to ensure effective communications with individuals with disabilities. This may include making notices available in alternative formats, such as Braille, large print, or audio.[77]

A covered entity must document compliance with the notice of privacy practices requirements and retain copies of each version of the notice for six years following the date it is last in effect. Written acknowledgment of receipt of the notice (or documentation of good faith efforts to obtain such acknowledgment), when required, also must be retained for six years.[78]

[B] Access

An individual has a right to access, inspect, and obtain a copy of his or her PHI.[79]

[1] Right to Access—Designated Record Set

An individual has a right to access, inspect, and obtain a copy of his or her PHI, but not necessarily all PHI held by the covered entity. This right applies only to information held by the covered entity in a designated record set. A *designated record set* comprises those records used to make decisions about the individual.[80] For providers, this includes (but is not limited to) medical records and billing records. For health plans, this includes (but is not limited to) enrollment, payment, claims adjudication, and case management or medical management records. A covered entity is not required to provide access to other information that duplicates PHI in the designated record set.[81]

The covered entity is required to document the designated record sets that are subject to access by the individual, as well as the titles or offices of those responsible for receiving and processing requests for access.[82] The Privacy Regulations do not specify where this information should be documented.

[2] Right to Access—General Process

The covered entity may require that the request for access be submitted in writing if it informs individuals in advance. (The requirement of a written request would be appropriate to include in the notice of privacy practices.) A covered entity must act on a request within 30 days.[83] This time limit may be extended for another

---

[75] 65 Fed. Reg. 82,549 (Dec. 28, 2000); 78 Fed. Reg. 5625 (Jan. 25, 2013); see also Title VI of the Civil Rights Act of 1964; Policy Guidance on the Prohibition Against National Origin Discrimination as It Affects Persons with Limited English Proficiency, 65 Fed. Reg. 52,762 (Aug. 30, 2000) and Limited English Proficiency (LEP) Resources and Tools from OCR, available at http://www.hhs.gov/ocr/civilrights/resources/specialtopics/lep.

[76] Available at http://www.hhs.gov/ocr/privacy/hipaa/modelnotices.html.

[77] 78 Fed. Reg. 5625 (Jan. 25, 2013).

[78] 45 C.F.R. § 164.520(e).

[79] 45 C.F.R. § 164.524.

[80] 45 C.F.R. § 164.501.

[81] 45 C.F.R. § 164.524(c)(1).

[82] 45 C.F.R. § 164.524(e).

[83] Prior to the compliance date of the HITECH Regulations (i.e., prior to September 23, 2013), an additional 30 days was allowed if the information requested was not on site. Under the HITECH Regulations, this extra time was no longer deemed necessary. 78 Fed. Reg. 5637 (Jan. 25, 2013).

30 days with written notice to the individual.[84] The time period for responding begins on the date of the request, even if time is subsequently spent clarifying the scope of the request, agreeing on electronic formats, etc.[85]

If the covered entity does not maintain the information requested, but knows where it is maintained, the covered entity must inform the individual where to direct the request for access.[86] The information must be produced in the form or format requested by the individual, if readily producible in that form or format. It may be provided in summary form if the individual agrees.[87]

When a health care provider, in the course of treating an individual, collects family medical history information, that information becomes part of the individual's medical record and PHI (and potentially a designated record set). The individual will have a right to access that information (or exercise rights with regard to that information) in a designated record set, but the family members referenced in that medical history do not.[88]

[3] Right to Electronic Copies

An individual has a right to access his or her PHI in a designated record set, regardless of the format in which that PHI is maintained. But, under the HITECH Regulations, some additional rules apply to electronic PHI. The HITECH Act states that, if the covered entity "uses or maintains an electronic health record," the individual has the right to obtain copies of these records in an electronic format.[89] This statutory language, which tied the individual's rights to an ill-defined "electronic health record," was deemed too narrow an approach by HHS. HHS wanted to create a uniform standard for access to electronic PHI that applied to both health plans and health care providers. The new requirements in the HITECH Regulations are based on a combination of the HITECH Act and HHS's general authority under the HIPAA statute to promulgate rules.[90]

Effective September 23, 2013, under the HITECH Regulations, if the individual requests an electronic copy of PHI (in a designated record set) that is maintained electronically by the covered entity, the covered entity must provide access to the information in the electronic form and format requested by the individual, if readily producible in that manner; or otherwise, in a readable electronic form and format agreed to by the covered entity and the individual.[91]

HHS, in the HITECH Regulations, also provides the following clarifications about the provision of these electronic copies:[92]

- A covered entity is not required to purchase or build new technology to accommodate a request for a particular electronic form or format that is not "readily producible" by the covered entity at the time of the request, provided another form of electronic copy can be provided.

- The covered entity must be able to produce at least one form of readable electronic copy of the requested information.

- If the covered entity has a legacy or other system that cannot produce any form of electronic copy, some investment may be needed to ensure the covered entity can meet the basic requirement of producing some form of electronic copy.

---

[84] 45 C.F.R. § 164.524(b).

[85] 78 Fed. Reg. 5637 (Jan. 25, 2013).

[86] 45 C.F.R. § 164.524(d)(3).

[87] 45 C.F.R. § 164.524(c)(2).

[88] OCR, FAQ: "Does the HIPAA Privacy Rule limit what a doctor can do with family medical history?", available at http://www.hhs.gov/ocr/privacy/hipaa/faq/covered_entities/511.html.

[89] HITECH Act § 13405(e).

[90] 78 Fed. Reg. 5566, 5631 (Jan. 25, 2013).

[91] 45 C.F.R. § 164.524(c)(2)(ii); 78 Fed. Reg. 5631 (Jan. 25, 2013).

[92] 78 Fed. Reg. 5631, 5633–5634 (Jan. 25, 2013).

- If the covered entity cannot provide the copies in the form and format requested by the individual, and the individual declines to accept the information in the form or formats that the covered entity can readily produce, the covered entity may provide the information in hard copy. This is the only instance in which providing a hard copy is an acceptable alternative.

- If the covered entity maintains some information electronically and other information on paper, it may respond to a request with a combination of media.

- PDF is a format that would satisfy the requirement, if it is requested by or agreed to by the individual.

- Though not a specific requirement under the Regulations, HHS expects covered entities, to the extent possible, to provide *machine-readable* copies (e.g., digital information in a standard format that can be processed and analyzed by computer). This could include, for example, MS Word, MS Excel, text, HTML, text-based PDF, or other similar formats.

- If the designated record set contains links to images or to other data, those data or images must be included in the electronic copy provided to the individual, although a covered entity may wish to discuss the scope of the request with the individual.

- The electronic copy provided must contain all of the requested information in the designated record set at the time the request is processed (not as of the date the request is received).

- A covered entity is not required to scan documents to create electronic copies, if the information is not otherwise in electronic form, but has the option to do so.

- A covered entity is not required to use electronic devices, such as flash drives, provided by the individual (due to the potential security risks).

- A covered entity may send the information to an individual via unencrypted e-mails, if it has advised the individual of the risk and the individual still prefers unencrypted e-mail. The notification of risk need only advise the individual that there is some level of risk that the e-mail could be read by a third party; no detailed explanation of encryption or information security is required.

[4] Sending Requested PHI to a Third Party

Under the HITECH Act, the individual may choose to direct the covered entity to transmit requested electronic PHI directly to a third party designated by the individual, provided that the choice is "clear, conspicuous and specific."[93] Under the HITECH Regulations, effective September 23, 2013, HHS implements this HITECH Act requirement and extends it to paper copies as well.[94] HHS has interpreted the "clear, conspicuous and specific" requirement to mean that the request must be in writing, be signed by the individual, and clearly identify the third party and where the copies are to be sent.[95] In addition, the covered entity must implement reasonable policies and procedures to verify the identity of the requestor.[96]

HHS distinguishes these requests by individuals from requests by a third party holding an authorization from the individual (See **§ 3.03[F]**), clarifying that these requests must clearly come from the individual rather than a third party.[97] An authorization alone, without more, such as a separate request letter from the individual, would therefore not meet this requirement.

---

[93] HITECH Act § 13405(e).
[94] 45 C.F.R. 164.524(c)(3)(ii); 78 Fed. Reg. 5634 (Jan. 25, 2013).
[95] 45 C.F.R. 164.524(c)(3)(ii); 78 Fed. Reg. 5634 (Jan. 25, 2013).
[96] 78 Fed. Reg. 5635 (Jan. 25, 2013). See **§ 3.01[B]** regarding verification of identity.
[97] 75 Fed. Reg. 40,868, 40,902 (July 14, 2010); 78 Fed. Reg. 5634–5635 (Jan. 25, 2013).

[5]   Denials of Requests

There are both unreviewable and reviewable grounds for denial of access.[98] The covered entity may deny access, without appeal, for the following types of information:

- Psychotherapy notes (but not other mental health records);[99]

- Information compiled in reasonable anticipation of a lawsuit;

- Information held by prisons on inmates, based on an assessment of the risks of providing access;

- Information held by a research entity, when the individual has agreed to a temporary limitation on access;

- Information for which access would be denied under the Privacy Act of 1974; and

- Information obtained from someone other than a health care provider under a promise of confidentiality, where access would likely reveal the source.

The covered entity may deny access, subject to appeal, if the request is for information that the covered entity believes to be reasonably likely to endanger the life or physical safety of the individual or another person, or to cause substantial harm to another person (or to cause substantial harm to the individual, if the request comes from a personal representative). These denials are subject to review by a licensed health professional who did not participate in the original decision to deny access.

A denial of access must be timely and in writing. The denial must include an explanation of the basis for the denial, an explanation of the individual's appeal rights, if applicable, a description of the complaint process, and contact information. The covered entity must, to the extent possible, provide the individual with access to other PHI requested.[100]

[6]   Fees for Copies of Records

The covered entity may charge the individual a reasonable cost-based fee but only for:

- Labor for copying the requested information, whether in paper or electronic form;

- Supplies for creating the paper copy;

- Electronic media, if the individual requested that an electronic copy be provided on portable media;

- Postage, if the individual requested that the information should be mailed; and

- Preparing an explanation or summary of the PHI, if agreed to by the individual.[101]

HHS recognizes that the labor costs associated with searching for and retrieving electronic PHI requested by the individual is not negligible (contrary to what it initially thought). In the HITECH Regulations, HHS clarifies that the labor costs included in a reasonable cost-based fee could include skilled technical staff time spent

---

[98] 45 C.F.R. § 164.524(a). Previously, reasons for denial included situations where the release of information was prohibited by the Clinical Laboratory Improvement Amendments (CLIA). The CLIA regulations (42 C.F.R. § 493.1291(f)) imposed limitations on direct patient access to certain lab results. This was changed by new regulations in 2014, which expand patients' rights to directly access their own lab test reports, with compliance required by October 2, 2014. 79 Fed. Reg. 7290 (Feb. 6, 2014).

[99] See **§ 3.04[D]** for a definition and discussion of psychotherapy notes.

[100] 45 C.F.R. § 164.524(d).

[101] 45 C.F.R. 164.524(c)(4). The fees specific to electronic copies are new with HITECH. 78 Fed. Reg. 5635 (Jan. 25, 2013).

creating and copying the electronic file, including extracting, compiling, scanning, and burning PHI to media, and distributing the media.[102]

Covered entities may not, however, charge any fees for retrieving or locating the information, whether structured as a standard fee or a cost-based fee, whether for paper or electronic records, and whether charged as part of a per-page fee or as a separate fee.[103] The cost of maintaining systems, capital costs for data access, storage, or infrastructure, and the cost of adopting new technology to produce PHI in electronic formats are also not allowable as part of the "reasonable, cost-based fees."[104] Covered entities may, however, charge an individual for preparing an affidavit to accompany the requested records, certifying that the information is a true and correct copy of the records. Preparation of such an affidavit is considered a separate service from the copying of the records and is, therefore, not subject to the "reasonable, cost-based fee" limitation.[105]

A covered entity's fees must be both reasonable and cost-based. When state laws provide limits on the fee that a covered entity may charge for PHI, this is relevant in determining whether a covered entity's fee is "reasonable." HHS has provided the following examples:

- If state law permits a charge of 25 cents per page, but a covered entity has a cost of 5 cents per page, then the covered entity may not charge more than 5 cents per page (the reasonable and cost-based amount).

- If a covered entity's cost is 30 cents per page, but state law limits the covered entity's charge to 25 cents per page, then the covered entity is limited to 25 cents per page (despite the 30-cent-per-page cost, the amount is not reasonable based on state law).[106]

Fees set by state law for costs that are allowed by the Privacy Regulations, such as copying and postage, are presumed to be reasonable.[107]

The Privacy Regulations do not address charge limitations in other situations, such as a disclosure under an authorization (see § 3.03[F]). Some courts have addressed this question and held that the charge limitations apply only to requests by individuals (or personal representatives) and do not apply when a third party, such as the individual's attorney, makes the request even though the attorney may be acting as the agent of the individual. Individuals may be able to circumvent this problem by requesting the records directly and then handing them over to their attorneys.[108] Or, under the HITECH Regulations, the individual can make a written request that the records be sent directly to a third party. (See § 3.02[B][4].)

[7] Guidance for Consumers

OCR has issued a guidance memo, directed at consumers, explaining the individual's right of access.[109] The memo provides links to videos and pamphlets that provide individuals with detailed information about their rights. OCR continues to develop consumer education materials.

---

[102] 78 Fed. Reg. 5636 (Jan. 25, 2013).

[103] 45 C.F.R. § 164.524(c)(4); 65 Fed. Reg. 82,557, 82,735 (Dec. 28, 2000); 78 Fed. Reg. 5636 (Jan. 25, 2013).

[104] 78 Fed. Reg. 5636 (Jan. 25, 2013).

[105] 78 Fed. Reg. 5636 (Jan. 25, 2013).

[106] 78 Fed. Reg. 5636 (Jan. 25, 2013)

[107] 45 C.F.R. § 164.524(c)(4); 65 Fed. Reg. 82,557, 82,735 (Dec. 28, 2000); 78 Fed. Reg. 5636 (Jan. 25, 2013).

[108] 65 Fed. Reg. 82,557 (Dec. 28, 2000); Webb v. Smart Document Solutions, 499 F.3d 1078 (9th Cir. 2007); Bugarin v. ChartOne, Inc., 38 Cal. Rptr. 3d 505 (Cal. App. 2 Dist. Jan. 27, 2006); but see also Espinoza v. Gold Cross Services, Inc., 234 P.3d 156 (Utah Ct. App., 2010).

[109] OCR Memorandum (May 31, 2012), available at http://www.hhs.gov/ocr/privacy/hipaa/understanding/consumers/righttoaccessmemo.pdf.

[C]   Amendments

An individual has the right to request that the covered entity amend PHI held by the covered entity in a designated record set.[110] The intent is to ensure that such information is accurate and complete. Amending the record need not mean altering existing information; a covered entity may instead append the amendment to the record or otherwise link the original and amended information.[111] This approach retains the integrity of the original medical record.

The covered entity may require that the request be submitted in writing with an explanation supporting the request if it so informs the individual.[112] (The requirement of a written request would be appropriate to include in the notice of privacy practices.) The covered entity must act on the request within 60 days. This time limit may be extended for another 30 days with written notice to the individual.[113]

The covered entity may deny the request under certain circumstances, such as if the covered entity did not create the PHI in question, or if the covered entity determines that the current information in the record is accurate and complete.[114] The denial must be in writing and must include the following:

- The basis for the denial;

- A statement of the individual's right to submit a statement of disagreement for the record and the process for doing so (such statement of disagreement must be included in future disclosures of the relevant PHI);

- A statement that if a statement of disagreement is not submitted, the individual may ask that the covered entity provide the request for and denial of the amendment with any future disclosures of the relevant PHI; and

- A description of the complaint process and contact information.

The covered entity may prepare a rebuttal to the individual's statement of disagreement.

The covered entity must identify the record or PHI that remains disputed and, as appropriate, link the request for amendment, denial of the request, statement of disagreement, and rebuttal to that record or PHI in the designated record set, so that these items are included in future disclosures.[115]

If an amendment is accepted, the covered entity must amend all affected records. In addition, the covered entity must make a reasonable effort to inform persons identified by the individual as having received the information that is to be amended and other persons the covered entity knows have the information and may rely on it (e.g., business associates of the covered entity).[116] Similarly, if the covered entity receives a notice of amendment from another covered entity, it is required to make the appropriate correction/amendment in its records.[117]

As with requests for access, the covered entity is required to document the designated record sets that are subject to amendment requests by the individual, as well as the titles or offices of those responsible for receiving and processing requests for amendments.[118]

---

[110] 45 C.F.R. § 164.526. See **§ 3.02[B][1]** for a definition of designated record set.

[111] 45 C.F.R. § 164.526(c)(1).

[112] 45 C.F.R. § 164.526(b)(1).

[113] 45 C.F.R. § 164.526(b)(2).

[114] 45 C.F.R. § 164.526(a)(2).

[115] 45 C.F.R. § 164.526(d).

[116] 45 C.F.R. § 164.526(c)(2)–(3).

[117] 45 C.F.R. § 164.526(e).

[118] 45 C.F.R. § 164.526(f).

[D] Accounting of Disclosures

[1] Current Requirements

An individual has the right to receive an accounting of disclosures of his or her PHI made by the covered entity.[119] Covered entities have been required to provide these "accountings," on request, since the original Privacy Regulations took effect in 2003. The HITECH Act made significant changes to the "accounting of disclosures" requirements, and HHS published proposed regulations in May 2011, which made even greater changes.[120] This section discusses the pre-HITECH regulations currently in effect. **Section 3.02[D][2]** discusses the proposed changes.

As noted, an individual may request an accounting of certain disclosures of his or her PHI made by the covered entity. A tracking mechanism will be required for all disclosures that are subject to this accounting requirement. For each disclosure, the following information must be tracked so that it can be provided to the individual upon request:

- Date of disclosure;

- Name of recipient (and address, if known);

- Brief description of the PHI disclosed; and

- Either a statement of the purpose of the disclosure (so as to reasonably inform the individual of the basis for the disclosure) or a copy of a written request for the disclosure (if any).[121]

An accounting of disclosures must include disclosures to or by the business associates of the covered entity if the disclosures are for purposes that are not excluded from the accounting requirement.[122] Business associates are required to track disclosures for an accounting under the terms of the business associate agreement.[123]

The accounting of disclosure requirement is not applicable to all categories of disclosures. In fact, it is not applicable to the most common types of disclosures, with the understanding that the individual knows or should know that his or her PHI is being disclosed for these purposes. Unfortunately, the Privacy Regulations described the accounting requirement in terms of what a covered entity *does not* need to account for, rather than what it *does* need to account for. The Privacy Regulations list the following disclosures as excluded from the accounting requirement:

(1) Disclosures for treatment, payment, or health care operations;

(2) Disclosures to the individual or his/her personal representative;

(3) Disclosures made pursuant to an authorization;

(4) Incidental disclosures;

(5) Disclosures for a facility directory or to family/caregivers;

(6) Disclosures for national security or intelligence purposes;

(7) Disclosures to law enforcement officials or correctional facilities; and

(8) Disclosures as part of a limited data set.[124]

---

[119] 45 C.F.R. § 164.528.

[120] HITECH Act § 13405(c); 76 Fed. Reg. 31,426 (May 31, 2011).

[121] 45 C.F.R. § 164.528(b)(2).

[122] 45 C.F.R. § 164.528(b)(1).

[123] See **§ 3.07**.

[124] 45 C.F.R. § 164.528(a)(1). These categories of disclosures are described in more detail in **§ 3.02**.

The remaining types of disclosures that *are* subject to this accounting requirement include disclosures made pursuant to 45 C.F.R. § 164.512 (other than those specifically listed above), disclosures to the Secretary of HHS, and mistakes and other disclosures made contrary to the Privacy Regulations. The following chart summarizes which categories of disclosures do and do not need to be tracked and included in an accounting.

Not Required for an Accounting

Disclosures named in the Privacy Regulations as excluded from the Accounting Requirement

- For treatment (changed by HITECH Act; see below).

- For payment (changed by HITECH Act; see below).

- For health care operations (changed by HITECH Act; see below).

- For a facility directory.

- Incidental disclosures. (Note: These are not the same as mistakes, which must be included in the Accounting.)

- Made based on the individual's written authorization.

- To the individual or his or her legal representative.

- Limited disclosures to persons (e.g., family) involved in the individual's care under § 164.510(b).

- For national security or intelligence purposes.

- To law enforcement officials or correctional institutions about an inmate or other individual in legal custody.

- As part of a limited data set, or information that has been de-identified.

- Made prior to April 14, 2003.

- Made more than six years prior to the date of the request.

Required for an Accounting

Other disclosures, not named in the Privacy Regulations as excluded, and therefore included in the Accounting Requirement

- To the Secretary of the federal Department of Health & Human Services. § 164.502

- Required by law (e.g., mandated reporting under state law). § 164.512(a)

- For public health activities/reporting. § 164.512(b)

- About victims of abuse, neglect, or domestic violence. § 164.512(c)

- For health oversight activities (e.g., licensure actions). § 164.512(d)

- In response to a court order. § 164.512(e)

- In response to a subpoena or discovery request. § 164.512(e)

- For law enforcement. § 164.512(f)

- To a medical examiner or funeral director, or for cadaver organ donations. § 164.512(g)-(h)

- For research without an authorization (i.e., under an IRB waiver). § 164.512(i)

- To avert a serious threat to health or safety. § 164.512(j)

- Certain specialized government functions (e.g., regarding armed forces personnel). § 164.512(k) (except not § 164.512(k)(2) or § 164.512(k)(5))

- For workers' compensation as authorized by and to the extent required to comply with workers' compensation laws. § 164.512(l)

- Disclosures not permitted by the Privacy Regulations (e.g., a disclosure without a valid authorization, when one is required).

- Any other disclosures not on the list of exclusions in the other column.

Covered entities have typically received few requests for accountings of disclosures. However, when necessary to respond to a request, a centralized record of disclosures is likely to make it easier to gather the required information. Some covered entities have required their business associates to periodically turn over their disclosure records to the covered entity, so that the covered entity can maintain consolidated disclosure-tracking information.

The covered entity must respond to an accounting request in writing, and for each applicable disclosure it must provide the elements described above: the date of disclosure, the name/address of recipient, a description of the PHI disclosed, and the purpose of the disclosure. Certain multiple disclosures may be summarized,[125] and special rules apply to accountings related to disclosures for research involving 50 or more individuals.[126]

The covered entity must act on the request within 60 days. This time limit may be extended for another 30 days with written notice to the individual.[127] In addition, under certain circumstances, the covered entity may temporarily suspend an individual's right to information about disclosures to a health oversight agency or law enforcement official.[128]

The covered entity must provide the first accounting in any 12-month period without charge but may charge a reasonable cost-based fee for additional accountings, provided the individual is informed of the costs and given an opportunity to modify the request to avoid or reduce the fee.[129] The Privacy Regulations do not specifically authorize the covered entity to require that a request for an accounting be in writing, but such a requirement is not prohibited, and would be appropriate to include in the notice of privacy practices.

The covered entity must document the information tracked for accounting purposes, the written accountings provided to individuals, and the titles or offices of those responsible for receiving and processing requests for accountings from individuals.[130]

[2] The HITECH Act and the Proposed Regulations

In 2009, the HITECH Act made significant changes to the "accounting of disclosures" requirements. Under the HITECH Act, if a covered entity uses or maintains an electronic health record with respect to PHI, the disclosures of that PHI *through that electronic health record* for treatment, payment, and health care operations (TPO) purposes will be subject to the accounting of disclosures requirement.[131] An "electronic health record (EHR)" was defined as "an electronic record of health-related information on an individual that is created, gathered, managed, and consulted by authorized health care clinicians and staff."[132] This language left open to interpretation the extent to which this statutory requirement applies other than in a traditional clinical setting.

For this expanded right to an accounting for disclosures made through an EHR for TPO purposes, the HITECH Act limited the accounting period to three years prior to the request, rather than the standard six years applicable to accounting for other disclosures. In addition, under the Act, the covered entity was given the choice to provide either an accounting that also included disclosures by its business associates or an accounting of the covered entity's own disclosures and a list of business associates for the individual to contact. The business associates would then be required to provide their own accountings upon direct request from the individual.[133]

Under the Act, the new right to an accounting of disclosures for TPO applies only to disclosures made through an EHR, and the effective date under the Act depended on when the covered entity acquired the EHR. For a covered entity that had acquired the EHR as of January 1, 2009, the Act states that the new requirements

---

[125] 45 C.F.R. § 164.528(b).

[126] 45 C.F.R. § 164.528(b)(4).

[127] 45 C.F.R. § 164.528(c).

[128] 45 C.F.R. § 164.528(a).

[129] 45 C.F.R. § 164.528(c)(2).

[130] 45 C.F.R. § 164.528(d).

[131] HITECH Act § 13405(c). See **§ 3.03[B]** for information about treatment, payment, and health care operations (TPO) purposes.

[132] HITECH Act § 13400(5).

[133] HITECH Act § 13405(c).

apply to TPO disclosures made on and after January 1, 2014. For a covered entity that acquires the EHR after January 1, 2009, the new requirements apply to TPO disclosures made on and after the later of January 1, 2011, or the date the covered entity acquires the EHR. HHS is permitted to extend these compliance dates.[134]

The HITECH Act required HHS to issue regulations for these new accounting of disclosures requirements that would balance the interests of individuals and the administrative burden on covered entities and business associates. In May 2011, HHS issued proposed regulations to implement the HITECH Act requirements but also used its broad regulatory authority under HIPAA to propose other significant changes.[135] HHS proposes a "split" of the individual's right to an accounting of disclosures into two separate but complementary rights. The original right to an accounting of disclosures would continue but in a more limited fashion, and a new "access report" right would be added to address the HITECH changes.

Under the proposed regulations, an individual's right to request an accounting of disclosures would be limited to disclosures from a designated record set (rather than a disclosure of any PHI) and would be available only for disclosures made within three years prior to the request, rather than the original six years.[136] Limitation to the designated record set makes this right more consistent with the individual's right to access and request amendments, which are also limited to the designated record set. The HITECH Act requirement relating to accounting of disclosures for TPO is addressed by HHS in the access report provisions, discussed below. For the accounting of disclosures, the list of disclosures to be accounted for would actually get shorter rather than longer under the proposed regulations. For example, HHS proposes that disclosures required by law, and for research or public health purposes (with certain exceptions), need not be included in an accounting.[137] HHS also proposes excluding accounting for disclosures that are impermissible disclosures under the Privacy Regulations, provided a breach notice has been sent to the individual.[138] HHS also requested comments on what other disclosures might be excluded.

HHS proposes changes to simplify the content of an accounting as well. For example, if the exact date of the disclosure is not known, HHS would allow an approximate date in some cases. HHS also proposes decreasing the required time period for responding to a request from 60 days to 30 days (still with one permitted 30-day extension). In addition, HHS clarifies that a covered entity can require that the individual make the request for an accounting in writing.[139]

HHS introduced the new access report requirement to implement the HITECH Act provision requiring an accounting of disclosures for TPO through an EHR. HHS rejects the statute's "through an EHR" language and proposes instead that the requirement should apply to any electronic PHI in a designated record set (hereinafter referred to as an e-DRS).[140] One result of this change is that under the proposed regulations, the access report requirement would clearly apply to all covered entities, not just to health care providers.

Under the proposed regulations, an individual would have a right to request an access report covering a period of up to three years prior to the request. This report would be generated using the raw data from the access logs of e-DRS systems.[141] HHS states that all covered entities and business associates must already have such access logs, because they are required by the Security Regulations.[142] This is a broad interpretation of the Security Regulations that assumes all covered entities and business associates meet the Security Regulations requirements in the same manner, that is, through the use of access logs that cover every system access of every individual record, and, moreover, that the content and retention periods for such access logs match HHS's

---

[134] HITECH Act § 13405(c).

[135] 76 Fed. Reg. 31,426 (May 31, 2011).

[136] 76 Fed, Reg. 31,430 (May 31, 2011).

[137] 76 Fed, Reg. 31,431–34 (May 31, 2011).

[138] 76 Fed, Reg. 31,431 (May 31, 2011).

[139] 76 Fed, Reg. 31,434–35 (May 31, 2011).

[140] 76 Fed, Reg. 31,436–37 (May 31, 2011).

[141] 76 Fed, Reg. 31,436 (May 31, 2011).

[142] 76 Fed, Reg. 31,437 (May 31, 2011) (citing the Security Regulation requirement at 45 C.F.R § 164.312(b)). Under the HITECH Act, business associates are also directly subject to the Security Rule; however, that did not take effect until February 2010.

proposed requirements. This is a controversial approach, as it seems contrary to the "flexibility and scalability" principle embedded in the Security Regulations.

Under the proposed regulations, the access report would identify each *access* to the individual's e-DRS records for any purpose, rather than each *disclosure* for TPO. HHS concluded that this access-based approach was more aligned with individuals' interests in the information and that the access logs of most covered entities' e-DRS systems could not currently distinguish between a use and a disclosure and could not identify the purpose of the access.[143]

The access report would be a reader-friendly version of the data in the access log and would include the following elements:

- Date and time of access;

- Name of the natural person if available; otherwise, the name of the entity accessing the e-DRS (user IDs are expected to be converted to people's first and last names for the report);

- Description of what information was accessed, if available; and

- Description of the action by the user (e.g., create, modify, delete), if available.[144]

This would be the first time that specific persons must be identified by name in such a report, and this raises employee/workforce privacy, safety, and other concerns.

In some cases, such as medical records related to a single complex hospital stay, the access report could include tens of thousands of records. The proposed regulations would not require any summary information or any additional content about the roles of the persons named.[145] Covered entities should, however, expect such questions to be asked and would need to develop an approach on how to respond. Responding to follow-up questions from individuals receiving voluminous access reports would require considerable resources.

HHS describes the individual's interest in knowing who accessed his or her PHI, focusing in particular on the interest in knowing whether a particular person inappropriately accessed that PHI. While it might be possible for the individual to glean this information from these access reports, it may be difficult for the individual to determine whether a particular access was "appropriate" or not. Individuals may be able to get this information more easily and efficiently by filing a complaint with the covered entity and asking the covered entity to determine whether a particular person impermissibly accessed the individual's records.

HHS recognized that the access report might identify access that meets the definition of "patient safety work product" under the Patient Safety and Quality Improvement Act[146] and as such is confidential and privileged. The proposed regulations would require covered entities to exclude these access records from an access report.[147] Comments to the proposed regulations will likely raise issues of other access records that should be excluded for similar reasons of privilege. Exclusion of records for reasons of privilege will be important, but it is not clear how the covered entity or business associate is supposed to do this. Concerns will certainly be raised to HHS about the potential need to modify systems or create manual processes to capture and identify any such access records that need to be excluded by user or by purpose (to the extent such exclusions are permitted or required by the final regulations).

As with an accounting of disclosures, HHS proposes that a covered entity would have 30 days to provide a requested access report (with one possible 30-day extension).[148] The covered entity may require that the individual's request be in writing. The access report must be provided in an electronic form and format requested by the individual if it is readily producible in that form and format. If not, and the individual does not agree to the

---

[143] 76 Fed. Reg. 31,436–37 (May 31, 2011).
[144] 76 Fed. Reg. 31,437–38 (May 31, 2011).
[145] 76 Fed. Reg. 31,440 (May 31, 2011).
[146] 42 C.F.R. Pt. 3.
[147] 76 Fed. Reg. 31,441 (May 31, 2011).
[148] 76 Fed. Reg. 31,440 (May 31, 2011).

electronic form and format offered by the covered entity, the covered entity must produce the access report in a readable hard copy form.[149] As with the accounting of disclosures, the individual may not be charged a fee for the first request in a 12-month period, and the individual must be notified if there will be a charge for a subsequent request.[150]

HHS would expect the covered entity to aggregate the access log data from all its e-DRS systems into a single report, which would also include the access reports of its business associates. Covered entities may find it difficult and expensive to aggregate raw access data across systems to create these reports. This "aggregate access report" differs from the HITECH Act approach, which would have given the covered entity the option of responding only for itself and providing the requesting individual with a list of business associates to contact. HHS rejected this as too burdensome for the individual.[151]

Because the right to an access report is new, information about this right would need to be added to the covered entity's notice of privacy practices. HHS considers this a material change to the notice, triggering distribution obligations (see § 3.02[A][3]). The final regulations may make an exception to the standard rules about providing updated notices to make this process less burdensome.[152]

HHS proposes separate compliance dates for the revised accounting of disclosures provisions and for the new access report requirements. For the revised accounting of disclosures provisions, HHS proposes a compliance date of 180 days after the effective date of the final regulations. For the access report requirements, covered entities and business associates would be required to comply with report requests beginning January 1, 2013, with respect to any e-DRS system acquired after January 1, 2009, and beginning January 1, 2014, for any e-DRS system acquired on or before January 1, 2009. HHS assumes covered entities and business associates will have the access log data going back three years from those compliance dates and appears to require that the access report be made available starting on the compliance dates and including access up to three years prior to the compliance date. This approach would be different from the HITECH Act, which stated that the requirement would apply to *disclosures made* on or after the effective date. In another change from the HITECH statute, the compliance dates for a covered entity or business associate could vary depending on the date it acquired each particular e-DRS system. HHS encourages the inclusion of data from all e-DRS systems during this transition period, even if not required by the regulation.[153]

The proposed regulations regarding the new access report have generated much controversy and discussion. It is expected that the volume of comments to HHS will be significant. There is the hope, if not the expectation, among covered entities that the final version of the new access report regulations will be considerably different from the proposed version and will better balance the burdens to covered entities and business associates with the value to the individual.

[E]   Restrictions and Confidential Communications

[1]   Restrictions

An individual has the right to request restrictions to the covered entity's uses and disclosures of the individual's PHI, with respect to uses and disclosures for treatment, payment, health care operations, and for certain uses and disclosures to persons involved in the individual's care or for notification purposes. In general, the

---

[149] 76 Fed. Reg. 31,440 (May 31, 2011).
[150] 76 Fed. Reg. 31,440 (May 31, 2011).
[151] 76 Fed. Reg. 31,439 (May 31, 2011).
[152] 76 Fed. Reg. 31,441 (May 31, 2011).
[153] 76 Fed. Reg. 31,441–42 (May 31, 2011).

covered entity may deny such a request; but if it grants the request, it is bound by any restriction to which it agrees (except in cases of emergency treatment), and these restrictions must be documented.[154]

The one exception to the covered entity's ability to deny a restriction request comes from the HITECH Act.[155] As implemented by the HITECH Regulations, effective September 23, 2013, a covered entity *must* comply with a request to restrict disclosures from health care providers to health plans if

(1)   the disclosure of PHI would be to a health plan for purposes of carrying out payment or health care operations;

(2)   the disclosure is not otherwise required by law; and

(3)   the PHI pertains solely to a health care item or service for which the health care provider involved has been paid in full, either by the individual or another person on behalf of the individual (but not by the health plan).[156]

The implementation of these restrictions on disclosures to health plans in these "self-pay" situations can be complex for providers. HHS recognized this, and has provided the following guidance:

- *Flagging the Record.* Providers are not required to create separate medical records or otherwise segregate the PHI subject to the restriction, but some method of flagging the restricted item or service in the record will be needed to avoid inadvertently disclosing the PHI to the health plan for payment or health care operations purposes (such as audits by the health plan). HHS has noted that, to comply with the minimum necessary standards, providers should already have mechanisms in place to appropriately limit the disclosure of PHI.[157]

- *No "All or None" Approach Permitted.* A provider may not impose an "all or nothing" approach and require that the restriction apply to all services received from the provider and, therefore, require out-of-pocket payment for all services.[158] Each restriction request is specific to a particular item or service that is paid for in full by, or on behalf of, the individual.

- *Split Visits.* HHS expects a provider to accommodate an individual's request for a restriction for specific health care items or services that are part of the same treatment encounter with other items or services, if they can be separated or unbundled. If a provider is able to unbundle the items or services, the provider should counsel individuals on the impact of the unbundling, for example, advising the individual that the health plan may be able to determine that the restricted item or service was performed based on the other services provided. After this counseling, if the individual still wants to request the restriction, the provider must comply with the individual's request. On the other hand, if the items or services cannot be unbundled, they will be treated as a single item or service. If the provider is not able to unbundle a group of items or services, the provider should inform the individual of this and give the individual the opportunity to decide whether he or she wants to pay for the entire bundle of items or services in order to restrict disclosures to the health plan.[159]

- *Timing of the Request.* HHS has recognized that a provider may not be able to implement the request for restrictions "if the individual waits until the care has been initiated" before making the request. The only example HHS provides is that of a hospital stay, stating that the PHI may have already been

---

[154] 45 C.F.R. § 164.522(a). If restricted PHI is disclosed to a provider for emergency treatment, the covered entity must request that the provider not further use or disclose the PHI. 45 C.F.R. § 164.522(a)(1)(iii)–(iv). The Regulations also specify the manner in which such a restriction may be terminated. 45 C.F.R. § 164.522(a)(2).

[155] HITECH Act § 13405(a).

[156] 45 C.F.R. § 164.522(a)(vi).

[157] 78 Fed. Reg. 5628 (Jan. 25, 2013).

[158] 78 Fed. Reg. 5626 (Jan. 25, 2013).

[159] 78 Fed. Reg. 5629 (Jan. 25, 2013).

disclosed to the health plan.[160] This issue can easily occur in other care settings as well. For example, when an individual checks in for a doctor's appointment in a clinic setting, that check-in may set in motion a billing process, even before the individual sees the doctor.

- *Paid in Full.* The service or item may be paid in full either by the individual or on behalf of the individual (e.g., by a family member or by *another* health plan).[161] An individual may choose to use a Flexible Spending Account (FSA) or Health Savings Account (HSA) to pay for the services that the individual wishes to have restricted from disclosure to another health plan, but the individual may not restrict disclosures to the FSA or HSA necessary for that payment.[162]

- *Bounced Checks.* If an individual's payment for the service or item in question is not honored (e.g., the check bounces), the provider may submit the claim to the health plan for payment. The dishonored payment would negate the restriction request, because the individual did not fulfill a necessary condition. HHS nevertheless expects the provider to make reasonable efforts to contact the individual to attempt to obtain payment prior to billing the health plan. The provider may establish its own policies with regard to this process. The provider may also choose to require payment in full at the time of the restriction request to avoid later difficulties. Pre-payment may also be advisable if the service requires health plan pre-certification (but it is not obtained due to the restriction request). In such a situation, if the provider is not paid by the individual, lack of the pre-certification may mean it is not possible to obtain payment from the health plan at a later time.[163]

- *Downstream Providers (Prescribing).* If the provider prescribes medication as part of the service/encounter, the provider typically would send that prescription electronically to the individual's pharmacy. If the individual also wants to restrict the pharmacy from disclosing the prescription to the health plan, there may be a timing problem, because the pharmacy may contact the health plan before the individual can reach the pharmacy. The provider is not required to notify "downstream providers" of restriction requests. HHS states that the physician would thus not be required to alert the pharmacy about the restriction. HHS encourages providers to counsel individuals on the need for the individual to take responsibility for contacting other providers to request a restriction on disclosures. HHS also notes that the provider could give a paper prescription to the individual, which could allow the individual time to request a restriction at the pharmacy and pay out of pocket for the item.[164] Note: HHS does not specifically address the situation where the pharmacy is part of the same covered entity as the prescribing physician. It is unclear whether, as part of the same covered entity, the pharmacy would be deemed to have notice of the restriction. In such cases, counseling of the individual and offering a paper prescription may be even more important.

- *Downstream Providers (Other).* HHS does not define "downstream provider," but other "downstream providers" could include consulting physicians, outside labs, specialists, pathologists, radiologists, and others. The provider is not required to notify any downstream providers of the restriction. That is the individual's responsibility. HHS encourages (but does not require) providers to counsel individuals on the individual's obligation to contact other providers to request a restriction. HHS also suggests that the provider could assist individuals in alerting downstream providers, when feasible.[165] Note: In some cases, such as in a large complex health system, it may seem more of a floodplain than a simple downstream flow, and individuals may have difficulty identifying the connections among providers and who to contact to request a restriction.

---

[160] 78 Fed. Reg. 5630 (Jan. 25, 2013).
[161] 78 Fed. Reg. 5626, 5629 (Jan. 25, 2013).
[162] 78 Fed. Reg. 5630 (Jan. 25, 2013).
[163] 78 Fed. Reg. 5629–5630 (Jan. 25, 2013).
[164] 78 Fed. Reg. 5629 (Jan. 25, 2013).
[165] 78 Fed. Reg. 5629 (Jan. 25, 2013).

- *Follow-up Services.* If the individual requests a restriction regarding a service and then has a follow-up visit but does not request a restriction, the restriction on the first visit will be deemed revoked to the extent the provider must disclose information to the health plan about the first service to get paid for the second. No authorization from the individual is required for the disclosure. HHS strongly encourages the provider to discuss this with the individual to ensure he or she realizes that the previously restricted PHI will be disclosed, unless the individual requests a new restriction for the follow-up care and pays for it in full.[166]

- *HMOs.* If an individual receives care in an HMO setting and requests a restriction, the provider should comply with the request, unless it would be inconsistent with state or other law to do so. Therefore, if a provider within an HMO is prohibited by law from accepting payment from the individual in excess of what would be the individual's normal co-pay or cost-sharing amount, the provider may advise the individual that he or she must seek out-of-network care in order to restrict the disclosure to the HMO. (If the provider is able to treat the service as out-of-network and comply with the requested restriction, it should do so.) In contrast, a contractual requirement for the provider to submit a claim or otherwise disclose information to the HMO does not relieve the provider from its obligation to honor requests for restrictions. HHS notes that HMOs have a 180-day compliance period to change their provider contracts accordingly.[167]

- *Impact on Plan Deductibles.* Because the individual is paying in full for the items or service, and no information is disclosed to the health plan, the individual should not expect that this payment would be counted toward any plan deductible or out-of-pocket limitations.[168]

- *Business Associates.* A provider may disclose restricted PHI to its own business associates for the provider's own purposes. The provider may not, however, disclose the restricted PHI to a business associate of the health plan, as such a disclosure would be considered equivalent to a disclosure to the health plan.[169]

- *Disclosures Required by Law.* Providers may continue to make disclosures that are required by law (essentially, court-enforceable mandates that compel the disclosure), even if a restriction is in place. For example, providers may continue to disclose the otherwise restricted PHI if mandated by Medicare conditions of participation.

  - *Medicaid/State Programs.* If a provider is required by state or other law to submit a claim for any service provided to the covered individual, and there is no "self-pay" exception, then the disclosure is required by law.

  - *Medicare.* In general, when a physician or supplier furnishes a Medicare-covered service, it is required to submit a claim to Medicare. However, there is an exception to the rule. If the Medicare beneficiary (or his or her legal representative) refuses of his or her own free will to authorize the submission of a claim to Medicare for Part B services, the physician or supplier is not required to submit a claim and may charge the individual directly for the service. The limitations on what a physician or supplier may collect from a Medicare beneficiary still apply, even though a claim was not submitted. Thus, the law does not require submission of the claim to Medicare in these particular circumstances, and the physician or supplier must honor the restriction request.[170]

---

[166] 78 Fed. Reg. 5630 (Jan. 25, 2013).

[167] 78 Fed. Reg. 5629 (Jan. 25, 2013).

[168] 78 Fed. Reg. 5626 (Jan. 25, 2013).

[169] 78 Fed. Reg. 5630 (Jan. 25, 2013).

[170] 78 Fed. Reg. 5628 (Jan. 25, 2013). HHS cites the provisions related to physicians and suppliers under Medicare Part B only. HHS is silent with regard to hospital and other facility charges under Part A, and whether submission of such claims would be required by law.

Even with this guidance from HHS, questions will continue to arise as to how to operationalize this new "self-pay" restriction requirement. For example, the restriction applies not only to the initial billing to the health plan for the item or service, but also to later health care operations, such as health plan claim audits. In addition, the requirement applies only to *disclosures* to a health plan, and it is unclear whether or how the requirement would apply in an integrated system where the provider and health plan are part of the same covered entity, and the communication to the health plan would be a *use* rather than a *disclosure*.

Although the *request* for restrictions is not required to be in writing, for these special "self-pay" restrictions on disclosures to health plans, a written request is advisable and may be combined with the required documentation about the agreed-to restriction. Providers may want to develop a standard form for these requests, which clearly explains matters such as the scope of the restriction, when payment is required, the patient's obligations with respect to downstream providers, and what happens in the event of a follow-up visit that requires disclosure of the restricted service. Much of the guidance provided by HHS recommends that the provider counsel the patient on the complexities and consequences inherent in these restriction requests. This is complicated for both the provider and the patient. Providers should have some type of written explanation to provide to patients to avoid misunderstandings.

[2]   Confidential Communications

Requests for confidential communications impact providers and health plans differently. A provider must accommodate reasonable requests by individuals to receive PHI communications from the provider at an alternative location or by alternative means. The provider may not require an explanation from the individual as to the basis of the request as a condition for complying, but it may require the request be in writing. The provider may also require that the individual provide additional information about how payment will be handled as a condition to agreeing to the confidential communications.[171]

A health plan must accommodate reasonable requests by individuals to receive PHI communications from the health plan at alternative locations or by alternative means only if the individual clearly states that the disclosure of all or part of that information could endanger the individual. The health plan may require that this statement regarding endangerment be included in a written request for such alternative communications.[172] The health plan may also require additional information about how payment will be handled as a condition to agreeing to the confidential communications. An example of a confidential communication request would be the individual asking that explanations of benefits and other claim correspondence be mailed to her work address rather than her home address. An example of endangerment could include an individual whose spouse will become physically abusive if he or she discovers the individual has sought treatment.

§ 3.03   USE AND DISCLOSURE OF PHI

The main principle of the Privacy Regulations is that PHI may be used or disclosed by a covered entity or business associate only as required or permitted under the Regulations.[173] The term *use* refers to the sharing, employment, application, utilization, examination, or analysis of PHI within the entity that maintains it. The term *disclosure* refers to any release, transfer, provision of access to, or divulging of PHI outside the entity maintaining it.[174]

---

[171] 45 C.F.R. § 164.522(b).

[172] 45 C.F.R. § 164.522(b).

[173] 45 C.F.R. § 164.502(a).

[174] 45 C.F.R. § 160.103.

[A] Required and Permitted Uses and Disclosures

The Privacy Regulations both *require* and *permit* uses and disclosures.

[1] Covered Entities

For a covered entity, the only two types of disclosures that are *required* are (1) to the individual in accordance with a request for access or request for an accounting of disclosures as described in **§§ 3.02[B]** and **3.02[D]**, respectively, and (2) when required by HHS to investigate a covered entity's compliance with the Administrative Simplification Regulations.[175]

The *permitted* uses and disclosures are more numerous and are categorized according to their purpose:

- To the individual;

- For treatment, payment, or health care operations, which in some cases requires a good faith effort to obtain the individual's written acknowledgement of receipt of the covered entity's notice of privacy practices;

- In the event of incidental disclosures, if applicable requirements are followed;

- For facility directories, provided the individual has been given an opportunity to opt out;

- For disclosures to family and other caregivers, provided the individual has been given an opportunity to opt out;

- For public health purposes, law enforcement purposes, and other limited purposes for which permission of the individual is not required;

- For limited data sets, subject to certain requirements; and

- For other purposes, pursuant to a valid authorization.[176]

Each of these categories applies in specific circumstances and is discussed in greater detail in **§ 3.03**. Other more specialized uses and disclosures are discussed in **§ 3.04**.

[2] Business Associates

A business associate is *required* to disclose PHI (1) when required by HHS to investigate the business associate's compliance with the Administrative Simplification Regulations; and (2) to the covered entity, individual, or individual's designee, as necessary, to satisfy the covered entity's obligations with respect to an individual's requests for access to electronic PHI in a designated record set.[177]

A business associate is *permitted* to use or disclose PHI only as permitted or required by its business associate agreement or as required by law.[178] The business associate may not use or disclose PHI in a manner that would violate the Administrative Simplification Regulations if the use or disclosure were made by the covered entity.[179]

---

[175] 45 C.F.R. § 164.502(a)(2).

[176] 45 C.F.R. § 164.502(a)(1). Certain other special categories, such as fundraising, sale of PHI, and marketing, are discussed in **§ 3.04**.

[177] 45 C.F.R. § 164.502(a)(4).

[178] 45 C.F.R. § 164.502(a)(3).

[179] 45 C.F.R. § 164.502(a)(3). An exception applies with regard to certain uses and disclosures related to the proper administration and management of the business associate, or to certain data aggregation services, to the extent these are permitted under the terms of the business associate agreement (see **§ 3.06**).

Provisions relating to business associates and business associate agreements, respectively, are covered in more detail in **§ 1.02[B]** and **§ 3.06**.

[B] Treatment, Payment, and Health Care Operations

Treatment, payment, and health care operations (sometimes called "TPO") are the most common functions of covered entities.

- *Treatment* includes provision, coordination, or management of health care and related services by one or more health care providers, including coordination or management of health care by a health care provider with a third party, consultation between health care providers relating to a patient, or the referral of a patient for health care from one health care provider to another.[180] In most cases, the treatment provided will be treatment of the individual, but the Privacy Regulations do permit the use or disclosure of PHI for the treatment of others.[181]

- *Payment* includes activities engaged in by a health plan to obtain premiums or to determine or fulfill its responsibilities to provide coverage or benefits; a health plan or provider providing or obtaining reimbursement for the provision of health care; determinations of eligibility or coverage; coordination of benefits; adjudication or subrogation of health care claims; billing; claims management; utilization review; collection activity; obtaining payment under a reinsurance contract; and review of health care services for coverage or medical necessity.[182]

- *Health care operations* means the following activities to the extent they are related to the covered functions of the covered entity: conducting quality assessment or improvement activities; reviewing the competence or qualifications of health care professionals; evaluating health plan performance; conducting health care practitioner and other training programs; accreditation, certification, licensing, or credentialing activities; underwriting, premium rating; medical review; legal services; auditing functions, including fraud and abuse detection and compliance programs; business planning and development; and business management and general administrative activities of the entity. Health care operations also includes a sale, transfer, merger, or consolidation of a covered entity with another covered entity and related transfers of records and due diligence.[183]

[1] Consent

Consent to use or disclose PHI for treatment, payment, and health care operations is permitted but not required under the Privacy Regulations.[184] Covered entities may, therefore, continue to follow consent processes mandated by state law. Covered entities that choose to have a consent process have complete discretion (under the Privacy Regulations) in designing that process.[185] The Privacy Regulations make a distinction between "consent" and "authorization." Uses and disclosures that require an authorization are discussed in **§ 3.03[F]**.

---

[180] 45 C.F.R. § 164.501.

[181] OCR, FAQ: "Under the HIPAA Privacy Rule may a health care provider disclose protected health information about an individual to another provider, when such information is requested for the treatment of a family member of the individual?", available at http://www.hhs.gov/ocr/privacy/hipaa/faq/disclosures/512.html.

[182] 45 C.F.R. § 164.501. Additional details regarding what constitutes payment are found in the regulation and should be referenced before making a final determination as to whether an activity falls into this category.

[183] 45 C.F.R. § 164.501. Additional details regarding what constitutes health care operations are found in the regulation and should be referenced before making a final determination as to whether an activity falls into this category.

[184] 45 C.F.R. § 164.506(b). Elimination of the consent requirement was a major change in the Privacy Regulations and was implemented in the modified version of the regulations published August 14, 2002, at 67 Fed. Reg. 53,182.

[185] 67 Fed. Reg. 53,211 (Aug. 14, 2002).

Consent may not be obtained in lieu of an authorization if an authorization is otherwise required under the Privacy Regulations.

[2]   Treatment, Payment, and Health Care Operations of the Covered Entity

A covered entity is not required to obtain consent (or authorization) to use and disclose PHI for its own treatment, payment, and health care operations. The Privacy Regulations provide "regulatory permission" for these activities.[186] The notice of privacy practices puts the individual on notice of these uses and disclosures (see **§ 3.02[A]**).

[3]   Treatment, Payment, and Health Care Operations of Another Entity

In addition to using and disclosing PHI for its own treatment, payment, and health care operations, a covered entity may, without consent (or authorization), use and disclose PHI for the treatment, payment, and certain health care operations purposes of another entity as follows:[187]

1. A covered entity may disclose PHI for the *treatment* activities of any health care provider.

2. A covered entity may disclose PHI to another covered entity or to any health care provider for the *payment* activities of that recipient.

3. A covered entity may disclose PHI to another covered entity for the *health care operations* of that other entity if that entity either has or had a relationship with the individual who is the subject of the information,[188] the PHI disclosed pertains to such relationship, and the disclosure is for one of the following subcategories of health care operations:

    • Conducting quality assessment and improvement activities (including outcomes evaluation and development of clinical guidelines, provided that obtaining generalized knowledge is not the primary purpose of any resulting studies); population-based activities relating to improving health or reducing health care costs; protocol development; case management and care coordination; contacting health care providers and patients with information about treatment alternatives; and related functions that do not include treatment;

    • Reviewing the competence or qualifications of health care professionals; evaluating practitioner and provider performance, and health plan performance; conducting training programs in which students, trainees, or practitioners in areas of health care learn under supervision to practice or improve their skills as health care providers; training of non–health care professionals; accreditation, certification, licensing, or credentialing activities; or

    • The purpose of health care fraud and abuse detection or compliance.

Disclosures for health care operations that do not meet these criteria require an authorization.

---

[186] 67 Fed. Reg. 53,211 (Aug. 14, 2002).

[187] 45 C.F.R. § 164.506(c).

[188] A covered entity, prior to making a disclosure allowed under this provision, is permitted to communicate with another covered entity as necessary to determine if this condition has been met. Where the relationship between the covered entity and the individual has ended, a disclosure of PHI about the individual is permitted to the extent the disclosure is related to the past relationship. For example, a health care provider may disclose PHI to a health plan for HEDIS (Health Plan Employer Data and Information Set) purposes, even if the individual no longer is covered by the health plan, provided that the period for which information is needed overlaps with the period for which the individual was enrolled in the health plan. For disclosures of PHI for quality and other health care operations where the covered entity requesting the information does not have a relationship with the individual, the provisions for limited data sets and data use agreements are intended to provide a mechanism for disclosures of PHI. 67 Fed. Reg. 53,217 (Aug. 14, 2002). *See* **§§ 1.03[C]** and **3.06** for discussions of limited data sets and data use agreements, respectively.

A covered entity that participates in an organized health care arrangement may disclose PHI about an individual to other participants in the organized health care arrangement for any joint health care operations activities of the organized health care arrangement.[189]

If the Privacy Regulations permit a covered entity to disclose PHI to another covered entity, the covered entity is also permitted to disclose PHI directly to a business associate acting on behalf of that other covered entity.[190] (See **§ 1.02[B]** and **§ 3.06** for more information regarding business associates and business associate agreements, respectively.)

[C] Opt-Out Approach

The individual's written permission is not required for uses and disclosures for the purposes described in this section, provided the covered entity informs the individual in advance and the individual has opportunity to object to or restrict these uses or disclosures.[191] Advising the individual of this right and the individual's response may be oral rather than in writing.

[1] Facility Directory

Under certain circumstances, a provider with a facility directory may include in that directory the individual's:

- Name;

- Location in the facility;

- General condition in terms that do not communicate specific medical information about the individual (e.g., fair, critical, stable, etc.); and

- Religious affiliation.[192]

The above information may be included in the directory if the individual does not object. The provider must inform the individual in advance what PHI may be included in the facility directory and to whom disclosures may be made, and give the individual a meaningful opportunity to opt out of the directory listing or to restrict some or all of the uses and disclosures in regard to the directory (e.g., omitting religious affiliation or general condition from the directory information). Subject to the individual's right to object, the provider may disclose the directory information (except religious affiliation) to anyone who asks for the individual by name. All directory information, including religious affiliation, may be disclosed to members of the clergy (including clergy who are part of the covered entity's workforce), and they need not ask for the individual by name.[193]

The Privacy Regulations allow such directory-type disclosures when individuals are incapacitated and in emergency treatment circumstances; in such situations, the provider must make the decision whether to include the individual's information in the facility directory in accordance with professional judgment as to the individual's best interests. The provider must, when it becomes practicable, inform the individual about its policies regarding the facility directory and provide the opportunity to object to the use or disclosure of PHI for the directory.[194]

---

[189] 45 C.F.R. § 164.506(c)(5). See **§ 1.02[C][3]** for more information on OHCAs.

[190] 67 Fed. Reg. 53,218 (Aug. 14, 2002).

[191] 45 C.F.R. § 164.510.

[192] 45 C.F.R. § 164.510(a); 65 Fed. Reg. 82,521 (Dec. 28, 2000).

[193] 45 C.F.R. § 164.510(a); 78 Fed. Reg. 5628 (Jan. 25, 2013) (clarifying that "clergy" does not exclude members of the workforce).

[194] 45 C.F.R. § 164.510(a).

[2] Family, Friends, and Current Caregivers

Covered entities may disclose to a person involved in the current health care of the individual (such as a family member, other relative, close personal friend, or any other person identified by the individual) PHI directly related to the person's involvement in the current health care of the individual or payment related to that health care. Covered entities may also use or disclose PHI to notify or assist in notification of family members, personal representatives, or other persons responsible for an individual's care with respect to an individual's location, condition, or death.[195]

When the individual is present at the time of disclosure and has the capacity to make his or her own decisions, a covered entity may use or disclose PHI only if it:

1. obtains the individual's agreement to disclose to the third parties involved in their care;

2. provides the individual with an opportunity to object to such disclosure and the individual does not express an objection; or

3. reasonably infers from the circumstances, based on the exercise of professional judgment, that the individual does not object to the disclosure.[196]

Situations in which providers may infer an individual's agreement to disclose PHI include, for example, when the individual brings his or her spouse into the doctor's office while treatment is being discussed or when a friend accompanies the individual to the emergency room for treatment.[197]

When the individual is not present or when the opportunity to agree or object to the use or disclosure cannot practicably be provided due to the individual's incapacity or an emergency circumstance, covered entities may, in the exercise of professional judgment, determine whether the disclosure is in the individual's best interests and, if so, disclose only the PHI that is directly relevant to the person's involvement with the individual's health care, payment for health care, or as needed for notification purposes. For example, this provision allows covered entities to inform relatives or others involved in a patient's care, such as the person who accompanied the patient to the emergency room, that a patient has suffered a heart attack and to provide updates on the patient's progress and prognosis when the patient is incapacitated and unable to make decisions about such disclosures.[198]

This permission to use professional judgment clearly applies in cases where the patient is unconscious.[199] Lack of capacity may also include situations where the patient is suffering from temporary psychosis or is under the influence of drugs or alcohol.[200] The provider should take into account the patient's desires, if previously communicated, as well as the current circumstances. And once the patient regains capacity, the provider should offer the patient the opportunity to object to future sharing of PHI.[201]

According to HHS, this provision of the Privacy Regulations is not intended to disrupt most current practices with respect to these types of disclosures. But permitting a covered entity to use its discretion has its limitations. The PHI disclosed should be only what is relevant to the circumstances, and the disclosure must be to someone close to the individual.[202]

---

[195] 45 C.F.R. § 164.510(b); 65 Fed. Reg. 82,522 (Dec. 28, 2000).

[196] 45 C.F.R. § 164.510(b)(2).

[197] 65 Fed. Reg. 82,523 (Dec. 28, 2000).

[198] 45 C.F.R. § 164.510(b)(3); 65 Fed. Reg. 82,523 (Dec. 28, 2000).

[199] HHS, "HIPAA Privacy Rule and Sharing Information Related to Mental Health" (Feb. 20, 2014), available at http://www.hhs.gov/ocr/privacy/hipaa/understanding/special/mhguidance.html (hereinafter, "OCR Guidance—Mental Health").

[200] OCR Guidance—Mental Health.

[201] OCR Guidance—Mental Health.

[202] 65 Fed. Reg. 82,523 (Dec. 28, 2000).

Covered entities are not required to verify the identity of the family member or other person involved in the individual's care. The individual's act of involving the person in the individual's care is sufficient verification of identity for purposes of this provision of the Privacy Regulations.[203]

The use of the terms "spouse" and "marriage" in the Privacy Regulations include persons in legally valid same-sex marriages, whether or not they live or receive services in a jurisdiction that recognizes the marriage. Legally married same-sex spouses are "family members" for purposes of this provision of the Privacy Regulations.[204]

A covered entity may also use or disclose PHI to a public or private disaster relief organization in order for that organization to locate a family member or other person involved in the individual's care.[205]

HHS has published two guidance documents, one for health care providers and one for patients, to help clarify this section of the Privacy Regulations, so that providers do not unnecessarily limit communications with a patient's family, friends, and caregivers.[206] This guidance provides the following examples:

- An emergency room doctor may discuss the patient's treatment in front of the patient's friend when the patient asks that the friend come into the treatment room.

- The patient's hospital may discuss the patient's bill with the patient's daughter who is with the patient at the hospital and has questions about the charges.

- The patient's doctor may talk to the patient's sister who is driving the patient home from the hospital about the patient keeping his foot raised during the ride home.

- The patient's doctor may discuss the drugs the patient needs to take with the patient's health aide who has accompanied the patient to an appointment.

- The patient's nurse may tell the patient that she (the nurse) is going to tell the patient's brother how the patient is doing, and then she may discuss the patient's health status with the patient's brother if the patient did not say that she should not.

- A surgeon who did emergency surgery on a patient may tell the patient's spouse about the patient's condition while the patient is unconscious.

- A pharmacist may give a prescription to a patient's friend whom the patient has sent to pick up the prescription.

- A hospital may discuss a patient's bill with her adult son who calls the hospital with questions about charges to his mother's account.

- A health care provider may give information regarding a patient's drug dosage to the patient's health aide who calls the provider with questions about the particular prescription.

But a health care provider is not required by the Privacy Regulations to share a patient's information when the patient is not present or is incapacitated, and can choose to wait until the patient has an opportunity to agree to the disclosure.[207] State law may also limit these disclosures.

---

[203] 65 Fed. Reg. 82,523 (Dec. 28, 2000).

[204] OCR, "HIPAA and Same Sex Marriage: Understanding Spouse, Family Member, and Marriage in the Privacy Rule (Sept. 2014), addressing the impact of the *United States v. Windsor* decision by the U.S. Supreme Court. Available at http://www.hhs.gov/ocr/privacy/ hipaa/understanding/special/samesexmarriage/index.html.

[205] 45 C.F.R. § 164.510(b)(4).

[206] See "A Health Care Provider's Guide to the HIPAA Privacy Rule: Communicating with a Patient's Family, Friends, or Others Involved in the Patient's Care," and "A Patient's Guide to the HIPAA Privacy Rule: When Health Care Providers May Communicate About You with Your Family, Friends, or Others Involved in Your Care," available at http://www.hhs.gov/ocr/privacy/hipaa/understanding/covere dentities/provider_ffg.pdf and http://www.hhs.gov/ocr/privacy/hipaa/understanding/consumers/consumer_ffg.pdf, respectively.

[207] "A Health Care Provider's Guide to the HIPAA Privacy Rule: Communicating with a Patient's Family, Friends, or Others Involved in the Patient's Care," available at http://www.hhs.gov/ocr/privacy/hipaa/understanding/coveredentities/provider_ffg.pdf.

In the HITECH Regulations, effective March 26, 2013, HHS modified these provisions with respect to deceased individuals, to permit a covered entity to disclose PHI to a family member, or other persons described above who were involved in the individual's health care or payment for health care prior to the individual's death, if relevant to the person's involvement, unless doing so is inconsistent with any prior expressed preference of the individual that is known to the covered entity.[208] Only relevant information should be provided, which generally will not include information about past, unrelated medical problems. In addition, these disclosures are permitted but not required, so a covered entity that questions the relationship of the person to the decedent, or otherwise believes the disclosure of the decedent's PHI would not be appropriate, is not required not make the disclosure.[209]

Examples given by HHS of how this provision could impact communications with friends and family of the decedent include:

- If the decedent's sister asks the decedent's provider about her sibling's death, the provider could describe the circumstances that led to the individual's death.

- A provider could disclose billing information to a family member of the decedent who is assisting in wrapping up the decedent's estate.[210]

HHS made these changes to permit access to health information about the decedent for involved persons who do not necessarily qualify as a personal representative of the decedent or decedent's estate. It is not intended, however, to change the authority of someone who is the decedent's personal representative.[211]

[D] Uses and Disclosures for Which No Permission Is Required

Certain uses and disclosures of PHI are necessary for public health, law enforcement, and the operation of the health care system. HHS determined that to require the individual's permission for these uses and disclosures would present an unacceptable obstacle to these public purposes. Therefore, uses and disclosures for the following purposes do not require the individual's consent, authorization, or an opportunity to opt out.[212]

For any use or disclosure permitted by any of the provisions in § 3.03[D], where the covered entity is required to inform the individual of, or where the individual may agree to, the use or disclosure, these communications may be oral rather than in writing, unless otherwise specified.

[1] Uses and Disclosures Required by Law

Covered entities may use and disclose PHI where required by law, provided the use or disclosure complies with and is limited to the relevant requirements of that law.[213] "Required by law" is a defined term, which is used here and in other provisions of the Regulations:

Required by law means a mandate contained in law that compels an entity to make a use or disclosure of protected health information and that is enforceable in a court of law. *Required by law* includes, but is not limited to, court orders and court-ordered warrants; subpoenas or summons issued by a court, grand jury, a governmental or tribal inspector general, or an administrative body authorized to require the production of information; a civil or an authorized investigative demand; Medicare conditions of participation with respect to health care providers participating in the program; and statutes or regulations that require the production of information,

---

[208] 45 C.F.R. § 164.510(b)(5). 78 Fed. Reg. 5615 (Jan. 25, 2013).

[209] 78 Fed. Reg. 5615 (Jan. 25, 2013).

[210] 78 Fed. Reg. 5615 (Jan. 25, 2013).

[211] 78 Fed. Reg. 5614-5615 (Jan. 25, 2013).

[212] 45 C.F.R. § 164.512.

[213] 45 C.F.R. § 164.512(a).

including statutes or regulations that require such information if payment is sought under a government program providing public benefits.[214]

Additional requirements apply if the purpose of the disclosures relates to victims of abuse, neglect, or domestic violence; disclosures for judicial or administrative proceedings; or disclosures for law enforcement.[215]

[2] Public Health Activities

Covered entities may disclose PHI for the following public purposes and to the following entities:[216]

1. *Public Health Reporting.* A covered entity may disclose PHI to a public health authority that is authorized by law to collect or receive such information for the purpose of preventing or controlling disease, injury, or disability. Examples include the reporting of disease, injury, vital events (such as birth or death), and the conduct of public health surveillance, public health investigations, and public health interventions; or, at the direction of a public health authority, to an official of a foreign government agency that is acting in collaboration with a public health authority.

2. *Child Abuse or Neglect.* A covered entity may disclose PHI to a public health authority or other appropriate government authority authorized by law to receive reports of child abuse or neglect.

3. *Food and Drug Administration (FDA) Regulation.* A covered entity may disclose PHI to a person subject to the jurisdiction of the FDA with respect to an FDA-regulated product or activity for which that person has responsibility, for the purpose of activities related to the quality, safety, or effectiveness of such FDA-regulated product or activity. Such purposes include, but are not limited to, the following activities and purposes: (A) to collect or report adverse events (or similar activities regarding food or dietary supplements), product defects or problems (including problems with the use or labeling of a product), or biological product deviations; (B) to track FDA-regulated products; (C) to enable product recalls, repairs, or replacement, or for lookback (including locating and notifying persons who have received products that have been withdrawn, recalled, or are the subject of lookback); and (D) to conduct post-marketing surveillance.

4. *Communicable Disease.* A covered entity may disclose PHI to a person who may have been exposed to a communicable disease or may otherwise be at risk of contracting or spreading a disease or condition if the covered entity or public health authority is authorized by law to notify such person as necessary in the conduct of a public health intervention or investigation.

5. *Employers.* A covered entity may disclose PHI to an employer about an individual who is a member of the workforce of the employer if four requirements are met: (A) the covered entity is a provider who provides health care to the individual at the request of the employer to conduct an evaluation relating to medical surveillance of the workplace, or to evaluate whether the individual has a work-related illness or injury; (B) the PHI that is disclosed consists of findings concerning a work-related illness or injury or a workplace-related medical surveillance; (C) the employer needs such findings in order to comply with its obligations under the Occupational Safety and Health Hazards Act (OSHA), or other federal or state law regarding workplace illness or injury or to carry out responsibilities for workplace

---

[214] 45 C.F.R. § 164.103.

[215] 45 C.F.R. § 164.512(a), referencing 45 C.F.R. §§ 164.512(c), (e), and (f).

[216] 45 C.F.R. § 164.512(b). The Federal Aviation Administration (FAA) has published a notice that, in light of its statutory duties with regard to medical and crash injury research, it is a public health authority within the meaning of the Privacy Regulations. 71 Fed. Reg. 8042 (Feb. 15, 2006). Similarly, the Consumer Product Safety Commission (CPSC) published a notice that it is a public health authority under the Privacy Regulations. The CPSC cites its authorization under federal law to collect certain health-related information in order to protect the public against unreasonable risks of injury from consumer products and, further, to promote research and investigation into the causes and prevention of harm to the public related to consumer products. 79 Fed. Reg. 11,769 (Mar. 3, 2014).

medical surveillance; and (D) the provider gives written notice to the individual that PHI relating to the medical surveillance of the workplace and work-related illnesses and injuries is disclosed to the employer, either by giving a copy of the notice to the individual at the time the health care is provided; or, if the health care is provided on the work site of the employer, by posting the notice in a prominent place at the location where the health care is provided.

6. *Student Immunizations.* A covered entity is permitted to disclose proof of immunization to a school, if the individual is a student or prospective student of the school, if the school is required by state or other law to have such proof of immunization prior to admitting the individual, and the covered entity obtains and documents agreement to the disclosure. This agreement may be obtained from the individual, if the individual is an adult or emancipated minor; otherwise, the agreement must be obtained from a parent, guardian, or another person acting *in loco parentis.*[217] This provision was added by the HITECH Regulations, because of the important role schools play in preventing the spread of communicable disease by ensuring students are vaccinated. Prior to the HITECH Regulations' effective date, March 26, 2013, an authorization was required to permit a covered entity to send immunization records directly to the school (although the covered entity could send the records to the individual or the individual's parents, as applicable, without a signed authorization). An authorization is no longer required, but if an oral rather than a written agreement is obtained, it must be documented.[218] The agreement must be an affirmative assent or request to the covered entity by the individual or parent (as applicable), not by the school. A signature is not required. The agreement is considered valid until revoked.[219]

If the covered entity also is a public health authority, the covered entity is permitted to use PHI in all cases in which it is permitted to disclose such information for public health activities, as described above.

[3] Victims of Abuse, Neglect, or Domestic Violence

A covered entity may disclose PHI about an individual whom it reasonably believes to be a victim of abuse, neglect, or domestic violence to a government authority, including a social service or protective services agency that is authorized by law to receive reports of such abuse, neglect, or domestic violence under the following circumstances:

- The disclosure is required by law and complies with and is limited to the relevant requirements of such law;

- The individual agrees to the disclosure; or

- The disclosure is expressly authorized by statute or regulation and (1) the covered entity, in the exercise of professional judgment, believes the disclosure is necessary to prevent serious harm to the individual or other potential victims; or (2) if the individual is unable to agree because of incapacity, a law enforcement or other public official authorized to receive the report represents that the PHI for which disclosure is sought is not intended to be used against the individual and that an immediate enforcement

---

[217] 45 C.F.R. § 164.512(b)(1)(6).

[218] OCR issued guidance on student immunizations, which give the following examples of such documentation: a copy of a written request from the parent for the disclosure or a notation in the child's medical record of a phone conversation where the parent made the request. OCR Guidance, Student Immunizations, available at http://www.hhs.gov/ocr/privacy/hipaa/understanding/coveredentities/studentimmunizations.html.

[219] 78 Fed. Reg. 5616-5618 (Jan. 25, 2013).

activity that depends upon the disclosure would be materially and adversely affected by waiting until the individual is able to agree to the disclosure.

However, reports of child abuse or neglect should be handled in accordance with **§ 3.03[D][2]**.

The covered entity must promptly inform the individual that such a report has been or will be made, except if the covered entity, in the exercise of professional judgment, believes that informing the individual would place the individual at risk of serious harm; or if the covered entity would be informing a personal representative, and the covered entity reasonably believes the personal representative is responsible for the abuse, neglect, or other injury, and in the professional judgment of the covered entity, informing such person would not be in the best interests of the individual.[220]

[4]   Health Oversight Activities

A covered entity may disclose PHI to a health oversight agency for oversight activities authorized by law, including audits; civil, administrative, or criminal investigations; inspections; licensure or disciplinary actions; or civil, administrative, or criminal proceedings or actions. Disclosure is also permitted for other activities necessary for appropriate oversight of the health care system; government benefit programs (for which health information is relevant to beneficiary eligibility); entities subject to government regulatory programs (for which health information is necessary for determining compliance with program standards); or entities subject to civil rights laws for which health information is necessary for determining compliance.

Such health oversight activity does not include an investigation or other activity in which the individual is the subject of the investigation or activity and such investigation or other activity does not arise out of and is not directly related to one of the following: the receipt of health care; a claim for public benefits related to health; or qualification for, or receipt of, public benefits or services when a patient's health is integral to the claim for public benefits or services.

If a covered entity also is a health oversight agency, it may use PHI for health oversight activities for which disclosure is permitted, as described above.[221]

[5]   Judicial and Administrative Proceedings

A covered entity may disclose PHI in the course of any judicial or administrative proceeding that is

- In response to an order of a court or administrative tribunal (but only to the extent expressly authorized by such order); or

- In response to a subpoena, discovery request, or other lawful process that is not accompanied by an order of a court or administrative tribunal, if the covered entity receives satisfactory assurance from the party seeking the information that reasonable efforts have been made by such party to ensure that the individual who is the subject of the PHI requested has been given notice of the request; or the covered entity receives satisfactory assurance from the party seeking the information that reasonable efforts have been made by such party to secure a qualified protective order.[222]

---

[220] 45 C.F.R. § 164.512(c).

[221] 45 C.F.R. § 164.512(d).

[222] 45 C.F.R. § 164.512(e). Refer to 45 C.F.R. § 162.512(e)(1)(iii)–(vi) regarding what will constitute "satisfactory assurances" and the requirements for a qualified protective order. Note that state law may require a court order and preempt this alternative. See **§ 3.04[G]** for additional information.

[6] Law Enforcement

A covered entity may disclose PHI for a law enforcement purpose to a law enforcement official if the following conditions are met, as applicable:[223]

1. *Pursuant to process and as otherwise required by law.* A covered entity may disclose PHI as required by law; for example, where state law requires a provider to report certain types of wounds or other physical injuries. (Except, with regard to child abuse or neglect, see **§ 3.03[D][2]**, and with regard to other abuse or neglect or domestic violence, see **§ 3.03[D][3]**). A covered entity may also disclose PHI in accordance with any of the following: a court order or court-ordered warrant, or a subpoena or summons issued by a judicial officer;[224] a grand jury subpoena; or an administrative request, such as an administrative subpoena or summons, a civil or an authorized investigative demand, or similar process authorized under law. The information sought must be relevant and material to a legitimate law enforcement inquiry. The request must be specific and limited in scope; and it must be the case that de-identified information could not reasonably be used.[225]

2. *Limited information for identification and location purposes.* In response to a law enforcement official's request for information for the purpose of identifying or locating a suspect, fugitive, material witness, or missing person, a covered entity may disclose the following limited PHI:

    - Name and address;

    - Date and place of birth;

    - Social Security number;

    - ABO blood type and rh factor;

    - Type of injury;

    - Date and time of treatment (including date and time of admission and discharge);

    - Date and time of death (if applicable); and

    - Description of distinguishing physical characteristics, including height, weight, gender, race, hair and eye color, presence or absence of facial hair, scars, and tattoos.

        Disclosure of the individual's DNA or DNA analysis; dental records; or typing, samples, or analysis of body fluids or tissue may not be disclosed for identification or location purposes. If a law enforcement officer requests that a covered entity notify the officer when a patient is discharged from (or is expected to be discharged from) a hospital or other facility, whether the covered entity may provide that notice will depend on the purpose of the request and whether it fits within one of the circumstances permitted by the Privacy Regulations, as well as applicable State law.

3. *Victims of a crime.* A covered entity may disclose PHI in response to a law enforcement official's request for information about an individual who is, or is suspected to be, a victim of a crime if the individual agrees to the disclosure. If the covered entity is unable to obtain the individual's agreement because of incapacity or other emergency circumstance, the PHI may be disclosed if the covered entity determines in its professional judgment that such disclosure is in the best interest of the individual and the law enforcement official represents that such information is needed to determine whether another

---

[223] 45 C.F.R. § 164.512(f). See also, HHS, "HIPAA Privacy Rule and Sharing Information Related to Mental Health" (Feb. 20, 2014), available at http://www.hhs.gov/ocr/privacy/hipaa/understanding/special/mhguidance.html.

[224] But see United States v. Zamora, 408 F. Supp. 2d 295 (S.D. Tex. 2006) (holding that a disclosure in response to a subpoena issued by a court clerk does not qualify for the law enforcement exception because a court clerk is not a judicial officer).

[225] See **§ 1.03[B]** for a discussion of de-identified information.

person has violated the law; such information is not intended to be used against the victim; and immediate law enforcement activity that depends upon the disclosure would be materially and adversely affected by waiting until the individual is able to agree to the disclosure.

4. *Decedents.* A covered entity may disclose PHI about an individual who has died to a law enforcement official for the purpose of alerting law enforcement of the death of the individual if the covered entity suspects that such death may have resulted from criminal conduct.

5. *Crime on premises.* A covered entity may disclose to a law enforcement official PHI that the covered entity believes in good faith constitutes evidence of criminal conduct that occurred on the premises of the covered entity.

6. *Reporting crime in emergencies.* A provider providing emergency health care in response to a medical emergency not on its own premises may disclose PHI to a law enforcement official if such disclosure appears necessary to alert law enforcement to the commission and nature of a crime; the location or victim of such crime; or the identity, description, and location of the perpetrator of such crime. If the provider believes that the medical emergency is the result of abuse or neglect of, or domestic violence against, the individual in need of emergency health care, this provision does not apply, and any disclosure to a law enforcement official is subject to **§ 3.03[D][3]**.

[7] Deceased Persons

A covered entity may disclose PHI to a coroner or medical examiner for the purpose of identifying a deceased individual, determining a cause of death, or other duties as authorized by law. A covered entity that also performs the duties of a coroner or medical examiner may use PHI for these purposes.[226]

A covered entity may disclose PHI to funeral directors, consistent with applicable law, as necessary to carry out their duties with respect to the decedent. If necessary for funeral directors to carry out their duties, the covered entity may disclose the PHI prior to, and in reasonable anticipation of, the individual's death.[227]

[8] Organ Donation

A covered entity may use PHI for, or disclose PHI to, organ procurement organizations or other entities engaged in the procurement, banking, or transplantation of cadaveric organs, eyes, or tissue for the purpose of facilitating organ, eye, or tissue donation and transplantation.[228]

[9] Research Purposes

The Privacy Regulations attempt to strike a balance between protecting the privacy of individually identifiable health information and ensuring that researchers continue to have access to medical information necessary to conduct vital research.[229] Currently, most research involving human subjects operates under the Common Rule (codified for HHS at Title 45 Code of Federal Regulations Part 46) and/or the FDA human subjects protection regulations. These other federal laws have some provisions that are similar to, but more stringent than and separate from, the Privacy Regulations' provisions regarding research. HHS is considering changes to the

---

[226] 45 C.F.R. § 164.512(g)(1).

[227] 45 C.F.R. § 164.512(g)(2).

[228] 45 C.F.R. § 164.512(h).

[229] See generally 45 C.F.R. § 164.512(i); HHS OCR Guidance on the Privacy Regulations, available at http://www.hhs.gov/ocr/privacy/hipaa/understanding/coveredentities/privacyguidance.html (hereinafter OCR Guidance); HHS National Institute of Health, "Protecting Personal Health Information in Research: Understanding the HIPAA Privacy Rule," available at http://privacyruleandresearch.nih.gov/pr_02.asp.

Common Rule, in part because increasing use of medical records, genetic information, stored biospecimens, and claims data in research has changed the nature of research risks. The risks are increasingly not just clinical or physical but also informational due to the risk of unauthorized uses or disclosures of patient data.[230] HHS has proposed establishment of HIPAA-like mandatory data security and information protection standards for all studies involving PHI or potentially identifiable data. This would encompass those research projects outside the scope of the Privacy and Security Regulations, where the researchers are not covered entities or business associates.[231]

Under the Privacy Regulations, a covered entity may always use or disclose de-identified information for research purposes or a limited data set under a data use agreement.[232] Furthermore, an authorization may be obtained from the individual to use or disclose his or her PHI for research purposes.[233] However, if the covered entity intends to use or disclose PHI without an authorization by the research subject, the following conditions must be met, as applicable:

1. For research without an authorization, the covered entity provides documentation that an Institutional Review Board (IRB) or a Privacy Board has approved an alteration or waiver of research participants' authorization for use/disclosure of their PHI for research purposes. This provision of the Privacy Regulations might be used, for example, to conduct records research when researchers are unable to use de-identified information and it is not practicable to obtain research participants' authorization.

    A valid waiver of authorization from the IRB or Privacy Board requires documentation of all of the following:

    •   A statement that the alteration or waiver of authorization was approved by an IRB or Privacy Board that was composed as described in the Privacy Regulations;

    •   A statement identifying the IRB or Privacy Board and the date on which the alteration or waiver of authorization was approved;

    •   A statement that the IRB or Privacy Board has determined that the alteration or waiver of authorization, in whole or in part, satisfies the following criteria:

        A. The use or disclosure of PHI involves no more than minimal risk to the privacy of individuals, based on, at least, the presence of the following elements:

            •   An adequate plan to protect the identifiers from improper use and disclosure;

            •   An adequate plan to destroy the identifiers at the earliest opportunity consistent with conduct of the research, unless there is a health or research justification for retaining the identifiers or such retention is otherwise required by law; and

            •   Adequate written assurances that the PHI will not be reused or disclosed to any other person or entity, except as required by law, for authorized oversight of the research study, or for other research for which the use or disclosure of PHI would be permitted by this subpart.

        B. The research could not practicably be conducted without the waiver or alteration;

        C. The research could not practicably be conducted without access to and use of the PHI.

    •   A brief description of the PHI for which use or access has been determined to be necessary by the IRB or Privacy Board;

---

[230] 76 Fed. Reg. 44,514 (July 26, 2011) (advanced notice of proposed rulemaking).

[231] 76 Fed. Reg. 44,514, 44,524 (July 26, 2011).

[232] See §§ 1.03[B] and 3.06 for a discussion of de-identified information and limited data sets, respectively.

[233] See § 3.02[F] for a discussion of authorizations.

- A statement that the alteration or waiver of authorization has been reviewed and approved under either normal or expedited review procedures as described in the Privacy Regulations; and

- The signature of the chair or other member, as designated by the chair, of the IRB or the Privacy Board, as applicable.

2. For reviews preparatory to research, the covered entity obtains representations from the researcher, either in writing or orally, that the use or disclosure of the PHI is solely to prepare a research protocol or for similar purposes preparatory to research, that the researcher will not remove any PHI from the covered entity in the course of the review, and that PHI for which access is sought is necessary for the research purpose. This provision might be used, for example, to design a research study or to assess the feasibility of conducting a study.

3. For research on decedents, the covered entity obtains representations from the researcher, either in writing or orally, that the use or disclosure being sought is solely for research on the PHI of decedents, that the PHI being sought is necessary for the research, and at the request of the covered entity, documentation of the death of the individuals about whom information is being sought. See **§ 3.04[E][3]** for additional discussion of the PHI of deceased individuals.

A number of guidance documents have been released by the National Institutes of Health relating to HIPAA and research.[234] These include:

- Protecting Personal Health Information in Research: Understanding the HIPAA Privacy Rule

- Health Services Research and the HIPAA Privacy Rule

- Research Repositories, Databases, and the HIPAA Privacy Rule

- Institutional Review Boards and the HIPAA Privacy Rule

- Privacy Boards and the HIPAA Privacy Rule.

[10] To Avert a Serious and Imminent Threat to Health or Safety

A covered entity may, consistent with applicable law and standards of ethical conduct, use or disclose PHI if it believes in good faith that the use or disclosure is necessary to prevent or lessen a serious and imminent threat to the health or safety of a person or the public and disclosure is to a person or persons reasonably able to prevent or lessen the threat, including the target of the threat; or is necessary for law enforcement authorities to identify or apprehend an individual, because of a statement by an individual admitting participation in a violent crime that the covered entity reasonably believes may have caused serious physical harm to the victim; or where it appears from all the circumstances that the individual has escaped from a correctional institution or from lawful custody. A covered entity's good faith is presumed if its beliefs in this regard are based upon actual knowledge or in reliance on a credible representation by a person with apparent knowledge or authority.

For example, a patient has stopped taking prescribed medication for a mental health condition, but the patient has capacity and objects to the provider notifying the patient's family. The provider, nevertheless, shares the information with a family member if doing so is consistent with applicable law and standards of ethical conduct and the provider has a good faith belief that the patient poses a serious and imminent threat to the health and safety of the patient or others (e.g., the patient becomes suicidal when the medication is not taken) and the family member is reasonably able to prevent or lessen that threat.[235]

---

[234] Available from HHS, National Institutes of Health, at http://privacyruleandresearch.nih.gov/healthservicesprivacy.asp.

[235] OCR Guidance—Mental Health.

In the case of a statement by an individual admitting participation in a violent crime, as described above, certain additional limitations apply. A disclosure made pursuant to such statement may only contain the statement made by the individual and any of the following limited PHI:

- Name and address;

- Date and place of birth;

- Social Security number;

- ABO blood type and rh factor;

- Type of injury;

- Date and time of treatment; and

- Date and time of death (if applicable).

Furthermore, use or disclosure is not permitted if the PHI is learned by the covered entity in the course of treatment to affect the propensity to commit such criminal conduct or in the course of counseling or therapy (or through a request by the individual to initiate or to be referred for such treatment, counseling, or therapy).[236]

[11] Specialized Government Functions

The covered entity may use and disclose PHI in various circumstances involving specialized government functions, including military and veterans' activities, national security and intelligence activities, protective services for the President and others, medical suitability determinations by the State Department, correctional institutions and other law enforcement custodial situations, and covered entities that are government programs providing public benefits.[237] The regulatory language should be consulted for additional information in these areas.

HHS has issued proposed regulations to remove unnecessary barriers under the Privacy Regulations that might prevent states from reporting information to the National Instant Criminal Background Check System (NICS). The Privacy Regulation would be changed to permit covered entities to disclose to the NICS the identities of individuals prohibited by federal law from possessing or receiving firearms for reasons related to mental illness.[238]

[12] Workers' Compensation

A covered entity may disclose PHI as authorized by and to the extent necessary to comply with laws relating to workers' compensation or other similar programs established by law that provide benefits for work-related injuries or illness without regard to fault.[239]

---

[236] 45 C.F.R. § 164.512(j). Following the mass shootings in Newtown, Connecticut, and Aurora, Colorado, OCR sent a letter to health care providers, reminding them of this section of HIPAA regarding disclosures intended to warn of a serious and imminent threat to a person or the public. Available at http://www.hhs.gov/ocr/office/lettertonationhcp.pdf (Jan. 15, 2013).

[237] 45 C.F.R. § 164.512(k).

[238] 79 Fed, Reg. 784 (Jan. 7, 2014).

[239] 45 C.F.R. § 164.512(l).

[E]   Incidental Uses and Disclosures

The Privacy Regulations are not intended to impede customary and necessary health care communications or practices, nor to require that all risk of incidental use or disclosure be eliminated.[240] The Privacy Regulations explicitly permit certain incidental uses and disclosures that occur as a result of a use or disclosure otherwise permitted by the Privacy Regulations.[241] Incidental uses or disclosures are permissible, however, only to the extent that the covered entity reasonably safeguards PHI to limit incidental uses and disclosures[242] and implements the minimum necessary standard.[243]

For example, a health care provider may instruct an administrative staff member to schedule a diagnostic procedure for a patient and may be overheard by one or more persons in the waiting room. Assuming that the provider made reasonable efforts to avoid being overheard and reasonably limited the information shared, an incidental disclosure resulting from such conversation is permissible under the Privacy Regulations.[244]

Areas of concern addressed by this provision include:

- Health care providers engaging in confidential conversations with other providers or with patients, where there is a possibility that they could be overheard;
- Using sign-in sheets in waiting rooms;
- Maintaining patient charts at bedside;
- Using X-ray lightboards except in isolated areas;
- Not immediately destroying empty prescription vials; and
- Calling out patient names in a waiting room.[245]

All of these actions and communications potentially involve incidental uses and disclosures of PHI, but may nevertheless be permissible if reasonable safeguards are used to limit uses and disclosures and minimum necessary standards are applied.

[F]   All Other Purposes—Authorization

For uses and disclosures that are not otherwise expressly permitted or required, covered entities must obtain the individual's authorization.[246] An authorization gives the covered entity permission to use particular PHI or disclose that PHI to a specified third party for a specified purpose. The covered entity must document and retain such signed authorizations.[247]

Covered entities may use only authorizations that meet the requirements of the Privacy Regulations, and any such use or disclosure will be lawful only to the extent it is consistent with the terms of such authorization. Thus, neither a voluntary consent document nor a written acknowledgement of the notice of privacy practices will constitute a valid permission to use or disclose PHI for a purpose that requires an authorization.[248]

---

[240] 67 Fed. Reg. 53,194 (Aug. 14, 2002); OCR Guidance (Incidental Uses and Disclosures).
[241] 45 C.F.R. § 164.502(a)(1)(iii).
[242] 45 C.F.R. § 164.530(c)(2)(ii).
[243] 45 C.F.R. § 164.514(d); see § 3.01[A].
[244] 67 Fed. Reg. 53,194 (Aug. 14, 2002).
[245] See 67 Fed. Reg. 53,193, 53,195 (Aug. 14, 2002).
[246] 45 C.F.R. § 164.508.
[247] 45 C.F.R. § 164.508(b)(6).
[248] 45 C.F.R. § 164.508(a); see 67 Fed. Reg. 53,220 (Aug. 14, 2002).

[1] Examples of When an Authorization Is Required

The following uses and disclosures, with limited exceptions, require the individual's authorization:

- A health care provider's direct disclosure of PHI relating to a child's physical examination to the child's school to permit the child's participation in sports activities;

- Sale of PHI, such as a patient list (e.g., an obstetrician's sale of patient names and addresses to a diaper service);[249]

- Disclosure of PHI to an employer;

- Disclosure of PHI to a life insurer for underwriting/eligibility for insurance;

- Disclosure to an attorney;[250]

- Use or disclosure of PHI for fundraising;[251]

- Use or disclosure of PHI for marketing;[252] and

- Use or disclosure of psychotherapy notes, except by the originator of the notes.[253]

Covered entities will need a process for determining whether the appropriate authorization has been obtained, what it specifically permits, and whether it is valid.

[2] Format and Content of an Authorization

An authorization is written in specific and customized terms. Incomplete, revoked, or expired authorizations are not valid.[254]

1. A valid authorization must contain the following elements:[255]

   - A description of the information to be used or disclosed that identifies the information in a specific and meaningful fashion;

   - The name or other specific identification of the person(s), or class of persons, authorized to make the requested use or disclosure;

   - The name or other specific identification of the person(s), or class of persons, to whom the covered entity may make the requested use or disclosure;

   - A description of each purpose of the requested use or disclosure (the statement "at the request of the individual" is sufficient if the individual initiates the authorization and does not provide a statement of the purpose);[256]

---

[249] See § 3.04[B] for a discussion of the sale of PHI.

[250] See § 3.04[G] for a discussion of attorneys and litigation.

[251] See § 3.04[A] for a discussion of fundraising.

[252] See § 3.04[C] for a discussion of marketing.

[253] See § 3.04[D] for a discussion of psychotherapy notes and mental health records.

[254] 45 C.F.R. § 164.508(b)(2).

[255] 45 C.F.R. § 164.508(c)(1).

[256] For research authorizations, HHS originally interpreted this to require study-specific authorizations. The concern was that individuals might not have sufficient information to make an informed decision about participating in future research studies. In the HITECH Regulations effective March 26, 2013, HHS clarified its position, stating that authorizations need not be study-specific, provided they effectively describe the future uses and disclosures to enable individuals to understand that their PHI may be used or disclosed for future research. 78 Fed. Reg. 5611–5612 (Jan. 25, 2013).

- An expiration date or an expiration event that relates to the individual or the purpose of the use or disclosure (e.g., the expiration event might be the initial release of the information, that is, a one-time release). For research purposes only, including the creation and maintenance of a research database or research repository, the statement "end of the research study" or "none" is sufficient; and

- Signature of the individual and date (if the authorization is signed by a personal representative of the individual, a description of such representative's authority to act for the individual is also required).

2. A valid authorization must also contain all of the following statements, written in a manner that is adequate to put the individual on notice of the substance of these statements:[257]

- A statement of the individual's right to revoke the authorization in writing and either (A) the exceptions to the right to revoke, together with a description of how the individual may revoke the authorization, or (B) to the extent this same information is included in the notice of privacy practices, a reference to that notice;

- A statement regarding whether or not treatment, payment, enrollment, or eligibility for benefits may be conditioned on the authorization, by stating either: (A) the covered entity may not condition treatment, payment, enrollment, or eligibility for benefits on whether the individual signs the authorization when the Privacy Regulations prohibit such conditioning of authorizations (see § 3.03[F][4]); or (B) the consequences to the individual of a refusal to sign the authorization when, in accordance with the Privacy Regulations, the covered entity can condition treatment, enrollment in the health plan, or eligibility for benefits on failure to obtain such authorization;

- A statement that information used or disclosed pursuant to the authorization may be subject to redisclosure by the recipient and no longer be protected by the Privacy Regulations (e.g., if the disclosure is to other than a covered entity). A general statement of this possibility is sufficient; no analysis of the risk of redisclosure is required.[258] A covered entity may provide additional information at its discretion; for example, when requesting an authorization for its own uses of PHI, the covered entity may provide assurances that the information will remain subject to the Privacy Regulations;[259] and

- If a communication is classified as a sale of PHI, or as marketing involving financial remuneration to the covered entity from a third party, a statement that there will be remuneration to the covered entity.[260]

3. A valid authorization must be written in plain language.[261]

4. A valid authorization may contain elements or information in addition to the elements listed above, provided that such additional elements or information are not inconsistent with the required elements.[262]

If the covered entity seeks authorization from the individual, the individual must be provided with a copy of the signed authorization.[263]

---

[257] 45 C.F.R. § 164.508(c)(2).

[258] 67 Fed. Reg. 53,221 (Aug. 14, 2002).

[259] 67 Fed. Reg. 53,222 (Aug. 14, 2002).

[260] 45 C.F.R. § 164.508(a)(3)(ii); 45 C.F.R. § 164.508(a)(4)(ii). See §§ 3.04[B] and 3.04[C] for additional information.

[261] 45 C.F.R. § 164.508(c)(3).

[262] 45 C.F.R. § 164.508(b)(1)(ii).

[263] 45 C.F.R. § 164.508(c)(4).

Authorization forms vary from covered entity to covered entity, yet each form will be valid if the requirements are met. A covered entity will need to determine whether or not it will accept authorization forms other than its own, and if it does, it will need a checklist of the required elements to verify that the authorization form received is HIPAA-compliant.

[3] Compound Authorizations

An authorization may not be combined with any other document to create a compound authorization, except as follows:[264]

1. An authorization for a research study may be in the same document as any other type of written permission for the same research study, including another authorization for the use or disclosure of PHI for such research or a consent to participate in such research. This provision was broadened, effective March 26, 2013, by the HITECH Regulations. This exception now includes combining an authorization for the use or disclosure of PHI for a research study with another authorization for the same research study or a different research study with an authorization for the creation or maintenance of a research database or repository, or with a consent to participate in research. If the covered entity has conditioned the provision of research-related treatment on one of the authorizations, any combined authorization must clearly distinguish the components that are a condition for receiving treatment and those that are not, so the individual understands which uses or disclosures can be declined while still receiving treatment.[265]

2. An authorization for a use or disclosure of psychotherapy notes may only be combined with another authorization for a use or disclosure of psychotherapy notes.

3. An authorization (other than for psychotherapy notes) may be combined with any other such authorization under this section, except when a covered entity has conditioned the provision of treatment, payment, or enrollment in the health plan, or eligibility for benefits on the provision of one of the authorizations.

[4] Conditioning of Authorizations

A covered entity may not condition the provision of treatment, payment, or enrollment in the health plan, or eligibility for benefits on the provision of an authorization, except as follows:[266]

1. A provider may condition the provision of research-related treatment on provision of an authorization for the use or disclosure of PHI for such research—that is, participation in a clinical trial may be conditioned on the patient providing an authorization to use PHI for the related research.

2. A health plan may condition enrollment in the health plan or eligibility for benefits on provision of an authorization requested by the health plan prior to an individual's enrollment in the health plan if (A) the authorization sought is for the health plan's eligibility or enrollment determinations relating to the individual or for its underwriting or risk rating determinations; and (B) the authorization is not for a use or disclosure of psychotherapy notes.

3. A covered entity may condition the provision of health care that is solely for the purpose of creating PHI for disclosure to a third party on provision of an authorization for the disclosure of the PHI to such third party. For example, a provider may have a contract with an employer to provide fitness-for-duty

---

[264] 45 C.F.R. § 164.508(b)(3).

[265] 45 C.F.R. § 164.508(c)(3)(i) and (iii). 78 Fed. Reg. 5610–5611 (Jan. 25, 2013).

[266] 45 C.F.R. § 164.508(b)(4).

exams for the employer's employees. The provider may refuse to conduct the exam if the individual refuses to authorize disclosure of the exam results to the employer.[267]

[5] Revoking an Authorization

An individual may revoke an authorization at any time, provided that the revocation is in writing, except (A) to the extent that the covered entity has taken action in reliance on the authorization; or (B) if the authorization was obtained as a condition of obtaining insurance coverage, and other law provides the insurer with the right to contest a claim under the policy or the policy itself.[268]

[6] Deceased Individuals

An authorization is valid until it expires or is revoked. OCR has informally confirmed that an authorization is not invalidated by the death of the individual.[269] A more restrictive state law could change this outcome.

[7] Transition Provisions

If express permission for use or disclosure of PHI was obtained before the Privacy Regulations' compliance date, the covered entity may rely on such permission after the compliance date (but must abide by its terms). This generally applies only with respect to information created or received prior to the compliance date.[270] Special transition provisions apply to research purposes.[271]

[8] Documentation

A covered entity must document and retain any signed authorization under this section for six years from the date of its creation or the date it was last in effect, whichever is later.[272]

§ 3.04 SPECIAL APPLICATIONS OF THE RULES RELATING TO USES AND DISCLOSURES

The following section provides additional explanation of certain uses and disclosures subject to special limitations under the Privacy Regulations.

[A] Fundraising

Fundraising is included in the definition of health care operations, but uses and disclosures of PHI for fundraising purposes are subject to special limitations. These fundraising rules are of particular importance to tax-exempt covered entities.

---

[267] 65 Fed. Reg. 82,516 (Dec. 28, 2000).

[268] 45 C.F.R. § 164.508(b)(5).

[269] American Bar Association, Technical Session Between the Department of Health and Human Services and the Joint Committee on Employee Benefits (May 10, 2007).

[270] 45 C.F.R. § 164.532.

[271] 45 C.F.R. § 164.532; 67 Fed. Reg. 53,248 (Aug. 14, 2002).

[272] 45 C.F.R. § 164.508(b)(6).

Although the general rule is that a signed authorization is required for uses and disclosures of an individual's PHI for fundraising purposes,[273] it is the exceptions to this rule that are of significance to fundraising organizations.

A special fundraising provision permits a covered entity to use PHI without authorization for fundraising *on its own behalf*, subject to certain limitations, including the individual's right to opt out of fundraising communications and limitations related to the categories of PHI that may be used to target solicitations.[274] Although "fundraising communication" is not defined in the Regulations, HHS has informally explained fundraising communications as including appeals for money, sponsorship of events, or similar support.[275]

[1] Right to Opt Out

The original Privacy Regulations required that fundraising materials sent to the individual explain how the individual may opt out of any further fundraising communications and also required that the covered entity make reasonable efforts to honor such requests. The HITECH Act made this a stricter standard, requiring that the opt-out notice be clear and conspicuous. Furthermore, the HITECH Act changed the original obligation of the covered entity to make a "reasonable effort to honor" such opt-out requests, and instead treats such opt-outs as the revocation of an authorization, making further fundraising communications simply prohibited.[276]

The HITECH Regulations expand on the Act's revisions to the fundraising requirements. These changes were effective March 26, 2013, with compliance required by September 23, 2013. The following new requirements apply regarding these communications:[277]

- With each fundraising communication to the individual, the covered entity must provide the individual with a clear and conspicuous opportunity to elect not to receive any further fundraising communications.

- The method of opting out of such communications may not create an undue burden on the individual or cause the individual to incur more than a nominal cost. The covered entities may, subject to this standard, select appropriate opt out methods. HHS suggests considering toll-free or local phone numbers and e-mails. HHS specifically identifies requiring an individual to write a letter to opt out as being unduly burdensome (but mailing a pre-printed prepaid postcard is okay).

- All fundraising communications, not just *fundraising materials sent* to the individual, are now subject to these fundraising rules. Prior to the HITECH Regulations, the language of the Regulations could reasonably be interpreted to not include telephone or in-person communications, because they were not materials sent to the individual. The HITECH Regulations eliminate that "materials sent" language and clearly include all fundraising communications to the individual, whether oral or written, and whether in person or by phone.

- Whether the opt-out opportunity applies to a particular fundraising campaign or to all future fundraising communications can be determined by the covered entity. But whichever approach is used, it should be made clear to the individual.

- If an individual has opted out, the covered entity *may not* make further fundraising communications to the individual. HHS, in the preamble to the HITECH Regulations, was unsympathetic to comments from covered entities that the previous "reasonable efforts" standard should be retained. Some

---

[273] *See* 45 C.F.R. §§ 164.514(f), 164.508(a)(1). The authorization must comply with the Privacy Regulations, and the scope of the authorization is limited by its terms and as otherwise restricted by law.

[274] 45 C.F.R. § 164.514(f). If the covered entity's fundraising communication is not *on behalf of* the covered entity, the use of the PHI requires a written authorization from the individual. 65 Fed. Reg. 82,546 (Dec. 28, 2000).

[275] 65 Fed. Reg. 82718 (Dec. 28, 2000); 78 Fed. Reg. 5621 (Jan. 25, 2013).

[276] HITECH Act § 13406(b).

[277] 45 C.F.R. § 164.514(f); 78 Fed. Reg. 5620–5622 (Jan. 25, 2013).

comments from covered entities indicated potential practical problems, such as an opt-out coming in during the lag time between the creation of a mailing list and the mailing itself, and difficulties with accurately identifying individuals on fundraising lists due to name changes, name variations, or multiple addresses. HHS's response was that strict adherence is required; fundraising communications require the same care and attention as any other handling of PHI.

- A covered entity may (but is not required to) provide individuals who have opted out with a method of opting back in. It must, however, be an affirmative election to opt back in. If an individual who has opted out makes a donation to the covered entity, that alone is not sufficient to be regarded as the individual's opting back in to future fundraising communications.

- A covered entity may not condition treatment or payment on the individual's decision whether or not to opt out.

- The covered entity's notice of privacy practices must contain a statement that the covered entity may contact the individual to raise funds for the covered entity and that the individual has a right to opt out of receiving such communications. See § 3.02[A].

[2] Targeted Solicitations—What PHI May Be Used

Health care providers often wish to solicit donations from patients to whom they have provided services. These fundraising programs are sometimes referred to as "grateful patient programs." Prior to the Privacy Regulations, these solicitations may have targeted patients who received certain types of services, received services from a particular department, or had a particular diagnosis or condition. Continuing such "targeted solicitations" has been restricted under the Privacy Regulations, which specifically limits the categories of PHI that may be used for fundraising communications.[278] For a covered entity to use any type of PHI other than what is specifically permitted by the Privacy Regulations for fundraising communications, the individual's authorization is required. Originally, the Privacy Regulations permitted the following information to be used in making a fundraising communication:

- Demographic information; and

- Dates of service of the health care provided to the individual.[279]

Covered entities raised concerns about these limitations, stating that they interfere with the ability of the covered entity to raise funds from willing and grateful former patients, because the covered entity is unable to target the fundraising requests. Being able to appropriately target the communications would help the covered entity avoid inappropriately sending the solicitation to individuals who had poor treatment outcomes and reduce the need to send the fundraising communication to all patients.[280]

Under the HITECH Regulations, effective March 26, 2013, the list of categories of PHI that may be used for fundraising communications has been expanded to:

- Demographic information relating to the individual (now defined to include name, address, other contact information, age, gender, and date of birth);

---

[278] 45 C.F.R. § 164.514(f).

[279] *Demographic information* was not defined under the original Privacy Regulations, but HHS had indicated informally that the term generally included the individual's name, address, other contact information (e.g., phone number), age, gender, and insurance status, but did not include any information about the individual's illness or treatment. 65 Fed. Reg. 82,718 (Dec. 28, 2000).

[280] 78 Fed. Reg. 5619 (Jan. 25, 2013). See also HHS National Committee on Vital and Health Statistics (NCVHS). Letter to Secretary Thompson—Findings and Recommendations on the Impact of the Privacy Rule on Fundraising, Sept. 2, 2004, available at http://www.ncvhs.hhs.gov/recommendations-reports-presentations/september-2-2004-letter-to-the-secretary-findings-and-recommendations-on-the-impact-of-the-privacy-rule-on-fundraising/; see also NCVHS, transcript of Sept. 1, 2004, meeting, available at http://www.ncvhs.hhs.gov/transcripts-minutes/transcript-of-the-september-1-2004-ncvhs-full-committee-meeting/.

- Dates of service of the health care provided to the individual;

- Department of service;

- Treating physician;

- Outcome information (including death); and

- Health insurance status.[281]

Being able to use these additional categories of PHI will allow covered entities to more effectively screen individuals and be more effective and efficient in their fundraising efforts. This can be a significant benefit for larger organizations that serve diverse populations and want to target subgroups of patients in their fundraising. For example, the covered entity can now create and use a mailing list of patients who have received services in a particular service department (e.g., an oncology clinic or maternity department).

[3] Use of Business Associates or Foundations

Under the exception described above, which permits covered entities to use and disclose PHI for fundraising (with certain limitations) without an authorization, the covered entity may disclose this limited PHI only to a business associate (or an institutionally related foundation). The special provision for institutionally related foundations was included due to certain tax code provisions that might not allow an institutionally related foundation to be a business associate of the covered entity.[282] The institutionally related foundation must qualify as a nonprofit charitable foundation under Code Section 501(c)(3) and must have a charter statement of its charitable purpose that contains a specific reference to the covered entity.[283] Having a similar mission to the covered entity is not sufficient. In the alternative, a business associate agreement is required.

[B] Sale of Protected Health Information

Prior to the HITECH Act, there was no general prohibition on the sale of PHI, although the Privacy Regulations imposed limits on the sale of PHI to another entity for that other entity's own marketing purposes. For example, under the marketing rules, a health care provider that sells a patient list to a drug manufacturer, so that the drug manufacturer can use the list to send advertising for a new drug directly to those patients, must obtain an authorization from every individual on that list.[284]

The HITECH Act expands this requirement to *any* sale of PHI, not just those for marketing purposes. Under the HITECH Act, a covered entity or business associate may not directly or indirectly receive remuneration in exchange for PHI, unless the covered entity obtains a valid authorization from the individual. The HITECH Act also included exceptions to this prohibition on the sale of PHI, relating, for example, to certain disclosures for public health activity, research, treatment, and other purposes.[285] The provisions of the HITECH Act were expanded and modified by the HITECH Regulations, as described below. Compliance with these HITECH Regulations limiting the sale of PHI is required by September 23, 2013.

Under the HITECH Regulations, the "sale of PHI" means "a disclosure of protected health information by a covered entity or business associate, if applicable, where the covered entity or business associate directly or indirectly receives remuneration from or on behalf of the recipient of the protected health information in exchange for the protected health information."[286] "Sale" is not limited to a transaction involving a transfer of

---

[281] 45 C.F.R. § 164.514(f).

[282] 65 Fed. Reg. 82,718 (Dec. 28, 2000).

[283] 45 C.F.R. § 164.514(f).

[284] OCR Guidance (Marketing), revised April 2003.

[285] HITECH Act § 13405(d)(1).

[286] 45 C.F.R. § 164.502(a)(5)(ii).

ownership of PHI, but also includes disclosures in exchange for remuneration under an access, license, or lease agreement.[287] A disclosure of PHI is not a "sale of PHI," if the purpose of the disclosure is for:

- Public health activities (including the disclosure of limited data sets);

- Research (including the disclosure of limited data sets), where the only remuneration received by the covered entity is a reasonable cost-based fee to cover the cost for preparation and transmittal of the data (which may include both direct and indirect costs, including labor, materials, and supplies for generating, storing, retrieving, and transmitting the PHI; labor and supplies to ensure the PHI is disclosed in a permissible manner; and related capital and overhead costs, but not fees that include a profit margin);

- Otherwise permitted disclosures for treatment and payment purposes (e.g., the sale of accounts receivables including PHI to a collection agency for payment purposes);

- The sale, transfer, merger, or consolidation of all or part of the covered entity, and for due diligence related to such activities, to the extent they are within the definition of health care operations and permitted by the Privacy Regulations as a disclosure for health care operations purposes;

- Disclosure to or by a business associate for activities that the business associate undertakes on behalf of the covered entity pursuant to a business associate agreement, where the only remuneration is provided by a covered entity to a business associate for performance of services under that agreement (or similarly, with regard to the activities of a subcontractor on behalf of the business associate);

- To provide an individual with a copy of the individual's PHI, in the individual's exercise of his or her rights under the Privacy Regulations with respect to access to PHI or an accounting of disclosures, where the fees charged are consistent with the Privacy Regulations;

- Disclosures of PHI required by law; or

- A disclosure of PHI permitted by and in accordance with the applicable requirements of the Privacy Regulations, where the only remuneration received by the covered entity or business associate is a reasonable, cost-based fee to cover the cost to prepare and transmit the PHI for such purpose or for a fee expressly permitted by other law. (A reasonable cost-based fee includes both direct and indirect costs, including labor, materials, and supplies for generating, storing, retrieving, and transmitting the PHI; labor and supplies to ensure the PHI is disclosed in a permissible manner; related capital and overhead costs; and costs in compliance with state law fee schedules or otherwise expressly permitted by other applicable law. Fees may not include a profit margin. HHS included this provision because it did not want to deter the disclosure of PHI for permissible purposes, just because the covered entity routinely receives remunerations equal to the cost of preparing, producing, and transmitting the PHI.)[288]

In addition, "sale of PHI" does not include payments a covered entity or business associate receives in the form of grants, contracts, or other arrangements to perform services, programs, or activities, such as a research study, because any provision of PHI is a byproduct of the service being provided. Similarly, the exchange of PHI through a health information exchange (HIE) that is paid for by fees assessed to the participants in the HIE is not a sale of PHI, because the fees are in exchange for the service provided, not the PHI itself. However, it would be a sale of PHI, if the covered entity or business associate is being compensated primarily to supply data it maintains in its role as a covered entity or business associate.[289]

Otherwise permissible uses of PHI within a single covered entity are not implicated by the prohibition on the sale of PHI, because it applies only to disclosures. Similarly, transfers of value among separate covered

---

[287] 78 Fed. Reg. 5606 (Jan. 25, 2013).

[288] HITECH Act § 13405(d)(2), as modified by the HITECH Regulations. 45 C.F.R. § 164.502(a)(5)(ii)(2). 78 Fed. Reg. 5605, 5606–5607 (Jan. 25, 2013).

[289] 78 Fed. Reg. 5606 (Jan. 25, 2013).

entities that have designated themselves as an affiliated covered entity (ACE), as described in § 1.02[C][2], are not implicated.[290]

As used in this section, with regard to the sale of PHI, "remuneration" means nonfinancial benefits (in-kind benefits) as well as financial benefits. For example, a covered entity is offered computers in an arrangement involving the covered entity disclosing PHI. The provision of PHI in exchange for the computers would not be considered a sale of PHI if the computers were solely used for the purpose of preparing and transmitting PHI to the recipient and were returned when the disclosure was completed. However, if the covered entity is permitted to use the computers for other purposes or to keep the computers after the disclosures have been made, then the computers are in-kind remuneration to the covered entity in exchange for the PHI, because it is more than what is needed to make the actual disclosures.[291]

References to direct and indirect remuneration relate to how the remuneration is received. That is, the remuneration to the covered entity or business associate could be received directly from the recipient of the PHI or could be received indirectly from someone else on behalf of the recipient of the PHI.[292]

An authorization is required, if after analysis of all the exceptions to the definition of "sale of PHI" discussed above, the disclosure of PHI for remuneration being contemplated by the covered entity or business associate is determined by the covered entity or business associate to be a sale of PHI. In addition to all the other requirements for a valid authorization, the authorization must state that the disclosure will result in remuneration to the covered entity. HHS does not provide specific wording required for this statement. Rather, the covered entity or business associate has the discretion to craft language appropriate to the circumstances, such as the specific type of remuneration received. HHS determined, under the HITECH Regulations, that it is not necessary, after all, to include the authorization language from the HITECH Act that related to whether the PHI could be further exchanged for remuneration by the entity receiving the PHI.[293]

HHS recognized that the new "sale of PHI" provisions had the potential for disrupting research studies and other activities already under way and included certain transition provisions to "grandfather in" prior authorizations. Thus, a covered entity may continue to rely on:

- An authorization obtained from the individual prior to September 23, 2013, even if remuneration is involved and the authorization does not state that the disclosure is in exchange for remuneration;[294]

- A documented waiver of authorization by an IRB or Privacy Board to release PHI for research, obtained prior to September 23, 2013, even if the covered entity receives remuneration in excess of a reasonable, cost-based fee to prepare and transmit the data;[295] and

- A data use agreement executed before January 25, 2013, under which the covered entity has been operating for purposes of disclosing a limited data set, and which complies with the Privacy Regulations but for the new prohibitions on the sale of PHI, until the earlier of September 22, 2014, or the date the agreement is renewed or modified on or after September 23, 2013.[296]

[C] Marketing

The rules for marketing communications are among the most complicated in the Privacy Regulations. The marketing rules address situations where a covered entity uses PHI to identify individuals to receive marketing communications. This Section describes the marketing rules under the new HITECH Regulations. The compliance date is September 23, 2013.

---

[290] 78 Fed. Reg. 5608 (Jan. 25, 2013).

[291] 78 Fed. Reg. 5607 (Jan. 25, 2013).

[292] 78 Fed. Reg. 5607 (Jan. 25, 2013).

[293] 45 C.F.R. § 164.508(a)(4); 78 Fed. Reg. 5604, 5608 (Jan. 25, 2013).

[294] 45 C.F.R. § 164.508(a)(4). 78 Fed. Reg. 5608 (Jan. 25, 2013).

[295] 45 C.F.R. § 164.508(a)(4). 78 Fed. Reg. 5608 (Jan. 25, 2013).

[296] 45 C.F.R. § 164.532(f).

The general rule is that authorization is required for uses and disclosures of PHI for marketing purposes.[297] The definition of *marketing* is quite broad, yet it has so many exceptions that many communications of a health care provider or health plan may not require authorization even though they might seem to be marketing-related activities. As defined by the Privacy Regulations, *marketing* generally means "to make a communication about a product or service that encourages recipients of the communication to purchase or use the product or service."[298]

The HITECH Act made changes that were intended to address arrangements where the covered entity is paid by a third party to use PHI to market the third party's products or services. The concern is that, although these may be health-related communications, the covered entity may be motivated more by commercial gain than by the individual's health care needs.[299] Certain uses of PHI for marketing purposes that were previously permitted without individual authorization may now require authorization if payments are made by a third party in exchange for those communications.[300] This Section explains how these changes are being implemented under the HITECH Regulations. Under the HITECH Regulations, the *use* of PHI for marketing-type communications to individuals now falls into four basic categories:

1. Authorization is not required.

2. Authorization is not required, *unless* the covered entity receives financial remuneration.

3. Subsidized communications regarding currently prescribed drugs (a special statutory category).

4. Authorization is required.

In addition, marketing arrangements in which the covered entity receives remuneration from, or on behalf of, a third party in exchange for a *disclosure* of PHI by the covered entity to the third party, for the third party's own purposes (marketing or otherwise), generally require authorization as a "sale of PHI."[301]

The types and categories of marketing communications are discussed in detail in this **§ 3.04[C]** and summarized in chart form in **Appendix B**.

[1] Authorization Is Not Required

Individual authorization is not required for the following communications, either because they are specifically not within the definition of "marketing" or because an exception applies.

1. *Face-to-Face Communications.* A covered entity may use an individual's PHI or disclose the PHI to the individual in a marketing communication with the individual in a face-to-face encounter. For example, an insurance company sells a health insurance policy in person to a customer and proceeds to also market a life insurance policy. These communications fall within the definition of marketing but are specifically exempted from the authorization requirement.[302] These face-to-face communications may be made orally or by handing materials to the individual; however, communications made over the phone or by e-mail are not face-to-face, and this exception would not apply.[303]

---

[297] 45 C.F.R. § 164.508(a)(3); 78 Fed. Reg. 5592 (Jan. 25, 2013).

[298] 45 C.F.R. § 164.501.

[299] HITECH Act § 3406(a); 78 Fed. Reg. 5592 (Jan. 25, 2013).

[300] HITECH Act § 3406(a). The 2010 proposed regulations from HHS would have created a special opt-out process for treatment communications if there were third-party payment. 75 Fed. Reg. 40,868, 40,884–87 (July 14, 2010). However, this was not made part of the final HITECH Regulations. 78 Fed. Reg. 5595 (Jan. 25, 2013).

[301] See **§ 3.04[B]** for further information on the sale of PHI.

[302] 45 C.F.R § 164.508(3).

[303] 78 Fed. Reg. 5596 (Jan. 25, 2013).

2. *Gifts of Nominal Value.* A covered entity may provide promotional gifts of nominal value to the individual (e.g., distributing sample products or pens/calendars with its own or another company's name or product name on them). For example, a hospital provides a free package of baby products to new mothers as they leave the maternity department, or a dentist provides a free toothbrush and dental floss sample to patients receiving dental check-ups. These communications fall within the definition of marketing but are specifically exempted from the authorization requirement.[304]

3. *A Communication That Promotes Health in a General Manner.* A covered entity may make a general communication that promotes health. Because the communication does not promote any particular product or service, it is not within the definition of marketing.[305] For example, a health care provider may send its patients a newsletter article about the health benefits of daily exercise or a general mailing regarding revised guidelines about the recommended frequency of mammograms.

4. *Communications About Government and Government-Sponsored Programs.* A covered entity may use and disclose PHI to communicate with individuals about eligibility and benefits under public programs, such as Medicare, Medicaid, and the State Children's Health Insurance Program (CHIP). Promotion of these programs is not considered marketing, because "there is no commercial component" to these communications.[306]

5. *Community Mailing Lists—Mailings Derived from Sources Other than Patient or Member Lists.* A mailing that does not contain PHI and is sent to all local residents, or based on some other criteria not involving the use of PHI, is not prohibited or limited by the Privacy Regulations. For example, a health care provider may send an announcement about its new clinic location to all local residents, using a community mailing list obtained from a third party. Although the mailing may reach current patients of the provider, no PHI was used to generate the mailing.

6. *Government-Mandated Communications.* Government-mandated communications are not considered marketing, because they are not commercial in nature. This is the case even if the communication is paid for by a third party whose product or service is being described. For example, if the Food and Drug Administration (FDA) determines that a particular drug requires certain communications to the patients about serious risks posed by the drug, such communications are not considered marketing, even if paid for by the drug manufacturer.[307]

[2] Authorization Is Not Required Unless There Is Financial Remuneration

Individual authorization is not required for the communications described in this section, related to treatment and health care operations, provided there is no financial remuneration, as defined below.[308]

1. *A Communication for Treatment of the Individual.* A communication for treatment of the individual by a health care provider.[309] For example, a primary care physician refers an individual to a specialist for a follow-up test, or a physician recommends a particular prescription drug to a patient.

2. *A Communication for Case Management, Care Coordination, or to Direct or Recommend Alternative Care for an Individual.* A covered entity's communications for case management or care coordination

---

[304] 45 C.F.R § 164.508(3); OCR, FAQ 288, available at http://www.hhs.gov/ocr/privacy/hipaa/faq/marketing/288.html.

[305] 78 Fed. Reg. 5597 (Jan. 25, 2013).

[306] 78 Fed. Reg. 5597 (Jan. 25, 2013); OCR, FAQ 293, available at http://www.hhs.gov/ocr/privacy/hipaa/faq/marketing/293.html.

[307] HHS, "The HIPAA Privacy Rule and Refill Reminders and Other Communications about a Drug or Biologic Currently Being Prescribed for the Individual" (Sept. 19, 2013), available at http://www.hhs.gov/ocr/privacy/hipaa/understanding/coveredentities/marketingrefillreminder.html (hereinafter, "OCR Refill Reminder Guidance").

[308] 45 C.F.R. §§ 164.501 and 164.508(a)(3)(i).

[309] 45 C.F.R. § 164.501.

for the individual, or to direct or recommend alternative treatments, therapies, health care providers, or care settings to the individual whether or not categorized as treatment.[310]

3. *A Communication to Describe the Covered Entity's Own Health-Related Products or Services—Health Care Providers.* A health care provider may send out a communication about its own services or products. For example, a hospital uses its patient list to announce that it has a new magnetic resonance imaging (MRI) machine.[311]

4. *A Communication to Describe the Covered Entity's Own Health-Related Products or Services—Health Plans.* A health plan may send out a communication about its own services or products. For example, a health plan sends a mailing to members approaching Medicare age with materials describing its Medicare supplemental plan and an application form. These communications are permitted to describe provision of or payment for a health-related product or service that is provided by, or included in a plan of benefits of, the covered entity making the communication. Additional examples include communications about:

- The entities who are participating in a health care provider network or health plan network (e.g., sending health plan members a list of participating providers);

- Replacement of, or enhancements to, a health plan; and

- Health-related products or services available only to a health plan member that add value to, but are not part of, a plan of benefits. These value-added items or services are common in managed care (e.g., a special health club discount or optical service discount available only to health plan members).[312]

If the covered entity will be receiving financial remuneration for making the communications described in this section, they will be considered marketing communications, and the covered entity is required to obtain the individual's authorization to use the individual's PHI for these communications. The authorization form must state that such remuneration is involved. If there is no financial remuneration, however, these communications are not considered marketing and no authorization is required.[313] The definition of financial remuneration is therefore key to the analysis of these communications.

Financial remuneration means "direct or indirect payment from or on behalf of a third party whose product or service is being described," but does not include payments for treatment of the individual.[314] Financial remuneration also does not include nonfinancial benefits, such as in-kind benefits.[315] Furthermore, the financial remuneration must be in exchange for a marketing communication about the third party's services or products. So, for example, this would not include a health care provider sending letters to its patients announcing a new, state-of-the art mammography machine, where the funds for the equipment were donated by a cancer foundation, because the funding was not in exchange for the mailing that publicizes the new equipment. In contrast, if the provider purchased the equipment, and the manufacturer of the equipment paid the provider to send the mailing, this would be a marketing communication in exchange for financial remuneration and would require an authorization.[316]

---

[310] 45 C.F.R. § 164.501.

[311] HITECH Act § 13406(a); 45 C.F.R. § 164.501.

[312] 45 C.F.R. §§ 164.501 and 164.508(a)(3)(i); OCR Guidance (Marketing), revised April 2003; 78 Fed. Reg. 5597 (Jan. 25, 2013).

[313] 45 C.F.R. § 164.501; 45 C.F.R. § 164.508(a)(3)(ii).

[314] 45 C.F.R. § 164.501, in paragraph (3) of the definition of marketing. "Payment" is also a defined term, but relates specifically to payment for health care, which is not intended to be included in the definition of financial remuneration for purposes of these marketing rules. 78 Fed. Reg. 5593 (Jan. 25, 2013).

[315] 78 Fed. Reg. 5596 (Jan. 25, 2013). "Financial remuneration" is a more narrowly defined term than the definition of "remuneration" used in the provisions related to the sale of PHI, which *does* include nonfinancial, in-kind benefits. See **§ 3.04[B]**.

[316] See examples at 78 Fed. Reg. 5593, 5595–5596 (Jan. 25, 2013).

In summary, the three key elements of the definition of financial remuneration are: (1) it covers financial but not other kinds of remuneration; (2) the payment must come directly or indirectly from the party whose services or products are being described; and (3) the payment must be in exchange for the marketing communication itself.

[3] Subsidized Communications—Currently Prescribed Drugs and Biologics

This is a special category that is similar to category [2], in that whether an authorization is required depends on whether there is financial remuneration, but the "subsidized communication" rules for this category are a little different and arise directly from the HITECH Act. HHS retained them in the final HITECH Regulations.[317]

"Marketing" does not include a communication that is made to provide refill reminders or otherwise communicate to the individual about a drug or biologic that is currently being prescribed for the individual, if any financial remuneration received by the covered entity in exchange for making the communication is reasonably related to the covered entity's cost of making the communication.[318] This three-part analysis is discussed in detail below.

First, is the communication about a drug or biologic currently being prescribed for the individual? HHS provides some flexibility in this definition. The communications may be about (1) refill reminders; (2) generic equivalents to the prescribed drugs; (3) encouraging individuals to take their prescribed medication as directed; (4) renewing prescriptions that have lapsed within the last 90 calendar days; and (5) for self-administered drugs or biologics, any aspect of the drug delivery system, including, for example, insulin pumps.[319] Communications about the following topics, however, are not included in this exception: (1) specific new formulations of a currently prescribed medicine; (2) specific adjunctive drugs related to the currently prescribed medicine; or (3) encouragement to the individual to switch from a prescribed medicine to an alternative medicine.[320]

Second, is any financial remuneration received by the covered entity in exchange for making the communication? Financial remuneration means payment and does not include nonfinancial or in-kind remuneration, such as supplies, computers, or other materials.[321] Furthermore, financial remuneration is considered to be in exchange for making the communication only if it is received from (or on behalf of) the third party whose product or service is being described.[322] A payment from someone else, such as a health plan, would not be considered relevant "financial remuneration."

Third, if there is financial remuneration (directly or indirectly) from a pharmaceutical manufacturer or other third party whose product or services is being described in the communication, is that remuneration reasonably related to the covered entity's cost of making the communication? The reasonable direct and indirect costs permitted include the costs of labor, supplies, and postage, and these costs must not involve any profit to the covered entity.[323] Related capital and overhead costs may also be permitted.[324] For example, a pharmacy may receive financial remuneration from a drug manufacturer to send refill reminders to patients currently taking a drug, if the remuneration only covers the pharmacy's costs of drafting, printing, and mailing those reminders. An authorization from the individual is required, if the financial remuneration to the covered entity in exchange for making the communication is not reasonably related to the covered entity's costs in making the communication.

---

[317] Although the compliance date for these regulations was September 23, 2013, HHS delayed enforcement of these refill-reminder rules until November 7, 2013. Notice from OCR (Sept. 19, 2013).

[318] 45 C.F.R § 164.501.

[319] 78 Fed. Reg. 5596; OCR Refill Reminder Guidance.

[320] OCR Refill Reminder Guidance.

[321] OCR Refill Reminder Guidance.

[322] OCR Refill Reminder Guidance.

[323] 78 Fed. Reg. 5597 (Jan. 25, 2013).

[324] OCR Refill Reminder Guidance.

Business associates may receive payment for assisting a covered entity in making these permitted refill-reminder communications, up to the fair market value of the business associate's services. The payment to the business associate may be made directly to the business associate by the drug manufacturer or other third party whose product or services are being described. The payment can also pass through the covered entity to the business associate.[325]

Finally, if these communications about currently prescribed drugs or biologics are made face-to-face (e.g., by the dispensing pharmacist), the provisions of category [1] apply, regardless of any financial remuneration.[326]

[4] Authorization Is Required

Individual authorization is required for the following communications, whether or not there is financial remuneration. However, if the covered entity receives financial remuneration from a third party, the authorization form must state that such remuneration is involved.[327]

1. *A Communication Promoting the Product or Service of a Third Party.* The marketing communication by the covered entity promotes the product or service of another entity; for example, a communication from a hospital, using its patient list to inform its patients about a cardiac facility (which is not part of the hospital) that can provide a baseline EKG for $39, when the communication is not for the purpose of individual treatment advice, requires an authorization.

2. *A Communication for a Non-Health-Related Product or Service.* The covered entity's communication promotes a service or product of its own, but it is not health-related; for example, a communication from a health insurer promoting a property and casualty insurance product offered by the same company requires an authorization.

3. *Use of PHI as Content of a Communication.* If a covered entity uses an individual's PHI as part of the content of a communication to third parties, for example in a brochure or a newsletter, whether these communications are classified as "marketing," "health care operations," or something else, an authorization is required relative to that content. For example, if a covered entity that is a rehabilitation facility sends a newsletter or other mailing to its patients regarding a new assistive technology and the communication contains a "success story" and photograph of a patient using the device, the patient who is featured in the story and photo must have signed an authorization for the use and disclosure of his or her PHI.

4. *Sale of PHI.* For the disclosure of PHI to a third party for the third party's marketing purposes, in exchange for remuneration, see **§ 3.04[B]** for additional information.

5. *Financial Remuneration.* For the communications described in **§ 3.04[C][2]** above, if there is financial remuneration (i.e., any direct or indirect payment from or on behalf of a third party whose product or service is being described in exchange for making the communication), authorization is required. For subsidized communications described **§ 3.04[C][3]** above, if the financial remuneration is in excess of what is permitted, authorization is required.

[5] Marketing and Other Laws

The fact that marketing and related communications are permitted without authorization under the Privacy Regulations does not mean that these practices do not violate other laws. For example, the federal anti-kickback statute, physician self-referral prohibition (Stark law), civil monetary penalties statute, as well as other federal

---

[325] OCR Refill Reminder Guidance.
[326] 78 Fed. Reg. 5597 (Jan. 25, 2013).
[327] 45 C.F.R. § 164.508(a)(3)(ii); OCR Guidance (Marketing).

and state laws, could be implicated by a covered entity's communications and marketing practices.[328] Reviewing the Privacy Regulations requirements should be just a part of a comprehensive legal review of proposed activities in this area.

[D] Mental Health Records and Psychotherapy Notes

The Privacy Regulations generally do not treat any category of PHI (e.g., mental health, substance abuse, or AIDS records) as more sensitive than any other.[329] There are, however, special rules relating to psychotherapy notes. The term *psychotherapy notes* refers only to the notes recorded (in any medium) by a health care provider who is a mental health professional documenting or analyzing a conversation during an individual, group, or family counseling session, which are separated from the rest of the individual's health record.[330]

Psychotherapy notes, by definition, are kept separate from the rest of the individual's medical record. Therefore, if the covered entity maintains a fully integrated medical record, it would likely not have psychotherapy notes, as defined by the Privacy Regulations. In addition, psychotherapy notes do not include records of medication prescription and monitoring, the start and stop times of the counseling sessions, the treatment modalities and frequencies, and results of clinical tests. Psychotherapy notes record the details of the counseling session and do not include summary information regarding diagnosis, functional status, treatment plan, symptoms, prognosis, or progress to date.[331]

If a mental health professional does maintain separate psychotherapy notes, these receive additional protection under the Privacy Regulations. In general, covered entities must obtain the individual's authorization in order to use or disclose psychotherapy notes.[332] See **§ 3.03[F]** for the standards for authorizations, which include a requirement that an authorization for use or disclosure of psychotherapy notes not be combined with an authorization relating to any other type of PHI. The following are the only circumstances in which such authorization is not required for psychotherapy notes:

1. To carry out the following treatment, payment, or health care operations:

   - Use (but not disclosure) by the originator of the psychotherapy notes for treatment purposes;

   - Use or disclosure by the covered entity for its own training programs in which students, trainees, or practitioners in mental health learn under supervision to practice or improve their skills in group, joint, family, or individual counseling; or

   - Use or disclosure by the covered entity to defend itself in a legal action or other proceeding brought by the individual.

2. For uses and disclosures:

   - Required by HHS to investigate compliance with the Administrative Simplification Regulations;

   - Required by law;

---

[328] 42 U.S.C. § 1320a-7b(b) (anti-kickback statute); 42 U.S.C. § 1395nn (Stark law); 42 U.S.C. § 1320a-7a (civil monetary penalties statute); OIG Special Fraud Alert (Aug. 2002) (regarding offering gifts and inducements to Medicare or Medicaid beneficiaries), available at http://oig.hhs.gov/fraud/docs/alertsandbulletins/SABGiftsandInducements.pdf.

[329] Any state law, however, that provides a higher level of protection to such records will generally still apply under the preemption analysis discussed in **§ 1.04**. There are also federal laws relating to protection of information relating to substance abuse treatment. See 42 C.F.R. Pt. 2. See also OCR Guidance—Mental Health.

[330] 45 C.F.R. § 164.501. HHS will study the question of whether certain test data, which is related to direct responses, scores, items, forms, protocols, manuals, or other materials that are part of a mental health evaluation, should be included in the definition of psychotherapy notes. HITECH Act § 13424(f).

[331] 45 C.F.R. § 164.501.

[332] 45 C.F.R. § 164.508(a)(2).

- To comply with a request from a health care oversight agency with respect to oversight of the originator of the psychotherapy notes;

- To coroners or medical examiners regarding a deceased individual; or

- To prevent or lessen a serious and imminent threat to the health or safety of a person or the public.[333]

[E] Underwriting

In general, PHI may be used or disclosed for underwriting, enrollment, premium rating, and other activities relating to the creation, renewal, or replacement of a contract of health insurance or health benefits, and ceding, securing, or placing a contract for reinsurance of risk relating to health care claims (including stop-loss and excess of loss insurance).[334] These activities are health care operations. Health plans receiving PHI for these purposes may not, however, use or disclose it for any other purpose, except as may be required by law, if the insurance or benefits contract is not placed with the health plan.[335] Health plans should develop a process to assure that the PHI is appropriately disposed of if the application for health insurance is unsuccessful.

Additional limits to underwriting activities arise from the Genetic Information Nondiscrimination Act of 2008 (GINA). GINA prohibits health plans and insurers from using or collecting genetic information for underwriting purposes and explicitly extends the definition of PHI to genetic information.[336] The HITECH Regulations update the Privacy Regulations to specifically include the GINA requirements by prohibiting a health plan from using or disclosing PHI that is genetic information for underwriting purposes.[337] This prohibition cannot be overcome by use of an authorization.[338] If the health plan intends to use or disclose PHI for underwriting purposes, its notice of privacy practices must state that it is prohibited from using or disclosing PHI that is genetic information of the individual for such underwriting purposes.[339]

The definition of health information under the Privacy Regulations was broad enough to encompass genetic information, but the HITECH Regulations update the definition to specifically reference genetic information.[340] Genetic information, as defined by GINA and now by the Privacy Regulations, means:

- With respect to an individual, information about:

  - the individual's genetic tests;

  - genetic tests of family members of the individual;

  - the manifestation of a disease or disorder in family members of such individual (e.g., family medical history); or

  - any request for, or receipt of, genetic services, or participation in clinical research that includes genetic services, by the individual or any family member of the individual.

---

[333] 45 C.F.R. § 164.508(a)(2).

[334] 45 C.F.R. § 164.501.

[335] 45 C.F.R. § 164.514(g).

[336] Genetic Information Nondiscrimination Act of 2008 (GINA), H.R. 493, 110th Cong. (2008); Pub. L. No. 110-233. Interim final regulations under GINA were issued October 1, 2009, and effective December 17, 2009. 74 Fed. Reg. 51,664 (Oct. 7, 2009). Final regulations were issued November 9, 2010, and were effective January 10, 2011. 75 Fed. Reg. 68,912 (Nov. 9, 2010).

[337] "Underwriting purposes," for the purpose of the prohibition related to genetic information, means, in summary: (1) rules related to plan eligibility or determination of plan benefits; (2) computation of premium or contribution amounts; (3) application of any pre-existing condition exclusion; and (4) other activities related to the creation, renewal, or replacement of a contract of health insurance or health benefits. "Underwriting purposes" does not include determinations of medical appropriateness where an individual seeks a benefit under the plan, coverage, or policy. 45 C.F.R. § 164.502(a)(5). See the full definition for additional detail.

[338] 78 Fed. Reg. 5666 (Jan. 25, 2013).

[339] 45 C.F.R. § 164.520(b)(1)(iii)(C).

[340] 45 C.F.R. § 160.103.

- With respect to an individual or family member of an individual, who is a pregnant woman, genetic information also includes:

  - information about any fetus carried by the individual or family member who is a pregnant woman; and

  - information about any embryo legally held by an individual or family member utilizing an assisted reproductive technology.

- Genetic information excludes information about the sex or age of any individual.[341]

These limitations on the use of genetic information for underwriting purposes will not be news to most health plans, because they have been complying with GINA's underwriting limitations for some time. However, the HITECH Regulations have a broader definition of "health plan" than GINA, so certain types of health plans not subject to GINA will be subject to these underwriting limitations for the first time through the HITECH Regulations. These health plans include employee welfare benefit plans, high risk pools, public benefit programs, and others.[342]

The prohibition does not apply to health care providers, who may use and disclose genetic information as necessary for treatment of the individual. For a covered entity, such as an HMO that has both provider and health plan functions, it may use genetic information for treatment purposes to determine the medical appropriateness of a benefit, and as otherwise permitted by the Privacy Regulations, but may not use genetic information for underwriting purposes.[343]

Compliance with these revised regulations is required as of the September 23, 2013 compliance date.[344] Thereafter, a use or disclosure of genetic information for underwriting purposes may be both a violation of GINA and a violation of the Privacy Regulations.

[F] Special Categories of Individuals

As detailed in this subsection, certain categories of persons receive special consideration under Privacy Regulations.

[1] Personal Representatives

A covered entity must treat a personal representative of an individual as the individual for purposes of the Privacy Regulations if such person is, under applicable law, authorized to act on behalf of the individual in making decisions related to health care.[345] This generally includes a court-appointed guardian and a person with a health care power of attorney but may also include other persons. This provision applies to persons empowered under state or other law (e.g., tribal law or military law) to make health-related decisions for an individual, whether or not the instrument or law granting such authority specifically addresses health information.[346]

---

[341] 45 C.F.R. § 160.103. Definitions have also been added to the Privacy Regulations for family member, genetic services, genetic test, and manifestation or manifested. 45 C.F.R. § 160.103. These definitions are generally consistent with the definitions of these terms in GINA. 78 Fed. Reg. 5661 (Jan. 25, 2013).

[342] 78 Fed. Reg. 5659–5660 (Jan. 25, 2013). These prohibitions regarding underwriting apply to all covered entities that are health plans, except for issuers of long-term care policies. 45 C.F.R. § 164.502(a)(5)(i).

[343] 78 Fed. Reg. 5667 (Jan. 25, 2013).

[344] 45 C.F.R. § 164.502(a)(5).

[345] 45 C.F.R. § 164.502(g); 65 Fed. Reg. 82,500 (Dec. 28, 2000); see also OCR Guidance (Personal Representatives), revised Sept. 19, 2013, available at http://www.hhs.gov/ocr/privacy/hipaa/understanding/coveredentities/personalreps.html.

[346] 65 Fed. Reg. 82,500 (Dec. 28, 2000); see also OCR Guidance (Personal Representatives), revised Sept. 19, 2013, available at http://www.hhs.gov/ocr/privacy/hipaa/understanding/coveredentities/personalreps.html.

The authority of a personal representative applies only to the extent that PHI is relevant to the matters on which the personal representative is authorized to represent the individual. For example, if under a limited health care power of attorney, a person's authority to make health care decisions for an individual is limited to decisions regarding artificial life support, such person is a personal representative and must be treated as the individual with respect to PHI related to that purpose. But the person may not be treated as the individual with respect to other purposes, such as unrelated treatment decisions or signing an authorization for the use of PHI for marketing purposes.[347]

A covered entity may choose not to treat a person as the personal representative of the individual if the covered entity reasonably believes in its professional judgment that the individual has been or may be subjected to domestic violence, abuse, or neglect by such person or that treating such person as the individual's personal representative could endanger the individual and it is not in the best interest of the individual to treat such person as the individual's personal representative.[348]

This addresses the question of who has the authority to act as the personal representative of the individual. See § 3.01[B] regarding the separate step of verifying the identity of a person claiming such authority.

[2]   Parents and Minors

In general, a person's right to control PHI is based on that person's right (under state or other applicable law) to control the health care itself. Because a parent usually has authority to make health care decisions about his or her minor child, a parent is generally a personal representative of his or her minor child under the Privacy Regulations and has the right to obtain access to health information about the child and exercise other such individual rights on behalf of the child. This may also be the case for a guardian or other person acting *in loco parentis* of a minor, subject to state law.[349] Being a divorced parent without physical custody of the child does not automatically mean that the parent is no longer a personal representative of the minor—this is a matter of state law and the terms of the divorce decree. Similarly, for parents who were never married, the rights of the father to his child's PHI will be governed by state law and factors such as whether a voluntary declaration of paternity has been filed.

There are three exceptions in which a parent might not be the personal representative with respect to certain health information about a minor child, and the minor has the authority to act as an individual in his or her own right. In the following situations, the Privacy Regulations defer to determinations under other law that the parent does not control the minor's health care decisions and therefore does not control the PHI related to that care.[350]

1.   When state or other law does not require consent of a parent before a minor can obtain a particular health care service, and the minor consents to the health care service, the parent is not the minor's personal representative under the Privacy Regulations. For example, when a state law provides an adolescent the right to consent to mental health treatment without the consent of his or her parent, and the adolescent obtains such treatment without the consent of the parent, the parent is not the personal representative under the Privacy Regulations for purposes of that treatment.

2.   When a court or a person (other than the parent) authorized by law makes treatment decisions for a minor, the parent is not the personal representative of the minor for the relevant services. For example, courts may grant authority to make health care decisions for the minor to an adult other than the parent, or to the minor, or the court may make the decision(s) itself. In order to not undermine these court decisions, the parent is not the personal representative under the Privacy Regulations in these circumstances.

---

[347] 65 Fed. Reg. 82,500 (Dec. 28, 2000); OCR Guidance (Personal Representatives), revised Sept. 19, 2013, available at http://www.hhs.gov/ocr/privacy/hipaa/understanding/coveredentities/personalreps.html.

[348] 45 C.F.R. § 164.502(g)(5).

[349] 45 C.F.R. §§ 164.502(g)(2), 164.502(g)(3); OCR Guidance (Personal Representatives), available at http://www.hhs.gov/ocr/privacy/hipaa/understanding/coveredentities/personalreps.html.

[350] 45 C.F.R. § 164.502(g)(3).

3. When a parent agrees to a confidential relationship between the minor and the provider, the parent does not have access to the health information related to that communication or relationship.[351]

Once children reach the age of majority (as defined by state law), they control their own records on the same basis as other individuals. A parent has no ongoing rights with respect to a child's PHI, even if the PHI relates to when the child was still a minor, unless the parent has been otherwise appointed a personal representative of the adult individual.

In addition, the Privacy Regulations do not preempt state law (including case law) specifically addressing disclosure of, or provision of access to, a minor's health information to a parent. This is true whether the state law permits, requires, or prohibits such disclosure or provision of access.[352] Thus, if a physician believes that disclosure of information about a minor would endanger that minor, but a state law requires disclosure to a parent, the physician may comply with the state law without violating the Privacy Regulations. Similarly, a provider may comply with a state law that requires disclosure to a parent and would not have to accommodate a request for confidential communications that would be contrary to state law.[353]

In the few cases in which the parent is not the personal representative of the minor, and state and other law about parental access is not explicit, a covered entity may provide or deny access to a parent provided that such discretion is permitted by state law or other law. The Privacy Regulations therefore do not prevent a covered entity from providing access to a parent if the covered entity would have been able to provide this access under state law or other applicable law. This discretion to provide or deny access to a parent may only be exercised by a licensed health care professional in the exercise of professional judgment.[354]

The Privacy Regulations defer to state law and reflect the HHS position that issues related to the rights of parents and minors with respect to health care and PHI are best left to the states.[355]

[3] Deceased Individuals

The PHI of deceased individuals is protected under the Privacy and Security Regulations. This § 3.04[F][3] summarizes the special considerations applicable to deceased individuals.[356]

The PHI of a deceased individual continues to be protected under the Privacy Regulations for 50 years following the death of the individual.[357] The addition of the 50-year time limit was part of the HITECH Act and HITECH Regulations, effective March 26, 2013.[358] See § 1.03[A] for more information about this change in the definition of "protected health information."

If under applicable law, an executor, administrator, or other person has authority to act on behalf of a deceased individual or the individual's estate, a covered entity must treat such person as a personal representative of the deceased individual with respect to PHI relevant to such personal representation.[359]

---

[351] 45 C.F.R. § 164.502(g)(3); OCR Guidance (Personal Representatives), available at http://www.hhs.gov/ocr/privacy/hipaa/understanding/coveredentities/personalreps.html.

[352] 45 C.F.R. § 164.502(g)(3)(ii).

[353] OCR Guidance (Personal Representatives), available at http://www.hhs.gov/ocr/privacy/hipaa/understanding/coveredentities/personalreps.html.

[354] 45 C.F.R. § 164.502(g)(3)(ii)(C).

[355] 67 Fed. Reg. 53,202 (Aug. 14, 2002).

[356] See also HHS, "Health Information of Deceased Individuals" (Sept. 19, 2013), available at http://www.hhs.gov/ocr/privacy/hipaa/understanding/coveredentities/decedents.html.

[357] 45 C.F.R. § 160.103; 45 C.F.R. § 164.502(f); 67 Fed. Reg. 53,201 (Aug. 14, 2002); 78 Fed. Reg. 5614 (Jan. 25, 2013).

[358] 78 Fed. Reg. 5614 (Jan. 25, 2013).

[359] 45 C.F.R. § 164.502(g)(4). See § 3.04[F][1]. See also Johnson v. Parker Hughes Clinics, No. Civ. 04-4130 PAM/RLR, 2005 WL 102968 (D. Minn. Jan. 13, 2005) (addressing but not resolving a question of HIPAA preemption and whether a surviving spouse was a personal representative of the deceased individual); Opis Management Resources LLC, et al., v. Secretary Florida Agency for Healthcare Administration, 713 F.3d 1291 (11th Cir. 2013) (holding that a Florida law requiring nursing homes to disclose patient records of deceased patients to a surviving spouse was preempted by HIPAA, on the grounds that the surviving spouse was not the personal representative of the deceased under that state law).

The following other special provisions permit disclosure of PHI of deceased individuals:

1. A covered entity may disclose PHI to a family member, or certain other persons who were involved in the individual's health care or payment for health care prior to the individual's death, unless doing so is inconsistent with a prior expressed preference of the individual that is known to the covered entity. This change was effective March 26, 2013, under the HITECH Regulations.[360]

2. A covered entity may disclose PHI about a deceased individual to a law enforcement official for the purpose of alerting law enforcement of the death of the individual, if the covered entity has a suspicion that such death may have resulted from criminal conduct.[361]

3. A covered entity may disclose PHI to a coroner or medical examiner for the purpose of identifying a deceased individual, determining a cause of death, or other duties as authorized by law. A covered entity that also performs the duties of a coroner or medical examiner may use PHI for these purposes.[362]

4. A covered entity may disclose PHI to funeral directors, consistent with applicable law, as necessary to carry out their duties with respect to the decedent. If necessary for funeral directors to carry out their duties, the covered entity may disclose the PHI prior to, and in reasonable anticipation of, the individual's death.[363]

5. A covered entity may use PHI for, or disclose PHI to, organ procurement organizations or other entities engaged in the procurement, banking, or transplantation of cadaveric organs, eyes, or tissue for the purpose of facilitating organ, eye, or tissue donation and transplantation.[364]

6. A covered entity may use and disclose PHI for research on decedents if the covered entity obtains representations from the researcher, either in writing or orally, that the use or disclosure being sought is solely for research on the PHI of decedents, that the PHI being sought is necessary for the research, and at the request of the covered entity, documentation of the death of the individuals about whom information is being sought.[365]

7. An authorization that has not expired by its terms and has not been revoked continues to be valid. OCR has informally confirmed that an authorization is not invalidated by the death of the individual.[366] A more restrictive state law could change this outcome.

[G] Litigation

HIPAA has changed the way medical records are requested and obtained during litigation by adding a layer of new federal rules over the existing state and federal rules in this area and by raising preemption issues. The Privacy Regulations come into play in cases relating to unlawful termination, medical malpractice, child custody, workers' compensation, and a variety of other causes of action where there is a need to obtain and use PHI in preparation for and during litigation.[367]

---

[360] 45 C.F.R. § 164.510(b). See also **§ 3.03[C]**.

[361] 45 C.F.R. § 164.512(f)(4). See also **§ 3.03[D][6]**.

[362] 45 C.F.R. § 164.512(g)(1). See also **§ 3.03[D][7]**.

[363] 45 C.F.R. § 164.512(g)(2). See also **§ 3.03[D][7]**.

[364] 45 C.F.R. § 164.512(h). See also **§ 3.03[D][8]**.

[365] 45 C.F.R. § 164.512(i)(1)(iii). See also **§ 3.03[D][9]**.

[366] American Bar Association, Technical Session Between the Department of Health and Human Services and the Joint Committee on Employee Benefits (May 10, 2007).

[367] See, e.g., Chapman v. Health and Hosps. Corps., 796 N.Y.S.2d 876 (N.Y. Sup. Ct., Mar. 24, 2005); Rigaud v. Garofalo, 2005 WL 1030196 (E.D. Pa. May 2, 2005) (employment termination, workers' compensation); Beard v. City of Chicago, 2005 WL 66074 (N.D. Ill. Jan. 10, 2005) (state tort claims, employment discrimination); Valentin Munoz v. Island Fin. Corp., 364 F. Supp. 2d 131 (D.P.R. Mar. 28, 2005) (state tort claims); University of Colo. Hosp. Auth. v. Denver Publ'g Co., 340 F. Supp. 2d 1142 (D. Colo. Aug. 2, 2004) (peer

The Privacy Regulations permit a covered entity to disclose an individual's PHI in the context of litigation, as covered in the sections below.[368]

[1] Disclosures to Covered Entity's Own Legal Counsel

A covered entity may, without the individual's authorization, use and disclose PHI for its own health care operations, which include performing or arranging for legal services.[369] This means that a covered entity may provide PHI to its in-house legal counsel or to its outside law firm as necessary for the performance of those legal services. The covered entity must, however, make reasonable efforts to limit such uses and disclosures to the minimum necessary to accomplish the intended purpose. This applies to any legal services for the covered entity, whether or not the covered entity is currently a party in a legal proceeding.

An outside law firm engaged to provide legal services and receiving PHI is a business associate of the covered entity, and a business associate agreement is required, as described in § 3.07. The law firm may, in turn, engage the services of others in furtherance of those legal services. These subcontractors might include other legal counsel, jury experts, file managers, investigators, litigation support personnel, or others hired by the law firm to assist in providing the legal services to the covered entity. If these subcontractors receive PHI, the law firm must execute business associate agreements with them that extend the same restrictions and conditions with regard to PHI as apply under the law firm's own business associate agreement.[370] Such an agreement is not required for the law firm to disclose PHI to opposing counsel, fact witnesses, or others who do not perform services that assist the law firm in performing legal services for the covered entity.[371] Similarly, the law firm would not need to enter into a subcontractor business associate agreement with an expert witness, because the expert witness is not performing legal functions that the law firm was engaged to perform.[372] Even when a business associate agreement is not required, a confidentiality agreement may be appropriate.

[2] Disclosures When Covered Entity Is a Party to Litigation

A covered entity that is a party to litigation may disclose PHI to an opposing party or its legal counsel as part of the covered entity's health care operations, subject to the minimum necessary rule as described in § 3.01[A]. The Privacy Regulations do not require such disclosures but will not impede them if required by state law or procedure.[373] The covered entity's legal counsel may seek a protective order to preserve the confidentiality of any PHI disclosed.

In addition to health care operations, a covered entity may be able to rely on other provisions of the Privacy Regulations in certain circumstances; for example, relying on the health oversight exception in a contested license revocation proceeding before a health oversight agency or relying on the payment exception in connection with legal proceedings in a debt collection action.[374] A covered entity should also be able to rely on the

---

review protections); *In re* Marriage of Kreiss, 19 Cal. Rptr. 3d 260 (Cal. App. 2 Dist. Sep. 29, 2004) (child custody); Mayer v. Huesner, 107 P.3d 152 (Wash. App. Div. 3, Feb. 24, 2005), *rev. denied*, 124 P.3d 659 (Wash. Nov. 2, 2005) (workers' compensation); Limbaugh v. State, 887 So. 2d 387 (Fla. App. Nov. 17, 2004), *rev. denied*, 903 So. 2d 189 (Fla. Apr. 28, 2005) (Florida "doctor shopping" statute).

[368] OCR HIPAA FAQs (formerly numbered 703 through 711), available at http://www.hhs.gov/hipaafaq/.

[369] 45 C.F.R. §§ 164.506(c)(1) and 164.501; OCR HIPAA FAQs (formerly numbered 704 and 705), available at http://www.hhs.gov/hipaafaq/.

[370] Some law firms take the position that these subcontractors should enter into a business associate agreement directly with the covered entity, rather than the law firm creating a subcontractor business associate arrangement. The correct approach may vary according the facts and circumstances.

[371] OCR HIPAA FAQ (formerly numbered 709), available at http://www.hhs.gov/hipaafaq/.

[372] 65 Fed. Reg. 82506 (Dec. 28, 2000).

[373] 45 C.F.R. §§ 164.506(c)(1), 164.501; OCR HIPAA FAQs (formerly numbered 704 and 705), available at http://www.hhs.gov/hipaafaq/.

[374] See OCR HIPAA FAQ (formerly numbered 704), available at http://www.hhs.gov/hipaafaq/.

provisions of the Privacy Regulations that would apply if it were not a party to the proceedings as described in **§ 3.04[G][3]**.

[3] Disclosures When Covered Entity Is Not a Party

Covered entities often receive subpoenas and other requests for PHI related to litigation in which the covered entity is not a party, but simply the owner or repository of records needed in a dispute. A covered entity that is not a party to the litigation may disclose PHI under the following conditions:

1. *Authorization.* A covered entity may disclose PHI in accordance with a HIPAA-compliant authorization, signed by the individual or his or her personal representative.[375] An individual's attorney is typically not an authorized personal representative for purposes of signing such an authorization.

2. *Court Order.* A covered entity may disclose PHI pursuant to a valid judicial or administrative order, provided that the covered entity discloses only the PHI expressly authorized by such order. This includes a subpoena or discovery request accompanied by a court order (i.e., an order signed by a judge or administrative hearing officer). No notice to the individual is required.[376]

3. *Subpoena or Discovery Request with Satisfactory Assurances.* A covered entity may disclose PHI pursuant to a subpoena, discovery request, or other lawful process that is not accompanied by a judicial or administrative order, but is accompanied by satisfactory written assurances regarding notice to the individual. These "assurances" require that the individual be given notice and an opportunity to object.[377]

4. *Subpoena or Discovery Request Accompanied by a Qualified Protective Order.* A covered entity may disclose PHI pursuant to a subpoena, discovery request, or other lawful process that is accompanied by a qualified protective order. The protective order must prohibit the use of the records for any purposes other than those for which the records were requested and must require that the records be returned to the covered entity or destroyed at the end of the legal proceeding.[378]

[4] Civil Investigative Demands

A civil investigative demand (CID), such as from a State Attorney General, is categorized by the Privacy Regulations as a law enforcement request. A covered entity may disclose PHI in response to a CID, provided the CID is accompanied by a written statement that the information requested is relevant and material to a legitimate law enforcement inquiry, specific and limited in scope to the extent reasonably practicable in light of the purpose for which the information is sought, and de-identified information cannot reasonably be used.[379]

[5] State Law

State law may be more restrictive than the Privacy Regulations with regard to requests for PHI in the situations described in **§ 3.04[G]** and may therefore preempt the Privacy Regulations. If so, all local rules and procedures must be followed. Published decisions concerning the application of the Privacy Regulations in

---

[375] 45 C.F.R. § 164.508.

[376] 45 C.F.R. § 164.512(e)(1)(i).

[377] 45 C.F.R. §§ 164.512(e)(1)(ii)(B), 164.512(e)(1)(iv)–(v). See § 164.512(e) for additional details. See also Chapman v. Health and Hosps. Corps., 796 N.Y.S.2d 876 (N.Y. Sup. Ct. Mar 24, 2005) (holding hospital not required to comply with petitioner's first subpoena for medical records because it did not meet HIPAA requirements, e.g., it did not limit use to the proceedings; the Court then issued its own HIPAA-compliant protective order to produce the relevant medical records).

[378] 45 C.F.R. § 164.512(e)(1)(ii)(B) and (iv)–(v). See § 164.512(e) for additional details.

[379] 45 C.F.R. § 164.512(f)(1)(ii)(C); OCR HIPAA FAQ (formerly numbered 505), available at http://www.hhs.gov/hipaafaq/.

litigation should be researched if requests for PHI are anticipated in litigation.[380] Covered entities will need to confer with legal counsel to make certain the court order, subpoena, or other documents received comply with the applicable requirements of the Privacy Regulations and state law and to ensure the covered entity's disclosures do not exceed the scope of the request.

[H] Emergency Preparedness

The Privacy Regulations permit a covered entity to disclose PHI in emergency situations under various provisions depending on the specific circumstances. HHS has provided a Decision Tool for Emergency Preparedness Planning, which discusses these options. The decision tool walks through different scenarios, involving disclosures for treatment, for public health, uses of a limited data set, and disclosures with an authorization.[381]

If the President declares an emergency or disaster *and* HHS declares a public health emergency, the Project Bioshield Act allows HHS to waive penalties against a hospital that does not comply with the following requirements of the Privacy Regulations:

- to obtain a patient's agreement to speak with family members or friends involved in the patient's care;
- to honor a request to opt out of the facility directory;
- to distribute a notice of privacy practices;
- to honor the patient's right to request privacy restrictions; and
- to honor the patient's right to request confidential communications.

The hospital must have instituted a disaster protocol, and this waiver applies only in the emergency area and for a limited emergency period, up to 72 hours.[382]

In November 2014, OCR issued a Bulletin that revisited the applicability of the Privacy Regulations "in light of the Ebola outbreak and other events."[383] The Bulletin was a reminder to covered entities and their business associates of the ways that PHI can be shared in an emergency, but that the Regulations still apply. The Bulletin does not contain new information, but it provides a good summary regarding disclosures for treatment, public health, communication with family and friends, prevention of imminent danger, facility directories, and the media. It also reviews the need to maintain safeguards on PHI and to limit information in accordance with the minimum necessary rule, even during an emergency.

§ 3.05 ADMINISTRATIVE REQUIREMENTS

To meet the requirements of HIPAA Privacy Regulations, a covered entity must create an organizational framework that includes a privacy official, training policies and procedures, a system for reporting noncompliance, and other administrative requirements as described in this section.[384]

---

[380] See, e.g., National Abortion Fed'n v. Ashcroft, 2004 WL 292079 (N.D. Ill. Feb. 6, 2004), *aff'd*, 362 F.3d 923 (7th Cir. 2004) (holding that a subpoena complied with HIPAA because a court order authorizing disclosure was attached, but that Illinois law nevertheless did not permit disclosure of the records, even if the identifying information was redacted, and granting a motion to quash the subpoena). See also, e.g., Webdale v. North Gen. Hosp., 796 N.Y.S.2d 861 (N.Y. Sup. 2005), *order aff'd*, 804 N.Y.S.2d 681 (N.Y.A.D. 1 Dept. 2005) (holding that criminal defendant's waiver of privilege and right to confidentiality of his medical records by relying upon them for his defense did not conflict with HIPAA, which permits disclosure for litigation).

[381] Available at http://www.hhs.gov/ocr/privacy/hipaa/understanding/special/emergency/decisiontoolintro.html.

[382] Project Bioshield Act of 2004, Pub. L. No. 108-276, § 9. See also http://www.hhs.gov/ocr/privacy/hipaa/faq/disclosures_in_emergency_situations/1068.html.

[383] OCR, "BULLETIN: HIPAA Privacy in Emergency Situations," (Nov. 2014), available at http://www.hhs.gov/ocr/privacy/hipaa/understanding/special/emergency/hipaa-privacy-emergency-situations.pdf.

[384] These administrative requirements are very similar to the organizational efforts required to develop a corporate compliance program in accordance with guidelines issued by the HHS Office of Inspector General (OIG). For information on how to integrate

[A]   Designation of Privacy Official and Contact Person

A covered entity must designate a privacy official who is responsible for the development and implementation of the policies and procedures of the covered entity. In addition, the covered entity must designate a contact person or office to be responsible for receiving complaints relating to the Privacy Regulations and to provide further information about matters covered by the covered entity's notice of privacy practices. The contact person may be, but need not be, the privacy official. Implementation varies widely, depending on the size and nature of the covered entity. Small entities may have a part-time privacy official or may assign this as an additional duty for a current staff person. In contrast, large organizations may have a full-time, dedicated privacy official.[385]

The designations of both the privacy official and the contact person must be documented.[386] The Privacy Regulations do not require any specific method for documenting these roles, but the documentation must be retained for six years from the date the designations were last in effect (as further discussed in **§ 3.05[J]**).

[B]   Training

A covered entity must train all members of its workforce (including volunteers, trainees, and others under direct control of the covered entity, whether paid or unpaid) on its policies and procedures with respect to PHI as necessary and appropriate to their job functions. Each new member of the workforce must be trained within a reasonable period of time after joining the covered entity's workforce. Subsequently, when there is a material change in a privacy policy or procedure, those whose jobs are affected must be retrained within a reasonable period of time. When there is a change in the Regulations, the affected workforce must be trained no later than the compliance date. The covered entity may determine the most effective means of achieving this training requirement for its workforce. However, the training must be based in the covered entity's own privacy practices and reflect its implementation of the Privacy Regulations. As a result, a covered entity cannot excuse workforce members from training on the basis that they previously received HIPAA training through another entity.

The covered entity must document that the mandated training has been provided.[387] Although not required, a covered entity may wish to have trainees sign a statement certifying that they received the privacy training and will honor all of the covered entity's privacy policies and procedures.

Training may also be advisable for individuals who are not members of the covered entity's workforce but work closely with the covered entity. For example, for business associates, attendance at training sessions could be part of their contractual obligations. For a hospital's medical staff, attendance at training could be required under the medical staff bylaws as a condition of obtaining and maintaining clinical privileges.

[C]   Safeguards

A covered entity must have in place appropriate administrative, physical, and technical safeguards to protect the privacy of PHI and reasonably safeguard it from any intentional or unintentional use or disclosure that is in violation of the Privacy Regulations.[388] This requirement applies to *all* PHI. For electronic PHI, this "mini-security rule" is just the beginning; the covered entity must coordinate these safeguards with those that are

---

HIPAA compliance with a corporate compliance program, see Carter, Patricia I., Applying Your Corporate Compliance Skills to the HIPAA Security Standard, Journal of Healthcare Information Management (Winter 2000) at 13; Carter, Patricia I., Integrating HIPAA Privacy and Security into your Corporate Compliance Program, paper presented at 2002 Annual Health Information Management Systems Society Conference, January 2002, available at http://www.himss.org/files/HIMSSorg/content/files/proceedings/2002/sessions/ses118.pdf

[385] See 65 Fed. Reg. 82,561 (Dec. 28, 2000).

[386] 45 C.F.R. § 164.530(a).

[387] 45 C.F.R. §§ 160.103 and 164.530(b).

[388] 45 C.F.R. § 164.530(c).

required under the Security Regulations (see **Chapter 4**).[389] The Security Regulations, although applicable only to electronic PHI, provide a useful framework for analyzing risks and structuring safeguards for nonelectronic PHI as well.

These safeguard requirements are intended to be scalable, because the nature of the required policies and procedures will vary with the size of the covered entity and the type of activities that the covered entity undertakes. A covered entity is not expected to guarantee the safety of PHI "against all assaults."[390] Circumvention of these safeguards may or may not signal a violation of the Privacy Regulations, depending on the circumstances and whether the covered entity had reasonable safeguards in place. Examples of appropriate safeguards include requiring that documents containing PHI be shredded prior to disposal, requiring that doors to medical records departments (or to file cabinets housing such records) remain locked, and limiting which personnel are authorized to have the key or key-code.[391]

The HHS Office of Civil Rights (OCR) has issued guidance on the appropriate disposal of PHI. Although the guidance does not require a particular method of disposal, it provides some examples of proper disposal methods.[392] These include:

- *Paper PHI.* Shredding, burning, pulping, or pulverizing the records so that PHI is rendered essentially unreadable, indecipherable, and otherwise cannot be reconstructed.

- *Electronic PHI.* Clearing (using software or hardware products to overwrite media with non-sensitive data), purging (degaussing or exposing the media to a strong magnetic field in order to disrupt the recorded magnetic domains), or destroying the media (disintegration, pulverization, melting, incinerating, or shredding). See **§ 4.02[B]**, *Standard 4.*

OCR has also advised that policies and procedures should be developed that address appropriate disposal of PHI by workforce members who use PHI offsite. Options could include returning the PHI to the covered entity for appropriate disposal, or if reasonable under the circumstances, permitting off-site secure disposal (such as shredding).[393]

When a disposal vendor is a business associate that picks up and shreds or otherwise destroys the PHI, the PHI waiting for disposal should be maintained in a secure area. In some cases, it may be appropriate to deposit PHI in locked dumpsters that are accessible only by authorized persons.[394]

[D] Complaints

Any person has the right to make a complaint to the covered entity and to OCR concerning the covered entity's privacy policies and procedures or its compliance with the requirements of the Privacy Regulations. A covered entity may not retaliate against the person for filing such a complaint.[395]

For complaints to the covered entity, the covered entity must provide a process for people to make complaints and must document all complaints received, and their disposition, if any.[396] The name of the designated contact person or office for such complaints, including a telephone number, must be provided in the covered

---

[389] 65 Fed. Reg. 82,561–62 (Dec. 28, 2000).

[390] 65 Fed. Reg. 82,562 (Dec. 28, 2000).

[391] 65 Fed. Reg. 82,562 (Dec. 28, 2000).

[392] HHS, OCR, Frequently Asked Questions About the Disposal of Protected Health Information, available at http://www.hhs.gov/ocr/privacy/hipaa/enforcement/examples/disposalfaqs.pdf.

[393] OCR HIPAA FAQ, available at http://www.hhs.gov/ocr/privacy/hipaa/faq/safeguards/579.html.

[394] HHS, OCR, Frequently Asked Questions About the Disposal of Protected Health Information, available at http://www.hhs.gov/ocr/privacy/hipaa/enforcement/examples/disposalfaqs.pdf.

[395] 45 C.F.R. §§ 164.520(b)(1)(vi) and 164.530(d). See also 45 C.F.R. § 164.502(j)(1) regarding whistleblowers.

[396] 45 C.F.R. § 164.530(d).

entity's notice of privacy practices.[397] If a covered entity has a reporting mechanism in place as part of a corporate compliance program, that same mechanism can generally be used for reporting HIPAA-related complaints. Anonymous reporting methods are not required, but it may be helpful to provide workforce members with an anonymous "hotline" to report privacy concerns.

No particular reporting mechanisms or response times are mandated by the Privacy Regulations. Nevertheless, a covered entity may wish to reserve the right to require that complaints be made in writing. And all complaints should be handled as promptly as possible. A prompt, courteous, and effective process for handling complaints internally will likely result in fewer complaints being filed with OCR.

Complaints to OCR must be filed in writing, identify the covered entity that is the subject of the complaint, and describe the acts or omissions believed to be a violation of the Privacy Regulations. The complaint must be filed within 180 days of when the complained-of act or omission became known to the individual. Complaints are to be sent to one of 10 regional OCR offices. The OCR encourages but does not require use of the OCR complaint form (which is now available in eight languages).[398]

[E] Sanctions

A covered entity must apply appropriate sanctions against members of its workforce who fail to comply with the privacy policies and procedures of the covered entity or the requirements of the Privacy Regulations. Written policies and procedures must describe these sanctions, and any sanctions that are applied must be documented. These sanctions do not apply to whistleblower activities.[399]

In general, a covered entity's HIPAA compliance program should set forth a progressive disciplinary policy for failing to comply with the organization's policies and procedures and applicable statutes and regulations. To the extent possible, this policy should be integrated with other disciplinary policies of the organization, including sanctions under the Security Regulations. Sanctions could range from oral warnings to suspension, termination, loss of clinical privileges, or financial penalties, as appropriate. Compliance policies should be consistently enforced, including, as appropriate, discipline of supervisors or managers for negligent failure to detect or correct an offense. Disciplinary policies and procedures should be communicated to all members of the workforce. Those affected should also be advised of the potential civil and criminal penalties for misuse or misappropriation of health information, and that such actions may be reported to law enforcement and regulatory, accreditation, and licensure organizations.

[F] Duty to Mitigate

A covered entity must mitigate, to the extent practicable, any harmful effect known to the covered entity of a use or disclosure of PHI in violation of its policies and procedures or the requirements of the Privacy Regulations by the covered entity or its Business Associate.[400] Mitigation steps may include, for example, offering identity theft protection or credit monitoring services to affected individuals, or taking steps to retrieve or limit further disclosures of improperly disclosed PHI.

Under the mitigation provision of the Privacy Regulations, the covered entity determines whether, under the circumstances, mitigation should include notice to affected individuals. One of the most significant changes under the HITECH Act, however, is the addition of specific requirements related to notification of breaches (see

---

[397] 45 C.F.R. § 164.520(b)(1)(vii).

[398] Notice of Addresses for Submission of HIPAA Health Information Privacy Complaints, 68 Fed. Reg. 13,711 (Mar. 20, 2003); see also "How to File a Complaint," at http://www.hhs.gov/ocr/privacy/hipaa/complaints/index.html.

[399] 45 C.F.R. § 164.530(e); 65 Fed. Reg. 82,562 (Dec. 28, 2000).

[400] 45 C.F.R. § 164.530(f).

Chapter 5). In addition, many states require individual notice in the event of certain breaches of privacy or security of personal information (especially Social Security numbers).[401]

[G] Refraining from Intimidating or Retaliatory Acts

A covered entity may not intimidate, threaten, coerce, discriminate against, or take other retaliatory action against:

1. Any individual for the exercise by the individual of any right under, or for participation by the individual in any process established by, the Privacy Regulations in regard to his or her PHI, including the filing of a complaint.

2. Any individual or any other person for:

   - Filing of a complaint with HHS;

   - Testifying, assisting, or participating in an investigation, compliance review, proceeding, or hearing under the Administrative Simplification provisions of HIPAA; or

   - Opposing any act or practice made unlawful by the Privacy Regulations, provided the individual or person has a good faith belief that the practice opposed is unlawful, and the manner of the opposition is reasonable and does not involve a disclosure of PHI in violation of the Privacy Regulations.[402]

[H] Waiver of Rights

A covered entity may not require individuals to waive their rights to file complaints with HHS as a condition of the provision of treatment, payment, or enrollment in a health plan, or eligibility for benefits.[403]

[I] Policies and Procedures

A covered entity must implement policies and procedures with respect to PHI that address each applicable standard in the Privacy Regulations. The policies and procedures must be reasonably designed, taking into account the size and type of activities that relate to PHI undertaken by the covered entity, to ensure such compliance. This reasonableness standard does not, however, permit or excuse an action that violates any other requirement of the Privacy Regulations.[404]

Whenever there is a change in law that necessitates a change to the covered entity's policies or procedures, the covered entity must promptly document and implement the revised policy or procedure. If the change in law materially affects the content of the covered entity's notice of privacy practices, the notice must be promptly revised.

When a covered entity changes a privacy practice that is stated in the notice of privacy practices and makes corresponding changes to its policies and procedures, it may make the changes effective for PHI that it created or received prior to the effective date of the notice revision if the covered entity has included in its notice a statement reserving its right to make such a change. If a covered entity has not reserved its right to change a privacy practice that is stated in the notice, the covered entity is bound by the privacy practices as stated in the notice with respect to PHI created or received while such notice is in effect, and the change will affect only PHI created

---

[401] See, e.g., Cal. Civ. Code § 1798.82; Minn. Stat. § 325E.61 and § 72A.502; N.C. Gen. Stat. § 75-60 *et seq.*; Wis. Stat. § 134.98; N.Y. Bus. Law § 899-aa.

[402] 45 C.F.R. § 164.530(g).

[403] 45 C.F.R. § 164.530(h).

[404] 45 C.F.R. § 164.530(i).

or received after the effective date of the revised notice. In either case, the covered entity may not implement a change to a policy or procedure prior to the effective date of the revised notice. A covered entity may make any other changes to policies and procedures at any time, if they do not materially affect the content of the notice, provided that the changes comply with the Privacy Regulations and are properly documented in advance of their effective date.[405]

[J]   Documentation

Creating and maintaining appropriate documentation is a key part of compliance with the Regulations. A covered entity must maintain the policies and procedures described in the preceding paragraph in written or electronic form. Other documentation requirements include:

- Designation of privacy official and contact person;
- Notice of privacy practices (including all revisions);
- Documentation of the designated record set;
- Titles/offices of those responsible for processing requests for access, amendments, and disclosures;
- Contents of an accounting of disclosures provided;
- Consents, authorizations, and related revocations;
- Documentation of resolutions of conflicts among authorizations;
- Training;
- Complaints received and their disposition; and
- Sanctions, including procedures and a record of sanctions applied.

If a communication is required by the Privacy Regulations to be in writing, the covered entity must maintain such writing or an electronic copy as documentation. If an action, an activity, or a designation is required by the Privacy Regulation to be documented, the covered entity must maintain a written or electronic record of such action, activity, or designation. A covered entity must retain these documents for six years from the date they were created or last in effect (the statute of limitations period for the civil monetary penalties).[406]

§ 3.06   BUSINESS ASSOCIATE AGREEMENTS AND DATA USE AGREEMENTS

Section 1.02[B] defines who is and is not considered a "business associate" for purposes of the Privacy and Security Regulations. The cornerstone of the relationship between a covered entity and its business associate, or between a business associate and its subcontractor, is the business associate agreement. This Section sets out the requirements for these agreements and discusses issues related to management and enforcement of these agreements.

The final part of this Section sets out the requirements for data use agreements. Data use agreements are similar to business associate agreements in that they set forth obligations that apply to PHI received from a covered entity, but the purposes are more limited and the PHI involved is always a limited data set.

---

[405] 45 C.F.R. § 164.530(i).

[406] 45 C.F.R. § 164.530(j); 65 Fed. Reg. 82,563 (Dec. 28, 2000).

[A] Business Associate Agreements—Content

Business associates are not permitted to use or disclose PHI in ways that would not be permitted by the covered entity itself. A written contract (a "business associate agreement") is required between the covered entity and the business associate that limits the business associate's uses and disclosures of PHI to those permitted by the contract and imposes certain security, inspection, and reporting requirements on the business associate. As described in **§ 1.02[B]**, under the HITECH Regulations, a business associate must also enter into a business associate agreement with any subcontractor business associates. That agreement must meet all the Privacy Regulations' and Security Regulations' requirements for other business associate agreements and must be at least as stringent as the business associate agreement with the covered entity. That is, each business associate agreement in a chain of business associate agreements must be at least as stringent as the agreement above it in the chain.[407]

Specific contract provisions are set forth in the Privacy Regulations and required in all business associate agreements.[408] Additional provisions, as noted, are required by the Security Regulations, if there is electronic PHI involved.[409] Certain changes to the provisions of business associate agreements are required as a result of the HITECH Act and HITECH Regulations, as noted. **Section 1.05[B]** explains the compliance dates for these new requirements, and the compliance timetable for amending or replacing existing business associate agreements.

[1] Required Provisions in Business Associate Agreements

The business associate agreement must contain provisions that address the following:[410]

1. The agreement must establish the permitted and required uses and disclosure of PHI by the business associate. While the contract need not detail each and every permitted use or disclosure of PHI, the contract should state the main purpose(s) for which the business associate may use or disclose PHI and generally indicate the reasons and types of persons to whom the business associate may make further disclosures.[411] This information may be included directly in the business associate agreement or may include a cross-reference to a services agreement between the parties that provides this information.

2. Except as described below, a business associate may not use or disclose PHI to the extent such use or disclosure would not be permitted if done by the covered entity. Similarly, a subcontractor may not use or disclose PHI to the extent such use or disclosure would not be permitted by the business associate.[412] This includes limiting the business associate's uses and disclosures of PHI to be "consistent with the covered entity's minimum necessary policies and procedures."[413]

3. There are two exceptions to the rule that the business associate cannot do what the covered entity could not do. If the business associate is to be permitted by the covered entity to do the following activities, the business associate agreement must state that the business associate may:

   - Use the PHI for proper management/administration of the business associate and to carry out the legal responsibilities of the business associate. PHI may also be disclosed for these purposes: (A) if the disclosure is required by law; or (B) the business associate (1) obtains reasonable assurances from the person to whom the information is disclosed that it will be held confidential and used or

---

[407] 45 C.F.R. §§ 164.314(a)(2)(iii); 164.502(e)(1); 164.502(e)(5); 78 Fed. Reg. 5599-5601 (Jan. 25, 2013).

[408] 45 C.F.R. § 164.504(e).

[409] 45 C.F.R. § 164.314(a).

[410] 45 C.F.R. § 164.504(e)(2).

[411] 45 C.F.R. § 164.504(e)(2)(i); 65 Fed. Reg. 82,505 (Dec. 28, 2000).

[412] 45 C.F.R. § 164.504(e)(2)(i); 78 Fed. Reg. 5601 (Jan. 25, 2013).

[413] 78 Fed. Reg. 5599 (Jan. 25, 2013). HHS does not characterize this as a change, but rather as a restatement of a principle.

further disclosed only as required by law or for the purposes for which it was disclosed to the person, and (2) is notified by the person of any instances of which he or she is aware in which the confidentiality of the information has been breached;[414] and

- Disclose the PHI for data aggregation services relating to the health care operations of the covered entity.[415] This data aggregation is the combining of the PHI of multiple covered entities by a party who is a business associate to each covered entity, to permit the analysis of data related to the health care operations of the respective covered entities (e.g., for quality assurance and comparative analyses, in cases where this combining of PHI for the respective health care operations of the covered entities would not be an activity that the covered entities could do themselves under the Privacy Regulations).[416]

4. The business associate agreement must state that the business associate has the obligation to:[417]

- Not use or further disclose PHI other than as permitted or required by the contract or as required by law;

- Use appropriate safeguards to prevent use or disclosure of PHI other than as provided for by its contract *and comply, where applicable, with the Security Regulations with regard to electronic PHI*[418] (Note: Italicized language added to conform to the HITECH Regulations.);

- Report to the covered entity any use or disclosure of PHI not provided for by its contract of which the business associate becomes aware, *including breaches of unsecured PHI as required by the breach notification requirements of the Breach Regulations*, and any security incidents of which it becomes aware.[419] (Note: Italicized language added to conform to the HITECH Regulations.);

- Ensure that any *subcontractor that creates, receives, maintains or transmits PHI on behalf of* the business associate agrees to the same restrictions and conditions that apply to the business associate with respect to such information[420] (Note: Italicized language modifies this provision to conform to the HITECH Regulations, which require that the business associate enter into a business associate agreement with its subcontractors that is at least as stringent as the business associate agreement with the covered entity.);

- Make available PHI to individuals in accordance with the Privacy Regulations' provisions regarding individual access;

- Make available PHI for amendment and incorporate any amendments to the PHI in accordance with the Privacy Regulations' provisions regarding an individual's right to have a covered entity

---

[414] 45 C.F.R. § 164.504(e)(2)(i)(A); 45 C.F.R. § 164.504(e)(4)(i).

[415] 45 C.F.R. § 164.504(e)(2)(i)(A).

[416] 45 C.F.R. § 164.504(e)(2)(i)(A); 65 Fed. Reg. 82,505 (Dec. 28, 2000).

[417] 45 C.F.R. § 164.504(e), § 164.314, changes arising from the HITECH Regulations, as noted.

[418] 45 C.F.R. §§ 164.504(e)(2)(ii)(D) and 164.314(a)(2)(i)(A).

[419] 45 C.F.R. §§ 164.504(e)(2)(ii)(C) and 164.314(a)(2)(i)(C). The definition of security incident is very broad and includes not only successful attempts to access or compromise the covered entity's PHI, but also unsuccessful attempts and incidents that may not involve the covered entity's PHI at all. For example, the definition could encompass every unsuccessful hit to the entity's firewall. As a result, the volume of reporting of all security incidents could overwhelm the covered entity. If so, a two-tiered approach to reporting may be advisable. For example, the agreement could require the business associate to immediately report to the covered entity any successful security incidents that involve the covered entity's PHI. For other incidents, periodic aggregate reporting may be sufficient.

This type of customized reporting has now been approved by HHS. HHS has issued guidance stating that the business associate contract may be used to establish the covered entity's specific reporting requirements, which should include requirements such as frequency, level of detail, and format. Furthermore, the parties may stipulate what is considered a "security incident" for reporting purposes. For example, the covered entity may determine that certain types of incidents could be reported in a periodic aggregate report with just the number of incidents during that period. OCR HIPAA FAQ, available at http://www.hhs.gov/ocr/privacy/hipaa/faq/securityrule/2002.html.

[420] 45 C.F.R. §§ 164.504(e)(2)(ii)(B) and 164.314(a)(2)(i)(B).

amend PHI. (Although business associates have direct liability for provision of copies of electronically maintained PHI requested by an individual, these copies may be provided to the covered entity, or directly to the individual or a designated third party, as specified in the business associate agreement.);[421]

- Make available an accounting of disclosures in accordance with the Privacy Regulations' provisions regarding an individual's right to receive an accounting of certain disclosures of his or her PHI made by the covered entity (or its business associates) (Note: Under the HITECH Act, additional accounting of disclosures and access report requirements may apply, but final regulations are pending. See **§ 3.02[D]**.);

- *To the extent the business associate is to carry out a covered entity's obligation under the Privacy Regulations, comply with the requirements of the Privacy Regulations that apply to the covered entity in the performance of such obligation.* (Note: Italicized language added to conform to the HITECH Regulations.) For example, if a group health plan's business associate agreement with a third-party administrator (TPA) delegates to the TPA the distribution of the plan's notice of privacy practices, the TPA would have to perform this service subject to the same rules that would apply if the covered entity handled the distribution;[422]

- Make available to HHS the business associate's internal practices, books, and records relating to the use and disclosure of PHI received from or created on behalf of the covered entity for purposes of determining the covered entity's compliance; and

- Return to the covered entity, or destroy, all PHI at the termination of the contract so that the business associate maintains no copies of the information in any form. If such return or destruction is not feasible, extend the protections of the contract to the retained information and limit further uses and disclosures to those purposes that make the return or destruction of the information infeasible.

5. The business associate agreement must authorize termination of the services contract and business associate contract by the covered entity, if the covered entity determines that the business associate has violated a material term of the business associate contract.

If both the covered entity and its business associate are governmental entities, special provisions apply. A memorandum of understanding is used in lieu of a business associate contract.[423]

For the original Privacy Regulations, HHS published guidance in the form of a Model Business Associate Agreement (which, after enactment of the HITECH Act, was withdrawn because it was no longer current). Following publication of the HITECH Regulations, HHS published a list of "sample business associate provisions." These are intended to provide guidance in drafting business associate agreements, but the specific language offered by HHS is not required.[424]

As an alternative to a business associate agreement, a covered entity may enter into a data use agreement with a business associate if the only PHI shared with the business associate is a limited data set to be used or disclosed for health care operations purposes.[425] See **§ 3.07[B]**.

---

[421] 45 C.F.R. § 164.502(a)(4)(ii); 78 Fed. Reg. 5598–5599, 5632 (Jan. 25, 2013).

[422] 78 Fed. Reg. 5600 (Jan. 25, 2013).

[423] 45 C.F.R. § 164.502(e)(3).

[424] 78 Fed. Reg. 5601 (Jan. 25, 2013). "Sample Business Associate Agreement Provisions (Published January 25, 2013)," available at http://www.hhs.gov/ocr/privacy/hipaa/understanding/coveredentities/contractprov.html. See also **Appendix D** for the list of sample provisions.

[425] 45 C.F.R. § 164.504(e)(3)(iv).

[2] Managing Business Associate Relationships

The persons responsible for vendor contracting should, by now, have integrated the business associate requirements with the entity's contracting process. Part of the routine in any new vendor relationship should be to assess whether or not the vendor is a business associate. Form agreements should incorporate the required terms or have standard amendments or exhibits to be attached if the vendor is a business associate. A covered entity should keep a current inventory of all of its business associates or a central file of its business associate agreements. This will be crucial to efficiently updating these agreements when necessary.

After years of negotiating these agreements, a typical covered entity will have a collection of business associate agreements that vary in their terms. Some of the differences may be minor; others may be significant. Any covered entity or business associate with "nonstandard" agreements must have a process for catching any "outlier" provisions that affect its operations. For example, perhaps its "standard" agreement requires notice of an unauthorized disclosure within five days, but other agreements specify 48 hours, or add that the notice must be in writing. The business associate will need reporting procedures that either reflect the most restrictive of these agreements or somehow capture the specific requirement for each relationship. The covered entity, for its part, needs to track what was agreed to in order to enforce the agreement.

A covered entity that knows of a pattern of activity or practice of the business associate that constitutes a material breach or violation of the business associate's obligations under the contract or other arrangement must take reasonable steps to cure the breach or end the violation and, if such steps are unsuccessful, must terminate the contract or arrangement, if feasible.[426] Whether termination of the agreement is feasible or not requires a case-by-case analysis and will depend on the specific facts. Termination is "not feasible" when terminating the contract would be "unreasonably burdensome" on the covered entity or when there are "no viable alternatives" to continuing a contract with that particular business associate. Termination is regarded as feasible even if it may inconvenience the covered entity or cost the covered entity more money to contract with other potential business associates.[427] In addition, a covered entity could pursue legal action against a business associate and potentially recover damages for the business associate's breach of the business associate agreement. A covered entity may also include an indemnification clause in the agreement that requires the business associate to indemnify the covered entity for third-party liabilities the covered entity incurs as a result of a contractual violation by the business associate.

Similarly, as of September 23, 2013, under the HITECH Regulations, a business associate that knows of a pattern of activity or practice that constitutes a material breach or violation of a subcontractor's obligation under the business associate agreement or other arrangement must take reasonable steps to cure the breach or end the violation. If such steps are unsuccessful, the business associate must terminate the contract or arrangement with the subcontractor business associate, if feasible.[428]

It is possible, because of the HITECH Act's imposition of direct responsibility and liability on business associates, that the relationship between covered entities and business associates will change. For example, in the past, deference may have been given to the covered entity with respect to the language of the business associate agreements or with respect to certain compliance processes because the covered entity was the party with the HIPAA obligations. Now, there may be more negotiation between the parties on such issues. In some cases, business associates may even reconsider whether they want to play this role and may want to restructure the services provided so PHI is no longer exchanged. If this is not feasible, there may be business associates who even choose to not provide services to covered entities.

---

[426] 45 C.F.R. § 164.504(e)(1)(ii). The HITECH Regulations, effective March 26, 2013, eliminated a prior requirement to report the problem to HHS if steps to correct the problem were unsuccessful and termination was not feasible. 78 Fed. Reg. 5598 (Jan. 25, 2013).

[427] 65 Fed. Reg. 82,505 (Dec. 28, 2000); 78 Fed. Reg. 5602 (Jan. 25, 2013).

[428] 45 C.F.R. § 164.504(e)(1)(iii). HITECH Act § 13404(b), the provision related to this requirement, was unclear and initially interpreted in a variety of ways, but finally clarified by the HITECH Regulations, at 78 Fed. Reg. 5600 (Jan. 25, 2013).

[B]   Data Use Agreements

As described in § 1.03[C], a limited data set is a special category of health information that is close to being de-identified information but is still PHI. A covered entity may use or disclose a limited data set only for the purposes of research, public health, and health care operations, and only if the covered entity obtains satisfactory assurances in the form of a data use agreement that the recipient will only use or disclose the limited data set for these limited purposes.[429] If a limited data set is disclosed to a business associate for health care operations purposes, a data use agreement is sufficient to satisfy the business associate agreement requirements and may be used in place of a business associate agreement.[430]

The data use agreement between the covered entity and the limited data set recipient must do the following:

1.   Establish the permitted uses and disclosures of such information by the recipient, which must be for purposes of research, public health, or health care operations. The data use agreement may not authorize the recipient to use or further disclose the information in a manner that would violate the requirements of the Privacy Regulations, if done by the covered entity;

2.   Establish who is permitted to use or receive the limited data set; and

3.   Provide that the recipient will:

   • Not use or further disclose the information other than as permitted by the data use agreement or as otherwise required by law;

   • Use appropriate safeguards to prevent use or disclosure of the information other than as provided for by the data use agreement;

   • Report to the covered entity any use or disclosure of the information not provided for by its data use agreement of which it becomes aware;

   • Ensure that any agents, including a subcontractor, to whom it provides the limited data set agrees to the same restrictions and conditions that apply to the limited data set recipient with respect to such information; and

   • Not identify the information or contact the individuals.[431]

The agreement should also include a termination provision, so that the covered entity can terminate the agreement if the recipient fails to comply with its terms.

A covered entity is not in compliance with the limited data set standards if the covered entity knew of a pattern of activity or practice of the limited data set recipient that constituted a material breach or violation of the data use agreement, unless the covered entity took reasonable steps to cure the breach or end the violation, as applicable, and if such steps were unsuccessful, discontinued disclosure of PHI to the recipient, and reported the problem to HHS.[432]

---

[429] 45 C.F.R. § 164.514(e)(3)–(4).

[430] 45 C.F.R. § 164.504(e)(3); 78 Fed. Reg. 5601 (Jan. 25, 2013). There is no similar "in lieu of" provision for disclosures of limited data sets to a business associate for research or public health purposes, because such disclosures would not otherwise require business associate agreements. 78 Fed. Reg. 5601–5602 (Jan. 25, 2013).

[431] 45 C.F.R. § 164.514(e)(4).

[432] 45 C.F.R. § 164.514(e)(4).

CHAPTER 4

SECURITY REGULATIONS

§ 4.01 GENERAL PRINCIPLES OF THE SECURITY REGULATIONS

The following section reviews general principles regarding the scope and implementation of the Security Regulations.

[A] Integration of Privacy and Security Compliance

Although the Security Regulations and Privacy Regulations were published separately and at different times, the Security Regulations are inextricably intertwined with the Privacy Regulations. The protection of the privacy of information depends, in many instances, on the existence of security measures, and the implementation of reasonable and appropriate security measures support privacy.[1] The stated objectives of the Security Regulations, in fact, specifically include protection against any reasonably anticipated uses or disclosures of such information that are not permitted or required under the Privacy Regulations.[2] According to HHS, if security standards are inadequate because they routinely permit reasonably anticipated but impermissible uses or disclosures of protected health information (PHI), and such disclosures could have been prevented by more appropriate security measures, a breach of privacy as well as a breach of security may have occurred.[3]

The Privacy Regulations protect PHI in *any form* and state only a general requirement about safeguarding the security of PHI. It is sometimes referred to as the "mini" security rule:

> "*Standard: safeguards.* A covered entity must have in place appropriate administrative, technical, and physical safeguards to protect the privacy of protected health information."[4]

In contrast, the Security Regulations provide specific guidance on safeguards for PHI in *electronic* form.

[B] Objectives of the Security Regulations

The Security Regulations require that covered entities and business associates meet four basic security objectives. The covered entity or business associate must:

1. Ensure the confidentiality, integrity, and availability[5] of all electronic PHI the covered entity or business associate creates, receives, maintains, or transmits;

2. Protect against any reasonably anticipated threats or hazards to the security or integrity of such information;

3. Protect against any reasonably anticipated uses or disclosures of such information that are not permitted or required under the Privacy Regulations; and

4. Ensure compliance with the Security Regulations by the covered entity's workforce.[6]

The use of the word "ensure" in the fourth objective reflects, according to the Department of Health and Human Services (HHS), Congress' intent to set "an exceptionally high goal for the security of electronic

---

[1] 68 Fed. Reg. 8341 (Feb. 20, 2003).

[2] 45 C.F.R. § 164.306(a)(3).

[3] 68 Fed. Reg. 8341 (Feb. 20, 2003).

[4] 45 C.F.R. § 164.530(c)(1).

[5] *Confidentiality* means that the data or information is not made available or disclosed to an unauthorized person or process. *Integrity* means that data or information has not been altered or destroyed in an unauthorized manner. *Availability* means that the data or information is accessible and usable upon demand by an authorized person. 45 C.F.R. § 164.304. Under the HIPAA statute, this standard included only confidentiality and integrity; availability was added by HHS in the Security Regulations. See 42 U.S.C. § 1320d-2(d)(2).

[6] 45 C.F.R. § 64.306(a).

protected health information."[7] Nevertheless, Congress also recognized that some trade-offs are necessary, and "ensuring" protection does not mean providing protection regardless of cost.[8] Therefore, when the Security Regulations require that the covered entity "ensure" the safety of information, the intent is that the covered entity "take steps, to the best of its ability, to protect that information."[9]

[C] Electronic Protected Health Information

The scope of health information to be safeguarded under the Security Regulations is limited to electronic PHI (sometimes referred to as "ePHI").[10] The definition of PHI is the same as for the Privacy Regulations, so it excludes Family Educational and Privacy Rights Act (FERPA) records and employment records.[11] Electronic PHI is PHI that is transmitted by or maintained in electronic media.[12] *Electronic media* means:

(1) Electronic storage material on which data is or may be recorded electronically, including, for example, devices in computers (hard drives) and any removable/transportable digital memory medium, such as magnetic tape or disk, optical disk, or digital memory card;

(2) Transmission media used to exchange information already in electronic storage media. Transmission media include, for example, the Internet, extranet or intranet, leased lines, dial-up lines, private networks, and the physical movement of removable/transportable electronic storage media. Certain transmissions, including of paper, via facsimile, and of voice, via telephone, are not considered to be transmissions via electronic media if the information being exchanged did not exist in electronic form immediately before the transmission.[13]

Under this definition, electronic PHI does not include paper-to-paper faxes, voice mail messages, or video-conferencing (provided the information was not in electronic form immediately prior to the transmission).[14] However, a computer-to-computer fax would be electronic PHI, because the information was in electronic form before being faxed. Electronic PHI also includes telephone voice response and faxback systems, because they are used as input and output devices for computers.[15] Although these examples from HHS are helpful, new technologies will continue to raise questions about what is and is not electronic PHI.

HHS has noted that, although the Security Regulations cover only electronic PHI, it may issue additional regulations with standards for nonelectronic PHI in the future.[16]

[D] Applicability to Business Associates

Business associates are persons or entities that receive, create, maintain, or transmit PHI (including ePHI) from or on behalf of the covered entity to perform services for the covered entity.[17] The criteria for determining whether a business associate relationship exists are the same under the Privacy Regulations and the Security Regulations, with the exception that under the Security Regulations, the PHI created, maintained, or transmitted

---

[7] 68 Fed. Reg. 8346 (Feb. 20, 2003).

[8] 68 Fed. Reg. 8346 (Feb. 20, 2003).

[9] 68 Fed. Reg. 8346 (Feb. 20, 2003)

[10] Under the HIPAA statute, security standards are required for *health information*, a term which is not defined in the statute. 42 U.S.C. § 1320d-2(d)(2). In the Privacy Regulations, HHS developed the narrower and more precisely defined term *protected health information*; this term is further limited to "electronic protected health information" for purposes of the Security Regulations.

[11] 45 C.F.R. § 160.103.

[12] 45 C.F.R. § 160.103.

[13] 45 C.F.R. § 160.103; 78 Fed. Reg. 5575 (Jan. 25, 2013).

[14] 45 C.F.R. § 160.103; 78 Fed. Reg. 5575 (Jan. 25, 2013).

[15] 45 C.F.R. § 160.103; OCR HIPAA FAQ, available at http://www.hhs.gov/ocr/privacy/hipaa/faq/securityrule/2010.html.

[16] 68 Fed. Reg. 8342 (Feb. 20, 2003).

[17] 45 C.F.R. § 160.103.

by the business associate must be electronic PHI.[18] See **§ 1.02[B]** for a discussion of what relationships qualify as business associate relationships.

Prior to the HITECH Act, the Security Regulations required business associates to provide contractual assurances that they would appropriately safeguard electronic PHI. Effective February 18, 2010, the HITECH act extended this obligation by specifically requiring business associates to comply with the sections of the Security Regulations regarding administrative, physical, and technical safeguards (see **§ 4.02**) and policies, procedures, and documentation (see **§ 4.03**).[19] The HITECH Regulations extend the liabilities of business associates further by including the general provisions relating to flexibility and scalability (see **§ 4.01[D]**), and the requirements regarding business associate agreements (see **§ 4.02[A]**).[20] Business associates are now directly liable for noncompliance with these requirements, and HIPAA civil and criminal penalties can be applied directly to business associates. See **§ 1.02[B]** for further discussion regarding the direct liability of business associates for compliance with the Security Regulations.

[E] Flexibility and Scalability

The Security Regulations have standards, which state what must be done, and implementation specifications, which provide more detailed explanations regarding how to achieve the standards.[21] The regulations do not provide a checklist of specific "to do" items, but rather a series of principles. The Security Regulations permit a covered entity or business associate to use any security measures that allow it to reasonably and appropriately implement the standards and the implementation specifications. In deciding which security measures to use, the covered entity or business associate must take into account the following four factors:

1. The size, complexity, and capabilities of the covered entity or business associate;

2. The entity's technical infrastructure, hardware, and software security capabilities;

3. The costs of the security measures; and

4. The probability and criticality of potential risks to the electronic PHI.[22]

No specific technologies are mandated. The standards focus on policy and process issues, not technology decisions. Technology decisions are left to the discretion of the covered entity, with the understanding that the rate of change in technology is too fast for technology-specific regulations to keep pace.

Some of the security standards have no implementation specifications; these standards must be implemented as stated. Many of the security standards, however, do have implementation specifications, which are either *required* or *addressable*. If an implementation specification is marked as "required," a covered entity or business associate must implement the specification as stated. If an implementation specification is marked as "addressable," a covered entity or business associate must assess whether the implementation specification is a "reasonable and appropriate safeguard in its environment" in light of its value in protecting the entity's PHI.[23] Based on this assessment, the covered entity or business associate has decisions to make. In the case of an addressable implementation specification, it must do one of the following:

1. *Implement the addressable implementation specification*—Applicable if the covered entity or business associate determines that the implementation specification is reasonable and appropriate to its particular circumstances.

---

[18] 45 C.F.R. § 164.308(b)(1).

[19] HITECH Act § 13401, referencing 45 C.F.R. §§ 164.308, 164.310, 164.312, and 164.316.

[20] 75 Fed. Reg. 40,868, 40,882–40,883 (July 14, 2010).

[21] 45 C.F.R. § 164.306(c)–(d).

[22] 45 C.F.R. § 164.306(b).

[23] 45 C.F.R. § 164.306(d).

2. *Implement one or more alternative security measures to accomplish the same purpose*—Applicable if the covered entity or business associate determines that the implementation specification is not reasonable and appropriate to its particular circumstances, but there are alternative measures that can be implemented to satisfy the security standard.

3. *Not implement either the addressable implementation specification or an alternative*—Applicable only if the covered entity or business associate determines that the implementation specification is not reasonable and appropriate to its particular circumstances and no equivalent alternative measure would be reasonable and appropriate either.[24]

The choice will depend on a variety of factors, such as risk analysis, risk mitigation strategy, evaluation of other security measures in place, and cost of implementation.

The covered entity or business associate must document its decision making regarding addressable standards. If the addressable standard is not implemented, the covered entity or business associate must document the reasons why it would not be reasonable and appropriate to do so. It must also document why the alternative selected (if any) is reasonable and appropriate. If the covered entity or business associate concludes that implementing the addressable specification is not reasonable and appropriate and that there is no reasonable and appropriate alternative, the documentation should show that this conclusion was reached after a thorough analysis and should explain both the reasons for this conclusion and how the standard will be met.

Despite, or perhaps because of, the flexibility and scalability incorporated into the Security Regulations, there are no "safe harbors." This flexibility and scalability make it easier for an organization to match its compliance strategy to its own risk assessment but also makes it more difficult to determine whether the security program developed is sufficient to meet the regulatory standards. The measures adopted by the covered entity or business associate will typically be judged after implementation, based on both outcomes and design decisions. Documenting the implementation decisions made and the reasons behind them will be a key factor in determining compliance. In addition, the organization must review and modify its security measures as needed to adapt its approach to changing circumstances.[25]

[F] Implementation Assistance

Many industry and government resources are available for guiding an organization through implementation of a security program. HHS provides many privacy and security tools, including "Reassessing Your Security Practices in a Health IT Environment: A Guide for Small Health Care Practices,"[26] and the OCR HIPAA Security Series, which includes the following useful guidance documents:[27]

- Security 101 for Covered Entities;

- Security Standards: Administrative Safeguards;

- Security Standards: Physical Safeguards;

- Security Standards: Technical Safeguards;

- Security Standards: Organizational Policies, Procedures and Documentation Requirements;

- Basics of Risk Analysis and Risk Management; and

- Security Standards: Implementation for the Small Provider.

---

[24] 45 C.F.R. § 164.306(c)–(d); see also OCR HIPAA FAQ, available at http://www.hhs.gov/ocr/privacy/hipaa/faq/securityrule/2020.html.

[25] 45 C.F.R. § 164.306(e).

[26] Available at http://www.healthit.gov/sites/default/files/small-practice-security-guide-1.pdf.

[27] Available at http://www.hhs.gov/ocr/privacy/hipaa/administrative/securityrule/securityruleguidance.html.

OCR has also provided Security Guidance on the following topics:[28]

- HIPAA Security Guidance for Remote Use of and Access to Electronic Protected Health Information;

- Guidance on Risk Analysis Requirements under the HIPAA Security Rule;

- Security Risk Assessment Tool (issued jointly with the Office of the National Coordinator for Health Information Technology); and

- Guide to Privacy and Security of Electronic Health Information (ver. 2.0) (issued jointly with the Office of the National Coordinator for Health Information Technology).

In addition, the National Institute of Standards and Technology (NIST), a federal agency, has published many reports on information security. Although not legally binding, NIST guidance can be very instructive. Some of the resources in the extensive catalog of NIST reports are:[29]

- An Introductory Resource Guide for Implementing the Health Insurance Portability and Accountability Act (HIPAA) Security Rule (SP800-66);

- Guide to Protecting the Confidentiality of Personally Identifiable Information (PII) (SP800-122).[30]; and

- NIST HIPAA Security Rule Toolkit (a self-assessment tool).

Finally, as discussed in **§ 6.09**, OCR published its audit protocols in 2012, identifying 165 areas of evaluation (77 of which pertain to the Security Regulations), which covered entities and business associates should be prepared to address with HHS, in the event of an onsite compliance review. Covered entities and business associates may also choose to use this "checklist" as one tool in conducting their own internal security assessments.

§ 4.02 SECURITY PROGRAM SAFEGUARDS

This section outlines the key principles of an effective security program for electronic PHI, as described in the Security Regulations.[31] The standards established in the Security Regulations are divided into three sections:

1. administrative safeguards,

2. physical safeguards, and

3. technical safeguards.

Each category in turn is addressed below.

[A] Administrative Safeguards

The Security Regulations' administrative safeguards are administrative actions, policies, and procedures to manage the selection, development, implementation, and maintenance of security measures to protect ePHI and

---

[28] Available at http://www.hhs.gov/ocr/privacy/hipaa/administrative/securityrule/securityruleguidance.html; http://www.healthit.gov/security-risk-assessment; http://www.healthit.gov/sites/default/files/pdf/privacy/privacy-and-security-guide.pdf.

[29] These and many other NIST publications are available for download at http://csrc.nist.gov/publications/nistpubs/; see also links to NIST guidance at http://www.hhs.gov/ocr/privacy/hipaa/administrative/securityrule/securityruleguidance.html. The HIPAA Security Rule Toolkit is available at http://scap.nist.gov/hipaa.

[30] These and many other NIST publications are available for download at http://csrc.nist.gov/publications/nistpubs/; see also links to NIST guidance at http://www.hhs.gov/ocr/privacy/hipaa/administrative/securityrule/securityruleguidance.html.

[31] **Appendix E** is a Security Matrix containing a high-level summary of the security standards and implementation specifications.

to manage the conduct of the covered entity's or business associate's workforce in relation to the protection of that information.[32]

Standard 1: Security Management Process

The cornerstone of any effective security program is the security management process, including risk analysis and risk management. This is the first and, arguably, the most important standard of the Security Regulations.

Standard

Implement policies and procedures to prevent, detect, contain, and correct security violations.[33]

Implementation Specifications

The following four implementation specifications are required and considered essential to a security management program:

1. *Risk Analysis.* [Required] Conduct an accurate and thorough assessment of the potential risks and vulnerabilities to the confidentiality, availability, and integrity of electronic PHI.

2. *Risk Management.* [Required] Implement security measures sufficient to reduce risks and vulnerabilities to a reasonable and appropriate level, so as to meet the objectives of the Security Regulations.

3. *Sanction Policy.* [Required] Apply appropriate sanctions against workforce members who fail to comply with the covered entity's (or business associate's) security policies and procedures.

4. *Information System Activity Review.* [Required] Review records of information system activity, such as audit logs, access reports, and security incident tracking reports.[34]

A covered entity or business associate must "take steps, to the best of its ability, to protect" electronic PHI.[35] A covered entity or business associate must do a risk analysis to identify the possible risks to, and vulnerabilities of, the information before it can take steps to eliminate or minimize those risks or vulnerabilities.[36] A *vulnerability* is defined as a "flaw or weakness in system security procedures, design, implementation, or internal controls that could be exercised (accidentally triggered or intentionally exploited)."[37]

The risk analysis may include inventorying all systems and applications that are used to access and store electronic PHI and classifying them by level of risk. The organization should identify reasonably anticipated threats to electronic PHI and vulnerabilities that, if exploited, would create a risk to the PHI. Threats that affect data and systems may be natural (e.g., earthquakes), human (unintentional or deliberate acts), or environmental (e.g., extended power failures, pollution). The risk analysis should consider what would be expected if the

---

[32] 45 C.F.R. § 164.304.

[33] 45 C.F.R. § 164.308(a)(1)(i).

[34] 45 C.F.R. § 164.308(a)(1)(ii). *Information systems* means an interconnected set of information resources under the same direct management control that shares common functionality. A system normally includes hardware, software, information, data, applications, communications, and people. 45 C.F.R. § 164.304.

[35] 68 Fed. Reg. 8346 (Feb. 20, 2003).

[36] 68 Fed. Reg. 8346 (Feb. 20, 2003).

[37] Guidance on Risk Analysis Requirements Under the HIPAA Security Rule (quoting NIST Special Publications 800-30), available at http://www.hhs.gov/ocr/privacy/hipaa/administrative/securityrule/rafinalguidancepdf.pdf (July 28, 2010). See also Guide for Conducting Risk Assessments (SP800-30 Rev-1), a refocused and expanded version of the NIST resource on risk assessments, available at http://csrc.nist.gov/publications/nistpubs/800-30-rev1/sp800_30_r1.pdf.

security measures were not in place, including the loss or damage of data and the anticipated consequences.[38] Risk assessment is not a one-time activity but an ongoing process. The covered entity must periodically review and update its risk assessment.

During a compliance review in 2009, CMS identified risk analysis to be a continuing weak area for covered entities. In particular, covered entities failed to perform or update the required risk assessments, missed areas of potential risk, and did not have formalized and documented risk assessment procedures.[39] In 2010, HHS chose *Guidance on Risk Analysis Requirements Under the HIPAA Security Rule* as the first topic of the annual security guidance documents it is required to issue under HITECH, confirming its focus on this key issue.[40]

In March 2014, HHS and the Office of the National Coordinator for Health Information technology (ONC) released a new Security Risk Assessment Tool (SRA Tool) to assist small- to medium-sized health care providers conduct their security risk assessments. Use of the SRA Tool is not required, but it is intended to help providers conduct their risk assessments in a thorough and organized manner.[41] The SRA Tool walks the provider through the Security Regulations' requirements by posing 156 yes/no questions about the provider. At each step, the provider can enter supplemental information and rank the likelihood of the threat and the level of potential impact as low, medium, or high. If a particular security measure is not in place, the provider is prompted to document the reason. The SRA Tool explains whether corrective action should be taken and provides additional resources for the provider. For each question, additional resources are available under "Things to Consider," "Threats and Vulnerabilities," and "Examples of Safeguards." A Glossary is also provided. All answers and risk remediation plans can be saved directly in the SRA Tool, and this information can be used to generate a report. A User Guide is available.

Risk management is the actual implementation of security measures to sufficiently reduce the covered entity's risk of losing or compromising its electronic PHI and to meet the security standards.[42] It involves establishing a balance between identifiable risks and vulnerabilities, expected relevant losses, and the cost of various protective measures and will vary depending on the size, complexity, and capabilities of the covered entity.[43] In 2011, NIST published *Managing Information Security Risk: Organization, Mission, and Information System View*, which NIST describes as its authoritative source of comprehensive risk management guidance, and which covered entities and business associates may find helpful.[44]

The sanctions policy required in connection with electronic PHI should be coordinated with the covered entity's sanctions policy regarding non-electronic PHI (required by the Privacy Regulations).[45] Furthermore, if the covered entity already has a general disciplinary policy in place, this may be adapted to incorporate the sanctions requirements of both the Security Regulations and Privacy Regulations.

---

[38] OCR HIPAA FAQs, available at http://www.hhs.gov/ocr/privacy/hipaa/faq/securityrule/2013.html and http://www.hhs.gov/ ocr/ privacy/hipaa/faq/securityrule/2022.html; Guidance on Risk Analysis Requirements Under the HIPAA Security Rule (quoting NIST Special Publications 800-30), available at http://www.hhs.gov/ocr/privacy/hipaa/administrative/securityrule/rafinalguidancepdf.pdf (July 28, 2010).

[39] CMS, *2009 HIPAA Compliance Review Analysis and Summary of Results*, available at http://www.hhs.gov/ocr/privacy/hipaa/ enforcement/cmscompliancerev09.pdf. CMS also provides some suggestions for improvement in these areas.

[40] HHS, *Guidance on Risk Analysis Requirements Under the HIPAA Security Rule*, available at http://www.hhs.gov/ocr/privacy/ hipaa/administrative/securityrule/rafinalguidancepdf.pdf (July 28, 2010).

[41] The SRA Tool is available at http://www.healthit.gov/providers-professionals/security-risk-assessment. See also HHS, Press Release, "HHS Releases Security Risk Assessment Tool to Help Providers with HIPAA Compliance (Mar. 28, 2014), available at http:// www.hhs.gov/news/press/2014pres/03/20140328a.html.

[42] OCR HIPAA FAQ, available at http://www.hhs.gov/ocr/privacy/hipaa/faq/securityrule/2013.html.

[43] 68 Fed. Reg. 8346–8347 (Feb. 20, 2003).

[44] Available at http://csrc.nist.gov/publications/nistpubs/800-39/SP800-39-final.pdf.

[45] See 45 C.F.R. § 164.530(e).

Standard 2: Assigned Security Responsibility

Standard

Identify the security official who is responsible for the development and implementation of the policies and procedures required by the Security Regulations.[46]

Implementation Specifications

None.

Responsibilities of the security official (or security officer) will include directing, monitoring, assessing, and training, both as an initial implementation project and on an ongoing basis. The security official should have sufficient authority to make recommendations regarding risk management issues, implement the necessary security policies and procedures, and enforce sanctions for noncompliance. For covered entities, the security officer will work closely with the covered entity's privacy officer. A multi-disciplinary security team should be considered for larger, more complex organizations.

Standard 3: Workforce Security

The Security Regulations require that the covered entity or business associate implement policies and procedures for authorizing access to electronic PHI that are consistent with the applicable requirements of the Privacy Regulations.[47] This is a two-step process. Standards 3 and 4 work hand in hand. First, there must be a process for determining the appropriate access to PHI for each member of the workforce, granting access based on job function and preventing access by unauthorized workforce members.[48] Second, policies and procedures for controlling that access must be established (e.g., controlled access to workstations, transactions, programs, processes, or other mechanisms).[49]

Standard

Implement policies and procedures to ensure that all workforce members have appropriate access to electronic PHI, as provided under Administrative Standard 4, and to prevent those workforce members who do not have such authorized access from obtaining access to electronic PHI.[50]

Implementation Specifications

1. *Authorization and/or Supervision.* [Addressable] Implement procedures for the authorization and/or supervision of workforce members who work with electronic PHI or in locations where it might be accessed.

2. *Workforce Clearance Procedure.* [Addressable] Implement procedures to determine that the access of a workforce member to electronic PHI is appropriate.

3. *Termination Procedures.* [Addressable] Implement procedures for terminating access to electronic PHI when the employment of, or other arrangement with, a workforce member ends or as required by

---

[46] 45 C.F.R. § 164.308(a)(2).

[47] 45 C.F.R. § 164.308(a)(4)(i).

[48] 45 C.F.R. §§ 164.308(a)(3)(i) and (ii)(B).

[49] 45 C.F.R. § 164.308(a)(4)(ii).

[50] 45 C.F.R. § 164.308(a)(3)(i).

determinations made as specified in the Workforce Clearance Procedure Implementation Specification above.[51]

Access rights must be documented, reviewed, and modified, as appropriate.[52] A set of guidelines for eliminating access to PHI by terminated workforce members in a timely manner is also a crucial part of a security program.[53] This includes de-activating computer access to electronic PHI, in addition to more traditional steps such as collecting ID cards, company documents, and keys from the terminated workforce member. Such procedures should be followed not only for employees, but also contractors, volunteers, and others.

Standard 4: Information Access Management

This standard makes it clear that controlling access to electronic PHI is part of the covered entity's or business associate's obligation to appropriately control access to *all* PHI.

Standard

Implement policies and procedures for authorizing access to electronic PHI that are consistent with the applicable requirements of the Privacy Regulations.[54]

Implementation Specifications

1. *Isolating Health Care Clearinghouse Functions.* [Required] If a health care clearinghouse is part of a larger organization, the clearinghouse must implement policies and procedures that protect the electronic PHI of the clearinghouse from unauthorized access by the larger organization.

2. *Access Authorization.* [Addressable] Implement policies and procedures for granting access to ePHI, for example, through access to a workstation, transaction, program, process, or other mechanism.

3. *Access Establishment and Modification.* [Addressable] Implement policies and procedures that, based upon the covered entity's or business associate's access authorization policies, under the Access Authorization Implementation Specification above, establish, document, review, and modify a user's right of access to a workstation, transaction, program, or process.[55]

Confidentiality agreements signed by workforce members are not required by HIPAA but are often advisable and, if used, should state that the confidentiality obligations continue after the termination of employment or other work arrangement.

Standard 5: Security Awareness and Training

Training is a critically important aspect of any effective security program. For covered entities, this security training can be successfully combined with training required under the Privacy Regulations.[56]

CMS, in its compliance reviews of covered entities, has found deficiencies in this area. Covered entities had no or inadequate policies and procedures relating to security awareness and training. In addition, covered

---

[51] 45 C.F.R. § 164.308(a)(3)(ii).
[52] 45 C.F.R. § 164.308(a)(4)(ii)(C).
[53] See 45 C.F.R. § 164.308(a)(3)(i)(C).
[54] 45 C.F.R. § 164.308(a)(4)(i).
[55] 45 C.F.R. § 164.308(a)(4)(ii).
[56] See 45 C.F.R. § 164.530(b).

entities did not conduct training prior to granting user access, did not conduct appropriate security refresher training, and did not maintain adequate documentation of the training.[57]

Standard

Implement a security awareness and training program for all members of the workforce (including management) of the covered entity or business associate.[58]

Implementation Specifications

1. *Security Reminders.* [Addressable] Periodic security updates.

2. *Protection from Malicious Software.* [Addressable] Procedures for guarding against, detecting, and reporting malicious software. Malicious software means software (e.g., a virus) designed to damage or disrupt a system.[59]

3. *Log-in Monitoring.* [Addressable] Procedures for monitoring log-in attempts and reporting discrepancies.

4. *Password Management.* [Addressable] Procedures for creating, changing, and safeguarding passwords (i.e., confidential authentication information composed of a string of characters).[60]

Each of these implementation specifications is addressable; therefore, they must be followed only as determined to be appropriate to the organization. Even if none of these particular implementation specifications is followed, however, security awareness and training are still required in some form to meet the standard.

All training should be documented and each person's attendance recorded. This is often most effectively coordinated by the Human Resources Department. In the event of a privacy or security incident, documented training records will provide evidence of the covered entity's or business associate's prevention efforts.

Standard 6: Security Incident Procedures

Standard

Implement policies and procedures to address security incidents.[61]

Implementation Specification

1. *Response and Reporting.* [Required] Identify and respond to suspected or known security incidents; mitigate, to the extent practicable, harmful effects of security incidents that are known to the covered entity or business associate; and document security incidents and their outcomes.[62]

A *security incident* is broadly defined as the attempted or successful unauthorized access, use, disclosure, modification, or destruction of information or interference with system operations in an information

---

[57] CMS, *2009 HIPAA Compliance Review Analysis and Summary of Results*, available at http://www.hhs.gov/ocr/privacy/hipaa/enforcement/cmscompliancerev09.pdf. CMS also provides some suggestions for improvement in these areas.

[58] 45 C.F.R. § 164.308(a)(5)(i).

[59] 45 C.F.R. § 164.304.

[60] 45 C.F.R. § 164.308(a)(5)(ii).

[61] 45 C.F.R. § 164.308(a)(6)(i).

[62] 45 C.F.R. § 164.308(a)(6)(ii).

system.[63] A covered entity or business associate should assess a security incident in the context of its risk assessment and risk management procedures.

The covered entity or business associate may determine that certain types of attempted or successful security incidents or patterns of incidents should lead to different responses. For example, a "ping" on the entity's firewall or an automated request for access to a communications network from an external source might require:

1. minimal, if any, response;

2. no mitigation actions (because little or no risk of a breach); and

3. brief documentation, such as tracking aggregate statistical data about such incidents.[64]

NIST has published a revised and updated *Computer Security Incident Handling Guide*, which offers practical guidelines for handling security incidents, including developing an effective incident response program.[65] Covered entities and business associates may find this useful.

The Security Regulations do not specifically require the covered entity or business associate to report security incidents to any outside person or entity, although some reporting requirements do arise from business associate agreements (see **§ 3.06**) and plan documents (see **§ 7.04**) and under state law. And, of course, if there is a related privacy breach, there are mitigation requirements under the Privacy Regulations and breach notification requirements under the Breach Regulations, as discussed in **§ 3.05[F]** and **Chapter 5**, respectively.[66]

Standard 7: Contingency Plan

Standard

Establish (and implement as needed) policies and procedures for responding to an emergency or other occurrence (e.g., fire, vandalism, system failure, or natural disaster) that damages systems that contain electronic PHI.[67]

Implementation Specifications

1. *Data Backup Plan.* [Required] Establish and implement procedures to create and maintain retrievable exact copies of electronic PHI.

2. *Disaster Recovery Plan.* [Required] Establish (and implement as needed) procedures to restore any loss of data.

3. *Emergency Mode Operation Plan.* [Required] Establish (and implement as needed) procedures to enable continuation of critical business processes for protection of the security of electronic PHI while operating in emergency mode.

4. *Testing and Revision Procedures.* [Addressable] Implement procedures for periodic testing and revision of contingency plans.

5. *Applications and Data Criticality Analysis.* [Addressable] Assess the relative criticality of specific applications and data in support of other contingency plan components.[68]

---

[63] 45 C.F.R. § 164.304.

[64] OCR HIPAA FAQ, available at http://www.hhs.gov/ocr/privacy/hipaa/faq/securityrule/2002.html.

[65] Available at http://nvlpubs.nist.gov/nistpubs/SpecialPublications/NIST.SP.800-61r2.pdf (Aug. 2012).

[66] See 45 C.F.R. § 164.530(d), (f); HITECH Act § 13402.

[67] 45 C.F.R. § 164.308(a)(7)(i).

[68] 45 C.F.R. § 164.308(a)(7)(ii).

To ensure continued business operations, any contingency plan should also address other critical information in addition to electronic PHI to the extent feasible for the organization.

Standard 8: Evaluation

Standard

Perform a periodic technical and nontechnical evaluation, based initially upon the standards implemented under the Security Regulations and subsequently in response to environmental or operational changes affecting the security of electronic PHI, which establishes the extent to which an entity's security policies and procedures meet the requirements of the Security Regulations.[69] With this Standard, we come full circle back to Standard 1, regarding risk analysis and management. These periodic evaluations are an integral part of that process.

Implementation Specifications

None.

This evaluation may be performed by the covered entity's or business associate's own staff or by an external organization. This standard may be difficult for small entities or those that do not have information technology staff and, in such cases, may require the use of an outside consultant. A covered entity or business associate may choose to have an external organization provide these evaluation services, but external certifications do not absolve the covered entity or business associate from its legal obligations under the Security Regulations or preclude HHS from finding a security violation.[70]

Standard 9: Business Associate Contracts

A covered entity is required to enter into a written contract ("business associate agreement") with its business associates to obtain satisfactory assurances that the business associate will appropriately safeguard the PHI.[71] In addition, business associates are required to enter into business associate agreements with their subcontractor business associates, if any, to obtain those same assurances. Only one business associate agreement is required to satisfy both the Privacy Regulations and Security Regulations. See **§ 3.06** for details on all the requirements for business associate agreements, but the special requirements arising under the Security Regulations can be summarized as follows. The business associate agreement must require that the business associate:

1. comply with all applicable requirements of the Security Regulations;

2. ensure that any subcontractor business associate also agrees to comply with the applicable requirements of the Security Regulations and enters into a business associate agreement; and

3. report to the covered entity any security incident of which it becomes aware, including breaches of unsecured PHI.[72]

As with the Privacy Regulations, if both the covered entity and business associate are governmental entities, special requirements apply; and, with respect to services on behalf of a group health plan by the plan sponsor, a plan amendment is required in lieu of a business associate agreement.[73]

---

[69] 45 C.F.R. § 164.308(a)(8)(i).

[70] OCR HIPAA FAQ, available at http://www.hhs.gov/ocr/privacy/hipaa/faq/securityrule/2003.html.

[71] 45 C.F.R. §§ 164.502(e), 164.504(e), 164.308(b), 164.314.

[72] 45 C.F.R. § 164.314.

[73] 45 C.F.R. § 164.314(a)(2)(iii); see **§ 7.05[A][4]**.

[B] Physical Safeguards

The Security Regulations' physical safeguards requirements are physical measures, policies, and procedures to protect a covered entity's or business associate's electronic information systems and related buildings and equipment from natural and environmental hazards and from unauthorized intrusion.[74]

Standard 1: Facility Access Controls

Standard

Implement policies and procedures to limit physical access to its electronic information systems and the facility or facilities in which they are housed, while ensuring that properly authorized access is allowed.[75]

Implementation Specifications.

1. *Contingency Operations.* [Addressable] Establish (and implement as needed) procedures that allow facility access in support of restoration of lost data under the disaster recovery plan and emergency mode operations plan in the event of an emergency.

2. *Facility Security Plan.* [Addressable] Implement policies and procedures to safeguard the facility and the equipment therein from unauthorized physical access, tampering, and theft.

3. *Access Control and Validation Procedures.* [Addressable] Implement procedures to control and validate a person's access to facilities based on their role or function, including visitor control and control of access to software programs for testing and revision.

4. *Maintenance Records.* [Addressable] Implement policies and procedures to document repairs and modifications to the physical components of a facility that are related to security (e.g., hardware, walls, doors, and locks).[76]

Facility means the physical premises and the interior and exterior of building(s).[77] If the covered entity or business associate occupies leased space, coordination with the owner may be required, not only to establish any physical security controls in the covered entity's or business associate's leased space but also to address building security and property management policies. Where the covered entity or business associate shares a building with other occupants, facility security measures taken by the building owner or manager (or even other occupants) must be considered and documented in the covered entity's or business associate's facility security plan, as appropriate.[78]

Standard 2: Workstation Use

There are two standards relating to workstations: Standard 2, which relates to workstation use, and Standard 3, which relates to workstation security.

---

[74] 45 C.F.R. § 164.304. Additional guidance is available as part of the HHS HIPAA Security series, *Security Standards: Physical Safeguards*, available at http://www.hhs.gov/ocr/privacy/hipaa/administrative/securityrule/physsafeguards.pdf.

[75] 45 C.F.R. § 164.310(a)(1).

[76] 45 C.F.R. § 164.310(a)(2).

[77] 45 C.F.R. § 164.304.

[78] See 68 Fed. Reg. 8353 (Feb. 20, 2003).

Standard

Implement policies and procedures that specify the proper functions to be performed, the manner in which those functions are to be performed, and the physical attributes of the surroundings of a specific workstation or class of workstation that can access ePHI.[79]

Implementation Specifications

None.

One such policy might require that users log off before leaving a workstation unattended. A "workstation" specifically refers to an electronic computing device (such as a desktop computer or a laptop computer or similar portable device) and electronic media stored in its immediate environment.[80]

Standard 3: Workstation Security

Standard

Implement physical safeguards for workstations that access ePHI in order to restrict access to authorized users.[81]

Implementation Specifications

None.

One such safeguard might be to locate workstations in an area not accessible to the public or to use privacy shields for computer monitors.

Standard 4: Device and Media Controls

Standard

Implement policies and procedures that govern the receipt and removal of hardware and electronic media that contain ePHI into and out of a facility and the movement of these items within the facility.[82]

Implementation Specifications

1. *Disposal*. [Required] Implement policies and procedures to address the final disposition of ePHI and/or the hardware or electronic media on which it is stored.[83]

2. *Media Re-use*. [Required] Implement procedures for removal of ePHI from electronic media before the media are made available for re-use.

3. *Accountability*. [Addressable] Maintain a record of the movements of hardware and electronic media and any person responsible therefore.

---

[79] 45 C.F.R. § 164.310(b).

[80] 45 C.F.R. § 164.304.

[81] 45 C.F.R. § 164.310(c).

[82] 45 C.F.R. § 164.310(d)(1).

[83] See **Chapter 5** regarding the HITECH Act breach notification requirements and the importance of properly disposing of PHI so that it is not considered "unsecured."

4. *Data Backup and Storage.* [Addressable] Create a retrievable, exact copy of ePHI, when needed, before movement of equipment.[84]

The HHS Office for Civil Rights (OCR) has issued guidance relevant to Implementation Specification 1, regarding the disposal of PHI. Although the guidance does not require a particular method of disposal, it provides some examples of proper disposal methods for electronic PHI:

- Clearing (using software or hardware products to overwrite media with nonsensitive data);

- Purging (degaussing or exposing the media to a strong magnetic field in order to disrupt the recorded magnetic domains); and

- Destroying the media (disintegration, pulverization, melting, incinerating, or shredding).[85]

Furthermore, if a disposal vendor (a business associate) is used to pick up and destroy the PHI, the PHI for disposal should be maintained in a secure area. In some cases, it may be appropriate to deposit PHI in locked dumpsters that are accessible only by authorized persons.[86]

[C] Technical Safeguards

Technical safeguards include both technology and the policy and procedures for its use that protect electronic PHI and control access to it.[87]

Standard 1: Access Controls

Technical policies and procedures for systems with electronic PHI that implement the access standards established under the administrative safeguards section.[88]

Standard

Implement technical policies and procedures for electronic information systems that maintain electronic PHI to allow access only to those persons or software programs that have been granted access rights as specified in the "Administrative Safeguards" section of the Security Regulations.[89]

Implementation Specifications

1. *Unique User Identification.* [Required] Assign a unique name and/or number for identifying and tracking user identity.

2. *Emergency Access Procedure.* [Required] Establish (and implement as needed) procedures for obtaining necessary ePHI during an emergency.

---

[84] 45 C.F.R. § 164.310(d)(2).

[85] HHS, OCR, Frequently Asked Questions About the Disposal of Protected Health Information, available at http://www.hhs.gov/ocr/privacy/hipaa/enforcement/examples/disposalfaqs.pdf. See **§ 3.05[C]** for more information about HHS guidance regarding disposal of PHI.

[86] HHS, OCR, Frequently Asked Questions About the Disposal of Protected Health Information, available at http://www.hhs.gov/ocr/privacy/hipaa/enforcement/examples/disposalfaqs.pdf.

[87] 45 C.F.R. § 164.304. Additional guidance is available as part of the HHS HIPAA Security series, *Security Standards: Technical Safeguards,* available at http://www.hhs.gov/ocr/privacy/hipaa/administrative/securityrule/techsafeguards.pdf.

[88] 45 C.F.R. § 164.312(a).

[89] 45 C.F.R. § 164.312(a)(1); see 45 C.F.R. § 164.308(a).

3. *Automatic Logoff.* [Addressable] Implement electronic procedures that terminate an electronic session after a predetermined time of inactivity.

4. *Encryption and Decryption.* [Addressable] Implement a mechanism to encrypt and decrypt ePHI.[90]
   See § 4.04[A] for additional discussion of encryption.

Standard 2: Audit Controls

Standard

Implement hardware, software, and/or procedural mechanisms that record and examine activity in information systems that contain or use electronic PHI.[91]

Implementation Specifications

None.

The covered entity's or business associate's risk assessment and risk analysis can help determine how intensive the entity's audit control function should be.[92]

Standard 3: Integrity

Standard

Implement policies and procedures to protect the integrity of electronic PHI and assure it is not improperly altered or destroyed.[93]

Implementation Specification

Mechanism to Authenticate electronic PHI. [Addressable] Implement electronic mechanisms to corroborate that electronic PHI has not been altered or destroyed in an unauthorized manner.[94]

HHS specifically cites digital signatures and check sum technology as examples of the "numerous techniques available."[95]

Standard 4: Person or Entity Authentication

Standard

Implement procedures to verify that persons or entities seeking access to electronic PHI are who they claim to be.[96]

---

[90] 45 C.F.R. § 164.312(a)(2). *Encryption* means the use of an algorithmic process to transform data into a form in which there is low probability of assigning meaning without use of a confidential process or key. 45 C.F.R. § 164.304.

[91] 45 C.F.R. § 164.312(b).

[92] 68 Fed. Reg. 8355 (Feb. 20, 2003).

[93] 45 C.F.R. § 164.312(c)(1).

[94] 45 C.F.R. § 164.312(c)(2).

[95] 68 Fed. Reg. 8356 (Feb. 20, 2003).

[96] 45 C.F.R. § 164.312(d)(1).

Implementation Specifications

None.

Personal authentication can be achieved through a variety of mechanisms, including biometric identification, passwords, personal identification numbers (PINs), telephone callbacks, token systems, or digital signatures.[97]

Standard 5: Transmission Security

Standard

Implement technical security measures to guard against unauthorized access to electronic PHI that is being transmitted over an electronic communications network.[98]

Implementation Specifications

1. *Integrity Controls.* [Addressable] Implement data integrity measures to ensure that electronically transmitted electronic PHI is not improperly modified without detection until disposed of.

2. *Encryption.* [Addressable] Implement a mechanism to encrypt electronic PHI whenever deemed appropriate.[99]

See § 4.04[A] for additional discussion of encryption.

§ 4.03 DOCUMENTATION, POLICIES, AND PROCEDURES

The Security Regulations require covered entities and business associates to implement and maintain written policies and procedures to comply with the standards, implementation specifications, and other requirements of the Security Regulations.[100] Documentation is also specifically required for certain actions, activities, and assessments, such as the risk assessment analysis.[101] These policies, procedures, and other documents must be made available to those persons responsible for implementing them.[102] Covered entities and business associates must maintain this documentation (on paper or electronically) for six years from the later of the date of its creation or the date when it last was in effect.[103] Documentation must be reviewed and updated periodically in response to environmental or operational changes affecting the security of PHI.[104]

During a compliance review in 2009, CMS identified this as a weak area for covered entities. CMS found that most of the covered entities it reviewed had few and inadequate policies and procedures, and the processes followed by the covered entities did not match their policies and procedures.[105]

---

[97] 68 Fed. Reg. 8356 (Feb. 20, 2003).

[98] 45 C.F.R. § 164.312(e)(1).

[99] 45 C.F.R. § 164.312(e)(2). *Encryption* means the use of an algorithmic process to transform data into a form in which there is low probability of assigning meaning without use of a confidential process or key. 45 C.F.R. § 164.304.

[100] 45 C.F.R. § 164.316 (Security Regulations). Additional guidance is available as part of the HHS HIPAA Security series, *Security Standards: Organizational, Policies and Procedures and Documentation Requirements*, available at http://www.hhs.gov/ocr/privacy/hipaa/administrative/securityrule/pprequirements.pdf.

[101] 45 C.F.R. § 164.316(b)(1)(i).

[102] 45 C.F.R. § 164.316(b)(1)(ii).

[103] 45 C.F.R. § 164.316(b)(2)(i).

[104] 45 C.F.R. § 164.316(b)(2)(iii).

[105] CMS, *2009 HIPAA Compliance Review Analysis and Summary of Results*, available at http://www.hhs.gov/ocr/privacy/hipaa/enforcement/cmscompliancerev09.pdf. CMS also provides some suggestions for improvement in these areas.

§ 4.04   SPECIAL TOPICS IN SECURITY

The following discussion concerns special applications of the Security Regulations.

[A]   Encryption

Encryption is an acceptable method of denying access to information in a file, whether the file is "at rest" or in transit,[106] by converting the original data into encoded text. *Encryption* means using an algorithmic process to transform data into a form in which there is low probability of converting the message into plain, comprehensible text without use of a confidential process or key, which should be held only by an authorized recipient.[107] Encryption varies in security level based on the strength of the underlying cryptographic algorithm. Consistent with HHS's initial commitment to avoiding technology-specific requirements, the Security Regulations do not identify any specific (or minimum) type or strength of encryption, which might soon be outmoded.[108]

Business practices and technology change, and the ease and availability of encryption also change. For example, in 2003, HHS concluded that no simple interoperable encryption tools existed for covered entities and business associates to communicate with patients by e-mail.[109] Since then, new tools have become available for secure electronic messaging.

In 2009, HHS set standards for what is considered "unsecured PHI," for purposes of the breach notification provisions of the HITECH Act. PHI that is "at rest" or "in motion" is considered to be unsecured, unless it is encrypted according to specific industry standards, but the standards stop short of imposing an encryption requirement under the Privacy or Security Regulations.[110] Under the Technical Safeguards of the Security Regulations, encryption remains addressable rather than required. Implementation of encryption must be based on the covered entity's or business associate's risk analysis. However, the breach notification requirement with respect to unsecured PHI under the HITECH Act is an important new factor in that risk analysis.

HHS strongly encourages covered entities to consider use of encryption technology for electronic PHI, whether at rest or in motion, but particularly for transmission over the Internet or data on mobile devices.[111] For example, because of the risk of data interception, HHS has suggested that a covered entity should consider mandating strong encryption methods for the electronic transmission of PHI.[112] If a risk analysis shows that electronic PHI transmitted from a covered entity or business associate would be at significant risk of unauthorized access, HHS expects these transmissions to be encrypted, as appropriate.[113] Furthermore, HHS guidance makes clear its view that, because of the risk of laptops or other portable devices being stolen, a covered entity or business associate should establish a policy that all portable devices that store PHI employ appropriately strong encryption technologies.[114] Covered entities and business associates should consult appropriate experts to determine reasonable and appropriate encryption measures.

---

[106] 68 Fed. Reg. 8355 (Feb. 20, 2003).

[107] 45 C.F.R. § 164.304.

[108] 68 Fed. Fed. 8357 (Feb. 20, 2003).

[109] 68 Fed. Reg. 8357 (Feb. 20, 2003).

[110] See § 5.02[C].

[111] See, e.g., 68 Fed. Reg. 8357 (Feb. 20, 2003).

[112] *HIPAA Security Guidance for Remote Use of and Access to Electronic Protected Health Information*, available at http://www.hhs.gov/ocr/privacy/hipaa/administrative/securityrule/remoteuse.pdf.

[113] 68 Fed. Reg. 8357 (Feb. 20, 2003).

[114] *HIPAA Security Guidance for Remote Use of and Access to Electronic Protected Health Information*, available at http://www.hhs.gov/ocr/privacy/hipaa/administrative/securityrule/remoteuse.pdf.

[B] Electronic Signatures

HHS issued proposed regulations in 1998 that would have established digital signatures as the standard for electronic signatures in health care.[115] HHS will not be issuing final regulations based on those proposed regulations but may issue a new electronic signature regulation at some time in the future.[116]

[C] E-mail

E-mail is commonly used in health care, both for internal communication and communication to outside parties (including patients). The Security Regulations do not prohibit the use of e-mail for sending electronic PHI, but the regulations do require that such e-mails be adequately protected. Risks associated with e-mails include interception, inadvertently sending the e-mail to the wrong recipient, inappropriately forwarding the e-mail, and unsecured storage.[117] Covered entities and business associates must assess their use of e-mail, identify the available means to protect electronic PHI as it is transmitted and stored, and choose an appropriate solution. This decision process must be documented.[118]

Only the minimum amount of PHI required for the intended purpose should be included in an e-mail. In fact, the PHI should be de-identified if feasible. Covered entities and business associates should also consider policies such as prohibiting the e-mail's subject line from containing any PHI, because this is the part of the message most likely to be inadvertently viewed by unauthorized persons. In addition, double-check before hitting "send," to ensure the recipient list is correct.

E-mails (and other means of Internet-based messaging) are increasingly being used as means of communication between patients and health care providers. These methods can be used to provide follow-up care, clarify instructions to patients, send test results, make appointments, or provide Web links to additional educational resources. Sometimes, these communications take the form of "e-visits," or structured electronic exchanges that replace in-person doctor visits. Although there can be many advantages to these e-mails or e-visits, they also raise concerns, including issues of privacy and security and obtaining informed consent from the patient. The American Medical Association and American Health Information Management Association are among the sources of practical guidelines in this area.

The use of encryption is not absolutely required under the Security Regulations. Encryption remains an addressable implementation specification. Alternative approaches are permitted if better suited to the covered entity's circumstances (see §§ 4.01[D] and 4.04[A]). However, if unencrypted e-mail is used, other safeguards should be applied, such as limiting the type or amount of PHI the e-mail contains.[119] Possible alternatives to encrypted e-mails include secure Web portals, secure messaging networks, and private networks. Renewed consideration should, however, be given to encryption of e-mails in light of the application of the Breach Regulations (see § 5.02[C]) to unsecured (i.e., unencrypted) e-mails and recent HHS guidance, discussed below, concerning putting individuals on notice of the risks on unencrypted e-mail.

Individuals may request to have the covered entity communicate with them by alternative means or at alternative locations, and the covered entity must comply if the request is reasonable (see § 3.02[E]). For example, a patient may ask that appointment reminders or other communications be sent by e-mail rather than through a postcard or phone call if e-mail is a reasonable alternative means for the covered entity.[120] HHS stated in its "Privacy and Security Framework: Safeguards" guidance that if the individual initiates communications with the covered entity using e-mail, the covered entity should be able to assume (unless the individual has

---

[115] 63 Fed. Reg. 43,256 (Aug. 12, 1998).

[116] 68 Fed. Reg. 8335 (Feb. 20, 2003).

[117] For additional information, see HHS, OCR, HIE Guidance, "Privacy and Security Framework: Safeguards," available at http://www.hhs.gov/ocr/privacy/hipaa/understanding/special/healthit (hereinafter "Privacy and Security Framework: Safeguards").

[118] OCR HIPAA FAQ, available at http://www.hhs.gov/ocr/privacy/hipaa/faq/securityrule/2006.html.

[119] "Privacy and Security Framework: Safeguards."

[120] "Privacy and Security Framework: Safeguards."

explicitly stated otherwise) that e-mail is an acceptable means of communication. However, if the covered entity feels the individual is unaware of the possible risks of unencrypted e-mail or has concerns about potential liability, the covered entity can alert the individual to those risks. The individual can then make an informed decision about whether to continue e-mail communications.[121] In guidance provided with the HITECH Regulations, HHS seems to take this a step further and establish a "duty to warn." HHS states that "covered entities are permitted to send individual unencrypted e-mails *if* [emphasis added] they have advised the individual of the risks associated with unencrypted e-mail."[122] HHS states that this warning is necessary but need not be an in-depth explanation of encryption technology and information security. However, the covered entity is expected to "notify the individual that there may be some level of risk that the information in the e-mail could be read by a third party."[123] HHS further indicates that if such notification is provided and the individual still prefers an unencrypted e-mail, and unauthorized access occurs during the transmission of the e-mail to the individual, the covered entity would not be held responsible.[124] It seems likely, however, that such a breach would be evaluated on a case-by-case basis.

If the patient has concerns about receiving PHI in an unencrypted e-mail, other means of communication, such as telephone or mail, should be offered. Methods of secure electronic communication, such as secure Web messaging, may also be an available alternative.[125]

[D]   Mobile Devices and Remote Access

Mobile devices, including portable computers, laptops, notebooks, smartphones, tablet computers, and digital cameras, are increasingly common in health care. Sometimes the device is provided by an employer; in other cases, it is owned by the user. These devices may or may not connect with the employer's other computer systems. If these devices contain PHI, security measures are required by the Security Regulations. Although security measures for mobile devices will overlap the covered entity's security measures for other computers, there are special risks related to mobile devices that will require special attention.

A covered entity or business associate also faces special challenges in applying the Security Regulations to workforce members who have remote access to electronic PHI (whether or not a portable device is involved), for example, staff who telecommute or work out of a home-based office, or physicians on the medical staff of a hospital who have remote access to the hospital's EHR. The covered entity or business associate should have a remote access policy, as additional risks apply in these situations as well.

Because of the additional risks inherent in mobile computing and remote access, and because of a number of well-publicized security incidents related to the loss of laptops containing electronic PHI, HHS issued the "HIPAA Security Guidance for Remote Use of and Access to Electronic Protected Health Information" in December 2006.[126] The purpose of the guidance is to set forth strategies that may be reasonable and appropriate for covered entities and business associates that (1) use portable media/devices, for example USB flash drives, that store electronic PHI, and (2) permit offsite access or transport of electronic PHI via laptops, tablets, smartphones, or home computers.

HHS is particularly concerned about laptops; home-based personal computers; smartphones; hotel, library, or other public workstations and Wireless Access Points (WAPs); USB flash drives and memory cards; CDs; DVDs; backup media; e-mail; smart cards; and remote access devices (including security hardware). Covered entities or business associates using any of these devices or modalities should review the guidance carefully.

---

[121] "Privacy and Security Framework: Safeguards."

[122] 78 Fed. Reg. 5634 (Jan. 25, 2013).

[123] 78 Fed. Reg. 5634 (Jan. 25, 2013).

[124] 78 Fed. Reg. 5634 (Jan. 25, 2013).

[125] "Privacy and Security Framework: Safeguards."

[126] "HIPAA Security Guidance for Remote Use of and Access to Electronic Protected Health Information," available at http://www.hhs.gov/ocr/privacy/hipaa/administrative/securityrule/remoteuse.pdf.

The HHS guidance begins with a discussion of risk assessment, stating that the covered entity (or business associate) should be "extremely cautious" about allowing the offsite use of or access to electronic PHI. And even then, access should be permitted only where "great rigor" has been taken to ensure that the necessary policies, procedures, and workforce training have been implemented consistent with the Security Regulations. The guidance also provides tables outlining possible risk management strategies in the areas of accessing electronic PHI, storing electronic PHI, and transmitting electronic PHI. Additional guidance regarding secure remote access is available in the 2007 NIST publication "User's Guide for Securing External Devices for Telework and Remote Access."[127]

In 2012, HHS issued guidance on the security of mobile devices as part of an initiative called "Mobile Devices: Know the RISKS. Take the STEPS. PROTECT & SECURE Health Information." The initiative offers educational materials, including videos, posters, and fact sheets. HHS features the following 11 basic steps for securing PHI when using a mobile device, such as a smartphone or tablet.[128]

1. Use a password or other user authentication.

2. Encrypt data stored on or sent by the device.

3. Install and activate remote wiping and/or remote disabling of the device, in case it is lost or stolen.

4. Disable and do not install file-sharing applications that let Internet users connect to each other's computers to share files.

5. Install and enable a firewall.

6. Install and enable security software to protect against malicious software, such as viruses.

7. Keep security software up to date.

8. Research apps before downloading.

9. Keep physical control of the device.

10. When using a public Wi-Fi network or hotspot to send or receive data, use adequate security.

11. Delete all stored PHI on the device before discarding or repurposing it.[129]

[E] Passwords

All covered entities and business associates must implement procedures to verify that persons or entities seeking access to electronic PHI are who they claim to be. Furthermore, password management is one of the addressable implementation specifications under the security awareness standard (Administrative Safeguards, Standard 5). Covered entities and business associates should have procedures for creating, changing, and safeguarding passwords.

User names and passwords are still the most common mechanisms used for personal authentication. HHS has suggested, however, that in some cases it may be appropriate to establish a two-factor authentication system. This process requires not only a username/password, but also an additional level of authentication, such as requiring users to answer a predetermined security question (e.g., What is your pet's name?).[130] This approach

---

[127] NIST Publ. 800-114, available at http://csrc.nist.gov/publications/nistpubs/800-114/SP800-114.pdf.

[128] See http://www.healthit.gov/providers-professionals/your-mobile-device-and-health-information-privacy-and-security; see also the December 12, 2012, HHS press release announcing the initiative, available at https://wayback.archive-it.org/3926/20150121155233/http://www.hhs.gov/news/press/2012pres/12/20121212a.html. In June 2013, NIST also published guidance on "Guidelines for Managing the Security of Mobile Devices in the Enterprise" (NIST Spec. Pub 800-124, Rev.1), available at http://csrc.nist.gov/publications/PubsSPs.html#800-124.

[129] Fact Sheet, "Take Steps to Protect and Secure Health Information When Using a Mobile Device," available at http://www.health it.gov/sites/default/files/fact-sheet-take-steps-to-protect-information.pdf.

[130] "HIPAA Security Guidance for Remote Use of and Access to Electronic Protected Health Information," available at http://www.hhs.gov/ocr/privacy/hipaa/administrative/securityrule/remoteuse.pdf.

has become common in the financial services industry. Also, especially for members of the workforce with remote access, consider methods such as providing a number-generating token (or comparable smartphone app) and requiring that number to be entered in addition to a password.

In its Security Information Series, HHS guidance related to usernames and passwords includes recommendations to:

- Train all users and establish guidelines for creating passwords and changing them periodically.

- Have policies in place that prevent workforce members from sharing their passwords with others.

- Advise workforce members to commit their passwords to memory. Take commonsense precautions, such as not writing passwords down and leaving them in areas that are visible or accessible to others.

- Monitor inappropriate or multiple attempted log-ins (e.g., when someone enters multiple combinations of usernames and/or passwords to attempt to gain system access).[131]

The Security Regulations do not specify detailed standards for creating passwords. However, it is generally advisable to have a password policy that establishes minimum length, complexity, and how often it must be changed. For example, CMS has established the following standards for user access to its own computer systems:

- Password must be 8 characters in length;

- Passwords must start with an alphabetical character;

- Password must contain at least one number;

- Password must contain at least one upper case letter and one lower case letter;

- Password must not contain your User ID.

- Passwords must not contain 4 consecutive characters of any of your previous 6 passwords;

- Passwords must be different from the previous 6 passwords;

- Passwords must not contain any of the reserved words or number combinations on a list specific to the organization. (The CMS list contains, e.g., PASSWORD, CMS, HCFA, LETMEIN, 1234, ORIOLES, etc.); and

- Passwords must be changed at least every 60 days.[132]

In its enforcement of the Security Regulations, CMS reported, as an example of a security complaint, a pharmacy that allowed employees to share login IDs and passwords to a system containing PHI. The practice was a violation of the pharmacy's written policies, but the process was overlooked in the pharmacy's risk assessment. The pharmacy re-issued unique user IDs and passwords for each user and agreed to a corrective action plan that required an updated risk analysis and reminders to all employees about the pharmacy's policy.[133] This example is a reminder that covered entities and business associates should not only establish password policies, but also need to ensure ongoing compliance.

---

[131] HHS Security Information Series, Part 2 (Administrative Safeguards) and Part 4 (Technical Safeguards), available at http://www.hhs.gov/ocr/privacy/hipaa/administrative/securityrule/securityruleguidance.html.

[132] Individuals Authorized Access to the CMS Computer Services (IACS), IACS User Guide, November 2013, § 8.0, available at http://cms.hhs.gov/Research-Statistics-Data-and-Systems/CMS-Information-Technology/IACS/Downloads/IACS-User-Guide.pdf.

[133] HIPAA Case Examples, formerly available at http://www.cms.hhs.gov/Enforcement/07_HIPAAComplaintExamples.asp.

[F] Security of Digital Copiers

In November 2010, the Federal Trade Commission (FTC) published tips for businesses on safeguarding data stored on digital copiers. These advanced copiers can print, scan, fax, and e-mail documents as well as copy them. To manage and store all this data, these copiers have hard drives. If the digital copier has been used on documents containing PHI, that PHI may remain on the copier's hard drive. The FTC guidance recommends evaluating and understanding your copier's security features, such as overwriting and encryption, and, when returning or disposing of a digital copier, taking appropriate steps to remove, destroy, or overwrite the data on its hard drive.[134]

In May 2010, HHS opened an investigation of a security breach at Affinity Health Plan, Inc., which involved electronic PHI on the hard drives of leased photocopiers. In 2013, Affinity entered into a Resolution Agreement with HHS regarding this matter. See § 6.05[O].

[G] Security of Peer-to-Peer File Sharing Software

Peer-to-peer (P2P) technology allows sharing of music, documents, and other files. Computers using the same or compatible P2P software can form a network and share files. If not configured properly, the P2P software may expose files not intended to be shared. The FTC has published guidance on these security problems.[135]

[H] Medical Identity Theft

Identity theft is an increasing problem in health care.[136] In "medical identity theft," someone uses another person's name or insurance information to obtain medical treatment, prescription drugs, or other health care services; or someone obtains the name and insurance information and uses it to submit and receive payment for fraudulent insurance claims. Medical identity theft can result in the thief's health information being mixed in with the victim's, which can result in treatment errors, in addition to creating insurance, credit report, and other financial problems.

The FTC has issued an FAQ addressing frequently asked questions related to medical identity theft.[137] The FTC identifies several ways people might discover that they are victims of medical identity theft, such as getting bills for medical services they did not receive, being told by their health plan that they've reached their limit on benefits, or being denied insurance because their medical records show a condition they don't actually have.[138]

The FTC sets forth a number of steps for a health care provider to take if it suspects a patient has been a victim of medical identity theft. The FTC recommends that the provider:

---

[134] FTC, "Copier Data Security: A Guide for Businesses," available at http://business.ftc.gov/documents/bus43-copier-data-security (Nov. 2010); also available through the OCR website at http://www.hhs.gov/ocr/privacy/hipaa/administrative/securityrule/index.html.

[135] FTC, "Peer-to-Peer File Sharing: A Guide for Business," available at http://business.ftc.gov/documents/bus46-peer-peer-file-sharing-guide-business (Jan. 2010); also available through the OCR website at http://www.hhs.gov/ocr/privacy/hipaa/administrative/securityrule/index.html.

[136] In April 2014, the FBI distributed a notice to health care providers warning that the health care industry is more vulnerable to cyber attacks than other industries, such as the financial and retail sectors. The notice also states that the health care industry can expect increased "cyber intrusions against health care systems," due to increased adoption of electronic health records (EHR), "lax cybersecurity standards, and a higher financial payout for medical records in the black market." FBI Cyber Division, Private Industry Notification, "Health Care Systems and Medical Devices at Risk for Increased Cyber Intrusions for Financial Gains," PIN # 140408-009 (Apr. 8, 2014).

[137] FTC, "Medical Identity Theft: FAQs for Health Care Providers and Health Plans," available at http://business.ftc.gov/documents/bus75-medical-identity-theft-faq-health-care-health-plan (Jan. 2011); also available through the OCR website at http://www.hhs.gov/ocr/privacy/hipaa/administrative/securityrule/index.html (hereinafter "FTC Medical Identity Theft FAQs").

[138] "FTC Medical Identity Theft FAQs."

- Conduct an investigation, including reviewing the patient's medical record for errors or inconsistencies;

- Understand its obligations under the Fair Credit Reporting Act with regard to the impact of the identity theft on its reporting of debt to credit reporting companies;

- Review its data security practices, even if the information used to commit the fraud did not come from that organization; and

- Provide any necessary breach notifications (e.g., if required under the Breach Regulations or state law).[139]

The FTC guidance also discusses what a provider should tell patients who have been victims of medical identity theft, including advising/reminding them of their rights to obtain copies of their medical records and request amendments, encouraging them to notify their health plan, and telling them how to file a complaint with OCR or the FTC.[140] The FTC has also issued guidance directed at consumers, regarding how to detect medical identity theft and how to respond.[141]

[I] Cloud Computing

Cloud computing is named after the cloud icon often used in technical diagrams to represent the Internet as a cloud through which transmissions or communications between parties occur. Cloud computing is an evolving concept with evolving definitions, but generally speaking, it can refer to any hosted service delivered over the Internet. NIST describes cloud computing as "a model for enabling ubiquitous, convenient, on-demand network access to a shared pool of configurable computing resources that can be rapidly provisioned and released with minimal management effort or service provider interaction."[142] That model has five essential characteristics:

1.   on-demand self-service;

2.   broad network access (e.g., available on phones and laptops);

3.   resource pooling (to serve multiple customers);

4.   rapid elasticity (scalable on demand); and

5.   measured services (metering).[143]

Cloud services can offer software, platforms or infrastructure, or a combination, and they can be public or private.

Cloud computing services are complex systems and thus are subject to flaws and failures, not all of which are unique to the cloud. When a covered entity or business associate uses a public cloud service, the data (including PHI) typically are physically controlled by the service provider. Cloud computing therefore raises special issues of confidentiality, data integrity, and availability. Fundamental security and privacy concerns include:

- physical location of the data;

- vulnerability of a highly complex system;

---

[139] "FTC Medical Identity Theft FAQs."

[140] "FTC Medical Identity Theft FAQs."

[141] FTC, "Medical Identity Theft" (Aug. 2012), available at http://www.consumer.ftc.gov/articles/0171-medical-identity-theft.

[142] NIST, *The NIST Definition of Cloud Computing* (SP800-145) (Sept. 2011), available at http://csrc.nist.gov/publications/nistpubs/800-145/SP800-145.pdf.

[143] NIST, *The NIST Definition of Cloud Computing* (SP800-145), available at http://csrc.nist.gov/publications/nistpubs/800-145/SP800-145.pdf.

- sharing of cloud resources among customers;

- logical but not physical separation of data between customers;

- administration of access controls;

- availability and reliability of the system; and

- loss of control over system administration and security decisions.[144]

In most cases, the cloud service provider will be a business associate of the covered entity. In the preamble to the HITECH Regulations, HHS discusses entities that store or maintain PHI on behalf of a covered entity, stating that such entities are business associates because they have an ongoing ("persistent" rather than "transitory") opportunity to access the PHI, even if they do not actually access or view the PHI.[145] The covered entity needs assurances that the cloud service provider is implementing appropriate administrative, physical, and technical safeguards and will cooperate with the covered entity to meet compliance and regulatory requirements. This will require more specific contractual commitments than in a standard business associate agreement; for example, relating to the encryption of data, location of the data (U.S. or foreign), access controls, and use of subcontractors. Furthermore, the covered entity must have a method of determining whether these commitments are being met on an ongoing basis.[146]

Although one of the biggest concerns with cloud computing is security, for a small provider or health plan with limited information technology and security staff using a good public cloud service could actually enhance security if appropriately managed. The cloud service provider may have resources and capabilities not otherwise available to a small covered entity.[147]

[J] The Internet of Things

A growing challenge for covered entities and business associates analyzing and managing risks to ePHI is the "Internet of Things." The "Internet of Things (IoT)" or "cyber-physical systems," generally refers to physical objects (not including smartphones, tablets, or laptop/desktop computers) that have embedded sensors and other technologies that connect to the Internet and send and receive data. There is not yet one commonly accepted definition. What is commonly accepted, however, is that the number of "things" connected to the Internet will continue to grow, and the IoT trend is massive and just beginning. In 2015, there were an estimated 25 billion devices connected to the Internet, and this is projected to grow to 50 billion by 2020.[148]

In health care, the Internet of Things often takes the form of health monitoring. For example:

- Sensors that collect data, such as blood pressure or glucose levels, and transmit the data to the person's health care provider for management of chronic diseases.

- Sensors that monitor breathing, temperature, or movement of an infant or an invalid and transmit that data to the smartphone of a parent or other family member.

- Wearable fitness devices that allow the user to share exercise and other wellness data with friends.

---

[144] NIST, *Cloud Computing Synopsis and Recommendations* (SP800-146), available at http://csrc.nist.gov/publications/nistpubs/800-146/sp800-146.pdf; NIST, *Guidelines on Security and Privacy in Public Cloud Computing* (SP800-144), available at http://csrc.nist.gov/publications/nistpubs/800-144/SP800-144.pdf.

[145] 78 Fed. Reg. 5572 (Jan. 25, 2013).

[146] For more information, also see NIST, *Cloud Computing Synopsis and Recommendations* (SP800-146), available at http://csrc.nist.gov/publications/nistpubs/800-146/sp800-146.pdf.

[147] See NIST, *Guidelines on Security and Privacy in Public Cloud Computing* (SP800-144), available at http://csrc.nist.gov/publications/nistpubs/800-144/SP800-144.pdf.

[148] Federal Trade Commission Staff Report, "Internet of Things: Privacy & Security in a Connected World," Jan. 2015 (hereinafter "FTC IoT Report"), available at https://www.ftc.gov/system/files/documents/reports/federal-trade-commission-staff-report-november-2013-workshop-entitled-internet-things-privacy/150127iotrpt.pdf.

All of these connected devices, remote access, sensors, and monitors raise concerns about privacy and security. And in many cases, they fall outside the scope of the HIPAA Regulations, because they are consumer products that do not involve a covered entity or business associate. But, depending on how they are used, e.g., by health care providers, they can trigger HIPAA obligations. It is a growing trend that covered entities and business associates will need to monitor and incorporate into their security compliance program.

HHS has recognized that mobile health technology is a growing field and additional guidance is needed, including guidance specific to cloud storage and related services.[149] HHS further stated that outreach to the mobile health technology industry is critical, and HHS is considering holding "listening" sessions about how HHS can help address privacy and security concerns through guidance.[150]

In the meantime, the Federal Trade Commission (FTC) has released a report, "The Internet of Things: Privacy and Security in a Connected World."[151] This FTC Staff Report identifies a number of potential security and privacy risks related to the Internet of Things, where these "things" might:

- Enable unauthorized access and misuse of personal information. If smart devices store sensitive health or financial information, security vulnerabilities in those devices could be exploited and lead to identity theft or fraud.

- Facilitate attacks on other systems to which the device is connected.

- Create risks to personal safety, such as hacking into a medical device and altering settings that endanger the user.

- Create privacy risks arising from the extensive collection and aggregation of personal information over time.[152]

The FTC Staff Report called for the adoption of new best practices to ensure privacy and security of consumer data, including:

- Security by Design—building security into the design of devices and testing those security measures rather than addressing security as an afterthought.

- Personnel Practices—adopting personnel practices that promote good security, including appropriate training for all personnel and assigning senior level responsibility for security.

- Third Party Service Providers—vetting vendors for good security practices and providing reasonable oversight of those vendors.

- Defense in Depth—when a risk is identified, implementing several levels of security measures, with encryption of sensitive information being particularly important.

- Access Control Measures—limiting access and providing for strong authentication.

- Monitor Products—monitoring products throughout their life cycle and patching known vulnerabilities.

---

[149] Sylvia Burwell, Secretary of HHS, Letter to U.S. Rep. Peter DeFazio, Nov. 21, 2014 (hereinafter "Burwell Letter").
[150] Burwell Letter.
[151] FTC IoT Report.
[152] FTC IoT Report.

- Data minimization—limiting the data collected and retained, and disposing of it when no longer needed, which would decrease the potential harm of a breach and also make the data a less attractive target for data thieves.[153]

Although the Internet of Things is growing rapidly, it is still in a relatively early stage. Ideas about best security practices are still forming and consensus still developing. In addition, debate continues regarding industry self-regulation versus new federal legislation. In the interim, further guidance from regulators on issues specific to the IoT can be expected.

---

[153] FTC IoT Report.

CHAPTER 5

BREACH REGULATIONS

§ 5.01   BREACH NOTIFICATION REGULATIONS

Prior to the HITECH Act, there was no explicit requirement under the Administrative Simplification Regulations to notify affected individuals of a privacy or security breach. Although the Privacy Regulations did impose a duty to mitigate any harmful effect known to the covered entity when there was an unauthorized use or disclosure of PHI (see **§ 3.05[F]**), the covered entity had considerable discretion in determining whether the mitigation would include notification to the affected individuals. The Privacy Regulations also required the covered entity to provide accountings of certain disclosures, including breaches (see **§ 3.02[D]**), but only if requested by the individual. In addition, there were state laws requiring notification in the event of certain security breaches (see **§ 5.10**), but these were often narrow in scope. None of these requirements led to a consistent process of notifying affected individuals of a breach of their PHI.

As explained in detail in this chapter, the HITECH Act and its implementing regulations require that individuals and HHS be notified of breaches of unsecured PHI. Shortly after passage of the HITECH Act, HHS issued interim final regulations with regard to the breach notification requirements, which were effective for breaches on or after September 23, 2009 (the "2009 Breach Regulations").[1] In 2013, the HITECH Regulations included final regulations on breach notifications (the "Breach Regulations"); these new Breach Regulations made a significant change to the 2009 Breach Regulations. This was a change to the risk assessment standards. The "risk of harm" analysis was replaced with a "low probability of compromise" analysis (see **§ 5.01[D]**). The new risk assessment standards must be applied to breaches on or after September 23, 2013.[2]

§ 5.02   ANALYSIS OF A BREACH

A covered entity must provide notification following a breach of unsecured PHI, unless there is a low probability of compromise of the PHI. This **§ 5.02** discusses the definition of "breach," exceptions to that definition, the impact to a breach analysis when the PHI is "unsecured," and the "low probability of compromise" analysis. See **Appendix C** for a flowchart summarizing this analysis.

[A]   Definition of a "Breach"

Under the HITECH Act, a breach is defined as the "unauthorized acquisition, access, use, or disclosure of protected health information which compromises the security or privacy of the PHI."[3] "Unauthorized," in this context, means "not permitted by the Privacy Regulations."[4] Therefore, the first question is whether the event was an acquisition, access, use, or disclosure of PHI that violated the Privacy Regulations.

A breach must involve PHI; therefore, an unauthorized use or disclosure of de-identified information would not be a breach for purposes of the breach notification requirements.[5] From September 23, 2009, through September 22, 2013, a disclosure of a limited data set that further excluded dates of birth and zip codes was not considered a breach because it was deemed to not compromise the security or privacy of the PHI under the 2009 Breach Regulations.[6] This exception was eliminated, effective September 23, 2013, by the new Breach Regulations.[7]

---

[1] HITECH Act § 13402. Interim final regulations were issued in August 2009. 74 Fed. Reg. 42,740 (Aug. 24, 2009).

[2] 78 Fed. Reg. 5638–5658 (Jan. 25, 2013).

[3] HITECH Act § 13400.

[4] 78 Fed. Reg. 5639 (Jan. 25, 2013). A violation of the Security Regulations does not itself constitute a breach, unless there is also a violation of the Privacy Regulations. 74 Fed. Reg. 42,740, 42,744 (Aug. 24, 2009).

[5] 74 Fed. Reg. 42,743 (Aug. 24, 2009); 78 Fed. Reg. 5642 (Jan. 25, 2013).

[6] 45 C.F.R. § 164.402 (under the 2009 Breach Regulations).

[7] 78 Fed. Reg. 5644 (Jan. 25, 2013).

[B]   Exceptions to the Definition of Breach

Under the Breach Regulations, a breach does *not* include the following circumstances:

1. Any unintentional acquisition, access, or use of PHI by a workforce member or person acting under the authority of a covered entity or a business associate, if such acquisition, access, or use was made in good faith and within the scope of authority and does not result in further use or disclosure in a manner not permitted under the Privacy Regulations.[8]

2. Any inadvertent disclosure by a person who is authorized to access PHI at a covered entity or business associate to another person authorized to access PHI at the same covered entity or business associate, or organized health care arrangement in which the covered entity participates, if the information received as a result of such disclosure is not further used or disclosed in a manner not permitted by the Privacy Regulations.[9]

3. A disclosure of PHI where a covered entity or business associate has a good faith belief that an unauthorized person to whom the disclosure was made would not reasonably have been able to retain such information.[10] Examples of this type of situation include a mismailed EOB (explanation of benefits) that is returned to the health plan without having been opened and a hospital nurse handing a patient the discharge papers of another patient, but quickly realizing her mistake and retrieving the papers, provided the nurse could reasonably conclude that the patient could not have read or retained the information.[11]

[C]   Unsecured PHI

A covered entity must provide breach notifications, as explained in this chapter, in the case of a breach of *unsecured* PHI that is discovered by the covered entity.[12] Unsecured PHI means PHI that is not rendered unusable, unreadable, or indecipherable to unauthorized persons through the use of a technology or methodology specified by HHS in annual guidance.[13] HHS has provided the following initial guidance on how to make PHI "secured" and thus making a breach of that PHI not subject to the notification requirements described in this chapter.[14] HHS has identified only two methods for making PHI into "secured PHI"—encryption and destruction:

1. *Encryption*: As defined in the Security Regulations, "encryption" means the use of an algorithmic process to transform data into a form in which there is a low probability of assigning meaning without use of a confidential process or key.[15] Successful encryption requires both a strong encryption algorithm and a secure decryption key or process that has not been breached. Under the HHS guidance

---

[8] 45 C.F.R. § 164.402. This exception would not cover "snooping employees," because such access would not be unintentional or in good faith. 78 Fed. Reg. 5640 (Jan. 25, 2013). If there is a "further use or disclosure" that is impermissible, that use or disclosure should be evaluated as a breach in its own right. 78 Fed. Reg. 5645 (Jan. 25, 2013).

[9] 45 C.F.R. § 164.402. These disclosures "at" a covered entity are intended to mean persons onsite, at the covered entity's facility, who are not workforce members. This would include physicians on the medical staff at a hospital. 78 Fed. Reg. 5645 (Jan. 25, 2013). If there is a "further use or disclosure" that is impermissible, that use or disclosure should be evaluated as a breach in its own right. 78 Fed. Reg. 5645 (Jan. 25, 2013).

[10] 45 C.F.R. § 164.402.

[11] 78 Fed. Reg. 5640 (Jan. 25, 2013).

[12] HITECH Act § 13402(a); 45 C.F.R. § 164.404.

[13] HITECH Act § 13402(h); 45 C.F.R. § 164.402. Initial guidance was issued at 74 Fed. Reg. 19,006 (Apr. 17, 2009) and is intended to be updated periodically.

[14] 74 Fed. Reg. 19,006 (Apr. 17, 2009), and incorporated into the interim final breach notification regulations at 74 Fed. Reg. 42,740 (Aug. 24, 2009).

[15] 45 C.F.R. § 164.304.

with regard to securing PHI for purposes of the breach notification provisions of the HITECH Act, the following encryption processes meet HHS standards:[16]

- Data at Rest: Valid encryption processes for data at rest that are consistent with *NIST Special Publication 800-111, Guide to Storage Encryption Technologies for End User Devices*.[17]

- Data in Motion: Valid encryption processes for data in motion that comply with Federal Information Processing Standards (FIPS) 140-2. These include, as appropriate, standards described in: NIST Special Publication 800-52, *Guidelines for the Selection and Use of Transport Layer Security (TLS) Implementations*; Publication 800-77, *Guide to IPsec VPNs*; or Publication 800-113, *Guide to SSL VPNs*, and may include others which are FIPS 140-2 validated.[18]

2. *Destruction*: PHI will be considered "secured" under the HHS guidance, if the media on which the PHI is stored or recorded has been destroyed in one of the following ways:[19]

- Hard copy media, such as paper or film, have been shredded or destroyed such that the PHI cannot be read or otherwise cannot be reconstructed; or

- Electronic media have been cleared, purged, or destroyed consistent with NIST Special Publication 800-88, *Guidelines for Media Sanitization*,[20] such that the PHI cannot be retrieved.

The methodologies and technologies identified in the HHS guidance are not merely examples; they are an exhaustive list of what makes PHI "secured" for purposes of the HITECH Act breach notification requirements.[21] No provision is made for an encryption-equivalent for paper records; therefore, they are "unsecured PHI," regardless of whatever other safeguards may have been implemented. Similarly, there is no method identified that would make oral records "secure."

[D] Compromising the Security or Privacy of the PHI

To be a "breach" requiring notification, the unauthorized acquisition, access, use, or disclosure must compromise the security or privacy of the PHI. The 2009 Breach Regulations interpreted the HITECH Act definition of breach such that "compromising the security or privacy of the PHI" meant posing a significant threat of financial, reputational, or other harm to the individual (the "harm standard").[22] The covered entity or business associate was required to conduct and document a fact-specific risk assessment to determine whether privacy or security was compromised under this harm standard.[23]

In 2013, the Breach Regulations revised the standards in two significant ways:

(a) An unauthorized use or disclosure is *presumed* to be a breach, unless the covered entity or business associate demonstrates that there is a low probability that the PHI has been compromised (or one of the other exceptions to the definition of breach applies).

(b) The harm standard is eliminated and replaced with a modified risk assessment intended to create a more objective standard, focused on the risk that the PHI has been "compromised." Notification is not required if the covered entity or business associate, through a risk assessment, can demonstrate that there is a low probability that the PHI has been compromised. The risk assessment must include at least the following four factors:

---

[16] 74 Fed. Reg. 19,009–10 (Apr. 27, 2009).

[17] Available at http://csrc.nist.gov/publications/PubsSPs.html.

[18] Available at http://csrc.nist.gov/publications/PubsSPs.html.

[19] 74 Fed. Reg. 19,010 (Apr. 17, 2009).

[20] Available at http://csrc.nist.gov/publications/PubsSPs.html.

[21] 74 Fed. Reg. 19,009 (Apr. 27, 2009).

[22] 45 C.F.R. § 164.402 (2009 Breach Regulations).

[23] 74 Fed. Reg. 42,740, 42,744–46 (Aug. 24, 2009); 78 Fed. Reg. 5640 (Jan. 25, 2013).

1. *What PHI was involved?* Consider the nature and extent of the PHI involved, including the types of identifiers and the likelihood of re-identification (e.g., Is the PHI of a more sensitive nature, such as Social Security numbers, credit card numbers, or other information that might increase the risk of identity theft? Does the PHI identify the nature of the services or other clinical information? What amount of detailed clinical information was involved? Could the PHI be used by an unauthorized recipient in a manner adverse to the individual or otherwise used to further the unauthorized recipient's own interests?);

2. *Who used or received the PHI?* Consider who was the unauthorized person who used the PHI or to whom the disclosure was made (e.g., Does the person have obligations to protect PHI, such as another covered entity? Does this person have the ability to re-identify PHI that may have few or no direct identifiers? Was it an impermissible use of the PHI, where there was no further impermissible disclosure outside the entity?);

3. *Was the PHI actually acquired?* Consider whether the PHI was actually acquired or viewed, or was there only the opportunity for the PHI to be acquired or viewed?; and

4. *To what extent have risks been mitigated?* Consider the extent to which the risk to the PHI has been mitigated (e.g., by obtaining satisfactory assurances from a unauthorized recipient that the PHI will not be further used or disclosed, by way of a confidentiality agreement or similar means, or that the PHI will be destroyed).[24]

HHS emphasizes that each of these four factors must be evaluated before coming to a conclusion.[25] No single factor is dispositive. Additional factors may also need to be considered in the risk assessment, depending on the circumstances.[26] Although HHS has provided four required factors to be considered in performing this more objective risk assessment to determine whether the PHI has been compromised, the Breach Regulations do not define what it means for PHI to have been "compromised."

In performing the risk assessment, covered entities and business associates are expected to evaluate the overall probability that the PHI has been compromised by considering all the factors in combination. These risk assessments must be thorough, completed in good faith, documented, and the conclusions reached must be reasonable. If an evaluation of the factors fails to demonstrate that there is a low probability that the PHI has been compromised, breach notification is required. (However, a covered entity or business associate may choose to provide the required notifications without performing a risk assessment.)[27] Whether applying an exception or the "risk of compromise" standard, the covered entity (or business associate, as applicable) has the burden of proof that notification was not required and must maintain documentation sufficient to meet that burden of proof.[28]

HHS has indicated that it will issue additional guidance to help covered entities and business associates in performing risk assessments with respect to "frequently occurring scenarios."[29] In the meantime, the preamble to the HITECH Regulations contains some examples of how HHS views the four factors in this new risk assessment, which may be instructive:

- If few or no direct identifiers are disclosed, the covered entity or business associate should determine whether there is a likelihood that the PHI could be re-identified based on the context and the ability to link the PHI to other available information.[30]

---

[24] 45 C.F.R. § 164.402 (HITECH Regulations); 78 Fed. Reg. 5641-5643 (Jan. 25, 2013). A covered entity has a duty to mitigate, to the extent practicable, any harmful effects known to the covered entity of a use or disclosure that is in violation of the Privacy Regulations or the entity's policies and procedures by the covered entity or its business associate. 45 C.F.R. § 164.530(f).

[25] 78 Fed. Reg. 5643 (Jan. 25, 2013).

[26] 78 Fed. Reg. 5642, 5643 (Jan. 25, 2013).

[27] 78 Fed. Reg. 5642 (Jan. 25, 2013).

[28] 78 Fed. Reg. 5640, 5641 (Jan. 25, 2013).

[29] 78 Fed. Reg. 5643 (Jan. 25, 2013).

[30] 78 Fed. Reg. 5642 (Jan. 25, 2013).

- If a covered entity misdirects a fax containing PHI to the wrong physician practice, but the receiving physician immediately notifies the covered entity and says he has destroyed it, the covered entity may be able to demonstrate (after performing a risk assessment) that there is a low risk that the PHI has been compromised.[31]

- If the covered entity impermissibly discloses a list of patient names, addresses, and hospital identification numbers, the PHI is clearly identifiable, and a risk assessment would likely conclude that there is more than a low probability that the information has been compromised, dependent on the other factors.[32]

- If the covered entity discloses a list of patient discharge dates and diagnoses, the entity would need to consider whether any of the individuals could be identified based on the specificity of the diagnosis, the size of the community served, or whether the unauthorized recipient may have the ability to combine the PHI with other available information to re-identify the individuals.[33]

- If the recipient of the impermissible disclosure is an employer, and the PHI contains dates of health care service and diagnoses of certain employees, the employer may be able to determine that the information pertains to specific employees based on other information available to the employer, such as dates of absence from work. In this case, there may be more than a low probability that the PHI has been compromised.[34]

- If a laptop computer was stolen and later recovered, and a forensic analysis shows that the PHI on the computer was never accessed, viewed, acquired, transferred, or otherwise compromised, the entity could conclude that the PHI was not actually acquired by an unauthorized individual even though the opportunity existed.[35] Entities in this situation may be able to demonstrate a low probability that the PHI has been compromised.[36]

- If a covered entity mailed information to the wrong individual, and the recipient opened the envelope and called the entity to report that she received the information in error, the unauthorized recipient viewed and acquired the information because she opened and read the information (as indicated by the fact she recognized it was mailed to her in error).[37]

- If a covered entity obtains the assurances of an employee, affiliated entity, business associate, or another covered entity that the entity or person destroyed PHI it received in error, the covered entity may be able to rely on such assurances. Similar assurances from other third parties may not be sufficient.[38]

A violation of the minimum necessary rule (see § 3.01[A]) can trigger breach notification obligations and must be evaluated under the same standards as any other impermissible use or disclosure. After analysis, covered entities and business associates may, for example, determine that a particular minimum necessary violation falls within the exceptions to the definition of breach. In addition, where a minimum necessary violation occurs in a disclosure to a business associate or as an internal use within a covered entity or business associate, the risk assessment can take into consideration the fact that the PHI was not acquired by a third party, which may mitigate the risk and help lead to a conclusion that there is a low probability that the PHI has been compromised.[39]

---

[31] 78 Fed. Reg. 5642 (Jan. 25, 2013).
[32] 78 Fed. Reg. 5642 (Jan. 25, 2013).
[33] 78 Fed. Reg. 5642-5643 (Jan. 25, 2013).
[34] 78 Fed. Reg. 5643 (Jan. 25, 2013).
[35] 78 Fed. Reg. 5643 (Jan. 25, 2013).
[36] 78 Fed. Reg. 5646 (Jan. 25, 2013).
[37] 78 Fed. Reg. 5643 (Jan. 25, 2013).
[38] 78 Fed. Reg. 5643 (Jan. 25, 2013).
[39] 78 Fed. Reg. 5644-5645 (Jan. 25, 2013).

§ 5.03 BREACH TREATED AS DISCOVERED

A breach is treated as "discovered" as of the first day on which the breach is known, or by exercising due diligence would have been known, to the covered entity.[40] The breach is considered discovered when the facts of the incident are first known, not when an investigation determines that the incident is a "breach" as defined by the Breach Regulations.[41] A covered entity shall be deemed to have knowledge of a breach if such breach is known or, by exercising reasonable diligence, would have been known, to any person, other than the person committing the breach, who is a workforce member or agent of the covered entity (determined in accordance with the federal common law of agency).[42] See § 5.08 for more about how this applies in the business associate context.

The covered entity is considered to have discovered the breach when anyone in its workforce (or certain business associates) discovers it. Therefore, training of all members of the workforce to promptly report any breaches to the privacy officer or other appropriate person is essential to meeting the notification timelines.

§ 5.04 TIMELINESS OF NOTIFICATION

All notifications required under the Breach Regulations must be made "without unreasonable delay and in no case later than 60 calendar days after the discovery of a breach" of unsecured PHI by the covered entity.[43] The covered entity is expected to make any required notifications as soon as reasonably possible, after the covered entity takes a reasonable amount of time to investigate the incident, and to develop the information that will be necessary to include in the notification. The 60-day mark is an outer limit, and notification may be considered late, even within those 60 days, if the delay is deemed unreasonable.[44] What is a "reasonable" delay is a fact-specific determination, and the only guidance offered by HHS is that relevant factors may include the nature of the breach, the number of individuals affected, and the covered entity's resources.[45]

The covered entity has the burden of demonstrating that all notifications were timely made as required, including evidence demonstrating the necessity of any delay (or demonstrating that the use or disclosure was not a breach of unsecured PHI).[46] If a law enforcement official determines that a breach notification, notice, or posting required to be made by the covered entity under the Act would impede a criminal investigation or cause damage to national security, such notification, notice, or posting will be delayed in the same manner as delays related to providing an accounting of disclosures.[47]

§ 5.05 INDIVIDUAL NOTIFICATION

The Breach Regulations set forth requirements both for the methods of notifying affected individuals about a breach and for the content of that notice.

---

[40] HITECH Act § 13402(c); 45 C.F.R. § 164.404(a)(2). "Exercising reasonable due diligence" is not defined here, but is used in the Enforcement Regulations at 45 C.F.R. § 160.401 (discussed in **Chapter 6**). In that context, it is intended to mean "the business care and prudence expected from a person seeking to satisfy a legal requirement under similar circumstances." 78 Fed. Reg. 5647 (Jan. 25, 2013).

[41] 78 Fed. Reg. 5648 (Jan. 25, 2013).

[42] HITECH Act § 13402(c); 45 C.F.R. § 164.404(a)(2).

[43] 45 C.F.R § 164.404(b).

[44] 78 Fed. Reg. 5648 (Jan. 25, 2013).

[45] 78 Fed. Reg. 5648 (Jan. 25, 2013).

[46] HITECH Act § 13402(d); 45 C.F.R. § 164.414.

[47] HITECH Act § 13402(g); 45 C.F.R. § 164.412. See **§ 3.02[D]** regarding the accounting of disclosures requirements.

[A] Individual Notification—Methods

Notice to affected individuals, with respect to a breach of unsecured PHI, must be provided promptly and use the following methods:[48]

- *Standard Notice*: Written notification by first-class mail to the individual at the last known address, or, if the individual agrees to electronic notification (and such agreement has not been withdrawn), by electronic mail. If covered entity knows the individual is deceased, and if it has the current address of the next of kin or personal representative, notification can be provided by first-class mail to the next of kin or personal representative (but not, apparently, by electronic means). If the affected individual is a minor or otherwise lacks capacity, the notification requirement is satisfied by notice to the parent or other personal representative. The notification may be provided in one or more mailings as information becomes available. A covered entity may mail the notification to an alternative address (e.g., a work address) if the covered entity has agreed to an individual's request that communications be sent to that address (see § 3.02[E][2]).

- *Substitute Notice*: If there is insufficient or out-of-date contact information that precludes a "standard notice" to the individual, a substitute form of notice reasonably calculated to reach the individual must be provided. The substitute notice should be provided as soon as reasonably possible after the covered entity realizes (e.g., by the return of undeliverable mail) that the contact information is deficient. However, prior to making a final determination as to how to provide substitute notice, the covered entity may try to update its contact information in order to provide a standard notice to more individuals, thus reducing the number for whom substitute notice is required. This is also important, because the number of these individuals determines the type of substitute notice required.

  If there are fewer than 10 individuals for which there is insufficient or out-of-date contact information, substitute notice may be provided by an alternative form of written notice, e-mail, website posting, telephone, or other means. If there are 10 or more individuals for which there is insufficient or out-of-date contact information, substitute notice must be in the form of a conspicuous posting (for a period of 90 days) on the home page of the covered entity's website, or conspicuous notice in major print or broadcast media in geographic areas where the individuals affected by the breach likely reside. Such a notice in media or web posting must include a toll-free phone number (available for at least 90 days) where an individual can learn whether his or her unsecured PHI is possibly included in the breach. For website notices, the home page or login page for account holders may display all the required notice information or may have a prominent hyperlink to the notice information. Substitute notice does not need to be provided to the next of kin or personal representative of a deceased individual, if only insufficient or out-of-date contact information is available.

- *Urgent Situations*: If the covered entity determines that urgent notification is needed because of possible imminent misuse of unsecured PHI, the covered entity may provide information to individuals by telephone or other means, as appropriate. This is in addition to other individual notification required under these provisions.

  Even in non-urgent circumstances, the covered entity may wish to contact the individual by phone. For example, if a health care provider is concerned that receiving the breach notification will cause the individual great distress due to the individual's circumstances, then the provider may telephone the individual or ask the individual to come to the provider's office to discuss the situation, prior to mailing the breach notification to the individual.[49] Under extremely limited circumstances (and not simply for the convenience of the covered entity), HHS may permit the breach notification to be provided orally in person or over the phone, if that is the only communication method the individual

---

[48] HITECH Act § 13402(e)(1); 45 C.F.R. § 164.404(d); 78 Fed. Reg. 5649, 5651 (Jan. 25, 2013).
[49] 78 Fed. Reg. 5651 (Jan. 25, 2013)

has agreed to, with the further expectation that the individual then come in to pick up the written notification.[50]

[B] Individual Notification—Content

The breach notification to an individual must include, to the extent possible, the following information (regardless of the method of notification):[51]

- A brief description of what happened, including the date of the breach and the date of the discovery of the breach, if known;

- A description of the *types* of unsecured PHI that were involved in the breach, such as full name, Social Security number, date of birth, home address, diagnosis, etc. (the notice is not required to include the actual PHI);

- Any steps individuals should take to protect themselves from potential harm resulting from the breach;

- A brief description of what the covered entity involved is doing to investigate the breach, to mitigate harm to the individuals, and to protect against any further breaches; and

- Contact procedures for individuals to ask questions or learn additional information, which must include a toll-free telephone number, an e-mail address, a website, or a postal address.

These content requirements give the covered entity some flexibility. The description of what happened may be a general description of the circumstances of the breach (and need not provide so much detail as to show someone how to perpetrate a future breach). Any employee sanctions imposed may be described generally ("appropriately disciplined") or more specifically ("promptly terminated"), and there is no requirement that the employee be identified. HHS is considering offering additional guidance with regard to notification content.[52]

The breach notification must be written in plain language. This means written at an appropriate reading level, using clear language and sentence structure. It should also not include extra information that distracts from the key notification messages.[53] A covered entity may also be subject to other laws relating to communications with individuals, which may, for example, require translating the notification into frequently encountered languages or providing the notification in alternate formats for individuals with disabilities.[54]

§ 5.06 MEDIA NOTIFICATION

In the event of discovery of a breach of the unsecured PHI of more than 500 residents of a state or jurisdiction, the covered entity must notify prominent media outlets serving that state or jurisdiction. The timing and content requirements are the same as for the individual notification (but, of course, would not identify the affected individuals).[55] This requirement supplements but does not replace the requirement to provide individual notice.

A press release posted on the covered entity's website does not satisfy this requirement. The media notification may be in the form of a press release, but it must be provided directly to prominent media outlets serving

---

[50] 78 Fed. Reg. 5651 (Jan. 25, 2013) (review this regulatory guidance for additional limits on this approach to breach notification).

[51] HITECH Act § 13402(f); 45 C.F.R. § 164.404(c)(1); 78 Fed. Reg. 5648-5649 (Jan. 25, 2013).

[52] 78 Fed. Reg. 5649 (Jan. 25, 2013).

[53] 45 C.F.R. § 164.404(c)(2); 78 Fed. Reg. 5648 (Jan. 25, 2013).

[54] 78 Fed. Reg. 5648 (Jan. 25, 2013).

[55] HITECH Act § 13402(e)(2); 45 C.F.R. § 164.406(c). Some breaches involving more than 500 individuals may not require media notice if they are residents of multiple states. See additional information on determining the appropriate geographic areas at 78 Fed. Reg. 5653 (Jan. 25, 2013).

the applicable geographic areas. The media outlets have no obligation to use, publish, or distribute the information it receives about the breach.[56]

§ 5.07 NOTIFICATION TO HHS

A covered entity must notify HHS following the discovery of a breach of unsecured PHI.[57]

- *Breach with respect to 500 or more individuals*: Notice must be provided to HHS at the same time as the individual written notices are sent and in the manner specified on the HHS website. For all breaches in this category, OCR will open an investigation.

- *Breach with respect to fewer than 500 individuals*: Covered entity must maintain a log or other documentation of the breach and submit such documentation annually to HHS within 60 days following the end of each calendar year for breaches discovered in that calendar year, and in the manner specified on the HHS website.

In 2015, OCR updated its online breach reporting portal.[58] It now requires users to submit information that was previously optional and collects more detailed information. Options available for selection, such as regarding safeguards in place prior to the breach, have been changed. It is now an adaptive "wizard" process that guides the user through the breach report.

HHS has also updated its website that lists all breaches involving the PHI of more than 500 individuals. For each breach, the list shows the name of the covered entity (and, if applicable, the business associate); the state; type of covered entity; the number of individuals affected; breach submission date; type of breach (e.g., theft, loss, unauthorized access, improper disposal); location of breached PHI (e.g., laptop, paper records, e-mail); and in some cases, a brief description of the incident.[59]

Beginning February 18, 2010, and annually thereafter, HHS will prepare and submit to the Committee on Finance and the Committee on Health, Education, Labor, and Pensions of the Senate and the Committee on Ways and Means and the Committee on Energy and Commerce of the House of Representatives a report containing the following information regarding breaches for which notice was provided to HHS.

- The number and nature of such breaches; and

- Actions taken in response to such breaches.[60]

The first of these reports was made to Congress in August 2011, covering 2009–2010. A second report was made in June 2014, covering 2011–2012. As required by the HITECH Act, these reports are available to the public on the OCR website.[61]

§ 5.08 BUSINESS ASSOCIATE REQUIREMENTS REGARDING A BREACH

Under the Privacy Regulations, business associates have always been required to report to the covered entity any use or disclosure of PHI not authorized under the business associate agreement of which the business associate becomes aware. In addition, under the Security Regulations, business associates have been required to

---

[56] 78 Fed. Reg. 5653 (Jan. 25, 2013).

[57] HITECH Act § 13402(e)(3); 45 C.F.R. § 164.408; 78 Fed. Reg. 5654 (Jan. 25, 2013).

[58] OCR Breach Portal, available at http://www.hhs.gov/ocr/privacy/hipaa/administrative/breachnotificationrule/brinstruction.html.

[59] HITECH Act § 13402(e)(4); 78 Fed. Reg. 5655 (Jan. 25, 2013). For the current listing, see https://ocrportal.hhs.gov/ocr/breach/breach_report.jsf.

[60] HITECH Act § 13402(i).

[61] See http://www.hhs.gov/ocr/privacy/hipaa/administrative/breachnotificationrule/breachreptmain.html.

report to the covered entity any security incidents of which they become aware. The business associate's duty to make these reports is not limited to uses, disclosures, or incidents involving breaches of unsecured PHI.

Now, under the Breach Regulations, if there is a breach of unsecured PHI, business associates have additional notice obligations. A business associate that discovers a breach of unsecured PHI must notify the covered entity of the breach, so that the covered entity can notify the affected individuals (and a subcontractor must notify its "upstream" business associate).[62] It is ultimately the covered entity's obligation to notify the individuals, although a covered entity could delegate this responsibility to a business associate under the terms of a business associate agreement.[63] In the case of a business associate that maintains PHI for multiple covered entities, the business associate need only report the breach to the covered entity whose PHI was involved. However, if the breach involves the unsecured PHI of multiple covered entities and it is unclear to which entity the PHI belonged, the business associate may need to notify many or all of the covered entities.[64]

As with a covered entity, a breach is treated as "discovered" as of the first day on which the breach is known to the business associate or, by exercising reasonable due diligence, would have been known to the business associate. A business associate shall be deemed to have knowledge of a breach if such breach is known or, by exercising reasonable diligence, would have been known, to any person, other than the person committing the breach, who is an employee, officer, or other agent of the business associate (determined in accordance with the federal common law of agency), including a subcontractor business associate.[65] If the business associate is acting as the agent of the covered entity, under the federal common law of agency, the business associate's discovery of the breach will be imputed to the covered entity. The covered entity's timeline for notification then starts on the date of the business associate's discovery of the breach, not on the date the business associate notifies the covered entity.[66] Similarly, discovery of a breach by a subcontractor business associate who is acting as the agent of the business associate would be imputed to the business associate. The notice by the business associate to the covered entity must be made without unreasonable delay and in no case later than 60 calendar days after the discovery of breach.[67]

The notice must include, to the extent possible, the identification of each individual whose unsecured PHI has been or is reasonably believed by the business associate to have been accessed, acquired, used, or disclosed in the breach. There may be situations where the business associate is unable to identify the individuals affected. For example, if a business associate is a record storage company that stores hundreds of boxes of paper records for the covered entity and one box is lost, the business associate may not be aware of which records are in the missing box.[68] The business associate must also provide the covered entity with any other available information that the covered entity is required to include in its notification to the individual, either at the time of the business associate's initial notice to the covered entity or promptly thereafter, as information becomes available to the business associate.[69] Incomplete information should not delay notice to the covered entity. The business associate has the burden of demonstrating that notifications to the covered entity were timely made or that the use or

---

[62] HITECH Act § 13402(b); 45 C.F.R. § 164.410(a)(1); 74 Fed. Reg. 42,753 (Aug. 24, 2009). The HITECH Regulations do not clearly state the obligations of a subcontractor business associate with regard to whom it must report a breach. Its contractual obligations will run to its "upstream" business associate (not to the covered entity). Therefore, it seems appropriate that the subcontractor business associate's notice obligations, in the event of a breach of unsecured PHI, would also run to its upstream business associate, not directly to the covered entity. The language of 45 C.F.R. § 164.410(a)(1), however, does not differentiate between subcontractor business associates and other business associates, and simply states that "a business associate shall . . . notify the covered entity of such breach." However, HHS did provide some guidance on this point in the Security Regulations section of the preamble to the HITECH Regulations. HHS stated that language that the reporting provisions would apply "in the same manner to subcontractors" means that a breach of unsecured PHI needs to be reported by a subcontractor "upstream" it its business associate and so on up the chain, until the covered entity is notified. 78 Fed. Reg. 5590 (Jan. 25, 2013).

[63] 78 Fed. Reg. 5650 (Jan. 25, 2013).

[64] 78 Fed. Reg. 5655 (Jan. 25, 2013); see also 78 Fed. Reg. 5651 (Jan. 25, 2013).

[65] HITECH Act § 13402(c); 45 C.F.R. § 164.410(a)(1).

[66] 78 Fed. Reg. 5655 (Jan. 25, 2013).

[67] 45 C.F.R. § 164.410(b).

[68] 78 Fed. Reg. 5655 (Jan. 25, 2013).

[69] HITECH Act § 13402(b); 45 C.F.R. § 164.410(c).

disclosure did not constitute a breach of unsecured PHI.[70] Questions of timely notification, control, responsibility, cooperation, costs, and sharing of information regarding the breach should be addressed in the business associate agreement. See **§ 3.06**.

§ 5.09 ADMINISTRATIVE REQUIREMENTS

[A] Documentation; Burden of Proof

As noted, the covered entity (and business associate, as applicable) has the burden of demonstrating that all required notifications were provided, or that the incident did not require notification. For all breaches reported to OCR that involve more than 500 individuals, OCR will open an investigation and will likely request additional information. The covered entity (and business associate, as applicable) should maintain documentation that all required notifications were made and all other requirements were met, including:

- A written description of all relevant facts of the incident and supporting documentation related to the investigation, such as policies and procedures, business associate agreements, security risk analysis and risk management reports, system activity reports, reports of forensic analysis, and training records.

- Determination of whether the incident met the definition of "breach," or if one of the three exceptions applied.

- Documentation that the PHI was not "unsecured," if applicable. This could include evidence regarding the encryption of electronic PHI.

- Documentation describing and analyzing *all four factors* in the "low probability of compromise analysis." This is especially important if the conclusion is that notification is not required.

- Date the breach was discovered (and how it was discovered).

- Copies of the individual notifications sent, date sent, and list of individual recipients.

- If substitute notice is used, documentation regarding which individuals required substitute notice and why, and how notice was provided.

- Copies of website notices used as substitute notices.

- If media notice was required, a dated copy of the press release and documentation of the media outlets that received it. If the individuals were from multiple jurisdictions, documentation of the determination regarding which media outlets to contact. Copies of resulting media coverage (if any) can provide additional evidence that the media notices were sent.

- Copy of the notification to HHS and the date sent.

- Documentation of mitigation, corrective action, and other follow-up actions, such as employee sanctions, additional training, adoption of new technologies, revised policies and procedures, updated risk management plans, and providing individuals with credit monitoring services.

[B] Notice of Privacy Practices

As discussed in **§ 3.02[A]**, the HITECH Regulations added a requirement that the covered entity's notice of privacy practices include a statement of the covered entity's duty to notify the individual following a breach of unsecured PHI. HHS believes that this advance notice of their rights will provide "helpful context" for

---

[70] HITECH Act § 13402(d); 45 C.F.R. § 164.414. As with notifications by a covered entity, if a law enforcement official determines that a breach notification by a business associate would impede a criminal investigation or cause damage to national security, delays are allowed in the same manner as for accountings of disclosures. HITECH Act § 13402(g); 45 C.F.R. § 164.412.

individuals who later receive a breach notification. A simple statement in the notice of privacy practices is sufficient.[71]

[C] Other Administrative Requirements

As discussed in § 3.05, the Privacy Regulations have administrative requirements that apply in the context of breach notification. These include having breach notification policies and procedures, training workforce members on these policies and procedures, employee sanctions for noncompliance, and the duty to mitigate, in the event of a breach.[72]

§ 5.10 RECONCILIATION WITH OTHER BREACH NOTIFICATION REQUIREMENTS

Almost all states require individual notification in the event of certain breaches of privacy or security of personal information (especially Social Security numbers).[73] In addition, CMS has issued security incident and privacy breach reporting procedures for its contractors (including Medicare Advantage Plans and Part D Prescription Drug Plans).[74] The scope of the Breach Regulations' breach notification requirements will often be broader than other laws, and notifications will be required under more circumstances. Covered entities and business associates will need to compare the Breach Regulations and state law regarding the timing, notification content, and other requirements. In most cases, covered entities and business associates will need to comply with both the Breach Regulations and state law. New federal breach notification laws are also being considered.[75]

---

[71] 78 Fed. Reg. 5624-5625 (Jan. 25, 2013).

[72] See § 3.05 for additional information; see also, OCR, Breach Notification Rule, available at http://www.hhs.gov/ocr/privacy/hipaa/administrative/breachnotificationrule/index.html.

[73] See, e.g., Cal. Civ. Code § 1798.82; Minn. Stat. § 325E.61 and § 72A.502; N.C. Gen. Stat. § 75-60 et seq.; Wis. Stat. § 134.98; NY Bus. Law § 899-aa.

[74] CMS, Letter re "Update on Security and Privacy Breach Reporting Procedures," Sept. 28, 2010.

[75] See, e.g., the Personal Data Notification & Protection Act, proposed by the White House in January 2015 at https://www.whitehouse.gov/sites/default/files/omb/legislative/letters/updated-data-breach-notification.pdf.

CHAPTER 6

ENFORCEMENT

§ 6.01 ENFORCEMENT

This chapter examines the enforcement of the Administrative Simplification Regulations. It reviews the policy and structure of the current compliance process, enforcement authority, civil investigations and penalties, criminal cases and penalties, audits and compliance reviews, and other ways the Regulations are used to enforce individual privacy rights. It also reviews the significant changes made to enforcement of the Regulations by the Health Information Technology for Economic and Clinical Health (HITECH) Act, Title XIII of the American Recovery and Reinvestment Act of 2009 (ARRA) and the HITECH Regulations.[1]

[A] Who Is Subject to Enforcement?

Originally only covered entities were subject to civil monetary penalties under the Administrative Simplification Regulations.[2] Under the HITECH Act, effective February 18, 2010, business associates are also subject to civil penalties for violation of the Regulations. Business associates are required to comply with the business associate provisions of the Privacy Regulations and with the Security Regulations and are subject to civil monetary penalties for violations of these requirements. See § 1.02[B] for details regarding the provisions of the Privacy and Security Regulations for which a business associate is now directly liable.[3]

[1] Multiple Covered Entities or Business Associates

If HHS determines that more than one covered entity or business associate is responsible for a violation, it will impose a civil monetary penalty against each covered entity or business associate. In the case of affiliated covered entities, each covered entity that is a member would be jointly and severally liable for a violation by the affiliation, unless it is established that another member of the affiliated covered entity was responsible for the violation.[4] Covered entities that are part of other types of joint arrangements, such as organized health care arrangements, are not, by virtue of such arrangements, automatically responsible for a violation by another covered entity in the arrangement. The relationship may, however, be a factor in HHS's analysis.[5]

[2] Liability for Acts of Agents, Employees, and Business Associates

As noted above, under the HITECH Act, effective February 18, 2010, business associates are subject to direct civil and criminal penalties for violation of the Administrative Simplification Regulations.[6] Covered entities and business associates may also become subject to liability *indirectly*.

A covered entity or business associate may be held vicariously liable for the acts or omissions of its agents, in accordance with the federal common law of agency, who are acting within the scope of that agency. The Enforcement Rule creates a presumption that a workforce member is an agent of the covered entity or business associate with respect to the workforce member's conduct under the Administrative Simplification Regulations, such as using and disclosing PHI.[7] Workforce members of a covered entity or business associate may include employees, independent contractors, volunteers, and trainees under the supervision of academic programs, among others, who are under the direct control of the covered entity (or business associate).[8]

---

[1] Pub. L. No. 111-5 (Feb. 17, 2009); HITECH Regulations, 78 Fed. Reg. 5577 (Jan. 25, 2013) (which included amendments to finalize the Enforcement Rule, previously issued as an interim final rule, at 74 Fed. Reg. 56,123 (Oct. 30, 2009).

[2] 45 C.F.R. § 160.402(a).

[3] HITECH Act §§ 13401(b), 13404(c); 78 Fed. Reg. 5577 (Jan. 15, 2013).

[4] 45 C.F.R. § 160.402(b).

[5] 71 Fed. Reg. 8402 (Feb. 16, 2006). See § 1.02[C] for more information about these organizational structures.

[6] HITECH Act § 13401(b), § 13404(c).

[7] 45 C.F.R. § 160.402(c); 71 Fed. Reg. 8403 (Feb. 16, 2006).

[8] 71 Fed. Reg. 8403 (Feb. 16, 2006).

The covered entity was previously able to insulate itself from vicarious liability for the acts of the business associate by entering into a HIPAA-compliant business associate agreement (provided that the covered entity either did not know of a practice or pattern of activity of the business associate that violates the Administrative Simplification Regulations or, upon learning of such pattern or practice, took the required steps to address the situation).[9] Effective with the HITECH Regulations, HHS has changed this approach.

Notwithstanding any business associate agreement, a covered entity is now liable for the acts or omissions of its business associates who are its agents, under the federal common law of agency. Similarly, a business associate is liable for the acts or omissions of its subcontractor business associates.[10] HHS states that this is necessary so that, where the covered entity has delegated a particular HIPAA obligation, such as distribution of its notice of privacy practices, the covered entity remains liable for the failure of its business associate to perform that obligation on the covered entity's behalf.[11] Although this is an understandable concern, this is a limited explanation for such a sweeping change. The only other explanation from HHS for eliminating the protection that a business associate agreement previously offered is that "a covered entity's liability for acts of its agents is customary under common law."[12]

The determination of whether a business associate is an agent of a covered entity (or whether a subcontractor is the agent of the business associate) under the federal common law of agency is a case-by-case determination, taking into account the terms of the business associate agreement but based on all the facts of the relationship, particularly the level of control over the business associate's conduct.[13] HHS describes the essential factor in determining whether an agency relationship exists as being the right or authority to control the business associate's conduct in the course of performing the services. A covered entity's right to give interim instructions or directions to the business associate is the type of control that distinguishes an agency relationship from a non-agency relationship.[14] For example, according to HHS, if with respect to the section of the business associate agreement relating to responding to requests from individuals for access to their PHI, the agreement says that the business associate will make this PHI available based on instructions to be provided by or under the direction of the covered entity, then an agency relationship is created for this activity.[15] This is because the covered entity retains the right to give additional, interim direction to the business associate as to how the services will be performed. It is worth noting that HHS indicates, in the preceding example, that agency is created for the particular activity, which implies that agency may not necessarily attach to other aspects of the relationship between the parties. Similarly, HHS also states that agency can be established even if the covered entity "does not retain the right or authority to control every aspect of its business associate's activities."[16] Furthermore, it is the authority to exercise control over the performance of the service that creates the agency relationship, even if the covered entity does not exercise that authority.[17]

Statements in a business associate agreement (e.g., disclaiming an agency relationship) or labels used (e.g., "independent contractor") do not settle the question. The manner in which the covered entity does (or does not) control performance of the service provided is the decisive factor.[18] HHS gives some examples to illustrate additional relevant factors important to the agency analysis:[19]

---

[9] 45 C.F.R. § 160.402(c) (prior to the HITECH Regulations' changes); 78 Fed. Reg. 5580 (Jan. 25, 2013).

[10] 45 C.F.R. § 160.402(c).

[11] 75 Fed. Reg. 40,868, 40,879–40,880 (July 14, 2010).

[12] 78 Fed. Reg. 5581 (Jan. 25, 2013).

[13] 78 Fed. Reg. 5581 (Jan. 25, 2013); 75 Fed. Reg. 40,868, 40,880 (July 14, 2010). The same analysis under the federal common law of agency applies to the relationship between a covered entity and business associate, and between a business associate and its subcontractor. For simplicity, it is discussed in this section in terms of a covered entity and its business associate.

[14] 78 Fed. Reg. 5581 (Jan. 25, 2013).

[15] 78 Fed. Reg. 5581 (Jan. 25, 2013).

[16] 78 Fed. Reg. 5582 (Jan. 25, 2013).

[17] 78 Fed. Reg. 5582 (Jan. 25, 2013).

[18] 78 Fed. Reg. 5581 (Jan. 25, 2013).

[19] 78 Fed. Reg. 5581–5582 (Jan. 25, 2013).

- *The type of service and skill level required to perform the service.* For example, a business associate that is hired to de-identify PHI for a small provider would likely not be an agent because the small provider likely would not have the expertise to provide interim instructions regarding how to perform de-identification.

- *Whether the covered entity is legally or otherwise prevented from performing the service or activity performed by its business associate.* For example, an accreditation agency (business associate) is likely not the agent of the covered entity, because the covered entity cannot perform the accreditation service and accredit itself.

Another key issue with regard to liability of a covered entity for the acts or omissions of the business associate (or liability of a business associate for the acts of a subcontractor) is the *scope* of any agency created. Under the federal common law of agency, for the principal to be liable, the agent must be acting within the scope of the agency.[20] This is also a "facts and circumstances" test. Important factors to consider in analyzing the scope of agency are:

- The time, place, and purpose of the business associate's conduct;

- Whether the business associate agent was engaged in a course of conduct subject to the covered entity's control;

- Whether the conduct is commonly done by a business associate to perform the service on behalf of a covered entity; and

- Whether the covered entity would reasonably expect that a business associate would engage in the conduct in question.[21]

HHS states that deviation from the terms of the business associate agreement does not automatically put the business associate's activities outside the scope of the agency. In fact, a business associate agent's conduct is generally within the scope of agency, if the conduct occurs during the performance of or incident to the assigned services. It does not matter that the services were performed carelessly, a mistake was made in the performance of the service, or even that the business associate disregarded specific instructions from the covered entity. HHS gives two examples to illustrate this. First, a business associate agent is likely within the scope of that agency if it impermissibly discloses more than the minimum necessary PHI, even if the disclosure is contrary to clear instructions from the covered entity. In contrast, if the business associate agent is doing something that is solely for its own benefit (or that of a third party), or other conduct not intended to serve any purpose of the covered entity, that conduct would generally be outside the scope of the agency.[22]

[3] Criminal Prosecution

Any person, whether a covered entity, a business associate, an employee of a covered entity, or any other person, can be subject to criminal prosecution under HIPAA, if he or she knowingly and in a manner contrary to HIPAA obtains or discloses PHI that is maintained by a covered entity.[23]

There had been debate over the scope of the criminal liability provision since 2005, when the DOJ Office of Legal Counsel published an opinion prepared for HHS and the U.S. Attorney General regarding who could be

---

[20] 78 Fed. Reg. 5582 (Jan. 25, 2013).

[21] 78 Fed. Reg. 5581 (Jan. 25, 2013).

[22] 78 Fed. Reg. 5582 (Jan. 25, 2013). In addition, in the guidance provided with the HITECH Regulations, HHS states that if a business associate agent fails to notify the covered entity of a violation of the Regulations, that agent may be acting outside the scope of its authority as agent, and in such a case, the agent's knowledge is not imputed to the principal. 78 Fed. Reg. 5587 (Jan. 25, 2013).

[23] HITECH Act § 13409 (effective Feb. 18, 2010). Under the HITECH Act, effective February 18, 2010, business associates are also specifically made subject to criminal liability for violation of the Privacy and Security Regulations. HITECH Act §§ 13401(b); 13404(c).

subject to criminal prosecution under the Administrative Simplification Regulations.[24] This "June 2005 Memorandum" concluded that only covered entities (and certain of their directors, officers, and employees) could be directly liable but that other persons could be indirectly liable under principles of conspiracy and aiding and abetting. Other opinions followed, interpreting the June 2005 Memorandum and discussing how it applied in the first HIPAA prosecutions and could be used to prosecute noncovered entities.[25] As of February 18, 2010, the question is settled by the HITECH Act, which clarifies that criminal liability for wrongfully obtaining or disclosing PHI can attach to any person who without appropriate authorization obtains or discloses PHI maintained by a covered entity, specifically rejecting any limitations suggested by the June 2005 Memorandum.[26]

See §§ **6.06** and **6.07** for more information on criminal penalties and enforcement actions.

[B] Enforcement Principles

The Department of Health and Human Services (HHS) has generally favored an approach of encouraging voluntary compliance and seeking informal resolution of complaints as a means of quickly and efficiently achieving compliance. To the extent practicable (and allowed by law), HHS seeks the cooperation of the covered entities and business associates in obtaining compliance and may provide technical assistance to help them comply voluntarily with the applicable Administrative Simplification Regulations.[27]

Although HHS will still generally try to correct noncompliance through voluntary corrective action, the HITECH Act now *requires* that HHS formally investigate complaints where a preliminary review of the facts indicates a possible violation due to "willful neglect."[28] In updating the Enforcement Rule in the HITECH Regulations, HHS noted that, "as a practical matter," this did not change anything, since they were already reviewing every complaint and initiating an investigation if that review indicated a possible violation of the Regulations.[29] Nevertheless, HHS retains the discretion as to whether or not to conduct a formal investigation in the event the preliminary review of the facts does not indicate willful neglect.[30]

HHS intends to conduct compliance reviews on a similar basis. A compliance review is an investigation of an allegation of a violation of the Regulations that comes to the attention of HHS other than through a complaint; for example, HHS sees a media account or receives a referral from another government agency.[31] As with complaints, HHS will conduct a formal investigation if a preliminary review of the facts indicates willful neglect.[32] See § **6.03** for additional information on complaints and § **6.09** for further information on compliance reviews and audits.

Finally, as detailed in § **6.07**, the number of HIPAA criminal prosecutions has been increasing. Both with regard to civil and criminal actions, the HITECH Act's expansion of the enforcement provisions has signaled a transformation of HHS's enforcement approach.

---

[24] Steve G. Bradbury, DOJ Office of Legal Counsel, Scope of Criminal Enforcement Under 42 U.S.C. § 1320d-6, Memorandum Opinion for the General Counsel HHS and Senior Counsel to the Deputy Attorney General (June 1, 2005) (hereinafter "June 2005 Memorandum"), available at http://www.justice.gov/sites/default/files/olc/opinions/attachments/2014/11/17/hipaa_final.htm.

[25] Winn, Peter A., "Criminal Prosecutions under HIPAA," The United States Attorneys' Bulletin (Sept. 2005); Smith DeWaal, Ian C., "Successfully Prosecuting Health Insurance Portability and Accountability Act Medical Privacy Violations Against Noncovered Entities," The United States Attorneys' Bulletin (July 2007) (hereinafter "Smith DeWaal").

[26] HITECH Act § 13409; Conference Report on H.R. 1, American Recovery and Reinvestment Act of 2009 (House of Representatives—Feb. 12, 2009), p. H1433 (Congress's conference committee report on HITECH).

[27] 45 C.F.R. § 160.304.

[28] HITECH Act § 13410(a); 45 C.F.R. § 160.306(c)(1).

[29] 45 C.F.R. § 160.306(c)(1); 78 Fed. Reg. 5578 (Jan. 25, 2013).

[30] 45 C.F.R. § 160.306(c)(2); 78 Fed. Reg. 5578 (Jan. 25, 2013).

[31] 78 Fed. Reg. 5579 (Jan. 25, 2013).

[32] 45 C.F.R. § 160.308; 78 Fed. Reg. 5578, 5579 (Jan. 25, 2013).

[C] Responsibility for Enforcement

[1] Federal Enforcement

The HHS Office of Civil Rights (OCR) is charged with administering and enforcing compliance with the Privacy Regulations, Security and Breach Regulations, and the HHS Centers for Medicare & Medicaid Services (CMS) is charged with administering and enforcing compliance with the Transaction Standards.[33] HHS enforces the civil monetary penalties, and the U.S. Department of Justice (DOJ) enforces the criminal penalties.[34]

OCR maintains a Privacy and Security Enforcement Website, and CMS maintains an Enforcement Website related to the Transaction Standards.[35] These Websites describe agency activities in enforcing the Regulations, the results of those activities, and enforcement statistics regarding complaints. The Websites also provide information on filing complaints and anonymous case examples of complaints and investigations for educational purposes. Beginning in 2009, OCR also posts information regarding breaches of unsecured PHI affecting 500 or more individuals, briefly summarizing each breach and identifying the covered entities and business associates involved.[36]

The Federal Trade Commission (FTC) can bring charges under the FTC Act to protect consumers against unfair and deceptive practices regarding collection, use, and security of consumers' personal information.[37] The FTC also enforces its own breach notification regulations, which are very similar to HHS's breach notification regulations but apply to vendors of personal health records (PHRs), PHR-related entities, and third party service providers (but not to covered entities or business associates).[38] The FTC enforcement initiatives are beyond the scope of this book.

[2] State Attorney General Enforcement

As a result of the HITECH Act, State Attorneys General now have the authority to bring a civil action under HIPAA on behalf of residents of their states in a U.S. district court to obtain injunctions or civil damages on behalf of those residents. The Attorney General must have reason to believe the interests of a state resident has been or is threatened or adversely affected by someone's violation of the Regulations.[39] This is in addition to any and all enforcement powers the Attorney General has under state law.

Damages are limited to amounts equal to the first tier of civil damages (described in §6.02[A]). With respect to the calculation of damages (including counting the number of violations and factors to be considered in determining the amount of damages) the State Attorney General must follow the same process established for HHS. In addition, the state action is subject to the same six-year statute of limitations as HHS actions. If the State Attorney General wins the case, the court may in its discretion award the costs of the action and reasonable attorney fees to the state.[40]

---

[33] 70 Fed. Reg. 15,329 (Mar. 25, 2005); 70 Fed. Reg. 20,226 (Apr. 18, 2005); 71 Fed. Reg. 8391 (Feb. 16, 2006); 74 Fed. Reg. 38,663 (Aug. 4, 2009). On July 27, 2009, HHS delegated authority for administering and enforcing the Security Regulations to OCR, transferring this authority from CMS. 74 Fed. Reg. 38,630 (Aug. 4, 2009).

[34] 71 Fed. Reg. 8390 (Feb. 16, 2006).

[35] See http://www.hhs.gov/ocr/privacy/hipaa/enforcement/index.html and http://www.cms.gov/Regulations-and-Guidance/HIPAA-Administrative-Simplification/ComplianceandEnforcement/.

[36] Available at https://ocrportal.hhs.gov/ocr/breach/breach_report.jsf. Also see **Chapter 5** regarding breach notification requirements.

[37] 15 U.S.C. §§41–58. Section 5 of the FTC Act prohibits unfair or deceptive acts or practices in the marketplace. The FTC also acts to protect consumers in privacy-related enforcement actions under the Gramm-Leach-Bliley Act, the Fair Credit Reporting Act, and the Children's Online Privacy Protection Act. See generally the FTC Privacy Initiatives site at http://business.ftc.gov/privacy-and-security.

[38] FTC Health Breach Notification Rule, 74 Fed. Reg. 42,962 (Aug. 25, 2009).

[39] HITECH Act §13410(e)(1). The authority of the State Attorneys General is effective for violations occurring after February 18, 2009. HITECH Act §13410(e)(3).

[40] HITECH Act §13410(e)(1).

Any such state action must be coordinated with HHS action on the same matter. The State Attorney General must provide advance written notice of any such civil action to HHS and provide HHS with a copy of the state complaint. If prior notice is not feasible, the state must provide notice immediately upon instituting legal action. HHS has the right to intervene in the action. If HHS has already instituted its own action against a person with respect to a specific violation of the Regulations, no State Attorney General may bring an action until the federal action is concluded.[41] To assist Attorneys General in their new enforcement authority under HIPAA, HHS awarded a $1.7 million contract for development of a series of training seminars for State Attorneys General.[42] In 2011, OCR held two-day seminars for State Attorneys General, which included a general introduction to the Privacy and Security Regulations, the impact of HITECH, a review of HIPAA and state law, investigative techniques for identifying and prosecuting potential violations, State Attorneys General roles and responsibilities, resources available to State Attorneys General in pursuing alleged HIPAA violations, and more.[43] In 2012, HHS made these training materials public, and they are available online.[44]

Only a few State Attorneys General have used these new enforcement powers under the HITECH Act. The first was the Connecticut Attorney General, who in January 2010 sued a health plan, Health Net, for allegedly failing to secure member medical records and financial information, in connection with a missing portable computer disk drive that contained the PHI of 1.5 million individuals, including 446,000 Connecticut enrollees.[45] A settlement was reached in July 2010, which included a $250,000 payment to the state and a corrective action plan.[46] The Attorney General of Vermont later filed a complaint against the health plan relating to the same incident because the data had included the records of 525 Vermont residents. A settlement was reached, which included a payment to the state in the amount of $55,000.[47] Two State Attorneys General issued complaints and entered into settlements with regard to this 2009 incident, but that does not account for all 1.5 million individuals, so there could have been legal action from other states. One lesson to covered entities is that if there is a breach involving residents of multiple states, be prepared for multiple State Attorney General actions.

The Massachusetts Attorney General was the next to bring charges under HIPAA against a covered entity and has been the most active State Attorney General enforcing HIPAA. The first Massachusetts case, as reported by the Attorney General, arose from a 2010 incident where South Shore Hospital shipped three boxes of unencrypted backup computer tapes to a vendor to be erased. Only one of the boxes arrived; the other two boxes were never recovered. There were no reports of unauthorized access to the data on the missing tapes, which included the PHI of 800,000 individuals, according to the Attorney General's statement. The Attorney General filed a lawsuit against the hospital, alleging violations of HIPAA and the State Consumer Protection Act, including failure to implement appropriate safeguards, policies, and procedures to protect consumer information; failing to have a business associate agreement in place with the vendor; and failing to properly train its workforce on privacy matters. The Attorney General also criticized the hospital for not informing the vendor that there was PHI on the tapes and for not determining whether the vendor had sufficient safeguards in place to protect the PHI. South Shore Hospital made no admissions, but in May 2012 entered into a settlement agreement with the

---

[41] HITECH Act § 13410(e)(1).

[42] HIPAA Enforcement Training for State Attorneys General, Solicitation #OS16885, awarded March 5, 2010.

[43] OCR, "HIPAA Enforcement Training for State Attorneys General," available at http://www.hhs.gov/ocr/privacy/hipaa/enforcement/sag/sagmoreinfo.html.

[44] HHS, "HIPAA Enforcement Training for State Attorneys General," available at http://www.hhshipaasagtraining.com.

[45] See Connecticut Attorney General's Office press release, "Attorney General Sues Health Net for Massive Security Breach Involving Private Medical Records and Financial Information on 446,000 Enrollees" (Jan. 13, 2010), available at http://www.ct.gov/ag/cwp/view.asp?A=2341&Q=453918.

[46] See Connecticut Attorney General's Office press release, "Attorney General Announces Health Net Settlement Involving Massive Security Breach Compromising Private Medical and Financial Info" (July 6, 2010), available at http://www.ct.gov/ag/cwp/view.asp?A=2341&Q=462754 (with a link to the settlement agreement).

[47] See Vermont Attorney General's Office press releases "Attorney General Settles Security Breach Allegations Against Health Insurer" (Jan. 18, 2011) and "Court Approves Attorney General HIPAA Settlement With Health Insurer," (Jan. 26, 2011) available, respectively, at http://ago.vermont.gov/focus/news/attorney-general-settles-security-breach-allegations-against-health-insurer.php and http://ago.vermont.gov/focus/news/court-approves-attorney-general-hipaa-settlement-with-health-insurer.php.

Attorney General, agreeing to pay a monetary settlement of $750,000. The settlement agreement also requires South Shore Hospital to take numerous steps to ensure future compliance, including requirements relating to business associate agreements and making inquiries into business associate security practices.[48] In 2013, in another case, the Massachusetts Attorney General entered into settlement agreements with the former owners of a medical billing company and four pathology groups, for a total of $140,000, which settled allegations that PHI for tens of thousands of patients were improperly disposed of at a public dump by the billing company. In addition to allegations based on state law, the Attorney General alleged violations of HIPAA by the four pathology groups, for failing to have appropriate safeguards in place to protect PHI they provided to the billing company.[49] These two Massachusetts cases are reminders that covered entities have an obligation under the Privacy and Security Regulations to securely dispose of PHI (see § 3.05[C]), and if the covered entity engages a vendor for disposal of PHI, that vendor is a business associate. Business associate agreements are required, and reasonable steps should be taken to ensure that the business associate can maintain appropriate security measures.

The third Massachusetts case also involved backup tapes. The Attorney General alleged that Women & Infants Hospital lost track of 19 unencrypted backup tapes from two of the hospital's locations, one in Massachusetts and one in Rhode Island, containing data (including patient names, Social Security numbers, and medical information) of more than 12,000 patients who were Massachusetts residents.[50] According to the Attorney General, the hospital shipped the computer backup tapes offsite in 2011 for the data to be transferred to a new system. Allegedly, the hospital did not realize the tapes were missing until 2012, due to an inadequate inventory and tracking system; and furthermore, the breach was not promptly reported due to deficient employee training and policies. The hospital entered into a settlement agreement, and although it made no admissions, agreed to pay $150,000 and take certain steps to ensure future compliance.[51] The Attorney General complaint raised both HIPAA and State law claims, and is of particular note because it demonstrates that an Attorney General will take actions to protect the PHI of her state's residents, even against a provider located in another state.

In late 2014, the Massachusetts Attorney General entered into two more settlement agreements, one with Beth Israel Deaconess Medical Center (BIDMC) and the other with Boston Children's Hospital (BCH), each involving a laptop stolen from a physician, which contained unencrypted patient PHI. In the BIDMC case, according to the Attorney General, in May 2012, an unauthorized person gained access to a BIDMC physician's office on the medical center campus and stole the laptop. The office was unlocked, the laptop was unattended on the desk, and it was unencrypted. The laptop was not BIDMC property but was regularly used by the physician for BIDMC business with BIDMC's knowledge. The Attorney General further alleged that the laptop contained the PHI of 3,796 patients and employees, and the physician and his staff were not following BIDMC policy requiring the encryption and physical security of laptops containing PHI.[52] In the BCH case, the Attorney General alleged that, while a BCH physician was at a conference in Argentina in May 2012, his unencrypted

---

[48] Attorney General of Massachusetts, "South Shore to Pay $750,000 to Settle Data Breach Allegations" (May 24, 2012), Press Release, available at http://www.mass.gov/ago/news-and-updates/press-releases/2012/2012-05-24-south-shore-hospital-data-breach-settlement.html; Final Judgment by Consent of Defendant South Shore Hospital, C.A. 14-2332G (Mass. Sup. Ct. July 22, 2014).

[49] Attorney General of Massachusetts, "Former Owners of Medical Billing Practice, Pathology Groups, Agree to Pay $140,000 to Settle Claims that Patients' Health Information was Disposed of at Georgetown Dump," (Jan. 7, 2013), Press Release, available at http://www.mass.gov/ago/news-and-updates/press-releases/2013/140k-settlement-over-medical-info-disposed-of-at-dump.html.

[50] Attorney General of Massachusetts, "Women & Infants Hospital to Pay $150,000 to Settle Data Breach Allegations Involving Massachusetts Patients" (July 23, 2014), Press Release, available at http://www.mass.gov/ago/news-and-updates/press-releases/2014/2014-07-23-women-infants-hospital.html; Final Judgment by Consent of Defendant Women & Infants Hospital of Rhode Island, C.A. 14-2332G (Mass. Sup. Ct. July 22, 2014).

[51] Attorney General of Massachusetts, "Women & Infants Hospital to Pay $150,000 to Settle Data Breach Allegations Involving Massachusetts Patients" (July 23, 2014), Press Release, available at http://www.mass.gov/ago/news-and-updates/press-releases/2014/2014-07-23-women-infants-hospital.html; Final Judgment by Consent of Defendant Women & Infants Hospital of Rhode Island, Civ. 14-2332G (Mass. Sup. Ct. July 22, 2014).

[52] Attorney General of Massachusetts, "Beth Israel Deaconess Medical Center to Pay $100,000 Over Data Breach Allegations" (Nov. 21, 2014), Press Release, available at http://www.mass.gov/ago/news-and-updates/press-releases/2014/2014-11-21-beth-israel-data-breach.html; Final Judgment by Consent of Defendant Beth Israel Deaconess Medical Center, Inc., Civ. 14-3627G (Mass. Sup. Ct. Nov. 20, 2014).

BCH-issued laptop was stolen. It contained the PHI of 2,159 BCH patients, including names, dates of birth, and medical information, which the physician had received in an e-mail from a colleague. Despite BCH policies, the laptop was not encrypted.[53] Both BIDMC and BCH entered into settlement agreements regarding both State law and HIPAA charges and, without any admissions, agreed to pay $100,000 and $40,000, respectively, and take certain steps to ensure future compliance, including properly tracking portable devices such as laptops as well as encrypting and physically securing those devices. The lessons from these two cases are familiar but worth repeating: Have clear written policies regarding encryption of portable devices containing PHI, and make certain that the policies are followed and the devices are appropriately encrypted.

The Minnesota Attorney General, in a lawsuit filed in January 2012, was the first to file HIPAA charges directly against a business associate.[54] The Minnesota case arose from the theft of a laptop. Accretive Health was the business associate of two covered entities, Fairview Health Services and North Memorial Hospital. The complaint states that the PHI of at least 23,531 patients of these hospitals was downloaded to the unencrypted laptop of an Accretive Health employee, and the laptop was stolen from the backseat of the employee's rental car in July 2011.[55] The Minnesota Attorney General's complaint alleges violations of HIPAA, as well as violations of state consumer protection, debt collection practices, and medical records laws. Count I of the complaint relates to HIPAA. The Attorney General begins by explaining that under the HITECH Act, a business associate is directly subject to the Security Regulations and can be held liable under HIPAA for civil and criminal penalties. The complaint then alleges that Accretive Health, as a business associate, violated HIPAA by failing to comply with HIPAA standards, including several enumerated administrative, physical, and technical security provisions of the Security Regulations.[56] The complaint asks for civil penalties under HIPAA and attorneys' fees and costs.[57] Accretive Health vociferously defended itself, and what followed was a series of public hearings, motions to dismiss, and amended complaints, followed by a Settlement Agreement in August 2012.[58] Under the Settlement Agreement, Accretive Health agreed to pay about $2.5 million to the State of Minnesota and to cease business operations in the State for two years. If Accretive Health wishes to return to Minnesota in the four years after that, it must seek a Consent Decree from the Attorney General. Accretive Health was also required to destroy or return to its Minnesota hospital clients all patient information in its possession (a standard business associate process for when a business associate agreement terminates). Accretive Health admitted no liability or wrongdoing.[59] In 2014, Accretive Health entered into a settlement agreement with the Federal Trade Commission (FTC) to settle charges that it had "unfairly exposed sensitive consumer information to the risk of theft or misuse because of its inadequate data security measures." Under the terms of the 20-year agreement, Accretive

---

[53] Attorney General of Massachusetts, "Boston Children's Hospital Settles Data Breach Allegations" (Dec. 19, 2014), Press Release, available at http://www.mass.gov/ago/news-and-updates/press-releases/2014/2014-12-19-boston-childrens.html; Final Judgment by Consent of Defendant Boston Children's Hospital, Civ. 14-3955B (Mass. Sup. Ct. Dec. 19, 2014).

[54] This action was brought after the HITECH Act established direct liability for business associates, but before publication of the final HITECH Regulations.

[55] Minnesota v. Accretive Health, Inc., Civil File No. 12-145, Complaint (D. Minn. Jan. 19, 2012); Office of Attorney General, "Attorney General Swanson Sues Accretive Health for Patient Privacy Violation," Press Release (Jan. 19, 2012), formerly available at http://www.ag.state.mn.us/Consumer/PressRelease/120119AccretiveHealth.asp.

[56] Minnesota v. Accretive Health, Inc., Civil File No. 12-145, Complaint (D. Minn. Jan. 19, 2012). The Minnesota Attorney General also issued a separate six-volume "Compliance Review of Fairview Health Services' Management Contracts with Accretive Health, Inc." (Apr. 2012), available at http://www.ag.state.mn.us/Consumer/Health. Volume 4 of this report is titled "Privacy Violations" and alleges "multiple violations of patient privacy rights under federal and state law."

[57] Minnesota v. Accretive Health, Inc., Civil File No. 12-145, Complaint (D. Minn. Jan. 19, 2012). The Attorney General moved to amend its complaint to add new allegations, including an allegation that Accretive Health and North Memorial did not enter into a business associate agreement. Minnesota v. Accretive Health, Inc., Civil File No. 12-145, Second Amended and Supplemental Complaint (D. Minn. June 19, 2012).

[58] See, e.g., Minnesota v. Accretive Health, Inc., Civil File No. 12-145, Motion to Dismiss (D. Minn. Apr. 30, 2012); Minnesota v. Accretive Health, Inc., Civil File No. 12-145, Second Amended and Supplemental Complaint (D. Minn. June 19, 2012); Minnesota v. Accretive Health, Inc., Civil File No. 12-145, Motion to Dismiss Second Amended Complaint (D. Minn. July 3, 2012). Minnesota v. Accretive Health, Inc., Civil File No. 12-145, Settlement Agreement, Release and Order (D. Minn. Aug. 7, 2012).

[59] Minnesota v. Accretive Health, Inc., Civil File No. 12-145, Settlement Agreement, Release and Order (D. Minn. Aug. 7, 2012).

Health will be required to establish a comprehensive security program, which will be evaluated initially and then every two years, by a certified third party.[60]

Finally, another Attorney General action regarding disposal of patient records was settled in 2015 in Indiana. This was Indiana's first enforcement action under HIPAA. The Indiana Attorney General filed a lawsuit against an Indiana dentist for improperly disposing of records of more than 5600 patients, alleging violations of State law and HIPAA. According to the Attorney General, the dentist hired a vendor to dispose of his patient records. More than 60 boxes of patient records were discarded in a dumpster. The dentist agreed to a settlement, requiring payment of a $12,000 penalty.[61] As in the Massachusetts cases discussed above, this is yet another reminder about the care that must be taken to dispose of PHI securely, and the importance of engaging business associates who understand the HIPAA requirements.

§ 6.02   HIPAA CIVIL PENALTIES

The Enforcement Rule, which applies to all the Administrative Simplification Regulations, was published on February 16, 2006, and became effective March 16, 2006.[62] It set policies for determining violations and calculating civil monetary penalties and established rules of procedure for imposition of civil monetary penalties.[63] As explained in this chapter, substantial changes were made to HIPAA enforcement under the HITECH Act. HHS issued a revised Enforcement Rule to conform to these statutory changes on October 30, 2009, and changes were effective November 30, 2009.[64] HHS further revised the Enforcement Rule under the HITECH Regulations, which were effective March 26, 2013.[65]

[A]   Tiered Penalties

For violations prior to the February 18, 2009, effective date of the HITECH Act, the old Enforcement Rule remains in effect. This means civil penalties for a covered entity's noncompliance with the Administrative Simplification Regulations prior to February 18, 2009, could result in maximum penalties of up to $100 per violation, with a maximum of $25,000 for all violations of an identical requirement by the same person in a calendar year.[66]

For violations occurring on or after February 18, 2009, the HITECH Act establishes a new four-tier penalty structure based on knowledge and intent, and applies to business associates as well as covered entities. The penalties increase with each tier, based on level of culpability, as follows:[67]

---

[60] FTC, "FTC Approves Final Consent Settling Charges That Accretive Health Failed to Adequately Protect Consumers' Personal Information," Press Release (Feb. 24, 2014), available at https://www.ftc.gov/news-events/press-releases/2014/02/ftc-approves-final-consent-settling-charges-accretive-health; Federal Trade Commission, Decision and Order, Dkt No. C-4432 (Feb. 24, 2014), available at https://www.ftc.gov/system/files/documents/cases/140224accretivehealthdo.pdf.

[61] Attorney General of Indiana, "State Settles with Former Dentists Accused of Dumping Patient Files" (Jan. 9, 2015), Press Release, available at http://www.in.gov/activecalendar/EventList.aspx?fromdate=1/1/2015&todate=12/31/2015&display=Year,Month&type=public&eventidn=203146&view=EventDetails&information_id=210192&print=print; Consent Judgment, Joseph Beck individually and dba Beck Family Dentistry, 49D10-1412PL041613 (Marion Circuit/Superior Court, Jan. 5, 2015).

[62] 71 Fed. Reg. 8390 (Feb. 16, 2006).

[63] 45 C.F.R. § 160.300; 71 Fed. Reg. 8390 (Feb. 16, 2006).

[64] 74 Fed. Reg. 56,123 (Oct. 30, 2009) (interim final rule).

[65] 78 Fed. Reg. 5566 (Jan. 25, 2013).

[66] 45 C.F.R. § 160.404(b)(2) (prior to modification by the Oct. 30, 2009, revisions to the Enforcement Rule); 78 Fed. Reg. 5582 (Jan. 25, 2013).

[67] HITECH Act § 13410(d); 45 C.F.R. § 160.404; 74 Fed. Reg. 56,123, 56,126–28 (Oct. 30, 2009); 78 Fed. Reg. 5583 (Jan. 25, 2013). Definitions of "reasonable diligence," "reasonable cause," and "willful neglect" can be found at 45 C.F.R. § 160.401, and HHS intends to publish guidance on their application. 78 Fed. Reg. 5580 (Jan. 25, 2013). The definition of "reasonable cause" was modified by changes to the Enforcement Rule under the HITECH Regulations. The prior definition of "reasonable cause" was based on "circumstances that would make it unreasonable for the covered entity, despite the exercise of ordinary business care and prudence, to comply with the provision violated." This was modified to include a knowledge element. 78 Fed. Reg. 5580 (Jan. 25, 2013).

CIVIL PENALTY TIERS

Tier	Level of Culpability	Penalty per Violation	Maximum Penalty for All Violations of an Identical Requirement in a Calendar Year
1	**Did Not Know** The covered entity or business associate did not know (and by exercising reasonable diligence would not have known) that it violated the provision of the Administrative Simplification Regulations. "Reasonable diligence" means the business care and prudence expected from a person seeking to satisfy a legal requirement under similar circumstances.	$100 to $50,000	$1.5 Million
2	**Reasonable Cause** The violation was due to reasonable cause and not to willful neglect. "Reasonable cause" means an act or omission in which a covered entity or business associate knew, or by exercising reasonable diligence would have known, that the act or omission violated a provision of the Administrative Simplification Regulations, *but* in which the covered entity or business associate did not act with willful neglect.	$1000 to $50,000	$1.5 Million
3	**Willful Neglect—Corrected** The violation was due to willful neglect, but the violation is corrected during the 30-day period beginning on the first date the liable person knew (or by exercising reasonable diligence would have known) of the failure to comply. "Willful neglect" means conscious, intentional failure or reckless indifference to the obligation to comply with the provision violated.	$10,000 to $50,000	$1.5 Million
4	**Willful Neglect—Not Corrected** The violation was due to willful neglect, and the violation is not corrected as described in Tier 3.	$50,000	$1.5 Million

Except as described above for cases of willful neglect,[68] no civil penalty may be imposed by HHS if the failure to comply is corrected within the 30-day period beginning on the first date the liable party knew (or by exercising reasonable diligence would have known) that the failure to comply occurred.[69] Notably, this 30-day period begins on the date the covered entity or business associate knew or should have known that *a violation* occurred, not merely that the facts of the situation occurred.[70]

This 30-day period may be extended as determined appropriate by HHS, based on the nature and extent of the violation.[71] If HHS determines that the covered entity or business associate was unable to comply, HHS may provide technical assistance to the entity during the described "correction period."

Enforcement action must be commenced by HHS within six years from the date of the violation.[72] Subject to the affirmative defenses discussed in **§ 6.02[D]**, if a complaint or compliance review cannot be

---

[68] 45 C.F.R. § 160.401; 74 Fed. Reg. 56,123 (Oct. 30, 2009).

[69] 45 C.F.R. § 160.410.

[70] 78 Fed. Reg. 5587 (Jan. 25, 2013).

[71] HITECH Act § 13410(d)(3); 45 C.F.R. § 160.410. See **§ 6.02[D]** regarding Affirmative Defenses.

[72] 45 C.F.R. § 160.414.

settled informally and HHS finds a violation, HHS must impose a civil penalty.[73] Under the HITECH Act, this requirement has been extended. Effective with penalties imposed on or after February 18, 2011, if the violation involves willful neglect, HHS is required to impose a penalty (as well as formally investigate any complaint if a preliminary investigation indicates a possible violation due to willful neglect).[74] However, HHS does have some discretion in determining the number of violations and the amount of the civil penalties. In the case of a failure to comply that is not due to willful neglect, HHS may waive penalties to the extent payment of the penalty would be excessive relative to the violation.[75] Furthermore, HHS may continue, in its discretion, to provide technical assistance, obtain corrective action, and resolve possible noncompliance by informal means where the possible noncompliance is due to reasonable cause and in cases where the person did not know (and by exercising reasonable diligence would not have known) of the violation.[76]

[B] Calculation of the Number of Violations

HHS will determine the number of violations of an identical requirement or prohibition (identical violations) based on the nature of the covered entity's or business associate's obligation to act (or not act) under the provision violated.[77] If there are violations of more than one requirement of the Regulations, HHS may separately calculate the penalties for each.[78] For example, if a covered entity enters into five business associate agreements that each authorize the business associate to use PHI in a manner not permitted by the Privacy Regulations, and each agreement also omits the provision requiring business associates to use appropriate safeguards to protect PHI, the covered entity may be calculated to have committed five violations of each of the two separate requirements relating to business associate agreements under the Privacy Regulations.[79]

In general, if multiple individuals are affected by an impermissible use or disclosure, the number of violations will likely be based on the number of individuals.[80] For example, if a covered entity impermissibly allows a workforce member to access the PHI of 20 patients stored in electronic health records, this constitutes 20 violations. The covered entity has an obligation with respect to each of the 20 patients, and each sharing of a patient's PHI constitutes a separate impermissible use and violation with respect to each patient.[81] Similarly, in most breach cases, there will be not only one or more impermissible uses or disclosures, but also one or more security or safeguards violations, and penalties may be calculated separately for each violation.[82]

With respect to continuing violations, a separate violation will be deemed to occur on each day such a violation continues.[83] For example, implementation of required security policies is an ongoing obligation; thus, failure to meet this requirement would be a continuing violation, measured by the number of days the obligation is not met. Similarly, a covered entity must provide an individual access to his or her PHI within 30 days of a request. Each day beyond this 30-day period during which the covered entity continues to fail to provide such access would be a separate violation.[84]

---

[73] 45 C.F.R. § 160.402(a).

[74] HITECH Act § 13410(a). See also **§ 6.03[D]**.

[75] 42 U.S.C. § 1320d-5(b)(3); 45 C.F.R. § 160.412; 78 Fed. Reg. 5586 (Jan. 25, 2013).

[76] HITECH Act § 13410(f); 74 Fed. Reg. 56,123, 56,128 (Oct. 30, 2009).

[77] 45 C.F.R. § 160.406.

[78] 78 Fed. Reg. 5584 (Jan. 25, 2013).

[79] 71 Fed. Reg. 8406–8407 (Feb. 16, 2006).

[80] 78 Fed. Reg. 5584 (Jan. 25, 2013).

[81] 71 Fed. Reg. 8406–07 (Feb. 16, 2006).

[82] 78 Fed. Reg. 5584 (Jan. 25, 2013).

[83] 45 C.F.R. § 160.406; 78 Fed. Reg. 5584 (Jan. 25, 2013).

[84] 71 Fed. Reg. 8407 (Feb. 16, 2006).

Penalties will not be imposed for duplicative provisions in the same subpart of the Regulations, where both a general and specific provision are violated (e.g., a security standard and a corresponding implementation specification).[85] HHS may use statistical sampling to establish prima facie evidence of the number of violations.[86]

The Cignet Health case involved a civil monetary penalty of $4.3 million. Section **6.04** describes this case in detail, including calculation of the civil monetary penalty.

[C] Mitigating and Aggravating Factors in Calculating Civil Penalties

HHS must consider certain factors in determining the amount of any civil monetary penalty.[87] These factors may be either aggravating factors or mitigating factors, and HHS has some discretion in how to apply them:[88]

(1) The nature of the violation, which may include consideration of the number of individuals affected, and the time period during which the violation occurred;

(2) The nature and extent of the resulting harm, which may include consideration of whether the violation caused physical harm, financial harm, or reputational harm to the individual, or interfered with the individual's ability to obtain health care;

(3) The covered entity or business associate's history of prior compliance or prior violations of the Administrative Simplification Regulations, which may include consideration of whether the current violation is the same or similar to previous indications of noncompliance, whether and to what extent there has been an attempt to correct prior indications of noncompliance, how the covered entity or business associate has responded to technical assistance from HHS in the context of a compliance effort, or how the covered entity or business associate has responded to prior complaints;

(4) The financial condition of the covered entity or business associate, which may include consideration of financial difficulties that affect the ability to comply, whether a civil monetary penalty would jeopardize the ability to continue to provide or pay for health care, and the size of the entity; and

(5) "such other matters as justice may require."[89]

[D] Affirmative Defenses

The Enforcement Rule provides for the affirmative defenses listed below. If the covered entity (or business associate, as applicable) can establish that one of these affirmative defenses exists with regard to the violation, HHS may not impose a civil monetary penalty.

- The covered entity establishes that it did not have knowledge of the violation and by exercising reasonable diligence would not have known that the violation occurred, but only with respect to violations occurring prior to February 18, 2009.[90]

---

[85] 45 C.F.R. § 160.404(b)(2); 71 Fed. Reg. 8404 (Feb. 16, 2006).

[86] 45 C.F.R. § 160.536; 71 Fed. Reg. 8420 (Feb. 16, 2006).

[87] 45 C.F.R. § 160.408.

[88] 45 C.F.R. § 160.408, as modified by 78 Fed. Reg. 5584-5585 (Jan. 25, 2013) (providing additional details about these factors). With regard to reputational harm, under factor 2, HHS states that the unlawful disclosure of PHI (even sensitive PHI) alone does not establish reputational harm. This determination will be based on all the facts, such as whether the disclosure resulted in adverse effects on employment, community standing, or personal relationships. Also, note that, in factor 3, "indications of noncompliance" replaces "violation," to make clear that a formal finding of a violation is not required. Prior indications of noncompliance may relate to the number of complaints against the entity that HHS has investigated and resolved by informal means, such as voluntary corrective action. A "mere complaint" is not sufficient to constitute an indication of noncompliance, however. 78 Fed. Reg. 5585 (Jan. 25, 2013).

[89] 45 C.F.R. § 160.408, as modified by 78 Fed. Reg. 5584–5585 (Jan. 25, 2013).

[90] 45 C.F.R. § 160.410.

- Also with respect to violations occurring prior to February 18, 2009, the failure to comply is due to circumstances that would make it unreasonable for the covered entity to comply, despite the exercise of ordinary business care and prudence; the violation is not due to willful neglect; and the failure to comply is corrected within 30 days (or such additional period permitted by HHS).[91] (Even if not corrected, HHS may waive the penalty to the extent it would be excessive relative to the violation.)[92]

- For violations on or after February 18, 2009, the covered entity or business associate establishes that the violation is not due to willful neglect and is corrected within 30 days (or such additional period permitted by HHS).[93] (Even if not corrected, HHS may waive the penalty to the extent it would be excessive relative to the violation.)[94]

- For violations occurring prior to February 18, 2011, the violation is an act *subject to* criminal penalties under the HIPAA Administrative Simplification Regulations (regardless of whether such criminal penalties have been imposed).[95] The HITECH Act modifies this and, effective for violations occurring on or after February 18, 2011, no civil penalties (or State Attorneys General damages) may be imposed with regard to a violation if HIPAA criminal penalties *have been imposed*.[96]

The covered entity or business associate may also have a statute of limitations defense. No enforcement action may be taken under the Enforcement Rule unless it is commenced by HHS within six years from the date of occurrence of the violation.[97]

[E] Sharing Civil Penalties Collected

The HITECH Act makes two significant changes with respect to distribution of civil monetary penalties collected for HIPAA violations, which may influence the number of penalties assessed. First, effective February 18, 2009, any civil monetary penalty or monetary settlement collected with respect to HIPAA privacy and security will be transferred to HHS for purposes of further enforcement.[98]

Second, the HITECH Act intends that an individual harmed by a privacy or security violation that results in a civil monetary penalty or monetary settlement be allowed to share in the monies collected.[99] This may have been a compromise with those who would have liked to see a private right of action added under the Act (see § 6.10). The Act requires that the Comptroller General issue a report making recommendations regarding a methodology under which such harmed individuals may receive a percentage of any civil monetary penalties or monetary settlements collected. Then, no later than February 18, 2012, HHS was to have issued a regulation based on these recommendations. The report and regulation are still pending. Once the regulation is issued, that methodology regarding distributions to harmed individuals will apply to penalties or settlements imposed on or after the effective date of that regulation.[100]

---

[91] 45 C.F.R. § 160.410, as modified by 78 Fed. Reg. 5585–5586 (Jan. 25, 2013).
[92] 45 C.F.R. § 160.412.
[93] Pub. L. No. 104-191, § 262(a) (codified at 42 U.S.C. § 1320d-5); 45 C.F.R. § 160.410. For violations due to willful neglect, correction within 30 days does not constitute an affirmative defense but will change the penalty tier. See § 6.02[A].
[94] 45 C.F.R. § 160.410, as modified by 78 Fed. Reg. 5585–5586 (Jan. 25, 2013); 45 C.F.R. § 160.412.
[95] 45 C.F.R. § 160.410.
[96] HITECH Act § 13410(a); 45 C.F.R. § 160.410(a), as modified by 78 Fed. Reg. 5585–5586 (Jan. 25, 2013).
[97] 45 C.F.R. § 160.414.
[98] HITECH Act § 13410(c).
[99] HITECH Act § 13410(c).
[100] HITECH Act § 13410(c).

§ 6.03 CIVIL COMPLAINTS AND INVESTIGATIONS

For the most part, OCR and CMS have focused on education and voluntary compliance rather than imposing penalties. The 2006 Enforcement Rule reflected this approach. The HITECH Act may, however, result in more complaints, more formal investigations, and more penalties being imposed. OCR has stated that it intends to leverage its limited resources by focusing its investigations on "high-impact cases" that send "strong enforcement messages."[101]

[A] Filing Complaints

OCR and CMS have, in most cases, responded to complaints rather than independently initiated compliance reviews.[102] Any person who believes a covered entity or business associate is not complying with the Administrative Simplification Regulations may file a complaint with OCR or CMS. OCR and CMS each have established procedures for filing and processing of complaints.[103] Complaints must be filed in writing within 180 days of when the complainant knew or should have known of the act or omission complained of.[104]

[B] Initial Processing of a Complaint

CMS has outlined its complaint and investigation process in detail in a Federal Register notice.[105] This section generally outlines these CMS procedures, but because they are comparable to the process OCR has been following to date, they are referred to herein as HHS procedures.

When HHS receives a complaint, it will contact the person who submitted the complaint to ask questions, if necessary, and then HHS will determine whether to accept the complaint. If it appears, based on a preliminary review, that a compliance failure may have occurred, HHS will contact the covered entity (or business associate, as applicable). The first notice of a complaint will likely come to the covered entity or business associate in the form of a letter from the CMS or OCR regional office. Covered entities and business associates should educate their staff to be alert to these letters, which may not be addressed to a particular individual but just to the organization. This correspondence should be forwarded immediately to the Compliance Officer, Privacy Officer, Security Officer, or other designated person, who should contact legal counsel. The covered entity or business associate (or its legal counsel) should contact CMS or OCR promptly to obtain additional information needed for the covered entity or business associate to investigate the complaint and to develop a response and corrective action plan (if appropriate).

The first written communication from HHS to the covered entity or business associate must describe the basis for the complaint.[106] HHS will ask the covered entity or business associate to submit a written response to the complaint within a specified time period, such as 14 or 30 days. This response typically would include (1) a statement that the covered entity's or business associate's actions complied with the Regulations, including supporting evidence, as applicable; (2) a detailed statement of disagreement with the allegations, (e.g., that the facts are not as represented in the complaint), with supporting evidence, as applicable; or (3) a corrective action plan, demonstrating that, although there may have been noncompliance, the covered entity or business associate has taken prompt and effective corrective action.

---

[101] OCR, "Annual Report to Congress on HIPAA Privacy, Security and Breach Notification Rule Compliance (2011-2012)," available at http://www.hhs.gov/ocr/privacy/hipaa/enforcement/compliancereport2011-2012.pdf.

[102] 70 Fed. Reg. 20,226 (Apr. 18, 2005). To date, OCR has received more than 90,000 complaints. See OCR, "Complaints Received by Calendar Year," available at http://www.hhs.gov/ocr/privacy/hipaa/enforcement/data/complaintsyear.html.

[103] 70 Fed. Reg. 15,329 (Mar. 25, 2005) (CMS HIPAA complaint rule); OCR, "How to File a Complaint," available at http://www.hhs.gov/ocr/privacy/hipaa/complaints/index.html (OCR HIPAA complaint procedure).

[104] 45 C.F.R. § 160.306.

[105] 70 Fed. Reg. 15,329 (Mar. 25, 2005). See also OCR, "What OCR Considers During Intake & Review," available at http://www.hhs.gov/ocr/privacy/hipaa/enforcement/process/whatocrconsiders.html.

[106] 45 C.F.R. § 160.306(c).

[C] Investigations

The Enforcement Rule requires covered entities and business associates to cooperate with complaint investigations (and compliance reviews), including providing HHS with relevant information and records.[107] In investigating a complaint, HHS will provide the covered entity or business associate with a data request, asking for contact information; a detailed position statement in response to the allegations, including supporting documents; general information about the entity; copies of policies and procedures; and other information HHS deems necessary to the investigation.

The Enforcement Rule describes in detail how formal investigations are conducted, how testimony is given, and how evidence is obtained. HHS may issue subpoenas to require the attendance and testimony of witnesses and the production of any other evidence during an investigation or compliance review.[108]

Any testimony or other evidence that HHS obtains during its investigation may be used by HHS in *any* of its activities and also may be used or offered into evidence in *any* administrative or judicial proceeding.[109] This could include, for example, use in a fraud and abuse investigation or proceeding.[110]

[D] Informal Resolution

If, following an investigation or compliance review, the evidence indicates noncompliance, HHS may attempt to resolve the matter through informal means (except in cases of willful neglect).[111] Prior to the HITECH Regulations, the Enforcement Rule required HHS to attempt resolution by informal means, but now HHS may proceed directly to the civil monetary penalty process without trying to resolve the matter informally, "particularly in cases involving willful neglect."[112]

Informal resolution may include demonstrated compliance or a completed corrective action plan.[113] If HHS resolves the matter informally, it must provide written notice to the covered entity or business associate. If HHS concludes that the matter cannot be resolved informally, it must inform the covered entity or business associate in writing and provide the covered entity or business associate with an opportunity to submit written evidence of any affirmative defenses or mitigating factors.[114]

Both OCR and CMS have previously stated informally that their enforcement strategy will focus on achieving voluntary compliance through technical assistance.[115] Again, this approach may change with the implementation of the HITECH Act.

---

[107] 45 C.F.R. § 160.310.

[108] 45 C.F.R. § 160.314(a).

[109] 45 C.F.R. § 160.314(c); 45 C.F.R. § 160.310(c)(3); 78 Fed. Reg. 5579 (Jan. 25, 2013). OCR provides information on its website regarding how HHS cooperates with the Department of Justice and Federal Trade Commission, at http://www.hhs.gov/ocr/privacy/hipaa/enforcement. 78 Fed. Reg. 5579 (Jan. 25, 2013).

[110] See United States v. Metropolitan Ambulance, a False Claims Act case under which the DOJ obtained PHI under a protective order, which allowed the DOJ to use the PHI for health oversight but required the DOJ to return or destroy it after trial. The DOJ objected that this requirement would unduly restrict its oversight function and the court agreed. The court held that the protective order may not restrict DOJ's use of the PHI to this particular litigation. United States *ex rel.* Kaplan v. Metropolitan Ambulance & First-Aid Corp., 395 F. Supp. 2d 1 (E.D.N.Y. Oct. 26, 2005) (distinguished by United States v. University Hosp., Inc., 2006 WL 2612631 (S.D. Ohio July 28, 2006)).

[111] 45 C.F.R. § 160.312(a).

[112] 45 C.F.R. § 160.312(a); 78 Fed. Reg. 5579 (Jan. 25, 2013).

[113] 45 C.F.R. § 160.312(a).

[114] 45 C.F.R. § 160.312(a).

[115] With respect to CMS enforcement, see 70 Fed. Reg. 15,330 (Mar. 25, 2005) (CMS Procedures for Non-Privacy Administrative Simplification Complaints under HIPAA) and CMS HIPAA FAQ #1331, formerly available at http://questions.cms.hhs.gov. With respect to OCR enforcement, see "How OCR Enforces the HIPAA Privacy Rule," available at http://www.hhs.gov/ocr/privacy/hipaa/enforcement/process/howocrenforces.html.

[E]   Hearing and Appeals Process

If HHS intends to impose a civil monetary penalty, it must provide written notice to the respondent. This notice must state the statutory basis for the penalty, the facts developed and HHS's analysis, the amount of the penalty, and the applicable penalty tier.[116]

If a covered entity receives notice from HHS that a civil monetary penalty is to be imposed, the covered entity may seek an administrative hearing before an administrative law judge (ALJ). HHS and the covered entity may each be represented by counsel, conduct discovery, present relevant evidence, present and cross-examine witnesses, submit written briefs, and present oral arguments. The ALJ will conduct a fair and impartial hearing and then issue a decision based on the record, which will affirm, increase, or reduce the penalty imposed by HHS. The ALJ's decision may be appealed to the HHS Departmental Appeals Board. Following the Board's decision, a judicial appeal to the U.S. Court of Appeals is permitted.[117] These processes are addressed in detail in the Enforcement Rule.

[F]   Public Notice of Civil Penalties

When a civil monetary penalty becomes final, HHS will notify the appropriate state or local medical or professional organizations, the state agencies administering certain state health care programs (e.g., Medicaid), utilization and quality control peer review organizations, and state or local licensing agencies (including state survey agencies), as it deems appropriate.[118]

The Enforcement Rule also states that HHS will provide notice to the public generally.[119] HHS posts civil monetary penalties and other monetary settlements achieved through OCR's compliance activities on the OCR Enforcement Website (see **§ 6.05**).[120]

§ 6.04   CIVIL MONETARY PENALTY CASES

[A]   Cignet Health (2011)

In February 2011, nearly eight years after the compliance date for the Privacy Regulations, OCR imposed the first civil monetary penalty (CMP) for violation of the Regulations. OCR issued a Notice of Final Determination to a covered entity, Cignet Health of Prince George's County (Cignet), imposing a CMP of $4.3 million.[121] Of this, $1.3 million was for the underlying violation (failure to provide copies of medical records to individuals upon request), but the larger part, $3 million, was for Cignet's failure to cooperate with OCR.[122]

In its Notice of Proposed Determination on October 20, 2010, OCR found that Cignet is a covered entity and subject to the Privacy Regulations, which require it to provide individuals with access to and copies of their PHI within 30 days of a request.[123] According to OCR, 41 individuals requested copies of their medical records

---

[116] 45 C.F.R. § 160.420.

[117] 45 C.F.R. § 160.500 *et seq.*

[118] 45 C.F.R. § 160.426.

[119] 45 C.F.R. § 160.426.

[120] 71 Fed. Reg. 8413 (Feb. 16, 2006); OCR Enforcement Website, available at http://www.hhs.gov/ocr/privacy/hipaa/enforcement/index.html. HHS could also publish this information in the Federal Register. 71 Fed. Reg. 8413 (Feb. 16, 2006).

[121] HHS, OCR, "Civil Monetary Penalty: Cignet Health Fined a $4.3 Million Civil Monetary Penalty for HIPAA Privacy Rule Violations," available at http://www.hhs.gov/ocr/privacy/hipaa/enforcement/examples/cignetcmp.html (hereinafter "HHS Statement—Cignet").

[122] HHS Statement—Cignet; OCR Notice of Proposed Determination—Cignet, available at http://www.hhs.gov/ocr/privacy/hipaa/enforcement/examples/cignetpenaltynotice.pdf (hereinafter "Cignet NPD"); OCR Notice of Final Determination—Cignet, available at http://www.hhs.gov/ocr/privacy/hipaa/enforcement/examples/cignetpenaltyletter.pdf (hereinafter "Cignet NFD").

[123] Cignet NPD.

from Cignet, and Cignet failed to respond. Several of these individuals informed Cignet that they were requesting copies of their health records so they could obtain medical care elsewhere.[124]

In its Notice of Proposed Determination, OCR tells the following story of its investigation and of Cignet's substantial failure to respond to OCR over the course of many months.[125] OCR sent a letter to Cignet explaining that OCR was investigating 38 complaints related to the access requests of 41 individuals and requesting a response from Cignet. Cignet did not respond to this letter, to numerous follow-up attempts to contact Cignet by phone, or to two additional letters.[126] OCR issued a subpoena for the records (delivered to Cignet by certified mail), directing Cignet to produce the records for the first 11 complainants. Again, Cignet failed to respond. OCR then sent another certified letter, advising Cignet that OCR had not received the medical records as directed by the subpoena and if Cignet did not respond within 10 days, OCR would begin enforcement action. Cignet again failed to respond.[127]

OCR finally sought a court order to enforce the subpoena in February 2010. The court issued an order for Cignet to show cause and scheduled a hearing, but Cignet did not appear and did not respond to defend the action. The court granted a default judgment to OCR and ordered Cignet to produce copies of the full medical records (designated record sets) for the 11 individuals identified in the subpoena, giving Cignet about a week to comply. Cignet now responded. On the deadline date, April 7, 2010, Cignet delivered 59 boxes of original medical records to the attorney representing OCR. In these boxes were the records of the 11 individuals named in the subpoena, plus records of approximately 4,500 other individuals. OCR had made no request for the records of these additional 4,500 individuals, and as stated by OCR, Cignet "had no basis for the disclosure of their Protected Health Information to OCR."[128]

In August 2010, OCR sent a certified letter to Cignet, stating that OCR had concluded that Cignet had violated the Privacy Regulations and that OCR had attempted to resolve the complaints though informal means but had been unable to do so. Therefore, OCR was informing Cignet of the "preliminary indications of noncompliance" and providing Cignet an opportunity to introduce evidence of mitigating factors, raise affirmative defenses, or provide evidence in support of a waiver of a CMP. On receipt of the letter, Cignet did not respond to OCR. OCR sought the authorization of the U.S. Attorney General and then proceeded to impose a CMP, issuing the Notice of Proposed Determination in October 2010, which outlined Cignet's right to request a hearing. After Cignet failed to exercise its right to a hearing, OCR issued a Notice of Final Determination on February 4, 2011. If Cignet fails to pay the CMP, HHS can have it deducted from any funds owed to Cignet by the U.S. government (presumably such as Medicare payments, tax refunds, etc.) or by bringing a court action to recover the amount of the penalty.[129]

In August 2011, HHS began court proceedings to collect the $4.3 million CMP (offset by retention of Medicaid and Medicare reimbursements to Cignet of less that $4,000).[130] Cignet responded, claiming that it had not previously been notified of the CMP and had not had the opportunity to defend the action in any hearing.[131] Cignet further stated that the matter should be referred to another medical group, because the patients requesting records were patients of that other group and the records should be obtained from them.[132] Cignet stated in other court documents that it had provided to HHS all the medical records Cignet had obtained from the other medical group when Cignet responded to the February 2010 court order, and Cignet could not have provided any medical

---

[124] Cignet NPD.

[125] Cignet NPD.

[126] Cignet NPD; although, apparently, there was at least one conversation between OCR and the Cignet Administrator in January 2009, Declaration of Diana Vincenzo, attachment to Sebelius v. Uplift Medical, P.C., Motion to Dismiss and Counterclaim, Case 8:11-CV-02168 (D. Md. Mar. 20, 2012).

[127] Cignet NPD.

[128] Cignet NPD.

[129] Cignet NPD; Cignet NFD.

[130] *Uplift Medical*, Complaint, Case 8:11-CV-02168 (D. Md. Aug. 4, 2011). According to the Complaint, Cignet Health is one of the trade names under which Uplift Medical, P.C. operates. "Cignet" will continue to be used herein to refer to the organization.

[131] *Uplift Medical*, Correspondence re: Defendant's Answer, Case 8:11-CV-02168 (D. Md. Nov. 2, 2011).

[132] *Uplift Medical*, Correspondence re: Defendant's Answer, Case 8:11-CV-02168 (D. Md. Nov. 2, 2011).

records prior to that time because the records "were exhibits documents in a Criminal hearing of a Maryland case."[133]

HHS moved for summary judgment, asserting that Cignet is legally barred from challenging the CMP (on either substantive or procedural grounds) because the CMP is final, and Cignet did not exhaust its administrative remedies. HHS states that Cignet was given multiple opportunities to challenge the CMP, yet failed to do so.[134] Nevertheless, HHS did respond to some of Cignet's points. For example, HHS states that even if the records in question were exhibits in a criminal case, that is not a defense to the HIPAA violation asserted. If Cignet was not capable of responding to the patients' requests for records because Cignet temporarily did not have possession of the records, Cignet still had an obligation to respond to the patients and provide the reason for the denial of the request.[135] In other court documents, HHS further explains that the "fact that a patient's medical record may be the subject of litigation does not obviate the covered entity's obligation to provide copies of the medical records to the requesting individual."[136]

Cignet continued to contest the CMP on various grounds, claiming that there were "fundamental errors" in the OCR investigation.[137] Moreover, Cignet also filed a counterclaim against HHS for damages inflicted by HHS on Cignet.[138] On August 30, 2012, the court granted summary judgment to HHS and dismissed Cignet's counterclaims.[139]

Although the extreme circumstances of this case seem to make it an outlier, lessons can be learned:

- It is important to promptly respond to communications from OCR. Staff should know that these communications should be immediately forwarded to the organization's privacy officer or other designated person. Communications from OCR need due attention, even in the face of competing organizational priorities. The lines of communication to OCR need to be kept open.

- Covered entities must respond to individuals asking for copies of their records, even if that response is to deny access or advise of a delay. (See § 3.02[B] for more information on individuals' right to access their PHI.)

- Covered entities and business associates should become familiar with OCR's administrative processes, so they do not miss opportunities to raise defenses or negotiate outcomes.

This case also illustrates how HHS calculates a CMP. For failure of Cignet to provide the 41 individuals with copies, OCR calculated a penalty of $100 per individual per day. Since each day is a separate violation, and in most cases, the noncompliance ran for hundreds of days, the CMP added up to $1,351,600. OCR further stated that Cignet failed, with willful neglect, to cooperate in the investigation of 27 complaints during 2009 and 2010, and failure to cooperate in an investigation is itself a violation of the Privacy Regulations. OCR determined the penalty amount to be $50,000 per violation and calculated the total CMP amount based on the number of violations (27) and the number of days of noncompliance. Because there is maximum penalty of $1.5 million for all violations of the same requirement in a calendar year, Cignet's penalty was significantly reduced from hundreds

---

[133] *Uplift Medical*, Correspondence from Dan E. Austin, M.D. on behalf of Uplift Medical, P.C., regarding Complaint/Answer, Case 8:11-CV-02168 (D. Md. Nov. 22, 2011).

[134] *Uplift Medical*, Response in Support of Summary Judgment, Case 8:11-CV-02168 (D. Md. Dec. 9, 2011).

[135] *Uplift Medical*, Response in Support of Summary Judgment, Case 8:11-CV-02168 (D. Md. Dec. 9, 2011) (also disputing that the criminal proceedings actually would have prevented Cignet from providing the requested records to the patients). See also *Uplift Medical*, Motion to Strike, Case 8:11-CV-02168 (D. Md. Apr. 9, 2012).

[136] *Uplift Medical*, Motion to Strike, Case 8:11-CV-02168 (D. Md. Apr. 9, 2012) (citing the exception to the Privacy Regulations concerning records compiled in anticipation of, or for use in, litigation, and stating that this exception would not apply to the underlying medical records themselves).

[137] *Uplift Medical*, Motion to Dismiss and Counterclaim, Case 8:11-CV-02168 (D. Md. Mar. 20, 2012).

[138] *Uplift Medical*, Motion to Dismiss and Counterclaim, Case 8:11-CV-02168 (D. Md. Mar. 20, 2012).

[139] *Uplift Medical*, Memorandum Opinion and Order, Case 8:11-CV-02168 (D. Md. Aug. 30, 2012). Cignet appealed, but the court dismissed the appeal a few months later for "failure to prosecute" (i.e., failure to take necessary steps to proceed with the appeal). *Uplift Medical*, Order and Mandate, Case 8:11-CV-02168 (D. Md. Jan. 16, 2013).

of millions to $3 million. OCR also noted that it considered two aggravating factors in calculating the CMP: (1) Cignet's failure to provide patients with the PHI they requested hindered their ability to seek medical care elsewhere, and (2) OCR was forced by Cignet's inaction to issue a subpoena and then obtain a court order to compel production of the records.[140]

§ 6.05   RESOLUTION AGREEMENTS

Enforcement levels are ramping up, and HHS has now entered into more than 20 resolution agreements with covered entities since 2008 (about half of these in just the last couple of years). HHS describes the resolution agreement as a contract signed by HHS and the covered entity in which the covered entity agrees to fulfill certain obligations and make reports to HHS, generally for a period of three years. HHS monitors the covered entity's compliance with its obligations during this period. A resolution agreement also likely includes payment of a "resolution amount." HHS describes resolution agreements as being used "to settle investigations with more serious outcomes, when OCR has not been able to reach a satisfactory resolution through the covered entity's demonstrated compliance or corrective action through other informal means."[141]

Each of the resolution agreements makes clear that the entity entering into the agreement is not making any admission of liability, and the entities may, in fact, affirmatively state that they deny any liability, any violations of the Privacy or Security Regulations, or other wrongdoing. Furthermore, many of the entities entering into these agreements also disclaim any agreement with HHS's statement of the facts and findings.[142] Similarly, HHS will include a statement in the resolution agreement that the agreement is not a concession by HHS that there were not violations of the Regulations or liability for civil monetary penalties.[143] The following are summaries of each of these resolution agreements. Refer to the resolution agreements for more information.

Repeating themes in these enforcement actions are alleged violations of the Privacy and Security Regulations related to improper disposal of PHI, and theft or loss of laptops or other mobile devices. Lessons learned include: encrypt the data on laptops and other mobile devices; ensure physical security of mobile devices and any "offsite" PHI; train workforce members; conduct risk assessments and take appropriate risk management measures to address identified risks; and create a culture of compliance. Another lesson is that these resolution agreements can involve any covered entity or business associate—large or small, health plan or provider, nonprofit or for profit, government agency or private entity.

[A]   Providence Health (2008)

HHS entered into a resolution agreement with Providence Health & Services, a Seattle-based health system, to settle potential violations of the Privacy and Security Regulations relating to the loss or theft of electronic PHI on laptops and backup media. The investigation and resolution agreement were a joint effort between OCR and CMS. Under the July 16, 2008, agreement, Providence agreed to pay $100,000 and implement a corrective action plan relative to safeguarding electronic PHI (ePHI) against theft or loss. Providence's cooperation with OCR and CMS permitted informal resolution of the case without civil monetary penalties.[144]

According to HHS, Providence lost electronic backup media and laptop computers containing electronic PHI in 2005 and 2006:

---

[140] Cignet NPD.

[141] See HHS, OCR, Resolution Agreements, available at http://www.hhs.gov/ocr/privacy/hipaa/enforcement/examples/index.html.

[142] See, e.g., Massachusetts General Resolution Agreement, available at http://www.hhs.gov/ocr/privacy/hipaa/enforcement/examples/massgeneralracap.pdf.

[143] See, e.g., Resolution Agreement between HHS and CVS, available at http://www.hhs.gov/ocr/privacy/hipaa/enforcement/examples/cvsresagrcap.pdf.

[144] HHS, OCR, "HHS, Providence Health & Services Agree on Corrective Action Plan to Protect Health Information," available at http://www.hhs.gov/ocr/privacy/hipaa/enforcement/examples/providenceresolutionagreement.html (hereinafter "HHS Statement—Providence").

On several occasions between September 2005 and March 2006, backup tapes, optical disks, and laptops, all containing unencrypted electronic protected health information, were removed from the Providence premises and were left unattended. The media and laptops were subsequently lost or stolen, compromising the protected health information of over 386,000 patients. . . . OCR and CMS together focused their investigations on Providence's failure to implement policies and procedures to safeguard this information.[145]

Providence agreed to pay HHS a resolution amount of $100,000, and to enter into and comply with a corrective action plan. Provided Providence adheres to the corrective action plan, HHS released Providence from civil liability under the Privacy and Security Regulations, with regard to the identified incidents.[146]

The corrective action plan was for a three-year period and required Providence to undertake the following actions relative to policies and procedures, training, and auditing and monitoring:[147]

- *Policies and Procedures.* Revise its written policies and procedures regarding the conduct of a risk assessment and risk management plan related to off-site electronic PHI; physical safeguards governing off-site storage and transport of backup electronic media containing PHI; physical safeguards regarding the physical security of portable devices containing electronic PHI; technical safeguards governing encryption and other technical safeguards for backup electronic media and portable devices containing electronic PHI.

- *Training.* Train its workforce members on these physical and technical safeguards.

- *Monitoring.* Conduct audits, interviews, and unannounced site visits of its facilities to validate compliance with these policies and procedures.

- *Reports to HHS.* Submit compliance reports to HHS for a period of three years.

The resolution agreement with Providence is significant because it was the first public written resolution of a HIPAA privacy or security complaint and the first monetary payment (though not a civil monetary penalty and still an "informal resolution").

[B] CVS Pharmacy (2009)

On January 16, 2009, HHS entered into a resolution agreement with CVS Pharmacy, Inc., the nation's largest retail pharmacy chain, relating to disposal of PHI. Under the agreement, CVS was required to pay a $2.25 million settlement and enter into a corrective action plan. CVS also signed a consent order with the FTC. OCR and the FTC conducted a joint investigation.[148] This was the first joint investigation and resolution by OCR and the FTC.

OCR and the FTC opened their investigations into CVS following nationwide media reports that CVS pharmacies were throwing trash containing PHI into unsecured trash containers. The FTC stated that, according to reports:

[This trash] contained pill bottles with patient names, addresses, prescribing physicians' names, medication and dosages; medication instruction sheets with personal information; computer order information from the pharmacies, including consumers' personal information; employment applications, including Social Security numbers; payroll information; and credit card and insurance card information, including, in some cases, account numbers and driver's license numbers.[149]

---

[145] HHS Statement—Providence.

[146] Providence Resolution Agreement.

[147] Providence Resolution Agreement.

[148] HHS, OCR, "CVS Pays $2.25 Million & Toughens Disposal Practices to Settle HIPAA Privacy Case," available at http://www.hhs.gov/ocr/privacy/hipaa/enforcement/examples/cvsresolutionagreement.html (hereinafter "HHS statement—CVS").

[149] FTC, "CVS Caremark Settles FTC Charges," available at http://www.ftc.gov/opa/2009/02/cvs.shtm (hereinafter "FTC statement—CVS"). *See also* HHS statement—CVS.

The FTC and OCR coordinated their investigations and settlements. The OCR review, which focused on the Privacy Regulations, stated that CVS failed to:

- Implement adequate policies and procedures to reasonably and appropriately safeguard PHI during the disposal process;

- Adequately train employees on how to dispose of PHI properly; and

- Maintain and implement a sanctions policy for members of its workforce who failed to comply with its disposal policies and procedures.[150]

Similarly, the FTC's complaint charged that CVS failed to implement reasonable and appropriate procedures for handling personal information about customers and employees.[151] According to the FTC, CVS made claims such as "CVS/pharmacy wants you to know that nothing is more central to our operations than maintaining the privacy of your health information." The FTC alleged that the claim was deceptive and that CVS's security practices also were unfair. Unfair and deceptive practices violate the FTC Act.[152]

Under the resolution agreement, CVS agreed to pay a $2.25 million resolution amount and implement a three-year corrective action plan that required CVS to develop and implement policies and procedures regarding disposal of PHI, train workforce members, require internal reporting of noncompliance, and apply sanctions for workers who do not follow the policies and procedures. The plan also required internal monitoring and submission of compliance reports to HHS.[153]

The FTC order bars future misrepresentations of the company's security practices with respect to consumer information. It requires CVS to establish, implement, and maintain a comprehensive information security program designed to protect the security, confidentiality, and integrity of the personal information it collects from consumers and employees. It also requires the company to obtain, every two years for the next 20 years, an audit from a qualified, independent, third-party professional to ensure that its security program meets the standards of the order. CVS will be subject to standard record keeping and reporting provisions to allow the FTC to monitor compliance.[154]

[C] Rite Aid (2010)

On July 27, 2010, HHS announced that it had entered into a resolution agreement with Rite Aid Corporation and its 40 affiliated entities (Rite Aid), relating to the disposal of PHI. Under the agreement, Rite Aid, one of the country's largest drug store chains, agreed to enter into a corrective action plan and pay a $1 million settlement to HHS.[155] As in the CVS Pharmacy case, Rite Aid also signed a consent order with the FTC.[156] This was the second joint investigation and resolution by OCR and the FTC.

The alleged facts of the Rite Aid case are similar to those alleged in the CVS Pharmacy case described above. The OCR and FTC investigations began after news reports about Rite Aid's using unsecured trash

---

[150] HHS statement—CVS.

[151] FTC statement—CVS; FTC Complaint (Final) (June 23, 2009), available at http://www.ftc.gov/os/caselist/0723119/index.shtm.

[152] FTC statement—CVS; FTC Complaint (Final) (June 23, 2009), available at http://www.ftc.gov/os/caselist/0723119/index.shtm.

[153] CVS Resolution Agreement; HHS statement—CVS.

[154] FTC statement—CVS; FTC Agreement Containing Consent Order (Proposed) (Feb. 18, 2009) (hereinafter "FTC-CVS Agreement"); FTC Decision and Order (Final) (June 23, 2009) and FTC Complaint (Final) (June 23, 2009), all available at http://www.ftc.gov/os/caselist/0723119/index.shtm. See also 74 Fed. Reg. 12,870 (Mar. 25, 2009) (analysis of proposed consent order).

[155] HHS News Release, "Rite Aid Agrees to Pay $1 Million to Settle HIPAA Privacy Case" (July 27, 2010), available at http://www.hhs.gov/ocr/privacy/hipaa/enforcement/examples/riteaidresagr.html (hereinafter "HHS statement—Rite Aid"); Rite Aid Resolution Agreement, available at http://www.hhs.gov/ocr/privacy/hipaa/enforcement/examples/riteaidres.pdf.

[156] FTC press release, "Rite Aid Settles FTC Charges that It Failed to Protect Medical and Financial Privacy of Customers and Employees" (July 27, 2010), available at http://www.ftc.gov/opa/2010/07/riteaid.shtm (hereinafter "FTC statement—Rite Aid"); *In re* Rite Aid Corp., Agreement Containing Consent Order, available at http://www.ftc.gov/os/caselist/0723121/index.shtm.

containers to discard trash that contained prescriptions, labeled pill bottles, and other items containing individual information.[157] As in the CVS Pharmacy case, the FTC tied its complaint to claims made by Rite Aid regarding its privacy practices, alleging that Rite Aid's claims about protecting consumer health information were deceptive and that Rite Aid's security practices were unfair.[158]

Under the HHS resolution agreement, Rite Aid agreed to pay HHS a resolution amount of $1 million and comply with a three-year corrective action plan that addresses policies and procedures, training, monitoring, internal reporting, and reports to OCR.[159] These terms are very similar (if not identical) to those in the CVS Pharmacy resolution agreement.

The FTC and Rite Aid also entered into an Agreement/Consent Order, which was made final by an FTC Decision and Order in November 2010.[160] The FTC Decision and Order requires Rite Aid to establish a comprehensive information security program designed to protect the security, confidentiality, and integrity of the personal information it collects from consumers. In addition, every two years for the next 20 years, Rite Aid must obtain an assessment from a qualified, independent, third-party professional to ensure that its security program meets the standards of the order. The Decision and Order also prohibits future misrepresentations of the company's privacy and security practices.[161]

The CVS Pharmacy and Rite Aid cases described in this section both allege very similar situations relating to improper disposal of non-electronic PHI. In response, OCR has developed FAQs regarding proper disposal of PHI to provide guidance to other covered entities and business associates.[162]

[D] Management Services Organization (2010)

On December 23, 2010, HHS entered into a resolution agreement with Management Services Organization Washington, Inc. (MSO), relating to MSO's disclosures of PHI to a related company for marketing purposes. The resolution agreement included a settlement amount of $35,000 and a two-year corrective action plan.[163]

OCR opened an investigation of MSO in December 2009, based on a referral from the OIG and Department of Justice, which were investigating potential False Claims Act violations.[164] MSO provided practice management services to individual health care providers.[165] The OCR investigation also included Washington Practice Management, LLC (WPM), which is owned by the same company as MSO. WPM is a company that markets and sells Medicare Advantage plans to consumers (for which it earns commissions).[166] According to the OCR investigation, for four years (until November 2010) MSO impermissibly disclosed electronic PHI to WPM in order for WPM to market Medicare Advantage plans to those individuals. Furthermore, OCR alleged

---

[157] HHS statement—Rite Aid; FTC statement—Rite Aid; Rite Aid Resolution Agreement.

[158] FTC statement—Rite Aid.

[159] Rite Aid Resolution Agreement, available at http://www.hhs.gov/ocr/privacy/hipaa/enforcement/examples/riteaidres.pdf.

[160] FTC Decision and Order, In the Matter of Rite Aid Corporation, Docket No. C-4308 (Nov. 22, 2010), available at http://www.ftc.gov/os/caselist/0723121/index.shtm (hereinafter "FTC Decision—Rite Aid"). See also FTC Complaint, In the Matter of Rite Aid Corporation, Docket No. C-4308, available at http://www.ftc.gov/os/caselist/0723121/index.shtm.

[161] FTC statement—Rite Aid; In re Rite Aid Corp., Agreement Containing Consent Order, available at http://www.ftc.gov/os/caselist/0723121/index.shtm. See also FTC Decision—Rite Aid.

[162] OCR, "Frequently Asked Questions about the Disposal of Protected Health Information," available at http://www.hhs.gov/ocr/privacy/hipaa/enforcement/examples/disposalfaqs.pdf.

[163] HHS, OCR, "Resolution Agreement," statement available at http://www.hhs.gov/ocr/privacy/hipaa/enforcement/examples/msoresagr.html; MSO Resolution Agreement, available at http://www.hhs.gov/ocr/privacy/hipaa/enforcement/examples/msoresultionagreement.pdf.

[164] MSO Resolution Agreement.

[165] OCR, "Health Information Security Rule Trends in Enforcement," presented at NIST/OCR HIPAA Security Assurance Conference (May 11, 2011), available at http://csrc.nist.gov/news_events/HIPAA-May2011_workshop/presentations/day2_HIPAA-conference2011-OCR-Enforcement-Activities.pdf (hereinafter "OCR NIST presentation").

[166] OCR NIST presentation.

that MSO did not have reasonable and appropriate privacy and security safeguards in place to protect that electronic PHI.[167]

Under the resolution agreement, MSO agreed to implement a corrective action plan that required MSO to develop and implement policies and procedures regarding marketing disclosures and safeguards for electronic PHI. It also required internal reporting of noncompliance, internal monitoring, and submission of compliance reports to HHS.[168]

The MSO resolution agreement seemed to receive less industry attention than others, perhaps because of the relatively modest resolution amount. However, it deserves notice as the first resolution agreement relating to the disclosure of PHI for marketing purposes. It is also interesting as an example of interagency cooperation leading to an OCR privacy and security investigation.

[E] Massachusetts General Hospital (2011)

"Mass General," one of the oldest and largest hospitals in the United States, entered into a resolution agreement with HHS on February 14, 2011. The agreement, between HHS and The General Hospital Corporation and Massachusetts General Physicians Organization, Inc. (collectively, MGH), related to an incident in which an MGH employee left documents containing PHI on a subway train. MGH agreed to pay a $1 million resolution amount and enter into a three-year corrective action plan.[169]

According to the resolution agreement, the incident began on a Friday in 2009, when an employee of an infectious disease unit removed documents containing PHI from the MGH premises in order to work at home. The documents consisted of billing encounter forms, which contained name, date of birth, medical record number, health insurer and policy number, diagnosis, and name of provider, for 66 patients, plus an office schedule containing the names and medical record numbers of 192 patients. The following Monday, while commuting to work, the employee removed the documents from her bag and placed them on the subway seat beside her. She left them behind on the train, and they were never recovered.[170]

Under the resolution agreement, MGH agreed to implement a corrective action plan that requires MGH to develop and implement written policies and procedures regarding (1) physical removal and transport of PHI, and (2) laptop and USB drive encryption. Furthermore, MGH had to prohibit its workforce from physically removing any PHI from its premises, unless the workforce member had completed certain specified training.

In the interim, before these new policies were implemented, MGH was permitted to allow its workforce to physically remove PHI from the premises only for performance of their job duties and only with reasonable and appropriate safeguards. MGH was required to issue a communication to its workforce regarding these requirements, applicability of sanctions for failure to follow them, and to provide notice of the OCR corrective action plan.[171]

Finally, MGH was required to conduct internal monitoring, implement internal reporting of noncompliance, and submit compliance reports to HHS.[172]

The MGH resolution agreement does not provide any details of how the resolution amount was calculated. As discussed in § 6.02[B], however, the OCR would not look at this as a single incident but as 192 violations. Thus, even in a single event, when the PHI of many individuals is involved, penalties will add up very quickly.

---

[167] MSO Resolution Agreement.

[168] MSO Resolution Agreement.

[169] HHS News Release, "Massachusetts General Hospital Settles Potential HIPAA Violations" (February 24, 2011), available at http://www.hhs.gov/news/press/2011pres/02/20110224b.html (hereinafter "HHS statement—Mass General"); Massachusetts General Resolution Agreement, available at http://www.hhs.gov/ocr/privacy/hipaa/enforcement/examples/massgeneralracap.pdf (hereinafter "Mass General Resolution Agreement").

[170] HHS statement—Mass General; Mass General Resolution Agreement.

[171] HHS statement—Mass General; Mass General Resolution Agreement.

[172] HHS statement—Mass General; Mass General Resolution Agreement.

Another lesson from the MGH resolution agreement is that OCR remains very concerned about lack of controls when PHI is "off site." In 2006, CMS (responsible at that time for Security Regulation enforcement) responded to security incidents involving stolen and lost laptops with guidance about the security of ePHI on portable devices.[173] That guidance recommended "extreme caution" about allowing offsite use of or access to ePHI. The PHI in the MGH incident was in paper rather than electronic form, and it is a reminder to covered entities and business associates that appropriate policies and safeguards must also be in place for paper records taken off site. Furthermore, since ePHI can be secured though encryption, in some situations it may be advisable to convert paper PHI to encrypted ePHI for offsite use.

The OCR Director used the announcement of the MGH Resolution Agreement to emphasize that OCR is serious about HIPAA enforcement and that covered entities must ensure continuing compliance with the Regulations. OCR expects a covered entity to have a "robust compliance program that includes employee training, vigilant implementation of policies and procedures, regular internal audits, and a prompt action plan to respond to incidents."[174]

[F] UCLA Health System (2011)

The University of California at Los Angeles Health System (UCLAHS) entered into a resolution agreement with HHS July 6, 2011, resolving two separate complaints made on behalf of two celebrity patients who received care at UCLAHS. The resolution agreement requires UCLAHS to pay a $865,000 resolution amount to HHS and to enter into a three-year corrective action plan to remedy gaps in its Privacy Regulations compliance.[175]

OCR began its investigations in June 2009; the investigations covered periods from 2005 to 2009. OCR's investigations found that hundreds of members of the UCLAHS workforce accessed the ePHI of patients without a permissible reason. In addition, OCR found that UCLAHS (1) did not provide and/or did not document privacy and security training for its workforce, (2) failed to apply appropriate sanctions and/or document sanctions on workforce members who impermissibly viewed e-PHI, and (3) failed to implement "security measures sufficient to reduce the risks of impermissible access to electronic protected health information by unauthorized users to a reasonable and appropriate level."[176]

Under the resolution agreement, UCLAHS agreed to implement a three-year corrective action plan that included terms relating to policies and procedures, workforce training, third-party compliance monitoring, and submission of reports to HHS.[177]

In discussing this case, HHS has emphasized that covered entities are responsible for the actions of their employees and has stressed the importance of training and meaningful policies and procedures (including audit trails) as "part of the everyday operations of any health care provider."[178]

As stated by OCR, employees must understand that accessing patient records simply out of personal curiosity is "unacceptable and against the law."[179] Upon referral by OCR, the Department of Justice conducted a criminal investigation that resulted in one UCLAHS employee pleading guilty to obtaining PHI for personal gain. See § 6.07[A][8].

---

[173] See § 4.04[D] for more information.

[174] HHS statement—Mass General.

[175] HHS News Release, "University of California Settles HIPAA Privacy and Security Case Involving UCLA Health Systems Facilities" (July 7, 2011), available at http://www.hhs.gov/news/press/2011pres/07/20110707a.html (hereinafter "HHS statement—UCLAHS"); UCLAHS Resolution Agreement, available at http://www.hhs.gov/ocr/privacy/hipaa/enforcement/examples/uclahsracap.pdf (hereinafter UCLAHS Resolution Agreement).

[176] UCLAHS Resolution Agreement.

[177] UCLAHS Resolution Agreement.

[178] HHS statement—UCLAHS.

[179] HHS statement—UCLAHS.

[G] Blue Cross Blue Shield of Tennessee (2012)

Blue Cross Blue Shield of Tennessee (BCBST) entered into a resolution agreement with HHS in March 2012 in connection with the theft of computer equipment containing ePHI. This was the first enforcement action arising from a report to OCR of a privacy breach under the HITECH Breach Regulations. BCBST agreed to pay a $1.5 million resolution amount and enter into a corrective action plan.[180]

On November 3, 2009, BCBST submitted a breach notification report to OCR concerning a breach involving the theft of 57 unencrypted computer hard drives. OCR opened an investigation on January 8, 2010.[181] The following describes OCR's findings from its investigation. BCBST had vacated a particular office facility but maintained a lease on part of the space and was storing the 57 hard drives in a network data closet there. The network data closet was secured by biometric and keycard scan security with a magnetic lock. There was an additional door with a keyed lock. The property management company was also providing security services. A few weeks before the equipment was scheduled to be moved out of this location, the hard drives were stolen.[182]

The hard drives contained data from video recordings and audio recordings of BCBST customer service calls. The drives were unencrypted and contained the PHI of over one million individuals, including plan member names, Social Security numbers, dates of birth, diagnosis codes, and health plan ID numbers. To access the PHI, each call record would have to be individually and manually reviewed.[183]

OCR concluded, based on its investigation, that BCBST had failed to implement appropriate administrative safeguards by not performing the required security evaluation in response to operational changes (with respect to the equipment left at the facility). OCR also concluded that BCBST failed to implement appropriate physical safeguards by not having adequate facility access controls in place.[184]

In addition to payment of the $1.5 million resolution amount, BCBST agreed to implement a 450-day corrective action plan that required BCBST to develop and implement written policies and procedures regarding the conduct of a security risk assessment, the conduct of a risk management plan to implement security measures identified by the risk assessment, facility access controls, facility security plan, and physical safeguards governing the storage of ePHI. BCBST was also required to provide training, conduct internal compliance monitoring, and make compliance reports to HHS.[185]

[H] Phoenix Cardiac Surgery (2012)

In April 2012, a small surgical practice in Arizona, Phoenix Cardiac Surgery, P.C. (PCS), entered into a resolution agreement with HHS, related to PCS's allegedly making PHI publicly available on the Internet and otherwise lacking safeguards for electronic PHI. PCS agreed to pay a resolution amount of $100,000 and enter into a corrective action plan.[186] Unlike most of the covered entities that have entered into these resolution agreements with HHS, PCS is a small organization. In discussing PCS, OCR made it clear that it "expects full compliance no matter the size of the covered entity."[187]

---

[180] HHS News Release, "HHS Settles HIPAA Case Involving with BCBST for $1.5 Million" (Mar. 13, 2012), available at http://www.hhs.gov/news/press/2012pres/03/20120313a.html (hereinafter "HHS statement—BCBST"); BCBST Resolution Agreement, available at http://www.hhs.gov/ocr/privacy/hipaa/enforcement/examples/resolution_agreement_and_cap.pdf (hereinafter BCBST Resolution Agreement). See § 3.06 for more information about the HITECH breach notification requirements.

[181] BCBST Resolution Agreement.

[182] BCBST Resolution Agreement.

[183] BCBST Resolution Agreement.

[184] HHS statement—BCBST.

[185] BCBST Resolution Agreement.

[186] HHS News Release, "HHS Settles Case with Phoenix Cardiac Surgery for Lack of HIPAA Safeguards" (Apr. 17, 2012), available at http://www.hhs.gov/news/press/2012pres/04/20120417a.html (hereinafter "HHS statement—Phoenix Cardiac Surgery"); Phoenix Cardiac Surgery Resolution Agreement, available at http://www.hhs.gov/ocr/privacy/hipaa/enforcement/examples/pcsurgery_agreement.pdf (hereinafter Phoenix Cardiac Surgery Resolution Agreement).

[187] HHS Statement—Phoenix Cardiac Surgery.

PCS is a for-profit cardiothoracic surgical practice, co-owned by two physicians. According to OCR's investigation, from April 2003 to the time of the investigation, PCS did not provide and document training of its workforce on required policies and procedures regarding PHI. Furthermore, OCR asserts that PCS failed to have appropriate and reasonable administrative and technical safeguards to protect PHI, failed to timely identify a security official, and failed to conduct an accurate and thorough security risk assessment.[188]

Specifically with regard to Internet use, OCR alleges that PCS:

- posted more than 1,000 separate entries of PHI on a publicly accessible, Internet-based calendar;

- daily transmitted ePHI from an Internet-based e-mail account to workforce members' personal Internet-based e-mail accounts; and

- failed to enter into business associate agreements with the vendors of the calendar and e-mail services.[189]

These allegations indicate that OCR's position is that business associate agreements were required because these vendors stored and maintained ePHI on behalf of a covered entity. Thus, OCR appears to be distinguishing these hosted Internet services from services that act merely as a "conduit" for PHI. The HITECH Regulations, published after this resolution agreement, clarified HHS's position about the limitations of the "conduit exception" and the need for business associate agreements with vendors who store or maintain PHI for a covered entity. In addition, HHS clarified its position regarding encryption of e-mail. See **§ 1.02[B][1]** for additional information about the "conduit" concept, **§ 4.04[I]** for information about "cloud computing," and **§ 4.04[C]** for information about e-mail encryption.

In addition to payment of the $100,000 resolution amount, PCS agreed to implement a one-year corrective action plan that required PCS to do the following:[190]

- *Policies and Procedures.* Develop, maintain, and revise (as necessary) written policies and procedures regarding the conduct in the allegations, relating to administrative and technical safeguards and training of the workforce; specifically including risk assessment, risk management plans, security official, business associate agreements, access controls (especially remote access), technical security measures for transmitted ePHI (including encryption or other adequate safeguards for communications like text messages), and security awareness training and other workforce training on PCS privacy and security policies.

- *Risk Assessment.* Submit to HHS an accurate and thorough current security risk assessment, which includes, but is not limited to, when ePHI is (1) posted to an Internet-based calendaring system, (2) transmitted over an Internet-based electronic communications system, (3) accessed remotely, or (4) transmitted to or from, or stored on a portable device.

- *Risk Management Plan.* Submit to HHS a risk management plan, sufficient to reduce the risk and vulnerabilities to ePHI identified by the updated risk assessment.

PCS also agreed to provide training to all members of the workforce who use or disclose PHI and to submit an implementation report to HHS.[191]

[I] Alaska Department of Health and Social Services (2012)

The Alaska Department of Health and Social Services (ADHSS) is the state agency responsible for administering the Alaska Medicaid Program. In June 2012, OCR announced its first HIPAA enforcement action

---

[188] Phoenix Cardiac Surgery Resolution Agreement.
[189] Phoenix Cardiac Surgery Resolution Agreement.
[190] Phoenix Cardiac Surgery Resolution Agreement.
[191] Phoenix Cardiac Surgery Resolution Agreement.

against a state agency.[192] ADHSS (hereinafter "Alaska Medicaid") entered into a resolution agreement with HHS related to safeguarding the electronic PHI of its Medicaid beneficiaries, which arose from the theft of a USB hard drive. Alaska Medicaid agreed to pay a resolution amount of $1.7 million and enter into a three-year corrective action plan.[193] OCR has made it clear, through this action, that it expects full compliance from all covered entities, whether public or private.[194]

OCR received an October 2009 breach report from Alaska Medicaid, which advised OCR that a portable electronic storage device *potentially* containing ePHI had been stolen from the vehicle of an Alaska Medicaid computer technician.[195] This led to an OCR investigation, from which OCR concluded that Alaska Medicaid had not done the following, each of which is required by the Security Regulations:

- Completed a risk analysis;

- Implemented sufficient risk management measures;

- Completed security training for its workforce;

- Implemented device and media controls; or

- Addressed device and media encryption.[196]

In addition to payment of the $1.7 million resolution amount, Alaska Medicaid agreed to implement a three-year corrective action plan. Alaska Medicaid is required to develop policies and procedures for tracking, safeguarding, encrypting, and disposing of and/or re-using devices that contain ePHI; respond to security incidents; and apply sanctions to workforce members who violate these policies and procedures. Alaska Medicaid must also conduct and submit to HHS an accurate and thorough current security risk assessment, and implement security measures sufficient to reduce the risks and vulnerabilities to ePHI identified by the risk assessment to a reasonable and appropriate level. Training, compliance monitoring, and reports to HHS are also required.[197]

[J] Massachusetts Eye and Ear (2012)

In April 2010, the Massachusetts Eye and Ear Infirmary and Massachusetts Eye and Ear Associates, Inc. (collectively, "MEEI") entered into a resolution agreement with HHS, which was related to the theft of a personal laptop containing the unencrypted PHI of MEEI patients and research subjects. MEEI agreed to pay a resolution amount of $1.5 million and to enter into a corrective action plan.[198] OCR alleged that MEEI failed to comply with certain requirements of the Security Regulations (e.g., conducting a thorough risk analysis of the security and confidentiality of PHI on portable devices), and furthermore, that "these failures continued over an extended period of time, demonstrating a long-term, organizational disregard for the requirements of the Security Rule."[199]

MEEI comprises two nonprofit corporations organized as a single "affiliated covered entity" for HIPAA compliance purposes. On April 21, 2010, OCR received notification from MEEI of a breach of unsecured ePHI, and on October 5, 2010, OCR notified MEEI that it was investigating the incident. In OCR's

---

[192] HHS News Release, "Alaska Medicaid Settles HIPAA Security Case for $1,700,000" (June 26, 2012), available at http://www.hhs.gov/news/press/2012pres/06/20120626a.html (hereinafter HHS Statement—Alaska Medicaid).

[193] Alaska Department of Health and Social Services Resolution Agreement, available at http://www.hhs.gov/ocr/privacy/hipaa/enforcement/examples/alaska-agreement.pdf (hereinafter "Alaska Medicaid Resolution Agreement").

[194] HHS statement—Alaska Medicaid.

[195] Alaska Medicaid Resolution Agreement.

[196] Alaska Medicaid Resolution Agreement.

[197] Alaska Medicaid Resolution Agreement.

[198] HHS News Release, "Massachusetts Provider Settles HIPAA Case for $1.5 Million" (Sept. 17, 2012), available at http://www.hhs.gov/news/press/2012pres/09/20120917a.html (hereinafter, "HHS Statement—MEEI").

[199] HHS Statement—MEEI.

investigation, it asserted that MEEI did not demonstrate that it had conducted a "thorough" analysis of the risk to confidentiality of ePHI on portable devices before October 2009, did not "fully evaluate" the risks, did not document chosen security measures and their rationale, and did not maintain ongoing reasonable and appropriate security measures. Other shortcomings alleged by OCR included (1) that MEEI had no reasonable means of tracking personally owned MEEI portable media devices that contained MEEI PHI, within or outside the facility, and (2) that MEEI did not implement an equivalent, reasonable, and appropriate alternative to encryption, or document the rationale supporting the decision not to encrypt.[200]

In addition to payment of the $1.5 million resolution amount, MEEI agreed to implement a three-year corrective action plan that requires security policies and procedures, independent compliance monitoring, workforce training, and reports to HHS.[201]

While it is unclear from the official documents what previous measures MEEI may have taken to comply with the Security Regulations, OCR makes clear that, in its view, those measures were insufficient. OCR wants covered entities and business associates to not only conduct risk assessments, but the risk analysis must be *thorough* and *completely evaluate* the risks, must be well-documented, and must be revisited regularly. Although the calculation of the resolution amount is not explained, it is possible that the relatively large amount may be related to OCR's contention that MEEI was noncompliant "over an extended period of time." Or perhaps, it is simply another indication that OCR has lost patience with covered entities and business associates that do not encrypt and physically safeguard portable devices containing PHI.

[K] Hospice of North Idaho (2013)

In the first resolution agreement of 2013, the Hospice of North Idaho (HONI) agreed to pay HHS a resolution amount of $50,000 to settle potential violations of the Security Regulations. HONI regularly uses laptop computers containing PHI as part of its fieldwork. In June 2010, one of these laptops was stolen. It contained the unencrypted PHI of 441 patients. HONI reported the breach to OCR on February 16, 2011.[202]

OCR notified HONI in July 2011 that it was conducting an investigation. OCR alleged, based on its investigation, that prior to January 2012, the hospice provider had failed to conduct "an accurate and thorough analysis" of the risks to ePHI on an ongoing basis, particularly with regard to portable devices. OCR also alleged that HONI did not have adequate policies and procedures in place to address the security of mobile devices until May 2011.[203] OCR acknowledged, however, that since the discovery of the theft, HONI has taken extensive additional steps to improve its privacy and security compliance program.[204]

In addition to payment of the $50,000 resolution amount, HONI agreed to implement a two-year corrective action plan that requires HONI to promptly investigate if it receives information that a workforce member may have failed to comply with HONI privacy and security policies and procedures. If HONI determines that there was noncompliance, it must inform HHS within 30 days.[205] The corrective action plan under this Resolution Agreement is notably more limited in scope than most of the others. This may be due to HONI having already made significant improvements.

---

[200] Massachusetts Eye and Ear Infirmary and Massachusetts Eye and Ear Associates, Inc. Resolution Agreement, available at http://www.hhs.gov/ocr/privacy/hipaa/enforcement/examples/meei-agreement-pdf.pdf (hereinafter "MEEI Resolution Agreement").

[201] MEEI Resolution Agreement.

[202] HHS News Release, "HHS Announces First HIPAA Breach Settlement Involving Less than 500 Patients" (Jan. 2, 2013), available at http://www.hhs.gov/news/press/2013pres/01/20130102a.html (hereinafter HHS "Statement—HONI"); Hospice of North Idaho Resolution Agreement, available at http://www.hhs.gov/ocr/privacy/hipaa/enforcement/examples/honi-agreement.pdf (hereinafter "HONI Resolution Agreement"). Covered entities are required to report breaches of unsecured PHI to OCR. If the breach involves 500 or more individuals, it must be reported immediately; otherwise, it must be reported within 60 days following the end of the calendar year. See **§ 3.06** for a full discussion of breach notification requirements.

[203] HONI Resolution Agreement.

[204] HHS Statement—HONI.

[205] HONI Resolution Agreement.

[L] Idaho State University (2013)

Idaho State University (ISU) operates 29 outpatient clinics and provides those clinics with health information technology systems security. Some, but not all, of these clinics are covered entities. As reported by HHS, ISU discovered a security breach in which the electronic PHI of approximately 17,500 patients of ISU's Pocatello Family Medicine Clinic was unsecured for at least 10 months, as a result of the disabling of firewall protections at servers maintained by ISU. OCR opened an investigation after ISU notified OCR of the breach.[206]

Based on its investigation, OCR alleged that ISU did not apply proper security measures and policies to address risks to ePHI. Furthermore, ISU did not have procedures in place for routine information systems reviews, which could have led to a much earlier detection of the firewall problem. Specifically, OCR alleged that, from 2007 to 2012, ISU did not conduct an analysis of the risk to electronic PHI as part of its security management process; adequately implement security measures to reduce risks and vulnerabilities to a reasonable and appropriate level; or adequately implement procedures to regularly review records of system activity to determine if any PHI was inappropriately used or disclosed.[207]

To settle the alleged violations, ISU agreed to pay a resolution amount of $400,000 and enter into a two-year corrective action plan.[208] The corrective action plan requires ISU to do the following:

- *Designation as a Hybrid Entity.* Designate ISU as a hybrid entity under HIPAA (see **§ 1.02[C][1]**), and provide HHS with documentation of such designation and of all of ISU's components that have been designated as covered health care components;

- *Risk Management.* Provide HHS with ISU's most recent risk management plan, which will include specific security measures to reduce risks and vulnerabilities to a reasonable and appropriate level for all its covered health care components, and after approval by HHS, implement the risk management plan;

- *Information System Activity Review.* Provide HHS with documentation of implementation of ISU's policies and procedures regarding information system activity review for all its covered health care components (subject to HHS approval);

- *Compliance Gap Analysis.* Provide to HHS documentation of ISU's updated gap analysis activity ("Post Incident Risk Assessment"), as specified by HHS, indicating changes in compliance status regarding each provision of the Security Regulations; and

- *Workforce Compliance; Internal Investigations.* If ISU receives information that a workforce member may have failed to comply with ISU's privacy and security policies and procedures, ISU must promptly investigate; and if it determines that there was noncompliance, it must inform HHS within 30 days; and

- *Report to HHS.* Submit annual compliance reports to HHS.[209]

[M] Shasta Regional Medical Center (2013)

In June 2013, Shasta Regional Medical Center (SRMC) agreed to a comprehensive corrective action plan and to pay a $275,000 resolution amount to settle alleged violations of the Privacy Regulations. OCR notified SRMC on January 6, 2012, that it was initiating a compliance review of the facility, based on a Los Angeles Times article published a few days earlier on January 4, 2012. According to the article, two senior leaders from

---

[206] HHS News Release, "Idaho State University Settles HIPAA Security Case for $400,000" (May 21, 2013), available at http://www.hhs.gov/ocr/privacy/hipaa/enforcement/examples/isu-agreement-press-release.html.html (hereinafter "HHS Statement—ISU").

[207] HHS Statement—ISU; Idaho State University Resolution Agreement, available at http://www.hhs.gov/ocr/privacy/hipaa/enforcement/examples/isu-agreement.pdf (hereinafter "ISU Resolution Agreement").

[208] ISU Resolution Agreement.

[209] ISU Resolution Agreement.

SRMC had met with the media to discuss the medical services SRMC had provided to a patient, but did not have a valid authorization from the patient to disclose her PHI.[210]

Following its investigation, OCR alleged that, based on the following conduct, SRMC had failed to safeguard the patient's PHI from impermissible disclosure on multiple occasions.

> i) On December 13, 2011, SRMC sent a letter, through its parent company, to *California Watch*, responding to a story concerning Medicare fraud. The letter described the [patient's] medical treatment and provided specifics about her lab results. SRMC did not have a written authorization from the [patient] to disclose this information to this news outlet.
>
> ii) On December 16, 2011, two of SRMC's senior leaders met with *The Record Searchlight's* editor to discuss the [patient's] medical record in detail. SRMC did not have a written authorization from the [patient] to disclose this information to this newspaper.
>
> iii) On December 20, 2011, SRMC sent a letter to *The Los Angeles Times*, which contained detailed information about the treatment the [patient] received. SRMC did not have a written authorization from the [patient] to disclose this information to this newspaper.[211]

OCR also alleged impermissible use of the patient's PHI:

> i) On December 20, 2011, SRMC sent an email to its entire workforce and medical staff, approximately 785-900 individuals, describing, in detail, the [patient's] medical condition, diagnosis and treatment. SRMC did not have a written authorization from the [patient] to share this information with SRMC's entire workforce and medical staff.[212]

OCR further alleged that SRMC had failed to sanction its workforce members, under SRMC's policy, which requires that it sanction employees for HIPAA violations.[213]

The Resolution Agreement was entered into jointly by SRMC and 15 other health care providers that are covered entities and under the same ownership or operational control (referred to collectively in the Resolution Agreement as the "Covered Entities").[214] It is not clear from the Resolution Agreement whether these Covered Entities had formed a single "affiliated covered entity" for HIPAA compliance purposes (see § 1.02[C][2]). To settle the alleged violations, without any admission of liability, the Covered Entities agreed to pay a resolution amount of $275,000 and enter into a one-year corrective action plan.[215] The corrective action plan includes the following obligations for SRMC:

> • *Policies and Procedures.* Develop, maintain and revise (as necessary), and implement policies and procedures applicable to SRMC (and all of its facilities and subsidiaries) regarding (1) appropriate administrative, physical, and technical safeguards to protect PHI from intentional or unintentional use or disclosure for media inquiries; (2) permissible and impermissible uses and disclosures of PHI for media inquiries and to workforce members who are not involved in the individual's care; (3) instructions regarding what is PHI, communicating with and responding to the media (including with regard to patient-related inquiries), and sharing PHI within SRMC, such as with workforce members not involved in the provision of care or payment for care; and (4) protocols for training all members of the workforce who have access to PHI to ensure that they know how to comply with the policies and

---

[210] HHS News Release, "HHS Requires California Medical Provider to Protect Patients' Right to Privacy" (June 13, 2013), available at http://www.hhs.gov/ocr/privacy/hipaa/enforcement/examples/shasta-agreement-press-release.html (hereinafter "HHS Statement—SRMC"); Shasta Regional Medical Center Resolution Agreement, available at http://www.hhs.gov/ocr/privacy/hipaa/enforcement/examples/shasta-agreement.pdf (hereinafter "SRMC Resolution Agreement").

[211] SRMC Resolution Agreement.

[212] SRMC Resolution Agreement.

[213] SRMC Resolution Agreement.

[214] SRMC Resolution Agreement.

[215] SRMC Resolution Agreement.

procedures and application of appropriate sanctions against members of the workforce who fail to comply with policies and procedures.

- *Training.* All workforce members who use or disclose PHI must receive specific training on the policies and procedures described above within 90 days of implementation of the policies and procedures (or within 30 days of joining the workforce).

- *Workforce Compliance; Internal Investigations.* If SRMC determines that a workforce member has violated the above policies and procedures, SRMC must notify HHS in writing within 30 days.

- *Report to HHS.* Submit an implementation report and annual reports to HHS.[216]

In addition, the Resolution Agreement requires each of the other Covered Entities to submit to HHS an affidavit by its CEO and Privacy Officer, stating they understand:

(a) an individual's protected health information ("PHI") is protected by Privacy Rule even if such information is already in the public domain or even though it has been disclosed by the individual; and (b) disclosures of PHI in response to media inquiries are only permissible pursuant to a signed HIPAA authorization.[217]

The affidavits must be submitted to HHS within 60 days, and each of these Covered Entities will ensure that all members of their respective workforces are informed of this policy.[218]

OCR makes clear that, despite a covered entity's desire to control a media situation, disclosure of a patient's PHI to the media is not the appropriate response. Furthermore, senior executives in the organization are responsible for knowing and complying with the Privacy, Breach and Security Regulations, and are held to the same standards as the rest of the workforce.

[N] WellPoint (2013)

WellPoint, Inc. and other related health plans have designated themselves as an affiliated covered entity under HIPAA (hereinafter, "WellPoint"). In July 2013, WellPoint agreed to pay HHS $1.7 million to settle claims related to the potential exposure of the PHI of more than 600,000 individuals on the Internet.[219] In announcing the resolution agreement, HHS emphasized the importance, for both covered entities and business associates, of ensuring that security issues are appropriately considered when implementing changes to information systems, especially when Internet-based access is involved.[220]

On June 18, 2010, WellPoint notified HHS of a breach of unsecured electronic PHI. HHS started an investigation and notified WellPoint of this on September 9, 2010. Based on its investigation, HHS alleged:[221]

- Security weaknesses in an online application database left the PHI of 612,402 individuals accessible to unauthorized persons over the Internet, from October 23, 2009, to March 7, 2010.

- The data included names, dates of birth, addresses, Social Security numbers, telephone numbers, and health information.

---

[216] SRMC Resolution Agreement.

[217] SRMC Resolution Agreement.

[218] SRMC Resolution Agreement.

[219] HHS News Release, "WellPoint Pays HHS $1.7 Million for Leaving Information Accessible Over Internet" (July 11, 2013), available at http://www.hhs.gov/news/press/2013pres/07/20130711b.html (hereinafter "HHS Statement—WellPoint"); WellPoint Resolution Agreement, available at http://www.hhs.gov/ocr/privacy/hipaa/enforcement/examples/wellpoint-agreement.pdf (hereinafter "WellPoint Resolution Agreement").

[220] HHS Statement—WellPoint.

[221] HHS Statement—WellPoint; WellPoint Resolution Agreement.

- WellPoint failed to implement appropriate administrative and technical safeguards; specifically failing to:
  - Adequately implement policies and procedures for authorizing access to the online application database;

  - Perform an appropriate technical evaluation in response to a software upgrade;

  - Have technical safeguards in place to control access and verify identity of those persons seeking access to the online database.

Unlike other resolution agreements, there was no corrective action plan, just the $1.7 million resolution amount.

[O]   Affinity Health Plan (2013)

Digital copiers have hard drives and are capable of storing information that is photocopied, including PHI. On April 15, 2010, Affinity Health Plan, Inc. ("Affinity") reported a breach to HHS that involved this type of photocopier.[222] Affinity was notified of the breach by the CBS Evening News. CBS, as part of an investigative report, purchased a photocopier previously leased by Affinity, and discovered that the hard drive contained electronic PHI.[223]

On May 19, 2010, HHS notified Affinity that it was opening an investigation. Based on that investigation, HHS concluded that Affinity impermissibly disclosed the electronic PHI of up to 344,579 individuals by failing to properly erase the hard drives in photocopiers prior to returning them to the photocopier leasing company. HHS further concluded that Affinity had failed to assess and identify the potential security risks and vulnerabilities of PHI in the photocopier hard drives, and failed to implement appropriate policies for disposal of that PHI.[224]

In addition to payment of a $1,215,780 resolution amount, Affinity agreed to implement a short-term (120 days) corrective action plan. Within the first five days, Affinity was required to use its best efforts to recover any photocopier hard drives that had been leased to Affinity and were still in the possession of the leasing company and to safeguard that PHI. For any hard drives that could not be retrieved, Affinity was required to document its efforts and the reason it could not retrieve the hard drives. In addition, within the first 30 days of the corrective action plan, Affinity was required to conduct a comprehensive risk analysis that included all its electronic equipment and systems, and develop a plan to mitigate any security risks and vulnerabilities found.[225]

This case is a reminder that PHI may be in locations that covered entities and business associates are not routinely including in their risk assessments. Furthermore, policies and procedures for secure disposal of PHI are necessary and should include the secure removal of PHI from equipment before it is recycled, destroyed, returned, or sold.

[P]   Adult & Pediatric Dermatology (2013)

In December 2013, Adult & Pediatric Dermatology, P.C. ("APDerm"), a private practice providing dermatology services, agreed to a corrective action plan and to pay a $150,000 resolution amount to settle alleged

---

[222] HHS News Release, "HHS Settles with Health Plan in Photocopier Breach Case" (August 14, 2013), available at http://www.hhs.gov/ocr/privacy/hipaa/enforcement/examples/affinity-agreement.html (hereinafter "HHS Statement—Affinity"); Affinity Resolution Agreement, available at http://www.hhs.gov/ocr/privacy/hipaa/enforcement/examples/affinity_agreement.pdf (hereinafter "Affinity Resolution Agreement").

[223] HHS Statement—Affinity.

[224] Affinity Resolution Agreement. The Federal Trade Commission has provided guidance regarding the security of these digital copiers. See § 4.04[F].

[225] Affinity Resolution Agreement.

violations of the Privacy and Security Regulations, and for the first time, violation of the Breach Regulations.[226]

APDerm notified HHS on October 7, 2011, of a breach of unsecured electronic PHI. APDerm reported that an unencrypted thumb drive containing PHI related to the treatment of approximately 2,200 patients was stolen from the vehicle of a member of the APDerm workforce. The thumb drive was never recovered. APDerm notified the patients and provided media notice, as required by the Breach Regulations.[227]

HHS notified APDerm on November 9, 2011, that it was investigating. In its investigation, HHS found purported deficiencies in APDerm's security risk assessment and management process. HHS also alleged that APDerm did not reasonably safeguard the unencrypted thumb drive. Finally, HHS concluded that, although APDerm had provided timely breach notifications, it did not fully comply with the Breach Regulations requirements to have written breach notification policies and procedures and to train workforce members until February 2012.[228]

In addition to payment of a $150,000 resolution amount, APDerm agreed to implement a corrective action plan. First, within one year, APDerm must conduct a comprehensive, organization-wide risk analysis of its electronic PHI security risks and vulnerabilities. Then, it must develop a risk management plan to address and mitigate any such risks and vulnerabilities identified, and revise policies and procedures, as needed. APDerm must prepare an Implementation Report for HHS; once that is approved by HHS, the corrective action plan compliance period will end.

Once again, with this resolution agreement, the focus returns to the risk assessment and risk management processes for electronic PHI. Furthermore, it puts covered entities on notice that even if they follow correct procedures in responding to a breach, they can still be found deficient if they don't have appropriate written procedures and workforce training with regard to breaches.

[Q] Skagit County, Washington (2014)

In 2012, OCR entered into a resolution agreement with an Alaskan state agency (see § 6.05[I]), demonstrating that government agencies were subject to HIPAA enforcement actions. In 2014, OCR took this a step further, sending "a strong message about the importance of HIPAA compliance to local and county governments, regardless of size."[229] HHS entered into a resolution agreement with Skagit County, Washington, which has a population of about 118,000 people.[230]

Skagit County reported a breach of unsecured PHI to HHS on December 9, 2011, involving the PHI of seven individuals accessed by unknown persons after the information had been inadvertently moved to a publicly accessible server maintained by the County. On May 2012, HHS notified Skagit County that it was investigating, and HHS subsequently determined that over the course of about two weeks, the County had improperly disclosed the PHI of 1,581 individuals by providing access on its public web server.[231] HHS alleged that the County failed to provide notification to "all of the individuals for whom it knew or should have known"

---

[226] HHS News Release, "Dermatology Practice Settles Potential HIPAA Violations" (December 26, 2013), available at http://www.hhs.gov/news/press/2013pres/12/20131226a.html (hereinafter "HHS Statement—APDerm"); Adult & Pediatric Dermatology, P.C. Resolution Agreement, available at http://www.hhs.gov/ocr/privacy/hipaa/enforcement/examples/apderm-resolution-agreement.pdf (hereinafter "APDerm Resolution Agreement").

[227] APDerm Resolution Agreement.

[228] APDerm Resolution Agreement.

[229] HHS News Release, "County Government Settles Potential HIPAA Violations" (March 7, 2014), available at http://www.hhs.gov/news/press/2014pres/03/20140307a.html (hereinafter "HHS Statement—Skagit County").

[230] HHS Statement—Skagit County; Skagit County Washington Resolution Agreement, available at http://www.hhs.gov/ocr/privacy/hipaa/enforcement/examples/skagit-county-settlement-agreement.pdf (hereinafter "Skagit County Resolution Agreement").

[231] HHS Statement—Skagit County; Skagit County Resolution Agreement. The resolution agreement is not specific, but it could be that difference between seven individuals and 1,581 individuals might be the difference between the records know to have been accessed and the total records that were accessible to the public.

that their PHI was compromised as a result of it being made accessible on the County's public web server.[232] HHS also alleged general and widespread noncompliance with the Security Regulations.[233]

Skagit County agreed to a $215,000 resolution amount and an extensive three-year corrective action plan. The corrective action plan first requires the County to provide substitute notice (see § **5.05**) either through publication in major print or broadcast media, or by posting a notice on the County's website, and furthermore, to ensure that the disclosures of PHI in this incident are included in any accounting of disclosures reports (see § **3.02[D]**) provided to individuals involved. The corrective action plan then focuses on broader concerns. The County is required to prepare hybrid entity documents, which designate which parts of the County are "covered health care components" and subject to the Regulations (see § **1.02[C][1]**). The County must also conduct an accurate and thorough security assessment and implement appropriate security measures. The County must also prepare and adopt policies and procedures, and conduct training for all workforce members.[234]

[R]   QCA Health Plan (2014)

Another unencrypted laptop stolen from another employee's car, this time involving QCA Health Plan, Inc. of Arkansas ("QCA"), led to a resolution agreement in April 2014. QCA submitted a breach notice to HHS in February 2012 reporting the theft of an unencrypted laptop containing the PHI of 148 individuals.[235] HHS notified QCA on May 3, 2012, that it was investigating. HHS, based on its investigation, concluded that QCA did not implement necessary security policies and procedures. Furthermore, on October 8, 2011, QCA did not implement physical safeguards for workstations, and impermissibly disclosed the PHI of the 148 individuals.[236] HHS alleged that QCA failed to comply with multiple requirements of the Regulations, beginning in 2005.[237]

QCA agreed to a resolution agreement in April 2014, which included a resolution amount of $250,000, and a two-year corrective action plan that requires it to conduct an updated risk analysis and implement a corresponding risk management plan. QCA must also provide security awareness training.[238]

HHS continues to emphasize the significant risk to the security of PHI of storing PHI on unencrypted laptops and other mobile devices. Also of note in this case was the fact that the HHS investigation looked back to 2005 in identifying alleged compliance failures.

[S]   Concentra Health Services (2014)

Here again, in this case, a resolution agreement arose from an unencrypted laptop being stolen. On November 30, 2011, the laptop was stolen from a Missouri physical therapy center, part of Concentra Health Services ("Concentra"). Concentra reported the breach to HHS, as required, and a few months later, HHS opened an investigation. In April 2014, Concentra and HHS entered into a resolution agreement, requiring Concentra to pay a resolution amount of $1,725,220 and enter into a two-year corrective action plan.[239]

The HHS investigation indicated that Concentra "had previously recognized in multiple risk analyses that a lack of encryption on its laptops, desktop computers, medical equipment, tablets, and other devices containing

---

[232] Skagit County Resolution Agreement.

[233] HHS Statement—Skagit County.

[234] Skagit County Resolution Agreement.

[235] HHS News Release, "Stolen Laptops Lead to Important HIPAA Settlements" (April 22, 2014), available at http://www.hhs.gov/news/press/2014pres/04/20140422b.html (hereinafter "HHS Statement—Concentra-QCA").

[236] QCA Health Plan Resolution Agreement, available at http://www.hhs.gov/ocr/privacy/hipaa/enforcement/examples/qca_agreement.pdf (hereinafter "QCA Resolution Agreement").

[237] HHS Statement—Concentra-QCA.

[238] QCA Resolution Agreement.

[239] HHS Statement—Concentra-QCA; Concentra Health Services Resolution Agreement, available at http://www.hhs.gov/ocr/privacy/hipaa/enforcement/examples/concentra_agreement.pdf (hereinafter "Concentra Resolution Agreement").

electronic protected health information (ePHI) was a critical risk."[240] Some steps had been taken with regard to encryption; as of October 2008, 434 out of 597 laptops were encrypted, according to Concentra reports.[241] But HHS deemed these efforts "incomplete and inconsistent."[242]

Concentra's corrective action plan requires Concentra to complete a new risk analysis and a new risk management plan. Concentra is also required to provide to HHS evidence of all implemented and planned remediation actions. For planned remediation actions, Concentra must also provide specific timelines for completion and identify other controls to safeguard ePHI in the interim. Specifically with regard to encryption, Concentra must provide status reports to HHS within 120 days, and at the end of each of the two years of the corrective action plan. These status reports must identify the percentage of all devices encrypted, evidence that all new devices have been encrypted, and an explanation for whatever has not been encrypted.[243]

Encryption is an addressable standard and not an absolute requirement under the Security Regulations. (See § 4.04[A].) But Concentra had identified the lack of encryption as a risk, and failed to either "adequately remediate and manage" that risk, or in the alternative, document why encryption was not reasonable and appropriate and implement a reasonable and appropriate alternative.[244] The risks associated with unencrypted devices can be significant, and covered entities and business associates should carefully consider any decision to forego or delay encryption. If they choose not to encrypt, it is essential to implement an appropriate alternative and document the analysis behind these decisions. This resolution agreement is also a good reminder for covered entities and business associates that doing a risk analysis is not sufficient; a risk management plan and appropriate and timely implementation is also critical.

[T] New York and Presbyterian Hospital; Columbia University (2014)

Columbia University ("CU") faculty members serve as attending physicians at New York and Presbyterian Hospital ("NYP"). CU and NYP are separate covered entities, but they operate a shared data network, which links to NYP patient information systems that contain electronic PHI. The shared data network has a shared firewall that is administered by employees of both organizations.[245] NYP and CU submitted a joint breach report to HHS on September 27, 2010, relating to a disclosure of the electronic PHI of 6,800 individuals. The PHI included patient status, vital signs, medications, and lab results. HHS notified both entities on November 5, 2010, that it was investigating. According to the HHS investigation that followed, the breach was caused by a CU physician who attempted to deactivate a personally owned computer server on the network containing NYP patient PHI. Due to a lack of technical safeguards, this resulted in electronic PHI being accessible to Internet search engines. NYP and CU discovered the breach when they received a complaint from a person who found the PHI of a former NYP patient on the Internet.[246]

The HHS investigation concluded that neither NYP nor CU had made efforts (prior to the breach) to make certain the server was secure, and neither had conducted an accurate and thorough risk analysis for all the systems that access NYP electronic PHI. Further, because the risk analysis was deficient, they had not developed an adequate risk management plan. Finally, HHS concluded that NYP had failed to implement policies and

---

[240] HHS Statement—Concentra-QCA.

[241] Concentra Resolution Agreement.

[242] HHS Statement—Concentra-QCA.

[243] Concentra Resolution Agreement.

[244] HHS Statement—Concentra-QCA; Concentra Resolution Agreement. Concentra began encrypting all devices in June 2012. Concentra Resolution Agreement.

[245] HHS News Release, "Data Breach Results in $4.8 Million Settlements" (May 7, 2014), available at http://www.hhs.gov/news/press/2014pres/05/20140507b.html (hereinafter "HHS Statement—NYP-CU").

[246] HHS Statement—NYP-CU. See also Trustees of Columbia University in the City of New York Resolution Agreement, available at http://www.hhs.gov/ocr/privacy/hipaa/enforcement/examples/columbia-university-resolution-agreement.pdf (hereinafter "CU Resolution Agreement") and New York and Presbyterian Hospital Resolution Agreement, available at http://www.hhs.gov/ocr/privacy/hipaa/enforcement/examples/ny-and-presbyterian-hospital-settlement-agreement.pdf (hereinafter "NYP Resolution Agreement").

procedures for authorizing access to its databases and failed to comply with its own information access management policies.[247]

NYP and CU each entered into resolution agreements with HHS, which included resolution amounts and extensive three-year corrective action plans. CU paid $1.5 million. NYP paid $3.3 million, the largest resolution amount to date. The details of how responsibility was allocated and how the respective resolution amounts were determined are not provided in the published resolution agreements. However, a comparison of the two agreements shows only NYP being cited for the breach itself: "NYP impermissibly disclosed the ePHI of 6,800 patients to Google and other Internet search engines when a computer server that had access to NYP ePHI information systems was errantly reconfigured."[248] The CU agreement does not contain a comparable statement in its findings. In other respects, the two agreements are quite similar.

Both the CU and NYP corrective action plans impose requirements for:[249]

- A comprehensive and through risk analysis.

- Developing and implementing an organization-wide risk management plan.

- Review, revision, and implementation of policies and procedures on information access management.

- Development of a process to evaluate any environmental and operational changes that affect the security of electronic PHI.

- Review, revision, and implementation of policies and procedures on device and media controls.

- Workforce training.

- Initial and periodic reports to HHS.

One additional requirement for NYP, however, is that the workforce training include training of "affiliated staff," i.e., the medical personnel who are employees of CU, but are authorized to treat patients at NYP and have been granted access to NYP electronic PHI. And in particular, that workforce members and affiliated staff be trained "on the necessity and existence of prohibitions on the purchase, use, or administration of computer equipment that accesses NYP ePHI, except under the explicit management of NYP IT personnel."[250]

[U] Parkview Health System (2014)

Parkview Health System, Inc. ("Parkview") is a nonprofit system providing community-based health care services in Indiana and Ohio. In 2011, HHS opened an investigation of Parkview based on a 2009 complaint from a physician regarding the transfer or disposal of boxes containing medical records.[251]

HHS describes the facts as follows: In September 2008, Parkview received and "took custody and control" of the non-electronic medical records of approximately 5,000 to 8,000 of the patients of a retiring physician, Dr. Hamilton.[252] Parkview held the records while assisting Dr. Hamilton's transition of her patients to new providers and while Parkview considered purchasing some of Dr. Hamilton's practice.[253] Subsequently, in June 2009, Parkview employees left 71 cardboard boxes containing these medical records unattended on the driveway of

---

[247] HHS Statement—NYP-CU.

[248] NYP Resolution Agreement.

[249] CU Resolution Agreement; NYP Resolution Agreement.

[250] NYP Resolution Agreement.

[251] HHS News Release, "$800,000 HIPAA Settlement in Medical Records Dumping Case" (June 23, 2014), available at http://www.hhs.gov/news/press/2014pres/06/20140623a.html (hereinafter "HHS Statement—Parkview").

[252] Parkview Health System Resolution Agreement, available at http://www.hhs.gov/ocr/privacy/hipaa/enforcement/examples/hhs-parkview-resolution-cap.pdf (hereinafter "Parkview Resolution Agreement").

[253] HHS Statement—Parkview.

Dr. Hamilton's home, in a heavily trafficked area, although they had notice that Dr. Hamilton had refused delivery and was not at home.[254] Dr. Hamilton filed a complaint with OCR.

HHS stated that Parkview was obligated to appropriately and reasonably safeguard all PHI in its possession "from the time it is acquired through its disposition."[255] HHS entered into resolution agreement with Parkview, which included payment of an $800,000 resolution amount and a corrective action plan. The corrective action plan requires Parkview to revise their policies and procedures regarding administrative, physical, and technical safeguards to protect non-electronic PHI. Members of the Parkview workforce with access to PHI must receive training and copies of the revised policies and procedures. Violations of these policies and procedures must be reported to HHS within 30 days, and Parkview must provide a final implementation report to HHS.[256]

HHS used this case to emphasize the point that improper disposal or transfer of PHI can put patient information at risk, and that "it is imperative that HIPAA covered entities and their business associates protect patient information during its transfer and disposal."[257] HHS then directed covered entities and business associates to OCR's FAQs regarding the disposal of PHI.[258]

[V] Anchorage Community Mental Health Services (2014)

Anchorage Community Mental Health Services (ACMHS) is a nonprofit community mental health services provider serving Anchorage, Alaska, and the surrounding area. OCR received a breach notification from ACMHS on March 2, 2012. The breach involved the unsecured electronic PHI of 2,743 individuals "due to malware compromising the security" of ACMHS' technology resources.[259] The specific nature of the breach or the malware at ACMHS is not described. In general, malware (malicious software) is software used to gain access to computer systems, disrupt system operations, and/or gain unauthorized access to information. Tools used to protect against malware include firewalls, installing software patches for identified vulnerabilities and anti-malware software.

On June 3, 2012, OCR notified ACMHS of its investigation of the breach. According to OCR's investigation:

- ACMHS had adopted Security Regulations policies and procedures in 2005 but had not followed them. ACMHS had failed to conduct accurate and thorough assessments of its potential security risks and vulnerabilities and had failed to implement policies and procedures requiring security measures that would reduce those risks and vulnerabilities to a reasonable and appropriate level.

- ACHMS failed to implement technical security measures to guard against unauthorized access by "failing to ensure that firewalls were in place with threat identification monitoring of inbound and outbound traffic and that information technology resources were both supported and regularly updated with available patches."[260]

OCR characterizes the ACMHS breach as "the direct result of ACMHS failing to identify and address basic risks, such as not regularly updating their IT resources with available patches and running outdated, unsupported

---

[254] Parkview Resolution Agreement.

[255] HHS Statement—Parkview.

[256] Parkview Resolution Agreement. Parkview is identified in the Resolution Agreement as a covered entity (an affiliated covered entity), with no indication that its role was as a business associate in this case.

[257] HHS Statement—Parkview.

[258] HHS Statement—Parkview (citing http://www.hhs.gov/ocr/privacy/hipaa/enforcement/examples/disposalfaqs.pdf).

[259] HHS Bulletin, "HIPAA Settlement Underscores the Vulnerability of Unpatched and Unsupported Software" (Dec. 8, 2014), available at http://www.hhs.gov/ocr/privacy/hipaa/enforcement/examples/acmhs/acmhsbulletin.pdf (hereinafter "HHS Bulletin—ACMHS"); Anchorage Community Mental Health Services Resolution Agreement, available at http://www.hhs.gov/ocr/privacy/hipaa/enforcement/examples/acmhs/amchs-capsettlement.pdf (hereinafter "ACMHS Resolution Agreement").

[260] ACMHS Resolution Agreement.

software."[261] But OCR also stated that ACMHS had cooperated and had been responsive to technical assistance from OCR.[262]

HHS entered into a Resolution Agreement with ACMHS that requires ACMHS to pay a $150,000 resolution amount and enter into a two-year corrective action plan (CAP). ACMHS is required to conduct annual security risk assessments and document its risk management plan. The CAP also requires ACMHS to adopt Security Regulations policies and procedures that have been approved by HHS and provide HHS-approved security training to its workforce.[263]

HHS used the Bulletin announcing the ACMHS settlement to emphasize the need for "a common sense approach" to regular ePHI risk assessment and risk management, including "reviewing systems for unpatched vulnerabilities and unsupported software that can leave patient information susceptible to malware and other risks."[264] The Bulletin also noted that OCR and ONC make available a Security Rule Risk Assessment Tool, which assists small to mid-size providers in conducting regular security risk assessments. See Standard 1 under § 4.02[A].

[W] Cornell Prescription Pharmacy (2015)

Two of the earliest HHS settlement agreements under the Privacy Regulations, CVS Pharmacy (see § 6.05[B]) and Rite-Aid (see § 6.05[C]), involved large retail pharmacy chains, where OCR opened investigations after media reports of the pharmacies' disposal of trash containing PHI in unsecured containers. The facts regarding Cornell Prescription Pharmacy ("Cornell") are quite similar, except that Cornell is a small, single-location pharmacy. Cornell specializes in compounded medications and serves the Denver area. OCR received notification from the Denver NBC news affiliate on January 11, 2012, of non-shredded Cornell PHI being disposed of in a publicly accessible dumpster.[265]

OCR immediately opened a compliance review and investigation on January 13, 2012, and notified Cornell on February 27, 2012. According to the OCR investigation, Cornell failed to reasonably safeguard PHI, failed to implement written policies and procedures to comply with the Privacy Regulations, and did not provide or document training of its workforce.[266]

HHS and Cornell entered into a Resolution Agreement that requires Cornell to pay a $125,000 resolution amount and enter into a two-year corrective action plan (CAP). Among the requirements of the CAP are that Cornell develop written policies and procedures to comply with the Privacy Regulations, distribute them to the Cornell workforce, obtain certification from each workforce member that he or she has read, understands, and will follow the policies and procedures, and finally, train all members of the workforce on these policies and procedures. These policies and procedures must address specific content, including that "paper PHI intended for disposal shall be shredded, burned, pulped, or pulverized so that the PHI is rendered essentially unreadable, indecipherable, and otherwise cannot be reconstructed."[267]

Regardless of size, whether a covered entity is a large retail pharmacy chain or a small compounding pharmacy, the disposal of PHI must be handled in a secure manner. The HHS Bulletin announcing the Cornell settlement called attention to OCR's "Frequently Asked Questions About the Disposal of Protected Health Information," which is quoted in the Resolution Agreement.[268]

---

[261] HHS Bulletin—ACMHS.

[262] HHS Bulletin—ACMHS.

[263] ACMHS Resolution Agreement.

[264] HHS Bulletin—ACMHS.

[265] HHS Bulletin, "HIPAA Settlement Highlights the Continuing Importance of Secure Disposal of Paper Medical Records" (Apr. 27, 2015), available at http://www.hhs.gov/ocr/privacy/hipaa/enforcement/examples/cornell/cornell-press-release.html (hereinafter "HHS Bulletin—CPP"); Cornell Prescription Pharmacy Resolution Agreement, available at http://www.hhs.gov/ocr/privacy/hipaa/enforcement/examples/cornell/cornell-cap.pdf (hereinafter "Cornell Resolution Agreement").

[266] Cornell Resolution Agreement.

[267] Cornell Resolution Agreement.

[268] OCR, "Frequently Asked Questions About the Disposal of Protected Health Information," available at http://www.hhs.gov/ocr/privacy/hipaa/enforcement/examples/disposalfaqs.pdf.

§ 6.06   HIPAA CRIMINAL PENALTIES

HIPAA establishes a criminal penalty of up to $50,000 and/or imprisonment for up to one year for any person who knowingly and in violation of the Administrative Simplification provisions:

- Uses or causes to be used a unique health identifier;

- Obtains individually identifiable health information relating to an individual; or

- Discloses individually identifiable health information to another person.[269]

If such offenses are committed under false pretenses, the penalty may be increased up to $100,000 and/or imprisonment for up to five years. If the offense is committed with the intent to sell, transfer, or use individually identifiable health information for commercial advantage, personal gain, or malicious harm, the penalty is a fine of up to $250,000 and/or imprisonment for up to 10 years.[270]

SUMMARY OF CATEGORIES OF CRIMINAL PENALTIES

Level of Knowledge/Intent	Criminal Penalty
A person knowingly obtains or discloses PHI in violation of the Administrative Simplification Regulations	Up to: • $50,000, and/or • Imprisonment for up to 1 year
If such offense is committed under false pretenses	Up to: • $100,000, and/or • Imprisonment for up to 5 years
If such offense is committed with the intent to sell, transfer, or use PHI for commercial advantage, personal gain, or malicious harm	Up to: • $250,000, and/or • Imprisonment for up to 10 years

The Enforcement Rule does not address criminal penalties. OCR refers all potential criminal complaints to the DOJ for investigation and possible criminal prosecution.

§ 6.07   CRIMINAL PROSECUTION

As discussed in **§ 6.01[A]**, any person may be subject to criminal liability if the person knowingly obtains or discloses individually identifiable health information (or uses or causes to be used a unique health identifier) in violation of the Administrative Simplification provisions of HIPAA.[271] As shown in **§ 6.06**, the penalties escalate if, beyond the "knowing" standard, the offense is committed under false pretenses or with the intent to sell, transfer, or use PHI for commercial advantage, personal gain, or malicious harm.[272]

Despite the broad applicability of the criminal liability statute, it is important to remember that to be liable for criminal penalties under HIPAA, the person charged must have acted *knowingly*. The DOJ's position is that this means that the government only needs to prove knowledge of the facts that constitute the offense, but it does not need to prove knowledge that the conduct in question violated the HIPAA statute or regulations.[273] The U.S.

---

[269] 42 U.S.C. § 1320d-6.

[270] Pub. L. No. 104-191, § 262(a) (codified at 42 U.S.C. § 1320d-5).

[271] 42 U.S.C. § 1320d-6. See **§ 6.01** for more information regarding the broadened applicability of the HIPAA criminal penalties.

[272] Health Insurance Portability and Accountability Act of 1996, Pub. L. No. 104-191, § 262(a) (codified at 42 U.S.C. § 1320d-5).

[273] June 2005 Memorandum.

Court of Appeals (Ninth Circuit) recently issued a ruling in the *Zhou* case, discussed at **§ 6.07[A][9]**, which addresses this knowledge issue and affirms the government's position. The court stated that the plain language of the HIPAA statute shows that its application is not limited to defendants who knew their actions were illegal. The court found that the standard "knowingly *and* in a manner contrary to HIPAA" comprised two distinct elements. The "knowledge" element applies only to the obtaining of PHI, not to knowledge that such actions were in violation of HIPAA.[274]

The HIPAA criminal prosecutions to date have generally involved employees of covered entities, but have not resulted in charges against the covered entities themselves. These defendants have most often worked for health care providers, but have also worked for health plans and clearinghouses. The *Stewart* case, discussed in **§ 6.07[A][15]**, is a rare exception, involving a hospital visitor.

Another common theme is identity theft and using PHI for financial gain. But there is a developing line of cases where there was not necessarily a financial motive, but where the violation resulted from other personal motives or simple curiosity. The following is not an exhaustive list of HIPAA criminal cases, but it is intended to illustrate some parameters around the developing approach to criminal enforcement of HIPAA.

[A] Criminal Cases

In many of the cases cited below, the HIPAA charges were accompanied by other charges, such as identity theft or computer fraud. In a particular case, there may be several laws under which the person could be charged, and the prosecutors make choices about which are most appropriate and effective in the circumstances. Increasingly, charging a violation of HIPAA appears to be one of those choices and may, in some cases, be the only criminal charge.

The information below has been taken from public records, in particular, records of court proceedings, and the official statements of the U.S. Attorney's Office.

[1] *Gibson* Case (2004)

The *Gibson* case, the first criminal prosecution under HIPAA, was a 2004 identity theft case. Richard Gibson, a former employee of a Seattle health care provider, pled guilty in federal court to wrongful disclosure of PHI for economic gain. Gibson admitted obtaining a cancer patient's name, date of birth, and Social Security number for the purpose of fraudulently obtaining credit cards in the patient's name (and accumulating more than $9,000 in debt).[275] Under the terms of a plea bargain, Gibson was sentenced to 16 months in prison (followed by three years' supervised release) and must pay restitution to the credit card companies and the patient.[276]

[2] *Ramirez* Case (2005)

Liz Arlene Ramirez worked for a Texas doctor's office that was under contract to provide physicals and medical care to FBI agents. She allegedly arranged to sell the PHI of a patient who was an FBI agent for $500 to a person she thought was working for a drug trafficker—but who turned out to be also working for the FBI and who recorded their meetings. Ramirez pled guilty in March 2006 to a federal felony offense under HIPAA of wrongfully using a unique health identifier with the intent to sell PHI for personal gain. Ramirez was sentenced in August 2006 to six months' imprisonment (plus two years' supervised release) and was required to pay a $100 criminal penalty.[277] As in the *Gibson* case, the *Ramirez* case involved an employee of a covered entity.

---

[274] United States v. Zhou, 678 F.3d 1110 (9th Cir. May 10, 2012).

[275] United States v. Gibson, Plea Agreement No. CR04-0374 RSM (W.D. Wash. Aug. 19, 2004).

[276] U.S. Attorney press release (Aug. 27, 2004), U.S. Attorney's Office, Western District of Washington.

[277] U.S. Department of Justice, U.S. Attorney's Office, S.D. Texas, press release: Alamo Woman Convicted of Selling FBI Agent's Medical Records, Mar. 7, 2006. United States v. Ramirez, Indictment (Aug. 30, 2005) and Plea Agreement (Aug. 23, 2006), Case 7:05-CR-00708-001 (S.D. Tex. McAllen Div); and see also Smith DeWaal (*citing* United States v. Ramirez).

[3]   *Williams* Case (2006)

Linda D. Williams was employed as an insurance representative by a Delaware health care clearinghouse that provides billing services for hospitals. Williams was alleged to have conspired to steal the identities of more than 400 of the billing company's clients. According to the indictment, Williams accessed the company's computer system to print out patient identification and medical information and then supplied the information to an accomplice, who paid her for this information. The accomplice then allegedly used the stolen information to submit false federal tax returns. Williams pled guilty to identity theft and wrongfully obtaining PHI for personal gain. Williams was sentenced to 27 months' imprisonment (followed by three years' supervised release). Her accomplice pled guilty to bank fraud, identity theft, and false claim charges, and was sentenced to 75 months' imprisonment (and three years' supervised release) and was required to pay restitution to the Internal Revenue Service and to the billing services company.[278]

[4]   *Machado-Ferrer* Case (2006)

This was the first criminal prosecution under the Privacy Regulations that went to trial. It involved two defendants in Florida, Isis Machado and Fernando Ferrer. Machado was employed at the front desk of a medical clinic, a covered entity, and had access to PHI. Machado and Ferrer were charged with obtaining patient PHI, including Social Security numbers, addresses, and dates of birth, and conspiring to use the information to make fraudulent Medicare claims in excess of $2.5 million. The indictments alleged that Machado sold the PHI to her cousin Ferrer, who then used the PHI in connection with filing the fraudulent Medicare claims. In January 2007, Machado entered a guilty plea to criminal conspiracy to commit computer fraud, identity theft, and wrongful disclosure of PHI. She was sentenced to three years' probation (including six months' home confinement) and also ordered to pay restitution in the amount of $2.5 million. Following a jury trial, Ferrer was found guilty of conspiracy, identity theft, computer fraud, and HIPAA violations. In April 2007, Ferrer was sentenced to 87 months in prison (and three years of supervised release) and was ordered to pay restitution in the amount of $2.5 million (jointly and severally with Machado).[279]

The indictment in this case cited the federal "aiding and abetting" law as well as HIPAA. As discussed in **§ 6.01**, the DOJ took the position generally that although only covered entities could be prosecuted directly under HIPAA, others could be found guilty under principles of aiding and abetting and conspiracy.

In April 2008, additional indictments were unsealed against six other persons in this matter. These six persons are owners of clinics and durable medical equipment suppliers, who allegedly used the patient information from Machado and Ferrer to submit fraudulent claims to Medicare. No HIPAA charges were included in these indictments.[280]

[5]   *Hollern* Case (2007)

In February 2007, Paul Hollern, a licensed chiropractor, was indicted by a grand jury for allegedly scheming to defraud health care benefit programs and videotaping his patients without their knowledge or under false

---

[278] United States v. Williams, Grand Jury Indictment (Nov. 26, 2006), Judgment and Plea Agreement (Apr. 26, 2007), Case 06-CR-129-001-GMS, (Del. 2007); United States v. Adjei, Judgment (May 15, 2007), Case 06-CR-55-GMS (Del. 2007) (affirmed on appeal). See also U.S. Attorney's Office, District of Delaware, press release, formerly available at http://149.101.225.20/usao/de/press/2006/11_17_06_medicalidtheft.pdf (Nov. 17, 2006) (no longer available online, but available through U.S. Attorney's Office); Smith DeWaal (*citing* United States v. Williams).

[279] United States v. Machado, Superseding Indictment (Dec. 7, 2006) and Judgment (May 1, 2007), Case 06CR60261-COHN (S.D. Fla. 2007); United States v. Ferrer, Superseding Indictment (Dec. 7, 2006) and Judgment (Apr. 30, 2007), Case 06CR60261-COHN (S.D. Fla. 2007). *See also* U.S. Attorney's Office, Southern District of Florida, press release, formerly available at http://www.usdoj.gov/usao/fls (May 3, 2007).

[280] U.S. Attorney's Office, Southern District of Florida, press release, formerly available at http://www.usdoj.gov/usao/fls (Apr. 1, 2008).

pretenses, as they were treated by students in Hollern's Kentucky chiropractic business training program. The HIPAA allegations involved Hollern giving these videotapes to his students. Count 3 of the indictment alleged that Hollern knowingly disclosed PHI (via these videotapes) under false pretense and for commercial advantage and personal gain, in violation of HIPAA. The case went to trial in January 2008, and in February, Hollern was convicted by a jury on the charge of illegal electronic eavesdropping for the videotaping of patients, but not on the HIPAA count or the other charges.[281]

[6] *Smith* Case (2007)

In December 2007, Andrea Smith and her husband, Justin Smith, were indicted on charges of conspiracy to violate the Privacy Regulations and aiding and abetting disclosure of PHI for personal gain and malicious harm. Andrea Smith was employed as a licensed practical nurse at a clinic in Arkansas. According to the indictment, Andrea Smith accessed PHI of a patient at the clinic and disclosed the patient's information, including details of the patient's diagnosis, to her husband. The husband, Justin Smith, then allegedly contacted the patient, stating that he intended to use the PHI in "an upcoming legal proceeding." The clinic, which terminated Smith's employment, was not charged in the case. In April 2008, Andrea Smith pled guilty to aiding and abetting the wrongful disclosure of PHI for personal gain and malicious harm. The conspiracy count against her and the charges against her husband were then dropped.[282] Andrea Smith was sentenced to two years probation and 100 hours of community service.[283] In this case, there were no charges such as computer fraud or identity theft; the only charges stemmed from the HIPAA violation.

[7] *Howell* Case (2008)

Leslie Howell was an employee of a counseling center in Oklahoma. According to the April 2008 indictment, Howell provided more than 100 patient files to two persons, knowing they would use the information to commit access device fraud and identity theft. The only charge in the indictment against Howell was the HIPAA violation. In May 2008, Howell pled guilty to disclosing PHI with the intent to use that information for personal gain.[284] Howell was sentenced to 14 months' imprisonment, to be followed by two years of supervised release, and must pay restitution in the amount of $20,415.[285] According to the DOJ, the two persons to whom Howell disclosed the patients' PHI each pled guilty to fraudulently obtaining credit cards and aggravated identity theft.[286]

[8] *Jackson* Case (2008)

According to an April 2008 grand jury indictment, Lawanda Jackson was an administrative specialist employed at UCLA medical center and, in that capacity, had access to patient information. Jackson allegedly

---

[281] United States v. Hollern, Superseding Indictment (Feb. 5, 2007) and Verdict (Feb. 8, 2008), Case 3:06CR-82-S (W.D. Ky. 2008). See also U.S. Department of Justice and U.S. Attorney's Office, Western District of Kentucky, press release (Feb. 5, 2007); Smith DeWaal (*citing* United States v. Hollern).

[282] United States v. Smith (Andrea and Justin Smith), Indictment (Dec. 5, 2007), Change of Plea—Andrea Smith (Apr. 15, 2008), Order of Dismissal—Justin Smith (Apr. 16, 2008), Case 4:07CR00378-SWW (E.D. Ark.). See also U.S. Attorney's Office, Eastern District of Arkansas, press release (Apr. 15, 2008) and Federal Bureau of Investigation, Little Rock Field Division, press release (Apr. 15, 2008).

[283] United States v. Andrea Smith, Sentencing, Case 4:07CR00378-SWW (E.D. Ark. Dec. 3, 2008).

[284] United States v. Howell, Superseding Indictment (Apr. 15, 2008), Petition to Enter Plea of Guilty (May 5, 2008), Case CR-08-50-HE (W.D. Okla. 2008). See also U.S. Attorney's Office, Western District of Oklahoma, press release (May 8, 2008).

[285] United States v. Howell, Judgment, Case CR-08-50-HE (W.D. Okla. Aug. 22, 2008) (restitution is joint and several with her two co-defendants).

[286] U.S. Attorney's Office, Western District of Oklahoma, press release (May 8, 2008).

had a deal to provide a national media outlet with PHI about celebrity patients in exchange for payment totaling at least $4,600. The only charge against Jackson was violation of HIPAA's criminal provisions. Jackson pled guilty on December 1, 2008, but died prior to sentencing.[287] Court records indicate that this indictment was part of a larger investigation (see *Zhou* in **§ 6.07[A][9]**).[288]

[9] *Zhou* Case (2008)

Huping Zhou was a licensed cardiothoracic surgeon in China and was working as a research assistant for the UCLA Health System in 2003. The U.S. Attorney brought charges against Zhou in 2008, alleging that Zhou impermissibly accessed PHI concerning celebrity patients and co-workers through his employer's electronic health record system, in violation of the privacy provisions of HIPAA.[289] Zhou agreed to plead guilty to four specific misdemeanor counts of violating HIPAA, conceding that he did not have a valid job-related reason to access the PHI.[290] The U.S. Attorney alleged that Zhou's improper access far exceeded the four counts he admitted to, and, on or about the date that Zhou received notice of termination of his employment, he began accessing health records off-hours and nearly 200 times accessed records of celebrities, co-workers, supervisors involved in his termination, and others.[291] There was no evidence that Zhou improperly used or attempted to sell the PHI he accessed.[292] Zhou was sentenced to four months' imprisonment on each count (to be served concurrently) and a $2,000 fine ($500 for each count); in addition, following release, Zhou will be placed on supervised release for one year.[293] This is the first time misdemeanor HIPAA charges for "snooping" have resulted in jail time.

Under the Plea Agreement, Zhou reserved the right to appeal on certain grounds related to the "knowledge" element of the indictment. In his appeal, Zhou claimed he did not have "knowledge" because he did not know his conduct was illegal under HIPAA.[294] In 2012, the U.S. Court of Appeals for the Ninth Circuit issued its ruling, addressing this knowledge issue and denying Zhou's appeal. The court held that the plain language of the HIPAA statute shows that its application is not limited to defendants who knew their actions were illegal. The court found that the standard "knowingly *and* in a manner contrary to HIPAA" comprised two distinct elements. The "knowledge" element applies only to knowledge of the actions involving the obtaining of PHI, not to knowledge that such actions were in violation of HIPAA.[295]

Although not explicit with regard to the nature of the connection, the U.S. Attorney's Office notified the court that the *Zhou* case "may be related" to the *Jackson* case discussed above at **§ 6.07[A][8]**.[296]

---

[287] United States v. Jackson, Order Dismissing Indictment (May 8, 2008); Government's Motion to Dismiss (May 7, 2998); Change of Plea and Setting of Sentencing Date (Dec. 1, 2008), Case CR08-00430 (C.D. Cal. 2008).

[288] United States v. Jackson, Indictment (Apr. 9, 2008) and Application for Order Sealing Indictment (Apr. 9, 2008), Case CR08-00430 (C.D. Cal. 2008). See also U.S. Attorney's Office, Central District of California, press release, formerly available at http://www.usdoj.gov/usao/cac/pressroom/pr2008/049.html (Apr. 29, 2008). In 2008, California passed a new law to punish unauthorized viewing of medical records in health care settings, including increased penalties, a private right of action, and reporting to State authorities. Cal. SB 541 and AB 211.

[289] United States v. Huping Zhou, Case CR-01356, Information (Grand Jury) (C.D. Cal. Nov. 17, 2008); First Superseding Information (C.D. Cal. Nov. 9, 2009); and Plea Agreement (C.D. Cal. Jan. 8, 2010).

[290] *Zhou*, Plea Agreement, Case CR-01356 (C.D. Cal. Nov. 17, 2008).

[291] *Zhou*, Government's Concurrence with Defendant's Presentence Report and Sentencing Position, Case CR-01356 (C.D. Cal. Apr. 18, 2010).

[292] FBI Los Angeles, DOJ press release, "Ex-UCLA Employee Sentenced to Federal Prison for Illegally Peeking at Patient Records," available at http://www.fbi.gov/losangeles/press-releases/2010/la042710a.htm.

[293] *Zhou*, Judgment and Probation/Commitment Order, Case CR-01356 (C.D. Cal. Apr. 27, 2010).

[294] *Zhou*, Plea Agreement, Case CR-01356 (C.D. Cal. Nov. 17, 2008); United States v. Huping Zhou, Court of Appeals Docket # 10-50231 (May 12, 2010).

[295] United States v. Zhou, 2012 WL 1626109 (9th Cir. May 10, 2012).

[296] *Zhou*, Notice to Court of Related Criminal Case, Case CR-01356 (C.D. Cal. Jan. 8, 2010).

[10] *McPherson* Case (2008)

A former employee of a New York hospital, Dwight McPherson was arrested in April 2008 on charges relating to an alleged two-year scheme to steal the identities of nearly 50,000 patients and sell that information to others intending to commit fraud.[297] The federal grand jury indictment stated that McPherson was an admissions representative at New York-Presbyterian Hospital and agreed to sell confidential patient information to a co-conspirator. The charges included counts of identity fraud, computer fraud, conspiracy, and wrongful disclosure of PHI. With respect to the HIPAA count, the indictment alleged that McPherson accessed the records of tens of thousands of hospital patients and sold some of those records to others for personal gain.[298] McPherson pled guilty on all counts and was sentenced to two years' imprisonment, followed by three years' supervised release, and was ordered to pay $882,972 in restitution.[299]

[11] *Holland-Miller-Griffin* Case (2009)

These cases involved a physician and two former employees of a hospital in Little Rock, Arkansas. Each defendant was indicted and pled guilty in connection with inappropriately accessing patient records out of "curiosity" in connection with a sensational case involving a local celebrity.[300]

Dr. Jay Holland was a physician with access to patient PHI at St. Vincent Infirmary Medical Center (SVIMC) and was charged by the U.S. Attorney with a criminal violation of HIPAA for impermissible access to a patient record.[301] According to the U.S. Attorney, Holland admitted that after watching news reports on TV regarding a patient at SVIMC, he logged on to the SVIMC electronic health record system from home to look at the patient's records.[302] He admitted that it was wrong for him to look at the records and that it was a violation of HIPAA, and he did it because he was curious.[303] SVIMC suspended Holland's privileges for two weeks and required him to complete online HIPAA training.[304] Holland pled guilty to one misdemeanor criminal count under HIPAA. He was sentenced to one year's probation, a $5,000 fine, and 50 hours of community service to be spent giving speeches regarding the importance of HIPAA laws to other health professionals.[305]

Sarah Elizabeth Miller was an account representative at SVIMC. She was responsible for checking patients in and out of the clinic and processing patient bills and had access to SVIMC electronic patient records for her duties. She admitted that she accessed the patient's files inappropriately out of curiosity. SVIMC fired Miller.[306] Miller pled guilty to one misdemeanor criminal count under HIPAA and was sentenced to one year's probation and a $2,500 fine.[307]

Candida Griffin was the Emergency Room Coordinator at SVIMC, where she had secretarial-type duties, including ordering patient tests and data entry in patient medical records. She was apparently asked to set up an "alias" to protect the identity of a particular emergency room patient. According to the U.S. Attorney, after the

---

[297] U.S. Attorney's Office, Southern District of New York, press release, available at http://www.justice.gov/usao/nys/pressreleases/April08/mcphersonarrestpr.pdf (Apr. 14, 2008).

[298] United States v. McPherson, Indictment, Case CR-00635 (S.D.N.Y. July 11, 2008).

[299] *McPherson*, Judgment, Case CR-00635 (S.D.N.Y. Aug. 18, 2010); *McPherson*, Amended Judgment, Case CR-00635 (S.D.N.Y. Dec. 1, 2010); *McPherson*, Order of Restitution, Case CR-00635 (S.D.N.Y. Dec. 1, 2010).

[300] United States v. Jay Holland, M.D., Transcript of Sentencing Hearing, Case CR-00168 (E.D. Ark. Nov. 4, 2009).

[301] *Holland*, Information, Case CR-00168 (E.D. Ark. June 29, 2009).

[302] U.S. Attorney, E.D. Arkansas, press release, "Doctor and Two Former Hospital Employees Plead Guilty to HIPAA Violation," available at http://www.justice.gov/usao/are/news/2009/July/3plea_HIPAA_07202009.pdf (hereinafter "Doctor and Two Former Hospital Employees Plead Guilty").

[303] Doctor and Two Former Hospital Employees Plead Guilty.

[304] Doctor and Two Former Hospital Employees Plead Guilty.

[305] *Holland*, Information, Case CR-00168 (E.D. Ark. June 29, 2009).

[306] Doctor and Two Former Hospital Employees Plead Guilty; United States v. Miller, Information, Case CR-00170 (E.D. Ark. June 29, 2009).

[307] *Miller*, Judgment in a Criminal Case, Case CR-00170 (E.D. Ark. Oct. 26, 2009).

patient was moved to the Intensive Care Unit, Griffin became curious about the patient's status and accessed her medical record. SVIMC fired Griffin.[308] Griffin pled guilty to one misdemeanor criminal count under HIPAA and was sentenced to one year of probation and a $1,500 fine.[309]

These cases are significant because they illustrate to employees of covered entities, business associates, and others the potential consequences of "snooping" or accessing PHI merely out of curiosity. All too often, there are media stories about cases where employees of health care providers and other covered entities access PHI inappropriately. Not all cases of snooping result in criminal charges, but many cases do result in termination of employment.

[12] *Brown-Barbary* Case (2009)

In May 2009, Jacquettia L. Brown and Tear Renee Barbary were charged with criminal HIPAA violations and other crimes for allegedly stealing patient hospital records as part of a conspiracy to commit credit card fraud.[310] According to the indictment, Brown, a medical records administrator at a Florida hospital, took patient records containing PHI without authorization and used that information to obtain patients' credit card information.[311] Brown allegedly provided patient PHI and credit card information to Barbary, who used the information to make unauthorized credit card purchases.[312] Brown was sentenced to two years' imprisonment, and Barbary was sentenced to 11 months' imprisonment, followed in each case by three years' supervised release.[313]

[13] *Charette* Case (2010)

A Las Vegas man, Richard W. Charette, was charged by a federal grand jury in April 2010 with participating in a conspiracy to receive and disclose patient records from University Medical Center (UMC), with the intent to use the information to solicit business and clients for personal injury attorneys.[314] Charette was indicted on one count of conspiracy to illegally disclose PHI for personal gain in violation of HIPAA. According to the grand jury indictment, an employee in the UMC trauma unit obtained "Face Sheets" containing confidential information of UMC trauma patients and passed them on to Charette. Charette then allegedly used the information to solicit patients for the personal injury attorneys.[315] According to the indictment, Charette paid the UMC employee for each patient who engaged the services of a personal injury attorney with whom Charette was affiliated.[316] Charette pled guilty and was sentenced to 33 months' imprisonment followed by three years' supervised release and was required to pay a fine of $5,000.[317] Charrette appealed the sentence.[318] The Court of Appeals

---

[308] "Doctor and Two Former Hospital Employees Plead Guilty"; United States v. Griffin, Information, Case CR-00169 (E.D. Ark. June 29, 2009).

[309] *Griffin*, Judgment in a Criminal Case, Case CR-00169 (E.D. Ark. Oct. 26, 2009).

[310] United States v. Brown and Barbary, Indictment, Case CR-20442 (S.D. Fla. May 26, 2009).

[311] *Brown and Barbary*, Indictment, Case CR-20442 (S.D. Fla. May 26, 2009).

[312] *Brown and Barbary*, Indictment, Case CR-20442 (S.D. Fla. May 26, 2009).

[313] United States v. Brown, Judgment in a Criminal Case, Case No. 20442-01 (S.D. Fla. Oct. 30, 2010); United States v. Barbary, Judgment in a Criminal Case, Case No. 20442-02 (S.D. Fla. Oct. 30, 2010); U.S. Attorney's Office, Southern District of Florida, press release, "Palmetto General Hospital Employee and Accomplice Sentenced for Stealing Patient Records in Fraud Scheme" (Oct. 29, 2009), available at http://www.justice.gov/usao/fls/PressReleases/091029-02.html.

[314] United States v. Charette, Criminal Indictment, Case CR-00193 (D. Nev. Apr. 28, 2010); FBI Los Angeles, DOJ press release, "Federal Charges Filed in UMC Records Leak Investigation—Man Charged with Conspiring to Sell Patient Records to Personal Injury Attorneys," available at http://www.fbi.gov/lasvegas/press-releases/2010/lv042810.htm.

[315] *Charette*, Criminal Indictment, Case CR-00193 (D. Nev. Apr. 28, 2010).

[316] *Charette*, Criminal Indictment, Case CR-00193 (D. Nev. Apr. 28, 2010).

[317] United States v. Charette, Judgment in a Criminal Case, Case CR-00193 (D. Nev. May 4, 2011).

[318] Court of Appeals Docket No. 11-10228, U.S. Ct. Appeals, Ninth Circuit (Notice of Appeal filed May 9, 2011).

(Ninth Circuit) affirmed the sentence imposed by the district court, comparing Charette to his "co-conspirator," saying that Charette "was a leader of the criminal activity and did not cooperate with the government."[319]

[14] *Hall-Finnie* Case (2011)

A grand jury in Florida indicted 12 defendants on charges relating to a "massive identify theft and bank fraud scheme," according to the U.S. Attorney for the Southern District of Florida.[320] All 12 were charged with conspiracy to commit bank fraud and conspiracy to commit identity theft and access device fraud, thereby defrauding the victims of in excess of $1.2 million.[321] In addition, two of the defendants, Erica Hall and Sharelle Finnie, were charged with obtaining PHI with the intent to sell, transfer, and use it for personal gain, in violation of HIPAA. According to the indictment, Hall and Finnie were each employed in medical offices—Hall as an office assistant in Coral Springs and Finnie as a medical assistant or office assistant in Ft. Lauderdale—and each had access to patient PHI, including names, dates of birth, Social Security numbers, and other sensitive information. Allegedly, Hall and Finnie unlawfully obtained patient information and sold it to fellow defendants. In documents filed during sentencing, Hall stated that while working in the doctor's office, she was approached by her sister-in-law (another one of the 12 defendants), who suggested Hall could make some money by providing her with patient information, and Hall subsequently provided information on 65 patients.[322] The indictment identifies numerous cell phone text messages as the means by which Hall allegedly transferred PHI to her co-conspirators. According to the indictment, the stolen patient information was used in a scheme to impersonate the victims and deplete their bank accounts and incur substantial credit card charges.[323]

Finnie pled guilty to conspiracy to commit bank fraud and to wrongful disclosure of PHI. She was sentenced to one year in prison, followed by three years of supervised release, and was ordered to pay restitution in the amount of $30,231.[324] According to court documents submitted by Finnie during sentencing, she succumbed to pressure from her boyfriend (one of the other 12 defendants) to provide him with patient information. She asserted that she was motivated, not by financial gain, but by a desire to maintain her relationship with her boyfriend.[325]

Hall pled guilty to conspiracy to commit bank fraud, conspiracy to commit identity theft and access device fraud, and wrongful disclosure of PHI. Hall was sentenced to 14 months in prison, followed by two years of supervised release, and was ordered to pay restitution in the amount of $37,411.[326] Hall has appealed her sentence to the U.S. Court of Appeals.

[15] *Stewart* Case (2011)

According to court documents, while Chelsea Stewart was visiting someone at a Birmingham, Alabama hospital in 2011, she went into the hospital's one-day surgery department, which was closed and unstaffed. She climbed over a counter and gained access to an area where the hospital had stored surgery department logs and

---

[319] United States v. Charette, Memorandum, Case No. 11-10228, D.C. No. 2:10-cr-000193 (9th Cir. Mar. 12, 2012).

[320] U.S. Attorney, Southern District of Florida, press release, "Medical Office Assistants and Broward County School Board Employee Among Twelve Charged in Bank Fraud and Identity Theft Ring" (Apr. 5, 2011), available at http://www.justice.gov/usao/fls/PressReleases/110405-02.html.

[321] United States v. Hall, Rembert, Finnie, Bethea, Cook, Gissendanner, Johnson, Hough, Baldwin, Hough, Powell & Sermons, Indictment, Case No. 60047 (S.D. Fla. Mar. 15, 2010).

[322] United States v. Hall, Sentencing Memorandum, Case No. 60047 (S.D. Fla. Sept. 6, 2011).

[323] United States v. Hall, Rembert, Finnie, Bethea, Cook, Gissendanner, Johnson, Hough, Baldwin, Hough, Powell & Sermons, Indictment, Case No. 60047 (S.D. Fla. Mar. 15, 2010).

[324] United States v. Finnie, Judgment, Case No. 60047 (S.D. Fla. Sept. 22, 2011).

[325] United States v. Finnie, Objections to Presentence Investigation Report and Request for Variance and Sentencing Memorandum Pursuant to 18 U.S.C. § 3553, Case No. 60047 (S.D. Fla. Sept. 6, 2011).

[326] United States v. Hall, Judgment, Case No. 60047 (S.D. Fla. Sept. 29, 2011).

other records containing the PHI of more than 4,000 patients.[327] Stewart removed those records from the hospital. She allegedly planned to attempt to use those identities for fraudulent activity. Stewart was not able to complete these plans, because the local police department executed a search warrant at the residence (on an unrelated matter) and found the stolen records.[328] The records consisted of hundreds of pages that contained the names, dates of birth, and Social Security numbers of the hospital's patients.[329] According to court documents, until the police found the patient records, the hospital had not realized the records were missing.[330]

Stewart was indicted by a grand jury in June 2011 on one count of knowingly and unlawfully obtaining PHI with the intent to sell, transfer, and use that PHI for commercial advantage, personal gain, and malicious harm in violation of HIPAA. Under the same indictment, Stewart was charged with other, unrelated crimes, including attempted bank fraud and aggravated identity theft.[331] Stewart pled guilty and was sentenced, in February 2012, to 15 months imprisonment on the HIPAA charge (a total of 39 months due to other unrelated charges), followed by five years of supervised release.[332]

Chelsea Stewart was not a covered entity, a business associate, or an employee of either one. She was simply a person who entered the hospital facility. As the HITECH Act has made clear, *any* person obtaining PHI unlawfully from a covered entity can be charged under HIPAA. This case is also a reminder that the physical security of paper records is as important as encryption of electronic PHI.

[16] *Kaye* Case (2011)

In 2010, the Virginia Board of Medicine reprimanded Richard Alan Kaye, D.O. for what it concluded was a breach of patient confidentiality.[333] In 2011, Kaye was indicted on HIPAA charges relating to the same incidents, but was acquitted.[334] This case involved what is known as the "duty to warn." The concept arose in clinical psychology as an exception to the duty of confidentiality, requiring that the clinician breach confidentiality to warn of a danger to others.[335] Duty-to-warn laws vary from state to state, with regard to, for example, the nature of the threat and who should receive the warning. The Privacy Regulations address this issue as a disclosure "to avert a serious threat to health or safety." See § 3.03[D][10]. The standards under state law and the Privacy Regulations with regard to such disclosures are likely to differ, making the analysis complex, and the issue can be a very difficult one for providers.

According to the Board of Medicine, Kaye treated "Patient A" in 2007. Kaye learned in late January 2008 that Patient A had been hospitalized at another facility, where she was being treated by others. In early February 2008, Kaye contacted individuals at Patient A's employer, identifying Patient A and making statements about her being admitted to a psychiatric facility, discussing his prior treatment of her, and opining on her "current mental state."[336] These conversations were conducted without Patient A's knowledge or authorization. The Board of Medicine found that Kaye was unable to "fully articulate or justify" his violation of Patient A's privacy, other than "alleged concerns for public safety based on her access to a weapon."[337] The Board also found that, despite Kaye's claims that he was afraid for his own safety and that of his family, he could not cite any

---

[327] United States v. Stewart, Plea Agreement, Case No. CR-00254 (N.D. Ala. Nov. 28, 2011).

[328] United States v. Stewart, Plea Agreement, Case No. CR-00254 (N.D. Ala. Nov. 28, 2011).

[329] United States v. Stewart, Criminal Complaint, Case No. CR-00254 (N.D. Ala. June 2, 2011).

[330] United States v. Stewart, Plea Agreement, Case No. CR-00254 (N.D. Ala. Nov. 28, 2011).

[331] United States v. Stewart, Indictment, Case No. CR-00254 (N.D. Ala. June 28, 2011).

[332] United States v. Stewart, Plea Agreement, Case No. CR-00254 (N.D. Ala. Nov. 28, 2011). United States v. Stewart, Judgment, Case No. CR-00254 (N.D. Ala. Feb. 8, 2012).

[333] Virginia Board of Medicine, *In re* Richard Alan Kaye, D.O., Order (May 20, 2010), available at http://www.dhp.virginia.gov/Notices/Medicine/0102037142/0102037142Order05202010.pdf (hereinafter "Board of Medicine Order").

[334] United States v. Kaye, Indictment, Case No. CR-00099 (E.D. Va. June 21, 2011); United States v. Kaye, Judgment of Acquittal, Case No. CR-00099 (E.D. Va. Nov. 2, 2011).

[335] The seminal case is Tarasoff v. Regents of the University of California, 551 P.2d 334 (Cal. 1976).

[336] Board of Medicine Order.

[337] Board of Medicine Order.

specific threats made by Patient A, with regard to harming herself or others.[338] The Board concluded that Kaye had breached the confidentiality of Patient A and issued sanctions.[339]

In June 2011, a grand jury indicted Kaye on three counts of violating HIPAA, relating to these same disclosures to Patient A's employer.[340] The indictment alleged that Kaye had knowingly and in violation of HIPAA disclosed patient information without authorization to agents of the patient's employer. The indictment further alleged that the disclosures were made under false pretenses, because Kaye claimed that the disclosures were necessary because Patient A was a serious and imminent threat to the safety of the public, but that in fact, Kaye knew that this was not true.[341] A jury trial was held in November 2011. Following the conclusion of the prosecution's case, the judge ruled from the bench and dismissed the case, citing an insufficiency of evidence.[342] Thus, Kaye was acquitted without having to put on a defense.

This case is notable for several reasons. First, there was a jury trial, but an acquittal without the case having to go to the jury. Second, the case involved disclosures to the patient's employer (which are, in most circumstances, not permitted under the Privacy Regulations without the patient's authorization). And third, it involved the complex "duty to warn" doctrine.

[17] *Wright* Case (2011)

Autumn Lee Wright was a Mayo Clinic employee in Rochester, Minnesota. According to her own statements in court documents, Wright was suspicious that her boyfriend was cheating on her with another woman, who claimed to be pregnant with the boyfriend's baby.[343] In Wright's job at the Mayo Clinic, she had access to patient health records, including the records of the "other woman." She accessed the woman's medical records, determined that the woman had recently had a miscarriage, but was unable to determine whether her boyfriend had been the father.[344] Wright confronted her boyfriend, who reacted by assaulting the other woman.[345]

Wright was indicted in April 2011 for obtaining and disclosing PHI for personal gain and malicious harm.[346] She pled guilty to the first count regarding wrongfully obtaining PHI, and the government dismissed the second count (wrongful disclosure). Wright was sentenced to three years probation, during which time she must complete 300 hours of community service.[347]

Although this case involved "snooping" in health records for personal reasons, those reasons were more than simple curiosity about a celebrity. In addition, malicious harm to another person did result, even if that was unforeseen by Wright.

[18] *Michel* Case (2012)

Helene Michel, owner and operator of a medical equipment company in New York, was convicted after a three-week jury trial of health care fraud, conspiracy to commit health care fraud, and wrongful disclosure of PHI under HIPAA. The U.S. Attorney alleged that, over a period of four and a half years, Michel stole patient information from more than a dozen nursing homes on Long Island and then submitted thousands of fraudulent

---

[338] Board of Medicine Order.

[339] Board of Medicine Order.

[340] United States v. Kaye, Indictment, Case No. CR-00099 (E.D. Va. June 21, 2011).

[341] United States v. Kaye, Indictment, Case No. CR-00099 (E.D. Va. June 21, 2011).

[342] United States v. Kaye, Judgment of Acquittal, Case No. CR-00099 (E.D. Va. Nov. 2, 2011).

[343] United States v. Wright, Defendant's Amended Position Paper Regarding Sentencing, Case. No. CR-00135 (Minn. Mar. 15, 2012).

[344] United States v. Wright, Defendant's Amended Position Paper Regarding Sentencing, Case. No. CR-00135 (Minn. Mar. 15, 2012).

[345] United States v. Wright, Defendant's Amended Position Paper Regarding Sentencing, Case. No. CR-00135 (Minn. Mar. 15, 2012).

[346] United States v. Wright, Indictment, Case. No. CR-00135 (Minn. Apr. 12, 2011).

[347] United States v. Wright, Judgment, Case. No. CR-00135 (Minn. May 15, 2012).

claims to Medicare.[348] Michel allegedly impersonated a doctor, a nurse practitioner, and a wound care expert, and accompanied doctors on patient rounds.[349] The U.S. Attorney characterized Michel as "a con woman, deceiving patients and administrators alike as she trolled for the information she used to submit fraudulent claims to Medicare to support her extravagant lifestyle."[350] Furthermore, "her criminal history is replete with theft offenses including . . . a felony conviction for posing as a registered nurse . . . Clearly, defendant's history of using ruses to commit crimes is a lengthy one."[351]

Early in the proceedings, questions were raised as to Michel's competency to stand trial. A defense expert witness diagnosed Michel with dissociative personality disorder (aka multiple personality disorder).[352] The defense attorney reported to the court that during Michel's evaluation by the defense expert, Michel "changed into a totally new personality."[353] Michel's attorney argued that Michel would not be competent to stand trial while in a dissociative state, and she can pass in and out of dissociative states without knowing it is happening, so that the person appearing at the trial could be any one of Michel's personalities; therefore, Michel was not competent to stand trial.[354] The court ultimately did find Michel competent to stand trial, with steps to be taken to reduce the stress of the proceedings so as to avoid a lapse by Michel into a dissociative state, which could render her incompetent.[355]

At trial, Michel was found guilty of health care fraud, conspiracy to commit health care fraud, and wrongful disclosure of PHI under HIPAA.[356] Michel was sentenced to 12 years in prison, followed by 3 years of supervised release, and was also ordered to pay restitution in the amount of $4.4 million, and to forfeit $1.3 million seized at the time of her indictment.[357] The verdict and sentence were upheld on appeal.[358]

§ 6.08   MEDICARE EXCLUSION

In addition to the civil and criminal penalties in the HIPAA statute, the Administrative Simplification Compliance Act provides that a covered entity that was not in compliance with the Transaction Standards by October 16, 2002 (or October 16, 2003, if an extension was obtained) is subject to exclusion from participation in the Medicare program at the discretion of the Secretary of HHS.[359] Some limited exceptions may apply.

---

[348] U.S. Attorney, Eastern District of New York, press release, "Long Island Medical Supplier Convicted of $10.7 Million Medicare Fraud" (Aug. 15, 2012), available at http://www.justice.gov/usao/nye/pr/2012/2012aug15.html; United States v. Michel, Superseding Indictment, Case. No. CR-00889 (E.D.N.Y. Mar. 21, 2012); United States v. Michel, Sentencing Memorandum by USA, Case. No. CR-00889 (E.D.N.Y. Feb. 15, 2012).

[349] U.S. Attorney, Eastern District of New York, press release, "Long Island Health Care Provider Sentenced to 12 Years in Prison for $10 Million Medicare Fraud and HIPAA Identity Theft" (Apr. 10, 2013), available at http://www.justice.gov/usao/nye/pr/2013/2013apr10.html.

[350] U.S. Attorney, Eastern District of New York, press release, "Long Island Health Care Provider Sentenced to 12 Years in Prison for $10 Million Medicare Fraud and HIPAA Identity Theft" (Apr. 10, 2013), available at http://www.justice.gov/usao/nye/pr/2013/2013apr10.html.

[351] United States v. Michel, Sentencing Memorandum by USA, Case. No. CR-00889 (E.D.N.Y. Feb. 15, 2012).

[352] United States v. Michel, Competency Hearing Report and Recommendation, Case. No. CR-00889 (E.D.N.Y. June 30, 2009); United States v. Michel, Government Letter Re: Ordering and Funding a Competency Evaluation, Case. No. CR-00889 (E.D.N.Y. Mar. 5, 2008); see also United States v. Michel, Notice of Mental Defect Defense, Case. No. CR-00889 (E.D.N.Y. Oct. 19, 2010).

[353] United States v. Michel, Letter as to Helene Michel, Case. No. CR-00889 (E.D.N.Y. Jul. 22, 2008).

[354] United States v. Michel, Notice of Motion and Affirmation, Case. No. CR-00889 (E.D.N.Y. Feb. 4, 2009).

[355] United States v. Michel, Competency Hearing Report and Recommendation, Case. No. CR-00889 (E.D.N.Y. June 30, 2009); United States v. Michel, Order Adopting Report and Recommendation, Case. No. CR-00889 (E.D.N.Y. Aug.18, 2009).

[356] United States v. Michel, Judgment, Case. No. CR-00889 (E.D.N.Y. Apr. 10, 2013).

[357] United States v. Michel, Judgment, Case. No. CR-00889 (E.D.N.Y. Apr. 10, 2013); United States v. Michel, Final Order of Forfeiture, Case. No. CR-00889 (E.D.N.Y. Apr. 19, 2013)

[358] United States v. Michel, Summary Order, Case. No. CR-00889 (U.S. Ct. App. 2nd Cir. (Apr. 9, 2013)

[359] Pub. L. No. 107-105; 68 Fed. Reg. 48,805 (Aug. 15, 2003).

§ 6.09   PRIVACY AND SECURITY COMPLIANCE REVIEWS AND AUDITS

[A]   Security Compliance Reviews–Before HITECH

In addition to OCR and CMS, the HHS Office of Inspector General (OIG) may initiate audits or compliance reviews to determine a covered entity's compliance.[360] In 2008, the OIG audited the CMS HIPAA enforcement efforts and criticized CMS for not conducting HIPAA Security Regulation compliance reviews of covered entities.[361] The preliminary results of the audits OIG conducted of covered entities showed "numerous, significant vulnerabilities in the systems and controls intended to protect ePHI at covered entities."[362] The OIG recommended that CMS be more proactive in overseeing and enforcing implementation of the HIPAA Security Rule by focusing on compliance reviews.[363]

During 2008, as the OIG was preparing its final report, CMS did begin conducting onsite compliance reviews.[364] CMS, through its Office of E-Health Standards and Services (OESS), conducted ten onsite reviews, selecting covered entities based on complaints, media reports of security violations, and recommendations from OCR.[365] The report prepared by OESS discussed in detail six areas that seemed to give covered entities the most difficulty: (1) risk assessment; (2) policies and procedures being up-to-date; (3) security awareness and training; (4) appropriately determining workforce access to ePHI; (5) workstation security; and (6) encryption.[366]

In 2009, before the responsibility for enforcement of the Security Regulations was transferred to OCR, CMS performed five onsite compliance reviews.[367] These were not complaint-based reviews; rather, the covered entities to be reviewed were selected by covered entity type and location and included a mix of health plans, clearinghouses, and providers.[368] Vulnerabilities identified in 2009 included: (1) risk analysis; (2) policies and procedures being adequate and up-to-date; (3) business associate agreements; (4) encryption of ePHI on mobile devices; and (5) training.[369] Clearly, the key areas of concern in these compliance reviews overlapped significantly with the 2008 report.

The OIG issued a new report in May 2011, which again criticized the lack of onsite compliance audits. The OIG conducted a focused audit of seven hospitals. The report identified 151 vulnerabilities, of which it categorized 124 as "high impact," meaning they may result in high-cost losses, significant harm to the hospitals' reputational or other interests, or death or serious injury.[370] Some of these vulnerabilities were:

- Five of the seven hospitals had 15 wireless access vulnerabilities, including ineffective encryption, rogue access points, lack of firewalls between the wireless and wired networks, and no authentication required to enter the wireless network.

---

[360] The OIG's authority arises from the Inspector Generals Act of 1978. Pub. L. No. 95-542 (authorizing the OIG to conduct and supervise audits related to HHS programs).

[361] HHS OIG, "Nationwide Review of the Centers for Medicare & Medicaid Services Health Insurance Portability and Accountability Act of 1996 Oversight (October 2008)" available at http://oig.hhs.gov/oas/reports/region4/40705064.pdf (hereinafter "OIG Security Report 2008").

[362] OIG Security Report 2008.

[363] OIG Security Report 2008.

[364] CMS, OESS, "HIPAA Compliance Review Analysis and Summary of Results," available at http://www.hhs.gov/ocr/privacy/hipaa/enforcement/cmscompliancerev08.pdf (hereinafter CMS Security Report 2008).

[365] CMS Security Report 2008.

[366] CMS Security Report 2008.

[367] CMS, OESS, "HIPAA Compliance Review Analysis and Summary of Results (2009)," available at http://www.hhs.gov/ocr/privacy/hipaa/enforcement/cmscompliancerev09.pdf (hereinafter "CMS Security Report 2009"); HHS OIG, Nationwide Rollup Review of the Centers for Medicare & Medicaid Services Health Insurance Portability and Accountability Act of 1996 Oversight (May 2011), available at http://oig.hhs.gov/oas/reports/region4/40805069.pdf (hereinafter "OIG Security Report 2011"); Elizabeth Holland, CMS OESS, presentation titled "CMS Security Compliance Review Activities" at NIST HIPAA Workshop, May 18, 2009 (hereinafter "Holland presentation"), available at http://csrc.nist.gov/news_events/HIPAA-May2009_workshop/presentations.html.

[368] CMS Security Report 2009; Holland presentation.

[369] Holland presentation.

[370] OIG Security Report 2011.

- The seven hospitals had 38 access control vulnerabilities, including inadequate password settings, access to root folders, unencrypted laptops, and computers that did not log off after a period of inactivity.

- The seven hospitals had 21 integrity control vulnerabilities, including uninstalled critical security patches, unrestricted Internet access, and outdated anti-virus updates.

- One hospital had two facility access vulnerabilities. The main data center was unsecured due to an unsecured indoor window, and a data backup room's door lock had been taped over.

The report also addressed problems with audit controls, authentication issues, transmission security, device and media controls, security management and risk assessments, workforce access controls, security incident response procedures, and contingency plans. The OCR opened compliance reviews of these seven hospitals based on the OIG audits.[371]

The OIG report concluded that the CMS oversight and enforcement actions were insufficient to ensure that covered entities effectively implemented and complied with the Security Regulations. The OIG recommended that, once OCR took over responsibility for Security Regulations enforcement, that it continue the noncomplaint-based compliance audit process that CMS began in 2009 or initiate a more expansive audit process.[372]

The HITECH Act requires periodic audits of covered entities and business associates with respect to both the Privacy Regulations and Security Regulations.[373] The OIG conducted a review of OCR's enforcement of the Security Regulations under HITECH, publishing its report in November 2013.[374] The OIG credited OCR for having provided compliance guidance for covered entities and establishing an investigation process for responding to complaints, but criticized OCR for failing to meet other critical oversight and enforcement requirements.[375] The OIG stated that OCR had failed to fully implement periodic Security Regulations audits, as required by the HITECH Act. OCR responded that it had taken the initial steps of developing an audit protocol and conducting pilot audits.[376] (More about these early efforts by OCR can be found in § 6.09[B]). OCR further stated that no funds had been appropriated for it to maintain a permanent audit program. The initial HITECH Act funding ended at the end of 2012.[377] OCR will, however, be able to use funds from the escalating number of resolution agreements (see § 6.05) to support an ongoing audit program.

[B] OCR Privacy and Security Audits–After HITECH

The HITECH Act requires that HHS periodically audit covered entities and business associates with respect to compliance with both the Privacy Regulations and Security Regulations.[378] To prepare to conduct these audits, OCR looked at various audit methodologies.[379] OCR then contracted with KPMG to develop the audit protocol and to conduct an initial pilot program of privacy and security audits, under the guidance of HHS

---

[371] OIG Security Report 2011.

[372] OIG Security Report 2011.

[373] HITECH Act § 13411.

[374] HHS OIG, "The Office for Civil Rights Did Not Meet All Federal Requirements in Its Oversight and Enforcement of the Health Insurance Portability and Accountability Act of Security Rule" (November 2013), available at https://oig.hhs.gov/oas/reports/region4/41105025.pdf (hereinafter "OIG Security Report 2013").

[375] OIG Security Report 2013.

[376] OIG Security Report 2013.

[377] OIG Security Report 2013.

[378] HITECH Act § 13411.

[379] In June 2011, OCR contracted with Booz Allen Hamilton, a consulting firm, to create a process to identify audit candidates. Federal Business Opportunities: OCR HIPAA Audit Candidate Identification, contract award (solicitation #OS55726), available at https://www.fbo.gov/index?s=opportunity&mode=form&id=b05f6c10faa8145a42d02e4c3596b55c&tab=core&_cview=0.

staff.[380] Pilot audits ("Phase 1") began in November 2011. An initial set of 20 audits was conducted through March 2012 and was used to develop and test the audit protocols. Based on this experience, the audit protocols were revised for use in 95 more audits conducted through the end of 2012.[381] Although both covered entities and business associates are subject to the audits under HITECH, OCR selected only covered entities for audit during the pilot phase. These covered entities included health care providers, health plans, and clearinghouses, and both large and small organizations.[382] The initial findings of these audits include: Security was a larger problem than privacy. Providers had more problems than health plans. Small providers had more problems than large providers.[383]

In 2013, OCR evaluated its pilot program to determine the next steps for performance audits in 2014 and beyond. The initial audit protocols will be modified to reflect the changes made by the HITECH Regulations, and business associates can expect to be included in future audits. The following information is based on the pilot audits and what is currently known, or anticipated, about the next phase of audits, commonly referred to as "Phase 2." In 2015, OCR was still in the process of developing a revised protocol for Phase 2 audits, and the audits were delayed.

In February 2014, HHS issued a regulatory notice regarding its plan to evaluate up to 1,200 covered entities and business associates as *potential* audit candidates.[384] OCR planned to send pre-audit survey notifications to between 550 and 800 entities, covering a wide range of entity types. Within each type, the entities would be randomly selected, if possible. These entities would receive a pre-audit survey requesting information such as covered entity status, type of health care organization, size (by number of patients, members, or transactions), total annual revenue, use of technology, locations, business associate information, and contact information. OCR would then use this information to select approximately 350 covered entities and 50 business associates to audit. Business associates will be selected from among those identified by the covered entities receiving notifications.[385] The original timeline was for these pre-audit survey notifications to be sent in late 2014. In 2015, however, OCR was still in the process of developing a revised protocol for Phase 2 audits, and the audits were stalled due to delays in developing an online portal for the submission of audit-related documents by covered entities and business associates. Pre-audit survey notifications began going out in mid-2015.

OCR announced that its Phase 2 audits would focus on particular requirements of the Privacy and Security Regulations and "specific subsets of covered entities and business associates."[386] The anticipated breakdown was as follows:[387]

---

[380] Federal Business Opportunities: OCR HIPAA Protocol and Program Performance, contract award (solicitation #OS57605), available at https://www.fbo.gov/index?s=opportunity&mode=form&id=9e045aa4f7e6f8499c5b6f74d5b211e9&tab=core&_cview=0; U.S. Government Accountability Office, Report to Congressional Committees, "Prescription Drug Data: HHS Has Issued Health Privacy and Security Regulations but Needs to Improve Guidance and Oversight," GAO-12-605, p. 22 (June 2012) (hereinafter "June 2012 GAO Report").

[381] June 2012 GAO Report, p. 22; OCR, "HIPAA Privacy & Security Audit Program," available at http://www.hhs.gov/ocr/privacy/hipaa/enforcement/audit/index.html; HHS, "OCR Pilot Audit Program," Presentation December 1, 2011.

[382] OCR, "HIPAA Privacy & Security Audit Program," available at http://www.hhs.gov/ocr/privacy/hipaa/enforcement/audit/auditpilotprogram.html; HHS, "OCR Pilot Audit Program," Presentation December 1, 2011. For a list of the specific types and locations of entities included in the first 20 selected for the pilot, see http://www.hhs.gov/ocr/privacy/hipaa/enforcement/audit/listofentities.html.

[383] OCR, "2012 Privacy and Security Audits," available at http://csrc.nist.gov/news_events/hiipaa_june2012/day2/day2-2_lsanches_ocr-audit.pdf

[384] 79 Fed. Reg. 10158 (Feb. 24, 2014).

[385] Sanches, Linda, OCR, "OCR Audits of HIPAA Privacy and Security and Breach Notification, Phase 2," HCCA Compliance Institute presentation (Mar. 31, 2014); U.S. Office of Management and Budget, Information Collection Request, ICR Ref. No. 201405-0945-002.

[386] OCR, "Annual Report to Congress on HIPAA Privacy, Security and Breach Notification Rule Compliance (2011-2012)," available at http://www.hhs.gov/ocr/privacy/hipaa/enforcement/compliancereport2011-2012.pdf.

[387] Sanches, Linda, OCR, "OCR Audits of HIPAA Privacy and Security and Breach Notification, Phase 2," HCCA Compliance Institute presentation (Mar. 31, 2014).

Entity Type	Privacy Audit	Breach Audit	Security Audit
Covered Entities	**100**	**100**	**150**
- Health Plans	33	31	45
- Providers	67	65	100
- Clearinghouses	—	4	5
Business Associates	—	—	**50**
- IT Related	—	—	35
- Non-IT Related	—	—	15
Total	**100**	**100**	**200**

The Phase 2 audits are expected to cover areas where deficiencies were found during the pilot phase, such as:

Security: Risk analysis and risk management; devices and media controls; transmission security; encryption; facility access controls.

Privacy: Notice of privacy practices; access by individuals; training based on the entity's policies and procedures.

Breach: Content and timeliness of breach notifications.[388]

Entities that are selected for an audit will receive notification from OCR.[389] Covered entities and business associates should educate their staff to be alert to these notifications, which should be forwarded immediately to the compliance officer, privacy officer, security officer, or other designated person, who should contact legal counsel.

In the initial notification, the entity will be asked to provide documents to the auditors, who in Phase 2 will be HHS staff rather than contractors. Entities should expect a request for documentation demonstrating the entity's privacy, security or breach notification compliance and will have about 10 days to respond.[390] OCR will have an online portal for entities to submit the documents electronically.

The auditors will conduct a desk review of those documents. During the pilot phase, site visits were also part of the standard audit protocol and may also be conducted in Phase 2, as resources permit. During site visits, auditors would interview key personnel and observe the entity's processes and operations.[391] During the pilot, fieldwork also included:

---

[388] Sanches, Linda, OCR, "OCR Audits of HIPAA Privacy and Security and Breach Notification, Phase 2," HCCA Compliance Institute presentation (Mar. 31, 2014).

[389] For a sample of the pilot phase letter, see http://www.hhs.gov/ocr/privacy/hipaa/enforcement/audit/sample-ocr_notification_ltr.pdf.

[390] June 2012 GAO Report, p. 22; OCR, "HIPAA Privacy & Security Audit Program," available at http://www.hhs.gov/ocr/privacy/hipaa/enforcement/audit/index.html; HHS, "OCR Pilot Audit Program," Presentation December 1, 2011.

[391] OCR, "HIPAA Privacy & Security Audit Program," available at http://www.hhs.gov/ocr/privacy/hipaa/enforcement/audit/index.html; HHS, "OCR Pilot Audit Program," Presentation December 1, 2011.

- Interviews with leadership (CIO, privacy officer, legal counsel, health information management director, etc.);

- Examination of physical features and operations;

- Reviewing the consistency between the organization's policies and actual processes; and

- Reviewing compliance with regulatory requirements.[392]

Following conclusion of the desk audit, and fieldwork (if applicable), the auditors will prepare a draft report, which will be shared with the entity.[393] The entity will have the opportunity to review the draft report and respond to the auditor.[394] The auditors will submit a final report to OCR after receipt of the entity's comments. OCR will review the final report, including findings and actions taken by the audited entity to address those findings. OCR will use the audit reports to identify best practices, guide development of technical assistance, and to determine what types of corrective actions are most effective.[395] If the audit report identifies a serious compliance issue, OCR may initiate a compliance review to address it. Audit reports will be used to generate aggregate results, but OCR will not identify the audited entities.[396]

[C] Preparing for a Privacy and Security Audit

OCR intends to post revised audit protocols for Phase 2 on its Web site, once development is complete. In the interim, covered entities and business associates should review OCR's initial audit protocol, published in June 2012.[397] The 2012 protocol identifies a total of 165 areas of evaluation: 77 under the Security Regulations, 10 under the Breach Regulations, and 78 under the Privacy Regulations.[398] Nearly all sections of the Privacy and Security Regulations are represented, though not all parts of this comprehensive audit protocol will necessarily be used in every audit. This protocol should be closely reviewed by all covered entities and business associates in preparing for an audit and for self-assessment of their HIPAA compliance. Some example sections of the 2012 audit protocol are included in **Appendix G**. The complete 2012 audit protocols are on the OCR website.[399]

In addition, when CMS was doing HIPAA security audits, it published a sample information request, which can also be found in **Appendix G**. The CMS sample is instructive and detailed with regard to security matters. OCR's requests will be broader, however, since they are auditing for privacy and well as security compliance.

The audit protocols identify many documents that may be requested by OCR. These include:

- Documentation identifying the privacy officer and security officer;

- Up-to-date security risk assessments and risk management plans (in-depth and current);

- Documentation of privacy and security training of workforce, including copies of training materials;

- Notices of Privacy Practices;

- Written and up-to-date privacy and security policies and procedures;

---

[392] Federal Business Opportunities: OCR HIPAA Protocol and Program Performance, contract award (solicitation #OS57605), available at https://www.fbo.gov/index?s=opportunity&mode=form&id=9e045aa4f7e6f8499c5b6f74d5b211e9&tab=core&_cview=0.

[393] June 2012 GAO Report, p. 22; OCR, "HIPAA Privacy & Security Audit Program," available at http://www.hhs.gov/ocr/privacy/hipaa/enforcement/audit/index.html; HHS, "OCR Pilot Audit Program," Presentation December 1, 2011.

[394] June 2012 GAO Report, p. 22; OCR, "HIPAA Privacy & Security Audit Program," available at http://www.hhs.gov/ocr/privacy/hipaa/enforcement/audit/index.html; HHS, "OCR Pilot Audit Program," Presentation December 1, 2011.

[395] June 2012 GAO Report, p. 22; OCR, "HIPAA Privacy & Security Audit Program," available at http://www.hhs.gov/ocr/privacy/hipaa/enforcement/audit/index.html; HHS, "OCR Pilot Audit Program," Presentation December 1, 2011.

[396] OCR, "HIPAA Privacy & Security Audit Program," available at http://www.hhs.gov/ocr/privacy/hipaa/enforcement/audit/index.html; HHS, "OCR Pilot Audit Program," Presentation December 1, 2011.

[397] Available at http://www.hhs.gov/ocr/privacy/hipaa/enforcement/audit/protocol.html.

[398] HHS, Audit Program Protocol, available at http://www.hhs.gov/ocr/privacy/hipaa/enforcement/audit/protocol.html.

[399] HHS, Audit Program Protocol, available at http://www.hhs.gov/ocr/privacy/hipaa/enforcement/audit/protocol.html.

- Business associate agreements;

- Documentation of individual complaints, and any related investigations, findings, mitigation, and sanctions; and

- Documentation of breaches and risk assessments.

Covered entities and business associates can reasonably assume that OCR will focus at least some of its auditing activities on issues regarding which OCR has issued guidance in the past or where prior audits, complaints, or resolution agreements have suggested pervasive problems. For example:

- Security risk assessments and resulting risk management plans;

- Encryption–policies and their implementation;

- Physical security of mobile media and devices, and safeguards for paper PHI taken offsite;

- Security of wireless networks;

- Protocols for handling privacy breaches, including risk assessments;

- Security related to remote access to ePHI;

- Business associate relationships and agreements;

- Disposal of PHI or ePHI;

- Disclosure of PHI to individuals' family and friends; and

- Compliance with requests related to individuals' rights, such as amendment or access requests.

To be prepared for a potential HIPAA privacy and security audit, and for ongoing compliance, covered entities and business associates should, at a minimum:

- Review the audit process and protocols on the OCR website.

- Determine who should receive immediate notification of an audit notification letter from OCR/HHS;

- Identify key staff that the auditors may want to interview, such President/CEO, Compliance Officer, Privacy Officer, Security Officer, trainers, incident response teams, access control specialists, human resources representatives, etc.;

- Ensure that key compliance documents are readily accessible, because they may requested by the auditors on 10 days' notice;

- Update the documentation of the organization's risk assessment, which means an accurate and thorough assessment of the current potential risks and vulnerabilities to the security of ePHI, updated to address environmental or operational changes since the last security assessment;

- Update the written risk management plan. (For any vulnerabilities still needing to be addressed, at least have a written action plan, even if it has not been fully executed.);

- Confirm that there is documentation of how each Security Regulation standard is being met, especially with regard to addressable implementation specifications;

- Review privacy and security policies and procedures. Updated or expanded as needed (e.g., for changes under the HITECH Regulations);

- Confirm that there is good documentation of breach investigations (particularly risk assessments) and breach notifications;

- Confirm all workforce members have received appropriate training and address any gaps (e.g., to incorporate new policies and procedures needed after the HITECH Regulations);

- Know who your business associates are. Review business associate relationships and subcontractor relationships, as defined under the HITECH Regulations; and

- Audit business associate agreements to ensure that signed copies are accessible and updated to comply with the HITECH Regulations.

HIPAA compliance is an ongoing never-perfected process, but covered entities and business associates will be expected to know what their risk areas are and have plans to manage those risks.

§ 6.10 INDIVIDUAL CIVIL REMEDIES

Although HIPAA provides mechanisms for HHS to encourage compliance and to punish noncompliant covered entities and business associates, it provides no direct relief to an individual who is injured by the unauthorized use or disclosure of confidential information or other violation of the Administrative Simplification Regulations. However, as explained in § 6.02[E], the HITECH Act requires HHS to develop a process that allows a harmed individual to share in a civil monetary penalty or monetary settlement collected. No regulations have yet been issued to implement this. Meanwhile, as discussed in this Section, plaintiffs are pursuing civil remedies under State law.

[A] No Private Right of Action Under HIPAA

The federal courts have consistently held that HIPAA itself does not provide any private cause of action—that is, an individual may not bring a lawsuit against a covered entity to enforce HIPAA.[400] The state courts that have addressed this question have followed the federal cases and held that the plaintiff does not have a private right of action under HIPAA.[401]

[B] State Laws Creating a Private Right of Action

In the right combination of circumstances, however, a state law may make it possible to bring an action under HIPAA. In *Webb*, the Ninth Circuit Court of Appeals agreed with other courts that HIPAA itself provides no private cause of action. However, the plaintiffs in this case (which concerned limitations on the costs of records under the Privacy Regulations) raised state law claims, invoking a California unfair competition statute that makes violations of other state and federal laws independently actionable. Lack of a private right of action under HIPAA did not therefore foreclose the state law claim, and the state law directed the court to determine whether there was a violation of federal law. The court, therefore, had to interpret the Privacy Regulations to determine whether the defendant's actions were "unfair or unlawful" (i.e., a violation of the Privacy Regulations and therefore stated a valid claim under the California statute). Ultimately, however, the court concluded that because the plaintiffs did not successfully allege a HIPAA violation, they had not stated a claim under the California unfair competition statute.[402] A stronger claim of a HIPAA violation might have led to a private cause of action indirectly through the California statute.

Relying on the *Webb* case, patients in Utah brought action against an ambulance company for unjust enrichment, for allegedly overcharging them for copies of medical records. The patients sought to rely on

---

[400] Pub. L. No. 104-191, § 262(a) (codified at 42 U.S.C. § 1320d-5); 65 Fed. Reg. 82,566; Acara v. Banks, 470 F.3d 569 (5th Cir. 2006) (first federal appeals court ruling on the issue, holding no private right of action under HIPAA). See also, e.g., Valentin Munoz v. Island Fin. Corp., 364 F. Supp. 2d 131 (D.P.R. Mar. 28, 2005).

[401] See, e.g., Community Hosp. Group, Inc. v. Blume et al., P.C., 885 A.2d 18 (N.J. Sup. Ct. 2005), *cert. denied*, 901 A. 2d 952 (N.J. 2006).

[402] Webb v. Smart Document Solutions, LLC, 499 F.3d 1078 (9th Cir. 2007) (citing Cal. Bus. & Prof. Code §§ 17200–17210) (the court first addressed the jurisdiction issue, noting that when there is no federal private right of action, federal courts may not entertain a claim that depends on federal question jurisdiction; however, this case was before the court based on diversity jurisdiction, so lack of a private right of action under HIPAA did not foreclose the state law claim).

HIPAA as setting the standard for the allowable fees. The court first confirmed the opinions of other courts by concluding that the plaintiff patients had no private right of action under HIPAA. The court went on to say, however, that states may create their own HIPAA-related causes of action by statute, citing the example of the *Webb* case and the California unfair competition statute. Ultimately, however, this analysis did not help the plaintiffs, because the court concluded that Utah had not "statutorily created a private right of action to redress HIPAA violations."[403]

[C] HIPAA as the Standard of Care in State Law Claims

Even though HIPAA does not provide individuals with a right to sue if their PHI is misused or their rights are violated, a person or entity that uses or discloses health information about an individual without consent or authorization may risk liability under other state or federal law. Such causes of action will vary from state to state. For example, liability might be found under state privacy statutes or tort law. Statutory claims could arise under a state medical records act, consumer fraud act, or through a licensing complaint. For a government entity, claims could also arise under a government data privacy act. Tort claims could include claims of negligence, professional malpractice, breach of fiduciary duty, or invasion of privacy. Claims of breach of contract might also be raised. A lawsuit by an injured individual may include a combination of these types of claims.

In tort, contract, or other causes of actions under state law, plaintiffs may argue that even though there is no private cause of action, the Privacy Regulations establish a standard of care relative to confidentiality of patient information. Even before the compliance date for the Privacy Regulations, federal courts used the Privacy Regulations' standards as the basis for decisions about the disclosure of medical records.[404] In 2006, in *Acosta*, a widely reported North Carolina case, the state court of appeals reinstated a case after dismissal by the trial court, holding that it was permissible to use HIPAA as evidence of the appropriate standard of care with regard to medical records. A patient (and former employee) at a psychiatric clinic alleged that the clinic's owner permitted the clinic's office manager inappropriate access to her medical records (by using the owner's access code) and that the office manager then improperly disclosed those records to a third party. The patient sued the clinic's owner for negligent infliction of emotional distress. She did not allege a private cause of action under HIPAA. However, establishing a standard of care is a necessary element in a negligence case, and the court held that HIPAA could be used to provide evidence of the duty of care owed by the clinic owner with regard to the privacy of the patient's medical records.[405]

Following the *Acosta* case, a line of cases has slowly developed, where plaintiffs have sued under State law causes of action, such as negligence, but have attempted to rely on HIPAA as the standard of care, with increasing success. Examples of some of these cases are provided below.

In *Sorenson*, a Utah case, the results on this issue were less conclusive. A patient was injured in an automobile accident and filed a personal injury action against the driver's insurance company. The patient alleged that his former doctor had engaged in impermissible *ex parte* communications with defense counsel in that personal injury case and sued the doctor for breach of the covenant of good faith and fair dealing and for various tort claims. Although the patient did not rely on a HIPAA standard in his claims, the doctor raised HIPAA as a bar to tort liability because HIPAA does not provide for a private right of action. The appeals court cited HIPAA standards as applicable in determining the doctor's duty of confidentiality to his patients and allowed the tort claims for breach of professional duty to proceed. The state supreme court, however, did not rely on or reference HIPAA in its analysis, though it held that the health care fiduciary duty of confidentiality does

---

[403] Espinoza v. Gold Cross Servs., Inc., 234 P.3d 156 (Ct. App. Utah, June 10, 2010).

[404] United States v. Sutherland, 143 F. Supp. 2d 609, 612 (W.D. Va. 2001) (the Privacy Regulations "indicate a strong federal policy to protect the privacy of patient medical records, and they provide guidance to the present case"); United States *ex rel.* Mary Jane Stewart v. Louisiana Clinic, 2002 WL 31819130 (E.D. La. Dec. 12, 2002), *aff'd*, 2003 WL 21283944 (E.D. La. Jun. 4, 2003).

[405] Acosta v. Byrum, 638 S.E.2d 246 (N.C. Ct. App. 2006).

prohibit *ex parte* communications between a tort plaintiff's treating physician and defense counsel.[406] As a result, the case is unclear with regard to the value of arguing HIPAA as the standard of care.

In *Cain*, when a plaintiff sued the OCR alleging that it failed to properly investigate his HIPAA privacy complaint, he cited the *Acosta* case, arguing that HIPAA may form the basis for a lawsuit by a patient notwithstanding the lack of a private right of action. The federal district court in Montana disagreed, finding that the *Acosta* case was not applicable. First, in this case, the lawsuit was against the OCR, not a covered entity. Second, unlike in *Acosta*, where the plaintiff cited HIPAA as the standard of care in a tort claim, there was not a tort claim in this case.[407] *Cain* shows some potential limits in applying *Acosta* but leaves the door open in cases involving tort claims against covered entities.

In West Virginia, in the *St. Mary's Medical Center* case, a patient sued a hospital alleging several state law tort claims arising from the hospital's alleged unauthorized disclosure of the patient's medical and psychiatric information to the patient's estranged wife and her divorce lawyer. The patient's position was that he was not making an argument for a private right of action under HIPAA, but rather making state law claims. The hospital argued that, although the plaintiff's claim was "artfully drafted to not specifically assert claims labeled HIPAA," the court should "look beyond the labels" and see the claims as assertions of a private right of action under HIPAA, and that HIPAA preempts the state law causes of actions. The Supreme Court of Appeals of West Virginia disagreed with the hospital. The court reviewed a number of cases in which HIPAA violations had either been used as the basis for a claim of negligence *per se*, or in which HIPAA was used to establish the standard of care for other tort claims. The court held that HIPAA does not preempt claims under state law causes of actions for the wrongful disclosure of health care information, and that the lower court had improperly dismissed the claims. The court's decision permitted the case to proceed.[408]

The *Avery Center for Obstetrics & Gynecology* case involved allegations by a patient that the Avery Center improperly supplied copies of the patient's medical record in response to a subpoena in a paternity suit. The patient's claims were presented as state law claims, and she stated that she had not relied on HIPAA as the basis of her cause of action, but rather as evidence of the appropriate standard of care. The trial court stated, however, that although the patient "labeled her claims as negligence claims," this did not change their "essential character" as HIPAA claims; and there is no private right of action under HIPAA. The patient appealed the case to the Connecticut Supreme Court. The Connecticut Supreme Court, in its opinion, reviewed and summarized numerous cases on this issue. Similar to the *St. Mary's Medical Center* case, the Connecticut Supreme Court refused to dismiss the patient's negligence claims based on HIPAA preemption of state law causes of action. Further, in addition to permitting the case to proceed, the Connecticut Supreme Court signaled that HIPAA may be used to establish the standard of care in the right circumstances. The court held that "to the extent it has become the common practice for Connecticut health care providers to follow the procedures required under HIPAA in rendering services to their patients, HIPAA and its implementing regulations may be utilized to inform the standard of care applicable to such claims arising from allegations of negligence in the disclosure of patients' medical records pursuant to a subpoena." The case was remanded to the trial court for further proceedings.[409]

Hinchy v. Walgreen Co., an Indiana case, may represent the first significant jury award of damages in a state tort claim that relies on HIPAA to establish the standard of care with respect to confidentiality of patient information. In this case, a pharmacy customer filed suit against Walgreens and a Walgreens-employed pharmacist relating to the pharmacist's access to and disclosure of the customer's prescription history. The customer

---

[406] Sorensen v. Barbuto, 143 P.3d 295 (Utah Ct. App. 2006); *upheld on state law grounds by* 177 P.3d 614 (Utah 2008). See also 75 Fed. Reg. 40,868, 40,874 (July 14, 2010), where HHS states that the Privacy Regulations do not create a federal evidentiary privilege, nor do they give effect to state physician-patient privilege laws or provisions of state law relating to the privacy of PHI for use in federal court proceedings.

[407] Cain v. Mitchell, 2007 WL 4287866 (W.D. Mont. Dec. 6, 2007).

[408] R.K. v. St. Mary's Medical Center, Inc., 229 W.Va. 712 (W.Va. 2012), *cert. denied*, 133 S.Ct. 1738 (2013). The court also held that the State's Medical Professional Liability Act (MPLA) did not apply to claims for improper disclosure of medical records; therefore, the MPLA's limitations on non-monetary losses would not apply.

[409] Byrne v. Avery Center for Obstetrics and Gynecology, P.C., 102 A.3d 32 (Conn. 2014).

alleged that the pharmacist accessed the customer's confidential prescription information while at work, but for personal reasons, and further, that the pharmacist subsequently shared this information with her husband (the customer's ex-boyfriend).[410] The customer was able to successfully argue at trial that the pharmacist breached her common law duty of confidentiality, relying on HIPAA to show the standard of care. The customer's claims of negligence, professional malpractice, and invasion of privacy were also brought against Walgreens, as the pharmacist's employer, under a theory of vicarious responsibility. (Vicarious liability may be imposed on an employer if the harm was inflicted by an employee while acting within the scope of employment.) The jury awarded the customer $1.44 million in damages, holding Walgreens and the pharmacist jointly responsible.[411] Walgreens appealed.[412] The Court of Appeals examined Indiana law on vicarious liability and concluded that the jury could reasonably have determined that the pharmacist's actions were within the scope of her employment. The pharmacist was authorized to use the computer system and printer, look up customer information, review customer prescription information, and make printouts of that information. Furthermore, the pharmacist was at work and using her employer's equipment when she improperly accessed the records. The Court of Appeals viewed the pharmacist's conduct as being of the same general nature as her ordinary job duties and of the same general nature as duties authorized by her employer (even though the pharmacist's actions, in this case, were not for the benefit of the employer). The Court of Appeals upheld the jury verdict and the damages award.[413] Further appeal from Walgreens is expected.

The interplay of state law claims of negligence and HIPAA as the standard of care in handling individual health information will depend on the particular State's laws regarding negligence and professional liability. And from an employer's standpoint, the State's interpretation of vicarious liability doctrine will be significant. These cases do, however, show a trend of plaintiffs bringing suit under State law claims, based on the standards set forth in the Privacy Regulations.

---

[410] Hinchy v. Walgreen Co., Order re Walgreen's Motion for Summary Judgment, Sup. Ct. Marion County, Indiana, Civ 49D10-1108-CT-029165 (Nov. 6, 2012).

[411] Hinchy v. Walgreen Co., Verdict, Sup. Ct. Marion County, Indiana, Civ 49D10-1108-CT-029165 (July 26, 2013). The jury awarded a total of $1.8 million in damages; but the jury found 20% of the damages were attributable to the ex-boyfriend, who was not a party to the case.

[412] Walgreen Co. v. Hinchy, 21 N.E.3d 99 (Ct. App. Ind., Nov. 14, 2014) (aff'd on rehearing, 25 N.E.3d 748, Jan 15, 2015).

[413] Walgreen Co. v. Hinchy, 21 N.E.3d 99 (Ct. App. Ind., Nov. 14, 2014) (aff'd on rehearing, 25 N.E.3d 748, Jan 15, 2015).

CHAPTER 7

EMPLOYER-SPONSORED GROUP HEALTH PLANS

§ 7.01 APPLICABILITY

When the Health Insurance Portability and Accountability Act of 1996 (HIPAA) first became law, employers concentrated on the "portability" provisions relating to special enrollment periods, certificates of creditable coverage, and other provisions of Title I. Now employer attention also encompasses the Administrative Simplification provisions of Title II.

Health plans, including employer-sponsored group health plans, are covered entities. Employers are not directly subject to the regulations;[1] however, many employers sponsor employee health plans that *are* covered entities. The employer is often not only the plan sponsor but also the plan administrator and plan fiduciary under the Employee Retirement Income Security Act of 1974 (ERISA). HIPAA recognizes that, under ERISA, a group health plan and its plan sponsor must be separate legal entities.[2] But, in practical terms, it is the plan sponsor that typically acts on behalf of a group health plan. An ERISA-covered group health plan usually does not have its own employees and often will have no assets.[3] Therefore, it is the employer, as the plan sponsor and fiduciary, that will have to be responsible for assuring the plan's compliance with the HIPAA regulations. As explained further in this chapter, employers offering self-insured health plans will be the most directly affected and will be responsible for the plan's full compliance with the HIPAA regulations, even if they use a third-party administrator (TPA). For employers offering fully insured plans, many (perhaps most) of the compliance functions will be the responsibility of the insurer, but the employer will retain some responsibilities, particularly if, as plan sponsor, it uses, creates, or receives PHI.

§ 7.02 COVERED ENTITY HEALTH PLANS

A health plan is a covered entity if it is an individual or group plan that provides or pays the cost of medical care.[4] Covered health plans include "group health plans" that are employee welfare benefit plans, as defined by Section 3(1) of ERISA, that offer health care benefits, whether insured or self-insured and whether the medical care is provided directly or through insurance, reimbursement, or otherwise.[5]

An exception is made for group health plans that have fewer than 50 participants and are administered by the employer (i.e., not by a third party).[6] These very small, internally administered plans are not subject to the HIPAA Administrative Simplification Regulations.

Covered group health plans include, for example, medical plans, dental plans, vision plans, health flexible spending accounts (Health FSAs), and some employee assistance plans (EAPs).

Some Health Savings Accounts (HSAs) and wellness programs may be covered entity health plans under the Administrative Simplification Regulations, depending on the nature and extent of the employer's involvement with the plan. An HSA is a tax-favored savings account for paying qualified medical expenses, used in combination with a high deductible health plan. An HSA will generally not be an employee welfare plan under ERISA if employer involvement with the HSA is limited. And therefore, it will not be a covered entity under the Administrative Simplification Regulations.[7]

---

[1] 65 Fed. Reg. 82,496 (Dec. 28, 2000) (plan sponsors are not covered entities).

[2] 65 Fed. Reg. 82,507 (Dec. 28, 2000).

[3] 65 Fed. Reg. 82,507 (Dec. 28, 2000).

[4] 45 C.F.R. § 160.103 (definition of health plan).

[5] 45 C.F.R. § 160.103 (definition of group health plan). A church plan or government plan may satisfy the ERISA definition of an *employee welfare benefit plan*, and be subject to HIPAA, even though it is not covered by ERISA due to an exemption.

[6] With the possible exception of a Health FSA, few health plans are likely to qualify for this exemption, because of the requirement that the plan be administered by the employer. Note: When evaluating the "under 50" factor, the plan sponsor should look to its Form 5500 filings and plan documents to help determine how many separate plans there are.

[7] Health Savings Accounts were created by the Medicare Modernization Act, Pub. L. No. 108-173, in 2003. An HSA is a tax-favored savings account for paying qualified medical expenses, used in combination with a high deductible health plan. The U.S. Department of Labor has indicated that an HSA will not be an employee welfare plan under ERISA if employer involvement with the HSA is limited. U.S. Dept. of Labor Field Assistance Bulletin (FAB) No. 2006-02 (citing FAB 2004-01), available at http://www.dol.gov/ebsa/regs/

Similarly, whether a workplace wellness program is a covered entity health plan depends on how it is structured. If a wellness program is offered directly by the employer and not as part of the employer's group health plan (and is not an "employee welfare benefit plan" as defined by ERISA) it is not subject to the Privacy, Security and Breach Regulations.[8] The health information collected from employees is not PHI, but it may be protected by other state and Federal law.[9]

If the wellness program is, however, offered as part of a group health plan of the employer, the individually identifiable health information collected from or created about participants in the program is PHI under the Regulations.[10] Recent guidance from OCR indicates that employer "incentives or rewards related to group health plan benefits, such as reductions in premiums or cost-sharing amounts, in exchange for participation in the wellness program" are evidence that the wellness program is part of the covered entity health plan.[11]

The following are not covered entity health plans under the Administrative Simplification Regulations: Disability (income replacement) plans, accident-only coverage, life insurance plans, liability insurance (or supplements to liability insurance), automobile medical payment coverage, and workers' compensation plans.[12] Nevertheless, personal information related to these plans may be impacted by the Privacy Regulations. See § 7.03[B].

Each separate health plan offered by the employer is a separate covered entity. A plan sponsor should look to its annual Form 5500 filings and plan documents, and consult legal counsel if necessary, to determine how many separate plans there are. For compliance purposes, the concepts of affiliated covered entity, hybrid entity, or organized health care arrangement, discussed in § 1.02[C], may be useful.

§ 7.03 NON–HEALTH PLAN INFORMATION

[A] Employment Records

Employment records held by an employer that is a covered entity are not PHI, even if they contain health information about an employee.[13] Employment records are employer information rather than plan or patient information, and they are not subject to the Administrative Simplification Regulations. Employment records may include medical information needed for an employer to carry out its obligations under the Family and Medical Leave Act (FMLA), Americans with Disabilities Act (ADA), and other laws, as well as files or records related to occupational injury, sick leave requests, drug screening results, workplace medical surveillance, and fitness-for-duty tests of employees.[14] But this is not PHI.

For providers or health plans (which are covered entities) to disclose PHI to an employer, a signed authorization from the employee will usually be required (see § 3.03[F]). For example, if an employer/plan sponsor requests PHI from its group health plan in connection with the employer's administration of an FMLA leave, a

---

fab_2006-2.html. HHS has indicated that it may issue further guidance regarding whether an HSA is a covered entity/health plan and that it is leaning toward a conclusion that it is not. American Bar Association, Technical Session Between the Department of Health and Human Services and the Joint Committee on Employee Benefits (May 17, 2005), available at http://www.americanbar.org/content/dam/aba/migrated/2011_build/employee_benefits/2005_hhs.authcheckdam.pdf.

[8] American Bar Association, "Technical Session Between the Department of Health and Human Services and the Joint Committee on Employee Benefits" (May 6, 2008), available at http://www.americanbar.org/content/dam/aba/migrated/2011_build/employee_benefits/hhs_2008.authcheckdam.pdf.

[9] OCR, "HIPAA Privacy and Security and Workplace Wellness Programs," Apr. 16, 2015, available at http://www.hhs.gov/ocr/privacy/hipaa/understanding/coveredentities/wellness/index.html.

[10] 75 Fed. Reg. 21,663 (Apr. 20, 2015) (proposed Amendments to Regulations Under the Americans with Disabilities Act).

[11] OCR, "HIPAA Privacy and Security and Workplace Wellness Programs," Apr. 16, 2015, available at http://www.hhs.gov/ocr/privacy/hipaa/understanding/coveredentities/wellness/index.html.

[12] 45 C.F.R. § 160.103 (definition of Health Plan).

[13] 45 C.F.R. § 160.103. See also OCR, *Employers and Health Information in the Workplace*, available at http://www.hhs.gov/ocr/privacy/hipaa/understanding/consumers/employers.html.

[14] 67 Fed. Reg. 53,192 (Aug. 14, 2002).

signed authorization from the employee would be required. If a provider has been hired by the employer to conduct fitness-for-duty exams or similar services requested by the employer, the provider may refuse to conduct the exam if the employee-patient refuses to sign the authorization that would allow the results to be shared with the employer (see § 3.03[F]). However, a provider may make certain disclosures to an employer without the individual's authorization, if the disclosures are for public health purposes. The provider must be providing health care services to the individual, at the request of the individual's employer, to conduct an evaluation relating to medical surveillance of the workplace or to evaluate whether the individual has a work-related injury or illness. Certain other conditions must be met, including putting the individual on notice about the disclosure to the employer.[15]

Information held by the employer, even if not subject to the Privacy and Security Regulations, should be kept confidential as appropriate and to the extent required by other laws.

[B] Records of Non-HIPAA-Covered Health Plans

As explained in § 7.02, not all employer-sponsored plans are "health plans" under the Administrative Simplification Regulations. Employee medical information related to disability plans and other employer-sponsored plans that do not meet the definition of health plan are not PHI and are not governed by the Administrative Simplification Regulations. It should be noted, however, that such plans may need to obtain health information from covered entities. Disclosures of PHI by covered entities for purposes related to such plans will be subject to the Privacy and Security Regulations. For example, if a long-term disability plan needs PHI from a provider or a health plan in connection with determining benefits under the disability plan, it will generally be necessary to obtain the patient's signed authorization prior to the disclosure. Similarly, a workers' compensation plan (not a covered entity) may need information about an employee from a provider (a covered entity). However, in this situation, the Privacy Regulations permit disclosures of PHI for workers' compensation purposes without an authorization, as authorized by and to the extent necessary to comply with state law (see § 3.03[D][12]).

§ 7.04 TRANSACTION STANDARDS

Any health plan that engages in the standard transactions, whether directly or through a third party, must be prepared to conduct those transactions *electronically*, using the standardized format and content set forth in the Transaction Standards.[16] Most employer-sponsored group health plans rely on an insurer[17] or a TPA for compliance with the Transaction Standards. Employers should make certain they are doing business with an insurer or a TPA that can comply with the Transaction Standards. The administrative services agreement with a TPA should include a requirement that the TPA will comply with the Transaction Standards for any standard transactions it conducts on behalf of the covered entity. Self-insured plans that are directly administered by the employer will need to take their own steps to assure compliance.

Enrollment transactions represent a special case. While the health plan is generally considered to be the party conducting the standard transactions, transfers of enrollment information may be viewed as being originated by the employer rather than the employer-sponsored group health plan. Therefore, because the employer is not a covered entity, the enrollment information transmitted from the employer to its health plan is not subject to the Transaction Standards.[18] Once the insurer has the information, it becomes PHI (but it can be disclosed back to the plan sponsor to use for plan administration functions).[19]

---

[15] 45 CFR 164.512(b). See also § 3.03[D][2].

[16] 45 C.F.R. Pts. 160 and 162.

[17] As used in this chapter, *insurer* includes not only health insurance issuers but also HMOs.

[18] 65 Fed. Reg. 50,317 and 50,318 (Aug. 17, 2000).

[19] See American Bar Association, "Technical Session Between the Department of Health and Human Services and the Joint Committee on Employee Benefits" (May 6, 2008), available at http://www.americanbar.org/content/dam/aba/migrated/2011_build/employee_benefits/hhs_2008.authcheckdam.pdf.

§ 7.05 PRIVACY REGULATIONS

Employers offering self-insured group health plans are liable for full compliance with the Privacy Regulations, even if they delegate most plan administration functions to a TPA. Employers offering fully insured plans are able to delegate many compliance functions to the insurer, but the employer's group health plan will retain some HIPAA compliance responsibilities.

All health plans must limit employer access to PHI as described above and may not use health plan PHI for employment purposes. In addition, a health plan may not use or disclose PHI that is genetic information for underwriting purposes.[20]

[A] Self-Insured Health Plans

A self-insured group health plan (sometimes called a self-funded plan) is one in which the employer assumes the financial risk for providing health care benefits to its employees. The self-funded employer typically pays for each health expense or claim from its general assets, as it is incurred, rather than paying a fixed premium to a health insurance company. These employers usually contract with a third-party administrator (TPA) to administer the self-insured plan. Often the TPA is a health insurer that also offers these plan administration services.

In general, a self-insured group health plan sponsored by an employer must comply with *all* health plan requirements under the Privacy Regulations, as described throughout this book. In addition, explained below are some further requirements. **Sections 7.05[A][1]–[4]** relate specifically to self-insured group health plans, where the plan sponsor creates, receives, or maintains PHI. **Sections 7.05[A][5]–[12]** discuss issues that apply to all types of covered entities, but there are some special "twists" to how they apply to self-insured group health plans.

[1] Limited Employer Access to PHI

Employers may not access any health plan PHI for non-plan purposes, and especially not for employment-related purposes, without the individual's authorization.[21] For example, an employer may not reassign an employee to another job *based on information from the health plan* that the employee is being treated for alcoholism. An employer receives personal information about employees from a variety of sources, including directly from the employee. The concern of the Privacy Regulations, however, is information received from or through the employer's health plan. This information may be used by the plan sponsor only for plan administration purposes.

[2] Firewalls

Employers must establish a "firewall" between the self-insured health plan's uses of PHI and general corporate or employment-related uses of PHI.[22] Employers that have the same person(s) handling all benefit plans plus human resource matters should consider separating these functions. Ideally, the health plan administration functions should be handled by staff who do not handle employment functions (e.g., performance reviews, terminations, etc.). In small organizations, where having different staff members for these functions is not feasible, the employer should, at a minimum, establish policies and conduct training regarding the confidentiality of PHI, the need to restrict internal uses as well as disclosures, and the prohibition on using health plan PHI for non-plan purposes. In addition, health plan PHI should be stored separately from non–health plan information and personnel records (whether these records are on paper or electronic).

---

[20] 45 CFR § 164.502(a)(5)(i).
[21] 45 C.F.R. § 164.504(f)(3)(iv); 65 Fed. Reg. 82,508 (Dec. 28, 2000).
[22] 45 C.F.R. § 164.504(f)(2)(iii); 65 Fed. Reg. 82,508 (Dec. 28, 2000).

[3] Communication Issues

A TPA or other business associate contacting an employer about a group health plan will need to be careful about which staff members at the employer's office it communicates with, so that PHI is communicated only to authorized personnel. Covered entities and business associates will need to carefully consider the appropriate avenues of communication. TPAs have taken a variety of approaches, ranging from permitting disclosures only to staff members of the employer who are specifically identified by the plan sponsor in a plan amendment to requiring the individual's signed authorization for any disclosure.

Individuals who contact the plan (e.g., to discuss a claim) will also encounter procedures designed to comply with the Privacy Regulations. Individuals may, of course, receive PHI about themselves. And a parent should be able to obtain PHI from the health plan about a minor child, as the personal representative of the child. But a covered spouse seeking information about an employee claim or the claim of an adult dependent may be asked to provide a signed authorization from the individual before PHI is disclosed. However, the plan may be permitted to disclose PHI about the individual to a family member, relative, close personal friend of the individual, or other person identified by the individual, if the PHI is directly relevant to that person's involvement with the individual's care or payment for care and the individual does not object.[23] For example:

- A health plan disclosing relevant PHI to a beneficiary's daughter who has called to assist her elderly mother in resolving a claim or other payment issue. (Effective March 26, 2013, under the HITECH Regulations, such communications to the daughter may also continue after the mother's death. See § 3.03[C][2] for further information.)

- A health plan disclosing relevant PHI to a human resources representative who has called the plan either with the individual also on the line, or able to turn the phone over to the individual to confirm to the plan that the representative calling is assisting the individual.[24]

Furthermore, the plan may require the person requesting information to verify his or her identity.[25]

An interesting reference guide that provides very thorough health plan "call center" procedures is that prepared by Medicare, a covered entity/health plan responsible for more than 40 million beneficiaries. Medicare has developed a comprehensive matrix to guide call center staff in determining under what circumstances beneficiary-specific information may be disclosed over the phone and what type of verification of identity is required.[26]

[4] Plan Document

If the plan sponsor needs to receive PHI, other than enrollment information and summary health information,[27] from the group health plan for plan administration purposes, the plan

---

[23] See § 3.03[C][2]. See also HHS HIPAA FAQ 1067, available at http://www.hhs.gov/ocr/privacy/hipaa/faq/disclosures_to_friends_and_family/1067.html.

[24] HHS HIPAA FAQ 1067, available at http://www.hhs.gov/ocr/privacy/hipaa/faq/disclosures_to_friends_and_family/1067.html.

[25] See HHS HIPAA FAQ, available at http://www.hhs.gov/ocr/privacy/hipaa/faq/disclosures_to_friends_and_family/534.html. See also § 3.01[B].

[26] *Medicare Contractor Beneficiary and Provider Communications Manual*, 100-09, ch. 2, § 30, available at http://www.cms.hhs.gov/manuals/downloads/com109c02.pdf.

[27] Summary health information is information that summarizes the claims history, expenses, or types of claims by individuals enrolled in the group health plan. To be considered summary health information, the identifiers listed under the safe harbor for de-identification in 45 C.F.R. § 164.514(b)(2)(i) must be removed prior to disclosing the information to a plan sponsor, except that the data may be aggregated to the level of a five-digit zip code. 45 C.F.R. § 164.504(a). Summary health information does not constitute de-identified information because there may be a reasonable basis to believe the information is identifiable to the plan sponsor, especially if the number of participants in the group health plan is small. 65 Fed. Reg. 82,647 (Dec. 28, 2000). The group health plan may not disclose summary health information to the plan sponsor, however, if the information includes genetic information to be used for underwriting purposes. 78 Fed. Reg. 5667 (Jan. 25, 2013).

document[28] must include certain specific provisions, similar to those of a business associate agreement. See § 7.07. No disclosures from the health plan to the employer/plan sponsor are permitted unless the plan document contains the required provisions.[29]

The requirement is stated broadly enough that these provisions can be integrated directly into the ERISA plan document or drafted as a separate document. See § 7.07 for a complete listing of the plan provisions needed to satisfy both the Privacy and Security Regulations. Note that if the circumstances require this plan language, then they also require that the notice of privacy practices include a statement that the plan may disclose PHI to the plan sponsor for plan administration purposes. See § 3.02[A][1].

The provisions that follow in §§ 7.05[A][5]–[12] apply to all covered entities but raise special issues in the context of employer-sponsored group health plans.

[5] Consents and Authorizations

Under the Privacy Regulations, a health plan does not need an individual's consent or authorization to use or disclose PHI for its own treatment, payment, or health care operation activities. These activities include, for example, claim payment, eligibility determinations, case management, stop-loss claims, subrogation, evaluating plan performance, underwriting, auditing, utilization review, credentialing, and medical reviews.[30]

Some uses and disclosures of information by the health plan do require a written authorization from the individual. Examples of uses/disclosures that would require such authorization include any disclosures by the health plan to the plan sponsor for non-plan purposes and providing names of individuals covered by the medical plan to a long-term care insurer for that insurer's marketing purposes. Note that, if an authorization is required, it must be signed by the individual who is the subject of the PHI (or his or her personal representative). The employee is not automatically allowed to sign an authorization on behalf of a covered dependent.

[6] Notice of Privacy Practices

For a self-insured group health plan, the employer (as plan sponsor) is responsible for distribution of the notice of privacy practices, but this may be delegated to a TPA. Some TPAs may also offer to draft the notice for their clients and, although this may be convenient, the plan sponsor should review the proposed notice carefully to ensure that it meets the specific needs of the group health plan. The group health plan remains liable under HIPAA for the provision of compliant notices to individuals, even if it delegates drafting and distribution to a business associate, such as a TPA. Also, all notices will need to have been amended by September 23, 2013, to comply with the HITECH Regulations, and plan sponsors are accountable for ensuring this has been done.

It may be more efficient for an employer, as the sponsor of multiple health plans, to issue a combined notice for all its noninsured plans (which may include health plans not administered by the TPA). Notices may be combined for related plans under an organized health care arrangement (see § 1.02[C][3]). In addition, if the group health plan is a hybrid entity (see § 1.02[C][1]), the notice should be clear about which components are the covered components. For example, a flexible benefits plan may be a hybrid entity, offering a pre-tax premium benefit and a dependent care flexible spending account that are not covered components, and a health care flexible spending account that is a covered component. The notice should clearly identify which plans (or components) it covers, and if applicable, should state that the participant may receive separate notices from other plans.

---

[28] ERISA-governed plans must maintain certain plan documents. ERISA § 402 (29 U.S.C. § 1102). This is in addition to the requirement to provide participants with summary plan descriptions. ERISA § 104(b)(1) (29 U.S.C. § 1024(b)(1)).

[29] 45 C.F.R. § 164.504(f).

[30] 45 C.F.R. § 164.501 (definitions of health care operations, payment, and treatment).

If the health plan intends to disclose PHI to the employer, as plan sponsor, for plan administration functions, the health plan's notice of privacy practices must state this.[31] In addition, new limitations on uses and disclosures of PHI for underwriting purposes apply, if the PHI is genetic information. Those limitations must be added to the notice of privacy practices to comply with the HITECH Regulations. See § 3.02[A] for detailed information about the content and distribution of the notice of privacy practices.

[7] Requests for Access and Amendments; Accounting for Disclosures

The self-insured health plan must establish a procedure for handling requests from individuals for access, amendments, and accountings of disclosures. If most of the health plan PHI is held by a TPA, the TPA may perform these functions on behalf of the health plan (i.e., handle requests directly from individuals). If so, these services should be made a clear obligation of the TPA under the administrative services contract or business associate agreement, and appropriate policies and procedures should be developed. The notice of privacy practices should explain whether individuals should contact the TPA or the employer with these requests.

The HITECH Act[32] expands the scope of the accounting for disclosures requirement to include disclosures for treatment, payment, and health care operations (see § 3.02[D]). On May 31, 2011, HHS published proposed regulations that would make even more extensive changes to this requirement.[33] Plan sponsors and health plans should be alert to significant changes to the accounting of disclosures requirement and the proposed addition of an access report requirement.

[8] Complaints

The self-insured group health plan must establish a procedure to handle privacy complaints from individuals. The notice of privacy practices should explain whether individuals should contact the TPA or the plan sponsor with complaints. If the TPA is the direct contact, the administrative services agreement or business associate agreement may require the TPA to periodically provide a record or summary of these complaints to the plan sponsor.

[9] Business Associate Agreements

A self-insured group health plan will typically outsource some plan administration activities. Any outside entity that receives PHI from the health plan in order to perform functions on behalf of the health plan is a business associate of the health plan. Business associates may include, for example, TPAs, preferred provider organizations, utilization review companies, subrogation recovery firms, accounting firms, insurance brokers, consultants, and outside legal counsel. Stop-loss carriers are generally not classified as business associates.

The plan must enter into a business associate agreement with each business associate. The business associate provisions may be incorporated in another contract, such as an administrative services agreement with a TPA. The business associate may, in turn, have subcontractor business associates. Business associates must have business associate agreements with their subcontractors, if any.

It is also permissible for the business associates of the plan to share PHI with each other; for example, the group health plan, as the covered entity, may direct its TPA business associate to share PHI with the plan's broker, another business associate, for certain plan administration purposes, such as an analysis of plan performance. The services involved in these BA-to-BA disclosures should be in within the scope of each of the business associates' services under their respective business associate agreements. Furthermore, the plan sponsor making this request for a BA-to-BA transfer may be requested by the business associate making the

---

[31] 45 C.F.R. § 164.520(b)(1)(iii)(C).
[32] HITECH Act, Pub. L. No. 111-5, § 13405.
[33] 76 Fed. Reg. 31,426 (May 31, 2011). See § 3.02[D][2].

disclosure to verify in writing the business associate relationships, the scope and frequency of the PHI to be disclosed, that the disclosure meets the covered entity's minimum necessary standards, and that the disclosure is for plan administration purposes.

The HITECH Act made changes of critical importance to business associates, including imposing direct compliance requirements under the Privacy and Security Regulations and direct liability for noncompliance. See §§ 1.02[B] and 3.06 for more information about business associates and business associate agreements, respectively.

[10]   Administrative Requirements

A self-insured employer-sponsored group health plan is subject to all the Privacy Regulations' administrative requirements. For example, the plan must:

- Designate a privacy official;
- Document the plan's privacy policies and procedures;
- Conduct privacy training;
- Establish information safeguards;
- Establish a system for reporting noncompliance; and
- Establish and enforce sanctions for policy violations.

Even if some of these functions are contractually delegated to a TPA, the group health plan remains accountable for compliance. Typically, a plan sponsor that delegates most plan administration to a TPA will still appoint a privacy officer for the group health plan, conduct staff training, and have (at a minimum) certain key written policies and procedures of its own.

[11]   Breach Notification

The HITECH Regulations require covered entities to provide notification to affected individuals in the event of a breach of unsecured PHI. Business associates also have new requirements for reporting the breach to the covered entity. See **Chapter 5** for more information about breach notification. For plan sponsors, this requirement applies only to plan PHI, not to breaches of employment information.

[12]   Minimum Necessary

The minimum necessary standard, described in § 3.01[A], applies to the self-insured plan's uses and disclosures for plan administration. The plan must limit the PHI to the minimum amount required to accomplish the intended purpose. The plan should, for example, examine the content of reports and data files to ensure that only the minimum data needed are included.

Under the HITECH Act, if a business associate is disclosing, using, or requesting PHI, it must determine what constitutes the minimum necessary to accomplish the intended purpose of such disclosure, use, or request generally in accordance with minimum necessary policies established by the covered entity. This means, for example, that a TPA may need to inquire of the group health plan (or plan sponsor) what its minimum necessary standards are, with requests to certain situations to be handled by the TPA.

[B]   Insured Health Plans

Employer-sponsored group health plans that offer benefits through an insurance contract with a health insurer or HMO (Insured Plans) are also covered entities under HIPAA. For Insured Plans, however, most of the compliance responsibilities discussed above will fall on the insurer, not on the employer or plan sponsor. For example, the insurer will typically handle compliance with regard to the individual's right to access and amend their records, and to obtain an accounting of disclosures. The policy behind this limited-compliance approach for the Insured Plan is that the insurer will be responsible for these individual rights and privacy protections in its own role as a covered entity, and the incremental value of having the employer's Insured Plan duplicate these activities would not justify the additional burdens on the plan sponsor. The obligations of an Insured Plan with regard to HIPAA compliance are determined by the approach the plan takes to PHI (i.e., does the Insured Plan take a "hands off" or "hands on" approach).

[1] The Hands-Off Approach

Insured Plans can reduce their privacy obligations if they take a "hands off" approach to PHI. An employer-sponsored group health plan is not subject to most Privacy Regulations requirements if it provides benefits solely through an insurance contract. To qualify under this hands-off approach, the Insured Plan may not create or receive any PHI, except that it may receive from the insurer enrollment/disenrollment information and summary health information for the purpose of obtaining premium bids or modifying, amending, or terminating the plan.[34]

With this hands-off approach, the Insured Plan is exempted from nearly all of the requirements under the Privacy Regulations.[35] These Insured Plans must still, however, limit employer access to PHI, and the plan sponsor/employer may not use PHI for employment purposes. Furthermore, the Insured Plan may not retaliate against or intimidate an employee exercising his/her rights under the Privacy Regulations or require that an employee waive his/her right to file a complaint with HHS as a condition for eligibility or participation in the plan.

[2] The Hands-On Approach

If the Insured Plan does create or receive PHI in addition to enrollment/disenrollment and summary health information (i.e., it takes a "hands on" approach), it is generally subject to all of the Privacy Regulations requirements, including all of the administrative requirements discussed above, such as appointing a privacy official, documenting its policies and procedures, and providing training for its workforce. A plan amendment will be required if the plan sponsor is to receive such PHI, and this must be reflected in the notice of privacy practices (see §§ 7.05[A][4] and 7.05[A][6]). The extent to which other provisions of the Privacy Regulations apply, and to what degree, will vary depending on the Insured Plan's activities related to the PHI—that is, what information does it receive and for what purposes. Insured Plans taking a hands-on approach should review § 7.05[A] for applicable issues.

The hands-on Insured Plan's responsibilities with regard to the notice of privacy practices are limited, compared to other covered entities. The Insured Plan must prepare and maintain a notice of privacy

---

[34] For purposes of these provisions relating to disclosure of enrollment and disenrollment information from the health plan to the employer, the enrollment and disenrollment information may not include medical information about the individual above and beyond that which is required (or situationally required) by the HIPAA Transactions Standards. 67 Fed. Reg. 53,208 (Aug. 14, 2002).

Summary health information is information that summarizes the claims history, expenses, or types of claims by individuals enrolled in the group health plan. To be considered summary health information, the identifiers listed under the safe harbor for de-identification in 45 C.F.R. § 164.514(b)(2)(i) must be removed prior to disclosing the information to a plan sponsor, except that the data may be aggregated to the level of a five-digit zip code. 45 C.F.R. § 164.504(a). Summary health information does not constitute de-identified information because there may be a reasonable basis to believe the information is identifiable to the plan sponsor, especially if the number of participants in the group health plan is small. 65 Fed. Reg. 82,647 (Dec. 28, 2000). The group health plan may not disclose summary health information to the plan sponsor, however, if the information includes genetic information to be used for underwriting purposes. 78 Fed. Reg. 5667 (Jan. 25, 2013).

[35] 45 C.F.R. §§ 164.504(f), 164.520(a)(2)(iii), and 164.530(k).

practices and provide that notice upon request, but is not required to distribute the notice to all plan participants.[36]

§ 7.06   SECURITY REGULATIONS

In addition to the Privacy Regulations, an employer-sponsored group health plan is required to comply with the Security Regulations, to the extent the plan maintains or transmits any PHI in electronic media. As discussed above, employment records are not PHI subject to these requirements. Furthermore, to the extent enrollment information maintained by the employer can be reasonably regarded as held by the employer in its role as employer rather than on behalf of the plan, the Security Regulations would not apply to that information.

The Security Regulations do not make the same distinction as the Privacy Regulations with regard to self-insured plans and insured plans (or hands on versus hands off). All the requirements apply with respect to any electronic PHI maintained, received, or transmitted by any group health plan. The group health plan must evaluate each standard and implementation specification in light of the plan's contact with electronic PHI. The following requirements will necessitate action by all group health plans, self-insured or fully insured, and regardless of level of PHI access or use.

[A]   Assigned Security Responsibility

Every group health plan must identify a security official who is responsible for the development and implementation of the entity's security policies and procedures. For many group health plans, this will be the same person who serves as privacy officer.

[B]   Risk Assessment and Management

Every group health plan must take the critical first step of conducting an accurate and thorough assessment of the potential risks and vulnerabilities to the confidentiality, availability, and integrity of its electronic PHI. Some places that a group health plan may find electronic PHI are:

- Eligibility and enrollment data files (which may not be PHI in the hands of the employer, but are PHI in the hands of the group health plan);

- Records related to benefits administered by the plan sponsor (e.g., claims submitted under a Health FSA);

- Reports received from the group health plan's insurer, broker, or TPA (e.g., as e-mail attachments or downloaded from an extranet);

- Electronic databases or spreadsheets for analysis of claims data;

- Human Resources or Benefits Department logs related to complaints or claims issues;

- E-mails, with or without attachments;

- Faxes received or stored electronically; and

- Word processing documents (e.g., claim appeal records, denial of coverage letters).

After identifying its sources of electronic PHI and the risks to that PHI, the group health plan must select and implement security measures sufficient to reduce risks and vulnerabilities to a reasonable and appropriate level, so as to meet the objectives of the Security Regulations. For group health plans with very limited

---

[36] 45 C.F.R. § 164.520(a)(2)(ii).

electronic PHI access, these measures may be fairly limited. The group health plan must document how it has addressed each standard and implementation specification in the Security Regulations.

Risk assessment and management must be revisited on a periodic basis and when there are changes to the group health plan's systems or access to or use of electronic PHI.

[C] Sanction Policy

The group health plan must establish and apply appropriate sanctions against workforce members who fail to comply with the plan's security policies and procedures. This sanction policy may be integrated with the Privacy Regulations' sanctions policy or other company disciplinary policies.

[D] Group Health Plan Amendments

As described in the following section, if a plan sponsor needs to receive PHI for plan administration purposes, its plan documents must include certain specific provisions. If the PHI the plan sponsor creates or receives is *electronic* PHI, additional provisions are required by the Security Regulations.

§ 7.07 PLAN DOCUMENT REQUIREMENTS FOR PRIVACY AND SECURITY

If the plan sponsor needs to receive PHI other than enrollment information and summary health information from the group health plan for plan administration purposes, the plan document must contain the following provisions.[37] These provisions may be in the form of an amendment or incorporated directly into a new or restated ERISA plan document or as a separate document.

1. Establish the permitted and required uses and disclosures of plan PHI by the plan sponsor (such uses and disclosures must be consistent with the Privacy Regulations);

2. Provide that the group health plan will disclose PHI to the plan sponsor only upon receipt of a certification by the plan sponsor that the plan documents incorporate (or have been amended to incorporate) the required provisions;[38]

3. The plan sponsor may not use or further disclose the information other than as permitted or required by the plan documents or as required by law;

4. The plan sponsor must ensure that any agents to whom it provides PHI received from the group health plan agree to the same restrictions and conditions that apply to the plan sponsor with respect to such information;

5. The plan sponsor may not use or disclose the PHI for employment-related actions and decisions or in connection with any other benefit or employee benefit plan of the plan sponsor;

6. The plan sponsor must report to the group health plan any use or disclosure of the information that is inconsistent with the uses or disclosures provided for in this amendment of which it becomes aware;[39]

---

[37] 45 C.F.R. § 164.504(f). This applies to group health plans that receive PHI, whether they are self-insured plans or hands-on Insured Plans.

[38] There is no specific form of certification required. A statement of certification could be included in the amendment itself and a copy provided to an insurer or TPA, as needed. Or a letter of certification could be prepared. Some TPAs may have a form certification they require plan sponsors to sign.

[39] It is not clear how a plan sponsor makes a report to the group health plan where the plan sponsor is itself the plan fiduciary. But see OCR FAQ, available at http://www.hhs.gov/ocr/privacy/hipaa/faq/securityrule/2016.html (regarding reporting security incidents).

7. The plan sponsor must make available PHI for access by the individual in accordance with 45 C.F.R. § 164.524;

8. The plan sponsor must make available PHI for amendment and incorporate any amendments to PHI in accordance with 45 C.F.R. § 164.526;

9. The plan sponsor must make available the information required to provide an accounting of disclosures in accordance with 45 C.F.R. § 164.528;

10. The plan sponsor must make its internal practices, books, and records relating to the use and disclosure of PHI received from the group health plan available to HHS for purposes of determining compliance by the group health plan with the Privacy Regulations;

11. If feasible, the plan sponsor must return or destroy all PHI received from the group health plan that the sponsor still maintains in any form and retain no copies of such information when no longer needed for the purpose for which disclosure was made, except that, if such return or destruction is not feasible, the plan sponsor must limit further uses and disclosures to those purposes that make the return or destruction of the information infeasible;

12. The plan sponsor must ensure that adequate separation between the group health plan and the plan sponsor is established;

13. Describe those employees or classes of employees or other persons under the control of the plan sponsor to be given access to the PHI to be disclosed by the plan. Any employee or person who receives PHI in the ordinary course of business that relates to payment under the health plan, health care operations of the health plan, or other matters pertaining to the group health plan must be included in such description. Restrict PHI access and use by such persons to the plan administration functions that the plan sponsor performs for the group health plan; and

14. The plan sponsor must provide an effective mechanism for resolving any issues of noncompliance with these plan document provisions by any persons granted access to PHI for plan administration purposes in accordance with the preceding provision.

If the PHI to be disclosed to the plan sponsor is electronic PHI, additional plan provisions are required to comply with the Security Regulations. The plan document or amendment should first be drafted to comply with the Privacy Regulations by including the provisions listed above. If the PHI disclosed to the plan sponsor is maintained or transmitted in electronic media, the following minor adjustments will be needed to accommodate the Security Regulations:

1. *Safeguards.* The Privacy Regulations do not require the plan to address appropriate safeguards; but the Security Regulations do require it, so a provision such as the following must be added:[40]

> The Plan Sponsor shall implement administrative, physical, and technical safeguards that reasonably and appropriately protect the confidentiality, integrity, and availability of the electronic protected health information that it creates, receives, maintains, or transmits on behalf of the Plan.

2. *Separation.* The separation between employer functions and plan functions required by the Privacy Regulations must be supported by appropriate security measures for any electronic PHI. This must be addressed in the plan.[41] For example:

> . . . The Plan Sponsor shall ensure that this separation is supported by reasonable and appropriate security measures.

---

[40] 45 C.F.R. § 164.314(b)(2)(i).
[41] 45 C.F.R. § 164.314(b)(2)(ii).

3. *Agents.* The plan sponsor must ensure that its agents agree to implement reasonable and appropriate security measures to protect electronic PHI:[42]

> . . . The Plan Sponsor further agrees to ensure that such agent agrees to implement reasonable and appropriate security measures to safeguard electronic protected health information.

4. *Security Incidents.* Similar to the requirement under the Privacy Regulations that the plan sponsor report to the covered entity any uses or disclosures of PHI that are inconsistent with the privacy provisions of the plan, the Security Regulations extend this to the reporting of security incidents:[43]

> If the Plan Sponsor becomes aware of (1) any use or disclosure of protected health information that is inconsistent with the uses and disclosures provided for herein, *or* (2) *any security incident*, the Plan Sponsor shall report it to the Plan.

See **Appendix F** for sample plan document language.

Some TPAs will draft plan documents for their clients and will include these privacy and security provisions. Remember, however, that these provisions may need to be customized for the particular plan or plan sponsor (e.g., with regard to identifying the covered health plans or classes of employees having access to PHI). If the covered entity delegates the drafting of the document to the TPA, it must be reviewed carefully.

Application of the HIPAA Administrative Simplification Regulations to group health plans and plan sponsors remains one of the more complex areas of HIPAA Administrative Simplification, due to the lack of official guidance in this area.

---

[42] 45 C.F.R. § 164.314(b)(2)(iii).
[43] 45 C.F.R. § 164.314(b)(2)(iv).

KEY PROVISIONS OF THE 2013 HITECH REGULATIONS

In January 2013, HHS published what have been called the HITECH Regulations or Omnibus HIPAA Regulations. Most of the changes arose from the HITECH Act of 2009. Some were revisions of previously issued HITECH regulations, such as the Breach Regulations and Enforcement Rule. Others were new regulations addressing areas covered by the HITECH Act, such as business associates. Still other changes were initiated by HHS to update the original Privacy Regulations, such as new provisions relating to student immunizations and fundraising. The following is a summary of the principal changes included in these "Omnibus" Regulations, with references to where in this book additional detail can be found.

TOPIC	SECTIONS
COMPLIANCE DATES • Compliance dates for changes under the HITECH Regulations	1.05[B]
BUSINESS ASSOCIATE ISSUES • Expands definition of "business associate," most importantly to include subcontractors and revised interpretation of "conduit" • Business associates directly liable for compliance with requirements of the Privacy and Security Regulations and directly subject to HIPAA civil penalties • Requires modifications to business associate agreements	1.02[B] 6.01 3.06 Appendix D
BREACH NOTIFICATION • Changes the notification standard from "significant risk of harm to the individual" to "demonstration of a low probability that the PHI has been compromised" • Four specific factors required to assess whether the PHI has been compromised • Business associate obligations to report breaches	Chapter 5
DEFINITION OF PROTECTED HEALTH INFORMATION (PHI) • Revised definition of PHI (a) excludes information about individuals deceased for more than 50 years; (b) includes genetic information; and (c) clarifies meaning of "demographic information"	1.03[A]
NOTICE OF PRIVACY PRACTICES • Content changes to incorporate HITECH provisions, such as notification of breaches and fundraising opt outs • HITECH changes are *material* changes triggering redistribution rules • Changes to distribution requirements for health plans	3.02[A]
ACCESS TO PHI • New right of individual to obtain a copy of PHI in an electronic format • New option for individual to have covered entity send copies directly to a third party	3.02[B]

continues

RESTRICTION REQUESTS	3.02[E]
• New right of individual to require providers to comply with a patient's request to not disclose PHI to patient's health plan, if disclosure would be for payment or health care operations and patient has paid for the service out-of-pocket	
FUNDRAISING	3.04[A]
• Opt-out language required in fundraising communications must now be clear and conspicuous	
• Opt outs must be treated as a revocation of authorization	
• More PHI now permitted for use in targeting patients for fundraising efforts	
PROHIBITION ON SALE OF PHI	3.04[B]
• Covered Entity may not receive any remuneration for the disclosure of PHI (with limited exceptions)	
MARKETING COMMUNICATION USING PHI	3.04[C] Appendix B
• Marketing rules grow more complex	
• Previously excepted uses now require authorization if there is financial remuneration for the communication	
• New rules for communications about drugs currently prescribed for the individual	
GENETIC INFORMATION	1.03[A] 3.04[E]
• Genetic information included in definition of PHI	
• Use of genetic information by health plans for underwriting purposes is prohibited	
DECEASED INDIVIDUALS	1.03[A] 3.03[C][2] 3.04[F][3]
• Definition of PHI excludes information about individuals deceased for more than 50 years	
• Permitted disclosures of relevant PHI to family or others involved in the care of the individual (or payment for that care) can now extend after the death of the individual	
STUDENT IMMUNIZATIONS	3.03[D][2]
• Covered entity may disclose proof of immunization directly to the school, if state law requires the school to have the information, with parent's agreement	
RESEARCH AUTHORIZATIONS	3.03
• Allows use of compound authorizations for research purposes	
• Allows authorizations to be used for future research studies	
CIVIL ENFORCEMENT	1.02[B] 6.01[A]
• Direct liability of business associates	
• Covered entity liability for business associates who are agents, under the federal common law of agency	
• Higher, tiered civil penalties for violation of HIPAA	
• HHS will conduct periodic privacy and security compliance audits of covered entities and business associates	

SUMMARY OF THE HIPAA MARKETING PROVISIONS AFTER HITECH

Details of the current marketing rules can be found in Section 3.04[C]. The following chart provides a summary reference to these requirements.

Type of Communication for Which PHI Is Used	Financial Remuneration?	Authorization Required?	Detailed Explanation
Face-to-face communication		No	3.04[C][1]
Promotional gifts of nominal value		No	3.04[C][1]
Communication that promotes health in a general manner (does not promote any particular products or services)		No	3.04[C][1]
Communication about eligibility or benefits for public programs (such as Medicare, Medicaid, CHIP)		No	3.04[C][1]
Communication for Treatment of the Individual	No	No	3.04[C][2]
	Yes	Yes	
Communication for Case Management, Care Coordination, or to Direct or Recommend Alternative Care for an Individual	No	No	3.04[C][2]
	Yes	Yes	
Communication to Describe the Covered Entity's Own Products or Services	No	No	3.04[C][2]
	Yes	Yes	
Refill reminders and other communications about currently prescribed drugs or biologic	Yes, but limited to reasonably related costs	No	3.04[C][1]
Refill reminders and other	Yes, but *not* limited to	Yes	3.04[C][2]

continues

communications about currently prescribed drugs or biologic	reasonably related costs		
Refill reminders and other communications about currently prescribed drugs or biologic	No	No	3.04[C][1]
Communication promoting the product or service of a third party		Yes	3.04[C][3]
Communication for a non-health-related product or service		Yes	3.04[C][3]
Use of PHI as the content of a marketing communication		Yes	3.04[C][3]

Other Communications		Authorization Required?	Detailed Explanation
Use of community mailing lists (derived from sources other than PHI)		No	3.04[C][1]
Sale of PHI to a third party (disclosure of PHI)		Yes	3.04[B] 3.04[C][1] 3.04[C][3]

HIPAA BREACH NOTIFICATION ANALYSIS

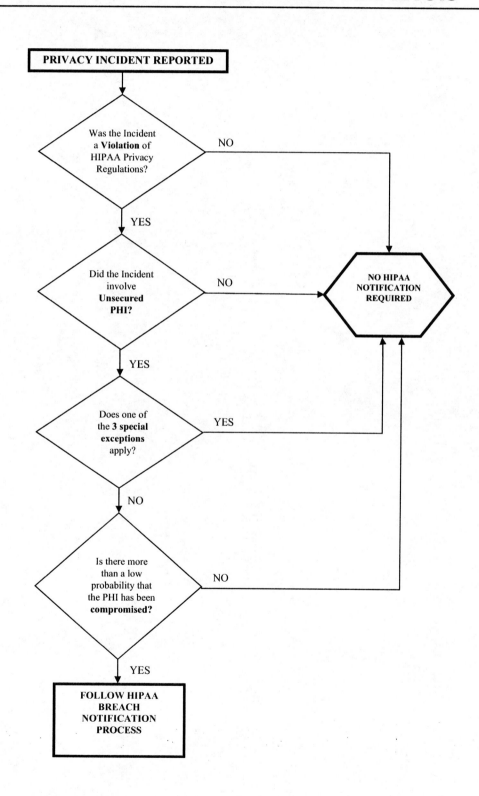

SAMPLE BUSINESS ASSOCIATE AGREEMENT PROVISIONS

HHS published the following sample provisions for business associate agreements, January 25, 2013, in conjunction with the HITECH Regulations. Although these contractual provisions arise from specific content requirements for business associate agreements, the specific language of these sample provisions is not mandated. They may be changed as needed for particular business arrangements between a covered entity and business associate, or business associate and subcontractor. Furthermore, other provisions will generally also be required to create a valid contract, and additional or more detailed provisions may be desirable. As noted by HHS, reliance on this sample may not be sufficient for compliance with state law and does not replace consultation with a lawyer or negotiations between the parties to the contract. See Section 3.06 for more information about business associate agreements.

The following sample provisions are available, along with other related material are available at http://www.hhs.gov/ocr/privacy/hipaa/understanding/coveredentities/contractprov.html.

Sample Business Associate Agreement Provisions

Words or phrases contained in brackets are intended as either optional language or as instructions to the users of these sample provisions.

Definitions

Catch-all definition:

The following terms used in this Agreement shall have the same meaning as those terms in the HIPAA Rules: Breach, Data Aggregation, Designated Record Set, Disclosure, Health Care Operations, Individual, Minimum Necessary, Notice of Privacy Practices, Protected Health Information, Required By Law, Secretary, Security Incident, Subcontractor, Unsecured Protected Health Information, and Use.

Specific definitions:

(a) Business Associate. "Business Associate" shall generally have the same meaning as the term "business associate" at 45 CFR 160.103, and in reference to the party to this agreement, shall mean [Insert Name of Business Associate].

(b) Covered Entity. "Covered Entity" shall generally have the same meaning as the term "covered entity" at 45 CFR 160.103, and in reference to the party to this agreement, shall mean [Insert Name of Covered Entity].

(c) HIPAA Rules. "HIPAA Rules" shall mean the Privacy, Security, Breach Notification, and Enforcement Rules at 45 CFR Part 160 and Part 164.

Obligations and Activities of Business Associate

Business Associate agrees to:

(a) Not use or disclose protected health information other than as permitted or required by the Agreement or as required by law;

(b) Use appropriate safeguards, and comply with Subpart C of 45 CFR Part 164 with respect to electronic protected health information, to prevent use or disclosure of protected health information other than as provided for by the Agreement;

(c) Report to covered entity any use or disclosure of protected health information not provided for by the Agreement of which it becomes aware, including breaches of unsecured protected health information as required at 45 CFR 164.410, and any security incident of which it becomes aware;

[The parties may wish to add additional specificity regarding the breach notification obligations of the business associate, such as a stricter timeframe for the business associate to report a potential breach to the covered entity and/or whether the business associate will handle breach notifications to individuals, the HHS Office for Civil Rights (OCR), and potentially the media, on behalf of the covered entity.]

(d) In accordance with 45 CFR 164.502(e)(1)(ii) and 164.308(b)(2), if applicable, ensure that any subcontractors that create, receive, maintain, or transmit protected health information on behalf of the business associate agree to the same restrictions, conditions, and requirements that apply to the business associate with respect to such information;

(e) Make available protected health information in a designated record set to the [Choose either "covered entity" or "individual or the individual's designee"] as necessary to satisfy covered entity's obligations under 45 CFR 164.524;

[The parties may wish to add additional specificity regarding how the business associate will respond to a request for access that the business associate receives directly from the individual (such as whether and in what time and manner a business associate is to provide the requested access or whether the business associate will forward the individual's request to the covered entity to fulfill) and the timeframe for the business associate to provide the information to the covered entity.]

(f) Make any amendment(s) to protected health information in a designated record set as directed or agreed to by the covered entity pursuant to 45 CFR 164.526, or take other measures as necessary to satisfy covered entity's obligations under 45 CFR 164.526;

[The parties may wish to add additional specificity regarding how the business associate will respond to a request for amendment that the business associate receives directly from the individual (such as whether and in what time and manner a business associate is to act on the request for amendment or whether the business associate will forward the individual's request to the covered entity) and the timeframe for the business associate to incorporate any amendments to the information in the designated record set.]

(g) Maintain and make available the information required to provide an accounting of disclosures to the [Choose either "covered entity" or "individual"] as necessary to satisfy covered entity's obligations under 45 CFR 164.528;

[The parties may wish to add additional specificity regarding how the business associate will respond to a request for an accounting of disclosures that the business associate receives directly from the individual (such as whether and in what time and manner the business associate is to provide the accounting of disclosures to the individual or whether the business associate will forward the request to the covered entity) and the timeframe for the business associate to provide information to the covered entity.]

(h) To the extent the business associate is to carry out one or more of covered entity's obligation(s) under Subpart E of 45 CFR Part 164, comply with the requirements of Subpart E that apply to the covered entity in the performance of such obligation(s); and

(i) Make its internal practices, books, and records available to the Secretary for purposes of determining compliance with the HIPAA Rules.

Permitted Uses and Disclosures by Business Associate

(a) Business associate may only use or disclose protected health information

[Option 1—Provide a specific list of permissible purposes.]

[Option 2—Reference an underlying service agreement, such as "as necessary to perform the services set forth in Service Agreement."]

[In addition to other permissible purposes, the parties should specify whether the business associate is authorized to use protected health information to de-identify the information in accordance with 45 CFR 164.514(a)-(c). The parties also may wish to specify the manner in which the business associate will de-identify the information and the permitted uses and disclosures by the business associate of the de-identified information.]

(b) Business associate may use or disclose protected health information as required by law.

(c) Business associate agrees to make uses and disclosures and requests for protected health information

[Option 1] consistent with covered entity's minimum necessary policies and procedures.

[Option 2] subject to the following minimum necessary requirements: [Include specific minimum necessary provisions that are consistent with the covered entity's minimum necessary policies and procedures.]

(d) Business associate may not use or disclose protected health information in a manner that would violate Subpart E of 45 CFR Part 164 if done by covered entity [if the Agreement permits the business associate to use or disclose protected health information for its own management and administration and legal responsibilities or for data aggregation services as set forth in optional provisions (e), (f), or (g) below, then add ", except for the specific uses and disclosures set forth below."]

(e) [Optional] Business associate may use protected health information for the proper management and administration of the business associate or to carry out the legal responsibilities of the business associate.

(f) [Optional] Business associate may disclose protected health information for the proper management and administration of business associate or to carry out the legal responsibilities of the business associate, provided the disclosures are required by law, or business associate obtains reasonable assurances from the person to whom the information is disclosed that the information will remain confidential and used or further disclosed only as required by law or for the purposes for which it was disclosed to the person, and the person notifies business associate of any instances of which it is aware in which the confidentiality of the information has been breached.

(g) [Optional] Business associate may provide data aggregation services relating to the health care operations of the covered entity.

Provisions for Covered Entity to Inform Business Associate of Privacy Practices and Restrictions

(a) [Optional] Covered entity shall notify business associate of any limitation(s) in the notice of privacy practices of covered entity under 45 CFR 164.520, to the extent that such limitation may affect business associate's use or disclosure of protected health information.

(b) [Optional] Covered entity shall notify business associate of any changes in, or revocation of, the permission by an individual to use or disclose his or her protected health information, to the extent that such changes may affect business associate's use or disclosure of protected health information.

(c) [Optional] Covered entity shall notify business associate of any restriction on the use or disclosure of protected health information that covered entity has agreed to or is required to abide by under 45 CFR 164.522, to the extent that such restriction may affect business associate's use or disclosure of protected health information.

Permissible Requests by Covered Entity

[Optional] Covered entity shall not request business associate to use or disclose protected health information in any manner that would not be permissible under Subpart E of 45 CFR Part 164 if done by covered entity. [Include an exception if the business associate will use or disclose protected health information for, and the agreement includes provisions for, data aggregation or management and administration and legal responsibilities of the business associate.]

Term and Termination

(a) Term. The Term of this Agreement shall be effective as of [Insert effective date], and shall terminate on [Insert termination date or event] or on the date covered entity terminates for cause as authorized in paragraph (b) of this Section, whichever is sooner.

(b) <u>Termination for Cause.</u> Business associate authorizes termination of this Agreement by covered entity, if covered entity determines business associate has violated a material term of the Agreement [and business associate has not cured the breach or ended the violation within the time specified by covered entity]. [Bracketed language may be added if the covered entity wishes to provide the business associate with an opportunity to cure a violation or breach of the contract before termination for cause.]

(c) <u>Obligations of Business Associate Upon Termination.</u>

[Option 1—if the business associate is to return or destroy all protected health information upon termination of the agreement]

Upon termination of this Agreement for any reason, business associate shall return to covered entity [or, if agreed to by covered entity, destroy] all protected health information received from covered entity, or created, maintained, or received by business associate on behalf of covered entity, that the business associate still maintains in any form. Business associate shall retain no copies of the protected health information.

[Option 2—if the agreement authorizes the business associate to use or disclose protected health information for its own management and administration or to carry out its legal responsibilities and the business associate needs to retain protected health information for such purposes after termination of the agreement]

Upon termination of this Agreement for any reason, business associate, with respect to protected health information received from covered entity, or created, maintained, or received by business associate on behalf of covered entity, shall:

1. Retain only that protected health information which is necessary for business associate to continue its proper management and administration or to carry out its legal responsibilities;

2. Return to covered entity [or, if agreed to by covered entity, destroy] the remaining protected health information that the business associate still maintains in any form;

3. Continue to use appropriate safeguards and comply with Subpart C of 45 CFR Part 164 with respect to electronic protected health information to prevent use or disclosure of the protected health information, other than as provided for in this Section, for as long as business associate retains the protected health information;

4. Not use or disclose the protected health information retained by business associate other than for the purposes for which such protected health information was retained and subject to the same conditions set out at [Insert section number related to paragraphs (e) and (f) above under "Permitted Uses and Disclosures By Business Associate"] which applied prior to termination; and

5. Return to covered entity [or, if agreed to by covered entity, destroy] the protected health information retained by business associate when it is no longer needed by business associate for its proper management and administration or to carry out its legal responsibilities.

[The agreement also could provide that the business associate will transmit the protected health information to another business associate of the covered entity at termination, and/or could add terms regarding a business associate's obligations to obtain or ensure the destruction of protected health information created, received, or maintained by subcontractors.]

(d) <u>Survival.</u> The obligations of business associate under this Section shall survive the termination of this Agreement.

Miscellaneous [Optional]

(a) [Optional] <u>Regulatory References.</u> A reference in this Agreement to a section in the HIPAA Rules means the section as in effect or as amended.

(b) [Optional] <u>Amendment.</u> The Parties agree to take such action as is necessary to amend this Agreement from time to time as is necessary for compliance with the requirements of the HIPAA Rules and any other applicable law.

(c) [Optional] <u>Interpretation.</u> Any ambiguity in this Agreement shall be interpreted to permit compliance with the HIPAA Rules.

SECURITY MATRIX

Summary of Security Regulations Standards and Implementation Specifications.[1]

Standards	45 CFR Sections	Implementation Specifications (R) = Required, (A) = Addressable
Administrative Safeguards		
Security Management Process	164.308(a)(1)	Risk Analysis (R)
		Risk Management (R)
		Sanction Policy (R)
		Information System Activity Review (R)
Assigned Security Responsibility	164.308(a)(2)	(R)
Workforce Security	164.308(a)(3)	Authorization and/or Supervision (A)
		Workforce Clearance Procedure (A)
		Termination Procedures (A)
Information Access Management	164.308(a)(4)	Isolating Health Care Clearinghouse Function (R)
		Access Authorization (A)
		Access Establishment and Modification (A)
Security Awareness and Training	164.308(a)(5)	Security Reminders (A)
		Protection from Malicious Software (A)
		Log-in Monitoring (A)
		Password Management (A)
Security Incident Procedures	164.308(a)(6)	Response and Reporting (R)
Contingency Plan	164.308(a)(7)	Data Backup Plan (R)
		Disaster Recovery Plan (R)
		Emergency Mode Operation Plan (R)
		Testing and Revision Procedure (A)
		Applications and Data Criticality Analysis (A)
Evaluation	164.308(a)(8)	(R)
Business Associate Contracts and Other Arrangements	164.308(b)(1)	Written Contract or Other Arrangement (R)
Physical Safeguards		
Facility Access Controls	164.310(a)(1)	Contingency Operations (A)
		Facility Security Plan (A)
		Access Control and Validation Procedures (A)
		Maintenance Records (A)
Workstation Use	164.310(b)	(R)
Workstation Security	164.310(c)	(R)
Device and Media Controls	164.310(d)(1)	Disposal (R)
		Media Re-use (R)
		Accountability (A)
		Data Backup and Storage (A)

continues

---

[1] 168 Fed. Reg. 8380 (Feb. 20, 2003).

Standards	*45 CFR Sections*	*Implementation Specifications (R) =* *Required, (A) = Addressable*
Technical Safeguards		
Access Control	164.312(a)(1)	Unique User Identification (R) Emergency Access Procedure (R) Automatic Logoff (A) Encryption and Decryption (A)
Audit Controls	164.312(b)	(R)
Integrity	164.312(c)(1)	Mechanism to Authenticate Electronic Protected Health Information (A)
Person or Entity Authentication	164.312(d)	(R)
Transmission Security	164.312(e)(1)	Integrity Controls (A) Encryption (A)

APPENDIX F
SAMPLE PLAN DOCUMENT AMENDMENT

*[To be customized to fit the specific circumstances, with advice of legal counsel.
Follow Plan procedures for adoption of amendments.]*

Drafting Note: The following amendment assumes there is a plan document that defines **Plan** (the group health plan) and **Plan Sponsor.** The Security provisions as well as the Privacy provisions have been incorporated.

PLAN AMENDMENT CONFIDENTIALITY OF PLAN INFORMATION

Plan Sponsor Certification: These provisions of the Plan are intended by the Plan and Plan Sponsor to comply with the provisions of the Health Insurance Portability and Accountability Act of 1996 ("HIPAA") privacy and security regulations at 45 C.F.R. § 164.504(f) and § 164.314(b)(2).

Uses and Disclosures of Individually Identifiable Health Information: The Plan Sponsor may use and disclose protected health information, as defined in 45 C.F.R. § 164.501, which it receives from the Plan, only as follows:

[Drafting Note: Describe Plan Sponsor's uses and disclosures of PHI for plan administration purposes.]

The Plan Sponsor shall not use or further disclose protected health information other than as permitted or required by the plan documents or as required by law.

Safeguards: The Plan Sponsor shall implement administrative, physical, and technical safeguards that reasonably and appropriately protect the confidentiality, integrity, and availability of the electronic protected health information that it creates, receives, maintains, or transmits on behalf of the Plan.

Agents of Plan Sponsor: The Plan Sponsor shall ensure that any agents to whom the Plan Sponsor provides protected health information agree to the same restrictions and conditions that apply to the Plan Sponsor with respect to such information. The Plan Sponsor further agrees to ensure that such agent agrees to implement reasonable and appropriate security measures to safeguard any electronic protected health information of the Plan created or received by the agent on behalf of the Plan.

Prohibited Uses and Disclosures: The Plan Sponsor shall not use or disclose protected health information received from the Plan for employment-related actions and decisions. The Plan Sponsor shall not use or disclose protected health information received from the Plan in connection with any other benefit or employee benefit plan of the Plan Sponsor. The Plan Sponsor will not use or disclose PHI that is genetic information for underwriting purposes.

Reporting: If the Plan Sponsor becomes aware of (1) any use or disclosure of protected health information that is inconsistent with the uses and disclosures provided for herein, or (2) any security incident, the Plan Sponsor shall report it to the Plan.

Individual Rights: The Plan Sponsor shall (A) make available protected health information to individuals in accordance with the access rights in 45 C.F.R. § 164.524; (B) make protected health information available for amendment and incorporate any amendments in accordance with 45 C.F.R. § 164.526; (C) make available the information required to provide an accounting of disclosures in accordance with 45 C.F.R. § 164.528.

HHS Audits: The Plan Sponsor shall make its internal practices, books, and records relating to the use and disclosure of protected health information received from the Plan available to the Secretary of Health & Human Services for purposes of determining the Plan's compliance with the HIPAA privacy regulations.

Information Retention: If feasible, the Plan Sponsor shall return or destroy all protected health information received from the Plan that the Plan Sponsor still maintains in any form and retain no copies of such information when no longer needed for the purpose for which the disclosure was made. If such return or destruction is not feasible, the Plan Sponsor shall limit further uses and disclosures to those purposes that make the return or destruction of the information infeasible.

Separation: The Plan and Plan Sponsor shall ensure that adequate separation is established between the Plan and Plan Sponsor. The Plan Sponsor shall ensure that this separation is supported by reasonable and appropriate security measures. The [*Drafting Note:* **Identify employees or classes of employees who may have access to PHI—Must include any employee or person who receives protected health information relating to (a) payment under the Plan, (b) health care operations of the Plan, or (c) other matters pertaining to the Plan in ordinary course of business.**] may have access to protected health information disclosed by the Plan. Such persons' access to and use of protected health information shall be limited to the Plan administration functions that the Plan Sponsor performs for the Plan. Noncompliance by such persons with the requirements of this paragraph may result in [*Drafting Note:* **Describe sanctions and other methods for resolving noncompliance.**].

APPENDIX G

SAMPLE OCR AUDIT PROTOCOLS AND COMPLIANCE REVIEW MATERIALS*

1. SAMPLE SECURITY AUDIT PROTOCOLS

Department of Health and Human Services—Office of Civil Rights

Section	Established Performance Criteria	Key Activity	Audit Procedures	Implementation Specification
§ 164.308	§ 164.308(a)(1): **Security Management Process**—(ii)(a) Conduct an accurate and thorough assessment of the potential risks and vulnerabilities to the confidentiality, integrity, and availability of electronic protected health information held by the covered entity.	Conduct Risk Assessment	Inquire of management as to whether formal or informal policies or practices exist to conduct an accurate assessment of potential risks and vulnerabilities to the confidentiality, integrity, and availability of ePHI. Obtain and review relevant documentation and evaluate the content relative to the specified criteria for an assessment of potential risks and vulnerabilities of ePHI. Evidence of covered entity risk assessment process or methodology considers the elements in the criteria and has been updated or maintained to reflect changes in the covered entity's environment. Determine if the covered entity risk assessment has been conducted on a periodic basis. Determine if the covered entity has identified all systems that contain, process, or transmit ePHI.	Required

continues

* These sample OCR Security, Breach and Privacy audit protocols are illustrative only and may not contain subsequent updates based on the HITECH Regulations. For complete (and the most current) audit protocols, go to: http://www.hhs.gov/ocr/privacy/hipaa/enforcement/audit/protocol.html. The Compliance Review materials, starting on page G-10, were published by HHS Office of E-Health Standards and Services, Feb. 20, 2008, and were formerly available at <http://www.cms.hhs.gov/Enforcement/Downloads/Information RequestforComplianceReviews.pdf>.

Section	Established Performance Criteria	Key Activity	Audit Procedures	Implementation Specification
§ 164.308	§ 164.308(a)(1)(i): **Security Management Process**—Although the HIPAA Security Rule does not require purchasing any particular technology, additional hardware, software, or services may be needed to adequately protect information. Considerations for their selection should include the following: -Applicability of the IT solutions to the intended environment; -The sensitivity of the data; -The organization's security policies, procedures, and standards; and -Other requirements such as resources available for operation, maintenance, and training.	Acquire IT Systems and Services	Inquire of management as to whether formal or informal policy and procedures exist covering the specific features of the HIPAA Security Rule information systems § 164.306(a) and (b). Obtain and review formal or informal policy and procedures and evaluate the content in relation to the specified performance to meet the HIPAA Security Rule § 164.306(a) and (b). Determine if the covered entity's formal or informal policy and procedures have been approved and updated on a periodic basis.	Required
§ 164.308	§ 164.308(a)(1)(ii)(D): **Security Management Process**—Implement procedures to regularly review records of information system activity, such as audit logs, access reports, and security incident tracking reports.	Develop and Deploy the Information System Activity Review Process	Inquire of management as to whether formal or informal policy and procedures exist to review information system activities, such as audit logs, access reports, and security incident tracking reports. Obtain and review formal or informal policy and procedures and evaluate the content in relation to specified performance criteria to determine if an appropriate review process is in place of information system activities. Obtain evidence for a sample of instances showing implementation of covered entity review practices. Determine if the covered entity policy and procedures have been approved and updated on a periodic basis.	Required

continues

Section	Established Performance Criteria	Key Activity	Audit Procedures	Implementation Specification
§ 164.308	§ 164.308(b)(1): **Business Associate Contracts and Other Arrangements**— Covered entities must enter into a contract or other arrangement with persons that meet the definition of business associate in § 160.103. The covered entity must obtain satisfactory assurance from the business associate that it will appropriately safeguard the information in accordance with § 164.314(a)(1) standards.	Written Contract or Other Arrangement	Inquire of management as to whether a process exists to ensure contracts or agreements including security requirements to address confidentiality, integrity, and availability of ePHI. Obtain and review the documentation of the process used to ensure contracts or arrangements including security requirements to address confidentiality, integrity, and availability of ePHI and evaluate the content in relation to the specified criteria. Determine if the contracts or arrangements are reviewed to ensure applicable requirements are addressed.	Required
§ 164.310	§ 164.310(a)(2)(ii): **Facility Access Controls**— Implement policies and procedures to safeguard the facility and equipment therein from unauthorized physical access, tampering, and theft.	Develop a Facility Security Plan	Inquire of management as to whether formal or informal policies and procedures exist to safeguard the facility and equipment therein from unauthorized physical access, tampering, and theft. Obtain and review formal or informal policies and procedures and evaluate the content in relation to the specified criteria for safeguarding the facility and equipment therein from unauthorized physical access, tampering, and theft. Determine if policies and procedures have been approved and updated on a periodic basis. If the covered entity has chosen not to fully implement this specification, the entity must have documentation on where they have chosen not to fully implement this specification and their rationale for doing so.	Addressable

continues

Section	Established Performance Criteria	Key Activity	Audit Procedures	Implementation Specification
§ 164.312	§ 164.312(a)(2)(iv): **Access Control**— Implement a mechanism to encrypt and decrypt electronic protected health information.	Encryption and Decryption	Inquire of management as to whether an encryption mechanism is in place to protect ePHI. Obtain and review formal or informal policies and procedures and evaluate the content relative to the specified criteria to determine that encryption standards exist to protect ePHI. Based on the complexity of the entity, elements to consider include but are not limited to: —Type(s) of encryption used. —How encryption keys are protected. —Access to modify or create keys is restricted to appropriate personnel. —How keys are managed. If the covered entity has chosen not to fully implement this specification, the entity must have documentation on where they have chosen not to fully implement this specification and their rationale for doing so. Evaluate this documentation if applicable.	Addressable
§ 164.312	§ 164.312(a)(2)(i): **Access Control**— Assign a unique name and/or number for identifying and tracking user identity. Ensure that system activity can be traced to a specific user. Ensure that the necessary data is available in the system logs to support audit and other related business functions.	Ensure That All System Users Have Been Assigned a Unique Identifier	Inquire of management as to how users are assigned unique user IDs. Obtain and review policies and/or procedures and evaluate the content in relation to the specified criteria to determine how user IDs are to be established and assigned and evaluate the content in relation to the specified criteria. Obtain and review user access lists for each in-scope application to determine if users are assigned a unique ID and evaluate the content in relation to the specified criteria for attributing IDs. For selected days, obtain and review user access logs to determine if user activity is tracked and reviewed on a periodic basis and evaluate the content of the logs in relation to the specified criteria for access reviews.	Required

2. SAMPLE BREACH AUDIT PROTOCOLS

Department of Health and Human Services—Office of Civil Rights

Section	Established Performance Criteria	Key Activity	Audit Procedures
§ 164.402	§ 164.402: **Definitions**— Breach means the acquisition, access, use, or disclosure of protected health information in a manner not permitted under subpart E of this part, which compromises the security or privacy of the protected health information. (1)(i) For purposes of this definition, compromises the security or privacy of the protected health information means poses a significant risk of financial, reputational, or other harm to the individual. (ii) A use or disclosure of protected health information that does not include the identifiers listed at § 164.514(e)(2), date of birth, and zip code does not compromise the security or privacy of the protected health information.	Risk Assessment of Breach	Inquire of management as to whether a risk assessment process exists to determine significant harm in a breach.
§ 164.404	§ 164.404(b): **Notice to Individuals**— Except as provided in § 164.412, a covered entity shall provide the notification required by paragraph (a) of this section without unreasonable delay and in no case later than 60 days after discovery of a breach.	Timeliness of Notification	Inquire of management as to whether a process exists for notifying individuals within the required time period. Obtain and review key documents that outline the process for notifying individuals of breaches. Verify, if any breaches have occurred, that individuals were notified within 60 days.

3.   SAMPLE PRIVACY AUDIT PROTOCOLS

Department of Health and Human Services—Office of Civil Rights

§ 164.506	§ 164.506: **Uses and disclosures to carry out treatment, payment, or health care operations**— (a) Except with respect to uses or disclosures that require an authorization under § 164.506(a)(2) and (3), a covered entity may use or disclose protected health information for treatment, payment, or health care operations as set forth in paragraph (c) of this section, provided that such use or disclosure is consistent with other applicable requirements of this subpart.	Permitted Uses and Disclosures	Inquire of management as to whether a process exists for the use or disclosure of PHI for treatment, payment, or health care operations provided and whether such use or disclosure is consistent with other applicable requirements. Obtain and review the process and evaluate the content relative to the specified criteria used for use or disclosure of PHI for treatment, payment, or health care operations provided to determine whether such use or disclosure is consistent with other applicable requirements. Obtain and review a sample of training programs and evaluate the content relative to the specified criteria to determine the use or disclosure of PHI for treatment, payment, or health care operations provided is consistent with other applicable requirements.
§ 164.514	§ 164.514: **Other requirements relating to uses and disclosures of protected health information**— (d)(2)(i) A covered entity must identify: (A) Those persons or classes of persons, as appropriate, in its workforce who need access to protected health information to carry out their duties; and (B) For each such person or class of persons, the category or categories of protected health information to which access is needed and any conditions appropriate to such access. (ii) A covered entity must make reasonable efforts to limit the access of such persons or classes identified in paragraph (d)(2)(i)(A) of this section to protected health information consistent with paragraph (d)(2)(i)(B) of this section.	Minimum Necessary Uses of PHI	Inquire of management as to whether access to PHI is restricted. Obtain and review a sample of workforce members with access to PHI for their corresponding job title and description to determine appropriateness. Obtain and review policies and procedures and evaluate the content relative to the specified criteria for terminating access to PHI. Select a sample listing of former employees to confirm that access to PHI was terminated. NOTE: The rule requires that the class/job functions that need to use or disclose PHI be determined, and the information be limited to what is needed for that job classification.

continues

| § 164.520 | § 164.520: **Notice of Privacy Practices for PHI**—
(c)(2) A covered health care provider that has a direct treatment relationship with an individual must
(i) Provide the notice: (A) No later than the date of the first service delivery, including service delivered electronically, to such individual after the compliance date for the covered health care provider; or (B) In an emergency treatment situation, as soon as reasonably practicable after the emergency treatment situation.
(ii) Except in an emergency treatment situation, make a good faith effort to obtain a written acknowledgment of receipt of the notice provided in accordance with paragraph (c)(2)(i) of this section, and if not obtained, document its good faith efforts to obtain such acknowledgment and the reason why the acknowledgment was not obtained;
(iii) If the covered health care provider maintains a physical service delivery site: (A) Have the notice available at the service delivery site for individuals to request to take with them; and (B) Post the notice in a clear and prominent location where it is reasonable to expect individuals seeking service from the covered health care provider to be able to read the notice.
(iv) Whenever the notice is revised, make the notice available upon request on or after the effective date of the revision and promptly comply with the requirements of paragraph (c)(2)(iii) of this section, if applicable. | Provisions of Notice— Certain Covered Health Care Providers | Specific requirements for certain covered health care providers: Inquire of management as to how the covered entity the notice to any person upon request. Obtain and review the formal or informal policies and procedures in place regarding the provision of the notice of privacy practices. Obtain and review an example acknowledgement of receipt of the notice and an example of documentation showing a good faith effort was made when an acknowledgment could not be obtained. For a selection of individuals who were new patients/new individuals, obtain and review documentation to determine if the initial date service corresponded with the date of the notice of privacy practices was received. If the dates do not correspond, determine if the initial service was an emergency situation or if there was another means or explanation. |
| § 164.524 | § 164.524: **Access of Individuals to PHI**—
(a)(1) Except as otherwise provided in paragraph (a)(2) or (a)(3) of this section, an individual has a right of access to review and obtain a copy of protected health information about the individual in a designated record set, for as long as the protected health information is maintained in the designated record set.
(b)(1) The covered entity must permit an individual to request access to review or to obtain a copy of the protected health information about the individual that is maintained in a | Right to Access | Inquire of management as to how an individual can access PHI. Obtain and review formal or informal policies and procedures to determine if a process is in place for individuals to access PHI. Obtain and review the notice of privacy practices to identify if an individual's right to access in timely manner is outlined in the notice. Determine whether fee charged meets criteria. |

continues

	designated record set. The covered entity may require individuals to make requests for access in writing, provided that it informs individuals of such a requirement. (b)(3) The covered entity must provide the access as requested by the individual in a timely manner as required by paragraph (b)(2) of this section, including arranging with the individual for a convenient time and place to review or obtain a copy of the protected health information, or mailing the copy of the protected health information at the individual's request. The covered entity may discuss the scope, format, and other aspects of the request for access with the individual as necessary to facilitate the timely provision of access. (b)(4) If the individual requests a copy of the protected health information or agrees to a summary or explanation of such information, the covered entity may impose a reasonable, cost-based fee, provided that the fee includes only the cost of: (i) Copying, including the cost of supplies for and labor of copying, the protected health information requested by the individual; (ii) Postage, when the individual has requested the copy, or the summary or explanation, be mailed; and (iii) Preparing an explanation or summary of the protected health information, if agreed to by the individual as required by paragraph (c)(2)(ii) of this section. (c)(3) If the covered entity does not maintain the protected health information that is the subject of the individual's request for access, and the covered entity knows where the requested information is maintained, the covered entity must inform the individual where to direct the request for access.		
§ 164.530	§ 164.530: **Administrative Requirements—** (b)(1) A covered entity must train all members of its workforce on the policies and procedures with respect to protected health information as necessary and appropriate for the	Training	Inquire of management as to whether training is provided to the entity's work force on HIPAA Privacy Standards. Obtain and review documentation to determine if a training process is in place for HIPAA privacy standards. Obtain and review documentation to

continues

	members of the workforce to carry out their functions within the covered entity. (b)(2)(i)(A) Training must be provided to each member of the covered entity's workforce by no later than the compliance date for the covered entity; (B) thereafter, to each new member of the workforce within a reasonable period of time after the person joins the covered entity's workforce; and (C) to each member of the covered entity's workforce whose functions are affected by a material change in the policies or procedures required by this subpart within a reasonable amount of time.		determine if a monitoring process is in place to help ensure all members of the workforce receive training on HIPAA privacy standards as mandated by § 164.530(b)(1) and § 164.530(b)(2)(i). For a selection of new hires within the audit period, obtain and review documentation showing training on HIPAA privacy compliance has been completed.
§ 164.530	§ 164.530: **Administrative Requirements**— (d)(1) A covered entity must provide a process for individuals to make complaints concerning the covered entity's policies and procedures required by this subpart and subpart D of this part or its compliance with such policies and procedures or the requirements of this subpart or subpart D of this part.	Complaints to the Covered Entity	Inquire of management as to whether formal or informal policies and procedures exist for receiving and processing complaints over the entity's privacy practices. Obtain and review formal or informal policies and procedures to determine how complaints are received, processed, and documented. From a population of complaints received within the audit period, obtain and review documentation of each complaint.
§ 164.530	§ 164.530: **Administrative Requirements**— (e)(1) A covered entity must have and apply appropriate sanctions against members of its workforce who fail to comply with the privacy policies and procedures of the covered entity or the requirements of this subpart.	Sanctions	Inquire of management as to whether sanctions are in place against members of the covered entity's workforce who fail to comply with the privacy policies and procedures. Obtain and review formal or informal policies and procedures to determine if sanctions are identified/described in the event members of the workforce do not comply with the entity's privacy practices. From a population of instances of individual/employee noncompliance within the audit period, obtain and review documentation to determine whether appropriate sanctions were applied. Obtain and review evidence that the policies and procedures are updated and conveyed to the workforce.

4. SAMPLE INTERVIEW AND DOCUMENT REQUEST FOR HIPAA SECURITY ONSITE INVESTIGATIONS AND COMPLIANCE REVIEWS

Department of Health and Human Services—Office of Civil Rights

1. Personnel who may be interviewed

   - President, CEO, or Director
   - HIPAA Compliance Officer
   - Lead Systems Manager or Director
   - Systems Security Officer
   - Lead Network Engineer and/or individuals responsible for:
     - administration of systems that store, transmit, or access Electronic Protected Health Information (EPHI)
     - administration systems networks (wired and wireless)
     - monitoring of systems that store, transmit, or access EPHI
     - monitoring systems networks (if different from above)
   - Computer Hardware Specialist
   - Disaster Recovery Specialist or person in charge of data backup
   - Facility Access Control Coordinator (physical security)
   - Human Resources Representative
   - Director of Training
   - Incident Response Team Leader
   - Others as identified . . .

2. Documents and other information that may be requested for investigations/reviews

   - <u>Policies and Procedures and Other Evidence That Address the Following:</u>
   - Prevention, detection, containment, and correction of security violations
   - Employee background checks and confidentiality agreements
   - Establishing user access for new and existing employees
   - List of authentication methods used to identify users authorized to access EPHI
   - List of individuals and contractors with access to EPHI to include copies of pertinent business associate agreements
   - List of software used to manage and control access to the Internet
   - Detecting, reporting, and responding to security incidents (if not in the security plan)
   - Physical security
   - Encryption and decryption of EPHI

- Mechanisms to ensure integrity of data during transmission—including portable media transmission (i.e., laptops, cell phones, BlackBerries, thumb drives)
- Monitoring systems use—authorized and unauthorized
- Use of wireless networks
- Granting, approving, and monitoring systems access (for example, by level, role, and job function)
- Sanctions for workforce members in violation of policies and procedures governing EPHI access or use
- Termination of systems access
- Session termination policies and procedures for inactive computer systems
- Policies and procedures for emergency access to electronic information systems
- Password management policies and procedures
- Secure workstation use (documentation of specific guidelines for each class of workstation (i.e., on site, laptop, and home system usage))
- Disposal of media and devices containing EPHI
- <u>Other Documents:</u>
- Entity-wide Security Plan
- Risk Analysis (most recent)
- Risk Management Plan (addressing risks identified in the Risk Analysis)
- Security violation monitoring reports
- Vulnerability scanning plans
    - Results from most recent vulnerability scan
- Network penetration testing policy and procedure
    - Results from most recent network penetration test
- List of all user accounts with access to systems that store, transmit, or access EPHI (for active and terminated employees)
- Configuration standards to include patch management for systems that store, transmit, or access EPHI (including workstations)
- Encryption or equivalent measures implemented on systems that store, transmit, or access EPHI
- Organization chart to include staff members responsible for general HIPAA compliance to include the protection of EPHI
- Examples of training courses or communications delivered to staff members to ensure awareness and understanding of EPHI policies and procedures (security awareness training)
- Policies and procedures governing the use of virus protection software
- Data backup procedures
- Disaster recovery plan
- Disaster recovery test plans and results

- Analysis of information systems, applications, and data groups according to their criticality and sensitivity
- Inventory of all information systems to include network diagrams listing hardware and software used to store, transmit, or maintain EPHI
- List of all Primary Domain Controllers (PDC) and servers
- Inventory log recording the owner and movement media and devices that contain EPHI

GLOSSARY OF HIPAA DEFINITIONS

(All **bold-faced** words found in each definition also are defined in this Glossary.)

ACCESS

As used in the **Security Regulations**, access is the ability or means necessary to read, write, modify, or communicate data/information or otherwise use any system resource.
[45 C.F.R. § 164.304.]

ADMINISTRATIVE SAFEGUARDS

Administrative safeguards are administrative actions and policies and procedures to manage the selection, development, implementation, and maintenance of **security measures** to protect **electronic protected health information**, and to manage the conduct of the **covered entity's or business associate's workforce** in relation to the protection of that information.
[45 C.F.R. § 164.304.]

ADMINISTRATIVE SIMPLIFICATION PROVISIONS

Administrative Simplification Provisions are those portions of **HIPAA** relating to **standard transactions**, privacy, and security and means any requirement or prohibition established by: (1) 42 U.S.C. 1320d-1320d-4, 1320d-7, 1320d-8, and 1320d-9; (2) Section 264 of Pub. L. No. 104-191; (3) Sections 13400-13424 of Public Law 111-5; or Code of Federal Regulations Title 45, Parts 160, 162, and 164, which includes the **Transaction Standards, Privacy Regulations, Security Regulations, Breach Regulations,** and **Enforcement Regulations**.
[45 C.F.R. Parts 160 - 164.]

AFFILIATED COVERED ENTITY (ACE)

Legally separate **covered entities** that are affiliated may designate themselves as a single **affiliated covered entity (ACE)** for purposes of compliance with the **Privacy Rules** and **Security Rules** if all of the **covered entities** designated are under **common ownership** or **common control**.
[45 C.F.R. § 164.105(b).]

AUTHENTICATION

Authentication is the corroboration that a person is the one claimed.
[45 C.F.R. § 164.304.]

AUTHORIZATION

An authorization is a specific form of permission, established by the **Privacy Rules**, to use and/or disclose an individual's **protected health information**. The authorization must satisfy the requirements set forth in the **Privacy Rules**, and it will permit **use** and/or **disclosure** either by the **covered entity** seeking authorization or by a third party.
[45 C.F.R. § 164.508.]

AVAILABILITY

Availability means that data or information is accessible and usable upon demand by an authorized person. [45 C.F.R. § 164.304.]

BREACH

Breach means the acquisition, access, use, or disclosure of **protected health information** in a manner not permitted under the **Privacy Rules** that compromises the security or privacy of the **protected health information**. Unless an exception applies, if there is an acquisition, access, use, or disclosure of **protected health information** in a manner not permitted under the **Privacy Rules**, a breach is presumed to have occurred, unless the covered entity or business associate, as applicable, demonstrates that there is a low probability that the PHI has been compromised based on a risk assessment of at least the following four factors:

(1) The nature and extent of the PHI involved, including the types of identifiers and the likelihood of re-identification;

(2) The unauthorized person who used the PHI or to whom the disclosure was made;

(3) Whether the PHI was actually acquired or viewed; and

(4) The extent to which the risk to the PHI has been mitigated.

The following exceptions apply, and breach does not include:

(i) Any unintentional acquisition, access, or **use** of **protected health information** by a **workforce** member or person acting under the authority of a **covered entity** or a **business associate**, if such acquisition, access, or **use** was made in good faith and within the scope of authority and does not result in further use or disclosure in a manner not permitted under the **Privacy Rules**.

(ii) Any inadvertent **disclosure** by a person who is authorized to access **protected health information** at a **covered entity** or **business associate** to another person authorized to access **protected health information** at the same **covered entity** or **business associate**, or **organized health care arrangement** in which the **covered entity** participates, and the information received as a result of such **disclosure** is not further **used** or **disclosed** in a manner not permitted under the **Privacy Rules**.

(iii) A **disclosure** of **protected health information** where a **covered entity** or **business associate** has a good faith belief that an unauthorized person to whom the **disclosure** was made would not reasonably have been able to retain such information.

[45 C.F.R. § 164.402.]

BREACH REGULATIONS

Regulations issued under **HITECH**, establishing notification requirements in the event of certain privacy breaches. These regulations, along with the **Transaction Standards, Privacy Regulations, Security Regulations**, and **Enforcement Regulations** make up the **Administrative Simplification** provisions of HIPAA.
[45 C.F.R. §§ 164.400–164.414.]

BUSINESS ASSOCIATE

Business associate means, with respect to a **covered entity**, a person who:

(i) On behalf of such **covered entity**, or of an **organized health care arrangement** (OHCA) in which the **covered entity** participates, but other than in the capacity of a member of the **workforce** of such

covered entity or OHCA, creates, receives, maintains, or transmits **protected health information** for a function or activity regulated by the **Administrative Simplification Provisions**, including claims processing or administration, data analysis, processing or administration, utilization review, quality assurance, patient safety activities listed at 42 CFR 3.20 (Patient Safety and Quality Improvement Act of 2005), billing, benefit management, practice management, and repricing; or

(ii)   Provides, other than in the capacity of a member of the **workforce** of such **covered entity**, legal, actuarial, accounting, consulting, **data aggregation**, management, administrative, accreditation, or financial services to or for such **covered entity**, or to or for an OHCA in which the **covered entity** participates, where the provision of the service involves the **disclosure** of **protected health information** from such **covered entity** or OHCA, or from another business associate of such **covered entity** or OHCA, to the person.

Business associate also specifically includes:

(i)   A Health Information Organization, E-prescribing Gateway, or other person who provides data transmission services with respect to **protected health information** to a **covered entity** and that requires access on a routine basis to such **protected health information**.

(ii)   A person who offers a personal health record to one or more individuals on behalf of a **covered entity**.

(iii)   A **subcontractor** who creates, receives, maintains, or transmits **protected health information** on behalf of the business associate.

Business associate does not include:

(i)   A **health care provider**, with respect to disclosures by a **covered entity** to the health care provider concerning the **treatment** of the **individual**.

(ii)   A **plan sponsor**, with respect to disclosures by a **group health plan** (or by a health insurance issuer or HMO with respect to a **group health plan**) to the **plan sponsor**, to the extent that the requirements of 45 CFR § 164.504(f) apply and are met.

(iii)   A government agency, with respect to determining eligibility for, or enrollment in, a government health plan that provides public benefits and is administered by another government agency, or collecting **protected health information** for such purposes, to the extent such activities are authorized by law.

(iv)   A covered entity by reason of its participating in an **organized health care arrangement** that performs services for the OHCA, even though those services would qualify as business associate activities if performed by a person or entity that is not a member of the OHCA.

[45 C.F.R. § 160.103).]

COMMON CONTROL

Common control exists if an entity has the power, whether directly or indirectly, to significantly influence or direct the actions or policies of another entity. Used to define **affiliated covered entity**.
[45 C.F.R. § 164.103.]

COMMON OWNERSHIP

Common ownership exists if an entity or entities possess an ownership or equity interest of 5 percent or more in another entity. Used to define **affiliated covered entity**.
[45 C.F.R. § 164.103.]

CONFIDENTIALITY

Confidentiality means the property that data or information is not made available or disclosed to unauthorized persons or processes.
[45 C.F.R. § 164.304.]

CONSENT

A consent is a general form of permission, established by the **Privacy Rules**, to use and/or disclose an individual's **protected health information**. Consent is not effective to permit a **use** or **disclosure** of **protected health information** when an **authorization** is required or when another condition must be met for such a **use** or **disclosure** to be permissible.
[45 C.F.R. § 164.506.]

CORRECTIONAL INSTITUTION

A correctional institution is any penal or correctional facility, jail, reformatory, detention center, work farm, halfway house, or residential community program center operated by, or under contract to, the United States, a State, a territory, a political subdivision of a State or territory, or an Indian tribe, for the confinement or rehabilitation of persons charged with or convicted of a criminal offense or other persons held in lawful custody. The term "other persons held in lawful custody" includes juvenile offenders adjudicated delinquent, aliens detained awaiting deportation, persons committed to mental institutions through the criminal justice system, witnesses, or others awaiting charges or trial.
[45 C.F.R. § 164.501.]

COVERED ENTITY

A covered entity is a **health plan**, a **health care clearinghouse**, or a **health care provider** that transmits information electronically in connection with a **covered transaction**.
[45 C.F.R. §§ 160.102, 160.103.]

COVERED FUNCTION

Covered functions are the activities performed by a **covered entity** that make it a **covered entity** as a **health plan**, **health care provider**, or **health care clearinghouse**. For instance, furnishing **health care** services and supplies is a covered function, because performing those activities makes an individual or organization a **health care provider** and, in most cases, a **covered entity**.
[45 C.F.R. § 164.103.]

COVERED PROVIDER OR COVERED HEALTH CARE PROVIDER

A covered provider is a **health care provider** that performs one or more **covered transactions** electronically and therefore becomes a **covered entity** under the **Privacy Rules**.
[45 C.F.R. §§ 160.102, 162.402.]

COVERED TRANSACTION OR TRANSACTION

A covered transaction is a transaction that is covered by **HIPAA**. A transaction is a transmission of information between two parties to carry out financial or administrative activities related to **health care**. It includes the following types of transmissions:

- **Health care** claims or equivalent encounter information.

- **Health care payment** and remittance advice.

- Coordination of benefits.

- **Health care** claim status.

- Enrollment and disenrollment in a **health plan**.

- Eligibility for a **health plan**.

- **Health plan** premium payments.

- Referral certification and authorization.

- First report of injury.

- Health claims attachments.

- **Health care** electronic funds transfers (EFTs) and remittance advice.

- Any other transactions designated by the Secretary of the **HHS**.

See also Standard Transaction.
[45 C.F.R. § 160.103.]

DATA AGGREGATION

Data aggregation is the combining of **protected health information**of two or more **covered entities** by a **business associate** to permit data analyses that relate to the **health care operations** of the respective **covered entities** that provided the **protected health information** to such **business associate**.
[45 C.F.R. § 164.501.]

DE-IDENTIFIED INFORMATION

De-identified information is **health information** that does not identify an individual and with respect to which there is no reasonable basis to believe that the information can be used to identify an individual. **Health information** is de-identified information if it meets the criteria of either of the following approaches:

1. Expert Approach: The determination of minimal risk of identification by a person with appropriate knowledge of and experience with generally accepted statistical and scientific principles and methods for rendering information not individually identifiable. The risk must be determined to be very small that the information could be used, alone or in combination with other reasonably available information, by an anticipated recipient, to identify the individual. **Or**

2. Safe Harbor Approach: The removal of all the following identifiers of the individual or of relatives, employers, or household members of the individual, and no actual knowledge on the part of the covered entity that the remaining information could be used alone or in combination with other information to identify the individual.

   - Names;

   - All geographic subdivisions smaller than a state, including street address, city, county, precinct, zip code, and equivalent codes. The first three digits of the zip code may be retained if certain conditions are met (i.e., the zip code area is not too sparsely populated);

   - All elements of dates (except year) for dates directly related to an individual, including birth date, admission date, discharge date, date of death; and all ages over 89 and all elements of dates (including year) indicative of such age, except that such ages and elements may be aggregated into a single category of age 90 or older;

- Telephone numbers;
- Fax numbers;
- E-mail addresses;
- Social Security numbers;
- Medical record numbers;
- Health plan beneficiary numbers;
- Account numbers;
- Certificate/license numbers;
- Vehicle identifiers and serial numbers, including license plate numbers;
- Device identifiers and serial numbers;
- Web addresses—Universal Resource Locators (URLs);
- Internet Protocol (IP) address numbers;
- Biometric identifiers, including fingerprints and voice prints;
- Full face photographic images and any comparable images; and
- Any other unique identifying number, characteristic, or code (except a re-identification code).

[45 C.F.R. § 164.514(a)–(c).]

DEMOGRAPHIC INFORMATION

Demographic Information generally includes the individual's name, address, other contact information (e.g., phone number), age, gender, and date of birth, but does not include any information about the individual's illness or treatment.
[45 C.F.R. § 164.514(f).]

DESIGNATED RECORD SET

A designated record set is a group of records maintained by or for a **covered entity** that: (1) contains the medical records and billing records about individuals maintained by or for a covered **health care provider**; (2) contains the enrollment, **payment**, claims adjudication, and case or medical management record systems maintained by or for a **health plan**; or (3) is used, in whole or in part, by or for the **covered entity** to make decisions about individuals. As used in this definition, "record" means any item, collection, or grouping of information that includes **protected health information** and is maintained, collected, used, or distributed by or for a **covered entity**.
[45 C.F.R. § 164.501.]

DIRECT TREATMENT RELATIONSHIP

A direct treatment relationship is a **treatment** relationship between an individual and a **health care provider** that is not an **indirect treatment relationship**.
[45 C.F.R. § 164.501.]

DISCLOSURE

Disclosure means the release, transfer, provision of, access to, or divulging in any manner of information outside the entity holding the information.
[45 C.F.R. § 160.103.]

ELECTRONIC HEALTH RECORD

An electronic health record, or EHR, as used under the privacy-related provisions of the HITECH Act, means an electronic record of health-related information on an individual that is created, gathered, managed, and consulted by authorized health care clinicians and staff.
[HITECH Act § 13400]

ELECTRONIC MEDIA

Electronic media means (1) electronic storage material on which data are or may be recorded electronically, including, for example, devices in computers (hard drives) and any removable/transportable digital memory medium, such as magnetic tape or disk, optical disk, or digital memory card; and (2) transmission media used to exchange information already in electronic storage media. Transmission media include, for example, the Internet, extranet or intranet, leased lines, dial-up lines, private networks, and the physical movement of removable/transportable electronic storage media. Certain transmissions, including of paper, via facsimile, and of voice, via telephone, are not considered to be transmissions via electronic media if the information being exchanged did not exist in electronic form immediately before the transmission.
[45 C.F.R. § 160.103.]

ELECTRONIC PROTECTED HEALTH INFORMATION

Electronic protected health information is **protected health information** that is transmitted or maintained in **electronic media**.
[45 C.F.R. § 160.103.]

ENCRYPTION

Encryption is the use of an algorithmic process to transform data into a form in which there is a low probability of assigning meaning without use of a confidential process or key.
[45 C.F.R. § 164.304.]

ENFORCEMENT REGULATIONS

Regulations regarding enforcement of the Administrative Simplification Regulations, including civil and criminal penalties. These regulations, along with the **Transaction Standards, Privacy Regulations, Security Regulations**, and **Breach Regulations,** make up the **Administrative Simplification** provisions of HIPAA.
[45 C.F.R. Part 160.]

FACILITY

Facility is the physical premises and the interior and exterior of a building(s).
[45 C.F.R. § 164.304.]

GROUP HEALTH PLAN

A group health plan is an employee welfare benefit plan (as defined by ERISA), including any insured or self-insured plan, that provides **medical care**, including items and services paid for as **medical care**, to employees or dependents either directly or through insurance, reimbursement, or otherwise, *if* (i) the plan has fifty or more participants, *or* (ii) is administered by an entity other than the employer that established and maintains the plan.

[45 C.F.R. § 160.103.]

HEALTH CARE

Health care is care, services, or supplies related to the health of an individual. It includes, but is not limited to, preventive, diagnostic, therapeutic, rehabilitative, maintenance, or palliative care, and counseling, service, assessment, or procedure with respect to the physical or mental condition (or functional status) of an individual or that affects the structure or function of the body. Health care also includes the sale or dispensing of a drug, device, equipment, or other item in accordance with a prescription.

[45 C.F.R. § 160.103.]

HEALTH CARE CLEARINGHOUSE

A health care clearinghouse is a public or private entity that either (1) processes or facilitates the processing of **health information** received from another entity in a nonstandard format or containing nonstandard data content into standard data elements or standard transactions or (2) receives a standard transaction from another entity and processes or facilitates the processing of **health information** into nonstandard format or nonstandard data content for the receiving entity. Entities such as billing services, repricing companies, community health management information systems or community **health information** systems, and value-added networks and switches are health care clearinghouses if they perform the functions in either (1) or (2).

[45 C.F.R. § 160.103.]

HEALTH CARE COMPONENT

A health care component is a component or combination of components of a **hybrid entity** designated by the **hybrid entity** in accordance with the **Privacy Rules**.

[45 C.F.R. § 164.103.]

HEALTH CARE OPERATIONS

Health care operations are defined as the following activities of a **covered entity**, to the extent such activities are related to **covered functions**. Health care operations also include these activities if they are conducted by an **organized health care arrangement** in which a **covered entity** participates.

- Conducting quality assessment and improvement activities, including—

    - outcome evaluation and development of clinical guidelines, provided that obtaining generalizable knowledge is not the primary purpose of any studies resulting from such activities;

    - patient safety activities (as defined in 42 C.F.R. § 3.20);

    - population-based activities relating to improving health or reducing **health care** costs, protocol development, case management and care coordination, and contacting **health care providers** and patients with information about **treatment** alternatives; and

    - related functions that do not include **treatment**.

- Reviewing the competence or qualifications of **health care** professionals; evaluating practitioner and **health care provider** performance; evaluating **health plan** performance; conducting health care training programs for students or practitioners; conducting training of non–health care professionals; and conducting accreditation, certification, licensing, or credentialing activities.

- Except as prohibited with regard to genetic information, underwriting, enrollment, premium rating, and other activities related to the creation, renewal, or replacement of a contract of health insurance or health benefits, and ceding, securing, or placing a contract for reinsurance of risk relating to claims for **health care** (including stop-loss insurance and excess of loss insurance).

- Conducting or arranging for medical review, legal services, and auditing functions, including fraud and abuse detection and compliance programs.

- Business planning and development, such as conducting cost-management and planning-related analyses related to managing and operating the entity, including formulary development and administration, development, or improvement of methods of **payment** or coverage policies.

- Business management and general administrative activities, including, but not limited to—

  - management activities relating to implementation of and compliance with **HIPAA**;

  - customer service, including the provision of data analyses for policy holders, plan sponsors, or other customers, provided that **protected health information** is not disclosed to such policy holder, **plan sponsor**, or customer;

  - resolution of internal grievances;

  - sale, transfer, merger, or consolidation of all or part of the **covered entity** with another **covered entity** or with an entity that will become a **covered entity** after such sale, transfer, merger, or consolidation is completed, as well as any due diligence related to the sale, transfer, merger, or consolidation;

  - creating **de-identified information** or a **limited data set** consistent with applicable requirements; and

  - fundraising for the benefit of the **covered entity** (consistent with applicable requirements).

[45 C.F.R. § 164.501.]

HEALTH CARE PROVIDER

A health care provider is a **provider of services** as defined under Medicare Part A, a provider of **medical or health services**, as defined under Medicare Part B, and any other person or organization that furnishes, bills, or is paid for **health care** in the normal course of business.
[45 C.F.R. § 160.103; 42 U.S.C. §§ 1395x(s), 1395x(u).]

HEALTH INFORMATION

Health information is any information, including genetic information, whether oral or recorded in any form or medium, that is created or received by a **health care provider**, **health plan**, **public health authority**, employer, life insurer, school or university, or **health care clearinghouse**; and the information relates to the past, present, or future physical or mental health or condition of an individual, the provision of **health care** to an individual, or past, present, or future **payment** for providing **health care** to an individual.
[45 C.F.R. § 160.103.]

HEALTH INSURANCE ISSUER

For purposes of defining a **health plan**, "health insurance issuer" means an insurance company, insurance service, or insurance organization (including an HMO) that is licensed to engage in the business of insurance in a State and is subject to State law that regulates insurance. Group health plans are not health insurance issuers.
[45 C.F.R. § 160.103.]

HEALTH OVERSIGHT ACTIVITY

A health oversight activity is an activity performed by a **health oversight agency** and includes audits; civil, administrative, or criminal investigations; inspections; licensure or disciplinary actions; or civil, administrative, or criminal proceedings or actions, or other activities necessary for appropriate oversight of the health care system and certain other regulated programs and entities.
[45 C.F.R. § 164.512(d).]

HEALTH OVERSIGHT AGENCY

A health oversight agency is an agency or authority of the United States, a State, a territory, a political subdivision of a State or territory, or an Indian tribe, or a person or entity acting under a grant of authority from, or contract with, such agency, including the employees or agents of such agency or its contractors or persons or entities to whom it has granted authority, that is authorized by law to oversee the **health care** system (whether public or private) or government programs in which **health information** is necessary to determine eligibility or compliance, or to enforce civil rights laws for which **health information** is relevant.
[45 C.F.R. § 164.501.]

HEALTH PLAN

A health plan is an individual or group plan that provides or pays for the cost of **medical care**. It *includes* the following, individually or in combination:

- A **group health plan**, a **health insurance issuer**, and an HMO.

- Part A or B of Medicare, Medicare Part D Drug Program, Medicare+Choice, Medicare Advantage Program, Medicaid, an issuer of a Medicare supplemental policy, and an issuer of a long-term care policy (excluding a nursing fixed indemnity policy).

- An employee welfare plan or other arrangement that offers or provides health benefits to the employees of two or more employers.

- The **health care** program for active military personnel, the veterans **health care** program, and the Civilian Health and Medical Program of the Uniformed Services.

- The Indian Health Service program, the Federal Employees Health Benefits Program, and approved state child health plans.

- Any other individual or group plan (or combination thereof) that provides or pays for the cost of **medical care**.

The term **health plan** *excludes*:

- Any policy or plan that provides or pays for excepted benefits. Excepted benefits are:
  - accident-only or disability income-only insurance (or combination thereof),
  - coverage issued as a supplement to liability insurance,

- liability insurance, including general liability and automobile liability insurance,
- workers' compensation or similar insurance,
- automobile medical payment insurance,
- credit-only insurance,
- coverage for on-site medical clinics, and
- other similar insurance coverage in which benefits for **medical care** are secondary or incidental to other insurance benefits (these may be specified in the Public Health Service Act regulations).
- A government funded program (other than a program specifically included in the list above)
  - whose principal purpose is something other than providing or paying for the cost of **health care** or
  - whose principal activity is the direct provision of **health care** to individuals or the making of grants to fund the direct provision of **health care** to individuals.

[45 C.F.R. § 160.103; 42 U.S.C. § 300gg-91(c) (excepted benefits).]

HHS

HHS is the U.S. Department of Health and Human Services. This is the federal agency that implements and oversees compliance with the **Administrative Simplification Provisions**.

HIPAA

HIPAA is the Health Insurance Portability and Accountability Act of 1996, and the regulations promulgated thereunder.

HITECH

HITECH is the 2009 Health Information Technology for Economic and Clinical Health Act (HITECH Act), and the regulations promulgated thereunder.

HYBRID ENTITY

A hybrid entity is a single legal entity that is a **covered entity**, whose business activities include both covered and noncovered functions and that designates **health care components** in accordance with the **Privacy Rules**.
[45 C.F.R. § 164.103.]

IMPLEMENTATION SPECIFICATION

An implementation specification means a specific requirement or instruction for implementing a standard.
[45 C.F.R. § 160.103.]

INDIRECT TREATMENT RELATIONSHIP

An indirect treatment relationship is a **treatment** relationship between an individual and a **health care provider** in which (1) the **health care provider** delivers **health care** to the individual based on the orders of another **health care provider**, and (2) the **health care provider** typically provides services or products, or reports the diagnosis or results associated with the **health care**, directly to another **health care provider**, who provides services or products or reports to the individual.
[45 C.F.R. § 164.501.]

INDIVIDUAL

An individual is the person who is the subject of the **protected health information**.
[45 C.F.R. § 160.103.]

INDIVIDUALLY IDENTIFIABLE HEALTH INFORMATION

Individually identifiable health information is information that is a subset of **health information**, including demographic information that is collected from an individual and that is created or received by a **health care provider**, a **health plan**, an employer, or **health care clearinghouse**. The information relates to the past, present, or future physical or mental health or condition of an individual. It also includes information concerning the provision of **health care** to an individual, or the past, present, or future **payment** for the provision of **health care** to an individual, when the information identifies the individual, or there is a reasonable basis to believe the information can be used to identify the individual.
[45 C.F.R. § 160.103.]

INFORMATION SYSTEM

An information system is an interconnected set of information resources under the same direct management control that shares common functionality. A system normally includes hardware, software, information, data, applications, communications, and people.
[45 C.F.R. § 164.304.]

INMATE

An inmate is a person incarcerated in or otherwise confined to a **correctional institution**.
[45 C.F.R. § 164.501.]

INTEGRITY

Integrity means the property that data or information have not been altered or destroyed in an unauthorized manner.
[45 C.F.R. § 164.304.]

LAW ENFORCEMENT OFFICIAL

A law enforcement official is an officer or employee of any agency or authority of the United States, a State, a territory, a political subdivision of a State or territory, or an Indian tribe, who is empowered by law (1) to investigate or conduct an official inquiry into a potential violation of law, or (2) to prosecute or otherwise conduct a criminal, civil, or administrative proceeding arising from an alleged violation of law.
[45 C.F.R. § 164.103.]

LIMITED DATA SET

A limited data set is **protected health information** from which the following sixteen specific direct identifiers of the individual or of relatives, employers, or household members of the individual have been removed:

1. Name;

2. Street address—postal address information, other than town/city, state, and zip code;

3. Telephone numbers;

4. Fax numbers;

5. E-mail addresses;

6. Social Security numbers;

7. Medical record numbers;

8. Health plan beneficiary numbers;

9. Account numbers;

10. Certificate/license numbers;

11. Vehicle identifiers and serial numbers, including license plate numbers;

12. Device identifiers and serial numbers;

13. Web addresses—Universal Resource Locators (URLs);

14. Internet Protocol (IP) address numbers;

15. Biometric identifiers, including fingerprints and voiceprints; and

16. Full face photographic images and any other comparable images.

[45 C.F.R. § 164.514(e).]

MALICIOUS SOFTWARE

Malicious software means software designed to damage or disrupt a system, such as a virus.
[45 C.F.R. § 164.304.]

MARKETING

Except as provided below, marketing means to make a communication about a product or service that encourages recipients of the communication to purchase or use the product or service.
Marketing does not include a communication made:

- To provide refill reminders or otherwise communicate about a drug or biologic that is currently being prescribed for the individual, only if any **financial remuneration** received by the covered entity in exchange for making the communication is reasonably related to the covered entity's cost of making the communication.

- For the following treatment and health care operations purposes, except where the covered entity receives **financial remuneration** in exchange for making the communication:

    - For treatment of an individual by a health care provider, including case management or care coordination for the individual, or to direct or recommend alternative treatments, therapies, health care providers, or settings of care to the individual;

    - To describe a health-related product or service (or payment for such product or service) that is provided by, or included in a plan of benefits of, the covered entity making the communication, including communications about: the entities participating in a health care provider network or health plan network; replacement of, or enhancements to, a health plan; and health-related products or services available only to a health plan enrollee that add value to, but are not part of, a plan of benefits; or

    - For case management or care coordination, contacting of individuals with information about treatment alternatives, and related functions to the extent these activities do not fall within the definition of treatment.

For purposes of the definition of marketing, "financial remuneration" means direct or indirect payment from or on behalf of a third party whose product or service is being described. Direct or indirect payment does not include any payment for treatment of an individual.

[45 C.F.R. § 164.501.]

MEDICAL CARE

For purposes of defining a **health plan** or **group health plan**, medical care refers to amounts paid for the diagnosis, cure, mitigation, treatment, or prevention of disease, or amounts paid for the purpose affecting any structure or function of the body. It also includes amounts paid for transportation primarily for and essential to such medical care, as well as amounts paid for insurance covering such medical care.

[42 U.S.C. § 300gg-91(a)(2).]

MEDICAL OR HEALTH SERVICES

For purposes of defining a **health care provider**, medical or health services are those items and services defined by Medicare at 42 U.S.C. § 1395x(s), and summarized below:

1. physicians' services;

2. services and supplies furnished incident to a physician's professional services;

3. hospital services incident to physicians' services rendered to outpatients and partial hospitalization services incident to such services;

4. diagnostic services, which are furnished to an individual as an outpatient by a hospital or by others under arrangements with them made by a hospital, and ordinarily furnished by such hospital (or by others under such arrangements) to its outpatients for the purpose of diagnostic study;

5. outpatient physical therapy services and outpatient occupational therapy services;

6. rural health clinic services and federally qualified health center services;

7. home dialysis supplies and equipment, self-care home dialysis support services, and institutional dialysis services and supplies;

8. antigens prepared by a physician for a particular patient;

9. services by a physician assistant, nurse practitioner, clinical psychologist, or clinical social worker furnished pursuant to certain Medicare contracts, and services and supplies furnished incident to such services;

10. blood clotting factors, for hemophilia patients, and items related to the administration of such factors;

11. prescription drugs used in immunosuppressive therapy furnished to an organ transplant patient;

12. services that would be physicians' services if furnished by a physician and that are (i) performed by a physician assistant under the supervision of a physician, or (ii) performed by a nurse practitioner or clinical nurse specialist working in collaboration with a physician; and services and supplies incident to such services;

13. certified nurse-midwife services;

14. qualified psychologist services;

15. clinical social worker services;

16. erythropoietin for dialysis patients;

17. prostate cancer screening tests;

18. an oral drug (approved by the FDA) prescribed for use as an anticancer chemotherapeutic agent;

19. colorectal cancer screening tests;

20. diabetes outpatient self-management training services;

21. an oral drug (approved by FDA) prescribed for use as an acute anti-emetic used as part of an anticancer chemotherapeutic regimen if the drug is administered by a physician (or as prescribed by a physician) as a full replacement for IV anti-emetic therapy;

22. screening for glaucoma;

23. medical nutrition therapy services for certain patients with diabetes or a renal disease;

24. diagnostic X-ray tests, diagnostic laboratory tests, and other diagnostic tests;

25. X-ray, radium, and radioactive isotope therapy, including materials and services of technicians;

26. surgical dressings, and splints, casts, and other devices used for reduction of fractures and dislocations;

27. durable medical equipment;

28. ambulance service where the use of other methods of transportation is contraindicated by the individual's condition;

29. prosthetic devices that replace all or part of an internal body organ (including colostomy bags and supplies directly related to colostomy care), including replacement of such devices, and including conventional eyeglasses or contact lenses furnished subsequent to cataract surgery with insertion of an intraocular lens;

30. leg, arm, back, and neck braces, and artificial legs, arms, and eyes;

31. pneumococcal vaccine and its administration; influenza vaccine and its administration; and hepatitis B vaccine and its administration;

32. services of a certified registered nurse anesthetist;

33. extra-depth shoes with inserts or custom molded shoes with inserts for certain individuals with diabetes, as prescribed by a qualified physician or podiatrist;

34. screening mammography;

35. screening pap smear and screening pelvic exam; and

36. bone mass measurement.

[42 U.S.C. § 1395x(s).]

OPERATING RULES

Operating rules are the necessary business rules and guidelines for the electronic exchange of information that are not defined by a **standard** or its implementation specifications.
[45 C.F.R. § 164.304.]

ORGANIZED HEALTH CARE ARRANGEMENT

An organized health care arrangement is defined as any of the following five types of arrangements:

• A clinically integrated care setting in which an individual typically receives **health care** from more than one **health care provider**, *e.g.*, a hospital and its medical staff.

- An organized system of **health care** in which more than one **covered entity** participates and the participating **covered entities** hold themselves out to the public as participating in a joint arrangement and participate in joint activities, including at least one of the following:

  — utilization review, performed by other participating entities or a third party on behalf of the participating entities,

  — quality assessment and improvement activities, assessed by other participating entities or a third party on behalf of the participating entities,

  — **payment** activities, if the financial risk for delivering care is shared by the participating **covered entities** through the joint arrangement and if **protected health information** created or received by a **covered entity** is reviewed by other participating **covered entities** or by a third party on behalf of the joint arrangement for the purpose of administering the sharing of financial risk.

- A **group health plan** and a health insurance issuer or HMO of the **group health plan**, but only with respect to **protected health information** created or received by the health insurance issuer or HMO that relates to individuals who are or who have been participants or beneficiaries in the **group health plan**.

- A **group health plan** and one or more other **group health plans**, each of which are maintained by the same **plan sponsor**.

- A **group health plan** and one or more other **group health plans**, each of which are maintained by the same **plan sponsor**, and a health insurance issuer or HMO of the **group health plans** maintained by the same sponsor, but only with respect to **protected health information** created or received by the health insurance issuer or HMO that relates to individuals who are or have been participants or beneficiaries in any of these **group health plans**.

[45 C.F.R. § 160.103.]

PASSWORD

Password is confidential **authentication** information composed of a string of characters.
[45 C.F.R. § 164.304.]

PAYMENT

Payment means activities that are undertaken by (1) a **health plan** to obtain premiums or to determine or fulfill its responsibility for coverage and provision of benefits under the **health plan** (subject to certain limitations on the use of genetic information for underwriting); or, (2) a **health care provider** or **health plan** to obtain or provide reimbursement for the provision of **health care**.

Such activities relate to the individual who receives the **health care** and include (but are not limited to):

- Eligibility or coverage determinations (including coordination of benefits or the determination of cost sharing amounts) and adjudication or subrogation of health benefit claims.

- Risk adjusting amounts due based on enrollee health status and demographic characteristics.

- Billing, claims management, obtaining payment under a contract for reinsurance (including stop-loss insurance and excess of loss insurance), and related **health care** data processing.

- Review of **health care** services for medical necessity, coverage under the plan, appropriateness of care, or justification of charges.

- Utilization review activities, including pre-certification, pre-authorization, and concurrent and retrospective review of services.

- **Disclosure** of the following **protected health information** to consumer reporting agencies relating to the collection of premiums or reimbursement:
  - — name and address,
  - — date of birth,
  - — Social Security number,
  - — **payment** history,
  - — account number, and
  - — name and address of **health care provider** and/or **health plan**.

[45 C.F.R. § 164.501.]

PERSON

Person means a natural person, trust or estate, partnership, corporation, professional association or corporation, or other entity, public or private.
[45 C.F.R. § 160.103.]

PERSONAL HEALTH RECORD

A personal health record, or PHR, is an electronic record of **PHR identifiable health information** on an individual that can be drawn from multiple sources and that is managed, shared, and controlled by or primarily for the individual.
[HITECH Act § 13400; 16 C.F.R. § 318.2.]

PERSONAL REPRESENTATIVE

A personal representative is a person who, under law, has authority to act on behalf of another individual in making decisions related to **health care**.
[45 C.F.R. § 164.502.]

PHI

PHI means protected health information.

PHR IDENTIFIABLE HEALTH INFORMATION

PHR identifiable health information means **individually identifiable health information** and, with respect to an individual, includes information that is provided by or on behalf of the individual and that identifies the individual or with respect to which there is a reasonable basis to believe that the information can be used to identify the individual.
[HITECH Act § 13407(f)(2)); 16 C.F.R. § 318.2.]

PHYSICAL SAFEGUARDS

Physical safeguards are physical measures, policies, and procedures to protect a **covered entity's** or **business associate's** electronic **information systems** and related buildings and equipment, from natural and environmental hazards, and unauthorized intrusion.

[45 C.F.R. § 164.304.]

PLAN ADMINISTRATION FUNCTIONS

Plan administration functions are administration functions performed by the **plan sponsor** of a **group health plan** on behalf of the **group health plan** and exclude functions performed by the **plan sponsor** in connection with any other benefit or benefit plan of the **plan sponsor**.

[45 C.F.R. § 164.504.]

PLAN SPONSOR

A plan sponsor is (1) the employer in the case of an employee benefit plan established or maintained by a single employer, (2) the employee organization in the case of a plan established or maintained by an employee organization, or (3) in the case of a plan established or maintained by two or more employers or jointly by one or more employers and one or more employee organizations, the association, committee, joint board of trustees, or other similar group of representatives of the parties that establish or maintain the plan.

[45 C.F.R. § 164.103; ERISA § 3(16)(B).]

PRIVACY REGULATIONS OR PRIVACY RULES

The Privacy Rules are the regulations regarding Privacy of Individually Identifiable Health Information promulgated by **HHS** under **HIPAA and HITECH**. These regulations, along with the **Transaction Standards, Breach Regulations, Security Regulations**, and **Enforcement Regulations** make up the **Administrative Simplification** provisions of HIPAA.

[45 C.F.R. Part 160 and Part 164, subparts A and E.]

PROTECTED HEALTH INFORMATION

Protected health information is **individually identifiable health information** that is transmitted by **electronic media**, maintained in **electronic media**, or transmitted or maintained in any other form or medium. It *does not* include **individually identifiable health information**:

- In education records covered by the Family Educational Rights and Privacy Act (FERPA) (20 U.S.C. § 1232g);
- In other records under FERPA described at 20 U.S.C. § 1232g(a)(4)(B)(iv) (relating to adult students);
- In employment records held by a **covered entity** in its role as employer; or
- Regarding a person who has been deceased for more than 50 years.

[45 C.F.R. § 160.103.]

PROVIDER OF SERVICES

A provider of services is a Medicare Part A term, used in the definition of **health care provider**, and includes a hospital, critical access hospital, skilled nursing facility, comprehensive outpatient rehabilitation

facility, home health agency, hospice program, or, in certain circumstances, a fund related to teaching hospital services.
[42 U.S.C. § 1395x(u).]

PSYCHOTHERAPY NOTES

Psychotherapy notes are notes recorded (in any medium) by a **health care provider** who is a mental health professional documenting or analyzing the contents of conversation during a private counseling session or a group, joint, or family counseling session and that are separated from the rest of the individual's medical record. Psychotherapy notes exclude medication prescription and monitoring, counseling session start and stop times, the modalities and frequencies of **treatment** furnished, results of clinical tests, and any summary of the following items: diagnosis, functional status, the **treatment** plan, symptoms, prognosis, and progress to date.
[45 C.F.R. § 164.501.]

PUBLIC HEALTH AUTHORITY

A public health authority is an agency or authority of the United States, a State, a territory, a political subdivision of a State or territory, or an Indian tribe, or a person or an entity acting under a grant of authority from, or contract with, such agency, including the employees or agents of such agency or its contractors or persons or entities to whom it has granted authority, that is responsible for public health matters as part of its official mandate.
[45 C.F.R. § 164.501.]

QUALIFIED PROTECTIVE ORDER

A qualified protective order is an order of a court or of an administrative tribunal or a stipulation by the parties to the litigation or administrative preceding that:

- Prohibits the parties from using or disclosing the **PHI** for any purpose other than the litigation or proceeding for which such information was requested and

- Requires the return or destruction of the **PHI** (including all copies made) at the end of the litigation or proceeding.

[45 C.F.R. § 164.512(e)(1)(v).]

REASONABLE CAUSE

Reasonable cause, in connection with the civil enforcement and affirmative defenses provisions, means an act or omission in which a **covered entity** or **business associate** knew, or by exercising reasonable diligence would have known, that the act or omission violated an **administrative simplification provision**, but in which the **covered entity** or **business associate** did not act with **willful neglect**.
[45 C.F.R. § 160.401.]

REASONABLE DILIGENCE

Reasonable diligence, in connection with the civil enforcement and affirmative defenses provisions, means the business care and prudence expected from a person seeking to satisfy a legal requirement under similar circumstances.
[45 C.F.R. § 160.401.]

REQUIRED BY LAW

Required by law means that a law contains a mandate compelling an entity to make a **use** or **disclosure** of **protected health information** and that the mandate is enforceable in a court of law. This includes, but is not limited to:

- Court orders and court-ordered warrants;

- Subpoenas or summons issued by a court, grand jury, a governmental or tribal inspector general, or an administrative body authorized to require the production of information;

- A civil or an authorized investigative demand;

- Medicare conditions of participation with respect to **health care providers** participating in the program; and

- Statutes or regulations that require the production of information, including statutes or regulations that require such information if **payment** is sought under a government program providing public benefits.

[45 C.F.R. § 164.103.]

RESEARCH

Research is a systematic investigation, including research development, testing, and evaluation, designed to develop or contribute to generalizable knowledge.
[45 C.F.R. § 164.501.]

SALE OF PHI

Sale of protected health information means a disclosure of protected health information by a covered entity or business associate, if applicable, where the covered entity or business associate directly or indirectly receives remuneration from or on behalf of the recipient of the protected health information in exchange for the protected health information.

Sale of protected health information does not, however, include a disclosure of protected health information:

(i) For public health purposes pursuant to 45 C.F.R. § 164.512(b) or § 164.514(e);

(ii) For research purposes pursuant to 45 C.F.R. § 164.512(i) or § 164.514(e), where the only remuneration received by the covered entity or business associate is a reasonable cost-based fee to cover the cost to prepare and transmit the protected health information for such purposes;

(iii) For treatment and payment purposes pursuant to 45 C.F.R. § 164.506(a);

(iv) For the sale, transfer, merger, or consolidation of all or part of the covered entity and for related due diligence as described in the definition of health care operations and pursuant to 45 C.F.R. § 164.506(a);

(v) To or by a business associate for activities that the business associate undertakes on behalf of a covered entity, or on behalf of a business associate in the case of a subcontractor, pursuant to 45 C.F.R. §§ 164.502(e) and 164.504(e), and the only remuneration provided is by the covered entity to the business associate, or by the business associate to the subcontractor, if applicable, for the performance of such activities;

(vi) To an individual, when requested under 45 C.F.R. § 164.524 or § 164.528;

(vii)   Required by law as permitted under 45 C.F.R. § 164.512(a); and

(viii) For any other purpose permitted by and in accordance with the applicable requirements of this sub-part, where the only remuneration received by the covered entity or business associate is a reasonable, cost-based fee to cover the cost to prepare and transmit the protected health information for such purpose or a fee otherwise expressly permitted by other law.

[45 C.F.R. § 164.502(a)(5)(ii).]

SECRETARY

References to the Secretary mean the Secretary of **HHS** or any other officer or employee of **HHS** to whom the authority involved has been delegated.
[45 C.F.R. § 160.103.]

SECURITY OR SECURITY MEASURES

Security or security measures mean all the **administrative**, **physical**, and **technical safeguards** in an **information system**.
[45 C.F.R. § 164.304.]

SECURITY INCIDENT

Security incident means the attempted or successful unauthorized **access**, **use**, **disclosure**, modification, or destruction of information or interference with system operations in an **information system**.
[45 C.F.R. § 164.304.]

SECURITY REGULATIONS OR SECURITY RULE

The Security Regulations are the regulations regarding security of **electronic protected health information** promulgated by **HHS** under **HIPAA and HITECH**. These regulations, along with the **Transaction Standards, Privacy Regulations, Breach Regulations**, and **Enforcement Regulations** make up the **Administrative Simplification** provisions of **HIPAA**.
[45 C.F.R. Part 160 and Part 164, subparts A and C.]

SMALL HEALTH PLAN

A small health plan is a **health plan** with annual receipts of $5 million or less.
[45 C.F.R. § 160.103.]

STANDARD

Standard means a rule, condition, or requirement (1) with respect to the privacy of PHI; or (2) describing the following information for products, systems, services, or practices: classification of components; specification of materials, performance, or operations; or delineation of procedures. **Operating rules** are not standards.
[45 C.F.R. § 160.103, as modified by Interim Final Regulations at 76 Fed. Reg. 40,495 (July 8, 2011).]

STANDARD TRANSACTION

A **covered transaction** that complies with the applicable standards and associated operating rules adopted under HIPAA.
[45 C.F.R. § 162.103, as modified by Interim Final Regulations at 76 Fed. Reg. 40,495 (July 8, 2011).]

STANDARD TRANSACTION REGULATIONS

Standards for the content and format of certain electronic transactions, including standard code sets and identifiers. These regulations, along with the **Privacy Regulations, Breach Regulations**, **Security Regulations,** and **Enforcement Regulations,** make up the **Administrative Simplification** provisions of **HIPAA**.
[45 C.F.R. Part 160 and Part 162.]

SUBCONTRACTOR

Subcontractor means a person to whom a **business associate** delegates a function, activity, or service, other than in the capacity of a member of the **workforce** of such **business associate**.
[45 C.F.R. § 160.103.]

SUMMARY HEALTH INFORMATION

Summary health information is information that may be **individually identifiable health information**, and (1) that summarizes the claims history, claims expenses, or type of claims experienced by individuals for whom a **plan sponsor** has provided health benefits under a **group health plan**, and (2) that has been de-identified by removing the identifiers listed in 45 C.F.R. § 164.514(b)(2), except that geographic data may be aggregated to the level of a 5-digit zip code.
[45 C.F.R. § 164.504.]

TECHNICAL SAFEGUARDS

Technical safeguards are the technology and the policy and procedures for its use that protect **electronic protected health information** and control **access** to it.
[45 C.F.R. § 164.304.]

TPO

TPO is shorthand for treatment, payment, or health care operations.

TRANSACTION

See Covered Transaction.

TREATMENT

Treatment is the provision, coordination, or management of **health care**and related services by one or more **health care providers**. It includes the coordination or management of **health care** by a **health care provider** with a third party, a consultation between **health care providers** relating to a patient, or the referral of a patient for **health care** from one **health care provider** to another.
[45 C.F.R. § 164.501.]

UNSECURED PROTECTED HEALTH INFORMATION

Unsecured protected health information means **protected health information** that is not rendered unusable, unreadable, or indecipherable to unauthorized persons through the use of a technology or methodology specified by the **Secretary** in the guidance issued under section 13402(h)(2) of HITECH.
[45 C.F.R. § 164.402.]

USE

Use means, with respect to **individually identifiable health information**, sharing, employing, applying, utilizing, examining, or analyzing such information within an entity (or, in a **hybrid entity**, a **health care component**) that maintains such information.
[45 C.F.R. § 160.103.]

USER

User is a person or entity with authorized **access** to **electronic protected health information**.
[45 C.F.R. § 164.304.]

VENDOR OF PERSONAL HEALTH RECORDS

A vendor of personal health records is an entity, other than a **covered entity** or **business associate**, that offers or maintains a **personal health record**.
[HITECH Act § 13400, as modified by 16 C.F.R. § 318.2.]

WILLFUL NEGLECT

Willful neglect means conscious, intentional failure or reckless indifference to the obligation to comply with the Administrative Simplification provision violated.
[45 C.F.R. § 160.401.]

WORKFORCE

Workforce means employees, volunteers, trainees, and other persons whose conduct, in the performance of work for a **covered entity** or **business associate**, is under the direct control of such **covered entity** or **business associate**, whether or not they are paid by the **covered entity or business associate**.
[45 C.F.R. § 160.103.]

WORKSTATION

Workstation is an electronic computing device, such as a laptop or desktop computer, or any other device that performs similar functions, and **electronic media** stored in its immediate environment.
[45 C.F.R. § 164.304.]

STATE-BY-STATE GUIDE TO MEDICAL PRIVACY STATUTES

¶ 10 Alabama

State	Health Care Privacy Statute/Provisions	Specific Disclosure Rules
ALABAMA	No general prohibition on disclosure of confidential medical information. Mental health patients have right of confidentiality of all information in mental health, medical, and financial records. Communications between mental health caregivers granted same status as attorney-client communications [Ala. Code §§ 34-26-2, 34-8A-21 (superseded in part by Ala. R. Evid. 503A), and 15-23-42].* An HMO may also claim privilege available to provider [Ala. Code § 27-21A-25]. Mental health patients have right to access records, absent clinical determination of detriment to health [Ala. Code § 22-56-4], but have no additional physician-patient privilege beyond general constitutional or statutory protections [Ala. Code § 22-56-10]. Health plans may not require genetic tests that show predisposition to cancer as condition of insurability, or use such tests to set premiums [Ala. Code § 27-53-2]. Recipients of drug test results or other related personal medical information must maintain that information in accordance with state and federal confidentiality laws [Ala. Code §§ 12-23A-5, 7, added by Act 2010-754]. Statewide trauma registry data are confidential pursuant to state and federal law [Ala. Code § 22-11-D(6), added by Act 2012-526]. Optometrists practicing telemedicine must provide notice of privacy practices consistent with HIPAA [Ala. Code § 34-22-83, amended by Act 2014-339].	• Apply to HMOs and utilization review agents [Ala. Code 27-3A-5] with exceptions. HMOs may not disclose health information without consent, except as necessary to carry out HMO legislation, to comply with court order, or when disclosure is pertinent to claim or litigation [Ala. Code § 27-21A-25]. • Apply to records of Board of Counseling Examiners concerning discipline of licensed counselors [Ala. Code § 34-8A-16, amended by Act 2010-545].* • Apply to specific medical conditions including information contained in reports submitted to statewide cancer or benign brain-related tumor registry, sexually transmitted diseases, and mandatory tuberculosis reports submitted to health agencies [Ala. Code §§ 22-13-33, 22-13-34, 22-11A-14, 22-11A-22, and 22-11A-9]. HIV test results for person charged with rape or sexual misconduct may not be disclosed to unauthorized persons [Ala. Code § 15-23-102, Act 2006-572]. • Affidavit of paternity is confidential record available in same manner as birth record [Ala. Code § 26-17-313, Act 2008-376].* Intentional unauthorized release of identifiable genetic specimen for purposes other than proceeding regarding parentage is misdemeanor [Ala. Code § 26-17-511, Act 2008-376].* • Power of attorney authorizes agent to act as principal's personal representative pursuant to HIPAA and applicable regulations [Ala. Code § 26-1A-213, Act 2011-683].

continues

State	Health Care Privacy Statute/Provisions	Specific Disclosure Rules
		• Board of Physical Therapy Wellness Committee records and proceedings pertaining to an impaired physical therapy licensee are confidential and usable only in the exercise of Committee's function and not available as public record, for court subpoena, or for discovery proceedings [Ala. Code § 34-24-193(e)(6), amended by Act 2012-387].* • A regional care organization of providers contracting with Medicaid must report all data as required by the Medicaid agency, consistent with the federal Health Insurance Portability and Accountability Act [Act No. 2013-261, § 2(g)]. • Access to minor's mental health records by parent or legal guardian follows HIPAA rules [Act 2015-476, Sec. 1].*

*Not limited to HIPAA-covered entities.

¶ 20 Alaska

State	Health Care Privacy Statute/Provisions	Specific Disclosure Rules
ALASKA	No general prohibition on disclosure of confidential medical information. Mental health records are confidential [Alaska Stat. §§ 47.30.590, 47.30.845], information maintained by a pharmacist in a patient record is confidential [Alaska Stat. § 08.80.315], and numerous health care provider-patient privileges exist [Alaska R. Evid. 504 and Alaska Stat. §§ 08.29.200, 08.63.200, 08.86.200, and 09.25.400]. Electronic medical records are allowed as long as the physical security of the records is protected from access by unauthorized persons [Alaska Stat. § 18.23.100]. Genetic tests may not be performed and the results may not be disclosed without the informed written consent of the person or person's representative [Alaska Stat. § 18.13.010, amended by 2004 Alaska Laws, ch. 176]. Standards to protect individually identifiable information contained in statewide electronic health information exchange must meet most stringent applicable federal and state privacy laws [Alaska Stat. § 18.23.310, added by 2009 Alaska Laws, ch. 24].	• Statute prohibiting HMOs from disclosing medical information about enrollees or applicants without consent, with exceptions for HMO legislation and court orders, repealed [Alaska Stat. § 21.86.280, repealed 2004 Alaska Laws, ch. 96, Sec. 53, effective June 5, 2004]. • Medical and financial information in possession of managed care entity regarding applicant or covered individual is confidential and is not subject to public disclosure. The provision does not apply to managed care entities [Alaska Stat. § 21.07.040, amended by 2004 Alaska Laws, ch. 96, Sec. 3, effective June 5, 2004]. • Data on birth defects, cancer, and infectious diseases that must be reported to the department of health are confidential, but Department of Health may use records for research [Alaska Stat. § 18.05.042].[*] • Medical records of patient who has been treated by emergency medical services (EMS) provider may be disclosed to that provider for purposes of evaluating performance of EMS personnel [Alaska Stat. § 18.08.087]. • Medical records held by public agencies are not subject to public inspection [Alaska Stat. § 40.25.120, amended by 2004 Alaska Laws, ch. 164, Sec. 4, effective July 24, 2004, and by 2007 Alaska Laws, ch. 22, Sec. 5, effective June 12, 2007].[*] • Medical records obtained for newborn and infant hearing screening by Department of Health and Social Services are confidential [Alaska Stat. § 47.20.320].[*] • Commissioner of Department of Health and Social Services shall adopt regulations establishing confidentiality and security standards for records received [Alaska Stat. § 18.05.040].[*] • Privacy of records in state controlled substance database must be maintained, with exceptions for board of pharmacy, licensed practitioners, pharmacists, law enforcement authorities, and individuals receiving controlled substance prescriptions [Alaska Stat. § 17.30.200, added by 2008 Alaska Laws, ch. 84, Sec. 2].[*]

continues

State	Health Care Privacy Statute/Provisions	Specific Disclosure Rules
		• Organ and anatomical gift procurement organization is allowed access to records to determine if decedent is donor; coroner or medical examiner may examine records relevant to anatomical gift from body over which either has jurisdiction [Alaska Stat. §§ 13.52.223, 13.52.257, amended by 2008 Alaska Laws, ch. 100, Sec. 1].*
		• Registry of patients and caregivers approved for medical marijuana use [Alaska Stat. § 17.37.010, amended by 2010 Alaska Laws, ch. 58].*
		• Disclosure of breach of security of personal information [Alaska Stat. § 45.48.010].*
		• Security standards for confidentiality of information in statewide electronic health information exchange system must meet most stringent applicable federal or state privacy law [Alaska Stat. § 18.23.310, added by 2009 Alaska Laws, ch. 24].
		• Board of Dental Examiners may inspect professional records of dentist to monitor compliance with licensing requirements [Alaska Stat. § 08.36.070, amended by 2012 Alaska Laws, ch. 53].*

*Not limited to HIPAA-covered entities.

¶ 30 Arizona

State	Health Care Privacy Statute/Provisions	Specific Disclosure Rules
ARIZONA	Medical records and the information they contain are confidential and privileged [Ariz. Rev. Stat. § 12-2292, amended by 2005 Ariz. Acts, ch. 0206, Sec. 1]. Privilege applies to physicians, dentists, hospitals, pharmacists, psychologists, health care service organizations, and others [Ariz. Rev. Stat. § 12-2291, amended by 2004 Ariz. Acts, ch. 191, Sec. 2]. Numerous health care provider-patient privileges exist [Ariz. Rev. Stat. §§ 12-2235, 32-2085, text repealed effective Jan. 1, 2011, and 38-3283, amended by 2006 Ariz. Acts, ch. 291, Sec. 1, text repealed effective Jan. 1, 2009]. Mental health records are confidential, with certain exceptions [Ariz. Rev. Stat. § 36-509, amended by 2005 Ariz. Acts, ch. 0206, Sec. 9]. Genetic test results are confidential [Ariz. Rev. Stat. § 12-2296, amended by 2011 Ariz. Acts, ch. 268, Sec. 3, and § 20-448.02]. Disclosure by insurers, including health care service organizations, of personal or privileged information about an individual collected or received in connection with an insurance transaction is restricted [Ariz. Rev. Stat. §§ 20-2101 to 20-2122]. A health professional must prepare a written protocol meeting specific requirements for the secure storage, transfer, and access of the medical records of the professional's patients [Ariz. Rev. Stat. § 32-3210, added by 2006 Ariz. Acts, ch. 236, Sec. 2].	• A provider may deny a request for access to medical records or payment records if access would likely cause substantial harm to the patient or another person, if the information was created or obtained in clinical research, consent to which included denial of access, or if the provider is a correctional institution [Ariz. Rev. Stat. § 12-2293, amended by 2012 Ariz. Acts, ch. 184, Sec. 1]. Providers may disclose medical records or payment records pursuant to written authorization signed by patient or patient's health care decision makers. Providers may disclose a patient's medical information without the patient's consent to: other current or previous health care providers for purposes of diagnosing or treating the patient; ambulance attendants providing care or transferring the patient; accrediting agencies; providers, for utilization review or peer review; billing, claims management or medical data processing entities; the provider's legal representative for securing legal advice; a deceased patient's administrator; third-party payors, with written authorization; the patient's health care decision maker, spouse, trustee, parent, guardian, adult child, or adult sibling at the time of the patient's death [Ariz. Rev. Stat. § 12-2294, amended by 2012 Ariz. Acts, ch. 184, Sec. 2]. • Medical records may be released to third parties pursuant to a subpoena when authorized by the patient or patient's health care decision maker, by court order, by a grand jury, by a health profession regulatory board, or when otherwise required by law. Providers may also deliver the records under seal under specified circumstances. A provider may not produce records pursuant to a subpoena that does not meet the statutory requirements, but must file the records under seal, object, or file a motion to quash or modify the subpoena [Ariz. Rev. Stat. § 12-2294.01, amended by 2005 Ariz. Acts, ch. 0206, Sec. 4].[*]

continues

State	Health Care Privacy Statute/Provisions	Specific Disclosure Rules
		• Insurance entities may disclose medical record information without the person's written authorization to prevent fraud or to verify insurance coverage; to conduct business when disclosure is reasonably necessary; to law enforcement agencies in situations involving fraud; under subpoena or court order; for marketing purposes, with certain restrictions. Disclosure is also authorized to a medical care institution or medical professional, with certain restrictions; to an insurance regulatory authority; for research purposes; to a party in connection with a sale or transfer of the insurer; to an affiliate, with certain restrictions; to a group insurance policyholder for claims review or audit; to a peer review organization; to a governmental authority for purposes of determining benefits eligibility; and to a policyholder regarding an insurance transaction [Ariz. Rev. Stat. § 20-2113].[*] • Mental health information may be disclosed to physicians and other providers treating or caring for the patient, individuals with consent of the patient, persons legally representing the patient, persons doing research or maintaining health statistics, in the case of prisoners, to the department of corrections, law enforcement to secure the return of patients absent without authorization, family members or persons participating in the patient's care, health care professional licensing agencies investigating malpractice claims; or pursuant to a court order. If the patient cannot object to disclosure because of incapacity or an emergency, the provider in the exercise of professional judgment may determine if disclosure is in the patient's best interests and may release the information. Disclosure may also be made to the patient's health care decision maker, to a third-party payer, or to an accreditation entity. Disclosure may also be made to the Department of Education or school district, a government agency, a properly appointed agent, human rights committees, and the Department of Public Safety [Ariz. Rev. Stat. § 36-509, amended by 2011 Ariz. Acts, ch. 268, Sec. 7].[*] • Cancer, birth defects, and other chronic diseases must be reported to the Department of Health Services to be used for certain limited purposes [Ariz. Rev. Stat. § 36-133].[*]

State	Health Care Privacy Statute/Provisions	Specific Disclosure Rules
		• Confidential HIV-related information obtained in processing insurance information may be disclosed only: to the protected person; to a person to whom disclosure is authorized in writing; to an authorized government agency; by court or administrative order; to the Industrial Commission for a claim [Ariz. Rev. Stat. § 20-448.01]. Similar restrictions apply to a person who obtains confidential communicable disease related information in the course of providing a health service. Confidential information may also be released if required by federal law, by the legal representative of the entity holding the information in order to secure legal advice, and for research in compliance with federal or state law [Ariz. Rev. Stat. § 36-664, amended by 2014 Ariz. Acts, ch. 222, Sec. 3].
		• A utilization review agent must file with the Insurance Director written procedures for assuring that patient information is maintained as confidential in accordance with applicable federal and state laws and is used solely for the purposes of utilization review and quality assurance [Ariz. Rev. Stat. § 20-2509].
		• Patient records kept by emergency medical service providers are confidential but must be available to the patient, the patient's guardian, or the patient's agent; prehospital incident history report is available to the public except for information protected from disclosure by state or federal law, including confidential patient treatment information [Ariz. Rev. Stat. § 32-2220, amended by 2012 Ariz. Acts, ch. 94].
		• Information obtained by Arizona health care cost containment system on insurer claims data reporting shall be maintained as confidential as required by HIPAA [Ariz. Rev. Stat. § 36-292, added by 2007 Ariz. Acts, ch. 263, Sec. 11].[*]
		• Board of Behavioral Health Examiners may establish confidential program for monitoring licensees who are chemically dependent and who enroll in qualified rehabilitation program [Ariz. Rev. Stat. § 32-3253, added by 2008 Ariz. Acts, ch. 134, Sec. 1].
		• Unprofessional conduct includes intentionally disclosing a professional secret or privileged communications [Ariz. Rev. Stat. § 32-1501, amended by 2008 Ariz. Acts, ch. 16, Sec. 1].[*]

continues

State	Health Care Privacy Statute/Provisions	Specific Disclosure Rules
		• Reports filed under uniform patient reporting system for hospital patient and emergency department services are public, but public access may not breach confidentiality of privileged medical information [Ariz. Rev. Stat.§ 36-125.05, amended by 2010 Ariz. Acts, ch. 36].
		• State may release child immunization records to a provider or associate subject to HIPAA confidentiality requirements [Ariz. Rev. Stat. § 36-135, amended by 2011 Ariz. Acts, ch. 268, Sec. 6].
		• Confidentiality exception created for entity providing services to provider under HIPAA confidentiality requirements [Ariz. Rev. Stat. § 36-364, amended by 2011 Ariz. Acts, ch. 268, Sec. 8].
		• Health information organizations may disclose individually identifiable health information in compliance with HIPAA privacy rules [Ariz. Rev. Stat. § 36-3805, added by 2011 Ariz. Acts, ch. 268, Sec. 9].
		• The result of a clinical laboratory test may be reported to a health care provider that has a treatment relationship with a patient, to a person or an entity that provides services to the provider and with whom the health care provider or the clinical laboratory has a business associate agreement that requires the person or entity to protect the confidentiality of patient information as required by HIPAA privacy standards, or to the patient or the patient's health care decision maker [Ariz. Rev. Stat. § 36-470, as amended by 2012 Ariz. Acts, ch. 184, Sec. 3].
		• Provision allowing religiously affiliated employer to exclude coverage for specific items or services because they are contrary to religious beliefs of employer offering health plan does not authorize a religiously affiliated employer to obtain an employee's protected health information or to violate HIPAA privacy rules [Ariz. Rev. Stat. §§ 20-826, 20-826AA, 20-1402N, 20-1404W, and 20-2329D, amended by 2012 Ariz. Acts, ch. 337 and 2014 Ariz. Acts ch. 215, Sec. 51].

State	Health Care Privacy Statute/Provisions	Specific Disclosure Rules
		• Person who has custody or control of medical records of a minor for whom a report of abuse, physical injury, neglect, and denial or deprivation of medical or surgical care or nourishment is required or authorized must make the records, or a copy, available to an investigating peace officer, child welfare investigator, or child protective services worker on a signed written request; records disclosed are confidential and may be used only in a judicial or administrative proceeding or investigation resulting from the report [Ariz. Rev. Stat. § 13-3620(G), amended by 2013 Ariz. Acts, ch. 5, Sec. 2].[*]
		• Medical examiner is entitled to all medical records of person for whom the medical examiner is required to certify cause of death [Ariz. Rev. Stat. § 11-594, amended by 2012 Ariz. Acts, ch. 60, Sec. 2].[*]
		• Controlled Substances Prescription Monitoring Program may release confidential prescription information to qualified hospital employee trained in HIPAA privacy standards [Ariz. Rev. Stat. § 36-2604, amended by 2014 Ariz. Acts, ch. 106, Sec. 1].

[*]Not limited to HIPAA-covered entities.

continues

¶ 40 Arkansas

State	Health Care Privacy Statute/Provisions	Specific Disclosure Rules
ARKANSAS	No general prohibition on disclosure of confidential medical information. Numerous health care provider-patient privileges exist [Ark. Rules of Evidence 503 (physician and psychotherapist-patient); Ark. Code Ann. §§ 17-27-311 (family therapist-client), 17-103-107 (social worker-client), and 17-97-105 (psychologist-patient)]; results of genetic research may not be disclosed without the subject's written consent [Ark. Code Ann. § 20-35-101 to 103, as amended by 2005 Ark. Act 1962]; Patient Medical Records Privacy Act requires that parties to litigation provide written notice of receipt of medical records to patient or patient's attorney [Ark. Code Ann. § 16-46-403, added by 2005 Ark. Act 1436, Sec. 1].* Authorization of public recording does not apply to the grounds of hospital or medical facility governed by HIPAA privacy rules [Ark. Code Ann. § 21-1-106, added by 2015 Act 1063, Sec. 1].	• HMOs may not disclose an enrollee's or applicant's medical information except as necessary to carry out the purposes of the HMO statute, with the person's express consent, pursuant to statute or court order, or a claim between the person and the HMO [Ark. Code Ann. § 23-76-129]. • State Hospital records and information compiled for purposes of mental health research and containing patient-identifying information may be used only for that purpose and may not be otherwise disclosed [Ark. Code Ann. § 20-46-104]. • Utilization review agents may not disclose confidential medical information obtained during UR activities without appropriate procedures for protecting the patient's confidentiality [Ark. Code Ann. § 20-9-913]. • Certain conditions must be reported to the state but must be treated as confidential by the facility, registry, or agency to whom reported, including actual or suspected cases of abuse or neglect of impaired adults [Ark. Code Ann. § 12-12-1717, amended by 2007 Ark. Act 283, Sec. 9],* cancer [§ 20-15-203], HIV/AIDS [§ 20-15-904], conditions reviewed for morbidity and mortality research [§ 20-9-304], trauma [§ 20-13-806, amended by 2009 Ark. Act 393], and venereal diseases [§ 20-16-504]. • Employers and insurers are prohibited from requiring genetic testing or using results of genetic tests as a condition of employment or insurance [Ark. Code Ann. §§ 11-5-403, 23-66-320].* • Department of Insurance privacy regulation restricts unauthorized disclosure of insurance consumer financial and health information [54 Code of Ark. R. & Regs. 074]. • Personal and medical information in public records may not be made public except on request of person records concern [Ark. Code Ann. § 14-14-110].* • Physician may release patient's medical records to guardian or attorney if disclosure would be detrimental to patient's health or well-being [Ark. Code Ann. § 16-46-106].

State	Health Care Privacy Statute/Provisions	Specific Disclosure Rules
		• Health Facility Infection Disclosure Act bars release of individually identifiable patient information [Ark. Code Ann. § 20-9-1206, added by 2007 Ark. Act 845, Sec. 1]. • Organ procurement organization may make a subsequent disclosure of the post-mortem examination results or other information received from the coroner or the state medical examiner only if relevant to transplantation or therapy [Ark. Code Ann. § 20-17-1222, amended by 2007 Ark. Act 839, Sec. 1]. • Records, including analyses, investigations, studies, reports, or recommendations, containing information relating to any Department of Health and Human Services risk or security assessment, known or suspected security vulnerability, or safeguard related to compliance with the Health Insurance Portability and Accountability Act or protection of other confidential Department information are confidential [Ark. Code Ann. § 25-19-105(b), added by 2007 Ark. Act 726, amended by 2009 Ark. Act 1291]. • Unsubstantiated child maltreatment report shall be confidential and shall be disclosed only to designated persons and entities. Any person or agency to whom disclosure is made shall not disclose to any other person [Ark. Code Ann. § 12-12-512(a), added by 2007 Ark. Act 284, Sec. 4].* • The Department of Human Services shall not release data that would identify person who made report to Child Abuse Hotline unless ordered by court, but information may be disclosed to law enforcement [Ark. Code Ann. § 12-18-502, amended by 2009 Ark. Act 749, Sec. 1].* • Information on a completed investigation of child abuse, including protected health information, pending due process shall be released upon request to: the alleged offender, the Department of Human Services, law enforcement, licensing authorities, facility directors, and legislators [Ark. Code Ann. § 12-18-710, amended by 2009 Ark. Act 749, Sec. 1].*

continues

State	Health Care Privacy Statute/Provisions	Specific Disclosure Rules
		• Records of children's advocacy centers are confidential, but may be released to attorney representing abused child, in authorized audit, to law enforcement, to licensing or registering authority, to grand jury, to court-appointed advocate, to Department of Human Services, or to person providing medical or psychiatric care to child [Ark. Code Ann. § 20-7-106, amended by 2009 Ark. Act 779].*
		• Reports, correspondence, memoranda, case histories, medical records, or other materials, including protected health information, compiled or gathered by the Department of Health and Human Services regarding a maltreated adult in the custody of the department or receiving protective services from the department shall be confidential and shall not be released or otherwise made available except to designated persons or entities. Except for maltreated adult, person or agency to whom disclosure is made may not disclose [Ark. Code Ann. § 9-20-121, added by 2007 Ark. Act 283]. Court may seal any records or parts of records concerning adult maltreatment and containing protected health information as defined by HIPAA [Ark. Code Ann. § 9-20-107, amended by 2009 Ark. Act 526].
		• Report of adult maltreatment that is determined to be founded, as well as any other information obtained, including protected health information, and a report written or photograph taken concerning a founded report in the possession of the Department of Health and Human Services shall be confidential and shall be made available only to designated persons or entities [Ark. Code Ann. § 12-12-1717, added by 2007 Ark. Act 283].
		• A screened out report or a pending report of adult maltreatment, including protected health information, shall be confidential and shall be made available only to designated persons or entities. Except for the subject of the report, no person or agency to which disclosure is made may disclose to any other person a report or other information obtained under this section [Ark. Code Ann. § 12-12-1718, amended by 2007 Ark. Act 283, Sec. 10].

State	Health Care Privacy Statute/Provisions	Specific Disclosure Rules
		• Data, records, reports, and documents collected or compiled by or on behalf of the Department of Health, the Trauma Advisory Council, or other authorized entity for the purpose of quality or system assessment and improvements must be treated in a manner consistent with all state and federal privacy requirements, including without limitation the HIPAA privacy rules [Ark. Code Ann. § 20-13-819, added by 2009 Ark. Act 393]. • Person who participates in the State Health Alliance for Records Exchange is not liable for damages that result solely from the person's use of or failure to use Exchange information or data imputed or retrieved under HIPAA and its regulations [Ark. Code Ann. § 25-42-106, added by 2011 Ark. Act 891]. • Power of attorney authorizes agent to act as principal's personal representative pursuant to HIPAA and applicable regulations [Ark. Code Ann. § 28-68-213, added by 2011 Ark. Act 805]. • Physician required to preserve fetal tissue extracted in abortion on child must redact protected health information as required by HIPAA privacy regulations before submitting tissue to state laboratory [Ark. Code Ann. § 12-18-108, added by 2013 Ark. Act. 725, Sec. 5]. • Arkansas Healthcare Quality and Payment Advisory Committee must treat data, records, reports, and documents in a manner consistent with state and federal privacy requirements, including HIPAA privacy requirements [Ark. Code Ann § 20-77-2107, added by 2013 Ark. Act 1266, Sec. 1]. • Arkansas Healthcare Transparency Initiative data is disclosable in manner that ensures privacy and security to insurers, employers, health care purchasers, researchers, state agencies, and providers; HIPAA notwithstanding, disclosed data may not include direct personal identifiers [26-61-907, added by 2015 Ark. Act 1233, Sec. 1].*

*Not limited to HIPAA-covered entities.

continues

¶ 50 California

State	Health Care Privacy Statute/Provisions	Specific Disclosure Rules
CALIFORNIA	The Confidentiality of Medical Information Act (CMIA) requires health care providers and employers to obtain written consent from patients before disclosing identifiable information, with numerous exceptions [Cal. Civ. Code § 56.10 exceptions applying to coroner's office added to this section as of Jan. 1, 2003]. Mental health information and records are confidential [Cal. Welf. & Inst. Code §§ 5328 (as amended to include exceptions for report of elder and dependent adult abuse effective Jan. 1, 2003) and 5540]. Privileges are recognized with respect to patients and their physicians, psychotherapists, psychologists, social workers, nurses, and sexual assault or domestic abuse counselors [Cal. Evid. Code §§ 990 through 1037.8]. Optometrists must comply with HIPAA and state law patient record protections [Cal. Bus. & Prof. Code § 3070.1, added by 2010 Cal. Stats. ch. 604]. The Office of Health Information Integrity in the California Health and Human Services Agency ensures the enforcement of California law mandating the confidentiality of medical information and imposes administrative fines for the unauthorized use of medical information; every provider of health care shall establish and implement appropriate administrative, technical, and physical safeguards to protect the privacy of a patient's medical information, and shall reasonably safeguard confidential medical information from any unauthorized access or unlawful access, use, or disclosure [Cal. Health & Saf. Code §§ 130200, 130203, added by 2008 Cal. Stats. ch. 602].	• Patient authorization for release of medical information is not required for disclosures related to the diagnosis, treatment, billing, emergencies, tissue transplants, licensing and accreditation, utilization review and quality assurance activities, pursuant to subpoenas or court orders, and other specified situations [Cal. Civ. Code § 56.10 (exceptions applying to coroner's office added to this section as of Jan. 1, 2003)]. • Exception to Confidentiality of Medical Information Act permits disclosure of medical information, consistent with applicable law and standards of ethical conduct, by a psychotherapist if the psychotherapist, in good faith, believes the disclosure is necessary to prevent or lessen a serious and imminent threat to the health or safety of a reasonably foreseeable victim or victims, and the disclosure is made to a person or persons reasonably able to prevent or lessen the threat, including the target of the threat [Cal. Civ. Code § 56.10(c)(19), amended by 2007 Cal. Stats. ch. 506, Sec. 1]. • Provider of health care may disclose medical information to a county social worker, a probation officer, or any other person who is legally authorized to have custody or care of a minor, as defined, for the purpose of coordinating health care services and medical treatment provided to the minor [Cal. Civ. Code §§ 56.10, 56.103, amended by 2007 Cal. Stats. ch. 552]. • Public guardian or a county's adult protective services agency, upon a showing of probable cause that a person is in substantial danger of abuse or neglect, may petition a court for orders in connection with an investigation of whether the appointment of the public guardian would be appropriate. These orders would provide for the authorized release of confidential medical information and financial information and would specify certain conditions to the release of medical information, including the obligation of the public guardian and adult protective services agency to keep information acquired under the order confidential [Cal. Civ. Code § 56.10, amended by 2007 Cal. Stats. ch. 553].[*]

State	Health Care Privacy Statute/Provisions	Specific Disclosure Rules
		• Providers and contractors may not disclose outpatient psychotherapy records without submitting a written request to the patient, except for disclosures made for the purpose of diagnosis or treatment [Cal. Civ. Code § 56.104, amended by 2013 Cal. Stats. ch. 444, Sec. 3].
		• A health care service plan (HMO) must file with the Director of the Department of Managed Health Care a copy of the plan's policies and procedures to protect the security of patient medical information to ensure compliance with the Confidentiality of Medical Information Act [Cal. Health & Safety Code § 1364.5].
		• Insurers need not obtain written authorization from patients before disclosing personal information to verify coverage or benefits, to inform a person of a medical problem, to detect fraud, or for marketing purposes, as long as no medical record or information about a person's character, personal habits, or reputation is disclosed subject to an opt-out provision [Cal. Ins. Code § 791.13].
		• An insurer may not disclose nonpublic personal medical record information about a consumer to affiliated or nonaffiliated third parties without the consumer's prior written authorization. The regulation does not prohibit disclosure of nonpublic personal medical record information as permitted by California Insurance Code Section 791.13 [Cal. Code Regs. tit. 10, § 2689.11].
		• Insurers and health plans must allow insured or enrollee to request confidential communication related to the receipt of sensitive services [Cal. Civil Code § 56.107; Cal. Health & Saf. Code § 1348.5; Cal. Ins. Code § 791.29; added by 2013 Cal. Stats. ch. 444, Secs. 4, 10, 18].
		• Various conditions must be reported to the state but must be treated as confidential by the agency, registry, or program that receives the report. Conditions include birth defects [Cal. Health & Safety Code § 103850], cancer [Cal. Health & Safety Code § 103885], and HIV/AIDS [Cal. Health & Safety Code §§ 120975 to 121022, 121024, amended by 2013 Cal. Stats. ch. 445]. Further disclosure of information on an HIV-positive person may be made by public health agency staff to the person or his or her provider, to the extent permitted by HIPAA [Cal. Health & Saf. Code § 121026, added by 2013 Cal. Stats. ch. 445].

continues

State	Health Care Privacy Statute/Provisions	Specific Disclosure Rules
		• Providers may obtain a patient's consent to post laboratory results by Internet posting or other electronic means. The results must be reviewed by the health care professional before posting, and access must be restricted by the use of a secure personal identification number [Cal. Health & Safety Code § 123148].
		• A health care provider choosing to utilize an electronic recordkeeping system must implement policies and procedures to include safeguards for confidentiality and unauthorized access to electronically stored patient health records, authentication by electronic signature keys, and systems maintenance [Cal. Health & Safety Code § 123149].
		• A person may not disclose genetic test results without written authorization [Cal. Ins. Code § 10149.1].[*]
		• Health practitioner who performs medical examination on a person in custody sought for commission or investigation of sexual assault must prepare a written report, subject to confidentiality requirements [Cal. Penal Code § 11160.1, added by 2005 Cal. Stats. ch. 133].
		• Hepatitis C screening of inmates is confidential [Cal. Penal Code § 5008.2, added by 2006 Cal. Stats. ch. 524].
		• Hearing loss tracking data on newborns is confidential [Cal. Health & Safety Code § 124119, amended by 2006 Cal. Stats. ch. 335, Sec. 4].
		• When patient refuses sharing of immunization information, physician may obtain it for purposes of patient care or protecting public health [Cal. Health & Safety Code § 120440, amended by 2006 Cal. Stats. ch. 329, Sec. 1].
		• Physician may release nonmedical information, including patient's name, address, age, sex, and general reason for treatment, to family or friends unless patient requests otherwise [Cal. Health & Safety Code § 56.1007; Cal. Health & Safety Code § 56.16, amended by 2013 Cal. Stats. ch. 444, Sec. 5].

State	Health Care Privacy Statute/Provisions	Specific Disclosure Rules
		• A clinic, health facility, home health agency, or hospice must prevent unlawful or unauthorized access to, and use or disclosure of, patients' medical information, and shall report any unlawful or unauthorized access to, or use or disclosure of, a patient's medical information to the Department of Health Care Services within five days, unless a law enforcement entity provides a statement that reporting would likely impede an investigation of the disclosure [Cal. Health & Safety Code § 1280.15, amended by 2010 Cal. Stats. ch. 501]. A clinic, health facility, home health agency, or hospice must delay reporting to affected patient or patient's representative unlawful or unauthorized access to, and use or disclosure of, patient's medical information beyond 5 business days if law enforcement agency or official states that compliance with that reporting requirement would impede agency's activities relating to the use or disclosure of patient's medical information [Cal. Health & Safety Code § 1280.15, amended by 2009 Cal. Stats. ch. 180].
		• Specialty mental health service contracts must require the entity awarded the contract to comply with all federal and state privacy laws, including HIPAA; the contract must prohibit the entity from using, selling, or disclosing client records for a purpose other than the one for which the record was given [Cal. Welf. & Inst. Code § 5778, added by 2008 Cal. Stats. ch. 320, Sec. 2].
		• For court-ordered involuntary blood tests, medical information regarding the HIV, hepatitis B, or hepatitis C status of the source patient shall be kept confidential and may not be further disclosed except as otherwise authorized by law [Cal. Health & Safety Code § 121065, amended by 2008 Cal. Stats. ch. 554].

continues

State	Health Care Privacy Statute/Provisions	Specific Disclosure Rules
		• Issuer of Medicare supplement contract must adhere to the requirements imposed by the federal Genetic Information Nondiscrimination Act of 2008 and may not request or require an individual or a family member of that individual to undergo a genetic test; the provision shall not be construed to preclude an issuer of a Medicare supplement contract from obtaining and using the results of a genetic test in making a determination regarding payment, as defined by HIPAA [Cal. Health & Safety Code § 1358.24, added by 2009 Cal. Stats. ch. 10].
		• Each provider of blood clotting products for home use shall comply with HIPAA privacy and confidentiality requirements [Cal. Health & Safety Code § 125286.25, amended by 2012 Cal. Stats. ch. 75].
		• Requirement that person or entity give notice of breach of confidentiality of unencrypted personal or medical information is deemed met if HIPAA-covered entity complies with HIPAA breach notification requirements [Cal. Civ. Code § 1798.82, amended by 2011 Cal. Stats. ch. 75].
		• Private entity conducting mental health services client record reviews for Department of Health Care Services must comply with state and federal privacy laws, including HIPAA [Cal. Welf. & Inst. Code § 5778, added by 2011 Cal. Stats. ch. 651].
		• Health plan and insurer contracts with provider may not restrict disclosure of claims data, but disclosure must comply with applicable privacy and data security law, including HIPAA [Cal. Health & Saf. Code § 1367.50, Cal. Ins. Code § 10117.52, added by 2012 Cal. Stats., ch. 869, Secs. 1-3].

*Not limited to HIPAA-covered entities.

¶ 60 Colorado

State	Health Care Privacy Statute/Provisions	Specific Disclosure Rules
COLORADO	No general prohibition on disclosure of confidential medical information. Restrictions on disclosure are found in statutes governing specific entities or conditions: psychologists, social workers, addiction counselors, and counselors [Colo. Rev. Stat. Ann. §§ 12-43-201 and 12-43-218, amended by 2011 Colo. Sess. Laws 285]; and HMOs [Colo. Rev. Stat. § 10-16-423]. Records and information regarding mental illness are confidential and privileged [Colo. Rev. Stat. Ann. § 27-10-120]. Licensed physical therapists must develop a written plan to ensure the security of patient medical records [Colo. Rev. Stat. Ann. § 12-41-115.5, added by 2011 Colo. Sess. Laws 172, Sec. 20]. Health care provider-patient privileges apply to physicians, surgeons, and registered nurses, and to psychologists, psychotherapists, social workers, professional counselors, and marriage and family therapists [Colo. Rev. Stat. Ann. § 13-90-107]. Disclosure provisions concerning health care cooperatives have been repealed [Former Colo. Rev. Stat. Ann. § 6-18-103, repealed effective Aug. 4, 2004].	• HMOs may disclose medical information as necessary to carry out the statutory provisions regarding HMOs, pursuant to statute or court order for production of evidence, or where there is a claim or litigation between a person and the HMO [Colo. Rev. Stat. Ann. § 10-16-423]. • Disclosure of genetic testing information without patient consent is allowed for diagnosis, treatment, or therapy and for scientific research if the test subject's identity is not released to a third party [Colo. Rev. Stat. Ann. § 10-3-1104.7]. • Health care professionals must report incidents of cancer, venereal and other communicable diseases, and cases of AIDS/HIV to health authorities, but such reports are strictly confidential and may not be released, shared with any agency or institution, or made public upon subpoena, discovery proceedings, or otherwise, except in limited circumstances [Colo. Rev. Stat. Ann. §§ 25-1-122, 25-4-402, 25-4-1404]. • Chiropractors may not disclose confidential communications made with patient in the course of the chiropractor's professional employment unless the patient gives his or her consent prior to the disclosure. Exceptions apply for consultations with another treating provider and for peer review [Colo. Rev. Stat. Ann. § 12-33-126]. • Insurers must implement a comprehensive written information security program that includes administrative, technical, and physical safeguards for the protection of consumer financial and health information. The safeguards included in the information security program must be appropriate to the size and complexity of the licensee and the nature and scope of its activities. The security program must be designed to: ensure the security and confidentiality of customer information; protect against any anticipated threats or hazards to the security or integrity of the information; and protect against unauthorized access to or use of the information that could result in substantial harm or inconvenience to any customer [3 Colo. Code Regs. § 702-6].

continues

State	Health Care Privacy Statute/Provisions	Specific Disclosure Rules
		• Immunization records may be released to the extent needed for the treatment, control, investigation, and prevention of vaccine-preventable diseases [Colo. Rev. Stat. Ann. § 25-4-2403, added by 2007 Colo. Sess. Laws 179, Sec. 6]. • All applicable confidentiality protections apply to telemedicine services, and the patient must have access to all medical information resulting from the services, as provided by applicable medical records access law [Colo. Rev. Stat. Ann. § 25.5-5-321, amended by 2007 Colo. Sess. Laws 282]. • Provider may not retaliate against health care worker for making a good faith disclosure, but provision does not grant immunity to worker for violation of state or federal patient confidentiality law [Colo. Rev. Stat. Ann. § 8-2-123, amended by 2007 Colo. Sess. Laws 67]. • Tuberculosis investigation records kept by Department of Public Health and Environment and local public health agencies shall be kept strictly confidential and shared only to extent necessary for investigation, treatment, and prevention, except that every effort shall be made to limit disclosure of personal identifying information to the minimal amount necessary to accomplish the public health purpose [Colo. Rev. Stat. Ann. § 25-4-511, amended by 2008 Colo. Sess. Laws 102]. • Assisted reproduction confidentiality rules amended to cover advanced practice nurse [Colo. Rev. Stat. Ann. § 19-4-106, amended by 2008 Colo. Sess. Laws 51]. • Licensed or certified addiction counselors subject to therapy confidentiality requirements, with exception for HIPAA covered entities [Colo. Rev. Stat. Ann. §§ 12-43-214, 12-43-218, amended by 2011 Colo. Sess. Laws 285]. • Department of Human Services and Department of Health Care Policy may share information but must comply with HIPAA privacy rules and Family Education Rights and Privacy Act of 1974 in Child Find activities to screen and evaluate children with disabilities [Colo. Rev. Stat. Ann. § 22-20-119, amended by 2007 Colo. Sess. Laws 360].

State	Health Care Privacy Statute/Provisions	Specific Disclosure Rules
		• Colorado Department of Public Health and the Environment must keep all medical records obtained during an inspection or investigation of a home care agency confidential, and the records are exempt from statutory disclosure as public records [Colo. Rev. Stat. Ann. § 25-27.5-105, amended by 2008 Colo. Sess. Laws 436].
		• A person who intentionally causes a peace officer, a firefighter, or an emergency medical technician to come into contact with blood, seminal fluid, urine, feces, saliva, mucus, vomit, or hazardous material may be ordered by court to submit to medical test for communicable disease, results of which shall be disclosed to victim on request; court review of test is closed and confidential [Colo. Rev. Stat. Ann. § 18-3-204, amended by 2009 Colo. Sess. Laws 305].*
		• Confidential registry of medical marijuana patients may be used to determine whether a physician should be referred to the Board of Medical Examiners [Colo. Rev. Stat. Ann. § 25-1.5-106, amended by 2010 Colo. Sess. Laws 356].
		• Release of medical records to person other than patient, and fees paid for release [Colo. Rev. Stat. Ann. §§ 25-1-801, 25-1-802, amended by 2014 Colo. Sess. Laws 124.
		• Emergency medical technicians, doctors, hospitals, nursing homes, pharmacies, home health agencies, health plans, and local health information agencies may engage in voluntary, secure, and confidential online exchange of forms containing advanced directives regarding a person's acceptance or rejection of life-sustaining medical or surgical treatment [Colo. Rev. Stat. Ann. § 25-1-1204, added by 2010 Colo. Sess. Laws 80].
		• Medical Treatment Decision Act declaration may include statement designating physician with whom provider may speak concerning life-sustaining procedures, and designation is deemed consistent with HIPAA privacy rules [Colo. Rev. Stat. Ann. § 15-18-104, added by 2010 Colo. Sess. Laws 113].

continues

State	Health Care Privacy Statute/Provisions	Specific Disclosure Rules
		• Electronic Prescription Drug Monitoring Program may answer queries on controlled substance prescription information to licensed pharmacists, law enforcement officials, state regulatory boards, and physicians [Colo. Rev. Stat. Ann. § 12-22-705, amended by 2011 Colo. Sess. Laws 230].
		• Medical Board, Nursing Board, and Department of Public Health and Environment shall not make further disclosures of peer review records disclosed by an authorized entity or its professional review committee; records of an authorized entity or its professional review Committee or governing board may be shared by and among authorized entities and their professional review committees and governing boards concerning the competence, professional conduct of, or the quality and appropriateness of patient care provided by a health care provider [Colo. Rev. Stat. Ann. § 1236.5104, amended by 2012 Colo. Sess. Laws, ch. 245].
		• Prescriptions, orders, and records are open for inspection only to federal, state, county, and municipal officers whose duty it is to enforce Colorado or federal law relating to controlled substances or the regulation of practitioners. Officer may not divulge his or her knowledge, except in connection with a prosecution or proceeding in court or before a licensing or registration board [Colo. Rev. Stat. Ann. § 27-80-212, formerly § 12-22-320, amended by 2012 Colo. Sess. Laws, ch. 281].
		• Prohibition against disclosure of mental health claims information by small group health plans repealed [Former Colo. Rev. Stat. Ann, § 10-16-104, repealed by 2013 Colo. Sess. Laws 38].
		• Restrictions on ability of government entity to access personal medical information [Colo. Rev. Stat. Ann. §§ 24-72-601, 24-72-603, amended by 2014 Colo. Sess. Laws 297].

*Not limited to HIPAA-covered entities.

¶ 70 Connecticut

State	Health Care Privacy Statute/Provisions	Specific Disclosure Rules
CONNECTICUT	No general prohibition on disclosure of confidential medical information. Specific prohibitions against disclosure apply to employers [Conn. Gen. Stat.§ 31-128f], insurance entities, including HMOs [Conn. Gen. Stat. §§ 38a-989 (technical amendments only, effective Oct. 1, 2002), 38a-976 (technical amendments only, effective Sept. 1, 2002), 38a-977], and pharmacists [Conn. Gen. Stat. § 20-626]. Health care provider-patient privileges exist for physicians, psychologists, psychiatrists, sexual assault counselors, and marital and family therapists [Conn. Gen. Stat. § 52-146b *et seq.*]. Board of Health Information Technology Exchange shall establish privacy standards no less stringent than those of HIPAA privacy rules [Conn. Gen. Stat. § 19a-750, amended by 2011 Conn. Pub. Acts 242]. Requirements for HIPAA authorization form to participate in pharmacy rewards program [Conn. Gen. Stat. § 20-633a, added by 2014 Conn. Pub. Acts 197].	• Insurers may not disclose personal or privileged information concerning an individual collected or received in connection with an insurance transaction unless the disclosure is made with the written authorization of the individual; reasonably necessary to enable a person to perform a business, professional, or insurance function for the disclosing insurance institution, or to provide information concerning eligibility or fraud; made to an insurance institution to detect criminal activity or for an insurance transaction involving the individual; made to a medical care institution or professional for the purpose of verifying coverage, informing an individual of a medical problem, or conducting an operations or services audit; made to an insurance regulatory authority; made to a law enforcement or other government authority; otherwise permitted or required by law; made in response to an administrative or judicial order; made for the purpose of conducting actuarial or research studies; made to a party for sale or transfer of the insurance institution; made to a person whose only use of such information will be in connection with the marketing of a product or service; made to an affiliate for auditing or marketing; made by a consumer reporting agency; made to a group policyholder for the purpose of reporting claims experience or conducting an audit; made to a peer review organization; made to a governmental authority for the purpose of determining the individual's eligibility for benefits; made to a certificate holder or policyholder for the purpose of providing information regarding the status of an insurance transaction; made to a lienholder, mortgagee, assignee, lessor, or other person with a legal or beneficial interest in a policy of insurance; or made pursuant to Section 53-445 [Conn. Gen. Stat. § 38a-988]. • Records of treatment of a patient's mental condition may be disclosed without the patient's consent to others involved in the patient's diagnosis or treatment; when there is a substantial risk of imminent physical injury by the patient to himself or herself or others; to place the patient in a mental health facility; and in other situations [Conn. Gen. Stat. § 52-146f].

continues

State	Health Care Privacy Statute/Provisions	Specific Disclosure Rules
		• Special disclosure rules apply to information obtained in connection with studies of morbidity and mortality [Conn. Gen. Stat. § 19a-25]; records of conception by artificial insemination [Conn. Gen. Stat. § 45a-773]; and HIV-related information [Conn. Gen. Stat. § 19a-583].[*]
		• Under an exception to the requirement that a provider give a patient records on request and notify the patient of test results indicating a need for further treatment, if the provider reasonably determines that the information is detrimental to the physical or mental health of the patient, or is likely to cause the patient to harm himself or another, the provider may withhold the information from the patient. The information may be supplied to an appropriate third party or to another provider who may release the information to the patient [Conn. Gen. Stat. § 20-7c].
		• Whenever a child is born who was conceived by the use of artificial insemination, the physician must file a statement with the probate court concerning the conception, and the statement may be disclosed only to the persons executing the consent, except upon order of the Probate Court for cause shown [Conn. Gen. Stat. § 45a-773].
		• Connecticut Health Information Network must adhere to strict confidentiality and privacy standards in creating Connecticut Community Health Data and Information Portal to provide access to public use datasets [Sen. Bill 1484, 2007 Conn. Pub. Acts 185].
		• Medical and health information on vital records of birth and fetal death must be recorded on the confidential portion of the record and may be used internally by the hospital for statistical and health and quality assurance purposes [Conn. Gen. Stat. § 7-48, amended by 2008 Conn. Pub. Acts 184].
		• Department of General Services mortality review process must operate in accordance with peer review provisions for medical review teams and confidentiality of records provisions [Conn. Gen. Stat. § 38a-395, 2008 Conn. Pub. Acts 42].

[*]Not limited to HIPAA-covered entities.

¶ 80 Delaware

State	Health Care Privacy Statute/Provisions	Specific Disclosure Rules
DELAWARE	No general statute protecting confidential medical information. Health care provider-patient privileges extended to physicians and psychotherapists [Del. Uniform Rules of Evidence, Rule 503], mental health counselors [Del. Code Ann. tit. 24, § 3017], and clinical social workers [Del. Code Ann. tit. 24, § 3913]. Mental health records are confidential, with certain exceptions [Del. Code Ann. tit. 16, § 5161]. Community mental health patient bill of rights includes confidential treatment of personal and medical records [Del. Code Ann. tit. 16, § 5192, added by 77 Del. Laws 387 (2010)]. Genetic information is confidential, with certain exceptions [Del. Code Ann. tit. 16, §§ 1201-1213, amended and renumbered by 78 Del. Laws 277 (2012)]. HIV-related test information may not be disclosed except as authorized [Del. Code Ann. tit. 16, § 717, amended and renumbered by 78 Del. Laws 277 (2012)]. New comprehensive statute restricts government use of protected health information to legitimate public health purposes, restricts its disclosure, and requires the information be expunged when its use no longer furthers the public health purpose [Del. Code Ann. tit. 16, §§ 1230, 1231, and 1232]. Requirements for safe destruction of documents containing personal identifying information exempt health insurer or health care facility that complies with HIPAA privacy standards [De. Code Ann. tit. 6, § 50c-104, added by 79 Del. Laws 287 (2014)].	• Managed care organizations (MCOs) may not disclose information about an enrollee's or applicant's diagnosis or treatment without the person's consent, except as required by statute, pursuant to court order, or in the case of a claim or litigation between the person and the MCO [Del. Code Ann. tit. 18, § 6412, amended by 75 Del. Laws 362 (2001)]. • Clinical social workers may disclose information obtained from a client without written consent in cases of threatened imminent violence, suspected child abuse, or if the person brings charges against the social worker [Del. Code Ann. tit. 24, § 3913].[*] • HIV test results may be disclosed without the subject's written consent to a health facility that procures, processes, or distributes blood [Del. Code Ann. tit. 16, § 717, amended and renumbered by 78 Del. Laws 277 (2012)]. Insurers are subject to specific laws governing HIV-related information [see Del. Code Ann. tit. 18, §§ 7404-7405]. • Hospitals and nursing homes must submit forms for all inpatient discharges to the state's health information database, which is confidential [Del. Code Ann. tit. 16, § 2001]. • Cancer cases must be reported to a state registry that may exchange information with cancer control agencies, preventing patients' confidentiality [Del. Code Ann. tit. 16, §§ 3202 and 3205]. • Birth defects must be reported to the Department of Health and Social Services. The reports of a birth defect may not be divulged or made public in any way that might tend to disclose the identity of the person or family of the person to whom it relates. However, patient identifying information may be exchanged among authorized agencies as approved by the Department and upon receipt by the Department of satisfactory assurances by those agencies of the preservation of the confidentiality of such information [Del. Code Ann. tit. 16, § 204].

continues

State	*Health Care Privacy Statute/Provisions*	*Specific Disclosure Rules*
		• Information pertaining to the diagnosis, treatment, or health of any enrollee obtained by a dental plan organization from the enrollee or any dentist shall be confidential and shall not be disclosed to any person except to the extent necessary to carry out the purposes of the dental plan laws, or with the consent of the enrollee, or pursuant to statute or court order. A dental plan organization may claim any statutory privileges against disclosure that the dentist who furnished the information is entitled to claim [Del. Code Ann. tit. 18, § 3820].
		• Insurers, including HMOs, are subject to the Privacy of Consumer Financial and Health Information regulation governing the treatment of nonpublic personal financial information about individuals by all licensees of the state insurance department. The regulation requires a licensee to provide notice to individuals about its privacy policies and practices; describes the conditions under which a licensee may disclose nonpublic personal financial information about individuals to affiliates and nonaffiliated third parties; and provides methods for individuals to prevent a licensee from disclosing that information [Del. Admin. Code tit. 18, § 904].
		• Physicians have a duty to report a willful violation of the confidential relationship or confidential communications of a patient [Del. Code Ann. tit. 24, § 1730].
		• Persons to whom data is submitted in accordance with newborn and infant screening requirements must keep the information confidential [Del. Code Ann. tit. 16, § 806A, added by 75 Del. Laws 116 (2005)].[*]
		• Agent of Board of Pharmacy may inspect pharmacy or place where drugs are manufactured, packaged, stocked, distributed, dispensed, or sold—all information gathered in inspection is to be kept confidential in accordance with state and federal privacy laws [Del. Code Ann. tit. 24, § 2534, amended by 76 Del. Laws 167 (2007)].

State	Health Care Privacy Statute/Provisions	Specific Disclosure Rules
		• Hospital infection data are privileged and not generally disclosable in legal or administrative proceedings—express intent of legislature is that patient's right of confidentiality shall not be violated, and patient, Social Security numbers, and any other identifiable patient information shall not be released, notwithstanding any other provision of law [Del. Code Ann. tit. 16, §§ 1006A, 1010A, amended by 76 Del. Laws 122 (2007)].
		• Department of Health and Social Services may require health insurer to provide eligibility and coverage information, and health insurer that provides data required by the Department, whether confidential or not, may not be held liable for providing the information to the Department or the Department's use of the information [Del. Code Ann. tit. 18, § 4005, amended by 76 Del. Laws 190 (2008)].
		• Person authorized under power of attorney to determine that principal is incapacitated may act as principal's personal representative pursuant to HIPAA [Del. Code Ann. tit. 49A § 109, amended by 77 Del. Laws 467 (2010)].
		• Records of the Emergency Medical Services for Children Advisory Committee and its quality care review committee and members are confidential and protected from discovery, subpoena, or admission into evidence in a judicial or administrative proceeding [Del. Code Ann. tit. 16, § 9707, amended by 78 Del. Laws 326 (2012)].
		• Department of Insurance may address competitive, trade secret, or health privacy concerns that arise from mandatory collection of carrier-specific workers' compensation insurance data [Del. Code Ann. tit. 19, § 2301E, amended by 78 Del. Laws 55, Sec. 1].

*Not limited to HIPAA-covered entities.

continues

¶ 90 District of Columbia

State	Health Care Privacy Statute/Provisions	Specific Disclosure Rules
DISTRICT OF COLUMBIA	No general prohibition on disclosure of medical information. Specific provisions against disclosure apply to certain entities [D.C. Code Ann. § 31-3426 (HMOs)] or medical conditions [D.C. Code Ann. § 31-1606 (AIDS testing)]. Disclosures of mental health information are prohibited [D.C. Code Ann. § 7-1201.01 *et seq.*]. Health care provider-patient privileges exist for physicians and mental health professionals [D.C. Code Ann. §§ 14-307, 7-1201.01 *et seq.*].	• HMOs may disclose medical information without consent to carry out the laws governing HMOs; where there is a claim or litigation between a person and the HMO; as needed to conduct business; and pursuant to statute or court order [D.C. Code Ann. § 31-3426]. • The amount and type of mental health information a provider may disclose to a third-party payor is limited, regardless of a valid authorization to disclose [D.C. Code Ann. § 7-1202.07]. Such information may also be disclosed as necessary to facilitate treatment; as required by law; in an emergency to a person's spouse, parent, guardian, police officer, or an intended victim; for scientific research or management or financial audits; and in certain court proceedings [D.C. Code Ann. §§ 7-1203.01 through 7-1203.06, 7-1204.01 through 7-1204.05]. • Mandatory cancer and communicable disease reports may be used only for statistical and public health purposes, and identifying information may be disclosed without written permission or a court order only if essential to protect the physical health of others [D.C. Code Ann. §§ 7-131, 7-302, 7-1605].[*] • With certain exceptions, insurers may not disclose nonpublic personal information about a consumer to a nonaffiliated third party unless the insurer has provided to the consumer an initial notice; the insurer has provided to the consumer an opt-out notice; the insurer has given the consumer a reasonable opportunity to opt out of the disclosure; and the consumer does not opt out [D.C. Regs. tit. 26, §§ 3600–3612]. • Mental health information and other protected health information concerning applicants for public assistance is privileged and confidential and may be disclosed only when the applicant consents or for specified purposes [D.C. Code Ann. § 4-209.04, amended by D.C. Act 16-63 of 2006].

State	Health Care Privacy Statute/Provisions	Specific Disclosure Rules
		• Organ procurement organization may acquire and use donor information from all available sources—personally identifiable information on the registry about a donor or prospective donor may not be used or disclosed without the express consent of the donor, prospective donor, or person that made the anatomical gift for any purpose other than to determine whether the donor or prospective donor has made, amended, or revoked an anatomical gift [Uniform Anatomical Gift Revision Act of 2008, D.C. Act 17-311 of 2008, Sec. 20b].
		• AIDS and HIV report records may be used for statistical and public health purposes only [D.C. Code Ann. § 7-1605, amended by D.C. Act 18-530 of 2010].

*Not limited to HIPAA-covered entities.

continues

¶ 100 Florida

State	Health Care Privacy Statute/Provisions	Specific Disclosure Rules
FLORIDA	Patients have a general right to privacy in health care [Fla. Stat. Ann. § 381.026]. A patient's records are confidential and may not be disclosed without written consent, nor may his or her medical condition be discussed with anyone other than the patient, his or her representative, or other providers involved in his or her care and treatment, with certain exceptions [Fla. Stat. Ann. § 456.057, amended by 2013 Fla. Laws, ch. 108]. There are numerous laws protecting the confidentiality of medical information held by various entities [e.g., Fla. Stat. Ann. §§ 400.022, 400.145 (nursing homes)] and government agencies [e.g., Fla. Stat. Ann. § 408.061 (Agency for Health Care Administration)]. Provider-patient privileges exist for psychotherapists and psychiatrists [Fla. Stat. Ann. §§ 90.503, 490.0147, 456.059].	• Health care providers may furnish records without patient consent as provided by law; pursuant to subpoena; for statistical or scientific research, if the patient's identity is protected. Providers may disclose medical information only to other providers involved in the patient's care; pursuant to subpoena and to the Health Department [Fla. Stat. Ann. § 456.057, amended by 2013 Fla. Laws, ch. 108], and to research groups and government agencies conducting morbidity and mortality studies [Fla. Stat. Ann. § 405.01]. • Insurers and HMOs may not disclose information regarding psychotherapeutic services, and such medical records are not subject to audit by the Insurance Department, but may be subpoenaed [Fla. Stat. Ann. §§ 627.4195, 641.59, 641.27, 636.039]. • Providers and facilities must maintain a record of all disclosures to a third party, including the purpose of the disclosure request, and keep it in the medical record [Fla. Stat. Ann. § 456.057, as amended by 2013 Fla. Laws, ch. 108]. • Hospitals may disclose patient records without patient consent to facility personnel and physicians in connection with the patient's treatment; for administrative, risk management and quality assurance or cost containment purposes; pursuant to subpoena; to organ procurement entities and tissue and eye banks; and to state agencies and entities as required by law [Fla. Stat. Ann. § 395.3025]. • Other specific disclosure rules apply to HIV testing [Fla. Stat. Ann. §§ 381.004, as amended by 2012 Fla. Laws, ch. 184; 456.061; 627.429; and 641.3007]; reportable and sexually transmitted diseases [Fla. Stat. Ann. §§ 381.0031; 119.07, as amended by 2005 Fla. Laws, ch. 251; and 384.29]; HIV tests [Fla. Stat. Ann. § 381.004, amended by 2012 Fla. Laws, ch. 184]; and substance abuse [Fla. Stat. Ann. § 397.501].

State	*Health Care Privacy Statute/Provisions*	*Specific Disclosure Rules*

- Unless waived by express and informed consent, the confidential status of clinical mental health records shall not be lost by either authorized or unauthorized disclosure to any person, organization, or agency. Release of the records is permitted when authorized by the patient or guardian, by the patient's counsel, by court order, or when the patient is committed and the committing agency requests the records. Information may also be disclosed in other circumstances, including when the patient has declared an intention to harm others [Fla. Stat. Ann. § 394.4615].

- Except for purposes of criminal prosecution, except for purposes of determining paternity, and except for purposes of acquiring specimens from persons convicted of certain offenses, DNA analysis may be performed only with the informed consent of the person to be tested. The results of such DNA analysis, whether held by a public or private entity, are the exclusive property of the person tested, are confidential, and may not be disclosed without the consent of the person tested [Fla. Stat. Ann. § 760.40, as amended by 2005 Fla. Laws, ch. 39].[*]

- Subject to specific exceptions, an insurer may not disclose nonpublic personal health information about a consumer or customer unless an authorization is obtained from the consumer or customer whose nonpublic personal health information is sought to be disclosed. The exceptions allow the insurer to use the information for insurance functions, including claims administration; claims adjustment and management; fraud investigations; underwriting; policy issuance; loss control; ratemaking; reinsurance; risk management; case management; disease management; quality assurance; peer review; research; grievance procedures; and other insurance activities, including those specifically authorized by the Department of Insurance [Fla. Admin. Code §§ 69J-128.001 through 696-128.025].

continues

State	Health Care Privacy Statute/Provisions	Specific Disclosure Rules
		• The Patients' Right-to-Know About Adverse Medical Incidents Act gives patients the right to have access to any records made or received in the course of business by a health care facility or health care provider relating to any adverse medical incident. In providing access to these records, the health care facility or health care provider may not disclose the identity of patients involved in the incidents and must maintain any privacy restrictions imposed by federal law [Fla. Stat. Ann. § 381.028, amended by 2007 Fla. Laws, ch. 5, Sec. 75].
		• Autopsy photographs and recordings are confidential but may be viewed by a surviving spouse, parent, or child [Fla. Stat. Ann. § 406.135, amended by 2006 Fla. Laws, ch. 263, Sec. 1].*
		• Provider who becomes aware through treatment-related blood test that person injured in motor vehicle crash has blood alcohol content above limit may notify law enforcement [Fla. Stat. Ann. § 316.1932, amended by 2006 Fla. Laws, ch. 247].
		• Information on medical facilities may be disclosed to a state or federal agency in order to prevent terrorism [Fla. Stat. Ann. § 381.95, amended by 2006 Fla. Laws, ch. 108].
		• A pharmacist administering influenza virus immunizations shall maintain and make available patient records using the same standards for confidentiality and maintenance of such records as those that are imposed on health care practitioners under § 456.057. These records shall be maintained for a minimum of 5 years [Fla. Stat. Ann. § 465.189, amended by 2007 Fla. Laws, ch. 152].
		• For purposes of reporting adverse medical incidents, "Privacy restrictions imposed by federal law" means the provisions relating to the disclosure of patient privacy information under federal law, including, but not limited to, the Health Insurance Portability and Accountability Act of 1996 (HIPAA), Pub. L. No. 104-191104-91, and its implementing regulations, the Federal Privacy Act, 5 U.S.C. § 552(a), and its implementing regulations, and any other federal law, including, but not limited to, federal common law and decisional law, that would prohibit the disclosure of patient privacy information [Fla. Stat. Ann. § 381.028, amended by 2007 Fla. Laws, ch. 5].

State	Health Care Privacy Statute/Provisions	Specific Disclosure Rules
		• Organ and tissue donor registry information that identifies a donor is confidential, but may be disclosed to procurement organizations [Fla. Stat. Ann. § 65.51551, added by 2008 Fla. Laws, ch. 222].
		• Medical information in foster parent application is exempt from disclosure as public record [Fla. Stat. Ann. § 409.175, amended by 2008 Fla. Laws, ch. 169].[*]
		• On receipt of HIPAA-compliant request, nursing home must furnish to competent resident or authorized representative copies of medical records [Fla. Stat. Ann. § 400.145, amended by 2014 Fla. Laws, ch. 83].
		• Nursing home adverse incident reports are confidential and not discoverable or admissible in civil or administrative proceedings except disciplinary hearings or regulatory board proceedings [Fla. Stat. Ann. § 400.147, amended by 2012 Fla. Laws, ch. 160].
		• Department of Health electronic database system has controlled substance prescriptions provided to it and provides prescription information to patient's health care practitioner and pharmacist who inform the Department that they wish the patient advisory report provided to them. The system must comply with HIPAA and all other relevant state and federal privacy and security laws and regulations. A pharmacy, prescriber, or dispenser may access the database for the purpose of reviewing the patient's controlled substance prescription history. Other access to the program's database is limited to the program's manager and staff [Fla. Stat. Ann. § 893.055, added by 2009 Fla. Laws, ch. 198, amended by 2011 Fla. Laws, ch. 141, and by 2011 Fla. Laws, ch. 5].
		• As a condition of Medicaid eligibility, Agency for Health Care Administration must ensure that Medicaid recipients consent to release of medical records to Agency and Medicaid Fraud Control Unit [Fla. Stat. Ann. § 409.963, added by 2011 Fla. Laws, ch. 134].

continues

State	Health Care Privacy Statute/Provisions	Specific Disclosure Rules
		• Prospective malpractice defendant or legal representative may interview the claimant's treating health care providers consistent with the authorization for release of protected health information, but provision does not require provider to submit to interview request [Fla. Stat. Ann. § 766.106, amended by 2013 Fla. Laws, ch. 108, Sec. 3]; statutory form authorizing release of protected health information shall be construed in accordance with HIPAA regulations [Fla. Stat. Ann. § 766.1065, amended by 2013 Fla. Laws, ch. 108, Sec. 4].

* Not limited to HIPAA-covered entities.

¶ 110 Georgia

State	Health Care Privacy Statute/Provisions	Specific Disclosure Rules
GEORGIA	No general prohibition on disclosure of confidential medical information. Specific prohibitions against disclosure apply to various entities and medical conditions, e.g., HMOs and insurance entities [Ga. Code §§ 33-21-23 and 33-39-14], information provided to research groups [Ga. Code § 31-7-6], and genetic testing [Ga. Code § 33-54-3]. There is no statutory physician-patient privilege, but there is a privilege extended to patients of psychiatrists, psychologists, clinical social workers, and marriage counselors [Ga. Code § 24-9-21]. A prescription drug order from a practitioner to a pharmacist is highly confidential and may not be compromised by unauthorized interventions [Ga. Code § 26-4-80, amended by 2006 Ga. Laws 588]. Georgia Drugs and Narcotics Agency must establish procedures to ensure privacy and confidentiality, and prescription information may be disclosed only in a manner that does not conflict with HIPAA requirements [Ga. Code § 16-30-60, added by 2011 Ga. Laws 229]. Identity of required report of abortion made to Department of Public Health is confidential [Ga. Code § 31-9B-3, amended by 2012 Ga. Laws 631]. Public Health and Alzheimer's Disease Registry established and regulated pursuant to patient confidentiality requirement of HIPAA [Ga. Code § 31-2A-16, added by 2014 Ga. Laws 646].	• HMOs may disclose enrollee or applicant medical information as necessary to carry out the law governing HMOs, pursuant to court order or statute, or in the event of claim or litigation by the person against the HMO [Ga. Code § 33-21-23]. • An insurance entity may disclose medical information without authorization to verify coverage benefits to a provider; as necessary to conduct the insurer's business; to law enforcement agencies, to prevent or prosecute fraud; pursuant to subpoena or search warrant [Ga. Code § 33-39-14]. • Physicians, pharmacists, hospitals, and health care facilities are required to release patient medical information to the Department of Human Resources as necessary for public health programs; where authorized or required by law; and pursuant to court order or subpoena [Ga. Code § 24-9-40]. • Specific disclosure rules apply to the records of patients in mental facilities [Ga. Code § 37-3-166], and to HIV status [Ga. Code § 24-9-47]. • The state health department may declare certain diseases, injuries, and conditions to be diseases requiring notice and to require reporting to the county board of health and the department. All such reports and data are deemed confidential, but the department may release such reports and data in statistical form or for valid research purposes. A health care provider, coroner, or medical examiner must report all known or presumptively diagnosed cases of persons harboring any illness or health condition that may be caused by bioterrorism, epidemic or pandemic disease, or novel and highly fatal infectious agents or toxins and that may pose a substantial risk of a public health emergency [Ga. Code § 31-12-2]. • Any medical information concerning a patient that was obtained by or released to an insurer from a pharmacy or pharmacist is confidential and privileged and may be released by the insurer to a third party for consideration only if such release is specifically authorized by the patient [Ga. Code § 33-24-59.4].

continues

State	Health Care Privacy Statute/Provisions	Specific Disclosure Rules
		• Insurers must comply with applicable state laws governing the collection, use, and disclosure of information gathered in connection with insurance transaction, and must also comply with Title V of the Gramm-Leach-Bliley Act (15 U.S.C. 6801*et seq.*) and other applicable federal laws to the extent said federal laws set forth standards that are either in addition to, or stricter than, the consumer protections in Georgia law [Ga. Admin. Comp. R. & Regs. Ch. 120-2-87-.04].
		• Ombudsman has authority to enter long-term care facility and view medical and social records of resident, with permission of resident or guardian, or when there is reason to believe guardian is not acting in resident's best interests [Ga. Code § 31-8-55, amended by 2007 Ga. Laws 48, Sec. 11].*
		• Office of Disability Services Ombudsmen may disclose confidential clinical records and protected health information as provided in code, protects confidential records and protected health information against further disclosure, and ensures compliance with HIPAA privacy rules [Ga. Code § 37-2-34, amended by 2008 Ga. Laws 418].
		• Provider must furnish complete and current copy of medical record to patient upon written request from patient or authorized party [Ga. Code § 31-33-2, amended by 2006 Ga. Laws 608, Sec. 2].
		• Disability services ombudsman may obtain but not further disclose confidential clinical records and protected health information, and ensures Department of Human Resources' compliance with HIPAA [Ga. Code § 37-2-34, amended by 2008 Ga. Laws 418].
		• Office of the Child Advocate for the Protection of Children is bound by all confidentiality safeguards provided in Georgia Code Sections 49-5-40 and 49-5-44. Records concerning child abuse or neglect received from the child abuse and neglect registry of any other state shall not be disclosed or used externally for any purpose other than conducting background checks to be used in foster care and adoptive placements [Ga. Code § 15-11-174, amended by 2007 Ga. Laws 248].*

State	Health Care Privacy Statute/Provisions	Specific Disclosure Rules
		• Requirement that hospital identified as primary stroke center annually report patient information shall not be construed to require disclosure of any confidential information or other data in violation of HIPAA [Ga. Code § 31-11-116, amended by 2008 Ga. Laws 772].
		• Health care agent in advance directive for health care is patient's personal representative for all purposes of federal or state law related to privacy of medical records, including HIPAA, and will have same access to medical records as patient and can disclose contents of records to others for patient's ongoing health care [Ga. § 31-32-4, amended by 2007 Ga. Laws 48].
		• Georgia Revised Uniform Anatomical Gift Act allows examination of medical and dental records of donor or prospective donor, and authorizes medical examiner to review medical records of decedent at request of procurement organization [Ga. Code §§ 44-5-152, 44-5-159.2, amended by 2008 Ga. Laws 545].
		• Law enforcement officers and medical examiners investigating deaths that may be result of medications administered or prescribed by a pain management clinic may send records to Georgia Composite Medical Board; records are confidential and may not be disclosed without Board's approval [Ga. Code § 43-34-290, added by 2013 Ga. Laws 128].*

* Not limited to HIPAA-covered entities.

continues

¶ 120 Hawaii

State	Health Care Privacy Statute/Provisions	Specific Disclosure Rules
HAWAII	Hawaii no longer has a general, comprehensive law prohibiting disclosure of private medical information. There are numerous laws concerning disclosure of medical information possessed by various entities [Haw. Rev. Stat. §§ 432D-21 (HMOs), 432E-10 (Managed Care Plans), 328-16 (Practitioners and Pharmacists), 329-104, amended by 2006 Haw. Sess. Laws 69 (Administrator of Electronic Prescription Accountability System), 334B-5 (Utilization Review Agents)]. State agencies are covered under the Uniform Information Practices Act [Haw. Rev. Stat.§ 92F-1 *et seq.*]. There are a number of health provider-patient privileges, applying to physicians, psychologists, and other counselors—subject to newly enacted exceptions for certain proceedings [Haw. Rev. Stat. Ann. § 626-1, amended by 2006 Haw. Sess. Laws 73, Haw. R. of Evid. 504, 504.1, 505.5]. Medical records may be destroyed after seven-year retention period or after minification in a manner that will preserve the confidentiality of the information [Haw. Rev. Stat. § 622-58]. Clinical laboratory test results may be provided to authorized person for any purpose permitted under HIPAA and applicable regulations [Haw. Rev. Stat. § 321-6.5, added by 2010 Haw. Sess. Laws 72]. HIPAA covered entities and their business associates that use or disclose health information in a manner permitted by and consistent with HIPAA's Privacy Rules are deemed to be acting in compliance with state privacy laws and regulations [Haw. Health Care Privacy Harmonization Act, Haw. Rev. Stat. § 323B1-4]. A person authorized by power of attorney to determine that principal is incapacitated may act as HIPAA personal representative to access health care information and communicate with provider [Haw. Rev. Stat. § ____-5, added by 2014 Haw. Acts. 22].	• Specific disclosure rules apply to HIV/AIDS status [Haw. Rev. Stat. Ann. § 325-101, amended by 2009 Haw. Acts. 11], cancer [Haw. Rev. Stat. Ann. § 324-22], communicable diseases [Haw. Rev. Stat. Ann. § 325-4], and mental health and mental retardation [Haw. Rev. Stat. Ann. §§ 324-12 and 324-13]. Insurers and HMOs may not require or disclose genetic information, subject to exceptions [Haw. Rev. Stat. §§ 431:10A-101, 431:10A-118, 432D-26]. • Records, and reports made for the purposes of treating mental health, mental illness, drug addiction, and alcoholism that are maintained, used, or disclosed by health care providers, health plans, or health care clearinghouses, and directly or indirectly identifying a person subject hereto, shall be kept confidential and shall not be disclosed except as allowed by HIPAA privacy rules; nothing in this section precludes application of more restrictive federal rules relating to confidentiality of alcohol and drug abuse patient records, or disclosure deemed necessary under the federal Protection and Advocacy for Mentally Ill Individuals Act of 1986, Public Law 99-319, to protect and advocate the rights of persons with mental illness who reside in facilities providing treatment or care [Haw. Rev. Stat. § 334-5, amended by 2014 Haw. Acts 214]. • For mental health treatment, disclosure of a person's treatment summary from a previous five year period from one provider to another may be deemed necessary for the purpose of continued care and treatment of the person, or for health care operations; provided that the health care provider seeking disclosure makes reasonable efforts to obtain advance consent from the person [Haw. Rev. Stat. § 334-1, amended by 2008 Haw. Acts 98, Sec. 1]. Nothing in the section governing confidentiality of mental health records shall preclude the application of more restrictive rules of confidentiality set forth for records covered by HIPAA relating to the confidentiality of alcohol and drug abuse patient records [Haw. Rev. Stat. § 334-5, amended by 2008 Haw. Acts 98, Sec. 2].

State	Health Care Privacy Statute/Provisions	Specific Disclosure Rules
		• Substance abuse on-site screening test information is confidential and may not be released without written informed consent of person being tested, except that it may be disclosed to the individual, a third party, the laboratory, and the decision maker in a proceeding initiated by or on behalf of the individual tested and arising from the test result [Haw. Rev. Stat. § 329B-5.5, amended by 2007 Haw. Acts 179].
		• A utilization review agent may not disclose individual medical or psychological records or any other confidential medical or psychological information obtained in the performance of utilization review or managed care activities [Haw. Rev. Stat. § 334B-5].
		• Except as otherwise authorized, an insurer may not disclose, directly or through any affiliate, any nonpublic personal financial information about a consumer to a nonaffiliated third party unless: the insurer has provided an initial notice and opt-out notice, the consumer has had the chance to opt out, and the consumer has not opted out [Haw. Rev. Stat. § 431:3A-301].
		• Administrator of state's Electronic Prescription Accountability System may not disclose information to the public, but may disclose to state personnel, law enforcement, and pharmacists [Haw. Rev. Stat. § 329-104, amended by 2006 Haw. Sess. Laws 69].
		• Health plan or provider that complies with HIPAA privacy and security standards is deemed to be in compliance with statute requiring notification of security breaches [Haw. Rev. Stat. § 487N-2, added by 2006 Haw. Acts. 135].
		• DNA samples, DNA profiles, and other forensic identification information collected by the Department of the Attorney General are exempt from public record disclosure provisions and may be released only to law enforcement agencies and to the person's defense counsel [Haw. Rev. Stat. § 844D-82].
		• Mental health counselor and associates may not be required to disclose information acquired in rendering mental health services, except as required by law, to prevent clear and imminent danger to a person or persons, in accordance with a waiver, or pursuant to a subpoena [Haw. Rev. Stat. § 453D-13].

continues

State	Health Care Privacy Statute/Provisions	Specific Disclosure Rules
		• Minor without support receiving primary medical care or services from a managed care plan may request that information regarding claims not be submitted to a spouse, parent, custodian, or guardian, and the plan may accommodate confidentiality requests of the minor by providing alternative services or services at alternative locations [2007 Haw. Acts 35]. • Medical records resulting from telemedicine services are part of a patient's health record, shall be made available to the patient, and shall be maintained in compliance with applicable state and federal requirements [Haw. Rev. Stat. § 453-1.3, added by 2009 Haw. Acts, ch. 20]. • Clinical laboratory test results may be provided to authorized persons for any purpose permitted under HIPAA and federal regulations promulgated thereunder; "authorized persons" include the provider ordering the test, or the provider's designee; and any HIPAA covered entity [Haw. Rev. Stats. § 321, added by 2010 Haw. Acts, ch. 72]. • Business may scan machine-readable zone of individual's Hawaii identification card or driver's license for purpose of recording, retaining, or transmitting information for a HIPAA-covered entity. [Haw. Rev. Stat. § 487J-6, amended by 2013 Haw. Acts 195].*

* Not limited to HIPAA-covered entities.

¶ 130 Idaho

State	Health Care Privacy Statute/Provisions	Specific Disclosure Rules
IDAHO	No general prohibition on disclosure of medical information. Privacy protections are contained in statutes governing specific medical conditions or entities. Grounds for medical discipline include failure of licensed provider to safeguard confidentiality of medical records or other medical information pertaining to identifiable patients [Idaho Code § 54-1814, amended by 2013 Idaho Sess. Laws 252]. Records of persons in mental facilities or assisted-living facilities are confidential [Idaho Code §§ 39-3315 and 39-3316]. A number of health care provider-patient privileges exist [Idaho Code §§ 9-203(4) (physician-patient); 54-2314 (psychologist-client); and 54-3410 (professional counselor-client)]. Information in the Time-Sensitive Emergency (TSE) Registry is confidential [Idaho Code 57-2006, amended by 2014 Idaho Sess. Laws 147].	• Alcohol and drug treatment facilities may make records available for research into treatment of substance abuse; researchers may not publish their information in a manner that identifies any patient [Idaho Code § 39-308].[*] • Cancer registry information may be exchanged with other states' registries, federal cancer control programs or health researchers [Idaho Code § 57-1706]. • Physicians and nursing homes must report suspected cases of abuse or neglect of vulnerable adults [Idaho Code § 39-5303]. • Specific disclosure rules apply to persons being treated for HIV/AIDS and venereal diseases [Idaho Code §§ 39-602 through 39-606]. • An exemption from disclosure applies to public records of hospital care, medical records, including prescriptions, drug orders, records, or any other prescription information that specifically identifies an individual patient, prescription records, records of psychiatric care or treatment and professional counseling, except as needed for background checks required by federal firearms laws [Idaho Code § 9-340C, amended by 2011 Idaho Sess. Laws 151 and 283]. • Managed care organizations performing utilization management must adopt procedures that protect the confidentiality of patient health records. The procedures may permit the organization to record a telephone conversation in the course of requesting patient medical information only if it complies with existing state and federal laws and the other party to the conversation is notified that he is being recorded [Idaho Code § 41-3930]. • Chiropractors may be disciplined for failure to safeguard the confidentiality of chiropractic records or other chiropractic information pertaining to identifiable clients, except as required or authorized by law [Idaho Code § 54-712].

continues

State	Health Care Privacy Statute/Provisions	Specific Disclosure Rules
		• Pharmacists must hold all prescriptions, drug orders, records or any other prescription information that specifically identifies an individual patient in the strictest confidence. No person in possession of such information shall release the information, unless requested by the Board of Pharmacy, the patient, the prescribing practitioner, a treating professional, authorized government representatives, or law enforcement authorities [Idaho Code § 54-1727, amended by 2007 Idaho Sess. Laws 140].
		• Acupuncturists may be disciplined for failing to maintain the confidentiality of records or other information pertaining to an identifiable client, except as required or authorized by law [Idaho Code § 54-4711, amended by 2007 Idaho Sess. Laws 220].
		• State mental health hospitals must keep all certificates, applications, records, and reports identifying a patient or former patient or an individual whose involuntary assessment, detention, or commitment is being sought. Such records may also be disclosed with the consent of the patient or attorney, if needed to carry out provisions of mental health treatment legislation, or if directed by a court [Idaho Code § 66-348].
		• Insurers are required under Privacy of Consumer Financial Information regulations to maintain a privacy policy that is clearly communicated to customers and, under certain circumstances to consumers, and that, subject to appropriate exceptions, no "nonpublic personal information" be disclosed to nonaffiliated third parties unless a consumer has been given a chance to "opt out" of having his information disclosed [IDAPA 18.01.48.001].
		• Durable power of attorney authorizes agent to release medical records and information governed by HIPAA [Idaho Code § 39-4510, amended by 2012 Idaho Sess. Laws 302].

State	Health Care Privacy Statute/Provisions	Specific Disclosure Rules
		• Physician may consent to blood or fluid testing of patient or deceased person for blood-transmitted or fluid-transmitted viruses or diseases if emergency or medical personnel have likely been exposed or if the patient is unconscious and incapable of informed consent. Protocols shall be established by hospitals to maintain confidentiality while disseminating the necessary test result information to persons who may have a significant exposure to blood or other body fluids and to maintain records of such tests to preserve the confidentiality of the test results. Hospitals must maintain confidentiality of the test results [Idaho Code § 39-4505, amended by 2007 Idaho Sess. Laws 196].
		• For purposes of external review, health care carrier must provide authorization form by which person covered by insurance authorizes health carrier and providers to disclose protected health information [Idaho Code § 41-5905, amended by 2009 Idaho Sess. Laws 87].
		• Licensed midwife or applicant for licensure may not disregard a client's dignity or right to privacy as to her person, condition, possessions, or medical record [Idaho Code § 54-5410, amended by 2009 Idaho Sess. Laws 65].[*]
		• Guardian of incapacitated person may give consents or approval for medical or professional care, and is automatically entitled to information governed by HIPAA [Idaho Code § 15-5-312, amended by 2014 Idaho Sess. Laws ch. 164].

[*] Not limited to HIPAA-covered entities.

continues

¶ 140 Illinois

State	Health Care Privacy Statute/Provisions	Specific Disclosure Rules
ILLINOIS	A patient's right to privacy and confidentiality in health care extends to information in the possession of physicians, medical providers, health services corporations, and insurers, including HMOs. The nature or details of services provided to a patient cannot be disclosed without written authorization [410 Ill. Comp. Stat. 50/3(d)]. A health care provider-patient privilege extends to a patient and his or her physician, surgeon, psychologist, nurse, mental health worker, therapist, and others, with certain exceptions [735 Ill. Comp. Stat. 5/8-802]. AIDS confidentiality laws restrict disclosure of HIV test results to health authorities, authorized health providers, and others [410 Ill. Comp. Stat. 305/9, amended by 2014 Ill. Laws 98-1046]. Insurance Commissioner must ensure confidentiality of claims for medical services submitted electronically, and adopt standards consistent with HIPAA and state law [820 Ill. Comp. Stat. 305/8.2a, added by 2011 Ill. Laws 97-18].	• Providers may disclose medical information without authorization to persons directly involved in treating the patient or processing payment for treatment; persons performing peer review or quality assurance functions; authorities in suspected child abuse or neglect cases, or incidences of sexually transmitted disease; or as otherwise required by law [410 Ill. Comp. Stat. 50/3(d)]. • Insurers and HMOs may disclose medical record information without authorization; to a medical professional to verify insurance benefits; to agents when necessary to conduct business; to law enforcement agencies, to prevent or prosecute fraud; and pursuant to search warrant or subpoena [215 Ill. Comp. Stat. 5/1014]. • Freedom of information rules do not permit disclosure of information in public records when disclosure would constitute a clearly unwarranted invasion of personal privacy, unless the subject consents to disclosure in writing [5 Ill. Comp. Stat. § 140/7, amended by 2005 Ill. Laws 94-280].[*] • Insurers must comply with Gramm-Leach-Bliley Act provisions concerning disclosure of personal information, including notice and "opt-out" provisions [Ill. Admin. Reg. tit. 50 §§ 4002.10 to 4002.240].[*] • Other specific disclosure rules apply to genetic testing [410 Ill. Comp. Stat. 513/15 and 513/30, amended by 2014 Ill. Laws 98-1046]; HIV/AIDS test results [410 Ill. Comp. 305/9, as amended by 2014 Ill. Laws. 98-1046]; mental health and developmental disabilities [740 Ill. Comp. Stat. 110/3, 110/5 through 110/14]; alcohol or drug abuse treatment programs [20 Ill. Comp. Stat. § 301/30-5]; cancer and hazardous substances treatment registry [410 Ill. Comp. Stat. § 525/4]; and sexually transmitted diseases [410 Ill. Comp. Stat. 325/8]. • After a mandatory report has been filed with the Department of Professional Regulation, an attorney seeking to recover damages for malpractice must provide patient records related to the physician involved in the disciplinary proceeding to the Department. Consent by the patient is not required for this disclosure [226 Ill. Comp. Stat. 60/24, amended by 2005 Ill. Laws 94-677; section scheduled to be repealed January 1, 2007].

State	Health Care Privacy Statute/Provisions	Specific Disclosure Rules
		• Anatomical gift donee may disclose test results confirming HIV exposure of gift only to donor's physician, who shall decide whether to notify person who executed gift [755 Ill. Comp. Stat. 50/5-45, amended by 2006 Ill. Laws 94-920].
		• Subject of HIV test or authorized representative shall be notified by personal contact whenever possible of the confirmed positive result of test. A health care provider is not in violation of this Section when an attempt to contact the test subject or representative at the address or telephone number provided does not result in contact and notification or where an attempt to deliver results by personal contact has not been successful [410 Ill. Comp. Stat. 305/9.5, amended by 2014 Ill. Laws 98-1046].
		• Mental health records of abused adult with disabilities are confidential [20 Ill. Comp. Stat. 2435/59, added by 2006 Ill. Laws 94-851].
		• Department of public health shall establish a network of human cord blood stem cell banks, which must establish a system of strict confidentiality to protect the identity and privacy of patients and donors in accordance with existing federal and state law and consistent with regulations promulgated under HIPAA for release of the identity of donors, the identity of recipients, or identifiable records. Bank must also have adequate systems for communication with other cord blood stem cell banks, transplant centers, and physicians with respect to the request, release, and distribution of cord blood units nationally, consistent with HIPAA, to track recipients' clinical outcomes for distributed units [20 Ill. Comp. Stat. 2310/2310-577, added by 2007 Ill. Laws 95-406].
		• Upon request of the reimbursing insurer, the provider under whose supervision habilitative services for children are being provided shall furnish medical records, clinical notes, or other necessary data to allow the insurer to substantiate that initial or continued medical treatment is medically necessary and that the patient's condition is clinically improving [Ill. Comp. Stat. 356z.14, amended by 2009 Ill. Laws 95-1049].

continues

State	Health Care Privacy Statute/Provisions	Specific Disclosure Rules
		• An entity that provides health insurance coverage under the Illinois Children's Health Insurance Program shall provide health insurance data match to the Department of Healthcare and Family Services for the purpose of determining eligibility for the Program. The Department of Healthcare and Family Services, in collaboration with the Department of Financial and Professional Regulation, Division of Insurance, shall adopt rules governing the exchange of information consistent with all laws relating to the confidentiality or privacy of personal information or medical records, including provisions under the federal HIPAA [215 Ill. Comp. Stat. 170/20; amended by 2014 Ill. Laws 98-651, to be repealed July 1, 2016].
		• Agent designated in power of attorney for health care has same access as principal to medical records and information governed by HIPAA and applicable regulations [755 Ill. Comp. Stat. 45/4-10, amended by 2014 Ill. Laws 98-1113].
		• Information collected by Department of Professional and Financial Regulation on wholesale drug distribution licensee or applicant is confidential and disclosable only to law enforcement officials, regulatory agencies, or the party presenting the subpoena [225 Ill. Comp. Stat. 120/173, added by 2012 Ill. Laws 97-804].*

* Not limited to HIPAA-covered entities.

¶ 150 Indiana

State	Health Care Privacy Statute/Provisions	Specific Disclosure Rules
INDIANA	No general prohibition on disclosure of confidential medical information. A number of health care provider-patient privileges exist: physician-patient [Ind. Code § 34-46-3-1]; psychologist-client [Ind. Code § 25-33-1-17]; social worker-client [Ind. Code § 25-23-6-6-1]; victim counselor-client [Ind. Code § 35-37-6-9]. Telehealth services must use secure technology that complies with HIPAA [Ind. Code § 25-22.5-14, added by 2014 Ind. Acts 1258].	• Health care providers are the owners of a patient's original health record and may use it without patient consent for legitimate business purposes, including submission of claims for payment from third parties, collection of accounts, litigation defense, quality assurance and peer review, and scientific, statistical and educational purposes [Ind. Code § 16-39-5-3]. • HMOs may access an enrollee's treatment records and other medical information during the time the person is covered by the HMO, and may disclose information as necessary to carry out the law governing HMOs, pursuant to statute or court order, or for litigation defense [Ind. Code § 27-13-31-1]. • Insurers may not disclose any nonpublic personal information about a consumer without complying with notice requirements and giving the consumer the opportunity to opt out of the disclosure [Ind. Admin. Reg. tit. 760 IAC 1-67-5 to 20]. • A provider may obtain a patient's health records from another provider without the patient's consent if the health records are needed to provide health care services to the patient [Ind. Code § 16-39-5-1]. • A patient's mental health record is confidential and shall be disclosed only with the consent of the patient except in specified circumstances [Ind. Code § 16-39-2-3]. • A utilization review agent must protect the confidentiality of the medical records of covered individuals [Ind. Code § 27-8-17-11]. • Hospital medical staff committees may access patient records for research, to gather statistics concerning prevention and treatment of diseases, and to reduce morbidity and mortality, but may not reveal patients' identity [Ind. Code § 16-39-6-1].

continues

State	Health Care Privacy Statute/Provisions	Specific Disclosure Rules
		• Other specific disclosure rules apply to pharmacists [Ind. Code § 25-26-13-15, Ind. Code § 25-26-16-3, amended by 2011 Ind. Acts 197]; the state cancer registry [Ind. Code §§ 16-38-2-1 through 16-38-2-7]; birth problems registry [Ind. Code §§ 16-38-4-1, 16-38-4-10, 16-38-4-11]; Department of Correction medical, psychiatric, or psychological data [Ind. Code § 11-8-5-2, amended by 2006 Ind. Acts. 12, 1155]; alcohol and drug abuse records [Ind. Code § 16-39-1-9]; HIV test results [Ind. Code § 16-41-6-1, amended by 2011 Ind. Acts 112]; and communicable disease reporting [Ind. Code §§ 16-41-2-1 and 16-41-8-1, amended by 2005 Ind. Acts 538].
		• Information that could be used to identify an opioid treatment program patient is confidential [Ind. Code §§ 12-23-18-5.6 and 12-23-18-5.7, amended by 2008 Ind. Acts 157].
		• The Health Informatics Corporation's plan to create the statewide health information exchange system must provide for procedures and security policies to ensure the following: compliance with HIPAA, protection of information privacy, and use of the information in the statewide health information exchange system only in accordance with HIPAA [Ind. Code § 5-31, added by 2007 Ind. Acts 111, ch. 6, Sec. 3; repealed effective July 1, 2012, by 2012 Ind. Acts 133, Sec. 50].
		• Requirement that database owner disclose security breach to person whose personal information may have been acquired by unauthorized person does not apply to a data-base owner that maintains its own data security procedures as part of an information privacy, security policy, or compliance plan under the federal Health Insurance Portability and Accountability Act (HIPAA) [Ind. Code § 24-4.9-2-2, amended by 2009 Ind. Acts 1121].[*]
		• Court may order proceeding closed during testimony of child witness or child victim if court finds that the testimony involves matters that would be protected under Health Insurance Portability and Accountability Act (HIPAA)

State	Health Care Privacy Statute/Provisions	Specific Disclosure Rules
		[Ind. Code § 31-32-6-4, amended by 2009 Ind. Acts 1210]. • Prehospital ambulance rescue or report record regarding an emergency patient that is utilized or compiled by an emergency ambulance service shall remain confidential and may be used solely for the purpose of compiling data and statistics [Ind. Code § 16-31-2-11, amended by 2012 Ind. Acts 1186].

*Not limited to HIPAA-covered entities.

continues

¶ 160 Iowa

State	*Health Care Privacy Statute/Provisions*	*Specific Disclosure Rules*
IOWA	Hospital records, medical records, and professional counselor records of the diagnosis, care, or treatment of a patient are confidential [Iowa Code § 22.7, amended by 2007 Iowa Acts 140, 202, 333, and 559]. A health care provider-patient privilege exists that extends to physicians, counselors, surgeons, physician's assistants, advanced registered nurse practitioners, mental health professionals, and their patients [Iowa Code § 622.10, amended by 2007 Iowa Acts 74]. Peer review reports are confidential [Iowa Code § 147.135, amended by 2007 Iowa Acts 74]. HIV status of provider is confidential [Iowa Code § 139a.8, amended by 2007 Iowa Acts 74]. Independent review organization must have quality assurance mechanism that ensures the confidentiality of medical and treatment records [Iowa Code § 514J-112, added by 2011 Iowa Acts 597]. Department of Public Health shall implement appropriate security standards, policies, and procedures to protect the transmission and receipt of protected health information exchanged through the Iowa Health Information Network, which shall, at a minimum, comply with the HIPAA security rule [Iowa Code § 135.156E, added by 2012 Iowa Acts 2318, amended by 2015 Iowa Acts 381].	• Apply to third-party payors (such as insurers) or peer review organizations with respect to mental health information [Iowa Code § 228.7]. • Apply to providers of mental health services [Iowa Code §§ 228.2 through 228.8]. • Apply to specific medical conditions including brain injury reports to the public health department [Iowa Code § 135.22]; communicable diseases [Iowa Code §§ 22.7(16) and 139A.3, amended by 2006 Iowa Acts 2322]; HIV status [Iowa Code §§ 141A.5 and 141A.11, amended by 2006 Iowa Acts 2543 and 2007 Iowa Acts 610]; and birth defects [Iowa Code § 136A.6]. • Apply to chemical and substance abuse treatment program records [Iowa Code § 125.37]. • Apply to HIV-related testing and records [Iowa Code § 141A.9, amended by 2007 Iowa Acts 610]. • A health maintenance organization is prohibited from releasing the names of its membership list of enrollees except to the extent necessary to HMO legislation or to conduct research or analyses regarding cost or quality issues [Iowa Code § 514B.30]. • Insurers may not disclose nonpublic personal health information about a consumer or customer unless an authorization is obtained from the consumer or customer [Iowa Admin. Code § 191 IAC 90.17(505)]. • Hospital or provider may release information to anatomical gift procurement organization as part of a referral or retrospective review of the patient as a potential donor, but information regarding the patient is confidential medical information that may not be disclosed without consent [Iowa Code § 142C.7, amended by 2007 Iowa Acts 509]. • A pharmacist, pharmacy, or prescribing practitioner who knowingly fails to comply with the confidentiality requirements or who delegates program information access to another individual is subject to disciplinary action by the appropriate professional licensing board [Iowa Code § 124.558, amended by 2007 Acts 333].

State	Health Care Privacy Statute/Provisions	Specific Disclosure Rules
		• The Iowa Department of Public Safety shall prescribe the form used when a law enforcement agency desires notification from a facility or hospital prior to discharge of a person admitted to the facility or hospital and for whom an arrest warrant has been issued or against whom charges are pending; the form must be consistent with all laws, regulations, and rules relating to the confidentiality or privacy of personal information or medical records, including HIPAA and its regulations [Iowa Code § 229.22, enacted March 24, 2010].
		• A patient shall have the opportunity to decline exchange of the patient's health information through the Iowa Health Information Network [Iowa Code § 135.156E, added by 2012 Iowa Acts 2318, amended by 2015 Iowa Acts 381]. A participant in the Iowa Health Information Network shall not release or use protected health information exchanged through the network for purposes unrelated to prevention, treatment, payment, or health care operations unless otherwise authorized or required by state or federal law; participants must limit use and disclosure in compliance with HIPAA privacy rules [Iowa Code § 135.156E(5), amended by 2012 Iowa Acts 1080, Sec. 14 and 2015 Iowa Acts 381].
		• Person authorized by principal in power of attorney may act as personal representative pursuant to HIPAA [Iowa Code § 633B.109, amended by 2014 Iowa Acts 2168, Sec. 11].

continues

¶ 170 Kansas

State	Health Care Privacy Statute/Provisions	Specific Disclosure Rules
KANSAS	No general prohibition on disclosure of confidential medical information. Privacy is addressed in statutes governing specific entities, such as HMOs [Kan. Stat. Ann. § 40-3226(a)], or medical conditions, such as sickle cell anemia [Kan. Stat. Ann. §§ 65-1,106]. Numerous health care provider-patient privileges exist [Kan. Stat. Ann. §§ 60-427 (physician-patient); 65-1654 (pharmacist-patient); 65-5601 and 65-5602 (mental health treatment personnel-patient); 65-5810 (professional counselor-client); 74-5323 and 74-5372 (psychologist-patient)].	• HMOs may disclose enrollee or applicant medical information as necessary to carry out the law governing HMOs, or as otherwise provided by law [Kan. Stat. Ann. § 40-3226(a)]. • Specific disclosure rules apply to utilization review organizations [Kan. Stat. Ann. §§ 40-22a09 and 40-22a10]. • Medical, psychiatric, psychological, or alcoholism or drug dependency treatment records that pertain to identifiable patients are not available under the state's public records law [Kan. Stat. Ann. § 45-221, amended by 2004 Kan. Acts, ch. 171, Sec. 30]. • Insurers are subject to the National Association of Insurance Commissioners' "Privacy of Consumer Financial And Health Information Regulation," which, with exceptions, is incorporated by reference in the insurance regulations [Kan. Admin. Regs. § 40-1-46].[*] • Specific disclosure rules apply to alcohol and substance abuse treatment records [Kan. Stat. Ann. § 59-29b79, amended by 2007 Kan. Acts H.B. 2528]; mental health patients [Kan. Stat. Ann. §§ 65-5601 through 65-5603, amended by 2005 Kan. Sess. Laws, ch. 27 and ch. 160]; HIV/AIDS status [Kan. Stat. Ann. § 65-6002]; and reporting of contagious diseases [Kan. Stat. Ann. §§ 65-118 and 65-119]. • Kansas Health Policy Authority Inspector General has access to confidential records of Authority facilities and personnel [added by 2007 Kan. Acts S.B. 11, Sec. 15]. • Information and records in State Board of Pharmacy prescription monitoring program database are privileged and confidential, and Board must maintain procedure to ensure that privacy and confidentiality of patients and patient information are maintained, except for disclosures for purposes of the Prescription Monitoring Act or Uniformed Controlled Substances Act [Kan. Stat. Ann. § 65-4101, amended by 2008 Kan. Acts S.B. 491].

State	Health Care Privacy Statute/Provisions	Specific Disclosure Rules
		• Office of Inspector General in Department of Health and Environment has access to confidential information of Department's contractors and health care providers and federal and state agencies that is necessary for Office to perform its duties. Inspector General and employees are subject to duty of confidentiality with respect to information [Kan. Stat. Ann. § 75-7427, amended by 2012 Kan. Acts H.B. 2416].[*]
		• HIPAA-covered entity must provide individual with access to his or her protected health information and also safeguard information from unauthorized disclosure, and may disclose information to state agency for public health purpose required by law, consistent with HIPAA privacy rules [Kan. Stat. Ann. §§ 65-6823-65-6829, amended by 2012 Kan. Acts, H.B. 2103].
		• Health plan predetermination of health care benefits request and response must meet HIPAA privacy standards. [Not yet codified, enacted by 2014 Kan. Acts A.B. 2668].

[*] Not limited to HIPAA-covered entities.

continues

¶ 180 Kentucky

State	Health Care Privacy Statute/Provisions	Specific Disclosure Rules
KENTUCKY	No general prohibition on disclosure of medical information. Privacy is addressed in statutes, which govern specific entities or medical conditions. Records of patients in state mental facilities are confidential, with certain exceptions, including treatment, payment, and health care operations under HIPAA [Ky. Rev. Stat. Ann. § 210.235, amended by 2014 Ky. Acts, ch. 12, Sec. 1]. No physician-patient privilege exists, but there are numerous mental health care provider-patient privileges [Ky. Rules of evidence 506 and 507 (counselor-client and psychotherapist-patient)]. No privilege exists for involuntarily hospitalized mental patients.	• An insurer or utilization review agent may not disclose or publish individual medical records or any other confidential medical information in the performance of utilization review activities except as provided in HIPAA and other applicable laws and regulations [Ky. Rev. Stat. Ann. § 304.17A-607, amended by 2011 Ky. Acts, ch. 24, Sec. 1236]. • Insurance utilization review agents may not disclose or publish individual medical records or any other confidential medical information in the performance of utilization review activities except as provided in the Health Insurance Portability and Accountability Act [Ky. Rev. Stat. § 304.17A-607, amended by 2010 Ky. Acts, ch. 24, Sec. 1236]. • Specific disclosure rules apply to reporting of cancer cases [Ky. Rev. Stat. Ann. § 214.556, amended by 2005 Ky. Acts, ch. 99, part B]; HIV test results [Ky. Rev. Stat. Ann. § 214.625(5)]; alcohol and drug abuse treatment records [Ky. Rev. Stat. § 222.271 and § 304.17A-555]; and sexually transmitted diseases [Ky. Rev. Stat. §§ 211.180, amended by 2004 Ky. Acts, ch. 102, Sec. 1, effective July 13, 2004, 214.410, and 214.420, amended by 2005 Ky. Acts, ch. 99, part B]. • Confidentiality rules do not preclude disclosure of preliminary positive HIV test to patient as basis to recommend options for prophylaxis or treatment [Ky. Rev. Stat. § 214.181, amended by 2008 Ky. Acts, ch. 150]. • Cabinet for Health and Family Services must establish procedures pertaining to confidentiality of data collected; staff with access to raw data and information shall sign a statement indicating that the staff person accepts responsibility to hold that data or identifying information in confidence and is aware of penalties under state or federal law for breach of confidentiality; data which, because of small sample size, breaches the confidentiality of individual patients, shall not be released [Ky. 2Rev. Stat. § 216.2925, amended by 2008 Ky. Acts, ch. 71].

State	Health Care Privacy Statute/Provisions	Specific Disclosure Rules
		• Data obtained through a trauma registry shall be confidential and for use solely by the Department for Public Health, the statewide trauma care director, or the advisory committee, and persons or public or private entities that participate in data collection for the trauma registry. Personal identifying information that is collected for use in the trauma registry shall not be subject to discovery or introduction into evidence in any civil action [Added by 2008 Ky. Acts, ch. 25].
		• Nonpublic personal health information may be provided to an employer-organized association health benefit plan and large group health benefit plan with 51 or more enrolled employees to cover entity transfer under HIPAA, provided that the health benefit plan certifies to the insurer that it has adopted HIPAA-required safeguards and will treat the nonpublic personal health information in accordance with HIPAA standards [Ky. Rev. Stat. § 304.17A-846, added by 2007 Ky. Acts, ch. 87].
		• A pharmacy may use the records of a hospital, physician, or other practitioner, transmitted by any means of communication, for purposes of validating pharmacy records with respect to orders or refills of a drug [Ky. Rev. Stat. § 304.17A-741, added by 2009 Ky. Acts, ch. 76, Sec. 2].
		• Medical laboratory results may be transmitted to a treating provider or an electronic health information exchange or network for the purposes of transmitting medical laboratory results to the ordering provider and to any other provider for the purposes of treatment, payment, or operations if patient consent has been obtained under HIPAA [Ky. Rev. Stat. § 333.150, amended by 2010 Ky. Acts, ch. 142].
		• Required reporting to Department for Public Health stroke database for quality improvement in stroke response and treatment does not require disclosure of confidential information in violation of HIPAA privacy rules [Ky. Rev. Stat. § 211.575, added by 2012 Ky. Acts, ch. 106].
		• Computer security breach notification requirements do not apply to person subject to HIPAA [Ky. Rev. Stat. § 365.732, added by 2014 Ky. Acts, ch. 84].

continues

¶ 190 Louisiana

State	Health Care Privacy Statute/Provisions	Specific Disclosure Rules
LOUISIANA	No general prohibition on disclosure of confidential medical information. Privacy is addressed in statutes covering specific entities or medical conditions. A health care provider-patient privilege exists pertaining to physicians, psychotherapists, pharmacists, hospitals, rape crisis counselors, and others [La. Code of Evidence Art. 510(a), La. Rev. Stat. Ann. § 13:3734]. Risk management information and information created by insurers, providers, and others to identify an underlying cause of an adverse patient outcome or a professional liability loss is deemed confidential and nondiscoverable [La. Rev. Stat. Ann. § 13:3715.5, 2005 La. Acts 63]. Health care provider communication to patients or their relatives and representatives expressing apology, regret, grief, sympathy, commiseration, condolence, compassion or benevolence does not constitute an admission and is not admissible to establish liability [La. Rev. Stat. Ann. § 13:3715.5, 2005 La. Acts 63]. Coroner must ensure that protected health information is obtained from providers in accordance with HIPAA [La. Rev. Stat. Ann. § 28:214.4, added by 2010 La. Acts 907]. Telemedicine records are subject to state and federal laws on privacy of health information [La. Rev. Stat. Ann. § 37:1271, amended by 2014 La. Acts 442].	• HMOs may not disclose any information about the diagnosis or treatment of an enrollee or applicant, with exceptions for disclosure of information necessary to carry out the HMO law, for court orders, and to defend against a claim or litigation by the enrollee or applicant [La. Rev. Stat. Ann. § 22:265 (former La. Rev. Stat. 22:2020); renumbered by 2008 La. Acts 415]. • Health insurer is not required to release information protected by HIPAA [La. Rev. Stat. Ann. § 22:978, amended by 2014 La. Acts 558]. • Louisiana has repealed the former provision limiting disclosure of confidential medical information or individual medical records obtained during utilization review activities [former La. Rev. Stat. Ann. § 40:2731, repealed by 2003 La. Acts, Act 200, approved June 5, 2003]. • State confidential medical records are exempted from disclosure under the Public Records Act, with certain specific exceptions [La. Rev. Stat. Ann. § 44:7]. • Specific disclosure rules apply to reports of communicable diseases [La. Rev. Stat. Ann. § 40:3.1]; genetic information [La. Rev. Stat. Ann. §§ 22-1023, renumbered by 2008 La. Acts 415, 40:1299.6]; mental retardation and developmental disability treatment records [La. Rev. Stat. Ann. § 28:454.2]; reports of cancer [La. Rev. Stat. Ann. §§ 40:1299.85, 40:1299.87]; prescription drug monitoring program information [La. Rev. Stat. § 40:1007, amended by 2015 La. Acts 22]; and HIV test results [La. Rev. Stat. Ann. § 40:1300.14]. • Identity of patient identified in provider licensing board investigation of provider is confidential [La. Rev. Stat. § 13:3715.1(J), amended by 2006 La. Acts 241].[*] • Medical records for workers' compensation claims are confidential [La. Rev. Stat. § 23:1293(A)(1), amended by 2006 La. Acts 16].[*]

State	Health Care Privacy Statute/Provisions	Specific Disclosure Rules
		• Medical malpractice review panel may obtain medical records through HIPAA-compliant authorization form [La. Rev. Stat. § 40:1299.47, amended by 2006 La. Acts 323].
		• Any health care provider or health plan and its directors, officers, employees, and agents thereof, acting in good faith, who voluntarily report or disclose information to a nonprofit health care quality improvement corporation which complies and functions in accordance with R.S. 13:3715.6, shall not be liable to any person for any injury, damage, or loss as a result of reporting or disclosing such information, unless the injury, damage, or loss was caused by willful or wanton misconduct [La. Rev. Stat. § 9:800.20, added by 2007 La. Acts 359].
		• In data collection, the Office of Public Health shall ensure confidentiality of patients by enforcing appropriate rules and regulations at least as stringent as those regulations applicable to covered entities promulgated under the HIPAA privacy regulations [La. Rev. Stat. § 1300.112, amended by 2014 La. Acts 7900].
		• Electronic prescription remittance advice may not contain any information that would cause a violation of the Health Insurance Portability and Accountability Act (HIPAA) and must follow the HIPAA Standard Transaction file format or any subsequent standards that are required [La. Rev. Stat. § 22:250.52, amended by 2008 La. Acts 755].
		• Personnel of the office of the coroner or the Coroner's Strategic Initiative for a Health Information and Intervention Program shall ensure that if any protected health information of an individual is to be obtained from any health care provider, the information is obtained in accordance with HIPAA [La. Rev. Stat. § 215.4, added by 2010 La. Acts 907].
		• A physician who determines that a medical emergency necessitating abortion exists with respect to a pregnant woman must certify in writing the specific medical conditions that constitute emergency; certification shall be placed in the medical file of woman and the files must be kept confidential as provided by law [La. Rev. Stat. § 1299.35.2, added by 2010 La. Acts 888].

continues

State	*Health Care Privacy Statute/Provisions*	*Specific Disclosure Rules*
		• Individual abortion reports completed by attending physician are confidential and shall not include name or address of woman [La. Rev. Stat. Ann. § 1299.35.10, amended by 2012 La. Acts 685].
		• Informed consent not required for HIV test of patient when hospital employee or physician, or law enforcement, fire service, or emergency medical response personnel, may have been exposed to patient's blood or bodily fluids; test results are confidential and may not be part of patient's medical record, except that hospital may inform exposed person or infectious disease control officer of law enforcement, fire service, or emergency medical response service of results [La. Rev. Stat. Ann. § 1299.39.7, added by 2012 La. Acts 759].

* Not limited to HIPAA-covered entities.

¶ 200 Maine

State	Health Care Privacy Statute/Provisions	Specific Disclosure Rules
MAINE	An individual's health care information is confidential and may not be disclosed by a health care practitioner or facility without the person's consent, except as provided by law [Me. Rev. Stat. tit. 22, § 1711-C]. Provider-patient privileges include those of patients of physicians and psychotherapists [Me. R. Rev. R. 503 (privilege expanded to remove rebuttal exceptions in criminal proceedings, April 11, 2002)], and social workers and marriage-family therapists [Me. Rev. Stat. tit. 32, §§ 7005 and 13862]. Person authorized as agent under power of attorney may act as principal's personal representative to access medical records [Me. Rev. Stat. tit. 18, § 5-909]. Protected health information submitted to Maine Health Data Organization is subject to HIPAA privacy standards. [Me. Rev. Stat. tit. 22, §§ 8702, 8705-A, 8708, and 8714 to 8717, as amended by 2014 Me. Laws, ch. 528].	• Health care practitioners or facilities may disclose information without consent: to other providers and facilities within and outside the original office or practice (except information about mental health services); in quality assurance, utilization or peer reviews; to family members, in certain situations; to third parties when there is a threat of imminent harm to an individual; pursuant to court order or subpoena; for scientific research purposes; and to regulators or those involved in accreditation or certification of a practitioner or facility [Me. Rev. Stat. tit. 22, § 1711-C]. • HMOs may disclose an enrollee's or applicant's health information without consent in order to comply with the HMO laws, pursuant to statute or court order, to assist health care review committees, and in response to a claim or litigation between an enrollee/applicant and the HMO [Me. Rev. Stat. Ann. tit. 24-A, § 4224]. • Insurers may not disclose personal information about a consumer collected or received in connection with an insurance transaction unless the disclosure is made with due consideration for the safety and reputation of all persons who may be affected by the disclosure, is limited to the minimum amount of personal information necessary to accomplish a lawful purpose, and is disclosed with authorization, to another insurer or health care provider, to a regulatory agency, for research purposes, for purposes of treatment, payment, or health care operations of the disclosing entity, or under other specific exceptions [Me. Rev. Stat. tit. 24-A, § 2215, amended by 2005 Me. Laws, ch. 127]. • Medical records and reports of municipal ambulance and rescue units and other emergency medical service units are not disclosable as public records [Me. Rev. Stat. tit. 1, § 402, amended by 2004 Me. Laws, ch. 614, Sec. 1].

continues

State	Health Care Privacy Statute/Provisions	Specific Disclosure Rules
		• Special disclosure rules apply to alcoholism and drug abuse treatment records [Me. Rev. Stat. tit. 24-A, § 2842]; child abuse incidents [Me. Rev. Stat. tit. 22, § 4015]; communicable disease reporting [Me. Rev. Stat. tit. 22, §§ 815, 821 through 824, amended by 2005 Me. Laws, ch. 383]; cancer reporting [Me. Rev. Stat. tit. 22, § 1404]; DNA records [Me. Rev. Stat. tit. 25, § 1577]; protection and advocacy agencies for persons with mental illness [Me. Rev. Stat. tit. 5, § 19507]; records of birth defects [Me. Rev. Stat. tit. 22, § 8943]; dentists [Me. Rev. Stat. tit. 32, § 1092-A]; behavioral and developmental services provider records [Me. Rev. Stat. tit. 34-B, § 1207, amended by 2005 Me. Laws, ch. 397 and 2006 Me. Laws, ch. 683, and Me. Rev. Stat. tit. 34-B, § 1223, amended by 2007 Me. Laws, ch. 356]; and HIV test results [Me. Rev. Stat. tit. 5, §§ 19203 and 19203-D, as amended by 2011 Me. Laws, ch. 347, Sec. 5].
		• A person who maintains computerized data that includes personal information must investigate a breach of the security of the system and notify the subject of the personal information if it is likely that the information has been or will be misused [10 Me. Rev. Stat. § 1348, amended by 2006 Me. Laws, ch. 503, Sec. 6].
		• Practitioner-specific quality data collected for the Maine Quality Forum is confidential and may not be disclosed by the forum prior to a determination of accuracy and completeness, but is not confidential after a determination of its accuracy and completeness is made by the Director of the Forum or a designee [24-A Me. Rev. Stat. § 6097, subsection 3, amended by 2006 Me. Laws, ch. 615, Sec. 3].
		• Credible allegations of fraud in MaineCare program are confidential until provider has been given notice of suspension of payments, except as necessary for investigation of fraud or administration of program [22 Me. Rev. Stat. § S1714-D, added by 2012 Me. Laws, ch. 687].
		• Managed care plan may not terminate or discipline provider for disclosing treatment information to patient [Me. Rev. Stat. tit. 24-A, § 4303, amended by 2007 Me. Laws, ch. 999, Sec. B-6].

State	Health Care Privacy Statute/Provisions	Specific Disclosure Rules
		• Provider specific quality data is confidential and may not be disclosed prior to determination of accuracy [Me. Rev. Stat. tit. 24-A, § 6907, amended by 2006 Me. Laws, ch. 615, Sec. 3].
		• A carrier or prescription drug information intermediary may not license, use, sell, transfer, or exchange for value, for any marketing purpose, prescription drug information that identifies directly or indirectly the individual [22 Me. Rev. Stat. § 1711-E, amended by 2007 Me. Laws, ch. 460, Sec. 1].
		• Department of Health and Human Services may approve a nursing facility certificate of need application when the applicant proposes capital expenditures for renovations and improvements that are necessary to comply with HIPAA and related patient privacy standards [22 Me. Rev. Stat. § 333-A, amended by 2008 Me. Laws, ch. 681, Sec. 5 and 2011 Me. Laws, ch. 90, Sec. Jx4].
		• Clinical review panel may review mental health patient's medical records to determine need for involuntary treatment [Me. Rev. Stat. tit. 34-5, § 3861, amended by 2008 Me. Laws, ch. 580].
		• Revised Uniform Anatomical Gift Act allows examination of donor's medical records, unless prohibited by law [Me. Rev. Stat. tit. 22, ch. 710-B, § 2953, added by 2008 Me. Laws, ch. 601].
		• A person authorized by the principal in the power of attorney to determine that the principal is incapacitated may act as the principal's personal representative pursuant to the federal HIPAA [Me. Rev. Stat. tit.18, §§ 5-909 through 5-943, amended by 2009 Me. Laws, ch. 292].
		• Newborn blood spot screening records that contain personally identifying medical information are confidential; these records include information on genetic, communicable, occupational or environmental disease entities, and information gathered from public health nurse activities, or any program for which the Department of Human Services collects personally identifying medical information [Me. Rev. Stat. tit. 22, § 42, subsection 5, amended by 2010 Me. Laws, ch. 514].

continues

State	*Health Care Privacy Statute/Provisions*	*Specific Disclosure Rules*
		• Data collected by Maine Emergency Medical Services may be released for research, public health surveillance, and linkage to electronic medical records if release is approved by EMS Board, Medical Direction and Practices Board, and EMS Director [Me. Rev. Stat. tit. 32, § 91-B, added by 2011 Me. Laws, ch. 271]. • Records of an independent review organization are confidential, except that a party to an external review may obtain a copy of the decision, and the Superintendent of Insurance shall distribute aggregate information on external review to the legislature and public [Me. Rev. Stat. tit. 24A, § 4312, added by 2013 Me. Laws, ch. 274, Sec. 1].

¶ 210 Maryland

State	Health Care Privacy Statute/Provisions	Specific Disclosure Rules
MARYLAND	Medical records are confidential and may be disclosed by health care providers only as provided by law [Md. Code Ann. Health-Gen §§ 4-302, amended by 2007 Md. Acts, ch. 8 and 2011 Md. Acts, ch. 534]. Maryland Health Care Commission shall adopt regulations for the privacy and security of protected health information obtained or released through a health information exchange, as required by HIPAA and other federal and state law [Md. Code Ann. § 4-302.2, added by 2014 Md. Acts ch. 615. Security breach notification requirements do not apply to personal information that, except for a medical record that a person is prohibited from redisclosing under Md. Ann. Code Health-Gen § 4-302, is disclosed in accordance with HIPAA privacy rules [Md. Ann. Code State Govt. § 10-302, amended by 2013 Md. Acts, ch. 304, Sec. 1]. A health care provider-patient privilege is extended only to psychiatrists or psychologists [Md. Court and Judicial Proceedings Code Ann. § 9-109].	• Providers may disclose information without consent to the provider's employees or agents to provide or seek payment for health care; to the provider's insurer and attorneys, in certain instances; in a health emergency; for educational or research purposes, evaluation of health care delivery systems, or for accreditation purposes; to other providers for purposes of treating the patient; and to organ and tissue procurement entities. Disclosure must be in accord with HIPAA privacy rules [Md. Code Ann. Health-Gen § 4-305, amended by 2012 Md. Acts, ch. 326]. Disclosure of the medical record is mandatory in some circumstances, including to a domestic violence fatality review team [Md. Code Ann. Health-Gen § 4-306, amended by 2005 Md. Acts, ch. 233, 503 and 2006 Md. Laws, ch. 44]. Providers may disclose medical records without authorization pursuant to compulsory process in Children in Need of Assistance Proceedings [Md. Code Ann. Health-Gen § 4-306(i), amended by 2008 Md. Acts, ch. 300]. • Insurers may disclose an insured's medical records to a medical review committee, accreditation board, or commission; pursuant to court order or subpoena; to a health service plan to coordinate benefits; to investigate possible insurance fraud; to evaluate an insurance application; to adjust a claim; and to evaluate a claim or suit for personal injury. Disclosure must be in accord with HIPAA privacy rules [Md. Code Ann. Insurance § 4-403, amended by 2012 Md. Acts, ch. 326]. • Insurers must accept Commissioner's standardized form for enrollee to request confidential communications in accordance with HIPAA standards [Md. Code Ann. Insurance § 15-141, added by 2014 Md. Acts ch. 72]. • Insurers must comply with notice and consent requirements concerning privacy of consumer financial and health information [Md. Admin. Code §§ 31.16.08.01 through 31.16.08.24]. • Nonprofit health service plans or Blue Cross/Blue Shield plans may disclose medical information under similar, but not identical, circumstances as above. Disclosure must be in accord with HIPAA privacy rules [Md. Code Ann. Insurance § 14-138, as amended by 2012 Md. Acts, ch. 326].

continues

State	Health Care Privacy Statute/Provisions	Specific Disclosure Rules
		• Specific disclosure rules apply to HIV/AIDS [Md. Code Ann. Health-Gen §§ 18-201.1, 18-207, and 18-215, as amended by 2007 Md. Acts, ch. 212; and Md. Code Ann. Health-Gen §§ 18-336, amended by 2008 Md. Acts, ch. 222, 18-338.1, and 13-338.2]; mental health records [Md. Code Ann. Health-Gen §§ 4-304, 4-307, amended by 2005 Md. Acts, ch. 503]; cancer reports [Md. Code Ann. Health-Gen § 18-204]; birth defects reports [Md. Code Ann. Health-Gen § 18-206, amended by 2008 Md. Acts, ch. 224]; genetic tests [Md. Code Ann. Insurance § 27-909]; child abuse [Md. Code Ann. Health-Gen § 4-306, amended by 2008 Md. Acts, ch. 300]; and reportable diseases [Md. Code Ann. Health-Gen § 18-205, amended by 2008 Md. Acts, ch. 270].
		• A person may not disclose a confidential research record to any person who is not engaged in the research or study for which it was assembled or obtained [Md. Code Ann. Human Serv. § 9-219, amended by 2007 Md. Acts, ch. 3].[*]
		• Rights of advocate of person with mental disorders or facilities do not include access to medical records or other confidential information that the advocate does not otherwise have access to under law [Md. Code Ann. Health-Gen § 10-701, amended by 2009 Md. Acts, ch. 621].[*]
		• Person authorized by the principal in the power of attorney to determine that the principal is incapacitated may act as the principal's personal representative to obtain access to principal's health care information and communicate with principal's health-care provider in accordance with Health Insurance Portability and Accountability Act [Md. Code Ann. Estates & Trusts § 17-111, added by 2010 Md. Acts, ch. 690].
		• Provider must disclose medical records in response to compulsory process unless "person in interest" objects within 30 days of required notice [Md. Ann. Code Health-Gen. §§ 4-301, 4-306, added by 2013 Md. Acts, ch. 287, Sec. 1].

[*] Not limited to HIPAA-covered entities.

¶ 220 Massachusetts

State	Health Care Privacy Statute/Provisions	Specific Disclosure Rules
MASSACHUSETTS	There is a statutory right of privacy that generally encompasses medical records and information [Mass Gen. Laws, ch. 214, § 1B], as well as other statutes governing specific entities and medical conditions. Hospital and other facilities' records are confidential to the extent provided by law, with certain exceptions [Mass. Gen. Laws, ch. 111, § 70E]. There is a health provider-patient privilege extended to psychiatrists, psychologists, and psychiatric nurse clinicians, as well as social workers [Mass. Gen. Laws, ch. 233, § 20B; Mass Gen. Laws, ch. 112, § 135B]. A mental health counselor has the privilege of refusing to disclose communication relative to diagnosis or treatment of client's mental or emotional condition [Mass. Gen. Laws, ch. 112, § 172A, added by 2007 Mass. Acts, ch. 142].	• Physicians, health care facilities, nursing homes, and other providers may disclose patient information without consent to establish eligibility for government benefits, for mandatory health department reports, or as required by any law [Mass Gen. Laws, ch. 112, § 12G]. • Provider's notification to parent or guardian of minor's treatment for drug or alcohol overdose must be conducted consistent with HIPAA privacy protections [Mass. Gen. Laws, ch. 112, § 12E1/2, added by 2012 Mass. Acts, ch. 244]. • Insurance entities may disclose information without a person's consent in order to verify insurance benefits; to conduct business when disclosure is necessary; to law enforcement agencies in fraud investigations; and pursuant to search warrant or subpoena [Mass. Gen. Laws, ch. 175I, § 13]. • Insurers may disclose any personal or privileged information about an individual collected or received in connection with an insurance transaction only in specific circumstances [Mass. Gen. Laws, ch. 175I, § 13]. • Rate filing materials submitted for review to Insurance Commissioner by insurers are deemed confidential and are not public records. [Mass. Gen. Laws, ch. 176J, § 6, amended by 2013 Mass. Acts, ch. 35].[*] • Personnel and medical files or information and other data relating to a specifically named individual, the disclosure of which may constitute an unwarranted invasion of personal privacy, are not disclosable under the Freedom of Information Act [Mass. Gen. Laws, ch. 4, § 7, amended by 2004 Mass. Acts, ch. 122, 149, and 349].[*]

continues

State	Health Care Privacy Statute/Provisions	Specific Disclosure Rules
		• Specific disclosure rules apply to HIV/AIDS testing [Mass. Gen. Laws, ch. 111, § 70F]; mental health information [Mass. Gen. Laws, ch. 112, § 129A; ch. 123, § 36; and ch. 176G, § 4B]; genetic testing [Mass. Gen. Laws, ch. 111, § 70G]; drug rehabilitation program records [Mass. Gen. Laws, ch. 111E, § 18]; psychologist's treatment records [Mass. Gen. Laws, ch. 112, § 129A]; pharmacists' emergency contraception reports [Mass. Gen. Laws, ch. 94C, § 19A]; and infectious disease reports [Mass. Gen. Laws, ch. 111D, § 6]. • Mental health counselor's privilege does not apply when there is a threat of imminent danger, in child custody cases, or in certain investigations [Mass. Gen. Laws, ch. 112, § 172A, added by 2007 Mass. Acts, ch. 142].

* Not limited to HIPAA-covered entities.

¶ 230 Michigan

State	Health Care Privacy Statute/Provisions	Specific Disclosure Rules
MICHIGAN	No general prohibition on disclosure of confidential medical information. Specific prohibitions against disclosure apply to certain entities and medical conditions. Information regarding mental health treatment is confidential, with certain exceptions [Mich. Comp. Laws § 330.1748]. Health care provider-patient privileges include psychiatrist or psychologist-patient [Mich. Comp. Laws §§ 330.1700 and 330.1750], physician-patient [Mich. Comp. Laws § 600.2157], licensed professional counsel or client [Mich. Comp. Laws § 333.18117], and dentist-patient [Mich. Comp. Laws § 333.16648]. Electronic prescriptions must protect patient confidentiality as required by applicable state and federal law, including HIPAA privacy rules [Mich. Comp. Laws § 333.17754, amended by 2013 Mich. Pub. Acts 2186 and 268]. Department of Mental Health shall develop standard release form for exchanging confidential mental health and substance use disorders, in accordance with HIPAA [Mich. Comp. Laws § 330.1141a, added by 2014 Mich. Pub. Acts 129]. Electronic prescriptions for expedited partner therapy to prevent spread of sexually transmitted disease must comply with HIPAA privacy rules [Mich. Comp. Laws § 333.17754, added by 2014 Mich. Pub. Acts 525].	• Nonprofit health care corporations may not disclose medical records without patient consent, except for claims adjudication or verifications, or as required by law [Mich. Comp. Laws § 550.1406]. • Third-party claims administrators may not disclose records that contain identifying information about a plan member's diagnosis or treatment without consent, except for claims adjudication or verification, for plan administration, for an ERISA audit, for excess loss insurance purchase or claims, to the insurance commissioner, or as otherwise required by law [Mich. Comp. Laws § 550.934]. • The Freedom of Information Act exempts from disclosure public records of medical, counseling, or psychological facts or evaluations concerning an individual if the individual's identity would be revealed by a disclosure of those facts or evaluation [Mich. Comp. Laws § 15.243]. • Insurers are restricted from disclosing nonpublic personal financial information about individuals who obtain or are claimants or beneficiaries of products or services primarily for personal, family, or household purposes [Mich. Comp. Laws § 500.501 through 500.547].

continues

State	*Health Care Privacy Statute/Provisions*	*Specific Disclosure Rules*
		• A hospital patient or resident is entitled to confidential treatment of personal and medical records, and may refuse their release to a person outside the health facility or agency except as required because of a transfer to another health care facility, as required by law or third-party payment contract, or as permitted or required under HIPAA [Mich. Comp. Laws § 333.20201, added by 2006 Mich. Pub. Acts 38]. Specific disclosure rules apply to HIV/AIDS [Mich. Comp. Laws § 333.5131 and § 333.5133, added by 2010 Mich. Pub. Acts 320]; cancer [Mich. Comp. Laws § 333.2619]; pharmacies [Mich. Comp. Laws § 333.17752]; substance abuse treatment [Mich. Comp. Laws §§ 333.6111 through 333.6113]; genetic tests [Mich. Comp. Laws § 333.17020]; psychologists [Mich. Comp. Laws § 333.18237]; health care facilities [Mich. Comp. Laws § 333.20201]; fetal death records [Mich. Comp. Laws § 2834, amended by 2012 Mich. Pub. Acts 499]; identity of person consenting to abortion [Mich. Comp. Laws § 17015, amended by 2012 Mich. Pub. Acts 499]; and medical research projects [Mich. Comp. Laws § 333.2631].
		• Entities that comply with HIPAA are deemed in compliance with security breach notification requirements [Mich. Comp. Laws § 445.72, added by 2006 Mich. Pub. Acts 566].
		• Health insurers and HMOs must provide to Department of Community Health information necessary to determine whether a health coverage recipient of the entity is also a medical assistance recipient [Mich. Comp. Laws § 550-283, added by 2006 Mich. Pub. Acts 593].
		• Records of elderly and vulnerable death review team are confidential and may be disclosed only to county medical examiner, prosecutor, law enforcement, or other review team [Mich. Comp. Laws § 52.203, amended by 2012 Mich. Pub. Acts 171].[*]

[*] Not limited to HIPAA-covered entities.

¶ 240 Minnesota

State	Health Care Privacy Statute/Provisions	Specific Disclosure Rules
MINNESOTA	Health care providers may not release a patient's health records to anyone without patient consent unless specifically authorized by law, with certain exceptions [Minn. Stat. § 144.293, subd. 2, renumbered and amended by 2007 Minn. Laws, ch. 147, Sec. 15]. Medical records maintained by hospitals and other medical facilities are confidential, with certain exceptions [Minn. Stat. § 144.651 subd. 16, amended by 2004 Minn. Laws, ch. 198, Sec. 10]. A health care provider-patient privilege is extended to physicians, nurses, dentists, chiropractors, psychologists, and sexual assault counselors and their patients and clients [Minn. Stat. § 595.02 subd. 1, amended by 2007 Minn. Laws, ch. 54, Sec. 4, and 2008 Minn. Laws, ch. 302, Sec. 1]. Social workers must maintain client confidentiality [Minn. Stat. § 148E.230, added by 2007 Minn. Laws, ch. 123]. Interoperable electronic health record systems must meet security standards that ensure confidentiality and integrity [Minn. Stat. § 144.3345, added by 2007 Minn. Laws, ch. 147].	• Providers may release health records without consent in a medical emergency, to other providers within related entities for treatment of the patient, to researchers for medical or scientific research and to a law enforcement agency with which the patient is involved in an emergency interaction [Minn. Stat. § 144.293, subd. 2, renumbered and amended by 2007 Minn. Laws, ch. 147, Sec. 15]. • Hospitals and other health facilities, including outpatient surgical centers, may disclose without consent where required by third-party payment contracts, in complaint inspections and health department inspections, and as otherwise provided by law [Minn. Stat. § 144.651 subd. 16, amended by 2004 Minn. Laws, ch. 198, Sec. 10]. • HMOs may disclose privileged information in some circumstances: to detect or prevent fraud; to verify insurance coverage, inform a person of a health problem, or conduct an operations audit; to insurance regulators; to law enforcement officials in the event of fraud or other illegal activities; and pursuant to a search warrant or subpoena [Minn. Stat. § 72A.502 subd. 2 through 11]. • Insurers may not disclose any personal or privileged information about a person collected or received in connection with an insurance transaction without the written authorization of that person except as authorized by the Insurance Fair Information Reporting statute. An insurer may not collect personal information about a policyholder or an applicant not relating to a claim from sources other than public records without a written authorization from the person [Minn. Stat. § 72A.502]. • Specific disclosure rules apply to genetic information [Minn. Stat. § 72A.139], cancer reporting [Minn. Stat. § 144.671], medical data from state-run facilities [Minn. Stat. § 13.384] genetic information [Minn. Stat. § 13.386, added by 2006 Minn. Laws, ch. 253, Sec. 40] anatomical gift registry [Minn. Stat. § 525A.20, amended by 2007 Minn. Laws, ch. 120, Sec. 20], and records maintained by the government [Minn. Stat. §§ 13.02 subd. 12, 13.04, 13.3805 subd. 1, amended by 2005 Minn. Laws, ch. 60].

continues

State	Health Care Privacy Statute/Provisions	Specific Disclosure Rules
		• Adult foster care license holder who creates, collects, records, maintains, stores, or discloses individually identifiable recipient data must comply with privacy laws and regulations, including HIPAA [Minn. Stat. § 245A.11, added by 2009 Minn. Laws, ch. 79, Sec. 5].
		• Effective January 1, 2011, all providers, group purchasers, prescribers, and dispensers must establish, maintain, and use an electronic prescription drug program that complies. This program must comply with the applicable standards in this section for transmitting, directly or through an intermediary, prescriptions and prescription-related information using electronic media; any pharmacy within an entity must be able to receive electronic prescription transmittals from outside the entity using the adopted NCPDP SCRIPT Standard, but this exemption does not supersede any HIPAA requirement that may require the use of a HIPAA transaction standard within an organization [Minn. Stat. § 62J.497, subd. 2, amended by 2009 Minn. Laws, ch. 102].

¶ 250 Mississippi

State	Health Care Privacy Statute/Provisions	Specific Disclosure Rules
MISSISSIPPI	No general prohibition on disclosure of confidential medical information. Specific prohibitions against disclosure apply to certain entities and medical conditions. Hospital records are privileged communications [Miss. Code Ann. § 41-9-67]. Health care provider-patient privileges extend to physicians, osteopaths, hospital, nurses, pharmacists, podiatrists, optometrists, and chiropractors and their patients [Miss. Code Ann. § 13-1-21], and to psychotherapists and psychologists [Miss. Code Ann. § 73-31-29, Miss. R.E. 503]. Peer review records are confidential [Miss. Code Ann. §§ 41-63-21 through 42-63-29]. Pharmacy records are confidential [Miss. Code Ann. § 73.21-121, 73-21-125, amended by 2006 Miss. Laws, ch. 533].	• HMOs and other benefit plans may disclose medical information without the person's consent to the extent necessary to follow the law governing such plans; pursuant to statute or court order; and in the event of claim or litigation between the person and the HMO [Miss. Code Ann. § 83-41-355, amended by 2006 Miss. S.B. 2729]. • Mental health records are confidential and may be released without patient consent only upon court order; when necessary for the patient's continuing treatment; when necessary to determine eligibility for benefits, compliance with statutory reporting requirements, or other lawful purpose; and when the patient has threatened imminent violence to an identifiable victim [Miss. Code Ann. § 41-21-97, amended by 2005 Miss. Laws, ch. 316 and 2006 Miss. S.B. 2729]. • A utilization review agent may not disclose or publish individual medical records or any other confidential medical information obtained in the performance of utilization review activities without the patient's authorization or a court order [Miss. Code Ann. § 41-83-17]. • Insurers may not disclose nonpublic personal health information about a consumer or customer unless an authorization is obtained from the consumer or customer whose information is sought to be disclosed [28-000-080 Miss. Code R. § 17]. • Specific disclosure rules apply to alcoholism treatment [Miss. Code Ann. § 41-30-33]; birth defects registry [Miss. Code Ann. § 41-21-205]; persons in need of mental treatment [Miss. Code Ann. § 41-21-97, amended by 2005 Miss. Laws, ch. 316 and 2006 Miss. S.B. 2729]; contagious and infectious diseases [Miss. Code Ann. § 41-23-1]; Hepatitis B or HIV status [Miss. Code Ann. § 41-34-7]; licensed professional counselors [Miss. Code Ann. § 73-30-17]; social workers [Miss. Code Ann. § 73-53-29]; health care review committees [Miss. Code Ann. § 83-41-355]; and cancer registry [Miss. Code Ann. § 41-91-5].

continues

State	*Health Care Privacy Statute/Provisions*	*Specific Disclosure Rules*
		• Submission of information to and use of information by the Department of Health registry program shall be considered a permitted disclosure required by law and for public health activities under HIPAA [Miss. Code. Ann. § 41-63-4, amended by 2008 Miss. H.B. 1023].
		• All persons providing information and data to the Mississippi Health Information Network shall retain a property right in that information or data, but grant to the other participants or subscribers a nonexclusive license to retrieve and use that information or data in accordance with the rules or regulations promulgated by the MS-HIN board and in compliance with the provisions of HIPAA; patients desiring to obtain a copy of their personal medical record or information are to request the copy from the health care provider who is the primary source of the information, and the MS-HIN shall not be required to provide this information directly to the patient [2010 Miss. H.B. 941 § 6, repealed effective July 1, 2014].
		• Identity of provider of mandatory reports of sex crimes against minors is confidential, except when court determines testimony is material in a proceeding or when identity is released to law enforcement and prosecutors [Miss. Code Ann. § 97-5-51, added by 2012 Miss. H.B. 16].[*]
		• Mississippi Health Information Network Board shall by rule ensure that patient-specific information be disclosed only in accordance with HIPAA [Miss. Code Ann. § 41-119-1, amended by 2014 Miss. H.B. 392, Sec. 7].
		• When patient or guardian designates lay caregiver, hospital must promptly request written consent to release medical information in accordance with state and federal law [Not yet codified, Miss. Gen. Laws 2015 Miss. S.B. 2108].[*]

[*] Not limited to HIPAA-covered entities.

¶ 260 Missouri

State	Health Care Privacy Statute/Provisions	Specific Disclosure Rules
MISSOURI	No general prohibition on disclosure of confidential medical information. A number of health care provider-patient privileges are extended [Mo. Rev. Stat. §§ 337.055 (psychologist); 337.540 (professional counselor); 337.636 (social worker); 337.736 (marital and family counselor); and 491.060 (physician, chiropractor, psychologist, and dentist)].	• HMOs may disclose an enrollee's or applicant's medical information without consent in order to follow the law governing HMOs; in response to a claim or litigation between the person and the HMO; and pursuant to statute or court order [Mo. Rev. Stat. § 354.515]. • Specific disclosure rules apply to mental health facilities and programs [Mo. Rev. Stat. § 630.140, amended by 2005 Mo. Laws 462 and 463]; pharmacies [Mo. Rev. Stat. § 338.100, repeated and replaced by 2010 Mo. Laws, S.B. 754]; epidemiological study data [Mo. Rev. Stat. § 192.067, amended by 2004 Mo. Laws, S.B. 179]; cancer reporting [Mo. Rev. Stat. §§ 192.650 and 192.655]; abuse and neglect of adults [Mo. Rev. Stat. § 660.263] and children [Mo. Rev. Stat. §§ 210.115 (reporting requirement expanded to include ministers) and 210.150, amended by 2004 Mo. Laws, H.B. 1453]; HIV/AIDS [Mo. Rev. Stat. §§ 191.653 and 191.656 (disclosure exception expanded to include prosecutors and victims of sexual offenses)]; pregnant woman substance abuse treatment [Mo. Rev. Stat. § 191.731]; psychologists [Mo. Rev. Stat. § 337.055]; marital and family therapists [Mo. Rev. Stat. § 337.736]; records of mental health residential facilities and day programs [Mo. Rev. Stat. § 630.050, amended by 2008 Mo. Laws 1081]; records of facility or program of Department of Mental Health [Mo. Rev. Stat. § 630.140, amended by 2008 Mo. Laws 1081]; and genetic and metabolic information [Mo. Rev. Stat. §§ 191.323, 375.1309]. • Health information organization may not restrict exchange of state agency data or standards-based clinical summaries for patients for HIPAA-allowable uses [Mo. Rev. Stat. § 191.237, amended by 2013 Mo. Laws, S.B. 89.

continues

¶ 270 Montana

State	Health Care Privacy Statute/Provisions	Specific Disclosure Rules
MONTANA	A provider may not disclose health care information about a patient to any other person without the patient's written authorization [Mont. Code Ann. § 50-16-525]. A number of provider-patient privileges are extended [Mont. Code Ann. §§ 26-1-805 (physician-patient), 26-1-806 (speech/language pathologist-client), and 26-1-807 (psychologist-client)]. Insurer disclosure requirements are limited for entities covered under the HIPAA privacy and security rules [Mont. Code Ann. § 33-19-105, amended by 2007 Mont. Acts, ch. 399]. Records of Board of Medical Examiners' physicians assistance program are confidential [Mont. Code Ann. § 37-3-208, added by 2007 Mont. Acts, ch. 271]. Telemedicine must use HIPAA-compliant technology [Mont. Code Ann. § 33-22-138, amended by 2013 Mont. Acts, ch. 164].	• A provider may disclose patient health information without consent to a person providing health care to the patient; for purposes of health care education, planning, quality assurance, peer review, or administrative services to the provider; to family members or close friends of the patient; to successor health care providers; for use in approved research projects; for an audit; to officials of a custodial institution in which the patient is detained; where there is a risk of immediate danger to an individual's health or safety; as required by law; or pursuant to subpoena or court order [Mont. Code Ann. §§ 50-16-529 and 50-16-530]. • Subsequent evaluation of event submitted to peer review, including incident or occurrence report, is privileged and confidential [Mont. Code Ann. § 50-16-201, amended by 2013 Mont. Acts, ch. 265]. • HMOs may not disclose any information about an enrollee's or applicant's treatment or health without express consent, with certain exceptions [Mont. Code Ann. § 33-31-113]. • Insurance entities may disclose a person's medical information only under certain circumstances: to verify insurance benefits; when necessary to conduct business; to law enforcement agencies in fraud situations; pursuant to search warrant or subpoena; and for marketing purposes, with certain restrictions [Mont. Code Ann. § 33-19-306; Mont. Admin. R. 6.6.6901 to 6904]. • Specific disclosure rules apply to HIV testing [Mont. Code Ann. § 50-16-1009]; infant mortality [Mont. Code Ann. § 50-16-102]; artificial insemination [Mont. Code Ann. § 40-6-106]; mental health [Mont. Code Ann. §§ 53-21-141, 53-21-166]; genetic information [Mont. Code Ann. § 33-18-904]; peer review committees [Mont. Code Ann. § 50-16-203, 204]; government health care information [Mont. Code Ann. § 50-16-603]; records of child abuse and neglect [Mont. Code Ann. § 41-3-206, amended by 2007 Mont. Acts, ch. 166]; state confidentiality rules do not apply to insurers covered under HIPAA standards [Mont. Code Ann. § 33-19-105, 2007 Mont. Acts, ch. 399]; and sexually transmitted diseases [Mont. Code Ann. § 50-18-109].

State	*Health Care Privacy Statute/Provisions*	*Specific Disclosure Rules*
		• Exceptions created for HIPAA covered entities with respect to state notice of privacy practices [Mont. Code Ann. § 33-19-105, amended by 2009 Mont. Acts, ch. 271].
		• A person authorized by the principal in the power of attorney to determine that the principal is incapacitated may act as the principal's personal representative pursuant to HIPAA and applicable regulations to obtain access to the principal's health care information and communicate with the principal's health care provider [Mont. Code Ann. § 72-31-348. Mont. Uniform Power of Attorney Act, Sec. 8, added by 2011 Mont. Acts, ch. 109].
		• Prescription drug registry information is confidential and may be provided only to prescriber or dispenser for treatment purposes, to individual requesting own data, to licensing or regulator, to coroner, to authorized individual, or to registry in another state [Mont. Code Ann. § 37-7-101, amended by 2011 Mont. Acts, ch. 24].

continues

¶ 280 Nebraska

State	Health Care Privacy Statute/Provisions	Specific Disclosure Rules
NEBRASKA	No general prohibition on disclosure of confidential medical information. Privacy protections are contained in statutes governing specific medical conditions and entities [Neb. Rev. Stat. §§ 44-7210 (health carrier); 44-32,172 (HMO); 44-4110.01 (preferred provider); and 44-4725 (prepaid limited health service)]. Physician-patient and professional counselor-client privileges exist [Neb. Rules of Evidence, Rule 504; Neb. Rev. Stat. § 27-504, amended effective Dec. 1, 2008 by 2007 Neb. Laws 463, § 1117]. A person authorized by power of attorney to determine that the principal is incapacitated may act as the principal's personal representative pursuant to HIPAA privacy rules to obtain access to the principal's health care information and communicate with health care provider [Neb. Rev. Stat. § 30-3408, amended by 2012 Neb. Laws 1113, § 47, effective Jan. 1, 2013; Neb. Rev. Stat. § 30-4009, added by 2012 Neb. Laws 113, § 9, effective Jan. 1, 2013].	• Health carriers and plans may only disclose enrollee/applicant health information without consent under limited circumstances: as necessary to carry out the laws governing the entity; pursuant to court order; and in order to defend against a claim or litigation by the covered person [Neb. Rev. Stat. §§ 44-7210, § 44-32, 172, 44-4110.01, and 44-4725]. • Insurers may not disclose nonpublic personal health information about a consumer or customer unless an authorization is obtained from the consumer or customer whose nonpublic personal health information is sought to be disclosed [Neb. Rev. Stat. § 44-916]. • Medical records held by state entities may be withheld from disclosure under public records laws [Neb. Rev. Stat. § 84-712.05, amended by 2007 Neb. Laws 389]. • Mental health professionals may disclose client or patient information without consent only pursuant to the rules of the Board of Examiners; when the person has brought charges against the provider; or when a patient has made a serious threat of violence against him or herself or an identifiable victim [Neb. Rev. Stat. §§ 71-1,335 amended and transferred to Neb. Rev. Stat. § 38-2136, effective Dec. 1, 2008, by 2007 Neb. Laws 463, § 753 and 71-1,336, amended and transferred to Neb. Rev. Stat. § 38-2137, effective Dec. 1, 2008, by 2007 Neb. Laws 463, § 754].

State	Health Care Privacy Statute/Provisions	Specific Disclosure Rules
		• Specific disclosure rules apply to pharmacists [Neb. Rev. Stat. § 71-1,147.36, amended and transferred to Neb. Rev. Stat. § 38-2868, effective Dec. 1, 2008, by 2007 Neb. Laws 463, § 964]; state registries for birth defects, brain injuries, and cancer [Neb. Rev. Stat. §§ 71-646, 81-669, 81-653 through 81-659, 81-642 through 81-647]; communicable diseases [Neb. Rev. Stat. §§ 71-502 through 71-503.01, 71-532, 71-507 through 71-511, amended by Neb. Laws 1115, §§ 36-37]; emergency medical services [Neb. Rev. Stat. § 71-5185, amended and transferred to Neb. Rev. Stat. § 38-1225, effective Dec. 1, 2008, by 2007 Neb. Laws 463, § 509]; approved researchers [Neb. Rev. Stat. § 81-666]; Department of Health and Human Services [Neb. Rev. Stat. § 81-671]; mental health commitment records [Neb. Rev. Stat. 71-961, amended by 2006 Neb. Laws 1119, § 52, transferred from Neb. Rev. Stat. 83-1068, effective July 1, 2004]; and morbidity/mortality studies [Neb. Rev. Stat. § 71-3402]. • Data collected for the statewide trauma registry are HIPAA protected health information and may be shared with emergency providers [Neb. Rev. Stat. § 71-8249, amended by 2008 Neb. Laws § 797]. • Access to immunization information is permitted pursuant to rules and regulations of the Department of Health and Human Services for purposes of direct patient care, public health activities, or enrollment in school or child care services [Nev. Rev. Stat. §§ 71-541, 544, amended by 2011 Neb. Laws § 591]. • Telehealth consultations must comply with HIPAA privacy and security rules [Neb. Rev. Stat. § 71-8506, amended by 2013 Neb. Laws 556, Sec. 6].

continues

¶ 290 Nevada

State	Health Care Privacy Statute/Provisions	Specific Disclosure Rules
NEVADA	No general prohibition on disclosure of confidential medical information. Restrictions on disclosure are found in statutes governing specific entities or conditions. A number of health care provider-patient privileges exist [Nev. Rev. Stat. §§ 49.225 and 49.215 (physician, dentist, osteopath, and psychiatric social worker); 49.209 (psychologist); 49.247 (marriage and family therapy); and 49.252 (social worker)]. Information on sentinel events collected by licensing boards must be kept confidential and is not subject to subpoena [Nev. Rev. Stat. § 630.30665, 2005 Nev. Stat. ch. 487, Sec. 1]. HIPAA-covered entities transmitting individually identifiable health information electronically are exempt from more stringent state laws; individuals may opt out [Nev. Rev. Stat. § 439.538, added by 2007 Nev. Acts, ch. 423]. Consistent with the federal HITECH Act, the Director of the Nevada Department of Health and Human Services will prescribe standards for the security and confidentiality of electronic health records, health-related information, and the statewide health information exchange system [Nev. Rev. Stat. § 313, added by 2011 Nev. Acts, ch. 313, § 7]. Health information exchange must comply with federal HITECH Act [Nev. Rev. Stat. § 439.587, amended by 2015 Nev. Acts, ch. 224].	• Mental health records of institutionalized patients are confidential, with certain exceptions [Nev. Rev. Stat. §§ 433A.360, 433.482(8), amended by 2007 Nev. Acts, ch. 423, § 3]. • Group insurers are prohibited from disclosing to the policyholder the fact that an insured is taking a prescribed drug or the identity of that drug [Nev. Rev. Stat. § 689B.280]. • Prepaid limited health service organizations may only disclose medical information of an enrollee without consent pursuant to statute or court order; to carry out the law governing such entities; or for a claim of legal action [Nev. Rev. Stat. § 695F.410]. • Specific disclosure rules apply to pharmacists [Nev. Rev. Stat. § 639.238, amended by 2007 Nev. Acts, ch. 423, §§ 24, 25]; reporting of communicable diseases [Nev. Rev. Stat. §§ 441A.150, 441A.220, amended by 2007 Nev. Acts, ch. 423, § 29, and 441A.230]; genetic information [Nev. Rev. Stat. §§ 396.521 and 396.523, § 629.171]; medical facility, facility for dependent, or home for individual residential care [Nev. Rev. Stat. § 449.720, amended by 2007 Nev. Acts, ch. 423, § 8]; treatment and rehabilitation of addicts [Nev. Rev. Stat. § 453.720]; cancer [Nev. Rev. Stat. § 457.270]; physicians, physician assistants, and practitioners of respiratory care [Nev. Rev. Stat. § 630.3065]; laboratories [Nev. Rev. Stat § 652.193]; and epilepsy [Nev. Rev. Stat. § 439.270]. • If the Health Division suspends the license of a medical facility or a facility for the dependent or if a facility otherwise ceases to operate, the Health Division may take control of and ensure the safety of the medical records of the facility. Subject to HIPAA provisions, the Health Division shall maintain confidentiality of the records, share records with law enforcement and regulators, and release records to the patient or patient's representative [Nev. Rev. Stat. § 449.171, added by 2009 Nev. Acts, ch. 153, Sec. 20].

State	Health Care Privacy Statute/Provisions	Specific Disclosure Rules
		• A person authorized by the principal in the power of attorney to determine that the principal is incapacitated may act as the principal's personal representative pursuant to HIPAA, and applicable regulations, to obtain a determination of incapacity [Nev. Rev. Stat. tit. 13, § 24, amended by 2009 Nev. Acts, ch. 64]. • Subject to HIPAA, custodian of provider's health care records may not prevent provider from physically inspecting or receiving copies of those records [Nev. Rev. Stat. § 629.___, added by 2015 Nev. Acts, ch. 318].

continues

¶ 300 New Hampshire

State	*Health Care Privacy Statute/Provisions*	*Specific Disclosure Rules*
NEW HAMPSHIRE	No general prohibition on disclosure of confidential medical information. Statutes governing specific entities or medical conditions contain restrictions on disclosure. Information in a patient's hospital clinical record is confidential [N.H. Rev. Stat. § 151:21 X]. Numerous health care privileges exist [N.H. Rev. Stat. §§ 329:26 (physician); 316-A:27 (chiropractor); § 326-B:35, amended by 2005 N.H. Laws, ch. 293 (nurse); 328-F:28 (allied health professional); and 330-A:32 (mental health practitioner)]. Prescription information must be kept confidential [N.H. Rev. Stat. §§ 328:1, 2, added by 2006 N.H. Laws, ch. 328]. Medical examiner's autopsy reports, investigative reports, and supporting documentation are confidential medical records [N.H. Rev. Stat. § 611-B:21, amended by 2007 N.H. Laws, ch. 324]. Cannabis alternative treatment center records are confidential health information and protected health care information for HIPAA purposes [N.H. Rev. Stat. § 126-W:7, added by 2013 N.H. Laws ch. 242].	• Health carriers offering managed care plans may not disclose health information of a covered person without consent except: to the extent necessary to carry out the law governing health carriers; pursuant to statute or court order; or in the event of claim or litigation between the person and the carrier [N.H. Rev. Stat. § 420-J:10]. • Insurers may not disclose nonpublic personal health information about a consumer or customer unless an authorization is obtained from the consumer or customer, or unless specific exceptions apply [N.H. Admin. Rules, Ins. 3005.01]. • State Right to Know Law exempts medical files [N.H. Rev. Stat. § 91-A:5].[*] • Specific disclosure rules apply to marketing of provider services; all medical information in the provider's medical records is deemed the property of the patient [N.H. Rev. Stat. § 332-I:1, amended by 2004 N.H. Laws, ch. 144, effective July 23, 2004]; pharmacists [N.H. Rev. Stat. § 318:29-a]; medical and scientific research [N.H. Rev. Stat. § 126-A:11]; HIV [N.H. Rev. Stat. §§ 141-F:7 and 141-F:8]; cancer reporting [N.H. Rev. Stat. §§ 141-B:7 and 141-B:8]; communicable diseases [N.H. Rev. Stat. §§ 141-C:7 and 141-C:8]; mental health services [N.H. Rev. Stat. § 135-C:19-a]; residential care facilities [N.H. Rev. Stat. § 151:21]; alcohol or drug abuse treatment [N.H. Rev. Stat. §§ 172:8-a and 330-C:12]; and genetic testing [N.H. Rev. Stat. § 141-H:2]. • No liability for breach of client confidentiality shall arise from the disclosure by a licensee of information related to reported sexual relations between a client and any mental health counselor or health care licensee of a state licensing or certifying agency when the disclosure is made in good faith and made to the board or any other state licensing or certifying agency [N.H. Rev. Stat. § 326-B:34, amended by 2005 N.H. Laws, ch. 293]. • Health care providers may not reveal confidential communications or information without consent of the patient, unless provided for by law or by the need to protect the welfare of the individual or the public interest [N.H. Rev. Stat. § 332-I:2, repealed and reenacted by 2006 N.H. Laws, ch. 250:2].

State	Health Care Privacy Statute/Provisions	Specific Disclosure Rules
		• Proceedings of residential care facility quality assurance programs are confidential [N.H. Rev. Stat. § 151:5-c, added by 2006 N.H. Laws, ch. 274:4].
		• Nurse fulfilling duty to warn of patient's violent acts not liable for breach of confidentiality [N.H. Rev. Stat. § 326-B:33, amended by 2006 N.H. Laws, ch. 297].
		• New Hampshire Birth Conditions Program [N.H. Rev. Stat. § 141-J:8, added by 2008 N.H. Laws, ch. 186].[*]
		• For the purpose of medical examination into cause and manner of death, where medical treatment has been provided to the decedent, upon written request of the supervising medical examiner any individual, partnership, association, corporation, institution, or governmental entity which has rendered such treatment shall provide the supervising medical examiner with all medical records pertaining to the decedent and the treatment rendered [N.H. Rev. Stat. § 611-B:14-a, added by 2008 N.H. Laws, ch. 197].
		• Commissioner of Health and Human Services shall have access to individually identifiable information relating to the occurrence of maternal deaths on a case-by-case basis where public health is at risk [N.H. Rev. Stat. § 132:31, added by 2010 N.H. Laws, ch. 129].
		• Information in the Controlled Drug Prescription Drug and Safety Program is confidential, is not a public record, is not subject to discovery or subpoena, and shall not be shared except with prescribers and dispensers, the patient, professional boards and regulators, law enforcement, and other states' programs [N.H. Rev. Stat. § 318-B:34, added by 2012 N.H. Laws, ch. 196].

[*] Not limited to HIPAA-covered entities.

continues

¶ 310 New Jersey

State	Health Care Privacy Statute/Provisions	Specific Disclosure Rules
NEW JERSEY	A hospital patient has a right to confidentiality of all records pertaining to his or her treatment except as otherwise provided by law or third-party payment contract [N.J. Stat. 26:2H-12.8]. Privacy protections are founded in statutes governing specific entities and medical conditions. A number of health care provider-patient privileges exist [N.J. Stat. §§ 2A:84A-22.1 and 2A:84A-22.2 (physician); 45:14B-28 (psychologist); and 45:8B-29 (marriage/family therapist)]. HMOs, dental plans, and prepaid prescription services may claim any privilege the original provider of the information is entitled to claim [N.J. Stat. §§ 17:48D-21, 17:48F-28 and 26:2J-27]; medical professionals are protected when they disclose medical errors in hospitals, nursing homes, and other providers—the reports are not public records or usable for adverse employment actions against the reporting professional [26:2H-12.25, effective Oct. 24, 2004].	• HMOs may disclose enrollee/applicant medical information without consent only to the extent necessary to carry out the law governing HMOs; pursuant to statute or court order; or in the event of claim or litigation between the person and the HMO [N.J. Stat. § 26:2J-27]. • An insurance entity may not disclose medical information about a person without consent, with certain exceptions: verifying insurance coverage benefits to a medical professional; to agents for purpose of conducting the entity's business when disclosure is necessary; to law enforcement agencies in fraud investigations; and pursuant to court order [N.J. Stat. § 17:23A-1 through 17:23A-18]. • Utilization review committees may disclose information they receive only to: a patient's attending physician; the CAO of the facility it serves; the facility's enforcement unit; government agencies in the performance of their duties; and the patient's insurer or plan, if authorized by the terms of coverage [N.J. Stat. § 2A:84A-22.8]. • Specific disclosure rules apply to state cancer and birth defects registries [N.J. Stat. §§ 26:8-40.23, 26:2-107]; genetic information [N.J. Stat. § 10:5-47]; HIV/AIDS [N.J. Stat. §§ 26:5C-7, 26:5C-8, and 26:5C-16, amended by 2007 N.J. Laws 218]; venereal disease [N.J. Stat.§ 26:4-41]; alcohol abuse treatment [N.J. Stat. § 26:2B-20]; nursing homes [N.J. Stat. § 30:13-5, amended by 2008 N.J. Laws 63]; behavioral health benefits and third-party payors [N.J. Stat. § 45:14B-32]; and institutionalized mentally ill persons [N.J. Stat. § 30:4-24.3]. • Medical records used in health claims processing, health care appeals, and utilization review are confidential and may be used only by the department involved, the organization, and the affected carrier for the purposes of the Health Claims Authorization, Processing and Payment Act [N.J. Stat. § 26:2S-12, added by 2005 N.J. Laws 352].

State	Health Care Privacy Statute/Provisions	Specific Disclosure Rules
		• Minors' treatment for drug use or abuse or for alcohol use or abuse that is consented to by a minor shall be considered confidential information between the physician, the provider, and the patient who may not be required to report the treatment except as may otherwise be required by law [N.J. Stat. § 9:27A-4, amended by 2005 N.J. Laws 342].
		• New Jersey Health Information Technology Commission recommends steps for the proper resolution of issues related to data ownership, governance, and confidentiality and security of patient information [N.J. Stat. § 26:1A-136, added by 2007 N.J. Laws 330].
		• The Commissioner of Health, in consultation with the Commissioner of Banking and Insurance, shall establish an advisory board to make recommendations to the Commissioners on Health Information Electronic Data Interchange Technology Policy, including a statewide policy on electronic health records, and measures to protect the confidentiality of medical information [N.J. Stat. § 26:1A-15.1, amended by 2012 N.J. Laws 17].
		• The Commissioner of Health shall make publicly available the identification number for the physician or physicians, as applicable, that appear on hospital billing forms and billing forms of ambulatory care facilities licensed to provide surgical services, to the extent that doing so is consistent with HIPAA [N.J. Stat. § 26:2H-5.1d, amended by 2009 N.J. Laws 263].
		• Hospital must request written consent of patient or guardian to release medical information to patient's designated caregiver, in compliance with HIPAA and state and federal laws [N.J. Stat. § 26:2H-5.26, added by 2014 N.J. Laws 68].

continues

¶ 320 New Mexico

State	Health Care Privacy Statute/Provisions	Specific Disclosure Rules
NEW MEXICO	No general prohibition on disclosure of confidential medical information. Privacy protections are found in statutes governing specific entities and medical conditions. Numerous provider-patient privileges exist [N.M.R. of Evid. 11-504 (physician and psychotherapist), R. 11-509 (social worker), N.M. Stat. Ann. §§ 31-25-3 (victim counselor), and 61-9-18 (psychologist), note: text of 61-9-18 will be repealed effective July 1, 2010]. Confidentiality of child's mental health and developmental disability information [N.M. Stat. Ann. § 32A-6-15, amended by 2007 N.M. Laws, ch. 162, § 24].	• HMOs may not disclose enrollee/applicant health information without consent, with certain exceptions: to the extent necessary to comply with the HMO law; pursuant to court order; or in order to defend against claims or litigation by the enrollee/applicant [N.M. Stat. Ann. § 59A-46-27, amended by 2007 N.M. Laws, ch. 218]. • All hospital records and health information that relates to and identifies specific persons as patients is confidential and not a matter of public record even if the information is in the custody or contained in records of a governmental agency; a custodian of confidential information may furnish it upon request to a governmental agency, a state educational institution, an association of licensed physicians, a licensed health facility, or staff committee [N.M. Stat. Ann. § 14-6-1]. • Insurers may not disclose nonpublic personal health information to any party, including affiliates, and may not disclose nonpublic personal financial information about a consumer to a nonaffiliated third party unless the insurer complies with notice and authorization requirements [N.M. Admin. Code, tit. 13 §§ 13.1.3.1 to 13.1.3.28]. • Specific disclosure rules apply to mental illness and developmental disabilities [N.M. Stat. Ann. § 43-1-19, amended by 2007 N.M. Laws, ch. 46]; sexually transmitted diseases and HIV [N.M. Stat. Ann. §§ 24-1-9.4, 24-2B-6, amended by 2013 N.M. Laws, ch. 72]; persons confined to an institution [N.M. Stat. Ann. § 14-2-1, amended by 2005 N.M. Laws, ch. 126]; Department of Health files [N.M. Stat. Ann. § 24-1-20]; voluntary alcohol and drug treatment [N.M. Stat. Ann. § 43-2-11, amended by 2005 N.M. Laws, ch. 198]; children's mental health and developmental disabilities [N.M. Stat. Ann. § 32A-6-15, amended by 2007 N.M. Laws, ch. 162]; and genetic information [N.M. Stat. Ann. § 24-21-3].

State	Health Care Privacy Statute/Provisions	Specific Disclosure Rules
		• Communications to the chiropractic board relating to potential disciplinary action are confidential, provided that information contained in a public file is subject to disclosure when the board acts on a complaint [N.M. Stat. Ann. § 61-4-10, amended by 2006 N.M. Laws, ch. 18, § 5, text repealed effective July 1, 2010].
		• A provider, health care institution, health information exchange or health care group purchaser shall not use or disclose health care information in an individual's electronic medical record to another person without the consent of the individual except as allowed by state or federal law [Electronic Medical Records Act, added by 2009 N.M. Laws, ch. 69].
		• Access to data in a health information system shall be provided in accordance with regulations adopted by the Health Policy Commission pursuant to the Health Information System Act; a data provider may obtain data it has submitted to the system, as well as aggregate data, but may not obtain data regarding an individual patient unless the data was originally submitted by the requesting provider [N.M. Stat. Ann. § 24-14A-6, amended by 2015 N.M. Laws, ch. 121]. Information collected and disseminated pursuant to the Health Information System Act is strictly confidential and not public record; data source is not liable for furnishing information [N.M. Stat. Ann. § 24-14A-8, amended by 2012 N.M. Laws, ch. 15].
		• Data collected by the Health Care Work Force Data Base shall be kept confidential; personally identifiable information may be released for state health planning purposes or to law enforcement for investigative purposes [N.M. Stat. Ann. § 24-14C-5, amended by 2012 N.M. Laws, ch. 16].
		• At the time a missing person report is made, the law enforcement agency to which the missing person report is given shall provide a dental record release form conforming to the requirements of the federal HIPAA to the custodian or immediate family member of the missing person; if a release form cannot be executed, the law enforcement agency shall seek disclosure of the dental records of a missing person directly from the records custodian pursuant to the provisions of HIPAA that allow disclosure of health information for law enforcement purposes [N.M. Stat. Ann. § 29-15-8, added by 2010 N.M. Laws, ch. 33].

continues

¶ 330 New York

State	Health Care Privacy Statute/Provisions	Specific Disclosure Rules
NEW YORK	No general prohibition on disclosure of confidential medical information. Nursing homes and facilities providing health services must adopt and publish a statement of a patient's right to have confidentiality in treatment of personal and medical records [N.Y. Pub. Health Law § 2803-c 3]. A number of health care provider-patient privileges exist [N.Y. C.P.L.R. §§ 4504 (physicians, nurses, dentists, podiatrists, chiropractors, medical corporations, professional service corporations, and university faculty practices); 4507 (psychologists); 4508 (social workers); and 4510 (rape crisis counselor)].	• Upon request of an insured or prospective insured, insurers must provide their procedures for protecting the confidentiality of medical records [N.Y. Ins. Law § 3217-a(b)(5)]. • When disclosing patient information to a person other than the patient, a health care provider must make a notation of the purpose of the disclosure, which must be as authorized by law, but a notation is not required for disclosure to practitioners or employees or agents of the facility or to government agencies inspecting the facility or investigating professional conduct [N.Y. Pub. Health Law § 18(6)]. These provisions also apply to HMOs [N.Y. Pub. Health Law §§ 18(1)(c), 4410]. • Department of Health shall implement protocols to ensure that information contained in Prescription Monitoring Program Registry is maintained in a secure and confidential manner and is accessible only by practitioners, pharmacists, or their designees for the Program's purposes; protocols will include a mechanism for the Department to monitor and record the identity of each authorized individual accessing the Registry and each controlled substance history accessed [N.Y. Pub. Health Law § 3343-a, added by 2012 N.Y. Laws, ch. 447, § 1]. • A health maintenance organization or its comprehensive health services plan may not disclose information acquired in the course of rendering professional services to a patient [N.Y. Pub. Health § 4410]. • An insurer may not disclose nonpublic personal health information about a consumer or customer unless an authorization is obtained from the consumer or customer or unless specific exceptions apply [N.Y. Comp. Codes R. & R. tit. 11 § 420.17]. • Utilization review agents must have written procedures assuring confidentiality of patient-specific information obtained during UR, and may disclose the information only as authorized by law [N.Y. Ins. Law § 4905(a)].

State	Health Care Privacy Statute/Provisions	Specific Disclosure Rules
		• Specific disclosure rules apply to child abuse reports by HMOs [N.Y. Pub. Health Law § 4410(3)]; records of mental health treatment [N.Y. Mental Hyg. Law § 33.13]; HIV/AIDS test results [N.Y. Pub. Health Law §§ 2781 and 2782]; communicable diseases including HIV [N.Y. Pub. Health Law §§ 2102, 2134-2135, amended by 2014 N.Y. Laws ch. 60, Sec. 2]; Alzheimer's disease [N.Y. Pub. Health Law § 2003]; cancer cases [N.Y. Pub. Health Law § 2402]; sexually transmissible diseases [N.Y. Pub. Health Law § 2306]; report of narcotics addiction [N.Y. Pub Health Law § 3372]; birth defects and genetic allied diseases [N.Y. Pub. Health Law § 2733]; long-term care [N.Y. Pub. Health Law, § 4403-f(7), amended by 2011 N.Y. Laws, ch. 59, § 41].

continues

¶ 340 North Carolina

State	Health Care Privacy Statute/Provisions	Specific Disclosure Rules
NORTH CAROLINA	No general prohibition on disclosure of confidential medical information, but disclosure of confidential medical information by insurance entities, including HMOs, and mental health facilities, is restricted by specific statutes. Several health care provider-patient privileges exist [N.C. Gen. Stat. §§ 8-53 (physician-patient), 8-53.3 (psychologist-client), 8-53.5 (licensed marital/family therapist-client), 8-53.7 (social worker-client), and 8-53.8 (professional counselor-client)]. Accreditation activities [N.C. Gen. Stat. § 131E-95(c), amended by 2006 N.C. Laws, ch. 114]. Disclosure of information in North Carolina Health Information Exchange must be consistent with HIPAA privacy rules and applicable state law [N.C. Gen. Stat. § 90-413.7, added by 2011 N.C. Laws, ch. 337]. Required reports on abortion are protected under HIPAA rules [N.C. Gen. Stat. § 14-45.1, amended by 2015 Laws, ch. 62].	• Medical records compiled and maintained by health care facilities in connection with individual patients are not public records and are not subject to inspection [N.C. Gen. Stat. § 131E-97]. • HMOs may not disclose enrollee/applicant health information without consent, except to the extent necessary to comply with the HMO law; pursuant to statute or court order; or in a claim or litigation between the person and the HMO [N.C. Gen. Stat. § 58-67-180]. • Insurance entities, including HMOs and medical service corporations, may not disclose a person's medical information without authorization, with limited exceptions: verifying insurance benefits; to conduct business when the disclosure is necessary; to law enforcement agencies in preventing or prosecuting fraud; and pursuant to a search warrant or subpoena [N.C. Gen. Stat. §§ 58-39-75(2) through (20)]. • Specific disclosure rules apply to pharmacies [N.C. Gen. Stat. § 90-85.36, amended by 2011 N.C. Laws, ch. 314]; mental health, developmental disabilities and substance abuse treatment facilities [N.C. Gen. Stat. §§ 122C-3, 122C-51 through 122C-56, amended by 2011 N.C. Laws, ch. 314, § 122C-25, amended by 2005 N.C. Sess. Law 276]; drug dependence treatment [N.C. Gen. Stat. § 90-109.1]; birth defects [N.C. Gen. Stat. § 130A-131.17]; cancer [N.C. Gen. Stat. § 130A-212]; adult care homes [N.C. Gen. Stat. § 131D-21]; nursing homes [N.C. Gen. Stat. § 131E-117]; and communicable diseases including HIV [N.C. Gen. Stat. §§ 130A-135 through 130A-140, 130A-143, amended by 2011 N.C. Laws, ch. 314]. • Child abuse and neglect reports to the Department of Health and Human Services are confidential [N.C. Gen. Stat. § 7B-311, amended by 2005 N.C. Sess. Laws 399, § 2, N.C. Gen. Stat. 8531.1, amended by 2007 N.C. Laws, ch. 353].* • Photographs and records made pursuant to an official autopsy are not public records, but the text of an official autopsy report is a public record [N.C. Gen. Stat.§ 132-18, added by 2005 N.C. Sess. Laws 393, § 1].*

State	Health Care Privacy Statute/Provisions	Specific Disclosure Rules
		• Confidential records disclosable to State Health Director for disease prevention [N.C. Gen. Stat. § 130A.15, added by 2007 N.C. Laws, ch. 353].
		• Records disclosed for law enforcement purposes [N.C. Gen. Stat. § 90-21.20B, amended by 2007 N.C. Laws, ch. 353].
		• Disclosure of emergency department data to CDC [N.C. Gen. Stat. § 130A-480, amended by 2007 N.C. Laws, ch. 8].

* Not limited to HIPAA-covered entities.

continues

¶ 350 North Dakota

State	Health Care Privacy Statute/Provisions	Specific Disclosure Rules
NORTH DAKOTA	No general prohibition on disclosure of confidential medical information. Privacy protections are found in statutes governing various entities and medical conditions. Several health care provider-patient privileges exist [N.D. Rules of Evidence, Rule 501, 503 (physician and psychotherapist-patient); N.D. Cent. Code §§ 31-01-06.3 (addiction counselor-client), and 43-47-09 (licensed professional counselor-client)]. Individually identifiable health information submitted to, stored in, or transmitted by Health Information Exchange is confidential [N.D. Cent. Code § 54-59, added by 2011 N.D. Laws S.B. 2037]. Peer review records are confidential and may be used for conducting a professional peer review, for reports and analyses, and by Department of Health to determine compliance with requirements of federal or state law [N.D. Cent. Code §§ 23-34-02 and 23-23-02.1, amended by 2011 N.D. Laws H.B. 1039]. Client information for substance abuse treatment program protected by HIPAA and other federal or state disclosure exclusions [N.D. § 50-31-06, amended by 2015 N.D. Laws S.B. 2237].	• Hospitals and other facilities providing maternity care may disclose the contents of their records in a judicial proceeding, to health or social agencies specifically interested in the patients, and to persons with a direct interest in the patient or infant's well-being [N.D. Cent. Code § 23-16-09]. • Insurers, HMOs, and other health plan entities must maintain procedures to ensure that all identifiable information regarding covered persons remains confidential, and may not disclose enrollee/applicant health information without consent, except: as necessary to follow the law governing the entity; pursuant to court order; or to defend against claims or litigation by the person [N.D. Cent. Code §§ 26.1-36-03.1, 26.1-36-12.4]. • HMOs may not disclose information pertaining to the diagnosis, treatment, or health of any enrollee or applicant obtained from the person or from any provider except to the extent that it may be necessary to carry out HMO legislation, or upon the express consent of the enrollee or applicant, or pursuant to statute or court order, or in the event of claim or litigation between the person and the HMO. An HMO may claim any statutory privileges against the disclosure that the provider who furnished the information to the health maintenance organization is entitled to claim [N.D. Cent. Code § 26.1-18.1-23]. • An insurer may not disclose nonpublic personal health information about a consumer or customer unless an authorization is obtained from the consumer or customer, or regulatory exceptions apply [N.D. Admin. Code § 45-14-01-17]. • Specific disclosure rules apply to abortion records [N.D. Cent. Code § 14-02.1-07, amended by 2011 N.D. Laws H.B. 1297]; HIV/AIDS [N.D. Cent. Code §§ 23-07-02.1 and 23-07-02.2]; congenital deformity reports [N.D. Cent. Code § 50-10-07]; research studies on morbidity and mortality [N.D. Cent. Code § 23-01-15]; public health authority [N.D. Cent. Code, §§ 23-01.3-02 and 23-01.3-08]; and sexually transmitted disease [N.D. Cent. Code §§ 23-07-03, 23-07-20.1].

State	Health Care Privacy Statute/Provisions	Specific Disclosure Rules
		• Physician health program records containing identifying information about a licensee participant are confidential and may be disclosed only for intervention, rehabilitation, referral assistance, or support services; or in a legal or administrative proceeding [N.D. Cent. Code § 43-17.3-07].
		• Pharmacy benefits manager must agree to allow provider or health care plan or carrier access to de-identified utilization information [N.D. Cent. Code § 26.1-27.1-05, amended by 2005 N.D. Laws 1332, § 2].
		• Access to prescription drug monitoring information [N.D. Cent. Code § 19-03.5-03, added by 2007 N.D. Laws, ch. 2134].
		• Abortion facilities and hospitals in which abortions are performed must keep a record of the number of women who received and viewed an ultrasound fetus image; records must remain confidential and may be used by the Department of Health only for gathering statistical data and ensuring compliance [N.D. Cent. Code § 14-02.1-07, amended by 2009 N.D. Laws, ch. 144].
		• Autism spectrum disorder database records are confidential, but Department of Health may provide records to other state agencies to effectuate purposes of database [2013 N.D. Laws, ch. 1038].*

* Not limited to HIPAA-covered entities.

continues

¶ 360 Ohio

State	Health Care Privacy Statute/Provisions	Specific Disclosure Rules
OHIO	No general prohibition on disclosure of confidential medical information. Privacy protections are found in statutes governing specific medical conditions or entities. Several health care provider-patient privileges exist [Ohio Rev. Code § 2317.02, amended by 2006 Ohio Laws 144, § 1 (physicians, dentists, chiropractors, professional counselors, social workers) and Ohio Rev. Code § 4732.19 (psychologists)].	• Insurance entities may not disclose a person's medical information without authorization except: to verify coverage benefits to a medical professional; to agents in conducting business when disclosure is necessary; to law enforcement agencies in order to prevent or prosecute fraud; pursuant to a search warrant or subpoena; and for marketing purposes, with certain restrictions [Ohio Rev. Code § 3904.13]. • Quality assurance and utilization review committees may use confidential records and information made available to them only in the exercise of committee functions [Ohio Rev. Code § 2305.24]. • Physicians, physician assistants, and psychologists may not disclose confidential communications, and may be subject to disciplinary action for doing so [Ohio Rev. Code §§ 4730.25, 4731.22, amended by 2004 Ohio Laws, H.B. 26, Sec. 1, 4732.17, and 4732.19]. • Specific disclosure rules apply to HIV/AIDS [Ohio Rev. Code § 3701.243]; long-term care resident records [Ohio Rev. Code § 173.20]; mental illness and mental retardation [Ohio Rev. Code § 5122.31, amended by 2005 Ohio Sess. Laws 66, part E]; birth defects [Ohio Rev. Code § 3705.32]; alcohol and drug addiction services [Ohio Rev. Code § 3793.13]; and cancer registry [Ohio Rev. Code § 3701.262]. • Board of Pharmacy may provide information from its drug database to law enforcement, pharmacist requesting the information, Medicaid managed care organizations, worker's compensation administrators, and other states' prescription monitoring programs [Ohio Rev. Code §§ 4739.79, 4739.80, amended by 2011 Ohio Laws 19].

State	Health Care Privacy Statute/Provisions	Specific Disclosure Rules
		• In accordance with HIPAA privacy rules, a state agency may exchange protected health information with another state agency relating to eligibility for or enrollment in a health plan or relating to participation in a government program providing public benefits if the exchange of information is necessary for operating a health plan, or coordinating or improving the administration of health care–related functions; for fiscal year 2013 only, a state agency also may exchange personally identifiable information with another state agency for purposes related to and in support of a health transformation initiative identified by the executive director of the Office of Health Transformation [Ohio Rev. Code § 191.04, added by 2012 Ohio Laws 487]. • Durable power of attorney may authorize attorney in fact to obtain information concerning principal's health, included HIPAA-defined protected health information, regardless of principal's capacity [Ohio Rev. Code § 1337.13, amended by 2013 Ohio Laws, H.B. 126].

continues

¶ 370 Oklahoma

State	Health Care Privacy Statute/Provisions	Specific Disclosure Rules
OKLAHOMA	No general prohibition on disclosure of confidential medical information. Privacy protections are found in statutes governing certain medical conditions or entities. Several provider-patient privileges exist [Okla. Stat. tit. 12, § 2503, amended by 2004 Okla. Acts, ch. 168, § 5 (physician and psychotherapist-patient); Okla. Stat. tit. 59, §§ 1261.6 (social worker-client), 1910 (licensed professional counselor-client), and 1925.11 (family therapist-patient)].	• Medical records and communications between a physician or psychotherapist and a mental health client are confidential and may not be disclosed without the patient's consent except by court order, or to other persons or agencies actively engaged in the patient's treatment or in related administrative work [Okla. Stat. tit. 43A, § 1-109, amended by 2004 Okla. Acts, ch. 113, § 3, 2006 Okla. Acts, ch. 16, § 20, 2006 Okla. Acts, ch. 20, § 2, 2013 Okla. Acts, ch. 37, § 2 (expanded to include drug or alcohol abuse treatment information, licensed drug and alcohol abuse counselors, and mandatory reporting of child abuse and other such crimes, and to allow patient access to records, with exceptions for certain information)]. • Records pertaining to diagnosis, treatment, or health of HMO enrollees or applicants may not be disclosed except to carry out the purposes of the Health Maintenance Organization Act of 2003, with the express consent of the enrollee or applicant, pursuant to a court order, or in the event of a claim or litigation between the person and the HMO [Okla. Stat. tit. 36, § 6927, added by 2003 Okla. Acts, ch. 197, § 27]. • Insurers may not disclose nonpublic personal health information about a consumer or customer unless an authorization is obtained from the consumer or customer, or specific exceptions to the nondisclosure rule apply [Okla. Admin. Code § 365:35-1-40]. • A psychologist may not disclose the fact that a patient is undergoing treatment, information acquired during treatment, or records of treatment without consent except in limited circumstances, such as when the patient has threatened to kill an identified person [Okla. Stat. tit. 59, § 1376, amended by 2004 Okla. Acts, ch. 168, § 14].

State	Health Care Privacy Statute/Provisions	Specific Disclosure Rules
		• Specific disclosure rules apply to information identifying persons with reportable diseases or who have participated in a public health investigation [Okla. Stat. tit. 63, § 1-502.2, amended by 2008 Okla. Acts, ch. 393]; genetic information [Okla. Stat. tit. 36, § 3614.1A, amended by 2009 Okla. Acts, ch. 144, § 3614.3]; dentists [Okla. Stat. tit. 59, § 328.32]; birth defects [Okla. Stat. tit. 63, § 1-550.2]; nursing homes [Okla. Stat. tit. 63, § 1-1918]; and the state tumor registry [Okla. Stat. tit. 63, § 1-551.1, amended by 2014 Okla. Acts, ch. 235].
		• Release of confidential information on person with reportable disease [Okla. Stat. tit. 63, § 1-502.2, amended by 2007 Okla. Acts, ch. 153].[*]
		• Existing confidentiality requirements apply to telemedicine [Okla. Stat. tit. 36, § 6804, amended by 2008 Okla. Acts, ch. 432].
		• District board of education must establish a procedure for school to request the disclosure of information concerning students who have received mental health care that indicates an explicit threat to the safety of students or school personnel, provided the disclosure does not violate the requirements and provisions of the Family Educational Rights and Privacy Act of 1974, HIPAA, or other state or federal confidentiality laws [Okla. Stat. tit. 70, § 24-100.3, added by 2009 Okla. Acts, ch. 276].[*]
		• Hospital shall promptly request written consent of patient or guardian to release medical information to patient's designated lay caregiver, in compliance with state and federal law [Okla. Stat. tit. 63, § 3113, added by 2014 Okla. Acts, ch. 253, § 2].

[*] Not limited to HIPAA-covered entities.

continues

¶ 380 Oregon

State	Health Care Privacy Statute/Provisions	Specific Disclosure Rules
OREGON	Personal medical information is exempt from public disclosure unless the public interest, by clear and convincing evidence, requires disclosure in a particular instance [Or. Rev. Stat. § 192.502, as amended by 2011 Or. Laws, ch. 424]. Several provider-patient privileges exist [Or. Rev. Stat. §§ 40.230 (psycho-therapists), 40.235, as amended by 2005 Or. Laws, ch. 353 (physicians and dentists), 40.240 (nurses), 40.250 (clinical social workers), and 40.262 (counselors)]; the Oregon Patient Safety Commission is required to establish a confidential, voluntary serious adverse event reporting system to identify serious adverse events [Or. Rev. Stat. § 442.820]. State-defined covered entity that is required to file annual financial statement must also file protection of health information report [Not yet codified, added by 2015 Or. Laws, ch. 133]. Hospital not required to have discharge policies that require disclosure of protected health information without consent [Or. Rev. Stat. § 441.___, added by 2015 Or. Laws, ch. 263].	• Insurers may not disclose any personal or privileged information about a person without written authorization, with certain exceptions: to verify insurance benefits; to conduct business when disclosure is necessary; to law enforcement agencies in preventing or prosecuting fraud; or pursuant to court order [Or. Rev. Stat. §§ 746.665(b) through (q)]. • Specific disclosure rules apply to alcohol and drug abuse treatment [Or. Rev. Stat. § 430.399]; cancer registry [Or. Rev. Stat. § 432.520]; genetic testing [Or. Rev. Stat. §§ 192.539, 192.547, amended by 2014 Or. Laws, ch. 45]; HIV status [Or. Rev. Stat. § 433.045, as amended by 2005 Or. Laws, ch. 516]; mental health records [Or. Rev. Stat. § 179.505, as amended by 2005 Or. Laws, ch. 498]; reportable diseases [Or. Rev. Stat. §§ 433.004 and 433.008]; nursing homes [Or. Rev. Stat. § 441.605]; immunization registries [Or. Rev. Stat. §§ 433.090, 433.092, amended by 2007 Or. Laws, ch. 196]; morbidity and mortality studies [Or. Rev. Stat. § 432.060]; and testing for HIV and hepatitis after law enforcement or emergency services personnel, health care provider, or firefighter contacts bodily fluids [Or. Rev. Stat. § 433.085, amended by 2012 Or. Laws, ch. 26]. • Provisions for continuation of health insurance coverage for a medical condition that a prudent layperson believes requires immediate attention does not require disclosure of otherwise privileged or confidential information [Or. Rev. Stat. § 743.839, amended by 2011 Or. Laws, ch. 500]. • The Oregon Department of Public Services and Prescription Drug Monitoring Advisory Program must establish and maintain a prescription monitoring program that complies with HIPAA and regulations and related federal alcohol and drug treatment confidentiality laws and regulations, and with state health and mental health confidentiality laws [Or. Rev. Stat. § 431.966, amended by 2014 Or. Laws, ch. 550].

State	Health Care Privacy Statute/Provisions	Specific Disclosure Rules
		• The Health Information Technology Oversight Council must ensure that health information technology applications have appropriate privacy and security controls and that data cannot be used for purposes other than patient care or as otherwise allowed by law [Or. Rev. Stat. §§ 431.301 through 431.308, 2008 Or. Laws, ch. 31, amended by 2009 Or. Laws, ch. 595 § 1171].
		• The person designated by power of attorney to determine whether the principal is financially incapable is the principal's personal representative for purposes of Oregon law and HIPAA privacy regulations [Or. Rev. Stat. § 127.005, amended by 2009 Or. Laws, ch. 46].

continues

¶ 390 Pennsylvania

State	Health Care Privacy Statute/Provisions	Specific Disclosure Rules
PENNSYLVANIA	No general prohibition on disclosure of confidential medical information. Privacy protections are found in statutes governing specific medical conditions or entities. A number of mental health care provider-patient privileges exist [42 Pa. Cons. Stat. §§ 5944 (psychiatrist/ psychologist) and 5945 (school nurses and school psychologists)]. There is also a narrowly drawn physician-patient privilege [42 Pa. Cons. Stat. § 5929]. A managed care plan and a utilization review entity must adopt and maintain procedures to ensure that all identifiable information regarding enrollee health, diagnosis, and treatment is adequately protected and remains confidential in compliance with all applicable federal and state laws and regulations and professional ethical standards [40 Pa. Cons. Stat. § 991.2131]. Disclosure of medical information to a health care agent does not waive confidentiality [20 Pa. Cons. Stat. § 5456, amended by 2006 Pa. Laws 179]. Limits on disclosure of Social Security Numbers inapplicable to HIPAA-covered entity [2006 Pa. Laws 60, § 4].	• Managed care plans and utilization review entities must maintain procedures to ensure that all identifiable information regarding enrollee treatment and health remains confidential. Disclosure is permitted to determine coverage, review complaints, conduct utilization review, or facilitate payment of a claim [40 Pa. Stat. §§ 991.2102, 991.2131]. • Insurers may not disclose nonpublic personal health information about a consumer unless an authorization is obtained from the consumer or unless specific exceptions apply [Pa. Admin. Code tit. 31, § 146b.11]. • Specific disclosure rules apply to alcohol and drug abuse treatment [71 Pa. Cons. Stat. § 1690.108]; suspected child abuse [23 Pa. Cons. Stat. §§ 6305, 6311, amended by 2-14 Pa. Laws 29]; cancer reporting [35 Pa. Cons. Stat. § 5636]; HIV/AIDS [35 Pa. Cons. Stat. § 7607, amended by 2011 Pa. Laws 59]; communicable diseases [35 Pa. Cons. Stat. §§ 521.4, 521.15]; health care facility reports of health care–associated infections [added by 2007 Pa. Laws 52, § 405]; and mental health [50 Pa. Cons. Stat. §§ 7103 and 7111]. • Peer review records are confidential and are not discoverable or admissible [40 Pa. Cons. Stat. § 1303.311].

¶ 400 Rhode Island

State	Health Care Privacy Statute/Provisions	Specific Disclosure Rules
RHODE ISLAND	The Confidentiality of Health Care Communications and Information Act provides a general, comprehensive prohibition against disclosure of confidential health care information [R.I. Gen. Laws §§ 5-37.3-3 and 5-37.3-4, amended by 2004 R.I. Pub. Laws, ch. 314, Sec. 1, effective July 3, 2004]. It includes information obtained from any health care service provider, including physicians, hospitals, dentists, optometrists, social workers, psychologists, and others. The physician-patient privilege is governed by the provisions of the Act.	• Confidential medical information may be released without patient consent under numerous circumstances, including: peer review boards; providers for coordinating health care services for the patient and for education and training within the facility; scientific research, with restrictions; news media (limited to the fact of a patient's hospital admission and general description of his or her condition); the provider's lawyer if the patient sues the provider for medical liability; and others [R.I. Gen. Laws § 5-37.3-4(b), amended by 2004 R.I. Pub. Laws, ch. 314, Sec. 1, effective July 3, 2004]. • Managed care entities and contractors are prohibited from providing any identifying information to any medical information data-base unless essential to compile statistical data regarding enrollees [R.I. Gen. Laws § 5-37.3-4(a), amended by 2004 R.I. Pub. Laws, ch. 314, Sec. 1, effective July 3, 2004]. • All information relating to a subscriber's health care history, diagnosis, condition, treatment, or evaluation shall be considered by the HMO to be confidential health care information and shall not be released or transferred except under the safeguards established by the Confidentiality of Health Care Information Act [R.I. Gen. Laws § 27-41-22]. • Medical records are exempt from disclosure under the Access to Public Records Act [R.I. Gen. Laws § 38-2-2].* • A utilization review agent may not disclose or publish individual medical records or any confidential medical information obtained in the performance of utilization review activities [R.I. Gen. Laws § 23-17.12-9, as amended by 2005 R.I. Pub. Laws, ch. 238]. • Insurers may not disclose nonpublic personal health information to an affiliate or nonaffiliated third party about an individual without obtaining an authorization from the individual, unless specific exceptions apply [R.I. Regs. R. 02-030-100].

continues

State	*Health Care Privacy Statute/Provisions*	*Specific Disclosure Rules*
		• Specific disclosure rules apply to genetic information [R.I. Gen. Laws § 28-6.7-1 (requirement of genetic testing or disclosure of genetic information generally prohibited; prohibitions greatly expanded, June 8, 2002)]; insurers and health plans prohibited from disclosing genetic information without authorization of individual [R.I. Gen. Laws § 27-18-52]; HIV/AIDS [R.I. Gen. Laws § 23-6-17 and § 23-13-19, amended by 2007 R.I. Laws, ch. 170, Sec. 2]; state cancer registry [R.I. Gen. Laws § 23-12-4]; alcoholism [R.I. Gen. Laws § 23-1.10-13]; sexually transmitted diseases [R.I. Gen. Laws § 23-11-9]; health care facilities [R.I. Gen. Laws § 23-17-19.1]; home care patients [R.I. Gen. Laws § 23-17.16-2]; emergency medical service workers [R.I. Gen. Laws § 23-4.1-19, amended by 2006 R.I. Pub. Laws, ch. 224]; prescriptions [R.I. Gen. Laws § 21-28-3.18, amended by 2006 R.I. Pub. Laws, ch. 176]; reports of abuse and neglect [R.I. Gen. Laws § 42-66-10, amended by 2007 R.I. Laws, ch. 209, Sec. 1]; and mental health [R.I. Gen. Laws §§ 40.1-5-26, amended by 2004 R.I. Pub. Laws, ch. 314, Sec. 2, effective July 3, 2004, and 40.1-5-27]. • Patients and health care providers have the choice to participate in the Rhode Island Information Exchange; participation in the HIE has no impact on the content of or use or disclosure of confidential health care information of patient participants that is held in locations other than the HIE; nothing in the HIE Act shall be construed to limit, change or otherwise affect entities' rights to exchange confidential health care information in accordance with other applicable laws [R.I. Gen. Laws § 5-37.7-4, added by 2008 R.I. Pub. Laws, ch. 466; R.I. Gen. Laws § 537.7-12, amended by 2014 R.I. Pub. Laws, ch. 277]. • Applications and supporting information submitted by qualifying medical marijuana patients are confidential and protected under HIPAA and are not subject to disclosure, except to authorized employees of the Department of Health as necessary to perform their official duties [R.I. Gen. Laws § 21-28-6.6, amended by 2010 R.I. Pub. Laws, ch. 110].*

State	*Health Care Privacy Statute/Provisions*	*Specific Disclosure Rules*
		• Minimum necessary disclosures are permitted by a provider to law enforcement personnel or to a person if the provider believes that a minor has been abused or neglected [R.I. Gen. Laws § 5-37.3-4, amended by 2010 R.I. Pub. Laws, ch. 85].*

* Not limited to HIPAA-covered entities.

continues

¶ 410 South Carolina

State	Health Care Privacy Statute/Provisions	Specific Disclosure Rules
SOUTH CAROLINA	No general prohibition on disclosure of confidential medical information. Privacy protections are found in laws governing specific medical conditions and entities. The physician-patient privilege is not recognized, but there is a mental health professional-client privilege [S.C. Code § 44-22-90].	• Physicians, hospitals, and other health facilities must provide the health department, upon request, access to their medical records, tumor registries, and other special disease record systems as necessary for its investigations [S.C. Code Ann. § 44-1-110]. • In responding to a request for medical information from an insurer, a physician may rely on the carrier's representation that the patient has authorized release of the information [S.C. Code § 44-115-50]. • A physician may sell medical records to another licensed physician or osteopath, but must first publish notice of his or her intention and of the patient's right to retrieve his or her records before a sale [S.C. Code § 44-115-130]. • HMOs may not disclose data or information pertaining to the diagnosis, treatment, or health of any enrollee or applicant obtained from such person or from any provider except to the extent that it may be necessary to carry out HMO legislation, or upon the express consent of the enrollee or applicant, or pursuant to statute or court order, or for a claim or litigation with the HMO. The HMO is entitled to claim any statutory privileges against disclosure that the provider who furnished the information is entitled to claim [S.C. Code Ann. § 38-33-260]. • Medical records, hospital staff reports, and similar records are not open for public inspection under the Public Records Act [S.C. Code Ann. § 30-4-20].[*] • Except as otherwise provided by law, a physician may not honor a request for the release of copies of medical records without the receipt of express written consent of the patient or person authorized by law to act on behalf of the patient [S.C. Code Ann. § 44-115-40]. • Patient authorization to have medical condition disclosed by provider or agent to designated individual, consistent with HIPAA [S.C. Code Ann. § 44-66-75, added by 2013 S.C. Acts 19].

State	Health Care Privacy Statute/Provisions	Specific Disclosure Rules
		• Insurers may not disclose nonpublic personal health information about a consumer or customer unless an authorization is obtained from the consumer or customer or a specific exception applies [S.C. Code Regs. 69-58 (2003)].
		• Specific disclosure rules apply to genetic information [S.C. Code § 38-93-30]; sexually transmitted diseases [S.C. Code §§ 44-29-70, 44-29-135, amended by 2011 S.C. Act 34, and 44-29-136]; mental health [S.C. Code § 44-22-90]; mental illness [S.C. Code Ann. § 19-11-95]; long-term care facilities [S.C. Code Ann. § 44-81-40]; evaluation of child for suspected abuse or neglect [S.C. Code Ann. § 63-7-380, amended by 2015 S.C. Acts. 75]; and cancer reports [S.C. Code § 44-35-40].
		• Hospital infection disclosure reporting requirements may not violate patient confidentiality and released reports may not include social security numbers or other identifying information; reporting is not deemed to waive privilege or confidentiality [S.C. Code Ann. 44-7-2450, 2006 Act 293, § 1].
		• Health care power of attorney includes HIPAA authorization [S.C. Code Ann. § 62-5-504(D), amended by 2006 S.C. Act 365].
		• Prescription drug monitoring information [S.C. Code Ann. § 44-53-1650, amended by 2014 S.C. Acts 244].
		• All information contained in organ and tissue donor registry is confidential and only may be accessed by procurement organizations that are licensed, accredited, or regulated under federal or state law, and only for the purpose of identifying a potential donor [S.C. Code Ann. § 44-43-1450, amended by 2007 S.C. Acts 92].
		• Information collected by Stroke Registry Taskforce must be in accordance with state and federal confidentiality provisions including HIPAA privacy requirements [S.C. Code Ann. § 44-61-670, added by 2011 S.C. Acts 62].
		• Hospital quality assurance review records are confidential and are not subject to discovery or subpoena and may not be used as evidence in a civil action unless the hospital waives confidentiality [S.C. Code § 44-7-392, added by 2012 S.C. Acts 275].

* Not limited to HIPAA-covered entities.

continues

¶ 420 South Dakota

State	Health Care Privacy Statute/Provisions	Specific Disclosure Rules
SOUTH DAKOTA	No general prohibition on disclosure of confidential medical information. Prohibitions are addressed in laws governing specific entities and medical conditions. There are several provider-patient privileges [S.D. Codified Laws §§ 19-13-6 and 19-13-7 (physician/psychoanalysts); § 36-27A-38 (psychologist/patient); § 34-20A-90 (alcohol and drug treatment facilities); § 36-26-30 (social workers); and § 36-32-27 (professional counselors)].	• HMOs may disclose enrollee/applicant health information without consent only to the extent necessary to follow the HMO law; pursuant to statute or court order; or in a claim or litigation between the person and the HMO [S.D. Codified Laws § 58-41-73]. • Information provided by Director of Division of Insurance by an HMO relative to risk-bearing entities is confidential, but may be disclosed to carry out purposes of HMO law and as allowed by state law [S.D. Codified Laws § 58-41-__, added by 2013 S.D. Laws, ch. 67]. • Specific disclosure rules apply to communicable diseases [S.D. Codified Laws § 34-22-12]; child abuse reports [S.D. Codified Laws § 26-8A-13, amended by 2007 S.D. Laws 1078. S.D. Codified Laws § 26-8A-13.1, added by 2007 S.D. Laws, ch. 166]; alcohol and drug abuse [S.D. Codified Laws § 34-20A-90]; venereal disease [S.D. Codified Laws § 34-23-2]; mental health information [S.D. Codified Laws § 27A-12-26]; medical research [S.D. Codified Laws § 34-14-1]; genetic tests [S.D. Codified Laws §§ 34-14-21 to 34-14-25]; pharmacies and pharmacists [S.D. Codified Laws § 36-11-69]; abortion [S.D. Codified Laws § 34-23A-7.1, amended by 2006 S.D. Laws, ch. 189, § 2]; records pertaining to minor children [S.D. Codified Laws § 25-5-7.3]; and cancer reports [S.D. Codified Laws §§ 1-43-11, 1-43-16 and 34-14-1].

¶ 430 Tennessee

State	Health Care Privacy Statute/Provisions	Specific Disclosure Rules
TENNESSEE	No general prohibition on disclosure of confidential medical information. Privacy is addressed in statutes governing specific entities and medical conditions. There is no physician-patient privilege, but a number of mental health care provider-patient privileges exist [Tenn. Code Ann. §§ 24-1-207 (psychiatrist-patient); 63-11-213 (psychologist/mental health professional-patient); 63-22-114 (marital/family therapist-client); and 63-23-107 (social worker-client)]. Records of a health care organization's quality improvement committee are privileged and confidential [Tenn. Code Ann. § 68-22-272, added by 2011 Tenn. Pub. Acts, ch. 67]. Records and reports regarding pregnant woman referred for drug abuse or drug dependence treatment shall be kept confidential [Tenn. Code Ann. § 33-10-104, added by 2013 Tenn. Pub. Acts, ch. 398, Sec. 2].	• Health care providers (including physicians, chiropractors, dentists, nurses, pharmacists, optometrists, professional counselors, and other licensed professionals) may not disclose a patient's name and address or other identifying information except in specified circumstances: statutorily required reports to health or government authorities; to third-party payors for utilization review, case management, peer reviews, or other administrative functions; and pursuant to subpoena [Tenn. Code Ann. § 63-2-101(b), as amended by 2005 Tenn. Pub. Acts, chs. 113 and 474]. • Hospitals and clinics may not disclose patient information except: mandatory reports to health authorities; for utilization reviews, case management or other administrative functions; pursuant to subpoena; or to providers treating the patient [Tenn. Code Ann. § 68-11-1502]. • HMOs must hold in confidence data or information pertaining to the diagnosis, treatment or health of any enrollee, or applicant, obtained from such person or from any provider. The information may be disclosed by the HMO only to carry out the purpose of HMO legislation, upon the consent of the enrollee or applicant; in the event of a claim or litigation between the enrollee or applicant and HMO; or when required by statute [Tenn. Code Ann. § 56-32-225]. • With respect to any information pertaining to the diagnosis, treatment, or health of any enrollee or applicant, a prepaid limited health service organization is entitled to claim any statutory privileges against disclosure that the provider who furnished the information is entitled to claim [Tenn. Code Ann. § 56-51-150]. • Medical records of patients in state, county, and municipal hospitals and medical facilities, and the medical records of persons receiving medical treatment at the expense of the state, county, or municipality, are confidential and not open as public records [Tenn. Code Ann. § 10-7-504, amended by 2007 Tenn. Pub. Acts, ch. 178]. • Utilization review agents must comply with all applicable laws to protect the confidentiality of individual medical records [Tenn. Code Ann. § 56-6-705].

continues

State	Health Care Privacy Statute/Provisions	Specific Disclosure Rules
		• An insurer may not disclose nonpublic personal information about a consumer to a nonaffiliated third party unless specifically authorized by regulation [Tenn. Comp. R. & Regs. R. 0780-1-72-.11 (2003)].

• Specific disclosure rules apply to abortions [Tenn. Code Ann. § 39-15-203 and Tenn. Code Ann. § 39-15-210, added by 2006 Tenn. Pub. Acts, ch. 845]; genetic information [Tenn. Code Ann. §§ 56-7-2702 and 56-7-2704]; sexually transmitted diseases and HIV [Tenn. Code Ann. §§ 68-5-703, 68-10-113, and 68-10-115]; mental health records [Tenn. Code Ann. § 33-3-104(10)]; birth defects [Tenn. Code Ann. § 68-5-506]; nursing homes [Tenn. Code Ann. § 68-11-901]; alcohol abuse prevention [Tenn. Code Ann. § 68-24-508]; pharmacists [Tenn. Code Ann. § 63-10-405, amended by 2006 Tenn. Pub. Acts, ch. 768]; public health authorities [Tenn. Code Ann. § 68-142-108, amended by 2007 Pub. Acts, ch. 588]; cancer registry [Tenn. Code Ann. §§ 68-1-1003 and 68-1-1006]; telemedicine [Tenn. Code Ann. § 63-1-___, added by 2015 Tenn. Pub. Acts, ch. 261]; and stroke registry [Tenn. Code Ann. § 68-1-1903, added by 2008 Tenn. Pub. Acts, ch. 1186].

• Confidentiality does not preclude providers from communicating during care or from responding to hospital request for records, consistent with HIPAA [Tenn. Code Ann. § 68-11-312, added by 2007 Tenn. Pub. Acts, ch. 391].

• Confidential information from Controlled Substance Database may be released to licensing board or regulator regarding dispensers, prescribers, health care practitioner extenders, or patients in investigation of controlled substance violations; information may also be released on court order [Tenn. Code Ann. § 53-10-308, amended by 2012 Tenn. Pub. Acts, ch. 880].

• Health care providers shall make their medical records available for inspection and copying by the department of health: (1) upon the presentation of a written authorization for release signed by the patient or the patient's legal representative; or (2) upon a written request made by the department of health investigators, inspectors, or surveyors who are performing authorized investigations, inspections, or surveys [Tenn. Code Ann. § 63-1-117, amended by 2009 Tenn. Pub. Acts, ch. 188].

¶ 440 Texas

State	Health Care Privacy Statute/Provisions	Specific Disclosure Rules
TEXAS	No general prohibition on disclosure of confidential medical information. Privacy is addressed in laws governing specific entities and medical conditions. A physician's treatment records and communications with a patient are confidential and may not be disclosed except as allowed by statute without the patient's consent [Tex. Occ. Code § 159.001 *et seq.*]. Numerous health care provider-patient privileges exist [Tex. R. Evid. 509 (physicians); Tex. Health & Safety Code §§ 611.002 and 611.003 (mental health professionals)].	• An insurer must obtain an authorization to disclose any nonpublic personal health information about a consumer to another party before making the disclosure, unless specific exceptions apply [Tex. Admin. Code tit. 28, § 22.53 (2003)]. • Hospitals may disclose a patient's health information without written consent only to a provider attending the patient; to an organ or tissue organization; and to specified others [Tex. Health & Safety Code §§ 241.152 and 241.153, amended by 2005 Tex. Gen. Laws, ch. 136]. • Specific disclosure laws apply to communicable diseases [Tex. Health & Safety Code §§ 81.041, 81.046, and 81.203, amended by 2009 Tex. Act. Sep. Bill 1171]; state cancer registry [Tex. Health & Safety Code § 82.009]; mental health records [Tex. Health & Safety Code §§ 611.002 and 611.004, amended by 2005 Tex. Gen. Laws, ch. 138]; sexual assault advocacy services [Tex. Health & Safety Code §§ 44.071 and 44.072]; HIV test results [Tex. Health & Safety Code § 81.103]; genetic information [Tex. Ins. Code § 546.102]; newborn and infant screening [Tex. Health & Safety Code §§ 33.0111-.0112, 33.017, and 47.003-.004, amended by 2012 Tex. Acts, ch. 1273]; peer review [Tex. Health & Safety Code § 161.0315]; and occupational conditions [Tex. Health & Safety Code §§ 84.001, 84.006]. • Disclosure of health plan eligibility and benefit information [Tex. Ins. Code § 8-1660, added by 2007 Tex. Gen. Laws, ch. 522]. • Fetal and infant mortality review information is confidential if disclosure would compromise the privacy of the decedent or the decedent's family [Tex. Health & Safety Code § 674.007, added by 2007 Tex. Acts, ch. 488].[*] • HIPAA covered entity must comply with HIPAA privacy standards; Health and Human Services Executive Director may adopt rules consistent with HIPAA; Texas Attorney General must adopt standards for notice and authorization for electronic disclosure of protected health information [Tex. Health & Safety Code §§ 181.004, 181.005, 181.154, amended by 2011 Tex. Acts, ch. 300].

continues

State	*Health Care Privacy Statute/Provisions*	*Specific Disclosure Rules*
		• Independent review organization may not publicly disclose HIPAA-protected patient information or transmit the information to a subcontractor that has not signed an agreement similar to the HIPAA business associate agreement [Tex. Ins. Code § 4202.002, amended by 2013 Tex. H.B. 2645].

* Not limited to HIPAA-covered entities.

¶ 450 Utah

State	Health Care Privacy Statute/Provisions	Specific Disclosure Rules
UTAH	No general prohibition on disclosure of confidential medical information. Records maintained by a governmental entity that contain individuals' medical information are private records and not open to public inspection, but must be disclosed under certain enumerated circumstances [Utah Code Ann. §§ 63-2-201 and 63-2-202]. Several provider-patient privileges exist [Utah Code Ann. §§ 78-24-8(4) (physicians) and 78-24-8(6) (sexual assault counselors); and Utah Rules of Evidence, Rule 506 (mental health therapists)].	• Psychologists, mental health therapists, and substance abuse counselors may disclose confidential communications with a patient without consent under certain limited circumstances: in reporting certain conditions as required by law; as part of an administrative, civil, or criminal proceeding; or under a professional or ethical standard that authorizes or requires disclosure [Utah Code Ann. §§ 58-61-602, 58-60-114, and 58-60-509]. • An insurer may not disclose nonpublic personal health information about a consumer or customer unless an authorization is obtained from the consumer or customer or unless exceptions to the nondisclosure regulation apply [Utah Admin. R. 590-206-17 (2003)]. • Specific disclosure rules apply to communicable diseases, including venereal diseases and HIV [Utah Code Ann. §§ 26-6-6, 26-6-3.5, 26-6-16, and 26-6-27, amended by 2012 Utah Laws, ch. 150]; sexual assault counseling [Utah Code Ann. § 78-3c-4]; genetic counselors [Utah Code Ann. § 58-75-502]; use of genetic tests [Utah Code §§ 26-45-101 to 106]; patient access to medical records [Utah Code § 78B-5-618, amended by 2015 Utah Laws, ch. 217]; state hospital and other mental health facilities [Utah Code Ann. § 62A-15-643]; confidentiality of HMO medical records and audits [Utah Code Ann. § 31A-8-405]; abortions [Utah Code Ann. §§ 76-7-302, 76-7-313]; medical records of deceased persons [Utah Code Ann. § 78-25-25.5, added by 2006 Utah Laws, ch. 238]; personal representatives under advance directives [Utah. Code Ann. § 75-2a-1112, added by 2007 Utah Laws, ch. 31]; and abuse or neglect of vulnerable adults [Utah Code Ann. §§ 62A-3-311 and 62A-3-311.1]. • Uniform electronic standards for insurance information will have to meet federal mandatory minimum standards following the adoption of national requirements for transactions in HIPAA [Utah Code Ann. § 3A-22-614/5, amended by 2010 Utah Laws, ch. 357].

continues

State	Health Care Privacy Statute/Provisions	Specific Disclosure Rules
		• Utah Department of Health Director may allow access to controlled substance database for scientific studies if identities of prescribers, patients, and pharmacies are de-identified in accordance with HIPAA rules and kept confidential [Utah Code Ann. § 58-37f-301, amended by 2014 Utah Laws, ch. 68].

¶ 460 Vermont

State	Health Care Privacy Statute/Provisions	Specific Disclosure Rules
VERMONT	No general prohibition on disclosure of confidential medical records. Privacy protections found in laws governing specific medical conditions and entities. Hospital patients have a right to privacy of their hospital records and communications [18 Vt. Stat. Ann. § 1852(a)]. Several health care provider-patient privileges exist, extending to a patient and his or her physician, chiropractor, dentist, nurse, psychologist, social worker, mental health counselor, or other mental health professional [12 Vt. Stat. Ann. § 1612; 18 Vt. Stat. Ann. § 7101(13); and Vt. Rules of Evidence, Rule 503]. Confidential records destruction requirements deemed met for HIPAA-compliant entity [9 Vt. Stat. Ann. 62-2445, added by 2006 Vt. Acts 162].	• Disclosure of hospital records without patient authorization is allowed only to medical personnel directly treating the patient, or to persons monitoring the quality of the treatment or researching its effectiveness [18 Vt. Stat. Ann. § 1852(a), amended by 2005 Vt. Acts 55]. • An insurer may not disclose nonpublic personal health information about a consumer or customer unless an authorization is obtained from the consumer or customer, or unless regulatory exceptions apply [Vt. Code Regs. 21-010-016 § 17 (2003)]. • Specific disclosure rules apply to research data [1 Vt. Stat. Ann. § 317(c)(23), amended by 2006 Vt. Acts 132, § 1]; communicable diseases and HIV reporting [18 Vt. Stat. Ann. § 1001, amended by 2007 Vt. Acts 73]; cancer and mammography registries [18 Vt. Stat. Ann. §§ 152 to 157]; venereal diseases [18 Vt. Stat. Ann. § 1099]; genetic testing [18 Vt. Stat. Ann. §§ 9331 to 9335]; nursing homes [33 Vt. Stat. Ann. § 7301]; emergency contraception [26 Vt. Stat. Ann. § 2078, added by 2006 Vt. Acts 101]; prescription drug information [18 Vt. Stat. Ann. § 4631, amended by 2008 Vt. Acts 89]; and mental illness [18 Vt. Stat. Ann. § 7103]. • Consistent with federal law, a professional providing a patient's medical home shall ensure access to a patient's medical records by the community health team members in a manner compliant with HIPAA [2010 Vt. Acts 128 § 704]. • Health care database maintained by Green Mountain Care Board is governed by applicable HIPAA privacy rule requirements [18 Vt. Stat. Ann. § 9410, amended by 2013 Vt. Acts 79 § 40].

continues

¶ 470 Virginia

State	Health Care Privacy Statute/Provisions	Specific Disclosure Rules
VIRGINIA	No provider or other person working in a health care setting may disclose a patient's records without his or her consent, except when permitted by statute [Va. Code Ann. § 32.1-127.1:03(A) and (D), amended by 2012 Va. Acts, chs. 386 and 402]. This includes records maintained by physicians, hospitals, dentists, pharmacists, psychologists, professional counselors, HMOs, nursing homes, state-operated health facilities, and others [Va. Code Ann. §§ 8.01-581.1, amended by 2006 Va. Acts 638 § 1, and 32.1-127.1:03(B), amended by 2011 Va. Acts, ch. 798]. Provider-patient privileges exist for physicians and other "licensed practitioner of the healing arts" [Va. Code Ann. § 8.01-399] and for licensed professional counselors, clinical social workers, and psychologists [Va. Code Ann. § 8.01-400.2].	• A provider may disclose a patient's records without consent under certain enumerated circumstances: pursuant to subpoena; as required by law including contagious disease, public safety, and reporting requirements for suspected abuse; in the normal course of business in a standard health services setting; to third-party payors or agents in connection with payment of bills; and others [Va. Code Ann. § 32.1-127.1:03(D), amended by 2012 Va. Acts, chs. 386 and 402]. • Insurance entities may not disclose a person's medical information without written consent, with certain exceptions: verifying coverage benefits to a medical professional; conducting actuarial or research studies; for conducting business when disclosure is necessary; to law enforcement agencies to prevent or prosecute fraud; and pursuant to court order, including search warrant or subpoena [Va. Code Ann. § 38.2-613]. • The state Freedom of Information Act excludes medical and mental health records, and records of abuse of persons receiving services, from public records open to inspection; records may be disclosed at custodian's discretion if otherwise permitted [Va. Code Ann. § 2.2-3705.5, amended by 2012 Va. Acts, ch. 507].* • Specific disclosure rules apply to cancer reports [Va. Code Ann. §§ 32.1-70 and 32.1-71]; genetic and metabolic diseases [Va. Code Ann. §§ 32.1-65, amended, with contingent effective date, by 2004 Va. Acts, ch. 760, and §§ 32.1-69, 38.2-508.4, and 38.2-612]; congenital anomalies [Va. Code Ann. §§ 32.1-69.1 and 32.1-69.2, amended by 2006 Va. Acts 699]; reporting of diseases [Va. Code Ann. § 32.1-36]; HIV testing [Va. Code Ann. § 32.1-36.1 and § 32.1-37.2, amended by 2008 Va. Acts 870]; emergency medical services patient care information system [Va. Code Ann. § 32.1-116.1:1, amended by 2007 Va. Acts, ch. 13 and by 2008 Va. Acts, ch. 563]; former provisions governing disclosure by mental health professionals of patient information to third-party payors were repealed

State	*Health Care Privacy Statute/Provisions*	*Specific Disclosure Rules*
		effective October 1, 2005 [former Va. Code Ann. §§ 37.1-225 to 37.1-233, repealed].
		• The pilot program for the use of biometric data to improve quality of care and efficiency for recipients of medical assistance must comply with state and federal requirements relating to interoperability and information security, including all requirements of HIPAA [2010 Va. Acts 870, § 3].
		• Ombudsman for health and related insurance for state employees may review health care records of covered employees in accordance with HIPAA privacy rules, and confidentiality shall be maintained in accordance with state law [Va. Code Ann. § 51.1-201, amended by 2014 Va. Acts ch. 631].

* Not limited to HIPAA-covered entities.

continues

¶ 480 Washington

State	Health Care Privacy Statute/Provisions	Specific Disclosure Rules
WASHINGTON	The Uniform Health Care Information Act [Wash. Rev. Code Ann. § 70.02.005 *et seq.*] governs disclosure of health care information maintained by health care providers, their employees and agents, and restricts them from disclosing such information about a patient to any other person without written authorization [Wash. Rev. Code Ann. § 70.02.020, amended by 2014 Wash. Laws, ch. 220]. A patient has the right to an accounting of disclosures of certain health care information by the provider [Wash. Rev. Code Ann. § 70.02.020(2), as amended by 2014 Wash. Laws, ch. 220]; a provider-patient privilege is extended to physicians [Wash. Rev. Code Ann. § 5.60.060, amended by 2006 Wash. Laws, chs. 30, 202, 259 and 2007 Wash. Laws, ch. 196], psychologists [Wash. Rev. Code Ann. § 18.83.110, amended by 2005 Wash. Laws, ch. 504, Sec. 706], and nurses [Wash. Rev. Code Ann. § 5.62.020], among others.	• Health care providers must disclose patient information without consent in certain circumstances: to health authorities as required by law or if needed to determine compliance with licensure laws or to protect the public health; to law enforcement authorities as required by laws; to coroners and medical examiners for investigations of deaths; and pursuant to compulsory process; a patient may receive an accounting of disclosures of some health care information made by the provider [Wash. Rev. Code Ann. § 70.02.050(2), as amended by 2014 Wash. Laws, ch. 220]. • Insurers must limit disclosure of any information, including health information, about an individual if the individual states in writing that disclosure could jeopardize the safety of the individual. Notwithstanding any insurance law requiring disclosure, an insurer may not disclose nonpublic personal health information concerning health services related to reproductive health, sexually transmitted diseases, chemical dependency, and mental health, if the individual makes a written request [Wash. Admin. Code § 284-04-510 (2003)]. • Public disclosure requirements for public records do not apply to personal information in any files maintained for patients or clients of public institutions or public health agencies, or welfare recipients [Wash. Rev. Code Ann. § 42.17.310, amended by 2005 Wash. Laws, chs. 33, 172, 274, 284, 312, 349, and 424, and 2006 Wash. Laws, chs. 75 and 302].[*] • Providers may disclose health information without patient consent under a variety of circumstances: to a person providing health care to the patient; to persons using the information for health care education, planning, quality assurance, peer review, administrative or other services to the provider; to a provider who previously treated the patient; to any person in the event of imminent danger to the health or safety of the patient or another person; to a patient's immediate family or close friend, if in accordance with good professional practice; to a successor provider; to an approved research project; for an audit; and others [Wash. Rev. Code Ann. § 70.02.050(1), amended by 2014 Wash. Laws, ch. 220].

State	*Health Care Privacy Statute/Provisions*	*Specific Disclosure Rules*
		• Specific disclosure rules apply to alcoholism and drug addiction treatment [Wash. Rev. Code Ann. § 70.96A.230]; reports of abuse [Wash. Rev. Code Ann. § 26.44.030]; medical research [Wash. Rev. Code Ann. §§ 42.48.010 through 42.48.040, amended in part by 2005 Wash. Laws, ch. 274]; HIV and sexually transmitted diseases [Wash. Rev. Code Ann. §§ 70.24.022 and 70.24.105]; suspected child abuse [Wash. Rev. Code Ann. § 74.13.280, amended by 2007 Wash. Laws, ch. 220]; Domestic Violence Fatality Review Panel records [Wash. Rev. Code § 43.235.040, amended by 2012 Wash. Laws, ch. 223]; cancer registry [Wash. Rev. Code Ann. § 70.54.230]; long-term care residents [Wash. Rev. Code Ann. § 43.190.110]; mental health [Wash. Rev. Code Ann. §§ 71.05.390 to 71.05.427, amended by 2005 Wash. Laws, ch. 504; §§ 71.05.620 through 71.05.690, amended by 2015 Wash. Laws, ch. 269]; treatment for alcoholism, drug addiction [Wash. Rev. Code Ann. § 70.96A.150]; adverse health events and incident reporting [Wash. Rev. Code Ann. §§ 70.56.020, 70.56.040, and 70.56.050, amended by 2008 Wash. Laws, ch. 136]; and others. • Reporting of medical errors to independent entity must preserve confidentiality [Wash. Rev. Code § 70.56.040, added by 2006 Wash. Laws, ch. 8]. • Disclosure of confidential information on mental health services for minors permitted only in specified circumstances, including for purposes of HIPAA [Wash. Rev. Code § 70.02.240, added by 2013 Wash. Laws ch. 200, Section 8]. • HIPAA-covered entity is deemed to comply with requirement for securing information for purposes of security breach notification statute [Wash. Rev. Code Ann. § 19.255.210, amended by 2015 Wash. Laws, ch. 64].

* Not limited to HIPAA-covered entities.

continues

¶ 490 West Virginia

State	Health Care Privacy Statute/Provisions	Specific Disclosure Rules
WEST VIRGINIA	No general prohibition on disclosure of confidential medical information. There is no statutory physician-patient privilege. Any physician-patient privilege is inapplicable in peer review proceedings [W. Va. Code § 30-3-9, amended by 2007 W. Va. Acts, ch. 573].	• Social workers and professional counselors may not disclose any confidential information acquired from clients without the client's consent, except in limited instances such as when the client is contemplating a crime or harmful act [W. Va. Code §§ 30-30-12, 30-31-13].
		• HMOs may not disclose enrollee/applicant health information without express consent, except to the extent necessary to follow the law governing HMOs, pursuant to statute or court order, or in a claim or litigation between the person and the HMO [W. Va. Code § 33-25A-26].
		• Insurers may not disclose nonpublic personal health information about a consumer or customer unless an authorization is obtained from the consumer or customer [W. Va. Regs. § 114-57-15].
		• Information pertaining to the diagnosis, treatment, or health of any enrollee or applicant obtained from that person or from any provider by any prepaid limited health service organization must be held in confidence and may not be disclosed except in specified circumstances [W. Va. Code § 33-25D-28].
		• The state Freedom of Information law excludes from public inspection information of a personal nature such as that kept in a personal, medical or similar file, if the public disclosure thereof would constitute an unreasonable invasion of privacy, unless the public interest by clear and convincing evidence requires disclosure. The exception does not preclude an individual from inspecting or copying his or her own personal, medical, or similar file [W. Va. Code § 29B-1-4, amended by 2007 W. Va. Acts, ch. 386].[*]

State	*Health Care Privacy Statute/Provisions*	*Specific Disclosure Rules*
		• Specific disclosure rules apply to the state cancer registry [W. Va. Code § 16-5A-2a]; pharmacists [W. Va. Code § 30-5-1b, amended by 2005 W. Va. Acts, ch. 184 and 2007 W. Va. Acts, ch. 1001]; Board of Pharmacy disclosure of confidential records from the West Virginia Controlled Substance Monitoring Program database [W. Va. Code § 60A-9-5, amended by 2012 W. Va. Acts, ch. 83]; HIV test results [W. Va. Code § 16-3C-3, amended by 2011 W. Va. Acts, ch. 488]; birth defects [W. Va. Code § 16-40-4]; social workers [W. Va. Code § 30-30-12]; licensed professional counselors [W. Va. Code § 30-31-13]; and mental health information [W. Va. Code § 27-3-1, amended by 2007 W. Va. Acts, ch. 3184].
		• West Virginia Health Information Network and Health Care Authority must comply with HIPAA privacy rules and confidentiality statutes [W. Va. Code § 16-29G-1 to 8, added by 2006 W. Va. Acts, ch. 107].
		• Person authorized in power of attorney to determine that principal is incapacitated may act as personal representative under HIPAA privacy rules to obtain access to principal's health care information and communicate with provider [W. Va. Code § 39B-1-109, amended by 2012 W. Va. Acts, ch. 199].
		• On designation of lay caregiver by patient or guardian, hospital shall promptly request written consent of patient or guardian to release medical information to lay caregiver, consistent with HIPAA rules [W. Va. Code § 16-5X-2, added by H.B. 2100 of 2015].[*]

[*] Not limited to HIPAA-covered entities.

continues

¶ 500 Wisconsin

State	Health Care Privacy Statute/Provisions	Specific Disclosure Rules
WISCONSIN	All patient health care records are confidential, and may be released only as provided by law, or with the patient's consent, or for purposes of health care operations, with certain exceptions [Wis. Stat. Ann. § 146.82, amended by 2003 Wis. Acts 281]. There is a broad health care provider-patient privilege, extending to physicians, registered nurses, chiropractors, psychologists, social workers, marriage/family therapists, and professional counselors and their patients/clients [Wis. Stat. Ann. § 905.04, amended by 2005 Wis. Acts 387, 434].	• Patient health care records must be released without the patient's consent in a number of situations: for management audits, program monitoring and accreditation; to providers or persons acting under their supervision; for billing, collection, or payment of claims; pursuant to court order; for research, with certain limitations; to government agencies that require reporting of certain conditions; to county officials in child abuse/neglect investigations; and to specified others [Wis. Stat. Ann. § 146.82, amended by 2005 Wis. Acts 187, 344, 387, 388, 434]. • An insurer may disclose a person's medical information without the person's consent to a health care facility or provider for verifying insurance coverage or benefits or for an operations or services audit; if necessary to a group policyholder for reporting claims experience; to pursue a subrogation of claim; and others [Wis. Stat. Ann. § 610.70(5), amended by 2005 Wis. Laws Act 22, § 165]. • Insurers may not disclose nonpublic personal health information about a consumer or customer unless an authorization is obtained from the consumer or customer, or unless disclosure is authorized by law [Wis. Adm. Code Ins. § 25.70]. • Specific disclosure rules apply to the state cancer registry [Wis. Stat. Ann. § 255.04]; genetic information [Wis. Stat. Ann. § 631.89]; HIV-related information [Wis. Stat. Ann. § 252.15(5), amended by 2005 Wis. Acts 155, 187, 266, 344, 387]; mental health, developmental disability, and drug/alcohol abuse treatment records [Wis. Stat. Ann. § 51.30, amended by 2005 Wis. Acts 344, 387, 388, 406, 434, 444, 449]; congenital disorders [Wis. Stat. Ann. § 253.13, amended by 2013 Wis. Act. 135]; evaluation of infants for fetal alcohol spectrum disorders [Wis. Stat. Ann. § 146.0257, added by 2013 Wis. Act 260]; and sexually transmitted diseases [Wis. Stat. Ann. § 252.11, amended by 2005 Wis. Act 187].

State	Health Care Privacy Statute/Provisions	Specific Disclosure Rules
		• A person authorized by the principal in a power of attorney to determine that the principal is incapacitated may act as the principal's personal representative, under HIPAA and applicable regulations, to obtain access to the principal's health care information and communicate with the principal's health care provider [Wis. Stat. Ann. § 244.08, added by 2009 Wis. Act 319].

continues

¶ 510 Wyoming

State	Health Care Privacy Statute/Provisions	Specific Disclosure Rules
WYOMING	No general prohibition on disclosure of confidential medical information. A number of health care provider-patient privileges exist [Wyo. Stat. Ann. §§ 1-12-101 (physician-patient); 33-27-123 (psychologist-client); and 35-2-610 (hospital-patient)].	• HMOs may not disclose any enrollee/applicant health information without express consent, except to carry out the purposes of the HMO Act; in a claim or litigation between the person and the HMO; to implement public medical assistance programs; and as required by statute [Wyo. Stat. Ann. § 26-34-130]. • A hospital may not disclose patient health information to any other person without the patient's consent, except to the extent a recipient needs to know the information, if the disclosure is to a person providing health care to the patient; for health care education or for planning, quality assurance, peer review or administrative or other services to the hospital; to immediate family members; or for approved research [Wyo. Stat. Ann. § 35-2-609, amended by 2006 Wyo. Sess. Laws, ch. 114]. • Insurers may not disclose nonpublic personal health information about a consumer or customer unless an authorization is obtained from the consumer or customer, or unless the disclosure is required for the performance of an insurance function or otherwise authorized by law [Weil's Code Wyo. R. 044-000-054, § 17 (2003)]. • Medical, psychological, and sociological data on individual persons, exclusive of coroners' autopsy reports, are not open to inspection under public records laws [Wyo. Stat. § 16-4-203]. • Hospitals may not disclose any hospital health care information about a patient to any other person without the patient's written authorization, except as otherwise authorized by law. A disclosure made under a patient's written authorization shall conform to the terms of that authorization [Wyo. Stat. § 35-2-606].

State	*Health Care Privacy Statute/Provisions*	*Specific Disclosure Rules*
		• Specific disclosure rules apply to mental health [Wyo. Stat. Ann. § 25-10-122, amended by 2006 Wyo. Sess. Laws, ch. 114]; Department of Health contractor treatment records [Wyo. Stat. Ann. §§ 9-2-125 and 9-2-126, added by 2007 Wyo. Sess. Laws, ch. 76]; coroner's reports [Wyo. Stat. Ann. § 7-4-105, added by 2011 Wyo. Sess. Laws, ch. 144]; child abuse reports [Wyo. Stat. Ann. § 14-3-214, amended by 2006 Wyo. Sess. Laws, ch. 114]; sexually transmitted diseases [Wyo. Stat. Ann. §§ 35-4-107, 35-4-130, 35-4-132]; sexual assault examinations [Wyo. Stat. Ann. § 6-2-309, amended by 2006 Wyo. Sess. Laws, ch. 77]; and physical therapists [Wyo. Stat. Ann. § 32-25-102, amended by 2009 Wyo. Sess. Laws, ch. 134]. • HIPAA covered entity or business associate is deemed to be in compliance with data security requirements for purposes of security breach notification statute [Wyo. Stat. § 40-12-502, 2015 Wyo. Sess. Laws, ch. 65].

INDEX

[References are to Sections and Appendices.]

R

S

V

W